W9-DBZ-888

Contents

HOW DOES YOUR COMPANY
MEASURE UP TO THE 100 BEST?

- After seven years, hourly workers at ADVANCED MICRO DEVICES get an extra week's vacation—and $3,000.

- FEL-PRO will help send your kid to college—with a $3,000 subsidy every year for four years.

- In 1992, one out of every five employees at MICROSOFT was a millionaire.

- MERCK, DU PONT, TANDEM COMPUTERS, and SYNTEX grant stock options to all employees.

- Three companies—BEN & JERRY'S, HERMAN MILLER, and SPRINGFIELD REMANUFACTURING—have in place salary caps limiting the amount of pay that the CEO can make to a multiple of the lowest wage in the company (7 times, 20 times, and 6 times, respectively).

- Companies owned 100 percent by employees include AVIS, PUBLIX, SPRINGFIELD REMANUFACTURING, and TD INDUSTRIES.

ROBERT LEVERING and MILTON MOSKOWITZ are coauthors, with Michael Katz, of five books about American business, including *Everybody's Business: A Field Guide to the 400 Leading Companies in America*. Levering is also the author of *A Great Place to Work*, and Moskowitz wrote *The Global Marketplace*. They live in the San Francisco Bay area.

The 100 Best Companies to Work For in America

ROBERT LEVERING
MILTON MOSKOWITZ

REVISED EDITION

A PLUME BOOK

PLUME
Published by the Penguin Group
Penguin Books USA Inc., 375 Hudson Street, New York, New York 10014, U.S.A.
Penguin Books Ltd, 27 Wrights Lane, London W8 5TZ, England
Penguin Books Australia Ltd, Ringwood, Victoria, Australia
Penguin Books Canada Ltd, 10 Alcorn Avenue, Toronto, Ontario, Canada M4V 3B2
Penguin Books (N.Z.) Ltd, 182–190 Wairau Road, Auckland 10, New Zealand

Penguin Books Ltd, Registered Offices: Harmondsworth, Middlesex, England

Published by Plume, an imprint of Dutton Signet, a division of Penguin Books USA Inc.
Published in a hardcover edition by Currency/Doubleday.

First Plume Printing, January, 1994
10 9 8 7 6 5 4 3 2 1

 REGISTERED TRADEMARK—MARCA REGISTRADA

LIBRARY OF CONGRESS CATALOGING-IN-PUBLICATION DATA
Levering, Robert, 1944–
    The 100 best companies to work for in America / Robert Levering,
Milton Moskowitz.
        p.   cm.
    Originally published: 1st Currency/Doubleday ed. New York :
Currency/Doubleday, 1993.
    ISBN 0-452-27123-1
    1. Personnel management—United States—Handbooks, manuals, etc.
2. Job satisfaction—United States—Handbooks, manuals, etc.
3. Corporations—United States—Handbooks, manuals, etc.
I. Moskowitz, Milton.   II. Title.   III. Title: One hundred best
companies to work for in America.
HF5549.2.U5L38   1994
331.2'0973—dc20   93–6406
                                                        CIP

Printed in the United States of America

For Abigail, who has a gentle spirit that's needed in every workplace.

For Peter Johnson, a true child of the light.

Acknowledgments

Our greatest debt is to the hundreds of employees who generously shared their work experiences with us. This book would not have been possible without their willingness to spend time explaining to us the ins and outs of their workplaces. Our understanding of these companies was helped immeasurably by Carol Townsend and Amy Lyman, who helped conduct the interviews, put penetrating questions, and offered innumerable insights reflected throughout these pages.

This project would have been hard to accomplish without the mighty boost we got from Seija Surr, our editorial assistant/researcher/scheduler/fact-checker extraordinaire. She unfailingly tracked down obscure details and buoyed our often jet-lagged spirits with her good humor and enthusiasm. We also are indebted to Kristin Denham, who helped Seija during the last stages of piecing the manuscript together, and Lee Townsend, whose quick wit helped us to characterize companies more deftly. And we can't say enough for our transcribers—John Erler, Bonnie Galvin, Maya Roth, and Karen Weeks—who turned the hours and hours of recorded interviews into readable documents of our conversations with employees.

As usual, we have received gems of advice and counsel from Michael Katz, our agent, friend, and coauthor on the last edition. Thanks too to our editors at Doubleday—Harriet Rubin, who came up with the original idea nearly a dozen years ago, and Janet Coleman, who was of immense help in guiding the book through the final stages of editing and production.

Preface to the Plume Edition

Today, when the air is rent with declarations that loyalty and job security are things of the past, and that perhaps the entire concept of the "good company" is obsolete, it's important to reaffirm the principle that work can be rewarding, not just for the people at the top of a company but for everyone employed there.

The companies we describe in this book have bonds with their employees that go beyond the paycheck. Job security is not a relic of the past for them. Nearly 20 have explicit or implicit policies that exclude mass layoffs. Two companies—Haworth and Physio-Control—managed not to sever a single employee from the payroll during periods of dramatic sales reversals. Others—Hewlett-Packard and Delta Air Lines—will pursue every possible avenue before deciding to let people go. And many of these firms are growing at a fast clip. During the first year after our hardcover edition appeared, 16 of these companies had hired a total of some 100,000 new workers. The smallest firm on our list, Great Plains Software, had nearly doubled its employment to almost 600.

It's true that the companies in this book offer extraordinary benefits. One has a free child care center. Another gives college-bound children of all employees tuition aid of $3,300 a year for four years. Three give free lunches—every day. Four offer stock options to all employees. But it's not specific practices or techniques that make these companies good places to work. It's the spirit underlying them that counts the most.

Lewis Platt, the CEO of Hewlett-Packard, expressed it well, we think, in a recent letter to employees. He had the sense that many HPers were worried that the company's core beliefs, set down in a document called "The HP Way," were being eroded. He said that those employees who talked about this erosion cited such things as the discontinuance of free coffee and doughnuts, the offering of voluntary severance packages to induce people to leave, and the shifting of employees to different locations. Platt pointed out that specific practices do not constitute the HP way. He said: "This is the definition of the HP way that I like: It simply means that we believe in people, and we believe people want to do a good job. It doesn't say anything about coffee and doughnuts."

Platt went on to tell employees that he visits "many companies where the top management clearly doesn't share this belief with us. They think the employees are going to rip them off anytime they get a chance. You know the companies that I'm talking about as well as I do. Our thinking about employees is a differentiator. So, I think we need to reaffirm it."

That's close to the way we feel about the companies in this book. They differ from the great mass of companies. IBM, for all the people it has let go because of horrendous miscalculations made by management, has not behaved in the callous manner of U.S. Steel, which failed to invest in its plants or its people and, as described by John Hoerr in his book *And the Wolf Finally Came*, told managers who had worked there for three decades: "Clean out your desk, this is your last day."

Most of us know—or, in our better moments, like to think we know—that money isn't everything, that the pursuit of power can be spiritually draining, and that happiness hinges crucially on a healthy inner spirit. Why, then, do we have to give up those beliefs when we come to work?

For this edition we have made corrections in the text to assure that the book is as accurate as possible. We have also paid close attention to the changes that have been taking place in our list of the 100 Best since the publication of the hardcover edition. Most of the companies have seen no significant changes, but 23 of them have. You will find our updates of those developments at the end of the book, immediately following the Epilogue.

Robert Levering
Milton Moskowitz
October, 1993

Introduction

No one who visits the Lincoln Electric plant in Cleveland can mistake where authority is located. Workers are clearly in charge here. They call the shots, including the decision as to how much time to spend with visiting reporters.

No one who spends the early morning hours after midnight in the Federal Express hub at the Memphis airport would miss the enthusiasm of men and women working in teams to unload packages from an armada of incoming planes, sort them by zip codes, and reload them onto planes that reach their destinations early enough to make a 10:30 A.M. delivery anywhere in the country. This is a charged-up work force.

Anyone who drops in at the landscaped, collegiate campus of SAS Institute near the Raleigh-Durham airport would be impressed to see two stand-alone buildings devoted entirely to the care of children from infants up to age six. Montessori teachers care for nearly three hundred kids of employees, who pay absolutely nothing for this on-site benefit.

First-time visitors to the USAA headquarters complex in San Antonio are stunned by the size of the place: it's the largest private office building in the world. Even more stunning is the world-unto-itself that this insurance company has created, a safe harbor where employees have incredible opportunities to learn new skills and move up.

And people who troop through the robotics factory of Odetics in Orange County, California, or apply for a job at Dallas-based Southwest Airlines, will not go very far without hearing the sounds of laughter. Fun is institutionalized at these two companies.

Those are the sights and sounds of the best workplaces in America. Found in all parts of the country and in all types of industry, they represent a signal departure from the hierarchical, authoritarian workplace that has prevailed for so long in American business. But they are also exceptional rather than typical. They stand out because they are so different. Most companies still offer dreadful work environments. This is true today, just as it was true in 1984 when we originally identified and described the nation's best workplaces in the first edition of *The 100 Best Companies to Work for in America*.

In our new search to find companies with exceptional workplaces, we have reached conclusions that run counter to much of the current wisdom about the American workplace. We found that even as the workplace has become traumatized by layoffs, job burnout, and shifting of more health insurance costs to the employee, the very best workplaces have become better. There were many more viable candidates for this book than for our list a decade ago. We had more than 400 nominations to begin with, more than double the last time. The 100 companies profiled in this book may account for only a small fraction of the total U.S. work force, but as exemplars they represent a growing force. They are magnets for people looking for meaningful work. They are models for companies trying to get it right. In those two important senses, they may herald the future.

Why are there better workplaces today—and more of them? One reason is adversity, which often brings out the best in people—and companies. American companies have been whipsawed in an increasingly competitive global environment. The quality of products turned out by American companies has been questioned, even held up to scorn. It wasn't until recent years that the perception sunk in that poor products may have something to do with bad workplaces, where employees were abused or ignored and considered little more than a cost of doing business. We have seen company after company where the quality movement has taken hold, which is often a key ingredient in the transition to a better workplace. (The quality movement is no panacea, however, as we have also seen workplaces that have changed little or have gotten worse after the introduction of quality processes.) Other factors which have contributed to an improvement in the quality of the workplace have been advancement of women and minorities into management ranks (they bring a fresh perspective to the work at hand), incorporation of environmental needs (workers need to breathe fresh air, too), and a greater health consciousness (reflected in gleaming fitness centers and health education programs). It's difficult to believe that it has taken so long, but at last we see companies which have actually posted it as a goal to become a good workplace. That kind of attitude was simply not in place in the early 1980s when we set out on our mission to find exceptional workplaces.

We have noted positive changes in five key areas:

• **More employee participation.** A rarity in the early 1980s, genuine employee involvement in decision-making about their jobs is a reality among the companies in this book. Ironically, this change has often occurred because of layoffs. With fewer supervisors, many companies have been forced to reorganize how work is accomplished. In some cases, the quality movement—the current management buzzword—has provided specific techniques for increasing employee participation.

• **More sensitivity to work/family issues.** Many of the companies in this book have made tremendous strides toward dealing with the problems of working mothers and fathers, offering a variety of child-care options and flexible work schedules.

• **More two-way communications.** Accessibility of the top executives is much more common today than in the early 1980s. Even many large firms offer employees opportunities to ask questions—and get answers— directly from their CEOs.

• **More sharing of the wealth.** Profit-sharing and gain-sharing programs have increased dramatically, as have ESOPs (employee stock ownership plans). Some companies are even extending stock options, typically reserved for a handful of top executives, to everyone in the ranks.

• **More fun.** Finally we saw many more companies where having fun seems to be part of the corporate mission. Fun is not inconsistent with operating a serious, profit-making business. Watch out for companies where there is no sense of humor.

There is a more fundamental characteristic of the new workplace style than quality teams, flextime, or profit-sharing plans. In the best workplaces, employees trust their managers, and the managers trust their employees. The trust is reflected in numerous ways: no time clocks, meetings where employees have a chance to register their concerns, job posting (so that employees have first crack at openings), constant training (so that employees can learn new skills), and employee committees empowered to make changes in policies, recommend new pay rates, or allocate the corporate charity dollars. Trust, in the workplace, simply means that employees are treated as partners and recognized as having something to contribute beyond brawn or manual dexterity or strong legs and arms.

There is more trust today because the authoritarian workstyle that has long been the standard operating procedure in American business has failed. It hasn't worked for employees, and it hasn't worked for employers. And that failure is at the root of the poor performance of American companies and the massive layoffs of the late 1980s and early 1990s. When management becomes disconnected from the people who work in the company, it becomes easy to fire them. And when workers are disconnected from what they are doing, it becomes easy for them not to care about the product or service they're delivering.

This failure has impelled companies to look for other options. It is our hope that by providing these concrete examples, employees and employers alike will see that this new work-style is not only possible but realistic and practical. This is true whether your company is big or small, old or young, high-tech or no-tech. The new work-style reflected in this book may be a harbinger of the American workplace in the next century.

Our Selection Process

During the last 10 years, we have kept our eyes and ears open for companies where the work experience is life-enhancing rather than life-deadening. One of us (Milton Moskowitz) has coauthored *Working Mother*'s annual survey of the best places for working mothers every year since 1986; the other (Robert Levering) wrote *A Great Place to Work: What Makes Some Employers So Good—and Most So Bad*; and we jointly coauthored a revision of *Everybody's Business: A Field Guide to the 400 Leading Companies in America*. Besides research for those projects, we obtained nominees for our list from many sources—magazine and newspaper articles, recommendations from friends, chance acquaintances, fellow business journalists. Some companies nominated themselves. Wherever we go, we always ask if people know of companies with reputations as good workplaces.

We gathered more than 300 new nominees through this process in addition to the 100 companies that were profiled in our previous book. We wrote all of these firms asking them to send us written materials that would show why they should be considered. The overwhelming majority responded to our request, sending us a small mountain of employee handbooks, benefits booklets, company newsletters, recruiting packages, annual reports, corporate histories, and videos. (The winner in terms of sheer weight was the 25-pound scrapbook we received from Great Plains Software.) After carefully culling through each of these packets, we selected 147 final candidates for site visits.

These site visits were crucial, as we've found you can only learn so much from written materials. It's hard to imagine what it's like to work in an iron foundry unless you are inside one and feel the heat. At each company, we spent extensive time talking to employees at all levels. Ours is a report refracted from the comments made to us by employees of these companies. For us the bottom line was always how employees answered these questions: Do you enjoy working here? Why? How does it compare with other places where you have worked?

Between September 1990 and January 1992, we visited each of our final candidates, located in 29 different states in every section of the country (racking up thousands of frequent flyer miles along the way). At each site, we normally ate in the employee cafeteria and took a tour of the plant or office facilities, stopping for impromptu conversations with as many employees as possible. We also typically conducted a minimum of four more formal interviews: with a group of a half-dozen to a dozen nonsupervisory employees; with a similar-sized group of first-line supervisors and middle managers; with a human resources executive; and with the CEO or other top officer of the company. We relied heavily on our skeptical journalistic instincts to detect whether the company's story held together. There were cases where the stories told by company executives and slick corporate brochures failed to match the accounts given by frustrated employees. (Those companies obviously are not in this book.) By the end of an exhausting day, we usually had a good feel for what it was like to work there and how the place compared with the others we'd seen.

Our roster has changed significantly. Of the 100 companies on the original list, only 55 survive in the new lineup. For the most part the other 45 are still good places to work. They have simply been replaced by better candidates (see the epilogue at the end of the book, "Why Levi Strauss Didn't Make It"). We have added young companies like Lotus, Valassis Communications, and Southwest Airlines, firms which were still in diapers when we began our research in the early 1980s. And we have added older companies like Avis, Alagasco, and UNUM, firms which have embraced new ways of working.

No two companies are alike, and we have among our 100 a diverse cast of characters. The companies range in employee size from 380,000 (Wal-Mart) to 430 (Great Plains Software). Thirteen have more than 50,000 employees; eight have fewer than 1,000. A greater number than in 1984— 31 as opposed to 20—are privately held firms or organized in such a way that there are no stockholders, which may be a commentary on the short-term outlook that is often imposed by a stock market listing. Good companies are finding it harder and harder to live with Wall Street. We have steel companies, drug companies, food and beverage purveyors, and a clutch of high-tech outfits. Once again we have included workplaces which are divisions or offshoots of larger corporations. We have our first law firm (we never thought we would see the day) and our first hospitals (three of them). Four of the companies on our list—Federal Express, IBM, Motorola, and Xerox—are Baldrige quality award winners.

If there was one issue that galvanized our selection process, it was job security. As we went around the country, companies were laying off people in droves. For a worker, there is nothing more traumatic than losing a job, especially at companies like Advanced Micro Devices, Digital Equipment, Eastman Kodak, Exxon, and Kellogg, firms which had previously promised employees, explicitly or implicitly, that they would never lose their jobs because of financial reverses. We therefore paid close attention to this issue. A no-layoff policy was not a ticket of admission to our roster. We have a number of companies—Cummins Engine, John Deere, IBM, Inland Steel, and Weyerhaeuser—that downsized their work forces considerably. In those cases, we looked to see how these cutbacks were handled. Was there adequate advance notice? Were the severance payments generous? Did affected employees get help in finding new jobs? We also asked employees for their reactions. One of the remarkable features of our roster is how many companies on it still adhere to a no-layoff policy: 18. Several companies—Federal Express and Haworth, for example—didn't resort to layoffs even when confronted with steep erosions in profits. IBM is a special case in point, having induced about 100,000 people to leave the company since 1985 without laying off people involuntarily. The practice of offering continuous employment is deeply ingrained at Big Blue, and we find it remarkable that the company has been able to continue to uphold that banner. Hewlett-Packard and Procter & Gamble have rarely separated people from their jobs without offering them a place somewhere else in the company, but both of these firms no longer want to be known as "no-layoff companies." What it comes down to, in the end, is not a simple numbers game. We recognize that companies may, at times, be forced to reduce payroll. The questions we ask relate to the treatment of employees during those rocky periods. That's our litmus test. And of course we still give our highest accolades to those companies which pledge not to lay off people.

Another issue that loomed larger in our deliberations this time was skyrocketing salaries for CEOs and other top officers. In 1980, salaries of CEOs were, on average, 40 times the lowest wages in the company; by the end of the decade, the ratio had soared to 100-to-1—and $1 million-plus paychecks had become commonplace. Most of the companies on our list are sensitive to this issue. Three of them—Ben & Jerry's Homemade, Springfield ReManufacturing, and Herman Miller—now have CEO salary caps in place. Others, like Cummins Engine and Delta Air Lines, have made a point of chopping executive compensation during adverse times. Managements which believe that this is not an issue of concern to employees are whistling in the dark; we heard it raised by employees in a number of companies where we interviewed. Indeed, Owen Gaffney, senior vice-president of human resources at Polaroid, believes that resentment is "like a time bomb clicking away in the American workplace."

It's tempting to make the generalization that good workplaces are superior because they help companies to succeed. It's an easy argument to mount here since nearly all the companies profiled in this book are highly successful. But it's a temptation we want to resist because we think it demeans the central thrust of our work, which is that there is something to be said, in and of itself, about providing a meaningful, healthy workplace for people. That should be enough motivation for anyone. What's more, we have found that employees can easily detect manipulators—those who use techniques common to good workplaces simply to enhance the bottom line. This was especially obvious to us as we saw companies jump on the quality movement bandwagon and institute employee-involvement programs without any attempt to change the managerial attitudes that characterize the old work-style. Managers might mouth all the right words, but employees can see through the techniques. They know when they are being used.

One feature about our roster surprised even us when we were toting up the ages of the "100 Best" companies. Many people might surmise that in a report on new work-styles, there would be a preponderance of young companies. But we discovered that no fewer than 21 of our companies were born in the last century. And if we extended our benchmark to the year 1912, picking up companies which are more than 80 years old, 26 companies—or more than a quarter of our list—are of that vintage. It says something for endurance, consistency, ability to change with the times, and—most of all—devotion to traditions of fair dealing that were set early in a company's history and have never been compromised. It makes us believe that the values that go with being a good workplace have extraordinary staying power.

Our Ratings

No company is perfect for everyone. This may be especially true in good places to work since these firms tend to have real character, or in business-jargon terms, their own culture. Companies with distinctive personalities tend to attract—and repel—certain types of individuals. We've tried to indicate what kinds of people do and don't fit into each company in our pluses and minuses at the top of each profile, as well as in the essays themselves.

Though none of these companies is perfect, we do believe that it's possible to spell out in general terms what an ideal workplace would be like. We've suggested what such a company would look like by rating each company on six different criteria. We reserved the top rating, five stars, for companies whose policies, practices, or traits met the following criteria:

★ ★ ★ ★ ★   Pay/Benefits

The company's policy is to pay at or near the top of its industry, and it offers unusual or unique benefits. Health and retirement plans are among the best in this industry. There is special sensitivity to work/family and health needs, exemplified by fitness centers and support for child care. (Note: This is *not* a relative ranking of pay and benefits among the "100 Best," since pay scales, even in the best-paying firms, are determined largely by industry norms.)

★ ★ ★ ★ ★   Opportunities

Training programs are numerous, enabling employees to learn new skills and advance in the ranks. There is a record of growth so that new openings are always being created. The company promotes from within so that it is possible to start in the lower ranks and work your way to the top. There are specific mechanisms for advancement (job posting, annual review, etc.). Women and minorities do well here.

★ ★ ★ ★ ★   Job Security

The company has a written or implicit no-layoff policy and recently went through a difficult period without resorting to layoffs. Four stars go to companies which have rarely if ever laid off employees, and to those firms which have gone through layoffs but have handled them without bruising their people.

★ ★ ★ ★ ★   Pride in Work/Company

Work is organized so that employees at all levels feel a direct connection with the product or service the company provides. People feel proud of their personal accomplishments, and they are recognized for their outstanding achievements. Employees feel they are helping to make their company a leader in its industry, and they cite the positive social contributions of the firm's products or services. They also feel good about the company's role as a corporate citizen.

★ ★ ★ ★ ★   Openness/Fairness

Top executives are accessible to everyone. The company has two-way communications vehicles that not only keep employees informed about what's going on but can transmit suggestions, criticisms, and complaints from employees to upper-level managers. And such critiques can be offered without fear of reprisal. The company has an explicit grievance system through which employees can challenge actions taken against them. Special perks for executives either don't exist or are held to a minimum.

★ ★ ★ ★ ★   Camaraderie/Friendliness

Employees talk about being part of a family, team, or special community that includes everyone at all ranks in the company. They clearly enjoy working (and playing) with one another. They socialize together at various functions during the year. There's laughter in the halls.

All of our 100 companies exhibit, to a greater or lesser degree, these characteristics. They are places where people thrive.

Recommendations and Comments

We've made every effort to be fair and accurate in our assessments of these companies. But we realize we're not infallible. So we welcome any comments from our readers. We also are constantly on the lookout for other good workplaces and would love to hear recommendations of other superlative employers. We can be reached at: 1537 Franklin Street #208, San Francisco, CA 94109.

Robert Levering
Milton Moskowitz
September 1992

Acipco

A **ACIPCO**

Acipco (American Cast Iron Pipe Company) is one of the world's biggest makers of iron pipes used to transport water and sewage. They also make valves, hydrants, ductile iron pipes, and other steel products. Employees: 2,500.

★★★★ Pay/Benefits
★★★ Opportunities
★★★★★ Job Security
★★★ Pride in Work/Company
★★★★★ Openness/Fairness
★★★★ Camaraderie/Friendliness

BIGGEST PLUS: On-site health care.
BIGGEST MINUS: You can get bogged down in the system.

One of the finest medical centers in Birmingham—a city known throughout the South for high-quality hospitals—sits on the north side of the city, only 300 yards from the largest iron foundry in the world. More than 200 people a day (nearly a third of them children) visit this center, which has eight full-time physicians (including three pediatricians), five full-time dentists, and 11 part-time medical specialists who regularly hold clinics there. Housed in a new building with brightly colored quilts on the walls, the center's only patients are the 10,000 current and former Acipco employees and their families (including spouses of deceased retirees).

Acipco provides what is arguably the best and most comprehensive employee health-care coverage of any company in America. Employees get a 75 percent discount on prescription drugs and only pay 15 percent of the doctor's fees when referred to an outside specialist. The company picks up the rest, including 100 percent of hospital bills. At a cost of more than $5,000 a year per employee, it is also one of the most expensive (the average large company spends $3,200 a year). Why does Acipco spend so much money on health care? Because that's what the employees want. Acipco's employees not only own the company—and have since 1924—but control it as well. The firm's board of directors includes top managers and four elected nonmanagement employees—an arrangement that also dates from 1924, when founder John J. Eagan died and left the company in the hands of its workers.

You can't escape hearing about Eagan at Acipco. His bronze statue greets you at the company entrance; his birthday, April 22, is celebrated every year; and his legacy is always mentioned in company sales literature. But what we heard most about during our visit to Acipco was his religious mission: to apply his understanding of Christian principles to business.

One of the specific ways Eagan applied his beliefs was providing employees with pensions, an almost unheard-of benefit at the time (1917). Eagan once said: "We have a pension fund. Industry has no right to take a man, use the best years of his life, and as old age approaches to throw him out and employ young men in his place. It is one of the real joys to see men who otherwise would be dependent on their families receiving monthly through this fund their own money which they have earned and which has been set aside in this fund."

During his lifetime Eagan was also one of the first employers to offer free medical and dental care, showers and clean towels (the foundry is hot and dirty), 24-hour hot food service, training and safety committees, and a no-layoff policy. He built houses for employees and opened a company store. The store still runs today, offering employees everything from groceries to VCRs and fishing gear. It has a markup of only 10 percent, and employees have up to 18 months to pay for major purchases through payroll deduction.

When Eagan died in 1923 he left all the company stock in a trust for the employees. The employee trust was, in effect, one of the earliest profit-sharing plans, as it paid dividends to employees based on the firm's profitability. In recent years, the quarterly bonus has added nearly 10 percent to an employee's base pay. And that is on top of a generous pay scale in the top 25 percent of comparable foundries. The average wage for unskilled laborers in 1992 was $11.71 an hour, and skilled tradespeople got an entry-level wage of $13.01 to $15.62 an hour. Welder Roger Huffstutler said: "We realize that if we don't put out, we don't get a bonus. It gives people more incentive."

Profit sharing heightens employees' sense of ownership. According to design engineer Mike Kitchens: "Most people do the job like they're spending their own money. You'll get a lot of input from guys in the shop. Being an engineer, I get questioned all the time: 'Why are you doing it this way?'

A lot of them know a lot more about it than I do. And I listen to them. We're all working for one common goal. Ultimately, it's a profit for the company, and it's also to perpetuate our existence and our income and everything else. It's also to respect each other and to apply Mr. Eagan's principle. It's not really Mr. Eagan's principle, it's our Lord and Savior's principle, Lord Jesus Christ, that this company was built on. Every penny we make, it comes back to us."

Another unique Eagan legacy is the board of operatives, composed of 12 employees elected to serve two-year terms. Two members of this board serve on the company's board of directors, as does a representative of the clerical workers and two members of the organization at large. Publicity manager Cynthia Lovoy explained that Eagan set up the board because he believed "that the workers and the management should communicate with each other, be able to sit down and listen to each other."

The board of operatives meets with works manager Eugene Langner at least every two weeks, and with the entire board of management (the top five executives) once a month to discuss any issues of concern. Grievances and discipline issues that cannot be resolved easily are brought to a committee of four board members (two white and two black) and four members of management. Before this committee can take any disciplinary action, the vote must be unanimous. If not, the issue is brought to the board of management, which makes the final decision. Langner told us that only one out of every 25 to 30 cases goes to the board of management.

The discipline committee is not the only one that has racial quotas. Two of the four hourly employees on most committees must be African-American. There is also a black charity committee and a white charity committee that solicit funds for different charities. Harvey Henley, a black board of operatives member, explained why: "At the time that it was established you had the two separate communities, and you still have some of that."

Even in a 100-percent-owned company, there can be labor-management problems. In 1983 the president, Carl Farlow, fired several board members over a dispute about cutting benefits to counter a slide in profits. The board members were reinstated the next day, and the president left Acipco in 1985 when reaching normal retirement age. According to 10-year board of operatives member James Frederick, relations between the board and management have been improving since then.

Machine shop employee Jack Praytor said: "I'm starting my third year on the board of operatives. I feel like our relationship with management is getting a lot better. There's always going to be a tug-of-war. To a certain degree it's just human: the man's always wanting more, the company's always trying to hold the costs down. So you are always going to have a little controversy there, which is not a real problem, but just human nature."

It was clear from our discussions at Acipco that, in general, management and labor have an open relationship. Thirty-five-year employee Ray Clayton, a foreman in mold maintenance, says: "I really like this word 'family,' because I feel that way. I have always felt like the people in high places here hear from the people out in the shop, and I still believe they care for me. I know that I can go talk to any of them whether it's the head of the company, or head of the medical department, or whoever, and there's a gentleman there that's going to listen to your problems and is going to do something about it. They're part of the Acipco family and not somebody to run from and hide from. I really think that our high officials enjoy coming out in the shop and do it at every opportunity. It's a very unique place."

The family feeling at Acipco is evident when you look at the company newsletter. This folksy monthly is usually filled with photos of recent Acipco social events like the open house, the Christmas party, or the buddy fishing tournament. The 1990 fishing tournament included 358 anglers who caught over 800 pounds of fish. At these fishing competitions, which are Acipco's largest employee activity, employees team up with a buddy and spend a day fishing on Lay Lake. Among the winners were Glenda and Don Schatz, who won $750 for catching the most fish (10 fish which together weighed 28.5 pounds) and $125 for winning in the husband-and-wife category. Live fish were returned to the water after the weigh-in.

Many of the Acipco family members are related. Don Hamlett, chief of dental staff in the medical clinic, is a second-generation Acipco employee. His father worked here as an electrician for 40 years. Today, more than 350 employees have been with the company more than 30 years. The average tenure is nearly 18 years, and annual turnover is about half a percent. Acipco may be the only company that records the number of births to employees and their spouses in their annual report. There were 88 in 1990.

Environmental chemist Ben Thomas is another second-generation Acipco employee. He thinks that like any good family, Acipco takes care of its own, and he told us this story to prove the point: "In the early '70s, my father got ill. He had Lou Gehrig's disease, which is incurable. At that time Dad was serving on the board of operatives and had to take an early retirement. Acipco did everything they possibly could to make him as comfortable as they could over those years. Mom and Dad moved to Florida because there's a clinic down there that has a special therapy for that disease. Dad took a turn for the worse while he was down there and the doctors had said that he could not survive an ambulance trip back to Birmingham. I called the director of employee relations at the time, who was Bobby Franklin. At that time I was still in college. I asked Bobby, 'What can we do to get Dad back home?' And he said, 'You don't worry about it, we'll take care of it.' That afternoon there was a jet plane, a private jet sitting here. They flew Dad home. That's the kind of company this is. The hospital bills were over $250,000, but we only paid $1,000. They don't forget their pensioners. They'll be here when you need them."

Types of jobs: Production—47 percent; executives, professionals, administration and clerical—22 percent; crafts—21 percent; technicians—5 percent; sales—3 percent; service—2 percent.

Main employment centers: Acipco's main office and plant is in Birmingham. Acipco owns smaller subsidiary plants in Alabaster, Alabama, and Beaumont, Texas. They also have sales offices in Sacramento, California; Dallas; Tulsa, Oklahoma; Minneapolis; Kansas City, Missouri; Chicago; Pittsburgh; New York City; Atlanta; and Orlando and Pompano Beach, Florida.

Headquarters: American Cast Iron Pipe Company
P.O. Box 2727
Birmingham, AL 35202
(205) 325–7701

Advanced Micro Devices

AMD is the fifth largest maker of silicon chips (semiconductors) in America. U.S. employees: 5,070.

★★★ Pay/Benefits
★★★★ Opportunities
★★★ Job Security
★★★ Pride in Work/Company
★★★ Openness/Fairness
★★★★ Camaraderie/Friendliness

BIGGEST PLUS: Dream vacations.
BIGGEST MINUS: You're working for a copycat.

Paul Olive worked for two other semiconductor companies in Silicon Valley —National Semiconductor and Intel—before coming to AMD in 1980, and he told us he was "impressed almost immediately when I walked in the door of this place. Instead of standing around and pointing your fingers at each other when something went wrong, the attitude was, 'We got a problem, let's get together and solve it.' That was such a refreshing thing that I haven't looked for a job since."

Olive's characterization of AMD as a place where people work together in harmony, almost as a family, jibed with other comments we heard in our visit to the company in 1991. This is no longer the brash and freewheeling high-tech superstar we described in our previous edition. But it has retained a people-oriented culture that separates the company from the hard-edge attitude that prevails in much of Silicon Valley. The 1980s had a chastening effect on AMD's arrogance, as intense Japanese competition delivered some powerful body blows to the American semiconductor industry. In the middle of the decade, AMD did the previously unthinkable and discarded its long-treasured no-layoff policy. By the early 1990s AMD was clearly middle-aged. Gone were the days of the huge Christmas bashes in San Francisco where thousands were entertained by well-known rock bands.

Still at AMD's helm in 1992 was Jerry Sanders, considered by many to personify the early go-go spirit of Silicon Valley. A former salesman for Fairchild Semiconductor, Sanders launched AMD in 1969 to act as a "second source" for semiconductors designed by other companies. Semiconductors are the chips at the heart of computers and other electronic devices, and AMD secured licenses to make them from the original designers. It then sought, through its own manufacturing processes, to come up with improved versions. It became so successful at marketing its chips that AMD started to design its own. Products designed by them accounted for 42 percent of their sales in 1991. In the early 1980s, when IBM introduced its personal computer, it chose a microprocessor made by Intel to power its PC. However, because it didn't want to be wholly dependent on Intel, IBM pressured Intel into licensing a second source. AMD became that second source, and that agreement later provoked a bitter court case that was still enfolding in 1992. Intel accused AMD of stealing its design, and AMD countersued, charging Intel with reneging on its agreements. Both sides have won victories in different court decisions—and the issue was still not resolved in mid-1992. Sanders told stockholders in the 1991 annual report: "AMD's fortunes are still closely tied to the outcome of pending litigation."

Sanders, long known for his lavish life-style, owns a mansion in Bel-Air (Nancy and Ronald Reagan live across the street). The day we visited, he was chauffeured to work in a Rolls-Royce. Sanders can maintain this life-style because he is paid well—over $1.5 million in cash in 1991, and in 1992 he was also granted an additional 300,000 shares of stock (worth nearly $3 million in 1992) and stock options for another 600,000 shares. But his personal life has toned down since the early 1980s. He has remarried, and he told us that he has little interest in his former showman's antics: "I am 55 years old. I am the founding CEO of a very successful, $1-billion company that is important to this nation, and while I am not taking myself too seriously, I am not going to put any damn lampshade on my head and do something silly either."

Always a great sloganeer, Sanders insists that the core of AMD is "People —Products—Profits," or in the expanded version: "If we take care of our people, products will be created, and profits will follow." Logic technology manager Ron Das told us: "If I look back at what AMD has gone through, especially in the last few years, it has been hard. But I would say that the people remain the most important aspect."

AMD's "people first" philosophy was demonstrated in how they handled layoffs. The company seems to have avoided the bitterness that often accompanies such traumatic events. This is especially significant considering how AMD, and Sanders in particular, had earlier so loudly proclaimed an adherence to a no-layoff policy. Sanders explained that the company's policy had always been that there would be no layoffs "unless the company's viability was at stake." By 1986, after AMD had lost millions of dollars, the company's "viability" was clearly at stake, and without layoffs the company would run out of cash. Employees seemed to handle the situation well, in part because AMD avoided any layoffs until after virtually every other competitor had resorted to them. Senior fab (fabrication) supervisor Paul Olive told us: "We had a no-layoff policy at one time. Jerry Sanders held out as long as he could, I think, but the industry changed so that we had to either lay people off or not exist anymore. They tried at first to do it with attrition. And eventually, it got so bad that they had to start doing layoffs. But the layoffs were done with good packages. Every time they had to do one, they did the next one a little better. And they didn't do any of them badly." In the layoffs in early 1991, employees received a week's pay for every year of service. Those with more than 10 years with the company received 1½ weeks' pay for every year of service. Benefits for laid-off employees were extended for 60 days.

And the company helped employees in other ways, too. Material distribution manager George McCarthy explained: "I have been with a lot of companies and I have never seen severance packages like they offered our people. They can come in and use the phones and type their résumés. We bent over backwards during the last three reductions in force to work with our people and we got them counseling if they needed counseling. And that just impressed the heck out of me. When we were losing money we spent a couple of million bucks to make sure our people had a chance at another job. That to me is very special." AMD spent $1 million on job retraining to help displaced workers, and nearly 300 workers have taken advantage of it. The company also sponsored a job fair for laid-off employees, and 50 former AMDers got jobs through the fair.

Another watershed event was the purchase in 1987 of Monolithic Memories, Inc. (MMI), struggling semiconductor maker. AMD went out of its way to welcome MMI employees into their family. Shipping clerk Roderick Marinas, for example, worked for MMI for one year before joining the military. When he left the military four years later, AMD gave him a job and five years of seniority, including 100 hours of vacation.

One benefit AMD incorporated from MMI was the sabbatical/dream vacation program. Through this program salaried employees get eight weeks off after seven years of service. The "dream vacation" is given to hourly employees every seven years. It consists of a week off with pay and $3,000 spending money. On her dream vacation, training specialist Judy Fen "went back home to New York and took my whole family." Maintenance support coordinator Lance Taylor told us: "I bought a new car. My wife works here, too. And we have both been here almost 10 years now, so when we got our trips we coordinated them both so that we could get them together, and with our money we bought a car." Roderick Marinas, who was about to get his "dream vacation" when we interviewed him, said: "What I plan to do is pay off the money I borrowed from my parents to purchase my house."

AMD was one of the first companies in "the Valley" to share its spoils with employees, establishing a profit-sharing program in 1972. Twice a year they distribute 10 percent of their pretax operating profits to employees (except when there are none, as in 1987 and 1991). In 1992 they distributed checks averaging $1,957 and $3,426 per employee. Domestic employees are also eligible for an attendance bonus: $75 a quarter for perfect attendance. To support employees with families, AMD entered a partnership with the YMCA in 1990 and opened a near-site preschool for their employees in Sunnyvale and Santa Clara, California.

The benefits are not the only thing that distinguishes AMD from other Silicon Valley companies. When we interviewed employees at AMD's headquarters in Sunnyvale, they described a family feeling. Senior clerk Lillian Albanoski, whose coworkers call her "Grams," told us: "There is a closeness here. You are like a brother, or a sister or a grandmother or a mother. I mean we are very close. And we have been a close-knit family here for many years. We have baby showers. If we know someone needs help, we help them as much as we can. In fact, there was one fellow who was working with us and there was going to be a Christmas party and he had gone out and he bought a new suit and shoes. His apartment got robbed and they took his new set of clothes for the Christmas party. So do you know what we did? We all got together and we bought him a new set of clothes."

Teamwork is promoted by an egalitarian atmosphere and accessibility of the top management. AMD has no executive dining rooms and no assigned parking spots (except for one company car). Doors in the executive suite are always open.

Arrogant people do not fit in at AMD. George McCarthy, with AMD since 1977, recalled: "There was one VP here who asked me to do something with some of the chemicals in the building that I didn't think was right. And I told him that I didn't think it was right. And he said, 'Do you know who I am?' And I said sarcastically, 'No, why don't you show me your American Express card?' And he never pulled that stuff again. His attitude was like, 'I am the VP and you are a peasant.' That won't go here anymore because we can get in to see anybody we want. I think everybody in this company can. If you want to go see [president and chief operating officer] Rich Previte, and you really got something that is bothering you, he will see you."

Accessibility has been institutionalized in recent years. Sanders holds "breakfast with Jerry" for AMD managers every quarter in both California and Texas. He gives news of the old quarter, lets them know what to expect from the upcoming months, and answers questions.

Rich Previte also dines with employees. He conducts meetings with about 15 employees in randomly selected groups from nonmanagement ranks. Previte reserves every Friday for one of these meetings, but sometimes the schedule gets a little out of hand. On one occasion, Previte ended up eating with employees four times in one day. He started off having breakfast with the swing-shift employees at 5:45 A.M., then joined a pizza party at 11:00, ate his regular employee luncheon at 1:00 with a randomly selected group, and finished off with another pizza party at 6:00.

Training is an important part of the AMD culture. Employees at all levels are eligible for AMD's tuition-reimbursement program. In the 1990–91 school year, 561 employees took part in the program. As part of a three-year specialized training effort begun in 1990, AMD has sent 90 employees through a college degree program at Mission College in Santa Clara, which cost the company $6,000 per employee. The full-time program lasts seven months and includes instruction in algebra, chemistry, and physics. AMD had spent $3.5 million on the Mission College program through mid-1992. One employee who completed the program in 1991, Paul Olive, explained: "When they closed my fab [section] down, they offered us the opportunity to go to Mission College and learn a new type of position. They gave us our salary every week just like it always comes and paid for everything at Mission College. All we had to do was find a way to get there in the morning."

Main employment centers: There are 3,800 employees at manufacturing facilities in Sunnyvale and Santa Clara, California, and 2,300 in San Antonio and Austin, Texas. AMD also has manufacturing facilities in Japan, Thailand, England, Malaysia, and Singapore.

Headquarters: Advanced Micro Devices, Inc.
901 Thompson Place
P.O. Box 3453
Sunnyvale, CA 94088
(408) 732-2400

Alagasco

Alagasco is the largest distributor of natural gas in Alabama with more than 410,000 customers. Employees: 1,300.

★ ★ ★ Pay/Benefits
★ ★ ★ ★ Opportunities
★ ★ ★ ★ ★ Job Security
★ ★ ★ ★ ★ Pride in Work/Company
★ ★ ★ Openness/Fairness
★ ★ ★ ★ Camaraderie/Friendliness

BIGGEST PLUS: Working here is a gas.
BIGGEST MINUS: Regulators can siphon your energy.

Mike Warren was sure of one thing when he became Alagasco's president in 1984. He knew that Alagasco did not deserve to be in the first edition of *The 100 Best Companies to Work For in America.* He was convinced, however, that with a lot of work he could make it into this edition. So he made that a corporate goal of this utility that provides natural gas to Birmingham, Montgomery, and other towns in central Alabama. It is part of Energen Corporation, which also produces methane gas from abandoned coal fields.

Construction supervisor Gordon Jones, who joined the company in 1952, thought Alagasco might have qualified for a list of the 100 worst places to work before Mike Warren came on board. His description sums up what many employees told us of pre-Warren days: "You were a piece of meat put out there to do a job and they expected it done the way they wanted it. This was true from the bottom all the way up to the vice-president. Everybody was fearful of their job. You had no input whatsoever. You were told what to do. You might be the smartest person in the United States, but your knowledge fell on deaf ears. Back then, if you were not of the white race, hang it in your ear, partner, you were as far as you were ever going to go. And if you were working for me and I didn't like the way you walked, you'd be gone the next day."

According to all reports, the company had a clearly delineated caste system. Managers were considered the brains, nonmanagement employees the brawn. Irving Hawkins, vice-president of marketing, described the attitude: "A lot of people felt that if you weren't the management class, then you had no bright ideas, everything you thought was stupid. It kept someone from wanting to raise their head up because they were always afraid that someone was going to knock them down." Managers motivated through fear. Several employees described the culture as, at best, one where "good deeds go unpunished."

Alagasco had a great many years to get set in its ways. Its roots can be traced back to 1852 when the Montgomery Gaslite Company provided that city with gas for street lighting. Realizing in 1984 that the 132-year-old Alagasco needed a "cultural revolution," Warren first met face-to-face with all 1,300 employees to tell them his vision. In the spring of 1985, he visited all the company's service areas and met with groups of from a dozen up to as many as 50 employees. According to Warren: "It was the first time they had that kind of meeting with the president of the company." Often he began by serving employees cheeseburgers that he grilled on a barbecue he carted around on the back of his car. At one location Warren took a half hour out of his schedule to play basketball with crewmen and servicemen on the company basketball court.

Warren told them of his goal to make Alagasco one of the 100 best companies to work for in America, and he emphasized that he wanted to get rid of the "utility mind-set." David Self, vice-president of human relations, defines the utility mind-set as "if it worked last year or five years ago or 10 years ago, then don't fix it. We've always done it this way and it's got us to where we are, so leave it alone."

Warren characterized this thinking as being a holdover from the age of the dinosaurs. He had a rubber dinosaur stamp made. Whenever a memo or a proposal came across his desk that reminded him of the utility mind-set, he stamped it with his dinosaur stamp and sent it back to the sender. This idea caught on and before long employees in the Montgomery office put together a 15-foot-long papier-mâché dinosaur, which made the rounds of company offices. In 1986 the union gave Warren the Dinosaur Killer of the Year Award.

Another Warren technique was "Hey Mike" cards. Secretary Theresa Martinez said: "Mr. Warren instituted the 'Hey Mike' program where he had these little cards on posters all over the company and if there was something you wanted to say, you could jot down a comment, a suggestion, a question, anything, and you didn't even have to sign it. And he responded to every single one of them." In 1985, during the first month of the program, Warren received 100 "Hey Mike" cards. "Hey Mike" suggestions that have been implemented include upgrades in company cars for lower-level management, a one-week orientation for new employees, and welcome packets for new customers.

One of those who responded to Warren's open management style was collector Dan Noojin, who said that during his first five years with Alagasco "I was miserable every day. I just came in and tried to do my job and keep my mouth shut and stay out of trouble. There was blatant chauvinism daily and racism. I remember when Mike Warren came to work here and it was filtered down to us that here was somebody with some new thinking that was going to change this company. And I remember I sat down at my word processor and I told my wife, 'I'm fixing to get fired. I'm fixing to write this guy a letter and tell him what I think about his company.' And I did. I told him, 'You've got good people in this company to start with, but this company is going to have to change because you've got some management that sucks like a bucket of ticks.' "

Noojin and others discovered that Warren really did intend to scrap the old ways. Noojin said: "I got this real friendly letter back saying, 'Wow. These are problems that we see and we're going to address.' And he did. For the first five years it was bad. For the last five years it's gotten better. It was dark when I came to work here and now you can see the sun coming up."

Business has been brighter, too. In 1991 their profits were nearly triple what they had been in 1985. And they have added an additional 50,000 customers.

Not all of Alagasco's managers embraced Warren's new philosophy. Warren gave them the chance to leave the company gracefully by offering two early-retirement plans. He replaced managers—whom some refer to as the "old dinosaurs"—with executives who espoused his employee-oriented philosophy. One of Warren's key appointments was Gary Youngblood, currently vice-president of the Birmingham service center.

To signal that he was instituting a culture change, Youngblood passed out a variety of business cards to his employees, saying things like: "Put some failure into the Birmingham District, try something," and "Beginning today every employee in the Birmingham District has the authority to give customer satisfaction." When Youngblood issued these cards, he said,

"This is your 'get out of jail free' card. If you try something and it fails, then you turn in this card and you're forgiven. And you see me and get another one."

Youngblood's attitude encouraged employees to take risks. Supervisor Carolyn Williams heard customers complain about the need for different payment envelopes. So she had them printed without getting her supervisor's approval—an unheard-of act in previous days. Office manager Barbara Harris, who has been with Alagasco since 1958, said: "They'll back us now; they may not agree with us, but they will still back the decision we made."

To make sure employees make good decisions, Alagasco opened its own training school, called Alabama Gas Company University, or AGCU. Since 1987 more than 250 employees have attended three-day sessions that combine both management and nonmanagement employees. Theresa Martinez called AGCU "the best learning experience I've had. I learned as much in those few days as I have in all of the other training experiences I've had combined." In addition to functional training, Alagasco was one of the first corporations to offer AIDS education to their employees, in 1988.

Alagasco reimburses employees for two-thirds of the cost of furthering their education, pays for half of fitness-center memberships and two-thirds of the cost of buying a personal computer (up to $2,000). They have also made an effort to promote women and minorities. Twenty-five percent of upper management is female, while 6 percent is black (23 percent of the work force is black).

Warren told his employees that to become one of the 100 best, they must have PRIDE. PRIDE is an acronym for Performance, Risk-taking, Innovation, Determination, and Enthusiasm. Employee morale is refired annually in a "We Take PRIDE" celebration, an indoor picnic held every summer since 1986. All employees and their families are bused into Birmingham for the event. The employees who have to work the Saturday of the picnic are treated to a special breakfast.

Another program that raised employee morale is Operation Assist. Alagasco hired 1,600 inner-city teenagers and weatherized the homes of 50,000 low-income customers between 1985 and 1991. Twenty-five Alagasco employees were reassigned to work on Operation Assist each summer, and 600 employees served as vocational advisors to the teenagers. Hazel Wheat, credit supervisor in Tuscaloosa, said: "Even at work you need caring personal relationships. I think that's what this whole program is about, passing on a knowledge of business but showing that you can care about people at the same time."

The sense of caring is palpable here. Engineer Tom Raines, with the company for 34 years, told us his story: "Five years ago I was in an accident and was burned severely. The first person I saw in the emergency room was Mike Warren. I was concerned about getting word to my wife and making sure she didn't get scared to death and things like that. He assured me that somebody would pick her up and get her to the hospital. And he told me if there was anything the company could do, they would do it. As a matter of fact, they put my wife up in the Hilton right next to the hospital, and my children that came from out of town, they put them up in the Hilton and gave them meal tickets and took care of all their needs while I spent two weeks in the burn unit. Most companies wouldn't do that."

Types of jobs: Clerical—34 percent; management—17 percent; craft—19 percent; operations—14 percent; technical—8 percent; service—5 percent; professional—3 percent.

Main employment centers: Alagasco has eight district offices in central Alabama.

Headquarters: Alabama Gas Corporation
2101 Sixth Ave. N.
Birmingham, AL 35203
(205) 326-8100

MOST STRONGLY UNIONIZED

Alagasco
Avis
Anheuser-Busch
Armstrong
Cooper Tire
Corning
Cummins Engine
John Deere
General Mills
Hershey Foods
Inland Steel
Johnson & Johnson
Kellogg
Knight-Ridder
Lyondell Petrochemical
Merck
Northwestern Mutual Life
Preston Trucking
J. M. Smucker
Southwest Airlines
U S West
Weyerhaeuser
Xerox

Anheuser-Busch

 ANHEUSER-BUSCH COMPANIES

Anheuser-Busch brews more beer than anyone else in the world, ranks as one of the nation's leading bread bakers, operates 10 theme parks, and owns the St. Louis Cardinals. U.S. employees 45,000.

★ ★ ★ ★	Pay/Benefits
★ ★ ★	Opportunities
★ ★ ★ ★	Job Security
★ ★ ★ ★ ★	Pride in Work/Company
★ ★ ★	Openness/Fairness
★ ★ ★ ★	Camaraderie/Friendliness

BIGGEST PLUS: Barrels of vacation time.
BIGGEST MINUS: This Bud may not be for you.

If braggadocio is what you are looking for, you've come to the right place. The brewer of Budweiser is as pugnacious as a company comes, always ready to put up its dukes. And in the barroom brawls that have characterized the beer industry, the Anheuser-Busch people have generally managed to score knockouts. They keep rolling out the barrels, determined to crush Miller, Coors, and anyone else who thinks he can sell beer to Americans. They have long been tigers about the quality of their brews, and they have long been elephants when it comes to promoting them—they crush opponents with advertising dollars. So if you want to join this juggernaut, you better like beer and be ready to promote it as a magical elixir that attracts a bevy of beautiful women. Beer is real serious business here.

Anheuser-Busch also has a reputation as one of the best employers in its hometown of St. Louis. Don Orf didn't know how good a reputation it had until the first Christmas after he was hired as a corporate buyer. He received a Christmas card from someone he had known only slightly from his previous job. "I opened up the card and a résumé fell out," Orf told us. "And there was a note on the back of the card saying, 'If there's an opening, even for a programmer, would you please forward my résumé and ask them to consider me?' "

Getting unsolicited résumés comes with the territory if you work here. Employees say that when they tell others that they work for Anheuser-Busch, the first question people ask is whether they are hiring. The same story in reverse can be heard from executive recruiters in the St. Louis area who reportedly get very excited if somebody from A-B indicates a willingness to leave the company, because it happens so rarely.

Anheuser-Busch's superlative reputation stems partly from offering high-paying jobs and a rich benefits package. And these jobs have been secure because even though U.S. beer consumption has been flat, A-B has steadily increased its market share. Indeed, a big plus of working here is that you are with a winner. Joyce Jasper, an executive secretary, told us: "I've worked most of my entire working career here at A-B. I worked for three years for another company and there was no comparison. A-B is a winning team and it's great to be a part of that winning team." Debbie Rogers, food technologist, said: "It makes me feel proud to be working here. It makes me feel like I want to do better. I want to be a part of the picture."

Employees have reason to be proud of A-B's record. Led by its flagship brand, Budweiser, the company is the largest brewer in the world and has been first in the United States since 1957. When we visited here in 1983, A-B held 34 percent of the American beer market; in 1992 it had 44 percent. Next in line is Miller Brewing, with 22 percent. The A-B steamroller has no plans to slow down. They hope to grab 50 percent of the market by 1995 by aggressive marketing of both old and new brews. In 1980 A-B produced five brands of beer; now there are 17. New brands have included Bud Light, Michelob Dry, Bud Dry, and O'Doul's, a nonalcoholic malt beverage introduced in 1990. This growth has led to more breweries. At the end of 1992, A-B had 12 breweries scattered across the country. A thirteenth was scheduled to open in Cartersville, Georgia, in 1993.

Aside from their heavy ad campaigns (more than $600 million a year on their brews), A-B employees strongly believe that the key to their success is quality. Bottler Ray Kickel said: "They make an excellent product. I think that's one thing we have a lot of pride in, the product. They're number one and they love it and they want to stay number one. It's a good feeling working for a place that's number one."

While quality has long been a byword of A-B's culture, employee involvement is a relatively recent phenomenon. In fact, a number of lower-level employees say that they used to feel left off this winning team until recent years. Brad Wood, a bottler in the St. Louis plant, said that the changes in the management's attitudes at headquarters have been slow to move into the plants: "Over in the plant it's just starting to filter down. We are starting to get new managers who are working with us. They want the plant to be more efficient and the workers to be happier. Before, you didn't see that. Now I enjoy coming to work. I didn't used to. They want to help out and they want to do everything to make it easier for everybody."

Just as teamwork has improved, so has communication from upper management to those in the lower ranks. Since the mid-1970s when he became CEO, August Busch III, great-grandson of the founder, has made it a practice to have annual meetings with groups of employees throughout the company. Every question is recorded. Most are answered on the spot, but for the ones that require follow-up, the name of the person who asked the question is noted and he or she gets a written response. Many of the questions and answers are printed in the company newsletter, the *Anheuser-Busch Eagle*. Plant managers also hold quarterly meetings with all their plant employees.

Greater employee involvement does not mean that someone other than a Busch family member is likely to rise to the top of this company. At least it hasn't happened in 130 years. The family that founded Anheuser-Busch in St. Louis in 1860 has produced five generations of leaders—and a sixth, August A. Busch IV, is in line to succeed his father. In 1990, at age 25, August IV was put in charge of the national launch of a new brand, Bud Dry. To make sure he wouldn't miss, they gave him an ad budget of $70 million. Such family continuity in an American company is highly unusual. No other major American company has a family management that goes back so long. In *Under the Influence*, an unauthorized biography of the Busch family (the company offered zero cooperation), Peter Hernon and Terry Ganey, two *St. Louis Post-Dispatch* reporters, pointed out: "While many scions and heirs of other huge fortunes have disappeared or have dissipated or squandered their fortunes and their companies, the Busches have endured through five tumultuous generations. The best among them have matched anyone's standard of hard work and pride of product. They have minded the store. Above all, they have remained true to their calling. They made beer—and if anyone thought that was too common or plebian, to hell with them."

This strong family heritage colors the workplace here. It's not the benign paternalism that holds forth at Hallmark Cards and Johnson Wax, but it is, in its own way, a source of pride to the people who work for the brewery. This is a pumped-up place. We remember the article that Bill Mueller, editor of the *Anheuser-Busch Eagle*, wrote eight years ago declaring: "I wonder if anyone else out there ever feels like I do when I see an Anheuser-Busch commercial. Sure, all the commercials make me proud to be a part of A-B, but the Christmas spot with the Clydesdales especially gives me a chill."

Busch family members are the biggest holders of A-B stock, but employees have been accumulating shares under stock-ownership plans that go back to the 1970s. In 1992 nearly three-quarters of the 45,000 people who worked for the Anheuser-Busch Companies owned stock. In the brewing company, 88 percent were stockholders. Lee Waltemade, vice-president of human resources, told us: "Some of the hourly folks in the St. Louis plant invested in the ESOP right off the bat, and their individual accounts are now in excess of $200,000. And that's in a span of less than 15 years." The huge payoff stemmed from the performance of A-B's stock, whose value went up by more than 10 times during the 1980s.

The people who work for Anheuser-Busch are well paid. In 1991 the average wage in the entire company was $50,000. The brewery workers are represented by the Teamsters, and their average hourly wage in 1992 was $18.95, with a boost to $19.45 an hour scheduled for March 1993. The unionized brewery employees also get great vacation benefits: four weeks after five years, six weeks after 10 years, and eight weeks after 15 years. On top of that, they get 15 paid holidays and six paid sick days a year. If they don't use the sick days, they can be cashed in at the end of the year.

Until 1981 Anheuser-Busch offered another perk—all the beer you could drink on the job. August Busch III stopped the practice, offering instead two free cases (24 cans or bottles each) of A-B products every month. For those who don't drink alcohol, the company offers two cases of O'Doul's.

In St. Louis in particular, where they own the St. Louis Cardinals, Anheuser-Busch has a good reputation for its philanthropy. They encourage their employees to be active in civic programs and civic affairs, and will make contributions to the organizations that their employees are involved in. They contribute over $25 million a year to hospitals, universities, symphonies, and other nonprofits. Executive vice-president Jerry Ritter said: "This company is bigger than life in St. Louis. And all of us are proud of that. The company gets the credit for being the most responsive, doing more for the community than anyone else in the city. It makes us feel good that we're thought of that way. And we get a little more respect from our peers and from our social acquaintances because we work here."

Thanks to the profits that have flowed from beer, Anheuser-Busch is more than St. Louis today—and more than beer. The Anheuser-Busch Companies include Dallas-based Campbell-Taggart, one of the nation's largest bakery companies; Eagle Snacks, third behind Frito-Lay and Borden in salted snacks; and Busch Entertainment Corp., a major theme park operator with Busch Gardens, Sea World, Cypress Gardens, Adventure Island, and Sesame Place. In 1992 the St. Louis Cardinals celebrated their 100th birthday. They have been owned by A-B since 1953.

Of the 45,000 people who work for all the A-B companies, only 20,000 are employed in the beer end of the business, which is the focus of our profile here. Beer is still the heart and soul of this company, and we were told that the companies outside the breweries do not have the same compensation and benefits package as in the breweries.

To counter the increasing social concern about the adverse effects of alcohol (more than 100,000 deaths a year are attributed to booze, including about 25,000 from drunk driving alone), Anheuser-Busch launched a major advertising campaign, spending about $1.5 million a year to support the message, "Know when to say when." The campaign is part of Anheuser-Busch's efforts to forestall increased labeling requirements on alcohol, comparable to the health warnings that the government has forced cigarette makers to carry. When Congress sought to double the excise tax on alcohol in 1990, Anheuser-Busch asked its employees to help lobby against it. Though that effort failed, Anheuser-Busch tells employees that they might be enlisted to help lobby against other threats to their industry.

Types of jobs: Brewery—44 percent; food products—44 percent; theme parks—8 percent; other (baseball, property management, transportation, and creative services)—4 percent.

Main employment centers: Breweries operate in St. Louis; Newark, New Jersey; Los Angeles; Jacksonville and Tampa, Florida; Houston; Columbus, Ohio; Merrimack, New Hampshire; Williamsburg, Virginia; Fairfield, California; Baldwinsville, New York; Fort Collins, Colorado; and Cartersville, Georgia. The company also operates can manufacturing plants in Jacksonville and Gainesville, Florida; Columbus, Ohio; and Arnold, Missouri. Anheuser-Busch also runs four Sea World parks in Orlando, San Diego, San Antonio, and Aurora, Ohio, and four theme parks in Tampa, Williamsburg, Dallas/Fort Worth, and Langhorne, Pennsylvania; and it's the proud owner of baseball's St. Louis Cardinals, nine-time winner of the World Series. A-B owns the nation's second largest baker, Campbell Taggart, which is headquartered in Dallas and operates more than 67 plants in the United States and Europe.

Headquarters: Anheuser-Busch Companies
One Busch Place
St. Louis, MO 63118
(314) 577-2000

Apogee Enterprises

Apogee Enterprises comprises a group of companies involved primarily in the fabrication, installation, and distribution of glass products. U.S. employees: 5,225.

★ ★ ★   Pay/Benefits
★ ★   Opportunities
★ ★   Job Security
★ ★ ★   Pride in Work/Company
★ ★ ★   Openness/Fairness
★ ★ ★ ★   Camaraderie/Friendliness

BIGGEST PLUS: A conglomerate with a personal touch.
BIGGEST MINUS: Glass is a fragile business.

The headquarters of Apogee Enterprises would not impress anyone. It was, when we visited there in 1991, a cramped, 6,800-square-foot space on the 19th floor of an ordinary-looking 24-story office building located just off state highway 494 in Bloomington, 12 miles southwest of Minneapolis. The furnishings were simple, and individual offices, including the one occupied by CEO Don Goldfus, were modest. Only 19 people worked here in 1992. This unostentatious style is in keeping with the way Apogee runs its businesses, which include glass shops to replace broken windshields and companies that fabricate glass and put up the curtainwalls that frame buildings. Apogee itself makes nothing. It's basically a holding company. But we were impressed by the warm feelings that sweep through the companies that make up the Apogee family. Among these units are Harmon Contract, Harmon Glass, Viracon, Marcon, and Wausau Metals. The most visible of the Apogee companies, to the consumer, is Harmon Glass. It has 275 automotive glass replacement shops in 33 states.

Typically, holding companies are financially driven, empire-building devices that focus narrowly on hard numbers. That's not the case with Apogee. Don Goldfus, who grew up in a poor neighborhood on the north side of Minneapolis and never graduated from college, is a very down-to-earth leader who has great rapport with the people who work in the operating companies. He joined Harmon Glass in 1959.

Now head of a company doing nearly $600 million a year, Goldfus defined for us the role of Apogee: "Our job is to explain what Apogee is and what we bring to the table. That is what I do. I go out and I talk a lot about what makes us different from our competitors and what kinds of standards we have and value systems. It's getting to be a very difficult job because when I started doing this, we had less than 100 employees, and now we have over 5,000." Goldfus still gets out to see the troops "as often as I can. For sure every week, someplace, even if it's just in the Twin Cities area, but I'm out there all the time, that is part of the job. I am the flag bearer for this Apogee concept, which is a difficult act because people do become very parochial about their area."

Goldfus said he has had many employees tell him "the reason they like working for us is because we know them. This really sounds simple, but it's amazing. I had a glazier one time, and we had a little get-together, and we were drinking a cup of coffee, and he said, 'I really love this company.' Now, this is one big rough guy. And I said, 'Why is that, Dan?' And he said, 'Because you know me.' This is the kind of thing I don't tell the security analysts because they'll think, 'Boy, is this guy soft.' But it was so emotional. He said, 'I've worked for all the glazing companies in town and I never knew the owner. Here we are in this big company and you know me personally.' What he was saying was, 'You have some respect for me as an individual. I have dignity.' "

Perhaps the most powerful force at Apogee is the strong sense of belonging. The company has been practicing employee involvement here long before the term was coined. The inside cover of the 1991 annual report said: "We don't believe in bureaucracy. Apogee's hallmark is decentralized management, and decisions are made as close to the customer as possible." Apogee has a track record for backing people who have ideas. In 1969 it supported a 29-year-old glass salesman, Jim Martineau, who saw an opportunity in glass fabrication. The division he started, Viracon, is now the nation's leading supplier of glass for commercial and institutional buildings. In 1987, in an interview in the American Management Association magazine, *Management Review*, Goldfus said: "The key word around here is trust. We subscribe to the Pygmalion Theory, or high-expectations management. We attract and hire people who want to be in business for themselves and put the financial strength of Apogee behind them. I can't possibly run all of these companies. Why, I don't know if I could run any of them. So you need people out there who will run them. That's the power of the system."

The people we talked to confirmed that this is how Apogee works. Larry Anderson, president of Harmon Glass, said: "We're entrusted, we're believed in as individuals that we have got something to offer and it's up to us to encourage that environment so the maximum number of people can live out their dreams." Anderson is a good example of Apogee values. A farm boy from Thief River Falls in Minnesota, he became a CPA without the benefit of a four-year college degree, and he joined Apogee in 1970 because he was impressed with its ethical standards. In his interview with former company president Russ Baumgardner, Anderson was told that "we pay the taxes that are due. We don't pay more than we owe, but we never cheat the government. And as long as we're on the subject: we never cheat our suppliers, or our employees, or our customers. If you cheat any of those people, you don't belong with Apogee." Recalls Anderson: "I really liked that message."

A nine-year employee, Bill Wiberg, told us: "They turn you loose and let you go ahead and do it." Benefits manager Pat Lamont added: "You can be what you want to be." And Rick Kraus, human resources director for Viracon/Curvlite, a unit that makes laminated automotive glass, explained that to work at Apogee "you have to have tolerance for a high degree of ambiguity. They'll tell you the objective, but you decide how you want to do that." Kraus noted that there is "a sign that we have had framed in our training room: 'Those closest to the work know the most about the work.' Managers know that they can't make the final decision without talking to the workers, or it's trouble. They want to participate in decisions that affect them, whether it's buying a new piece of equipment or staffing a new production line or whatever."

Many of the companies in this book owe their values to a legacy left by people who founded or built the business. Apogee is one of them. The company was born in 1949 as Harmon Glass, taking its name from the first location: 1112 Harmon Place in downtown Minneapolis. There were three founding partners, but two were gone within a year. The mainstay of the enterprise was Harold Burrows, a burly installer of automobile windshields who regularly worked 16 hours a day. He was joined in the early 1950s by a young St. Paul lawyer, Russ Baumgardner, who had invested $10,000 to keep Harmon afloat and who had also stepped in to buy the shares of the two partners no longer with the business. He ended up owning 70 percent of Harmon Glass, and according to the story told in *Windows of Opportunity*, a corporate history published in 1989: "This division of ownership didn't sit well with Russ Baumgardner. 'I'll tell you what we're going to do,' Baumgardner said to Burrows one day. 'I'm going to sell 20 percent of the company to you for $100. That way we'll be equal partners.' Later Baumgardner would explain, 'It didn't seem fair that Harold should own 30 percent of the company when he did 90 percent of the work.' "

That's one of the stories that make up the Russ Baumgardner legend at Apogee. He built up the company by hiring people and then giving them their head to find new opportunities. "Expect performance and you'll get it" was one of his mottos. Still another was: "I have a high tolerance for mistakes." Glass installer Harold Burrows retired from the company in 1963, and in 1968 Baumgardner renamed the company Apogee Enterprises, taking the name from an investment club to which he once belonged. He paid $1 for the right to use the name.

Wages at Apogee companies averaged $30,000 per employee in 1991. The top earner, at $312,500, was Goldfus. Incentive programs are widely in use at all levels. Sue Zufall, a customer service representative for Harmon Glass, said there is a shop-by-shop bonus plan. "If we hit so much over our budget, each person—not only the customer service rep but the shop installers as well—gets a bonus check. So there is an incentive to strive and work hard." Jim Carino, a plant manager at Viracon/Curvlite, told us that a bonus check is distributed "quarterly based on the performance of the individual plant. On average this year [1991], each of our employees is going to receive probably $2,000 in payouts." Viracon/Curvlite is a leading maker of replacement windshields for foreign cars.

Les Smith, an assistant manager at a Harmon Glass shop in Minneapolis, said that "we keep installers forever" because no one in the business pays a higher wage.

Apogee has a more broadly dispensed stock-option plan than most companies. In 1992 options were awarded to 490 people, including nonsupervisory employees. No-cost stock options enable the holders to profit from any appreciation in the price of Apogee shares. However, the most attractive incentive is reserved for the top 20 people in the company, who participate in a partnership plan under which they can defer up to half their bonus pay; this money is used to buy Apogee stock—and the company matches this purchase by contributing an equal number of shares. All employees can participate in a 401(k) savings plan under which Apogee will contribute 30 cents for every pretax dollar saved by an employee up to 6 percent of pay.

It's easy to be benevolent when sales and profits are steaming upward, as they were at Apogee during the 1980s. The company quadrupled in size during that decade. But the recession of 1991 tested the company. Apogee is heavily dependent on the construction business, which was in the doldrums. And the automotive glass business also deteriorated under pressure from insurance companies looking for cheaper installations. With two main prongs of its business under attack, Apogee saw profits decline by 50 percent. Two units in the West were closed, rendering 100 people jobless, and another 90 employees were laid off at Wausau Metals, an aluminum window fabricator in Wausau, Wisconsin.

However, most Apogee units did not resort to layoffs, and in August 1992 Goldfus told us that most of the 90 people laid off at Wausau had been recalled. Apogee has a long tradition of continuous employment, but the collapse of the commercial construction market hit like a sledge-hammer. Goldfus said that during this rough period the Apogee companies did try to continue to be mindful of employee needs, although, as he said, "we do have the shareholders to think about, too." Executive salaries at Apogee were cut by a third in 1991. The company's 1992 annual report featured "four ways to managing through a slowdown," none of them call-ing for work force reductions. More than 120 people have been here more than 20 years, which is amazing considering the fact that two-thirds of the employees were hired *after* 1980. And Don Goldfus knows many of those people. Benefits specialist Pat Lamont told us how the company once sent a mailing to employees announcing a new benefit. "I sent them all in for Don to sign," she said, "and they came back, many of them with handwrit-ten notes saying, 'His name is Wendell, but we call him Corky.' 'His name is Grant but we all call him Pete.' He knew all these people. They're all over the United States and he knows them and really cares about them."

Types of jobs: Factory and shop labor—75.6 percent; administration—11.9 percent; sales and marketing—6.4 percent; engineering—3.5 percent; man-agement—2.6 percent.

Main employment centers: Apogee has 941 employees at the window fab-rication facility in Wausau, Wisconsin; 981 employees in glass fabrication facilities in Owatonna, Minnesota, and Chicago, and over 2,000 employees in installation and distribution centers and sales offices throughout the United States.

Headquarters: Apogee Enterprises, Inc.
7900 Xerxes Ave. S.
Minneapolis, MN 55431
(612) 835-1874

BEST EMPLOYEE PUBLICATIONS

Leo Burnett
Hallmark Cards
Hewlett-Packard
IBM
Lotus Development
Merck
Publix Super Markets

Armstrong

Armstrong makes floor coverings (carpet and tile), ceilings, building products, and furniture. U.S. employees: 19,300.

★★★ Pay/Benefits
★★★★ Opportunities
★★★★ Job Security
★★★ Pride in Work/Company
★★★ Openness/Fairness
★★★★ Camaraderie/Friendliness

BIGGEST PLUS: You won't get the carpet pulled out from under you.
BIGGEST MINUS: You can't get to the ceiling without starting on the floorings.

When Bill Adams talks with groups of new employees at Armstrong Manor, he tells them that employees should never be asked to do something at Armstrong that they consider to be wrong. If that happens, Armstrong's CEO wants them to call him directly so that he can take care of the situation personally. He then gives them his personal phone number.

If you come to work here, you can be sure that ethics is not going to be treated lightly. Headquartered in the middle of Pennsylvania Dutch country, Armstrong looks for people who want to work for a company that still believes in old-fashioned values like honesty and integrity. They trace this concern to the middle of the 19th century, when founder Thomas Armstrong built his cork business on the slogan "Let the buyer have faith" in an era where most businesses operated according to the standard of "Let the buyer beware."

New employees can expect to be reminded of such traditions wherever they work in this Fortune 500 company, which has plants and offices throughout the world. But newly hired marketing and professional employees get especially heavy doses of the Armstrong history during their three-month training at the Armstrong Manor, a red brick farmhouse located a few miles from corporate headquarters. The manor serves as part dormitory, part training center. The last six presidents of Armstrong, including Bill Adams (class of '56), are graduates of Armstrong Manor. So are the five top executives and six of the company's 18 vice-presidents. Some still have their names engraved above the beds in third-floor dorm rooms.

This is a company where such traditions are important because people tend to stay around a long time. Management accountant Joe Haldeman explains: "When you come here, you're not really just coming for a specific job. I think we tend to look at it as if you're coming to really build a career with the company."

Because of this career orientation, many employees see the company as more than a place to spend their working hours. According to engineering administrative services supervisor Karen Donnelly: "I do think that a lot of people work hard for this company. But we are also encouraged to have fun. We have an engineering association, where we get together on a fairly regular basis. We have a picnic in the summer, a Christmas party in the winter, regular monthly meetings in between. And we have good turnouts because people get along very well with one another."

Celebrations like these are common here. Lancaster employees even have a Christmas songfest where they sing their own carol, "A Holiday Wish," which was written by an Armstrong employee. On other occasions they gather for square dancing, family movie nights, bowling, craft shows, and family outings to nearby Hershey Park.

Despite its old-fashioned flavor, Armstrong has become the nation's largest flooring and ceiling manufacturer by being aggressively up-to-date. Organization development manager Joe Rempe said: "It may seem a little sleepy here to some. But I'm sure our competitors would not say we're very sleepy. I compare Armstrong to Garrison Keillor's Lake Wobegon, where all the children are slightly above average. I don't think Armstrong is a corporation of geniuses. We're like the Lake Wobegon kids. We're slightly above average and we try awfully hard and we get along together very well."

Armstrong has a long history of promotion from within, so they do not directly recruit or hire for management positions from outside. In the 1920s, they began recruiting on college campuses, and they continue to regard colleges and universities as the major source for hiring of entry-level salaried positions, including sales and marketing, engineering, business information services, research and development, and accounting. Over the past several years, they have hired 70 to 75 college graduates a year. In 1992 the entry-level wage for someone with a bachelor's degree in a nontechnical field was just under $30,000. For someone with a bachelor's degree in industrial, electrical, mechanical, or chemical engineering, the starting salary can range from nearly $35,000 to almost $40,000.

To keep themselves up-to-date, Armstrong employs 700 people at the 620-acre Armstrong Innovation Center near Lancaster, which includes research and development, engineering, product styling and design, and a marketing development center.

Like many other major corporations, Armstrong became deeply involved in the quality movement during the 1980s. Outgoing-mail supervisor Mid Gockley told us: "When we used to get jobs, you weren't allowed to question anything. Now you can challenge everybody and say, 'Don't you think you should do it this way? You could save the company money doing this,' and so forth. It made us feel more part of the company."

Henry Overly, a production supervisor in the flooring plant, agrees: "Supervision has changed quite a bit in the last seven years. It's more of a cooperative-type situation now rather than me just telling people to do this or that. I think we work together more as a unit."

A recent company newsletter touted the success of the quality program in turning around the Jackson, Mississippi, tile plant that the company had considered closing in the 1970s. Employees there now rotate jobs, run their own meetings, and select their own training courses. Jackson plant finishing operator Cornelius Walker told *Armstrong World*: "I like that I'm trusted to do a good job, without anyone looking over my shoulder. I want to return that trust by doing the best job I can."

Armstrong's management tries hard to maintain this sense of trust. There is no executive dining room, and executives, including the CEO, often eat in the large employee cafeteria with workers from the flooring plant adjacent to the corporate offices. In 1989 Canada's Belzberg family made an effort to take over Armstrong. The company fought the takeover and eventually won. After the battle, Armstrong created an employee stock-ownership plan so that employees now own almost 15 percent of the company's stock.

During the takeover fight Armstrong went out of its way to keep employees informed. They received a constant stream of information. According to CEO Bill Adams: "In the absence of signals from management, people will supply their own. What we did was to supply copies of all relevant material written about the situation, pro or con, good or bad, including some terrible stuff that was inaccurate. But we said, 'We want you to read this and make up your own mind on it.' I think I can say that's behind us in part because of the way we handled it. I hope that people felt that they were trusted. And the one word I'd like to think characterizes this company is trust: trust us that we're doing the right thing; trust us, we'll keep you informed; trust that we're not going to tell you deep, dark secrets because they wouldn't be secrets anymore. And they understand that."

Perhaps because of the high degree of trust, Armstrong has been somewhat paternalistic in employee advancement. There is no companywide job posting system. So employees must rely on their annual job performance appraisals to make known their desires for new opportunities. They are equally old-fashioned when it comes to flexible hours. According to human resources planning analyst Dave Bendit: "Our lunch hour is variable, let's just put it that way. We have to be at work between 8:30 and 4:30. Flex hours would be the next step. But Armstrong is a conservative company and I'm not sure we're quite ready for that yet." Armstrong does, however, have a job-sharing program. In the customer response center, there are 23 employees who share jobs.

Along with the sense of trust comes a genuine caring attitude. Senior research technician Alex Vazquez told us his story: "My son was really ill one time. And I told my manager, 'I need some time to be with my son.' They gave me the time. They always kept in touch with me to see how things were. They gave me the time to go to the doctor."

Types of jobs: Production—88 percent; marketing—5 percent; research, engineering, and design—4 percent; business information services—1 percent; financial services—1 percent.

Main employment centers: Armstrong has 68 plants in 21 states and 22 countries. There are 4,500 employees in Lancaster, Pennsylvania, and 2,800 in Thomasville, North Carolina. About 4,700 Armstrong employees work outside the United States.

Headquarters: Armstrong World Industries, Inc.
P.O. Box 3001
Lancaster, PA 17604
(717) 397-0611

Avis

Avis is the world's second largest car rental company. U.S. employees: 13,000.

★ ★ ★ Pay/Benefits
★ ★ ★ ★ ★ Opportunities
★ ★ ★ ★ Job Security
★ ★ ★ ★ Pride in Work/Company
★ ★ ★ ★ Openness/Fairness
★ ★ ★ ★ Camaraderie/Friendliness

BIGGEST PLUS: You own the place.
BIGGEST MINUS: Owners work harder.

Two abbreviations—ESOP and EPG—tell the Avis story. Avis's ESOP (employee stock-ownership plan) owns the company, making it one of the largest employee-owned firms in the United States. Avis has trumpeted this fact in its advertising since 1987, when the employees bought the company. "At Avis Inc., our employees are acting like they own the place" and "Now when you rent from Avis Inc., you can deal directly with the owners" were two of these ads. And EPGs (employee participation groups) demonstrate why employee ownership is more than a catchy slogan at a company that coined one of the catchiest slogans in corporate America ("We try harder").

To understand the significance of ESOP and EPG at Avis, a little history is in order. Warren Avis founded this company in 1946 with the then novel idea of renting cars at airports. The company prospered, but employees had little sense of stability as the firm was constantly changing owners: Lazard Freres (1962), ITT (1972), Norton Simon (1977), Esmark (1983), Beatrice

(1984), Kohlberg Kravis Roberts (1985), and Wesray (1986)—a total of 11 different owners since 1954, including five in the five years before it became employee-owned.

Virginia Europe, who has worked in central billing at the Long Island headquarters since 1971, told us: "We changed owners like we changed our overcoats. We had a few Black Fridays, where people were laid off with no warning. And there was always that fear of, 'Gee, I wonder when the next one's coming down the road.' But since the ESOP that feeling has completely disappeared. Even in this recession that we're in, I've never heard layoffs mentioned or talked about."

From the management viewpoint, revolving-door ownership created a lot of problems. Tim Shanley, vice-president of financial planning and analysis, explained: "Certain decisions were being made by people who didn't understand the industry. We were a cash cow to them, and the decisions were being made for the sake of taking cash out of Avis. We had been very successful, but it all went to somebody else's pocket, not to the success of Avis."

Fortunately, Avis's last owner, Wesray, was willing to sell the firm to the employees. Led by CEO and chairman Joseph Vittoria, the employees bought the firm through an ESOP for $1.75 billion on September 25, 1987. Vittoria reserved about 15 percent of the stock for top managers. The other 85 percent was distributed among the other employees.

Employees like owning the company. Jay Jackson, who works in airlines marketing, said: "When a company is owned by employees, it provides you with a certain amount of security. It's like a family business. You have a part of the rock. You make decisions that make that company run."

Under the ESOP, each employee gets a certain number of shares every year based on the company's profits and his or her income. This stock can be a valuable benefit. In 1992 each employee got 6.5 shares of stock for each $1,000 in pay. So someone earning $20,000 would have received $2,714 in stock, or the equivalent of a bonus of nearly 14 percent. The stock has also been going up in value. A share in 1987 was worth $5.22; in 1992 it had risen to $20.88. Gerald McCormick, vice-president of compensation and benefits, estimates that a person who started in 1987 making $15,000 a year would have stock worth $51,000 after 10 years of service, assuming a modest 5 percent a year increase in the stock's value. The employee's stock awards are *in addition* to benefits like health insurance, pensions, and discounts on used cars and car rentals. And while unionized employees are often excluded from ESOPs, the Avis ESOP applies to *all* Avis employees, including the 35 percent of the hourly workers who belong to unions. Starting wages for entry-level jobs are between $7 and $12.75 an hour.

But money is only part of the story. According to senior vice-president Robert Salerno: "When you talk to people, the money is only the icing on the cake, not what the enthusiasm really is about. It's not about getting the stock certificate once a year. It's about being able to sit down and say, 'I have an idea and this is what I think.' And somebody listens to them and takes action on it. The fact that you get some money on top of that, that's just gravy."

Every month Avis employees get a chance to submit their ideas on how to improve the company—at 2:00 P.M. on the first Thursday of each month, to be precise. At that time Avis managers and employees throughout the company have their EPG meetings. At the 80-plus field locations, each group of rental sales agents, shuttle bus drivers, and mechanics elects its own representative to attend these EPG meetings for one year. These "quality leaders" in turn elect representatives to attend quarterly zone meetings, the semiannual regional meetings, and the annual EPG national meeting held at world headquarters on Long Island. About 20 elected employee-owners attend the annual meeting along with CEO Joseph Vittoria and other top managers.

Jay Jackson was impressed at how readily EPGs act on suggestions. After going through the company's orientation program, Jackson was still unclear about what each of the departments actually did. So, he says, "I went to my EPG group with the suggestion of putting together a directory that gives a blurb of what each department in this entire building does and make that available to the employees so that a fresh face can have an idea of what they're coming into. The idea was accepted, passed, and became a publication for this building."

Jackson contrasts Avis with his previous employer, Chase Manhattan Bank: "Chase tells you what they're going to do for the next quarterly period—and what part you'll play in that if you'll play any part at all. It's a dictatorship down. Here at Avis it's grass roots up."

EPGs generate literally hundreds of suggestions like Jackson's. Some other examples:

• In Hawaii, Avis's employee-owners decided that they wanted to dress in Hawaiian clothing. So they designed their own outfits (using Avis red and white colors), found a manufacturer in Hawaii, and now the uniforms include muumuus and Hawaiian tropical print shirts.

• In New York, EPGs developed a "job swap" program in which employees at the local airports and the world headquarters swapped jobs for short periods to learn more about each other's work.

• Avis sales staffers suggested saving on transaction fees by using an internal charge card instead of American Express when they rented Avis cars for their sales calls. Result: annual savings of $30,000 to $40,000.

Savings of $40,000 a year have real meaning for Avis employee-owners because they translate into higher profits, which in turn means a higher pool for the ESOP stock awards given at the end of the year.

Some employees were skeptical when the EPGs were introduced. Marcos Santiago, a shuttle bus driver at New York's JFK airport, told *Newsday:* "At first I didn't believe in it. I thought it was another gimmick to make us work harder. But after five or six months you see a different ball game."

Ownership has also given employees more gumption to question management. *Fortune* quotes Fort Lauderdale district manager Dan Falvey: "If I as a district manager decide to get a new carpet for the office, employees will now come up to me and say, 'Wait a minute, how much is this costing us?' They're half kidding, but the whole message of the ESOP is that you are an owner. We pay off the debt—we own a piece of this company."

According to CEO Joe Vittoria, the EPG meetings are only one way employees have more control over their jobs: "At Avis, unless it's something very significant, the employee will take care of that issue right on the spot. They feel the customer is being honest and straightforward, and we'll support the employee. So it might cost us $25 or $50. What they understand is, it's costing them as well. Therefore they're not just going to do this to make the customer happy. They're going to do it because they feel it was justified. Since these are true owners of the company, they can actually make decisions on their own."

Dramatic as the changes at Avis have been since the ESOP was created and the EPGs started meeting, employees stressed that Avis already had a pleasant working environment. About one-third of all full-timers have been with the company over 10 years. Some ascribe the longevity to Avis's family-oriented environment. Audrey Rosemond, supervisor of centralized commission services, said: "I think there's a lot of closeness and bonding here because people work here so long that they really care about each other. They make a lot of friends so that they become like a family."

David Stark added: "The family feeling is not only in this building, it's in the field also." Stark, a real estate attorney, ascribed the camaraderie to the fact that "there is no 'elite class' that I find. Everyone's door is open. Ninety-nine percent of the time, it's on a first-name basis. If you have a problem, if you need to see a senior manager or a senior VP, they say, 'Come on in, what's the matter, sit down.' Normally, you'll get an answer on the spot. If you sit in the cafeteria and look around, you can see the top officers sitting there having lunch with the rest of us. It's very open-door, it's shirt-sleeve."

Avis's top managers are accessible in more formal ways as well. CEO Vittoria has been holding early morning all-employee meetings (called "Vittles with Vittoria") in the cafeteria for many years. According to JoAnna Cuocco, who has been with the company since 1966: "You got to get there early, though, because it's packed. It's strictly optional. And everyone still goes. Most of the company starts at 9:00. He gives his little speech at 8:00. It's packed by 8:00. They stand in the hallway, they stand all over, you can't get in. People come early just to hear him. He presents the financials, the same figures that they give to the bankers who lend us all our money to buy our fleet. We don't disclose that publicly. But Vittoria will stand up there and tell everybody here what we're doing. And he's very joyful. As far as I'm concerned, he seems to be very down-to-earth. Not a lot of companies see the president of their company. We know what he looks like. We know him. We could talk to him if we wanted to talk to him."

Vittoria and other top managers also meet regularly with rank-and-file employees when they visit rental sites and the big reservations office in Tulsa. The company also has an electronic mail system for registering complaints, ESOP hot lines to answer questions, and a "One More" program, a postage-paid postcard that can be sent directly to CEO Vittoria with suggestions. Vittoria also often blocks out two to three hours of time, or even whole days, for drop-in visitors.

Avis also has a strong tradition of promotion from within. A third of all managers started in entry-level jobs. Avis has a job posting program through an electronic mail system that lists entry-level management jobs throughout the country. According to Carol Riley of the human resources department: "If there's a shift manager job open in Atlanta, and some rental sales agent in Omaha is interested in it, he or she can apply for that position."

Because of these policies, Avis offers many opportunities for advancement. According to Virginia Europe: "I came to work here almost 19 years ago after I had raised my five children. I came through a temporary agency because I had no skills whatsoever. I came here for a three-month assignment and ended up being hired as a grade-two clerk. And here I am still here 19 years later, and very happy. I enjoy what I do. I'm comfortable with the people I work with. I'm so comfortable here that I refuse to retire."

Types of jobs: Field operations—80 percent; sales and marketing—11 percent; staff—8 percent.

Main employment centers: 1,100 work at Avis headquarters on Long Island, New York. Another 1,025 work at their reservations center in Tulsa, Oklahoma. There are Avis field offices in every major airport in the country.

Headquarters: Avis Rent A Car System, Inc.
900 Old Country Rd.
Garden City, NY 11530
(516) 222-3000

Baptist Hospital of Miami

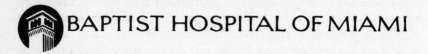

BAPTIST treats more patients than any other private hospital in the Miami area. Employees: 2,200.

★★★ Pay/Benefits
★★★★ Opportunities
★★★★★ Job Security
★★★★ Pride in Work/Company
★★★★ Openness/Fairness
★★★★ Camaraderie/Friendliness

BIGGEST PLUS: It looks more like a resort than a hospital.
BIGGEST MINUS: It's not stress free.

Nurse Mary Sue Nugent still remembers the first time she saw Baptist Hospital: "About 12 years ago I was driving down Kendall Drive and saw this pink hospital and palm trees and lakes, and I thought, 'What a beautiful place it would be to work there.'" Nugent had previously worked at hospitals in Illinois and in Washington, D.C., but had never seen a hospital like Baptist.

Indeed, Baptist looks more like a South Florida resort hotel than a big-city hospital. The first sign you see when entering the main driveway is "Slow—Duck Crossing," adjacent to one of the small lakes. The lake itself is encircled by a steady stream of joggers and walkers. The driveway leads to the Spanish-style main building with a colonnade surrounding a circular courtyard and a large fountain with a huge bronze pineapple in the middle. The pineapple is an ancient symbol of hospitality.

The first stop for many employees is Baptist's child-care center located behind the main building. Nearly 200 children are cared for by a staff of 31. Baptist has one of the country's oldest child-care centers. It opened in 1963 —*two decades* before most companies that consider themselves "pioneers" in the field were providing this benefit. Corey Gold, the center's director, was excited about a new benefit for sick children called "work and watch." Parents can take their sick children to the hospital's pediatrics ward at a cost of $1.25 an hour. Children who are not enrolled in the center can also be cared for under "work and watch" for $2.50 an hour. Another unusual feature of the center is that it is open from 6:30 A.M. to midnight, seven days a week.

Diana Phillips, a nurse from Scotland, had a six-month-old baby at the center when we visited. She said: "It has been a great source of peace of mind for me to have my child here on campus so that during my lunch break I can always go over and visit her."

Having peace of mind is important, because Baptist is one of the busiest hospitals in the state, serving 20,000 patients a year and another 50,000 in the emergency room. While many local hospitals are suffering from empty beds, Baptist has been turning away patients attracted by its reputation for high-quality care. It has been building new facilities on its 70-acre campus almost continuously since it was founded in 1956 by a group of Baptist ministers and laypeople on land donated by Arthur Vining Davis, former head of Alcoa. (Baptist cut its links with the Baptist Church in 1967, though five Baptist ministers still serve on the board.)

Baptist became even busier in August and September 1992 in the aftermath of Hurricane Andrew. The emergency room saw about 600 patients a day as opposed to the normal load of about 150. The hospital also came through for its own employees, about half of whom lost their homes as a result of the storm. More than 50 employees and their families actually lived in the hospital for several weeks, and others lived in campers and trailers on the hospital grounds. The hospital also provided workers with water and ice, food and clothing (including 60,000 pairs of underwear donated by Jockey), and raised more than $500,000 to help employees who needed help.

Even before the hurricane, Baptist had a hectic work environment. "There is never a dull moment around here," Cindy Mitchell, a secretary in the materials management department, told us. Mitchell likes the environment because "if there's one thing I don't like, it's to be bored." In a recent survey 82 percent of employees agreed with the statement "My job is very stressful," and 56 percent of employees agreed with the statement "Co-workers or those around me exhibit obvious signs of stress." The hospital has a stress task force, composed of a cross section of employees and managers, working on ways to relieve the pressures. They run an annual Less Stress Contest in which teams of employees can win gift certificates or have parties to celebrate new stress-relieving programs. Baptist also has a Less Stress Hot Line that operates 24 hours a day.

Though Baptist employees work hard, they still have time for fun. Anne Streeter, administrative director of women's services, explained: "It is legitimate to have fun here. It is institutionalized humor. I always love to see a new person come to department manager meetings because I know they are going to be in for it. It is probably nothing like they have ever been to because there are always at least two or three jokes. We make fun of each other."

Every month or so, Baptist sponsors a "monotony breaker day," where an auditorium is open for employees to socialize around such themes as Scottish poet Robert Burns's birthday (in January) or Spring Fling (in April) or Oktoberfest. These feature special menus and cafeteria entertainment (bagpipers for the Robert Burns event). Two free movie tickets are given as incentives to attend these gatherings. Three times a year Baptist puts on a Family Fun Night for employees' families and friends featuring free Disney movies and popcorn. They also set up trips to Orlando's Disney World, Epcot Center, and Universal Studios. The trips usually last a weekend and cost $100, which covers food, lodging, and admission.

Birthdays are big events here. Employees receive two free movie tickets and a card from Brian Keeley, the hospital's president, who explained: "There is so much stress and nasty things happening in the world, so we try to focus on some fun things. Celebrating a birthday requires zero energy but it invigorates everybody."

Keeley, who was 47 in 1992, joined the hospital as an administrative resident in 1972 and worked his way up to CEO in 1986. He said that Baptist makes a conscious effort to hire only "friendly" and "fun-loving" people. In the early 1980s, one of the nation's leading cardiovascular surgeons was working at Baptist. Keeley described him as having "tremendous dexterity and an IQ of 210, a walking encyclopedia, but when he is doing major open-heart surgery he is yelling at people, cursing, throwing his instruments against the wall like a little Hitler." According to Keeley: "Finally we said, 'Why do we allow people to act like little children?' So we decided we were just not going to tolerate things like that." The surgeon is no longer working at Baptist.

Employees talk about the friendly atmosphere. Child-care assistant Dorothy Mulley said: "You walk down the hallway and everybody has a greeting for you like 'Good morning' or 'Good afternoon,' always with a friendly smile." Environmental technician Eva Mae Fulton added: "The people are like one big family, the doctors, nurses, and everybody. I walk around the hospital and everybody is friendly. When you walk in the door, you can't smell it. You know how some hospitals have that smell when you get to the door. You don't have it here, this is the cleanest one ever." Secretary Lili Martin compares Baptist to her former employer, the University of Miami School of Medicine: "We are more like a family here. You know just about everybody by name."

Part of the family feeling Fulton and Martin are talking about is understandable. In 1991 there were 45 married couples working and close to 200 others who are related.

To inculcate the Baptist culture, new employees go through a training process. Baptist encourages all employees to think of the patients as "guests" and issues them wallet cards to remind them of how guests should be treated (see box). Vice-president Charlotte Dison explains: "We also defined a 'guest' as anyone whom we come in contact with, not only the visitors or vendors but patients' families, physicians, coworkers, volunteers." The standard they are seeking to achieve is that of Florida's only five-star hotel, the Ritz-Carlton, across the peninsula in Naples. They have even sent employees to spend a night at the Ritz to experience how guests are treated there.

Wallet Card Issued to Baptist Employees:

YOU ARE BAPTIST HOSPITAL

- You are what people see when they arrive here.
- Yours are the eyes they look into when they're frightened and lonely.
- Yours are the voices people hear when they ride the elevators, when they try to sleep and when they try to forget their problems.
- Yours are the comments people hear when you think they can't.
- Yours is the intelligence and caring that people hope they'll find here.
- No visitors, no patients can ever know the real you—unless you let them see it. All they can know is what they see and hear and experience.
- And so we have a stake in your attitude and in the collective attitudes of everyone who works at the hospital. We are judged by your performance. We are the care you give, the attention you pay, the courtesies you extend.

Thank you for all you're doing.

New employees attend a four-hour GREAT—Guest Relations Education and Training—session during their two-day orientation. This is followed by a two-and-a-half-hour refresher course, "Still GREAT," after they've been on the job for one year. The GREAT program started in the early 1980s and has been expanded to a number of other areas. There is a GREAT committee composed of 15 employees. It puts on the annual employee picnic and chooses the GREAT employee of the quarter, who receives a check for $250 and a parking space of his or her choice for a year. Employees can also nominate their coworkers for a Pineapple Award, which is instant recognition for a job well done.

The management ranks here are filled with people who started at the bottom. And women are well represented. Seventy-five percent of officials and managers are women, including three of the eight officers and three of the six vice-presidents. (Eighty percent of Baptist's employees are female.) Baptist received the Employer of the Year Award from the Florida Nurses Association for four out of the past five years. Nursing turnover is extremely low—with a vacancy rate of 4 percent versus the national average of 14 percent.

Barbara Russell, a nurse who has been promoted to director of infection control, said: "Many of us came through the ranks. You are encouraged and supported and given what you need to advance yourself, whether it is into management or just into more information in your specialty or whatever. There is tuition support and the like, but there is that other type of support here that you need from the management, which is always saying, 'Go for it! Go for it!' and 'What can we do to help you?' It is really nurturing."

Besides tuition support, Baptist offers a number of other benefits. Pay is good, ranking in the 90th percentile among local hospitals, according to vice-president Dison. Managers' compensation and advancement are tied to their evaluations by nonmanagement staff people.

Other advantages that come from working here include: a fitness center open 24 hours a day, seven days a week; free parking; a car wash; dry-cleaning service; and 50 percent discounts at local movie houses. Employees can also cash in unused sick days. Called the Holiday Bonus Option, 1,682 employees cashed in sick days worth $368,000 in 1990. In 1991, 300 employees had perfect attendance. Employees kick into a fund called the Sunshine Fund that is used to help other employees in need. Every dollar that an employee puts up is matched by the hospital. In the year ended June 30, 1991, the fund raised $35,290 and dispensed loans and gifts totaling $63,474—to employees in need.

Retirees also receive perks, according to personnel director Frank Stump: "When they leave Baptist Hospital they receive a hospital ID card, which allows them to continue to eat in the dining room and buy drugs at the pharmacy at the employee discount rate."

Benefits aside, many employees insist that the main attraction is the pride they feel in the work itself. In a recent survey 91 percent of employees agreed with the statement "I am trusted to do my job without someone unnecessarily checking on me." Medical technologist Kay Farris gave two examples: "Our ideas and our suggestions are taken seriously. My supervisor, Dr. George Karaboyas, has a very open and democratic way of handling the lab. At this time we are looking at replacing the workhorse of the laboratory. It is just a very important piece of equipment and we like it, but it is nearing the end of its useful life. So rather than just accept the opinion of the experts—which he does seek—he also asks our opinion."

Materials management director Frank Fernandez summed up feelings expressed by other employees: "I feel like I am getting challenged to do little things and to respond to new challenges and opportunities. We are allowed a lot of freedom. There is not some power that is watching over our shoulder to see what we do. We are allowed to make mistakes, and we do make mistakes and we learn from those mistakes. The level of autonomy that we have is quite remarkable. That makes us grow and be more confident in what we do."

Types of jobs: Professional—36 percent; clerical—22 percent; service—20 percent; technicians—16 percent; management—4 percent; laborers—2 percent.

Main employment center: Miami.

Headquarters: Baptist Hospital of Miami
8900 North Kendall Drive
Miami, FL 33176
(305) 596-1960

BEST FOR JOB SECURITY

Acipco
Alagasco
Donnelly
Erie Insurance
Federal Express
H. B. Fuller
Hallmark Cards
Haworth
Hewitt Associates
SC Johnson Wax
Lincoln Electric
Northwestern Mutual Life
Physio-Control
Rosenbluth International
Southwest Airlines
USAA
Worthington Industries

BE&K

BE&K is one of the nation's 25 largest construction companies, specializing in industrial process plants like pulp and paper mills, chemical plants, and steel mills. Employees: 6,000.

★ ★ ★ ★ Pay/Benefits
★ ★ ★ ★ Opportunities
    ★ ★ ★ Job Security
★ ★ ★ ★ Pride in Work/Company
★ ★ ★ ★ Openness/Fairness
★ ★ ★ ★ Camaraderie/Friendliness

BIGGEST PLUS: Soft hearts in a hard hat.
BIGGEST MINUS: Be prepared to move.

The construction industry is notoriously unstable. One day dozens or even hundreds of people are busily working on a project. The next day the project is built and most of those people are out on the streets looking for another job.

Here's a big contractor that tries to put some stability into that boom-and-bust cycle. For 20 years, BE&K has made it a policy to continue paying its construction supervisors during lulls between projects. Procurement manager Sam Nation said: "With other companies, when the job is over, if they don't have another immediate assignment, they may pay your medical benefits, but they don't pay your salary. BE&K pays their supervisors 80 percent of their salaries during an unassigned time. They give them the opportunity to be at home, take some time off."

Supervisors aren't the only ones given job security. In 1991, in the midst of a construction industry recession, BE&K became the first construction company to guarantee pay to hundreds of skilled craftsworkers. In return for having their pay guaranteed for a year, whether or not they actually worked, the craftsmen—electricians, pipefitters, carpenters, instrumentation technicians—promised to be at the beck and call of BE&K when projects came up. The offer was extended to 700 craftspeople—and 550, nine percent of them women, accepted. (They did, however, downsize their engineering department in 1992, affecting about 100 jobs that were not covered by the job guarantee. But even then BE&K went to extraordinary lengths not to throw people onto the streets, finding jobs for all but two people within the company or at other firms.)

Founded in 1972 by Peter Bolvig, Bill Edmonds, and Ted Kennedy, former vice-presidents at Rust Engineering in Birmingham, BE&K's initial contracts were to build pulp and paper mills. They have since branched out to design, construct, renovate, or maintain anything from industrial bakeries in Arkansas to oil and gas separation plants in Wyoming. BE&K owns engineering and construction subsidiaries throughout the South as well as in Finland and Luxembourg. Not one of BE&K's companies is unionized, which in recent years has led unions to picket their job sites in Minnesota and Maine.

BE&K has always gone about its business with a special attitude toward the people who work there. Michael Goodrich, BE&K's president, describes the philosophy as: "We take care of our own."

In 1990 BE&K became the first construction company to offer child care at a construction site. Their revolutionary center, called BEKare, is made of five modular units which are dismantled when the project is completed. It caters to the odd hours of construction workers who often work up to 12 hours a day. Six months after opening in Port Wentworth, Georgia, the center was caring for 65 children, from ages six months to 10 years, and was open 90 hours a week. Workers paid $51 a week for this care. In 1992 the center was moved to headquarters, where BE&K plans to build a permanent center on a nearby hilltop.

Largely because of its approach to child care, BE&K was listed among the top 16 companies in *Companies That Care: The Most Family-friendly Companies in America*, by Hal Morgan and Kerry Tucker. One woman told the authors: "This is my first construction job, and I don't think I could have taken it if they hadn't had the child-care center. The pay is better than at other jobs I've had too. And there's a chance to move up here."

BE&K has made their mark as the most hospitable construction company in the nation for women workers. Thanks to their recruiting and training efforts, BE&K boasts a 10 percent female work force in an industry where the average is 2 percent. A magazine once headlined a story about BE&K this way: "More Women Will Enter Construction if BE&K Has Anything to Do with It." Chairman Ted Kennedy told the authors of *Companies That Care* that because construction has become more mechanized, brute strength is no longer a basic requirement. "We found that women are actually better at some jobs, like welding, that require particularly dexterous handiwork," he said. BE&K plans to open a women's welding center at Saginaw, Alabama, to encourage women to learn this trade.

Another BE&K innovation is ombudsmanlike meetings at construction sites, open to *women only*. These gatherings began at Canton, North Carolina, where BE&K was working on a Champion paper mill, and allowed all women on the site—laborers, engineers, support people—to let off steam about anything that was bothering them. And they did, complaining about everything from sexual harassment to the belt buckles that were given out as safety awards—the women wanted (and got) smaller buckles so that they could wear them, too. One gripe at Canton led to an improvement in working conditions for all employees. The women objected to the filthiness of the portable johns at the work site. As a result, the supplier was replaced.

BE&K was one of the first construction companies to develop an on-site job training program. A typical training class is two hours a night, two nights a week, at no cost to the employee. BE&K pays supervisors to teach these courses. Tools and equipment manager Frank Cotton cited the example of a site in Columbus, Mississippi, where BE&K put up a pulp and paper mill for Weyerhaeuser and where it was difficult to find qualified workers: "Most of the people had maybe a fourth- or fifth-grade education. We offered pre-employment training for anyone in the community. We taught them the basic skills that a laborer would need: how to operate a jackhammer and an air compressor, how to pour grout, safety skills. There was no guarantee of employment, but those who had gone through this training were the first people we hired. After they were hired, they had additional opportunities to train. The individuals who went through welding training came out as certified welders in about three months. So, in six months we took individuals who had probably a fifth-grade education with no skills whatsoever and qualified them to make journeyman's rates. At that time it was $12.50 an hour. And this was all at no cost to them, only a little bit of time and a little bit of dedication." More than 50,000 people have graduated from one of BE&K's 400 on-site training courses.

At BE&K, taking care of their own goes beyond child care and training. When we visited their headquarters in a Birmingham office park, we heard numerous personal stories. When Mike Wheeler's brother was injured in a car accident, BE&K chartered a jet to fly him to his brother's side before he died. President Mike Goodrich explained: "They picked up the phone and said, 'We need a plane if Mike is going to see his brother before he dies. We've got to get him up there.' And nobody blinked an eye. We didn't have a plane available so we went out and chartered it [for $5,000]. That's just part of the company."

BE&K let accounting clerk Karen Driver work part-time so she could care for her son, who was born with cerebral palsy. Driver said: "I'm just an accounting clerk and the company has been great. Most of my friends who work for other companies are just astounded. They say they would have lost their jobs. They can't believe that BE&K worked with me as well as they have."

BE&K's sense of caring extends to the communities in which they do projects. Goodrich explained: "We'll get involved where no one else will."

BE&K people also pitch in with their own time. Project engineer Mike Jones cited examples of spouses who work as teachers' aides and employees who help to build playgrounds or new buildings for schools and communities. Jones said: "BE&K's method of helping out the local school is to roll up your sleeves and go to work. The multinational corporation's method of helping the local school is shaking their hand and giving them a check for $50,000 while getting their picture taken for the local newspaper."

It is no surprise, then, that there's a strong family feeling here. There are golf and fishing tournaments, quarterly luncheons, and job-site picnics. BE&K also flies employees and their spouses from remote job sites to Birmingham for a banquet at every fifth year of service.

In addition, the company makes a concerted effort to communicate with employees. They publish quarterly and monthly magazines, and executives travel to remote job sites to take employees and their spouses out to dinner. When it came time to schedule a dinner with the 150 salaried employees in International Falls, Minnesota, Frank Cotton explained: "It was intentionally done in February. Some thought that it should have been scheduled in October or November, but we said, 'Hey, these guys here are fighting the whole winter, at least we can go up in the midwinter for a night out.'" This is especially meaningful because of the nature of the business, where people can be working on a project for a year in Minnesota, then find themselves a year later in Florida and then in Oregon the following year.

Many people seem to thrive on the freedom that work life at BE&K offers. Mechanical engineering group leader David Templin told us: "One of the good qualities here is they are willing to let you take as much responsibility as you're willing to take and there are no rigid job descriptions."

Sometimes that freedom means people work extremely long hours. Templin said: "BE&K shows a willingness to sacrifice for the employees, therefore the employees are willing to sacrifice for BE&K. It's not an easy place to work by any means. It requires a lot of long hours and sometimes field assignments where you have to work 80, 90, or 100 hours in a week in order to meet the schedule."

Although they expect employees to put in long hours, BE&K is flexible. Goodrich says: "We do a lot of traveling to jobs all over the United States and we try to encourage employees to take time off. If you had to work a weekend, there's nothing wrong with taking a Monday or a Tuesday off. At the same time, you know that if you have a personal bind and need to be with your family you can pick up the phone and call somebody, and we'll cover for each other. That goes on all the time."

Types of jobs: Professional—44 percent; skilled crafts—43 percent; administration—6 percent; craft supervision—5 percent; management—2 percent.

Main employment centers: 600 work in the Birmingham headquarters. Other offices are in Mobile, Alabama; Baton Rouge, Louisiana; Charlotte and Raleigh, North Carolina; Portland, Oregon; Albany, New York; Wilmington, Delaware; Bucks County and Chichester, Pennsylvania; Lynn Haven, Florida; and Houston. Most of their project sites are in the Southeast or East Coast, although there are several in the Midwest and West.

Headquarters: BE&K, Inc.
2000 International Park Dr.
P.O. Box 2332
Birmingham, AL 35201
(205) 969-3600

Ben & Jerry's Homemade

BEN&JERRY'S®

Ben & Jerry's makes super premium ice cream, ice cream novelties, and frozen yogurt, and also franchises scoop shops. Their factory is one of the most popular tourist attractions in the state of Vermont, with over 200,000 visitors a year. Employees: 499.

★ ★ ★ Pay/Benefits
★ ★ ★ ★ Opportunities
★ ★ ★ ★ Job Security
★ ★ ★ ★ ★ Pride in Work/Company
★ ★ ★ ★ Openness/Fairness
★ ★ ★ ★ ★ Camaraderie/Friendliness

BIGGEST PLUS: Save the world while making ice cream.
BIGGEST MINUS: You need good humor to tolerate the chaos.

To say that Ben & Jerry's is fun is an understatement. Where else would you find an official Joy Gang presided over by a Minister of Joy? Where else would Mr. T, Mr. Clean, and Ralph Nader speak at employee meetings? And what other company celebrates events like Barry Manilow Day or Elvis Day, where they serve Elvis's favorite food—greasy hamburgers and peanut-butter and marshmallow sandwiches?

Alice Blachly, who works in consumer affairs, put it well: "I always come to work with a smile on my face because I just can't wait to see what's going to happen around here today. It's always something new. I knew I wanted to work here when I walked in the door and saw all these funny cartoonlike things around, and it just made me smile."

The sense of fun even permeates the production floor where employees churn out such unique flavors as Cherry Garcia, New York Super Fudge Chunk, Dastardly Mash, and Chunky Monkey. Alice Houghton describes a typical day: "When I'm doing the food feeder on a Cherry Garcia, the music is just a-blarin' and we sing. We do a lot of dancing and panto-mime." Accounts payable employee Mike Atwood, who used to work in production, added: "You can't act like a regular human being in there. You have to sort of let loose and say you're a kid again."

Ben & Jerry's has always been a fun place if for no other reason than cofounders Ben Cohen and Jerry Greenfield are funny guys who never pass up the opportunity to do the outrageous. At one annual meeting Habeeni Ben Coheni, dressed in a turban and sari, broke a cinder block over Green-field's belly. When Pillsbury tried to block Ben & Jerry's distribution to protect their premium ice cream, Häagen-Dazs, Greenfield formed a one-man picket line outside a Pillsbury plant carrying a sign reading, "What's the Dough Boy afraid of?"

Greenfield often expresses his business philosophy as, "If it's not fun, why do it?" He heads the Joy Gang, a committee whose mission is spread-ing joy in the workplace. He told us: "It's hard to figure out how to inte-grate joy into your daily business activities, but we recognize that it's some-thing that is central to our beliefs and we want to do it." With an annual budget of $10,000, the Joy Gang has been known to rent skates to use in the hallways, and give employees cardboard figures of the face of former CEO Fred "Chico" Lager for a "Disfigure Fred's Head" contest. The Joy Gang is responsible for scheduling massages during one of two annual mas-seuse visits.

Workers at Ben & Jerry's main plant and offices in Waterbury, Vermont, appreciate the attitudes behind such activities. According to real estate manager Carol Hedenberg: "When you think 'Joy Gang,' Jerry instantly pops into your head. He is what the Joy Gang is all about. He cares about each and every one of us, he really does."

Ben & Jerry's has more to recommend it than humor. In strictly business terms, it has been a winner. Started in 1978 as a two-man ice cream shop in a converted gas station in downtown Burlington, Vermont, Ben & Jerry's has grown to be the second largest seller of super premium ice cream (butter fat content of 15 percent), selling about one-fourth of this nation's supply of this artery-clogging favorite. They opened a second plant in eco-nomically depressed Springfield in southern Vermont in 1988, and will be-gin construction in 1993 of a third Vermont manufacturing plant in St. Albans.

Despite the growth, Ben & Jerry's has retained its open communications and zaniness. Executives hold quarterly meetings to keep employees up-to-date. These sessions are far from your run-of-the-mill presentations. In the past they have had midnight meetings to accommodate the third shift, where everyone else comes dressed in pajamas. When communication was chosen as the theme of one employee meeting, every employee received a set of wax lips. At some meetings they turn on the strobe light and dance to rock-and-roll music after business is done. Ben & Jerry employees even arranged for two of former CEO Chico Lager's idols, Mr. Clean and Mr. T, to speak at employee meetings. Mr. T had such a good time that he flew the rest of his family to Vermont and stayed for the annual meeting/music festival.

At Ben & Jerry's, the barriers between managers and employees have been as invisible as those between work and play. Roy Cook, a production supervisor, said: "I can tell my manager anything, even if I'm disagreeing with him." Alice Blachly added: "I feel that I am trusted and respected. And I trust the managers. They're really different from the people you'd find in usual management. They're not stuffed shirts at all." They do wear shirts at Ben & Jerry's but it's almost impossible to see anyone with a tie or jacket. During the winter months the standard uniform seems to be jeans and plaid shirt. The plaid shirts give way to T-shirts in the summer months. The Waterbury headquarters office looks like an elongated mobile home.

Ben & Jerry's was quick to address the issue of balancing work and family needs. They opened a child-care center adjacent to the Waterbury plant in 1990, and in 1991 they expanded benefits to include six weeks of maternity leave at full pay, two weeks of paid paternity leave, and four weeks of paid adoptive leave if you are the primary care-giver. Employees pay nothing for health insurance, and the company picks up 90 percent of the premium for dependent coverage. Alternative treatments like acupuncture and homeopathic care are covered by the policy. Ben & Jerry's is also one of the few U.S. companies to extend benefits to gay partners of employees and to heterosexual unmarried partners.

Just as growth hasn't diminished humor or informality, Ben & Jerry's has not lost the social mission in its founding charter. Cofounder Ben Cohen was eloquent on the subject when we interviewed him: "Businesses tend to exploit communities and their workers, and that wasn't the way I thought the game should be played. I thought it should be the opposite—that business had a responsibility to give back to the community, that because the business is allowed to be there in the first place, the business ought to support the community. What we're finding is that when you support the community, the community supports you back. When you give love, you receive love. I maintain that there is a spiritual dimension to business just as there is to the lives of individuals. When you put out good vibes, you get back good vibes, and I think that is what's happening."

Ben & Jerry's incorporates social consciousness into day-to-day activities.

Their annual report includes a social audit along with the traditional financial data. Managers are told to keep the social mission in mind when they make business decisions. This emphasis has led to flavors like Rainforest Crunch, which uses nuts from the Amazon rain forest purchased from a company that donates 60 percent of its profits to environmental organizations. Chocolate Fudge Brownie has brownies baked by the Greystone Bakery in Yonkers, New York, a company that uses its profits to house the homeless and train them as bakers. And they buy blueberries from the Passamaquoddy Indians in Maine for their Wild Maine Blueberry ice cream. In 1992 they introduced Wavy Gravy ice cream, named for the counterculture hero who was emcee at the Woodstock Music Festival in 1968.

Ben & Jerry's also has its own "Green Team," which meets twice a month. They have sponsored activities like the Green Flea Market (profits go to the Environmental Federation), Merry Mulching (Christmas tree recycling), reforestation projects (Ben & Jerry's plants 118 trees a year to replace those used to make the sticks for their Peace Pops), and a column ("The Daily Planet") for the company's monthly newsletter.

Philanthropy is also well above the norm here. They set aside 7.5 percent of pretax profits ($528,000 in 1991) for community groups. That's at least seven times the level prevailing at most companies. In 1991 funded groups included the Native American Community Board in South Dakota, the Kentucky Alliance Against Racist and Political Repression, and the Central Mass Safe Energy Project.

Ben & Jerry's social mission has also led to an unusual compensation system. Nobody who works for Ben & Jerry's can make more than seven times what the lowest-paid employee makes. In 1992 entry-level ice cream producers were earning $18,500 a year, which means executives were technically eligible to earn up to $129,000. However, the board of directors capped executive salaries at $100,000 until the lowest level passes $20,000 in salary and benefits. Cohen gave this rationale: "Just because one person has the skill of filling ice cream containers with ice cream and another person happens to have the skill of talking on the phone and selling ice cream, doesn't mean that one person should get paid all that much more than the other one. People are working just as hard. It's just that they have different skills, and I don't think one skill is worth more than another."

The cap has made it difficult to recruit top executives. Dave Barash, who was human resources director from 1988 to 1991 before becoming director of social ventures, gave this example: "When I hired a CFO [chief financial officer] we were offering 75 to 76 grand. That job elsewhere would get up to $200,000 or $300,000 a year." Ben & Jerry's advertised for the position in the New York Times and in small liberal magazines like the Utne Reader, Mother Jones, The Nation, and New Age. They searched for 18 months before finding Fran Rathke to fill the job. Barash, however, sees the silver lining: "The good news is that people who come into the top of the company subscribe to a set of values. People will come here for reasons other than money, and that will often mean that the commitment is deeper."

It's clear, from every employee survey taken, that the overwhelming majority of people at Ben & Jerry's like working here and buy into the social mission. At the same time, it's not all peaches-and-ice-cream. Explosive growth has brought problems of its own. A certain amount of chaos is tolerable when you're small; it can get counterproductive when you're growing. A Total Quality program has been installed, and one now hears the dreaded word "process" to describe new procedures.

New people have come in, too, on both the business and the sociopolitical side. Tall, bearded Chuck Lacy came here in 1988 from United Health Services, an upstate New York chain of nonprofit hospitals. He became president and chief operating officer in 1991. Liz Bankowski joined the company in 1990 after serving as chief of staff to Vermont governor Madeleine Kunin. In 1992 she was named director of social mission development, a position that it's safe to say doesn't exist at any other corporation in the land. In Ben & Jerry's humble hierarchy, it ranks on a par with the CFO (chief financial officer), in keeping with the company's determination to have what it calls a "two-part bottom line." Bankowski sees her job as one of spurring people to be involved in social mission activities so that they feel "like they are doing more here than just making a pint of ice cream." One who clearly feels that way is communications coordinator Maureen Martin, who told us that the social mission is what brought her to Ben & Jerry's. She explained: "It's not separate from our lives. I think that's what makes us work with a smile on our face. You don't feel like you're just working for a company. I feel like every day I'm working to educate people about different issues, I'm working to save the rain forests."

Types of jobs: Production—30 percent; distribution center—14 percent; marketing—13 percent; sales and retail—11 percent; shipping and receiving—8 percent; administration—8 percent; tours—4 percent; facilities—4 percent; finance—3 percent; maintenance—3 percent; questions and answers—2 percent.

Main employment centers: Ben & Jerry's has plants in Waterbury and Springfield, Vermont, and a distribution center in Bellows Falls, Vermont. They plan to build a third plant in St. Albans, Vermont, in 1993.

Headquarters: Ben & Jerry's Homemade, Inc.
Rte. 100
Box 240
Waterbury, VT 05676
(802) 244-5641

Beth Israel Hospital Boston

================================

Beth Israel Hospital Boston

Beth Israel operates a 510-bed (and 60-bassinet) hospital affiliated with Harvard Medical School. Employees: 5,100.

★★★★ Pay/Benefits
★★★★ Opportunities
★★★★ Job Security
★★★★★ Pride in Work/Company
★★★★★ Openness/Fairness
★★★★ Camaraderie/Friendliness

BIGGEST PLUS: They're getting rid of the hospital caste system.
BIGGEST MINUS: Some doctors don't want the caste removed.

Hospitals, by definition, are care-giving institutions, but for employees (doctors, nurses, lab technicians, maintenance people), they can be hellish places. It was therefore a revelation for us to meet the happy, enthusiastic crews at Boston's Beth Israel Hospital. Jammed into a crowded medical corridor in Brookline, just a little south of Fenway Park, Beth Israel is an enclave of vibrancy. It's the kind of hospital about which you say, "If I'm going to be sick, this is where I want to be."

At Beth Israel, warm feelings bubble up from the bottom. It's not a place where bosses—a doctor, head nurse, or maintenance supervisor—browbeat staff members. Deborah Saslon, an administrative secretary, told us Beth Israel is "a human place. You are given respect. I was tired of working where it's us versus them. This is the best place I have ever worked." Dr. Nancy

Oriol interned at Beth Israel and elected to stay on because she saw how happy people were. Another factor in her decision was that the women's locker room was as big as the men's. (Twenty-five percent of Beth Israel's doctors are female.) Joanne Ayoub, a training specialist, said she knows perhaps 100 people at the hospital, but when tragedy struck her family recently (her sister died), she heard from more than 400 employees. "People care here. I can't leave Beth Israel," she said. Tammy Barkyoumb, a nurse who grew up on a Vermont dairy farm, commutes a long way to Beth Israel and said to us: "My friends are sick and tired of hearing how much I like my job." Even the telephone operators we talked to sang the praises of Beth Israel. Telecommunications services manager Fannie Mabry said: "I live here, I go home to work." And Sandra Fenwick, vice-president of clinical planning, told us: "There is something about Beth Israel. You can feel the warmth in the walls."

All hands agree that the spirit that reigns here stems from the man at the top, Dr. Mitchell Rabkin, president of Beth Israel since 1966. An endocrinologist who might just as likely be caught reading the *Harvard Business Review* as the *New England Journal of Medicine*, Dr. Rabkin has pioneered on a number of fronts. In 1972 he had Beth Israel issue a patient's Bill of Rights, a document spelling out precisely what a patient has a right to expect from the hospital, including privacy, personal dignity, and respect (no one at Beth Israel addresses a patient by his or her first name without first getting permission). Every incoming patient—and every employee—receives a copy. The idea is to foster the independence of patients. In 1991 one wing of Beth Israel introduced a program of self-medication by patients. Nurse Katy Connell explained: "Our patients often go home on many new and confusing drugs. If they can learn to manage their medication while still in the hospital, they can go home feeling much more secure."

Nurses are treated with great respect here. Each incoming patient is assigned a registered nurse, who assumes 24-hour responsibility for overall care. A nurse, typically, has four patients under her care. She sits down with each one, takes a full-scale history, and maps out a complete care plan. For the patient, it removes some of the impersonal bureaucracy from the hospital routine. For the nurse, it makes her a colleague of the physician rather than a handmaiden. And as Dr. Rabkin is quick to point out: "In the hospital, it's not the doctor who's important, it's the nurse."

Dr. B. Lacklan Forrow, a physician who recently returned to Beth Israel after a hiatus of six years ("Not every hospital is like this one," he assured us), related that one of the first moves Mitch Rabkin made after becoming president was to eliminate the separate, white-tablecloth dining area for physicians in the hospital cafeteria. After he tore down the curtain, doctors complained that they needed, for professional reasons, to have a place where they could talk to one another over lunch. Dr. Rabkin told them: "You want to eat together, fine! Just sit down at the same table."

The cafeteria is a benefit by itself. "We love to eat," Joanne Ayoub said, to which another employee added: "We come to work here for the food." A bustling place crackling with energy and good humor, the Beth Israel cafeteria on the ground floor of the hospital feeds 2,200 people a day, offering up a dazzling variety of dishes. Broccoli cheese soup, Indonesian chicken, mushroom pizza, rice pilaf, zucchini and julienne carrots were all on the menu one day early in 1992—and if you didn't want any of that, you could get spaghetti and meatballs at the grill or a chicken salad and avocado sandwich at the deli bar. Beth Israel also has a renowned in-house bakery. Every day, on average, the cafeteria sells 720 chocolate-chip cookies, 156 oatmeal cookies, and 60 peanut-butter cookies. And for holidays, they sell pies—more than 400 were taken home for Thanksgiving Day in 1991. If you have to work on Thanksgiving or Christmas, you're entitled to a free meal in the cafeteria—and you may also invite members of your family to join you there, compliments of Beth Israel.

Once a year there's a free meal at the cafeteria for every employee. That happens during Employee Appreciation Week, usually the first week in February. A series of events unfurl that week to celebrate long-term employees, and on one of those days employees can cash in a ticket distributed with their last paycheck for a free meal—breakfast, lunch, or dinner.

Thanksgiving pies aren't the only goodies employees get. Entry-level clerks bring home $15,200 a year, secretaries $19,840, registered nurses $38,577—and they tap into a strong benefits package, including a wide array of training programs. The hospital has an earned-time program that entitles each employee to 34 days off each year—it combines vacation time, sick leave, and holidays into one bank. Beth Israel has been particularly strong about work/family benefits, and in 1991 the hospital managed to find precious space to open its own child-care center. Admission was by lottery, and it was quickly filled to capacity: 115 children.

Mitchell Rabkin is a very visible presence in this hospital. "He pops up everywhere," said Beryl Chapman, a nurse who worked in operating rooms for 23 years before moving to a clinic. Lois Amirault, a telephone operator, whose mother had also been a telephone operator here, told us that if she fields a complaint from a caller, she has no hesitation about giving out Dr. Rabkin's extension, because she knows he will take care of it. In his book about Beth Israel, *Drawing the Line*, Samuel Gorovitz wrote that Dr. Rabkin once had some young doctors dress in the uniforms of the maintenance staff and move about the hospital to get a feel for how the support staff is treated.

Dr. Rabkin helps to keep this place together with an informal, weekly newsletter that he writes himself. The polar opposite of slick, the letter looks like it was run off on an old-fashioned mimeograph machine that needs ink. It's one sheet printed on both sides, and it's distributed in the hospital every Friday—in English, Spanish, and French. The author has, of course, complete editorial control. He might note the death of a longtime employee, someone's promotion, special events, or new programs available to employees. Once, just before Thanksgiving, he explained how to carve up a turkey, a skill that he pointed out was important to have, to keep up Beth Israel's reputation.

One of the most remarkable programs launched here, in 1989, was PRE-PARE/21, an acronym for Participation, Responsibility, Education, Productivity, Accountability, Recognition, and Excellence for the 21st Century. PREPARE/21 is Beth Israel's version of the Scanlon Plan, a share-the-wealth scheme that has enabled workers at Donnelly Corp., Herman Miller, and Dana Corp. to organize themselves into teams and come up with ways to cut costs and improve operations. They then share directly in productivity gains achieved by their companies. Beth Israel put the program in a hospital setting. Dozens of teams now function in the hospital, generating ideas on how to improve quality and enhance efficiency as well as reduce costs. Thirteen times a year the hospital issues a "gain report" that discloses figures on admissions and discharges, revenues and expenditures, calculating the difference between budget projections and actual performance. The gains, if any, are split with employees. In the first year of PREPARE/21, the gains were on the order of $2 million, half of which was paid out to employees. In the second year, the gains were $1.74 million—and $870,000 was distributed to employees. Beth Israel is the first organization outside the manufacturing sector to embrace the Scanlon Plan, and it's a striking example of how employees here are expected to act as "owners."

Since Dr. Rabkin's arrival here, turnover has decreased dramatically. Nationally, turnover of nurses runs 19 percent; at Beth Israel, it's 6.7 percent. In 1990 *Boston* magazine surveyed nurses in and around Boston, asking them where else, aside from their present job, they would like to work. Beth Israel received the most votes, 65, the next most desirable hospital, 36.

Beth Israel was founded by the Jewish community of Boston in 1916, intended from the start to be a hospital for "all races, creeds and colors." It's a nonsectarian institution, but its major donors have been Jews, and until 1989 its board of trustees was entirely Jewish. However, most of its patients and support staff are non-Jewish. It was originally located in the Boston neighborhood of Roxbury—then largely Jewish, today largely black —and moved in 1928 to Brookline near Harvard Medical School. Today, it's still in the same location but has spread out to 16 buildings, part of the 175-acre Longwood medical area. Within a short distance are 15 colleges and hospitals, including Brigham Hospital, the world-famous Dana Faber Cancer Institute, and Simmons College.

Some people might say "a hospital is a hospital." But Dr. Rabkin's achievement has been to invest *meaning* in the workplace so that Beth Israel is different. Nuggets of his philosophy can be found everywhere— he's always dropping them. In the winter of 1992 he explained, in a letter to the *Harvard Business Review*, his conception of management-employee partnerships:

"Not only must workers learn and be motivated to do so, managers must learn as well. Indeed, workers teaching their peers has value; nobody knows the details of a job as well as those doing it, and workers often best perceive a job's problems. However, if workers cannot inform managers—and managers cannot learn and respond—workers' insights have no credibility, and the notion of their partnerships with management becomes empty verbiage."

Types of jobs: Registered nurses—25 percent; secretarial and clerical—17 percent; service and maintenance—16 percent; physicians and Ph.D.'s—10 percent; house staff and fellows—9 percent; other health professionals—7 percent; supervisors and managers—6 percent; technicians—5 percent; administration—5 percent.

Main employment center: Boston.

Headquarters: Beth Israel Hospital Boston
330 Brookline Ave.
Boston, MA 02215
(617) 735-2800

Leo Burnett

LEO BURNETT COMPANY · INC.

Leo Burnett is the largest advertising agency in the United States. U.S.
employees: 2,300.

★★★★★ Pay/Benefits
★★★★ Opportunities
★★★ Job Security
★★★★ Pride in Work/Company
★★★ Openness/Fairness
★★★★ Camaraderie/Friendliness

BIGGEST PLUS: As American as apple pie.
BIGGEST MINUS: But that includes the Marlboro man.

Most of the people who work here never met the founder, Leo Burnett.
That's because they're too young. Leo Burnett died in 1971. But that
doesn't mean they don't know him. In a death-defying move, the people
who run this ad agency have kept his name and memory alive in big ways
and small ways so that virtually every employee understands what he stood
for:

"Good advertising lifts up, not tears down."

"Nothing is ever good enough around here."

"Clichés are unacceptable."

"We want people to say, 'What a great product,' not 'What a great ad.' "

Burnett never misses a chance to remind their people of the precepts—
and idiosyncrasies—of the founder. It's the glue that holds the place together. Burnett gives away 1,500 apples a day, following a tradition that

goes back to the birth of the agency in 1935, in the midst of the Depression. Visitors used to walk away munching apples, some of them saying, "It won't be long before Leo Burnett is selling apples on the street corner instead of giving them away." This wisecrack ended up in a Chicago newspaper column, and, as the agency explains today, "We became more determined than ever to make better and better ads and give away more and more apples." The apple-giving is not confined to the headquarters office. Every floor in every Burnett office in the world displays a bowl of apples, free for the taking.

Also still widely in use at Burnett are the stubby, black No. 2 pencils that Leo favored to mark up ads. His likeness is everywhere, too. The 22nd floor of the agency, where the top people sit, has a wall of photographs and drawings. In most companies, it would be a "rogues' gallery" of former presidents and chairmen. At Burnett, all the images are of one man: Leo Burnett. When they moved into their new building on Chicago's Wacker Drive in 1989, there was no question what it would be called—the Leo Burnett Building—and the guest of honor was Leo's widow, Naomi, who died the following year at age 96.

The people who work here feel close to one another. Arlo Oviatt, a copywriter who joined the agency in 1989, has friends in the ad business who have changed jobs several times and who keep asking him, "Are you going to be a Burnetter for life?" He tells them: "The morning that I wake up and say I don't want to do this anymore, that will be the day that I'll leave. And of course there have been days when I said, 'I don't want to go to work today.' But it's never been something I dreaded. And I can't imagine, in talking to some of my friends, the realm of opportunity anywhere else that I've found here."

It's not just the ad makers who are happy here. Joyce Wilson, who runs the all-important mailroom, told us: "What hit me about Burnett is that everybody was so friendly. It's like you weren't at work. It's like a big party here on eight [the eighth floor, where the mail department is located]. After six years, I still have Burnett stars in my eyes." (Burnett's symbol, from the start of the agency, is a hand reaching for the stars with the legend "When you reach for the stars, you may not always get one, but you won't come up with a handful of mud either.")

Sam Armando, a media research assistant, related that when his father died in 1991, "it's incredible the people I work with, how they picked up the slack for me. I found out that some people covering my desk were here until like 10:30, 11:00 at night, just to do my stuff so I didn't have to worry about it." There were tears in his eyes when he told that story.

Tears also flowed at Burnett in 1991 when the agency's beloved production chief, Al Lira, died of a heart attack. Tributes poured in from all over the world—and more than two dozen were printed in Burnett's crackerjack house magazine, *theBurnettwork*. Our favorite letter was the one from Chicago staffer Jerry Reitman, who recalled an argument he had with Al several years ago, an argument he lost. "And I didn't lose gracefully," Reitman continued. "Al sensed it. Finally, one day as we were walking towards each other from opposite ends of the hall, without a word, he grabbed me in a bear hug, kissed me on the cheek, and walked away. I learned a little humanity from him that day."

Burnett does tend at times to be a big, soppy place, in keeping with the corny, heart-tugging commercials they execute for such clients as McDonald's, Kellogg's, United Airlines, Hallmark Cards, and Maytag. They don't go in for hard-edge advertising. This is an all-American place, midwestern, old-fashioned, friendly, down-to-earth. They do terrific ads and the people who work here are not arrogant yuppie types. Tim Leahy, who recruits account management people for the agency and whose uncle once worked for Burnett, said: "When you meet the people within the company, they just tend to be smart, aggressive, like all-American people that you could relate to."

Burnett's success—it became the largest advertising agency in the United States during the 1980s—testifies to the wisdom of a company going its own way. While other agencies diversified into peripheral areas— public relations, market research, sales promotion—Burnett stuck to its guns: it did advertising, period. (There has been only one merger in its history, with a Detroit agency, D. P. Brother, in 1967.) While other agencies sold stock to the public, Burnett insisted on remaining private. And they are adamant about this decision. Hal "Cap" Adams, head of Burnett from 1986 to 1992, said: "Going public makes a few people very wealthy and screws it up for the others for the rest of the agency's life." Adams also told us that because the agency is privately held, it was able to hold the fort and not fire anyone in 1990, when the ad business suffered one of its worst downturns in many years. "That," said Adams, "was not a decision you could have sold to a group of outside owners. But we could sell it to ourselves. It's our money." Between June 1990 and June 1991 the number of jobs at U.S. ad agencies declined 3.7 percent; at Burnett, the number of jobs increased 7.4 percent.

Another of Burnett's stubborn streaks is loyalty to its hometown, Chicago. The center of the advertising business is New York City, but Burnett will have none of it. They maintain a contact office there, but all of its work is done in Chicago. And most of the people in the upper ranks of the agency are midwesterners. Many are native Chicagoans.

The advertising agency business has a reputation for volatility, with people and clients coming and going. You'd never know it from Burnett. When we interviewed here in 1983, we met Adele Zine, who worked in accounting and was coming up on her 40th year with Burnett, and Marcia Garrett, who left schoolteaching 19 years earlier to become a receptionist at Burnett. When we revisited in 1991, they were both still there, happy and enthusiastic. Because we were visiting on August 5, the agency's birthday, Garrett was handing out envelopes and a present for everyone who came through the door on her floor. This is another Burnett tradition—every August 5 there's a birthday celebration in which every employee receives $1 for every year the agency has been in business. In 1991 that meant $56 for every person—and not only in the United States but in the 54 offices in 47 other countries. It amounted to a one-day payout of $362,800. On that day, Burnett also gives special presents to people who are marking their fifth, 10th, 15th, and 20th years with the company—and the company makes a point of simultaneously giving presents to spouses of celebrating employees. The gift for employees marking their 25th anniversary is substantial: $2,000.

Burnett, in 1991, had 26 people who had been with the agency for 30 or more years, 123 with service between 20 and 30 years, and 364 who had been with the agency between 10 and 20 years. That same loyalty obtains on the client side. Burnett only has 33 clients, all of them major national advertisers. It works for the four largest advertisers in the nation: Philip Morris, Procter & Gamble, General Motors, and Sears, Roebuck. Nearly all of its client relationships go back more than 10 years, and it has been doing ads for 13 clients for more than 25 years.

Burnett's largest client is Philip Morris. The agency does the ads for Marlboro, Merit, Benson & Hedges, and Virginia Slims cigarettes as well as for the Philip Morris-owned Miller beers (both High Life and Lite). This means, of course, that you won't find any smoking-cessation programs in place here, nor any restrictions beyond what the law requires. It's in sharp contrast to the spanking, state-of-the-art fitness center, called Revisions, which Burnett installed for its people on the second floor of a building across the way from its own. We had heard that it wasn't easy for someone to refuse to work on a cigarette account, but that was denied by employee relations manager Patti Haidu, who told us: "I think your supervisor considers your own personal feelings about, not just cigarettes, but a variety of products and they take that into account. It's not held against you. We have enough clients here and enough products that you could find an assignment if you are uncomfortable working on something." Is anyone going to object to working on the Green Giant vegetables or Heinz ketchup?

Burnett has a super pay and benefits package. There's a profit-sharing plan that has paid out the maximum allowed by the IRS—15 percent of your pay—every year except one (1942). There's an annual bonus, a pension plan, medical and dental insurance, and a sick-time benefit that is probably unique: employees with at least two years' service receive full salary whenever they are sick. Period. No conditions. No time limits. (After 56 days, the company's long-term disability insurance kicks in.)

But it's the Leo Burnett mythology that makes this place work. There's a story they tell of a time in the 1960s when Leo was on the elevator in the Prudential building (where the agency was then ensconced) with a young man who wore sandals, dark glasses, and had hair down to his waist. After the man left the elevator on a Burnett floor, Leo, with his famous quivering lip, turned and said, "If he's ours, he better be good." That man, Richard Fizdale, rose to creative chief, and in 1992 he became the chief executive of the agency, succeeding Cap Adams.

Every new employee of the agency sits down on his or her first day to view the film of one of Leo Burnett's last talks to the troops, given on December 1, 1967, at the annual December breakfast where the year is reviewed and bonus checks are handed out. It's called, "When to Take My Name off the Door," and it's a real tear-jerker. Burnett told his people that they should remove his name when "you spend more time trying to make money and *less* time making advertising," when "you compromise your integrity," when "you lose your humility and become big-shot weisen-heimers . . . a little too big for your boots."

Burnett never stops brainwashing its people with these thoughts. And in 1991, when they were pitching the $35-million Sony advertising account, they screened the "When to Take My Name off the Door" film for the prospective client. They got the account, which prompted this comment from the runner-up, Jerry Della Femina: "We were pitching Sony, and I walked in there at the end, as chairman of my agency, and explained to them how much I really wanted their business, and how closely involved I would be, personally. And then the Burnett people came in and they popped in this video of Leo talking. It was just Leo talking about the philosophy of advertising. And he beat me. Sony would rather work with Leo dead than me alive. That's how powerful he is—he's one of the few people in this business who started an agency who really got to live for-ever."

Types of jobs: Creative—29 percent; client services—22 percent; media—19 percent; research—7 percent; integrated communications—2 percent.

Main employment centers: Chicago, 2,200. Small contact offices in New York, Detroit, and Los Angeles, 100. Another 3,300 work in overseas offices.

Headquarters: Leo Burnett Company, Inc.
35 W. Wacker Dr.
Chicago, IL 60601
(312) 220-5959

60

Chaparral Steel

Chaparral produces steel faster than any other steel mill in America. Employees: 930.

★★★★ Pay/Benefits
★★★★★ Opportunities
★★★★ Job Security
★★★ Pride in Work/Company
★★★★★ Openness/Fairness
★★★★ Camaraderie/Friendliness

BIGGEST PLUS: You set your own pay rate.
BIGGEST MINUS: You have to bring your own lunch.

Nine hundred and thirty people work at Chaparral Steel, and there are 930 different rates of pay. No two people are paid the same here because Chaparral has created an unusual way of paying workers, based on their job, seniority, versatility, skills, and training credits. The system may drive the payroll department crazy, but employees love it.

Most employees work in Chaparral's steel mill located outside Midlothian, Texas (population 5,000), about a half hour's drive south of Dallas. Chaparral, named after a species of roadrunner, makes various steel products like beams for skyscrapers and concrete reinforcing rods from junked automobiles and other sources of scrap metal. Adjacent to the mill stands a huge car shredder that reduces autos to usable scrap in 18 seconds. Chaparral workers heat the scrap metal to temperatures of 3,000 degrees Fahrenheit and pour it into various shapes. According to *Fortune*, Chaparral produces steel faster than any other mill in America. Work in the mill is hot and dirty. But it's not monotonous, because Chaparral makes sure workers use their minds as well as their brawn. Or, as Chaparral's president and CEO Gordon Forward told us: "We see our company being more of a 'mentofacturing' as opposed to a manufacturing company—'manual' means hand and 'mento' means mind. We're going to take the grunt out of steelmaking."

One of the more dramatic ways Chaparral has found to engage workers' minds is by taking them on sales calls. Before leaving on such trips, the company provides the workers with their own business cards. Melt shop operator Brad Cowan accompanied two sales representatives to Los Angeles, San Diego, and Mexico. "It was interesting to see where your stuff ends up after it leaves here. I got to talk with the people who run the companies and tell them that if they had complaints to let us know."

Chaparral steelworkers also go to other steel mills to study new or different processes. Bart Peugh, a bar mill machinist, told us he went to Pittsburgh and Chicago on such missions. And he said that once his entire crew of 40 went to Tulsa, Oklahoma, to study a plant that used a "sucker rod" to forge steel. A different crew was sent to Japan, where they worked in a Japanese mill for five weeks. A crew also went to Germany.

On a more mundane level, Chaparral engages employees' minds through on-the-job training and classroom education. Employees can learn every job in their department by spending time doing each task. In the casting department, for instance, there are three "torchman" positions and two operator positions in the casting tower. Instead of an employee staying in one of those positions until there is an opening elsewhere, he (96 percent of the steelworkers are men) will spend time in each position. They get credit (translated into higher pay rates) for the time they spend learning other jobs.

Similar cross-training takes place in other areas of the company. Shipping clerks, for instance, learn how to answer credit questions. Security guards are trained as paramedics and to enter accounting data into a computer. Jim Stamey, a crane operator who had been with the company less than a year when we were there, said: "Everyone learns everyone else's job. That's one of the beautiful things about Chaparral."

Besides getting higher pay for learning other jobs, employees also get credit for the training they take. An employee can take 22 different courses ranging from basic skills like mathematics, safety, and health, to advanced mechanical training. About 85 percent of Chaparral's employees participate in this training. In addition to higher pay rates for completing courses, the company pays workers $20 for each four-hour training session, which they take before or after shifts or during a day off.

Chaparral also reimburses tuition costs for employees who pursue their own education. Senior operator Tom Hanley, who has been here for eight years, has taken advantage of this benefit: "When I started here I was a high school dropout. I had no personal goals, no company goals, no nothing. I was a nobody. I came here and they said, 'Why don't you try doing this?' So I buzzed through high school, and I'm going to college now, and they're paying for that also."

Gordon Forward said that the emphasis on cross-training and education is only part of treating employees as adults, or as he sometimes puts it facetiously, "management by adultery." He explained how it worked: "We don't dock pay at all. We try to treat employees as adults. What we're doing is based on trust. Docking pay doesn't solve problems, it's a distrust system. Time clocks also show distrust. They say the company doesn't trust you at 8:00 in the morning, and they still don't trust you at 4:00 in the afternoon."

Trust goes beyond the absence of time clocks. It extends to deciding the hours of shifts. Some of the steelworkers put in eight hours a day, but others have 12-hour shifts and work 14 days straight and are off the next 14 days. Still others work combinations of eight- and 14-hour shifts. According to human resources manager Jeff Roesler: "You name a shift, we have it. The departments really decide what shifts they want to work. Really it's the guys that say, 'This is what we would like to do.' "

Forward has the same attitude with managerial employees, most of whom, including Forward, normally wear sport shirts to work. He recalled that when the company was started and he was vice-president of operations, he used to come to work dressed without a tie because he spent so much time in the construction area. He told the other managers that they did not have to wear a tie. The then president of the company liked the idea and suggested instituting a company policy that nobody wears a tie. Forward told him that he had "missed" the point "because if you put that policy out tomorrow, we would all wear ties. What we want is no policy. You want to trust people to use their judgment."

He has the same attitude about putting down rules. According to Forward: "The managers' time is their own. I try to avoid the stultifying structure-type stuff. They don't have to write trip reports. If they feel like it, fine, but the best thing is, if you've been on a trip and you saw something you liked, then go out and try it and see if we can do it. That kind of freedom helps on the stress side. We try not to shackle them with speckled crap, unnecessary meetings, long meetings."

Hourly workers observe a similar attitude. Brad Cowan worked in a wire mill before coming to Chaparral Steel. At the wire mill, "I got paid a lot less and the management was always on top of you to produce more. Down here management in the melt shop, they just leave you alone and let you do your job. When they can see that something you're doing could be done a little different to produce more steel and better quality, they'll come in and tell you. Basically, they leave it up to the individuals to make decisions."

Senior operator Jerry Forsythe has been at Chaparral since 1975, when the area where the mill is now located "was just a muddy field." Because the company has grown so much, he said, "we're not as close to management as we used to be, but it's better than anyplace I worked before. The main thing that makes me happy about getting up in the morning and coming to work is the fact that I like what I do and I have freedom. You're free to do your job, take complaints or recommendations to your supervisors, and they listen. You can order your own parts, take care of everything, and carry it on through. It makes it a lot more pleasant to be in a job when it's like that and not just being crammed down your throat."

Unlike many companies, Chaparral doesn't believe in employee suggestion programs. Forward believes they undermine teamwork: "I enjoy brainstorming. But if you have a suggestion scheme, it works counter to brainstorming. Whose idea was it? We don't give a damn whose idea it was, let's see if we can make something happen."

Instead of paying for suggestions, he believes in profit sharing, where everybody shares in the rewards of productivity improvements. Unlike some other mini-mills, Chaparral has no other incentive systems, such as piece rates, to motivate workers. Forward said: "I see profit sharing as part of a holistic approach. When you pay piecemeal, it says nothing about quality and it says nothing about how many people you have. When you pay piecemeal what you want is more people to make it run faster." Employees are given 8.5 percent of the company's gross profits in two profit-sharing checks a year, one at Christmastime and one in the summer. However, when there are no profits, there's no profit sharing—and that was the case in 1992 when the mill was losing money, thereby producing a loss for Dallas-based Texas Industries, a cement and concrete producer that owns 81 percent of Chaparral.

Chaparral does not have a company cafeteria. Employees either bring their own lunches to eat in break rooms or take a short drive to Midlothian to eat in one of the diners. (Dee Tee's coffeehouse is a favorite for managers and workers alike.) They do have free coffee, free hot chocolate, free Gatorade. In the clean and well-lit locker room, steelworkers can put on the green overalls, boots, and prescription safety glasses the company provides.

What counts most, however, is the human concern employees sense at Chaparral. Senior operator Tom Hanley gave us a personal example: "I was going through some financial problems. I went bankrupt and I needed some money to make a house payment and it was the end of the line. And I went to my boss and I said, 'Look, I'm having a problem, I need some money and I'm tapped out at the credit union.' Twenty minutes later I had a check for $600 in my hand. I wouldn't think it was a policy, but it's their way of taking care of you. Whatever it takes, they make sure you're happy so you don't come to work with problems."

Types of jobs: Manufacturing and sales—83 percent; administration—17 percent.

Main employment center: Midlothian, Texas.

Headquarters: Chaparral Steel Company
300 Ward Rd.
Midlothian, TX 76065
(214) 775-8241

Compaq Computer

COMPAQ

COMPUTER CORPORATION

Compaq makes desktop and portable computers that are IBM-compatible. U.S. employees: 6,500.

★ ★ ★   Pay/Benefits
★ ★   Opportunities
★ ★   Job Security
★ ★ ★   Pride in Work/Company
★ ★ ★   Openness/Fairness
★ ★ ★   Camaraderie/Friendliness

BIGGEST PLUS: Decisions are in your lap.
BIGGEST MINUS: They might delete your job.

The scene was a large community church in northwest Houston, where the quarterly, all-employee meeting of Compaq was just concluding. Top executives, dressed in sport shirts, kicked beach balls carrying the names of Compaq's rivals (IBM, Apple, Tandy, Dell, AST) into the crowd. Then, with Beach Boys music blaring over loudspeakers, the executives jumped down from the stage and joined employees in batting the beach balls around the big auditorium.

The event was notable because it occurred in the summer of 1992, nearly a year after Compaq went through the most traumatic ordeal in its 10-year history. In October 1991 a boardroom coup ousted founder Rod Canion and led to the first layoffs in the company's history. One of the people kicking the beach balls in the 2,000-seat Metropolitan Baptist Church two miles from Compaq headquarters was Eckhard Pfeiffer, a tall German national who had replaced Canion as CEO. We had visited Compaq a month before the October purge, and the concern we had was: will the new CEO dismantle the remarkable culture that had been planted and nurtured by the Rod Canion team since Compaq was founded in 1982? We put the question to Pfeiffer in the summer of 1992, and he said the main change in the company has to do with the way it competes in the fast-moving computer market, not in the culture. "We're not the first company who has stumbled on its course," he told us. "I remember when Apple stumbled. I remember when Sun [Microsystems] stumbled. I remember when many other companies have stumbled—HP [Hewlett-Packard]—and I don't think you would doubt today that HP is a good company."

Compaq had made its mark by selling premium-priced IBM-compatible computers to big companies. It was known as the Cadillac of the IBM clones. Now it wants to be the Chevrolet as well. Discount computer makers like Dell Computer and AST Research had gouged huge market shares out of Compaq's hide, and the company had been slow to react. Exit Canion, enter Pfeiffer, whose mission is to turn Compaq into a street-fighting, price-competitive computer warrior. To do that will require a committed work force—and that's something Compaq has had from its founding. Canion, Pfeiffer, and a number of other top Compaq executives came out of Texas Instruments, an engineer-dominated electronics company that is known for its rigidity. And while Canion and his cofounders took some ideas from their old employer, they were determined to create a company with a much more open work-style.

The fact that Pfeiffer still holds the quarterly employee meetings is one sign that he recognizes the importance of preserving the culture so identified with Compaq. These meetings are more than rah-rah affairs. They include a no-holds-barred question-and-answer period. Compaq employees are therefore encouraged that they still have the freedom to confront management in this manner. When Pfeiffer took over, speculation was rife that he would introduce a more autocratic style. The upbeat beach ball gathering indicated that Compaq retains the spirit that made the company a shooting star of the 1980s.

Compaq's story is already a legend in the annals of contemporary American business. Soon after IBM introduced its first personal computer in 1981, Canion and Jim Harris, another Texas Instruments engineer, came up with the idea of a similar, but smaller, portable machine (hence the company name). A copy of the original sketch is still on display at corporate headquarters. Their machine was an instant hit, selling more than 50,000 in the first year. By 1985 Compaq's sales catapulted it onto the Fortune 500 roster, faster than any company in history. Two years later, Compaq became the first company to reach $1 billion in sales in only five years.

In the process, Compaq also became a high-quality place to work. Employees were pampered with many perks, exemplified by free Coke machines and an annual outing to the Astro World amusement park where employees and their families were admitted free and given $15 spending money. In the cost-cutting Pfeiffer regime, these were two perks that went by the boards. The Astro World trip was eliminated, and the Cokes went to 35 cents.

Still in place, of course, is the magnificent headquarters complex built by Canion. Set back from the highway in a secluded grove of huge pine trees with jogging trails, it features sleek, silver-colored buildings with reflective glass windows. The buildings are interconnected by enclosed walkways so that employees do not have to step outside into the hot and humid Houston weather. And the assembly lines on the campus are light and airy, brightened by potted trees and plants. It's the Texan version of Silicon Valley.

Also still in place here is the "consensus management" style adopted at the start of the company to avoid the hierarchical style of Texas Instruments. Canion had told us that the founding group was made up of engineers who had little business experience. They simply used "common sense" to solve problems and make decisions. He told us: "In our culture, consensus is a management tool for reaching a better decision than you would have reached by yourself." Pfeiffer told us that consensus management continues to operate at Compaq, except that he has tried to get more accountability into the process. In the end, he explained, after the meetings and discussions, managers must realize they "have to make the decision."

Canion and the other cofounders had also established a strong benefits program, and it remains in force although the cost containment that came in with the Pfeiffer regime has brought some cutbacks. For example, employees now have to pick up more of the tab for medical expenses, and the program that used to award stock options to every employee was replaced in 1992 by a profit-sharing plan that pays out twice a year.

Compaq employees themselves gave us a graphic picture of the workstyle. Benefits manager Jean Gibson told us: "Every position at the company is valued equally, and the contribution that everybody makes is important." Jim Ganthier, an electrical engineering supervisor, said: "It's not just the team concept alone that helps make Compaq's success. I worked for two corporations, GTE and Northern Telecom, which were very auto-cratic kinds of organizations. One of the things that is nice here is that it's a very flat organization. And there's the open door policy. You can talk to the CEO or send him a B-Mail." In keeping with Compaq's egalitarian ethos, they have no executive dining rooms, no reserved parking spaces, and no large, plush offices. On the other hand, Compaq is not a hang-loose kind of place from the standpoint of dress code. In this respect, they follow the TI model. Employees dress conservatively, in suits and ties and dresses. Compaq also prohibits the serving of alcoholic beverages at any company function.

Compaq's concern for employees was demonstrated when they laid off employees in 1991. According to the *Houston Post*, employees leaving the company were given one and a half to two weeks' pay for every year of service plus one week's pay for every $5,000 of their final salary. There was a minimum severance of two months' pay. Some 1,400 people were severed from the payroll in this cutback.

Departing CEO Rod Canion didn't get treated too shabbily either. His severance pay was $3.6 million, payable over 16 months. The new CEO, Eckhard Pfeiffer, earned $1.6 million in 1991 and is working with a con-tract that guarantees him severance pay of four times his salary. Pfeiffer, who was 50 in 1992, has been with the company since 1983, ever since Canion called him up at Texas Instruments and asked him to come on over and spearhead Compaq's invasion of Europe. (The German-born Pfeiffer had worked 20 years at TI, joining the company after graduating from Southern Methodist University in Dallas.) Pfeiffer did a sensational job for Compaq in Europe, pushing its sales there to $1.8 billion and second only to IBM in the personal computer market. In January 1991, Pfeiffer was recalled from Europe and installed by Canion as Compaq's president and chief operating officer. Before the year was out, he had Canion's job.

There was, understandably, a tremendous loyalty in this company to Rod Canion. After he was fired, about 100 employees picketed their own com-pany with signs that said, "We love you, Rod." Since his elevation to CEO, Pfeiffer has worked hard to reestablish trust. In his first 10 months as CEO, he resorted to the company's electronic mail system (B-mail) 10 times to describe changes and lay out his plans for the future, including a special anniversary message on Compaq's 10th birthday in February 1992. And he has continued to preside over the quarterly company meetings, where he gives a direct report on the state of Compaq. When we interviewed him in the summer of 1992, Pfeiffer said that he felt that with the company's new thrust to take on all comers in the rough-and-tough computer market, Compaq had been revitalized. "All of a sudden," he told us, "it's back. People feel again that we have a direction, a course of action. We have strategic thinking behind it. We're developing new visions for the future, and the company is returning and building on its tradition of strength, which is really the people."

Another Rod Canion institution that Pfeiffer has retained is the Association of Compaq Employees or ACE, although funding for its many activities has been cut. ACE organizes the annual company picnic, intramural sports teams, and 26 different clubs devoted to hobbies ranging from bridge to mountain climbing. The company used to fund all these programs; now employees who participate must pay the full cost. ACE used to have a full-time staff of six; now it has two. Employees used to be able to call an ACE hotline to talk to a human being about upcoming events; now the number is answered by an automated message. Thirteen employees from all levels of the company serve on the ACE board of directors. Also still available to Compaq employees and their families on holidays and weekends is the 50-acre recreation park on the campus.

We talked with Mark Ruck, ACE's employee-elected president, in mid-1992, and he gave us this assessment of Compaq: "Free Cokes are gone. But in the vast scheme of things, where can you go to buy a Coke for 35 cents? Not many places. So it's not subsidized to the same extent it was before, but it's not like you've been stripped bare. Before a lot of people had the feeling of being on the gravy train. We were getting paid very nicely, and we're living in an area of the country that has a very low cost of living and we were making out like bandits. And we still are. No one's pay got cut except for those whose jobs got cut. The perks were adjusted, but not below what was competitive in the industry. I think that the overall sense is that it is still a very good place to work and the future looks bright." An engineer with Texas Instruments before joining Compaq, Ruck said: "Even at TI's best, it was never as good as Compaq at its worst."

Main employment centers: Houston is where most of the 6,500 U.S. employees work. Another 2,500 work at plants in Singapore and Scotland.

Headquarters: Compaq Computer Corp.
20555 SH 149
Houston, TX 77070
(713) 370-0670

Cooper Tire

Cooper Tire, the world's ninth largest tire maker, makes replacement tires and industrial rubber products. Employees: 6,545.

★★★★ Pay/Benefits
★★★ Opportunities
★★★★ Job Security
★★★★★ Pride in Work/Company
★★★ Openness/Fairness
★★★ Camaraderie/Friendliness

BIGGEST PLUS: You could retire a millionaire.
BIGGEST MINUS: You may go flat before you get there.

From the outside, Cooper tires look very much like their competitors'. But there's something very special about the inside of Cooper's tires. The tire builder, the worker who tends the machine that blends together the various layers of rubber, stamps his own name (or her name—there are 65 female tire builders) inside the tire. The workers' signatures have been a long tradition here, and the company once promoted it in an advertising slogan: "The tire with two names."

Having workers sign their tires illustrates the pride that pervades Cooper Tire. There is much to be proud of. For one, Cooper Tire remains an independent company. Only one other American tire maker—Goodyear—can say that. All the others have either folded or been bought out by foreigners (Japan's Bridgestone bought Firestone, France's Michelin took over Uniroyal Goodrich, Germany's Continental makes General). Cooper now has the only passenger tire plant in Ohio, once the tire capital of the world. And in an industry that saw more than 40 plants close during the

1980s, Cooper continues to grow. They opened three new plants during the 1980s, nearly doubling the work force.

Pride is something they talk about here. Assistant advertising manager Joyce Huber said: "It seems like everyone associated with Cooper, from the people who build the tires right on down to the independent tire dealers who sell them, feel the pride that's associated with being part of Cooper." Administrative manager Tom Lause, who worked at the Texarkana facility, said: "When you sign a check and they ask, 'Where's your place of employment?' and you say, 'Cooper Tire,' they're impressed."

Headquartered in Findlay, Ohio, 45 miles south of Toledo, Cooper is anything but slick. Their 30-year-old brick headquarters building is spartan. There are no famous sculptures or other artworks in the lobby, just old Cooper tires and the company creed encased in glass. Executives' offices have cheap paneling and heavy metal desks. The company uses only black-and-white photos in their annual report, and unlike other tire companies, they only advertise in magazines and on the Paul Harvey radio show (Harvey uses Cooper tires on his limousine).

Cooper Tire's other U.S. plants are located in small towns in the South —Albany, Georgia; Tupelo and Clarksdale, Mississippi; and Texarkana and El Dorado, Arkansas. This small-town atmosphere helps lend an air of collegiality. According to former president Bill Fitzgerald: "Whether it's the bowling league, the golf team, the community activities, there's some interface between people outside the work environment in the community at large. I think our people are proud that they are Cooper employees. I think that stands for something in the communities in which we operate."

Long tenure also adds to the family feeling. An employee since 1949, Harold Copus, who buffs the sides of whitewall tires, said: "I think the reason they call it family-oriented is because of the seniority. Most people have grown with the company. It was small in the beginning, and it's just expanded from about 1956 on." The family feeling doesn't end with retirement. Retirees are invited to a dinner every year and receive cards from the chairman, Ivan Gorr, on their birthday.

Although Cooper's plants are unionized by the United Rubber Workers (including those in the South), management and labor both feel part of the same family. Findlay plant foreman Jim De Puy explained: "We have golf outings that include anybody from Ivan Gorr to the guy in the plant who cleans the rest rooms. I'm a good friend of the vice-president of the union here. He knows I have a job to do, I know he has a job to do. We negotiate that stuff at work. We've had some good disagreements, too. But at night we're down in his garage painting a car together. Down there we paint cars and it's not Cooper. Here it's Cooper and we don't think cars." There was a brief, three-week strike at the Findlay plant in late 1991 as a result of a dispute over a medical benefits clause in the contract but it doesn't appear to have had any lingering effect.

Communication between blue- and white-collar workers at Cooper has an open and honest flavor. Traffic and transportation manager Ron Lee, who has been at Cooper since 1966, explained: "If you really don't agree with something that's going on, you're not intimidated to voice a negative opinion. They'll listen. Job security is not threatened by having to agree with your boss."

Communications have improved over the years. Lee said: "The old philosophy was that you really didn't let people know how you were doing because you were scared that they were going to ask for higher wages." Now employees have monthly meetings on the factory floor, which include business updates and opportunities to offer suggestions and complaints.

Most supervisors know what it's like in the lower ranks because they came from there. Mechanical drafter Melanie Thomas told us: "I started in the mailroom and had enough opportunities and challenges that now I'm in engineering. That's quite a ways to go for someone with just a high school education. They paid for all my schooling, and I get to graduate this year. And my bosses have been very flexible. If I have a class at 5:00 o'clock, I'm allowed to come in and work from 7:00 to 4:00 or make up the time on the weekends." Several senior managers also started their careers as hourly production employees, including vice-president John Fahl and managers Paul Smith, Jack Adams, and Mike Delaney.

The conviviality here does not mean that people don't work hard. Tire factories are, by nature, hot and dirty, and the process involves difficult manual labor. It can also be stressful because Cooper pays factory workers on a piece-rate system. Sidewall tire buffer Harold Copus said: "Our pay is figured daily and we get paid once a week. We figure our own pay according to how many units you've built and various other options like if your machine broke down or if you're out of material."

Union steward Dick Lane, a tire builder at Findlay, said his brother built tires for about a year but quit "because he couldn't take the stress. When you work piece-rate, you're in there wanting to make as much money as you can make and still build a quality product. Most people can take the stress, but there's a few that can't."

Cooper employees put in a lot of overtime. Lane explains: "In my 30 years of working for Cooper, I've only had five years during which I've worked five days a week. For probably 25 of my years with Cooper I've worked six or seven days a week. That's by their choice. We need production."

Since Cooper usually needs a high level of production, layoffs are rare. Lane says he has been laid off only four weeks during his 30-year tenure. Operations supervisor Jim Miller cited Cooper's reluctance to eliminate jobs. He said: "I've been involved in the fact-finding and decision-making that keeps our plants operating. Just because it's a dying market doesn't mean that they're going to close that plant and put 130 people out of a job.

We have an investment in those people. The building and the equipment are not what's valuable to the company, it's the people."

Cooper shows that it values its people in the best way possible—it compensates them well. In addition to their base compensation, salaried employees can participate in a savings and profit-sharing plan in which the company matches dollar for dollar the first 6 percent of pay saved by an employee. Fifteen-year employee Tony Brinkman, a senior product engineer, explained: "Cooper may not be the best place to start, but it's a fantastic place to retire from. I can go to Du Pont and make probably 20 percent more than I'm making right now. I get calls from headhunters periodically, but I haven't left yet in 15 years. The money is out there if I want to go and pursue it, but I'm building up for the retirement part of it. With our retirement plans, our profit sharing, you won't find anybody that will match it."

By directing their savings into Cooper stock, a number of retirees have left with millions through the profit-sharing program. Here's an example: if an employee who was hired in 1965 at a salary of $6,811 had retired in 1991 with a salary of $36,774 and had invested 6 percent of his or her pay in Cooper stock (matched dollar for dollar by Cooper), he or she would now own 43,807 shares of Cooper stock, worth $2.2 million in 1992. This is in addition to the salaried retirement plan. Cooper stock rose 6,800 percent in the 1980s alone. The employee trust is Cooper's largest shareholder, owning 13 percent of the company.

Union and hourly employees cannot participate in the profit-sharing plan. (Seventy percent of the employees are hourly, the remainder are salaried.) Instead, hourly employees are offered a company-funded retirement plan and a 401(k) savings plan, which they can invest in cash, mutual funds, or stock.

Turnover is low and Cooper is quite selective in hiring. In 1992, 11 percent of the employees had been with Cooper for 25 years or more, 19 percent 15 to 25 years, and 41 percent had at least a five-year tenure. Distribution director Tom Wills, who was hired in 1987, said: "I got a top-secret military clearance in the Air Force in a shorter period of time than it took to get into this company. This company prides itself on being a real pain in the butt to get in with. I think six months had lapsed from the first time I had talked to the industrial relations people until I was given an offer. And at one point I think the manager involved in the activity sensed my frustration and he said, 'The good news is that when people come to Cooper they hardly ever leave.' And that's been my experience. I think they go above and beyond to make sure you're going to fit in the culture. There are very few square pegs in round holes here."

Types of jobs: Production—70 percent; administrative—15 percent; marketing—5 percent; technical/engineering—4 percent; information systems

—2 percent; financial—2 percent; part-time and college work programs—2 percent.

Main employment centers: Cooper has plants in Albany, Georgia (150 employees); Clarksdale (200) and Tupelo (1,040), Mississippi; Auburn, Indiana (680); El Dorado (330) and Texarkana (1,580), Arkansas; Bowling Green (470) and Findlay (1,660), Ohio. They have regional distribution centers in Albany, Georgia; Moraine and Findlay, Ohio; Buena Park, California; Texarkana, Arkansas; Elk Grove Village, Illinois; North Brunswick and New Brunswick, New Jersey; Dallas; Kansas City, Missouri; Tupelo, Mississippi; and Fife, Washington.

Headquarters: The Cooper Tire Company
P.O. Box 550
Lima & Western Aves.
Findlay, OH 45839
(419) 423-1321

OLDEST COMPANIES

Du Pont (1801)
John Deere (1837)
Procter & Gamble (1837)
J. P. Morgan (1838)
UNUM (1848)
Corning (1851)
Alagasco (1852)
Northwestern Mutual Life (1857)
Anheuser-Busch (1860)
Armstrong (1860)
Goldman Sachs (1869)
Tennant (1870)
Morrison & Foerster (1883)
Johnson & Johnson (1886)
SC Johnson Wax (1886)
A. G. Edwards (1887)
Merck (1887)
Springs (1887)
McCormick (1889)
Rosenbluth International (1892)
Inland Steel (1893)
J. M. Smucker (1897)

Corning

CORNING

Corning makes glass products including optical fibers, cookware, ceramic cores for catalytic converters in cars, Steuben glass, and Serengeti sunglasses. They also own Metpath, a large chain of clinical testing labs. U.S. employees: 28,000.

★★★ Pay/Benefits
★★★ Opportunities
★★★★ Job Security
★★★★ Pride in Work/Company
★★★★ Openness/Fairness
★★★★ Camaraderie/Friendliness

BIGGEST PLUS: Crystal-clear communications.
BIGGEST MINUS: They still have a glass ceiling.

Gary Vogt was happy even though he was about to lose his job. When we met him in late 1990, Vogt was operations manager of Corning's Erwin, New York, ceramics plant. A committee of employees, a majority of them union members, had decided to eliminate his job, the number two position in the plant. Vogt was pleased with this turn of events because he had helped set up this committee to make precisely this sort of cost-savings recommendation.

Employees voting to eliminate a manager's job exemplifies the remarkable changes that have taken place here during the past decade. This is one of those rare companies where the buzzwords of the late 1980s—"quality," "empowerment," and "diversity"—have become a way of life. This is especially notable since Corning is one of America's oldest companies, founded in 1851. Its name is associated with glass. (Corning's formal name was

Corning Glass until 1989, when it was changed to Corning, Inc.) The Corning Glass Center, adjacent to the corporate headquarters, is upstate New York's second most popular tourist attraction (first is Niagara Falls), with nearly a half million visitors a year. Visitors can observe some of Corning's workers on the job when they see the Steuben glassblowers create their exquisite—and expensive—vases, bowls, and other etched-glass objects.

Corning doesn't just make glass, though. Their 40 plants churn out everything from cookware (Corningware, Pyrex, Visions, Corelle) to space shuttle windows to light bulbs for turn signals to laboratory hot plates. Corning owns 50 percent of Dow Corning, makers of the controversial silicon gel breast implants. But the two companies are run independently, and Dow Corning is headquartered in Midland, Michigan, the home of Dow Chemical, which owns the other half of the company.

People at Corning trace the company's transformation to 1984, when CEO Jamie Houghton took a training course on quality. Houghton is the great-great-grandson of Corning's founder. His brother and former CEO, Amory Houghton, Jr., represents the district encompassing Corning in Congress. For years the Houghton family had run Corning somewhat paternalistically, providing good benefits and job security but not giving middle managers or other employees much of a say in how things were to be run.

Corning's style changed with the introduction of the total quality movement. Top management went through a two-and-a-half-day training session first, and then sent the trainers on the road for the two years it took to train the rest of the work force. In total, Corning has given quality training to 26,000 employees in six languages. This was only the first wave. Corning subsequently sent the work force through classes in statistical process control, problem-solving techniques, and group dynamics. Every year employees at all levels spend at least 5 percent of their time in training.

Diesel manufacturing section supervisor Ann Sphon said training did make a difference: "Now that the hourly employees are aware of quality, they come right back at you and say, 'You've got the quality principles posted up here, but you are asking me to do this, and this isn't a quality job.' They throw it right back at you. Power has been pushed down, and now we're starting to push back up." Sphon herself has been pushed up—promoted to senior product engineer soon after we met her.

When we visited Corning, we heard numerous stories of how employees are involved. When the telecommunications department moved into a new building in 1986, a team of secretaries told management they wanted to help set up their new work space. Management agreed and the secretaries chose the wall colors, set up service centers and kitchens, and organized the move. Secretary Kathy Foley, who has been here since 1966, explained: "You can voice your opinion and you are heard. When I first started with the company, you weren't asked your opinion and you didn't dare bring it up on your own. Now if you're not heard, it's your own fault for not taking the initiative."

The Erwin Ceramics Plant Vision Statement

We, the people of Erwin Ceramics Plant, have a set of beliefs and rights that we value and are fundamental to our future.

It is the Right of all Employees to:

- Work in a clean, safe and healthy environment.
- Work in a facility free of drugs and alcohol.
- Be fully trained and equipped with the proper tools.
- Work with fully trained, competent and dedicated people.
- Access information that will improve their understanding of our business.
- Challenging and meaningful work with systems that provide an opportunity for growth.
- Be treated with dignity and respect, free of harassment and intimidation.
- Participate in decisions that affect their worklife.
- Expect long-term employment.

Employees in the administrative center also took the initiative when they were asked to interview candidates for a job opening. After the interviews were over, the human resources department thanked the employees but told them their department was going to make the final decision. The workers wouldn't hear of it. They made the decision, and their candidate was hired. One of the employees involved, executive secretary Penny Schoonover, told us: "Everybody listens to me more than they used to."

The most dramatic changes can be seen in plants where production workers now perform tasks formerly done only by supervisors and managers. In some plants, workers set their own shifts, schedule their own vacations, make job assignments, and run production meetings. In 1988, at the Erwin ceramics plant, where they make catalytic converters, operations manager Vogt assembled eight salaried employees and eight union members to draft a vision statement. They asked all of the plant employees to list three words to describe the kind of plant they would like to work in. These lists were then used to create a new vision statement for the plant. After completing this statement, they organized a design team of 12 union and four salaried people to implement it. Result: they decided to eliminate 80 jobs, including Vogt's. However, no one will be laid off. The eliminations will be handled through attrition. Vogt himself moved up to plant manager when his former boss was promoted to headquarters. Another result was that in the first year, defects decreased by 38 percent and were running 50 percent fewer than in older plant lines using more traditional work methods.

Denny LeBaron, a member of the design team, had previously worked for Corning for a year and a half, leaving in 1974 because he thought it was run like "a dictatorship." He returned in 1986, and feels the most dramatic change has been the cooperation between management and union employees. Because of the quality training, he believes, "the barriers started breaking down between 'we' and 'they.'"

In addition to sharing decision-making with employees, Corning offers all employees a corporate performance bonus based on the company's profits and all salaried employees an extra two weeks of vacation every five years. Another advantage of working for Corning is its location, a small town (population 12,000) of the same name nestled in the foothills of the Appalachian Mountains near the scenic Finger Lakes. Kathy Foley told us: "Part of the fun is that the people that I work with are people that I want to play with. I enjoy seeing them outside of work." Because Corning is the major employer in this small community, many members of the same family end up working together. Fifteen-year employee Penny Schoonover told us: "I always thought that Corning was the place to work. My parents, grandparents, aunts, cousins, they all work here, so I thought I had to. The week after I graduated from high school I started with Corning."

There are some drawbacks to small towns, especially for minorities. Between 1980 and 1987 one of every six black professionals working here left the company, citing lack of career opportunities as their reason for departure. Up until 1988 African-Americans who worked for Corning were driving 98 miles to Rochester to get a haircut. Corning has tried to make life more attractive for minority employees in recent years. Not only have they recruited a black hairdresser, but the company helped bring in a new cable channel, the Black Entertainment Network, and encouraged the local radio station to widen their music selection. Corning managers have been told that retention and promotion of women and minorities will figure in promotion decisions, and managers spend two days in workshops designed to teach them about racism and sexism. Corning's hard work has started to pay off. BusinessWeek reported that in 1987 the attrition rate for black employees was 15.3 percent. In 1992 that rate had gone down to 6.2 percent. Change does come slowly. Of the 40 vice-presidents, only two are female. However, they do have an exemplary child-care program. The Corning Children's Center opened in 1980, and construction began in 1992 on a new $1.2-million child-care center that will accommodate 150 children.

There's still one touch of the old company that employees still appreciate. During the week before Christmas, Jamie Houghton and other top executives walk through the hallways of every Corning facility in the area to thank employees for their contributions that year and to wish them happy holidays.

Main employment centers: Corning has 25 plants in the United States and another 11 internationally. States with Corning plants include New York, Pennsylvania, Virginia, California, Ohio, Illinois, Kentucky, West Virginia, and North Carolina. About 6,000 work in the Corning, New York, area.

Headquarters: Corning, Inc.
Houghton Park
Corning, NY 14831
(607) 974-9000

Cray Research

Cray Research is the leading maker of supercomputers. U.S. employees: 4,659.

★★★★ Pay/Benefits
★★★ Opportunities
★★★ Job Security
★★★★ Pride in Work/Company
★★★★ Openness/Fairness
★★★★ Camaraderie/Friendliness

BIGGEST PLUS: On the cutting edge of computer power.
BIGGEST MINUS: You have to live and breathe supercomputers.

To some extent, all companies are defined by the products they make or the services they offer. But at Cray Research, identification with the prod-

ucts—supercomputers—is intense. Employees at all levels understand that
the mission of this company is to design, build, and sell the world's fastest
and most powerful computers, machines with awesome computational
power that can be used to solve very complex problems and come with
price tags of up to $30 million. Employees not only understand that, they
feel that the work they do has a direct influence on Cray's efforts to remain
the leader in supercomputing.

As is the case with other companies in the computer industry, these
efforts are sometimes framed grandiloquently. Cray's CEO, John A.
Rollwagen, who has an electrical engineering degree from MIT and an
M.B.A. from the Harvard Business School, likens working at Cray to being
on "a mission for God," meaning that the supercomputers designed here
will play prime roles in helping scientists come up with answers to such
scourges as AIDS and the hole in the ozone layer. The supercomputer has
made life easier for a lot of users. Auto companies, for example, no longer
have to crash cars to test their safety. As human resources vice-president
Deborah Barber told us: "It's a different thing than attaching yourself to a
tube of toothpaste." Koushik Ghosh, a senior programmer-analyst, said: "I
sometimes come in on Saturday and Sunday mornings so that I can have
the entire machine to myself. We have the world's best computers. That's
why I came to Cray."

Supercomputers are the only products made by Cray. Treasury manager
John Allen cites this single-product lens as a "unifying influence," pointing
out that Cray doesn't make radios or television sets or camcorders, the
profits from which can fund other lines of business. "We only have one
product line," he said. "We do supercomputers and we don't have the
resources that some of our would-be competitors have. It does away with a
lot of bureaucratic crap because everybody knows there isn't a lot of time or
money to waste."

To carry out its mission, Cray has fostered an open environment characterized by flexibility, independence, and risk-taking. At its new campus in
Eagan, just south of Minneapolis, informality reigns. There are no reserved
parking spots, no executive dining rooms, but there is a wonderful glass-
walled cafeteria, where a chef was cooking pasta to order the day we were
there. The standard uniform seemed to be jeans and plaid shirts. Cray feels
that workplace qualities, among them pride, diversity, and having fun, are
so important that they have been documented in a statement called "The
Cray Style." Every new employee receives a copy so that he or she will
know what to expect.

Employees shared with us their experiences with Cray culture—and they
didn't always agree. Dissent and open discussion are encouraged here,
along with a recognition that sometimes you make a mistake or fail. Barb
Norton, a senior program supervisor at Cray's Rice Lake plant, said: "You
feel like you live at Cray. It's like my address because I'm there more than I

am at home." To which Elaine Frankowski, a biochemist who came to Cray in 1990 from Honeywell, retorted: "I don't. This is a very important part of my life, this is not my life. I have a family, I have friends, I have children, I have community organizations, I have outside interests. I come in here in the morning and I work flat out for more hours than I would for any other company, but I go home and this is not my address." Frankowski, when we saw her, was doing something that had never been tried before at Cray—developing a software applications program in computational chemistry to run on non-Cray machines; it's part of the company's efforts in network supercomputing. She left Honeywell for Cray because she wanted to pursue the technical route rather than the managerial path, and it's possible to do that here because of a strong parallel career program that extends recognition, titles, and money to technical and professional people who don't want to be top managers.

"At Honeywell," said Frankowski, "if you're not in management, you're nothing." She described Cray "as a company where grown-ups work," relating that John Rollwagen "came up to me a couple of weeks ago and said he had a bone to pick with me and told me what it was, and I said, 'Don't whine at me, it's not my fault.' At Honeywell, when the CEO walked around, he had this phalanx of little men in gray suits that looked like they were carved out of soap around him and you couldn't even talk to him. So I'm an adult in the sense that I can tell the CEO that I know the reason that this is happening and it has nothing to do with what I am doing. And I know that two days later he talked to a group of people, and he had actually heard what I said."

Various people we talked to emphasized that this is not a place for people who need to be told what to do. Instead, they said, Cray is a company where people are expected to seize the initiative. Since 1989 the company has been giving annual awards for leadership and innovation to employees nominated by their peers. In 1991, 14 individuals and six teams with a total of 49 people won awards. Award winners have come from all wings of the company. Winners and their guests attend a day-long event in Minneapolis, including small group meetings with senior management, and each winner gets a crystal obelisk and 25 shares of Cray stock (valued at up to $1,000 in 1991). Five of them are also awarded sabbaticals of three to six months. Those who are chosen for the sabbatical continue to receive their pay and benefits, and get an additional $5,000 for expenses. In 1990 a task force of employees crafted a statement on what leadership means here. The statement said: "Leadership often is confused with management, but while not everyone is a manager, everyone certainly can be a leader."

Volatility is one of the hallmarks of the fledgling computer industry, and Cray has not been immune to it. In three years, 1987 to 1990, the company lost three key people, including its founder, Seymour Cray, who went off to pursue his supercomputing dreams in a new company, Cray Computer, and its president, Marcelo A. Gumucio, who was fired by Rollwagen over differences in style. Steve Chen, one of the technical leaders of the company, also left to start a company funded by IBM.

The Gumucio dismissal in 1990 was handled in classic Cray style. First, employees got the news. Then the company shared with the media what it had told employees (Cray has a unique press-release policy: it sends a memo to employees, copies the memo, and sends it out to the media), inviting reporters to Cray to interview Rollwagen and Gumucio in adjacent offices. Four days later, Rollwagen, dressed in a green plaid shirt and slacks, invited 900 employees at corporate headquarters to the cafeteria, where he explained why Gumucio had left and fielded questions from the audience. This session was videotaped and sent off to other Cray facilities. The brunt of Rollwagen's message was that he and Gumucio had different operating styles, resulting in confusion in the ranks. Gumucio's style was depicted as being "more formal" and "structured," while Rollwagen has a more "intuitive" approach. "We ran into trouble trying to marry my management style and Marcelo's at the head of the organization," said Rollwagen. "After talking to a lot of people, I realized there was something happening that absolutely was intolerable: the growth of fear and blame. If we get in a mode where we're afraid to take a risk or extend ourselves, both individually and collectively, we're not going to stay at the leading edge."

Another jolt to the system came in late 1989, when Cray had its first layoffs since the company was founded in 1972. Some 430 people left the company, most of them from the main manufacturing plant in Chippewa Falls, Wisconsin, Seymour Cray's hometown. However, Cray offered such an attractive package to induce employees to leave that only 30 people were fired. The rest volunteered for a package that offered three weeks' severance pay plus two weeks' pay for every year of service. In addition, Cray gave departing full-time employees tuition aid of $4,000 to pursue any educational program they desired. Departing part-time employees were eligible for $2,000 in tuition aid. In total, 193 employees had their tuitions paid by the company. As the main employer in Chippewa Falls, Cray felt it was important to help employees gain skills in other fields.

So 430 people—and Seymour Cray—left the company in 1989. Rod Anderson, a training supervisor in Chippewa Falls, said: "When Seymour left, it was devastating because we were Seymour. And then when Seymour left, there was a healing process, and it wasn't getting rid of the bad because he was not the bad, it was knowing that we could survive without. It was growth because we can survive without Seymour, we can survive without a figurehead, the top design engineer, because we are Cray Research, we are not one person, we are everybody from the lowest person right up to John Rollwagen."

Rollwagen, a Zen-like character who was Cray's first salesman, has been running the company since 1981. He likes to tell stories to create a mythology that holds the company together. For many years, he told "Seymour stories." And he still tells them even though Seymour has left. One story has it that every summer Seymour Cray would build a sailboat and then destroy it in the fall, the point being that one shouldn't copy from one's previous work. It's not clear whether Seymour actually did this—maybe he did it once, one employee told us—but that doesn't stop Rollwagen from telling the story.

Rollwagen has created some mythology of his own. The company's old headquarters in Minneapolis had a fountain in front that was created by a local artist, Andrew Leicester. Many Cray employees hated the structure and vented their feelings by placing rubber ducks in the fountain. Rollwagen accepted the prank by starting a tradition called Ducky Days, a company picnic featuring outrageous duck awards, duck tug-of-war, duck hot dogs, duck beer. When Cray moved to its new campus setting in Eagan, the despised fountain, called Octal, was moved there. At the first company meeting of employees, executive vice-president Bob Ewald, who's usually dressed in jeans, appeared at the podium in a three-piece suit to introduce Rollwagen. The CEO came out dressed in a yellow duck suit, as did other members of the executive team. Rollwagen explained that Cray had spared no expense to hire the finest designers to come up with duck suits that henceforth would be the dress code at the company. Then Rollwagen introduced the fountain architect, Leicester, "who created the beloved Octal, which we couldn't bear to leave behind." They went out on the deck overlooking a pond where Leicester was going to dedicate the blessed fountain. The artist walked up to the railing, pushed a detonator—and blew the fountain into smithereens.

How do you get an artist to blow up his own work? Rollwagen said he told Leicester, "I want to make you as famous as Seymour Cray." In fact, it turned out to be a devastating experience for Leicester. Although he had agreed to do it, he failed to realize how it would affect him. Rollwagen said Leicester's face turned white with shock—and for more than a year after that, the artist was still angry at having been dragooned into destroying his fountain.

But now it's part of the mythology at Cray Research. The annual picnic is still called Ducky Days, and at the quarterly meeting that followed Gumucio's dismissal, Rollwagen and other top executives conducted the entire meeting dressed in duck suits. Human resources vice-president Deborah Barber puts it this way: "John believes that one of his roles as CEO is to create symbols, because that is what people rally around. The burning of the fountain was symbolic of how we stay at the creative edge. The idea is you burn everything that went before and you keep starting over with a fresh sheet. You don't want to be pulled down by old thoughts that are no longer creative." Pow!

Dayton Hudson

═══════════════════════════

Dayton Hudson
Corporation ▓

Dayton Hudson, the nation's fourth largest general merchandise retailer, operates Target, Mervyn's, Dayton's, Hudson's, and Marshall Field stores in 33 states. U.S. employees: 168,000.

★ ★ ★ Pay/Benefits
★ ★ ★ ★ Opportunities
★ ★ ★ Job Security
★ ★ ★ ★ Pride in Work/Company
★ ★ ★ Openness/Fairness
★ ★ ★ Camaraderie/Friendliness

BIGGEST PLUS: Opportunities are in stock.
BIGGEST MINUS: You're part of a huge inventory.

In 1984 we had this to say about Dayton Hudson: "They doubled their work force in the past five years—and may double it again in the next five." Well, they didn't quite manage to do that, but they weren't far off. This Minneapolis-based store operator had 90,000 employees then; in early 1992 they had 168,000. It was a notable achievement in view of the disasters suffered by many of the biggest players in retailing: Federated Department Stores, Associated Dry Goods, Allied Stores, Carter Hawley Hale, R. H. Macy. In this minefield, Dayton Hudson proved to be nimble. With an assist from the Minnesota legislature, they staved off a takeover bid and emerged, at the end of the 1980s, as one of the Titans of U.S. retailing, outsold only by Wal-Mart, Sears, K mart, and J. C. Penney.

For someone looking for new opportunities, Dayton Hudson is a company to consider. In the past five years they have opened 312 new stores. In mid-1992 they were operating nearly 800 stores in 33 states. And this expansion is not over. More than 50 new stores were on the drawing boards for 1992, and another 300 are planned by the end of 1995.

Dayton Hudson itself is not where the jobs are. This is a holding company that occupies three floors in the IDS Tower in downtown Minneapolis, across the street from the Dayton's department store from which this retailing empire sprang. Only 170 people work for Dayton Hudson at their headquarters. The jobs are in the stores, especially on the sales floors, where 62 percent of employees work.

There are three distinctly different types of stores within Dayton Hudson. Each division of the chain has its own history, its own culture, and even some of its own operating practices. Dayton Hudson is the glue that holds them together, maintaining a set of core values common to all three wings.

The dowager of the chain is the department store division—Dayton's, Hudson's, and Marshall Field—where there are cultures within cultures. It's now the smallest of the three parts. Here we have the old-line, gracious, spacious emporiums that used to anchor the downtowns of our major cities. Each part has its origins in a big midwestern city. George D. Dayton opened his Dayton Dry Goods store in Minneapolis in 1903. Joseph Lowthian Hudson opened a men's and boys' haberdashery in the old Detroit Opera House in 1881. And Marshall Field founded his store in Chicago in 1852. At the turn of the century, Marshall Field was the largest dry goods establishment in the world. Its flagship store in Chicago's Loop reflects the quiet, commodious elegance of a bygone era. Today, this division has 62 department stores, the biggest concentrations being in Chicago (14 Marshall Field stores), the Twin Cities (10 Daytons), and Detroit (nine Hudsons).

The next biggest link in the Dayton Hudson chain is Mervyn's, started by Mervyn Morris in California in 1949. Mervyn's specializes in selling moderately priced clothing to middle-class customers. When it was acquired by Dayton Hudson in 1978, Mervyn's had 47 stores. At the end of 1991, it had 245 stores in 15 states.

Dayton Hudson's biggest unit is the Target discount store chain. Started by Dayton's from scratch in 1962, it now encompasses close to 500 stores in 32 states.

It's clearly different working in an elegant, high-fashion place like Dayton's or Marshall Field from working in a more casual, family atmosphere like Mervyn's or in the more rambunctious, supermarketlike din of a Target. Steve Watson, who rose from the department store side to president of Dayton Hudson, talked to us about the differences. "This company," he said, "believes in giving people the ability to run their own businesses. We have always described ourselves as autonomous. Target runs its business, Mervyn's runs its business, and the department stores run their business— and they don't run them in exactly the same way."

The common theme we heard from employees is that Dayton Hudson runs a hassle-free environment where individuality is respected—and ideas are sought from all levels. Target appears to be more free-swinging than the two older divisions, but they all seem to share the same values about people. Fred Donath, a sales manager at the Dayton's store in Southdale, just south of Minneapolis, said to us: "I like working for this company. It is a real open company and I am treated as if I have a brain. I can take that attitude of 'get involved' and I hate to say 'down' to the lowest level because we don't consider the hourly people the lowest level. They are critical to our success and we expect them to have good ideas and to serve those ideas up and be entrepreneurial in their little piece of the business. Every idea is valued. Not every idea is a good idea, but it is valued."

Central credit collections manager Debbie Lynch agreed: "I think what stands out about this company is the culture and value that they place on challenging individuals and letting them run their business. I am responsible for a lot of dollars that are past due with the company. I have a staff of 70 people and we have been successful and our company isn't in deep trouble and I think the reason is because we rely on our employees to come up with the ideas for us to collect better and do our job better. People have such great ideas and the thing that I find interesting is that I am not expected to be the driver of the business, I am the facilitator."

A recently hired Target employee, Debra Davis, who works in college relations, told us that in the latest annual employee survey conducted by the company, hourly people complained about the 10 percent discount card they were getting with their paychecks—it was good for just one week. They asked why they couldn't get the same card received by salaried people —it's good for a year. "And we got it like that, right away," said Davis. "It's a permanent card. They listen to what we say."

Efforts to involve people have been growing apace here. The department store division has a performance-plus plan enabling sales consultants—the term Dayton Hudson uses for salespersons—to set sales goals geared to their hourly rate and collect commissions on sales above that level. At Target stores, when there's a question about the price of an item, the cashier in the checkout lane is empowered to ask the customer what the price is and, if it sounds reasonable, simply ring it up without getting any okays. The department stores are also promoting more sales consultants into management track positions. This change is reflected in the advance of women in management ranks. In 1980 only 7 percent of Dayton Hudson officers were female; today 20 percent are. But they still have a way to go. The work force here is 75 percent female.

Dayton Hudson companies, like all retailers, employ a lot of part-timers, and flexible schedules play important roles. Target and Mervyn's have more alternative work programs than the department stores. Dan Glynn, a Target warehouse worker who has been with the company for 18 years, explained how it worked in his area: "They have two classifications. Flex regulars have to be available to work up to 40 hours a week and last year most of them averaged at least 32 hours. Part-timers work up to 20 hours a week and the company can't force them to work more than 20 hours. When times are really busy, they ask them to volunteer. So people who don't want to work that many hours have a choice of staying on as a part-timer as opposed to becoming a flex regular."

According to Glynn: "At the warehouse level everybody makes $14 an hour on the floor, even part-timers, who work up to that level in about three years. A lot of our part-time help has been here 10 or 12 years. A lot of them have even been through college. In fact, I was looking at our wage statements, and a lot of those part-timers made $26 or $28 an hour last year. One of the updated benefits we have had in the last two years is that they have access to medical insurance and to our savings and stock-purchase plan, which now has gone up to a dollar-for-dollar match."

While those might be prevailing rates in the warehouse, the entry-level wage here—say for a telephone operator or sales consultant—is $6 an hour. There is an annual merit increase. A management trainee will start at about $22,000 a year. The benefits are good but they vary by division. For example, at Mervyn's and the department store division, part-timers need to work at least 24 hours a week to gain access to benefits. However, at Target, benefits are based on length of service and grade. This means that part-timers do not have to work a minimum number of hours to get health insurance, a unique benefit. Nancy Laagard, director of compensation and benefits for Target, explained the rationale as follows: "One of the reasons we did that is because there are so many people in the retail industry who work part-time who have been with us seven or eight years and was it fair to say to these people, 'Sorry, but just because you are a dedicated cashier who only works on Saturdays and Sundays, you don't get any benefits'?"

Other benefits also vary by division. New mothers who want to take extra time off after the birth of a child can get a 24-week leave with a job-back guarantee at Target; at Mervyn's, it's 16 weeks; at the department stores, it's six weeks. Department store employees who adopt a child can get Dayton Hudson support up to $1,200—that's not a benefit available to Target or Mervyn's people. But parents who work at Target headquarters in downtown Minneapolis may now place their children in a Montessori grade school that was opened a few blocks away as part of the city's public school system. Target pays the lease on the space and helps to pay the salaries of the two teachers. Thirty-eight Target children were enrolled there in 1992. Jenny Radcliffe, who edits the sprightly employee publications at Target, said the school was why she joined Target.

A number of employees we talked to expressed pride at working for a company whose commitment to the communities where it operates has made it an exemplar of social responsibility in business. Most big companies in America contribute about 1 percent of pretax profits to philanthropic purposes. Following a policy adopted by the Dayton family after World War II, Dayton Hudson allocates 5 percent *every year*. That meant contributions of $27 million in 1991. Monica Kenney, who manages the Target store in Knollwood, a Minneapolis suburb, related how four years ago "Target loaned me out to the United Way from July until November. They paid my salary but I worked for the United Way and helped run the Minneapolis campaign." Paul Singer, vice-president for merchandise planning and control, said: "When *Sesame Street* comes on, you can see that it's sponsored by Dayton Hudson department stores or Target. My kids tell their friends, 'My daddy works for Target.' "

Reggie Walton, alterations manager for Dayton's, said: "It is very important to me that I give back to the community. I do a lot of volunteer work, and the company has been very supportive of that. I take a week from my vacation to do volunteer work, but if there is any extended time, the company has always said, 'We have no problem with that, you do what you feel you have to do.' "

Walton, a black man who came here six years ago from Omaha, where he worked for another retail chain, conceded that he was uneasy about making this move because Minneapolis—and Dayton Hudson—seemed to be so white. "It was very white and still is," he said, "but I have found that I am not looked upon as a minority. I am looked upon as an employee. I have a boss who gives me the freedom to run the business as I see fit. I am allowed to make all the changes I want." Walton runs the alterations business for 14 Dayton stores. More than 200 people work for him. "They are of all nationalities," he said. "I call it my United Nations."

Types of jobs: Target: store operations—92 percent; distribution—5 percent; administration—3 percent. Dayton Hudson: store operations—81 percent; distribution—10 percent; administration—9 percent. Mervyn's: store operations—89 percent; distribution—5 percent; administration—6 percent.

Main employment centers: With stores in 33 states, Dayton Hudson is everywhere in the U.S. except for the Northeast. Its biggest states are: California (39,950 employees), Minnesota (22,900), Michigan (15,800), Illinois (10,500), Texas (14,500), and Florida (5,500).

Headquarters: Dayton Hudson Corp.
777 Nicollet Mall
Minneapolis, MN 55402
(612) 370-6948

John Deere

John Deere is the largest producer of farm machines like tractors and harvesters. They also make construction and forestry equipment and lawn mowers for golf courses and homeowners. Employees: 36,000.

★ ★ ★ ★   Pay/Benefits
★ ★ ★   Opportunities
★ ★ ★   Job Security
★ ★ ★ ★ ★   Pride in Work/Company
★ ★ ★ ★   Openness/Fairness
★ ★ ★   Camaraderie/Friendliness

BIGGEST PLUS: A proud history rooted in America's heartland.
BIGGEST MINUS: Your job may be harvested.

The 1980s brought almost nothing but bad news to John Deere. The bottom fell out of the farm equipment business. In 1982 demand for farm machinery was less than one-quarter of what it had been the previous year. Deere reacted by "downsizing"—encouraging employees to take early retirement and laying off others. Numbers tell the story: in 1981 Deere had 61,000 workers; by 1991 they were down to 36,000. And in 1986 Deere suffered a five-and-a-half-month strike by the United Auto Workers, the longest in the company's 150-year history.

That's the bad news. The good news is that Deere survived the decade. That was no mean accomplishment in an industry in which every other farm machinery equipment maker has either been merged, sold, or went bankrupt. But Deere didn't just survive the 1980s. They did so in a way that made Deere a much better place to work. They entered new businesses, and instead of closing down factories, Deere kept all of them open, which earned them goodwill in the small Midwest towns where Deere has plants. Also, their relations with the UAW are better than ever, according to both management and labor, who have embarked on numerous experiments in participatory management. In 1991 Deere and the UAW signed a new contract without much fuss. The UAW then offered a similar contract to Caterpillar, where management refused to accept it, provoking a bitter strike in early 1992 that ended with the capitulation of the union.

We visited Deere's huge Harvester Works plant in Moline, Illinois, where they make the world's largest harvesters—all painted in the distinctive Deere shade of green. Their top-of-the-line Model 9600 stands 13 feet 10 inches tall, cuts 12 rows of corn at a time, and sells for $135,000. Like all of Deere's plants, Harvester Works had far fewer people in 1991 (3,200) than they had in 1981 (6,800). But in meeting with employees, we didn't feel that we were talking with survivors of a disaster. Quite the opposite. They talked enthusiastically about dramatic changes that have given more authority to lower-level employees.

Ray Sprouse, Jr., has been working on the assembly line at Harvester Works for nearly 30 years. In recent years, the company has trained supervisors and assembly-line workers to work more cooperatively, which means lower-level employees now have more control over their work and supervisors have changed into coordinators. Here's how Sprouse sees these changes: "I like the idea of the company trusting us and letting us do our job. Everybody is starting to listen to the people who are actually doing the job. Nobody knows better what they are doing than the person doing it. Our jobs are a lot harder than what they were, so it also gives you a challenge. It lets you use your mind. Ten or 15 years ago the philosophy was park your brains at the gate when you come in, just do what you are told. Now you work as an individual."

When we asked Sprouse for an example of the changed work environment, he told a story about a defective combine that had been shipped to Minnesota. The company sent Sprouse to check into the problem. He recalls: "I went into the dealership up there, and the people were totally astounded that somebody from the assembly line was there to help them." Sprouse, too, was astounded by Deere's willingness to send him there. Letting an assembly-line worker deal directly with customers was simply unimaginable in the past.

When we toured the plant, we saw many examples of the new Deere. Soon after we entered the plant, we spied an unusual sight. A welder on the assembly line put down his blowtorch, flipped up his mask, pulled a cellular phone from his belt, and started talking to someone. After he completed his call, we asked the welder, Gary Versluis, to explain what he was doing. He said that he was talking to someone in another part of the plant who supplies parts for the axles. He told us that a few months earlier he had noticed how much time he spent walking to various parts of the plant—to confer with others, get needed parts, find out the status of particular items. He told his supervisor that he thought it would save him time, and the company money, if he could have a phone. Much to Versluis's surprise, his supervisor quickly authorized the $1,200 purchase.

Workers regaled us with such stories. Deere people see themselves as working for the premier company in their industry, with a tradition of high-quality products. Pay and benefits are second to none in the industry. They're also proud of Deere's long history, one that's deeply rooted in the soil of the nation's Farm Belt. Deere's vintage two-cylinder tractor, produced between 1918 and 1960 and known as Poppin' Johnny or Johnny Popper, has a fan club, with more than 13,000 members. When the club held an expo of antique tractors several years ago in Waterloo, Iowa, an estimated 100,000 visitors showed up to see the 175 fully restored Poppin' Johnnys.

You can also get a sense of Deere's proud history by visiting the corporate headquarters in Moline. Surrounded by 1,200 acres of cornfields, the headquarters was designed by Eero Saarinen, who used unpainted steel to express what he called "the big, forceful, functional character of [Deere's] products. No brashly modern or pretentious building would have been right." Called by some the "Versailles of the cornfields," the building overlooks several ponds replete with swans, carp, and numerous fountains. The fountains are not just for landscaping. They also cool water for the building's air-conditioning system. A Henry Moore sculpture rests on an island in the larger pond, and the interior of the building houses an extensive art collection of works from Japan, Turkey, Brazil, New Guinea, and the United States.

In addition to being a wonderful environment for the nearly 2,000 people who work there, the headquarters is also a major tourist attraction for farmers and others, about 30,000 a year, who come to see the extensive collection of farm equipment. A highlight of the exhibit is a three-dimensional mural made up of more than 2,000 historical items of rural Americana from 1837 to 1918. Of particular interest is a replica of the first successful self-cleaning steel plow, which John Deere developed in 1837 when he started the company.

One other remarkable aspect of Deere's headquarters is that most offices, including those of the top officers, have glass walls and doors, which are rarely closed. Accounting department employee Judy Finnessy, who previously worked at the Harvester Works plant, said: "There is an open-door policy at Deere. There are no doors on the offices; you can pretty much go in when you want to, talk to your boss or his boss, with anybody."

Employees feel free to call top managers by their first names, but people don't dress informally here. It's mostly dark suits and white shirts for men, conservative-looking suits for women.

The headquarters attire reflects Deere's midwestern character. President

David Stowe told us: "It takes a certain type of person to work for this company. It has a unique set of customers—contractors and farmers. These are very independent men, very entrepreneurial men who take risks every year in their businesses. These are demanding people and have a right to be demanding. You don't dictate to them but you do develop interchanges and ways of working with them. To enjoy this kind of work you have to have a natural feel for machinery and people who work with machinery. I wouldn't say you have to like living in the Midwest to work for Deere, because we have plants and sales units all over the country. But this is the heartland. If you are a swinging New Yorker or L.A. surfer and can't give that up, you better not come to work for Deere."

John Leinart, who works in the industrial engineering department, insists that being firmly rooted in the Midwest implies a "midwestern value system. The value system for the whole country is changing, but we are going back to staying home on Saturday nights with your families instead of the me, me, me stuff. The coasts are changing but we never changed."

Integrity is an important component of this value system. Commercial systems manager John Boten said: "I started out in accounting and have a good memory. I saw an invoice where it was obvious that the company which had billed us had made a mistake and substantially undercharged us. There was no question about it, we paid the vendor the amount that was due. Like Abraham Lincoln, it was taught to me early in my career that I had to have integrity in everything that I do here."

As homespun as this philosophy sounds, it's useful to keep in mind that the architect of the modern Deere was William Hewitt, a sophisticated San Franciscan who married into the Deere family and took the helm of the company in 1955 after his father-in-law, Colonel Charles Deere Wiman, great-grandson of the company founder, died of cancer. Hewitt ran Deere from 1955 to 1982, presiding over significant innovations in farm machinery and expansion of the company beyond the United States. And it was Hewitt who went to Eero Saarinen and asked him to build the sophisticated headquarters building in the middle of Illinois cornfields.

Main employment centers: Deere has factories in Kansas, Iowa, Illinois, Tennessee, Wisconsin, and New Jersey. They also have plants in Canada, France, Germany, Mexico, Argentina, Spain, and South Africa.

Headquarters: John Deere & Company
John Deere Rd.
Moline, IL 61265
(309) 765-8000

Delta Air Lines

Delta is the third largest airline in the United States. U.S. employees: 64,000.

★★★★★ Pay/Benefits
★★★★ Opportunities
★★★★ Job Security
★★★★★ Pride in Work/Company
★★★★ Openness/Fairness
★★★★★ Camaraderie/Friendliness

BIGGEST PLUS: You'll get first-class treatment.
BIGGEST MINUS: It has its ups and downs.

In 1984 we described the relationship between Delta and its employees as one of the most publicized love affairs in the corporate world. We're happy to report that it's still going strong.

This is quite a feat, since Delta went through a lot of changes in the past decade. In 1987 they took over Western Airlines and its 11,700 employees. Four years later they took over many Pan Am routes and another 7,800 employees. By 1992 Delta's work force had doubled, it had become a major international carrier, with extensive routes to both Europe and the Far East, and it was vying with American and United for the title of the nation's largest airline.

Despite these changes, employees still refer to the Delta "family." Not only do longtime Delta workers use this term but former Western and Pan Am employees talk about being part of the family. Joanne Wells, who came to Delta in the Western merger, said: "There is something a little bit different here from Western. I noticed it when I first came, like when you go down the hallway, for example, people would say hello to you, even if they had never seen you before."

Terrell Jones, a former Pan Am pilot who now flies Delta's Boston-New York-Washington shuttle routes, had been through an earlier takeover when he was flying for National Airlines, which was taken over by Pan Am in 1979. The ensuing decade was a nightmare, marked by constant conflicts. By contrast, Jones said he is delighted with the reception he's received from his Delta counterparts. He called Delta "pilot heaven."

The Delta family feeling surfaces in many ways. Roger Todd, a worker at Atlanta's Hartsfield International Airport, told us this story: "In 1985 my dad passed away and was buried about 80 miles away, almost to Alabama. Ten or 12 guys, coworkers, came to the funeral. Later on we went back to my mom's house, and neighbors and others just couldn't believe that so many people had driven that far. It does make a big difference. We are getting mighty big but I still think we're family. We're just a bigger family." At Delta headquarters receptionist Lawanda Oswalt sends flowers to employees and their families who are ill or have a death in the family. In 1991 she sent 2,980 flower arrangements.

Delta's president, Whit Hawkins, who started here in 1955, said: "I have friends here. They are not just people I work with. I enjoy them. Our families have grown up together. Every time I get off an airplane somewhere, I probably am going to run into someone I know. It's a feeling that is very good. Let me tell you another example: I had a friend who said he'd like to have one of our bumper stickers to put on his car. And I said, 'Fine. But why?' And he said, 'Because if I have a flat tire out here on the interstate there is a darn good chance somebody from Delta is going to come by and help me.' "

Delta's family has always had a Southern flavor, as the airline has deep roots in the red soil of the Deep South. It still holds its annual stockholders meetings in the Mississippi Delta town of Monroe, Louisiana, where the company was founded in 1926. Many of the firm's executives, including the chairman and the president, are Southerners. There's a touch of Southern conservatism in the strict dress code. Men are not permitted to wear earrings nor can women wear miniskirts. *The Wall Street Journal* reported that Delta refused to release an old billboard photo of model Marla Maples to the media after her affair with Donald Trump became public.

Getting into this family isn't easy. Delta conducts extensive interviews and gives potential employees a psychological test. And the competition is fierce. In 1991 Delta received over 10,000 applications for flight attendant jobs every month. Of those, 200 were hired.

Besides the family environment, Delta has other drawing cards. It pays better than any other airline. In 1991 Delta's average salary was $44,000, with pilots averaging more than $110,000 and flight attendants more than $33,000. Delta pays top dollar even though none of its workers, aside from the pilots and flight dispatchers, belongs to a union in a heavily unionized industry. Delta's benefits also top those of other airlines. They offer one that is a rarity in corporate America: survivor benefits. If a Delta employee dies, the spouse or beneficiary receives either a lump sum of up to $50,000 or a monthly check of 70 percent of the employee's average earnings for as long as 30 years. This benefit is in addition to life insurance payments. Like other major airlines, Delta employees receive pass privileges. After 10 years employees get passes for unlimited free flights anywhere Delta flies in the United States.

Another reason Delta is the preferred employer among the major airlines has been its no-layoff policy. Even though this industry is notoriously cyclical, Delta has avoided layoffs of permanent workers since 1952. In mid-1992, after posting huge losses, Delta announced it was reducing its work force by 5 percent. But they avoided eliminating any permanent employees by cutting 2,000 to 3,000 temporary workers and allowing normal attrition to reduce other positions.

These policies have a big impact. Cargo handler Roger Todd said: "You know that management is going to treat you the way they would expect to be treated if they were in the work force and you were in management. They treat you fairly. I'm in cargo now but spent 20-something years in passenger service. And it is easy to go out and do a little extra for a passenger when you know that the company is going to take good care of you."

During tough times Delta's top managers have cut their salaries first before taking any actions that affect the rest of the troops. During the cutbacks of 1992, CEO Ron Allen reduced his salary by $100,000 to $475,000, and Hawkins, along with eight senior vice-presidents, agreed to take a 5 percent cut in pay.

Like most Delta executives, Allen came up through the ranks. He started in 1963 as a part-time methods analyst in the personnel department while he was a student at Georgia Tech. Hawkins started his career as a ramp agent. Three senior vice-presidents started out in entry-level jobs, and 11 out of the 18 vice-presidents started out on the bottom rung of the corporate ladder.

Delta uses the term "personnel" instead of "employee." Hawkins explained why: "We think it sounds more informal, less structured. With the word 'employee,' you have established that there are two groups. With 'personnel,' everybody belongs in that group. That is the way we feel about it. We don't do things that make it sound like we have two groups of people here. I think it is important. We like to say the last person hired by the personnel department today could be the next chairman of the board. There is nothing to keep that from happening."

At least once every 18 months Delta convenes personnel meetings to allow employees to get things off their chests. Top managers meet with groups of two to three dozen employees, who get a chance to fire away. Issues raised at these sessions have ranged all over the place. Delta recently eliminated smoking in all its facilities as a result of concerns raised at the personnel meetings. To ease the way, the company offered in-house no-smoking classes at every U.S. station.

Personnel meetings help clear the air of potential problems. But employees also talk about a positive environment that encourages them to try out ideas. Those who provide exceptional service are saluted in the company magazine. There's an Above and Beyond Award for outstanding customer service whose winners get a walnut plaque, lapel pin, and $100 savings bond.

Employees whose ideas do not work out are not punished. One employee called it a "climate of approval." Supervisor Fred Elsberry explained: "One thing that helps us to admit we have made a mistake is that the people who are above us don't hold it against us. In this company, if you make a mistake and you recognize it and something positive comes out of that, that's a positive for the company, it is a positive for you, it is a positive for the employee, because as a manager, my main job is to keep my people happy. There is support from above to know that we are free to try things and make mistakes and it is not going to be our career on the line."

Delta employees testify to the lengths the company goes to to keep their spirits up. Flight attendant Rhett Dobbs told this story: "One morning I woke up and had a lot of problems. I had lost some family members and I could not get on that flight attendant smile. It just wouldn't come on. I just couldn't handle it. But I got in my car. I had friends I could go to. I had family I could go to. I started driving and I realized I was driving to Delta. And I parked across the street and I had no idea who I was going to talk to. It really didn't matter. And I started walking down the hall and a supervisor walked out who knew me by face but that was about all and she came up to me and said, 'Rhett, are you okay?' I said, 'No, I am not.' She said, 'Can I help?' and she took me into her office and canceled all of her appointments. Delta has a lot of support groups that they can direct you to. Mine was just an afternoon breakdown! After I got to cry on her shoulder I was perfectly happy and ready to go on the airplane."

Types of jobs: Reservations and customer service agents—36 percent; flight attendants—21 percent; managers and professionals—13 percent; mechanics—13 percent; pilots—12 percent; other—5 percent.

Main employment centers: Delta flies to 213 cities in 33 countries. They are the largest private employer in Georgia, with 23,686 employees at their Atlanta hub. 6,535 employees work at the Dallas/Fort Worth hub, 4,309 in Salt Lake City, 4,145 in Los Angeles, and 3,307 in Cincinnati. 16,000 work overseas.

Headquarters: Delta Air Lines
Hartsfield International Airport
Atlanta, GA 30320
(404) 715-2600

Donnelly

═══════════════════════════

Donnelly

Donnelly makes glass products for motor vehicles (rearview mirrors, modular windows, interior lighting) and coated glass used in LCD displays and computer terminals. U.S. employees: 2,160.

★ ★ ★ Pay/Benefits
★ ★ ★ ★ Opportunities
★ ★ ★ ★ ★ Job Security
★ ★ ★ ★ Pride in Work/Company
★ ★ ★ ★ ★ Openness/Fairness
★ ★ ★ ★ Camaraderie/Friendliness

BIGGEST PLUS: Windows of opportunity.
BIGGEST MINUS: Only if you follow the rules.

To see what may be the most democratic company in the United States, check out Donnelly Corporation in western Michigan, where the Calvinist work ethic is alive and strong. Among the earliest settlers of this region were members of the Dutch Reformed Church, and their influence lingers. A number of companies in the area—Steelcase, Herman Miller, Haworth—feed off this tradition, but the one that does the most, in terms of giving *every* employee a say in what goes on, is Donnelly, a major maker of glass products, especially for the automobile industry.

It's a safe bet that the rearview mirror in your car was made by Donnelly. They own more than 90 percent of this market. They also developed the modular glass window that can be shipped directly to auto plants and slipped into the body of the car as it moves down the assembly line. To do that requires fine-precision work. At Donnelly, craftsmanship is a driving force. They have a joint venture at Mount Pleasant, Tennessee, with the big Japanese glassmaker, Asahi Glass, supplying modular windows for GM's Saturn—and unlike the GM-Toyota partnership at NUMMI Motors in California, in this case it's the American company (Donnelly) teaching the Japanese (Asahi). "We held their feet to the fire to get the tolerances right," a Donnelly engineer said to us.

Donnelly's Top-Rated Suggestion Program

Posters like this one help stimulate suggestions at Donnelly Corp. They are up at all plants.

1. What made you mad today?
2. What took too long?
3. What was the cause of any complaints?
4. What was misunderstood?
5. What cost too much?
6. What was wasted?
7. What was too complicated?
8. What is just plain silly?
9. What took too many people?
10. What job involved too many actions?

A new hire at Donnelly is told right away that "you are not being hired to do just one job." Donnelly people work in teams—a typical one has 10 or 12 members—and they set their own goals. And while you may be assigned to a primary task, you're expected to learn the jobs of everyone else on the team. We asked Paul Prescott, who works on the modular window line, how Donnelly differed from the Pennsylvania glass company where he worked before 1987. "There's a world of difference," he said. "Here I can go on to other jobs. When I worked at the other place, I worked the same job for eight years with no chance of getting another job. Now I can bid on jobs every year. I can get advancements, I can talk to any manager about anything, right up to the president. I always felt like I was the underdog, but now I feel like I can say something and it's being heard."

This feeling of empowerment is something we heard frequently in talking to Donnelly employees. Keith Gillette, a second-shift section leader in the modular systems group, told us: "The pride we take in our work reflects that we don't have to be necessarily supervised. We can actually function as human beings who have brains and we can sort of monitor one another."

To which a nearby worker added: "I think it's contagious. There's an extra sense of pride with people around here." Or as another put it: "If I come to work at 7:30 instead of 7:00 in the morning, he's going to be watching me saying, 'You've got your hand in my pocket, my bonus is going to be less because you weren't performing.' So everybody turns into little supervisors and it tends to make you accountable."

Imagine working for a company organized along the lines of a representative government. That's Donnelly. It has an elaborate structure to resolve grievances and set the policies and guidelines that govern the way people work here. Think of it as a three-tier system. At the first level is the work team; everyone at Donnelly, whether in the factory or office, belongs to a work team. The work teams elect representatives to serve on an equity committee: that's the second tier. Equity committees meet monthly to settle disputes and interpret personnel policies. The third—and highest—level is the Donnelly Committee, consisting of 15 members, nearly all of them elected by the equity committees. One of the members is the president of the company or another senior officer. The Donnelly Committee makes the final policies for the entire company, and it also has the responsibility of recommending an annual wage and benefits package to the board of directors of the company. There are other subsets to this structure, but that's the basic outline. It's democracy in a corporate setting, except that instead of majority rule, at Donnelly all decisions by these committees must be unanimous to "prevent the formation of divisive groups."

Before decisions are made, the issues are researched to death. The company probably spent $150,000 before coming up with a policy banning smoking. And in 1991 the committees spent three exhaustive months studying the question of drug testing. They finally arrived at a decision to do random testing. Fairness is a concept that's paramount in these discussions. Donnelly refused to adopt the two-tier wage system (paying newcomers less than old-timers for the same work) embraced by other western Michigan employers. A few years ago it did bring in new factory employees at $7.40 an hour, but after they worked for a year alongside others doing the same work but getting higher pay, the issue of fairness was raised by the employee committees—and the entry-level wage was raised to $8.47 an hour. During the discussions a number of employees said it was not fair to ask people to live on $7.40 an hour. It's safe to say that discussions of this kind are not going on at other companies in the United States. Nowhere else is fairness elevated to the plane it occupies at Donnelly. And nowhere else do rank-and-file employees have such a direct influence on company policies. This is a company that prides itself on having a self-managed work force. As they explained to their shareholders in 1990: "The Donnelly Management System is based on fundamental assumptions about people—that people are intelligent, creative, and motivated when goals are clearly articulated and understood."

In most companies, employees have no idea what the phrase "return on investment" means. At Donnelly, they do because quarterly bonuses are pegged to this measure, which tells how much money the company earns on the investment by shareholders. Quarterly bonuses are paid once the return exceeds 5.2 percent. Between 1984 and 1991, the bonuses ranged from a low of 1 percent to a high of 7 percent. The idea of having workers share in the profits this way stemmed from Donnelly's adoption, in 1952, of the Scanlon Plan, a scheme worked out by the late Joseph Scanlon to overcome management-labor hostility. It was years ahead of its time. When John F. Donnelly brought the Scanlon Plan into the company, his counterparts in western Michigan business circles suspected he was some kind of communist. J. Dwane Baumgardner, who holds a Ph.D. in optics and who became chief executive at Donnelly in 1983, told us it's not the bonus that's important but the concept. He explained: "When people come in here they ask, 'What kind of bonus plan do you have?' And they focus on the bonus plan only. They lose sight of the basic principles behind the plan, the ones of identity, participation, equity, competence. It's a way of conducting the business, it's a way of life. The philosophy is important."

That philosophy—emphasizing participation, fairness, and self-management—shows up in a lot of other ways at Donnelly. Twice during recent years they have won a national award for having the most suggestions per employee of any company in the country. In 1989 some 2,400 suggestions —or 1.4 per employee—were turned in. Donnelly's concern for fairness extends to its one overseas plant in Ireland, which has operated for 24 years with only one day lost because of a labor dispute. (That's an unheard-of record for an Irish plant.) Job security is also high on the agenda here. Anyone who has put in five years at Donnelly doesn't have to worry about losing a job. In the event of a layoff, five-year veterans have bumping rights over those with less seniority, and they are guaranteed 90 percent of their pay for one year if laid off or demoted. Workers are not displaced by technology. If an employee's job is eliminated, he or she gets a chance to move to another area. That was the case in 1991 when Donnelly phased out a longtime operation where exterior mirror components were chrome-coated. No one in this department was laid off. Instead, they were retrained and integrated into other wings of the company.

People rise in the ranks here through on-the-job training. In 1992 some 550 employees in the modular window group were attending week-long workshops in team-building skills. The company has a tuition-reimbursement program that gives employees up to $1,000 to pay for courses—and they do not have to be job-related and you do not need approval from your supervisor. Women have also done well here, holding about half the jobs, an unusually high proportion for a company manufacturing parts for automobiles.

While it's a leader in the practice of industrial democracy, there is noth-

ing hit-or-miss about the way Donnelly operates. On the contrary, it's almost rigid in the way it devises the rules of the game. They are meticulously spelled out in a 170-page handbook devoid of any sense of humor.
Here, for example, is the section dealing with "Christmas gift":

"As a token of appreciation for another year of service, and in the spirit
of the season, Donnelly presents every employee with a ham at Christmas
or a turkey at Thanksgiving on alternate years."

That doesn't even do justice to this company benefit. Employees we
interviewed said that the great feature of this tradition was that the ham or
turkey was passed out to employees by the top executives of the company,
and it lifted everyone's spirits "to see Dwane Baumgardner standing on a
loading platform at 5:00 A.M. passing out turkeys."

One change at Donnelly has been the sale of stock to the public. That
happened in 1988 because some members of the founding family wanted
to cash in their shares and/or establish a market value for their holdings. So
Donnelly's shares are now publicly traded, but the Donnelly family members (and there are many of them) continue to control the company; the
shares they hold have 93 percent of the voting power. One family member,
John F. Donnelly, Jr., son of the John F. Donnelly who brought the Scanlon Plan into the company in 1952, is a vice-president. He was paid
$173,000 in 1991. Dwane Baumgardner was paid $354,000, modest by
CEO pay scales in America.

One ironic consequence of being a publicly owned company is that employees tend to get a little less information than they did when Donnelly
was privately owned. That's because of the regulations of the Securities and
Exchange Commission, which require that shareholders receive all the per-
tinent information released about the company. In the past, the company
might, for example, tell its employees how things looked for the next six
months, hazarding even a guess about how sales and profits will come in.
Now that cannot be done unless the shareholders are told the news at the
same time. So it tends to put a damper on the release of information inside
the company.

It has never been easy getting a job at Donnelly because their reputation
is so good. They have 10,000 applications on file. When they do announce
that they are in a hiring mood, people in western Michigan get their sleep-
ing bags to spend the night so that they can get their applications in early
the next morning. They make a point of looking for people who are comfortable working in teams. Communications manager Maryam Komejan
told us that "we've had people who couldn't stand the sharing of decisions." That type will not be comfortable here.

Donnelly must be doing something right. While their major customers,
automakers, have been in the doldrums, laying off thousands of employees,
Donnelly has been spurting ahead. Since we last looked at the company, in
1985, sales have tripled and the number of employees has doubled. It's a

function of the company coming up with improved products, entering new areas (coated glass), and forging alliances with other companies. Donnelly puts between 5 and 6 percent of its revenues into research and development. Advanced research labs are maintained at Holland and Tucson, Arizona. Donnelly's prowess is reflected in the fact that virtually every car manufacturer in the world has, at one time or another, been a customer.

Types of jobs: Factory workers—59 percent; research—11 percent; administration—11 percent; skilled trades—9 percent; managers/supervisors—9 percent; marketing/sales—1 percent.

Main employment centers: 2,100 people work in 12 facilities in western Michigan. Another 180 are employed at its joint venture with Asahi Glass in Mount Pleasant, Tennessee, and 350 are employed at the plant in Naas, Ireland.

Headquarters: Donnelly Corporation
414 E. 40th St.
Holland, MI 49423
(616) 786-7000

MOST UNUSUAL BENEFITS

FREE CHILD CARE: SAS Institute
STOCK OPTIONS FOR ALL EMPLOYEES: Du Pont, Merck, Syntex, Tandem
BENEFITS FOR GAY AND LESBIAN PARTNERS: Ben & Jerry's Homemade, Lotus
$3,000 A YEAR FOR CHILDREN OF EMPLOYEES IN COLLEGE: Fel-Pro
FREE INCOME-TAX PREPARATION: Fel-Pro
TUTORING FOR SCHOOL-AGE CHILDREN: Fel-Pro
WEEK'S VACATION FOR NEWLYWEDS: Johnson & Johnson
THREE-YEAR JOB-PROTECTED FAMILY LEAVE: IBM
FOUR TICKETS FOR EVERY GAME: Los Angeles Dodgers
THREE-DOLLAR HAIRCUTS: Worthington Industries
THIRTY PERCENT OF PAY IN ONE LUMP SUM IN JANUARY: UNUM
$2,000 FOR GETTING COLLEGE DEGREE: H. B. Fuller
UNLIMITED SICK PAY (FULLY PAID): Leo Burnett, Syntex

Du Pont

Du Pont is the nation's largest maker of chemical products used in every-thing from apparel to electronics, building construction, and agriculture. It also owns Conoco, a large petroleum company. U.S. employees: 95,200.

★★★★ Pay/Benefits
★★★★ Opportunities
★★★★ Job Security
★★★ Pride in Work/Company
★★★ Openness/Fairness
★★ Camaraderie/Friendliness

BIGGEST PLUS: Explosive opportunities.
BIGGEST MINUS: A bulletproof bureaucracy.

This is easily the oldest company on our list. Founded in 1802 to make explosives, Du Pont is now a multinational chemical and oil giant. It has a long paternalistic tradition of taking care of its own, which has translated into a comfortable place to work with a rich package of benefits and an unwritten pact of lifetime employment. But Du Pont's paternalism has also historically meant hierarchical control by a small group of white men. Two Du Pont institutions that long symbolized this control were the Executive Committee, composed of a handful of top officers, and the annual Eagle Lodge retreat, where the top 60 executives would meet to hash out the company strategy.

Neither of those institutions exists today, thanks to Edgar Woolard, Du Pont's CEO, who has embarked on what some insist is nothing less than a cultural revolution. The Eagle Lodge retreat, for instance, was named after the site in Pennsylvania where the all-male group of executives would meet, golf, and play tennis. Not only did Woolard eliminate the retreat in 1989, his first year as CEO, but he replaced it with an entirely new kind of gathering called the Corporate Leadership Conference. At the first gathering in Palm Beach, 45 people, or 15 percent of the 300 attendees, were female or minorities. The next year 25 percent were *not* white males. At the same time, Woolard opened up the gathering to managers who were not in the top ranks. Brenda Thomas, a black marketing supervisor, was invited even though both her boss and her boss's boss were not. (Since 1980 Du Pont has doubled the number of women and nonwhites in professional and management jobs.)

Woolard has also broken with Du Pont tradition by making himself more accessible to the troops. For instance, twice a month he meets over breakfast or lunch with different groups of employees. Woolard always ends the sessions with the same question: "If you were in my job, what would you do?"

The Corporate Leadership Conference and the breakfast meetings are tips of the iceberg of change at today's Du Pont. Woolard is determined to reduce the weight of the hierarchy, especially in the plants where most Du Ponters work. These plants churn out a vast array of chemical products. They're perhaps best known for fibers (Du Pont invented nylon; Lycra, used in the popular spandex athletic wear; and Kevlar, used in bulletproof vests). Their plants also make such items as Teflon coating, synthetic rubber and resins, pesticides, and polymers (used in building products, automotive paints, and separation systems). To keep a steady stream of new products on line, Du Pont spends more than $1 billion a year on research and development.

At the plant level, Woolard has encouraged changes that will allow employees to make many decisions formerly reserved for higher-level managers. In 1992 *The Wall Street Journal* wrote about one of Du Pont's most efficient plants located along the Delaware River near Wilmington. The plant produces titanium dioxide, a pigment used in paper and paint. In a program started in 1991, management has paid about $18,000 to workers for actions that have saved the company money. Walt Zerbe received a bonus of more than $1,000 for rejecting a contractor's bid to paint the plant's buildings and equipment—the contractor came back a few days later with a bid 20 percent lower.

We heard similar stories when we interviewed employees at Du Pont's headquarters in downtown Wilmington, Delaware, in late 1990. According to Bill Harvey: "People are really beginning to feel empowered. I'm doing things I never thought I would do because I don't feel the barriers are there anymore, both personally and business-wise. I'm willing to take more risks." Harvey, who manages building services personnel, cited a recent meeting in which employees from lower levels got together to discuss ideas. Harvey told us that 10 years ago it would have been impossible to hold such a meeting without bringing in all the bosses.

Another, more subtle, attempt to change Du Pont's culture revolves around the concept of risk-taking. John Himes, vice-president of human resources, related an example of a group in his department that failed abysmally when they attempted to do something by computer that had formerly been done by hand. Rather than ignore the mistake, Himes said, "We decided we'd hold a recognition celebration for the failure and we called it 'a good try.'" Himes recalled that a woman came up to him and said, "You know, I've worked here 35 years, and that's the most meaningful thing that's ever happened in my work career."

The employees we met were clearly aware of the efforts being made to turn Du Pont into a more flexible, less hidebound company. And they approve. One of them said to us that in the past Du Pont "has been very exclusive and very white and male dominated, and Woolard has shown that this is not going to be the corporation of the future." Another said: "Woolard's style has taken the secrecy out." Still another said that in the old days Du Pont used to "take care of lame managers and if you ended up working for one of those clowns, it was bad news." And still another reported that when she had trouble with managers, her colleagues would say, "Don't worry, he'll either die or retire soon." And Marjorie Doyle, a Du Pont female lawyer who previously worked 10 years at Conoco, the oil company acquired by Du Pont in 1981, told us that when she was at Conoco she had to put up with a boss who couldn't "see somebody in a bra being general counsel of the company." She applauded Woolard's steps to shake up Du Pont, characterizing his approach this way: "He's basically said, 'I mean it. And those of you in upper management who don't believe it, I'd be happy to find you jobs elsewhere.'" Another employee in our group said that while they have talked about diversity at Du Pont for a long time, it's only since Woolard became CEO that it has taken on some substance. He said: "Woolard has really walked the talk. He has said that 'Diversity does not just mean black and white, men and women. It means anything you do, behavioral attitude, ethnic culture.' He has put definition to that word."

Du Pont is not a case of a bad workplace becoming good. Rather it is a case of a good workplace becoming better. They have a long history of providing top-flight benefits. Du Pont came out with a pension and retirement plan in 1904, company-paid life insurance in 1919, paid vacations in 1934, health insurance in 1936, and a disability pay plan in 1937. In 1991 Du Pont granted all employees around the world options to buy 100 shares of stock. Du Pont thus became the largest company ever to give to its entire work force a perk that's almost always reserved for the upper reaches of management. Options give the holders a no-cost opportunity to benefit from a rise in the stock price.

Du Pont has also emerged as one of the most pro-family companies in the nation under the leadership of Faith A. Wohl, a grandmother whose position is director of work force partnering. Wohl, who was 56 in 1992, has spearheaded initiatives which have included $1.5 million to build and renovate child-care centers near Du Pont work sites, $250,000 to set up a child-care referral system for the state of Delaware, $225,000 to help 45 child-care centers gain accreditation, unpaid family leave of six months *after* paid maternity leave, and flexible work schedules. Few companies have put as much clout behind this thrust as Du Pont. Wohl has a staff of 19, running a gamut of programs, and her activity has mushroomed into active work/family committees at 50 Du Pont locations. Du Pont has a work force that is 24 percent female, and in 1992 they had one woman vice-president out of 75. In the upper management ranks, people making over $150,000 a year, women held 20 of the 475 positions.

Safety has long been another area in which Du Pont shines. It is perhaps the most safety-obsessed company in the land. For years every Du Pont CEO has required a written report on his desk within 24 hours of any injury accident that occurs in a company plant anywhere in the world. Every month, every work group in the company sits down and discusses a safety-related issue, often with a video or a speaker. This is not confined to those who work in dangerous jobs in the chemical plants. One office worker mentioned how she has become extremely conscious of the potential hazards of file drawers. Another said: "Safety is number one here. You could probably get into more trouble for violating a safety rule than you can for almost anything else." However, in 1991 Du Pont suffered 15 employee fatalities, up from three in 1990, and the company made a point of highlighting this record in its annual report, noting that it considered any fatality "unacceptable" and was "working to reverse these trends immediately." Eight lives were lost when a company jet crashed in Borneo. Another was killed in a commercial airline crash and another in a car crash.

Though Du Pont no longer offers lifetime employment, it has avoided the massive layoffs that have characterized other big American corporations in recent years. They've slimmed down, however. In July 1991, when Du Pont announced that it was going to reduce annual expenditures by $1 billion, CEO Woolard wrote a letter to all employees, saying: "I am also aware that some people will say that this action is inconsistent with our commitment to value and respect employees. I strongly disagree. If we don't act now, we increase the chances that several struggling businesses will be unsuccessful, thereby decreasing security for all our employees." He assured them that the company would do everything in its power to avoid involuntary layoffs and said: "We will offer outplacement services to help people find other jobs. Because of the high skill level and reputation of Du Pont employees, an average of 95 percent of the people outplaced in the past have found employment."

By mid-1992 Du Pont had reduced its work force by 6,500. But not one of the people who left had done so involuntarily. They all had accepted one of the generous early retirement or severance packages. Those age 50 with 15 years of service or age 45 with 25 years of service were eligible for an early retirement package which included an enhanced pension that could be taken early without reduction. The pension was calculated by multiplying years of service and pay by 1.5 percent and subtracting half of the Social Security benefit. For those who did not qualify for early retirement, Du Pont offered two weeks' pay for every year of service for the first five years and four weeks' pay for every year of service after five years and an extension of medical, dental, and life insurance for one year.

Changing a big company is a challenging task, especially in Du Pont's case because it has long been an exemplar of how a big corporation is supposed to run. It wrote the book on how managers can effectively govern a multidivisional organization—and it did it not just here but at General Motors, which it once controlled. Most business historians agree that without Du Pont's hand on the wheel, General Motors would have collapsed in the 1920s. But it's also true that Du Pont has long been the bête noire of public interest groups, which have regarded it as a laggard in social responsibility areas. In 1992 the Council on Economic Priorities, which gives annual corporate conscience awards to companies, gave Du Pont a dishonorable mention award, identifying the company as "by far the nation's largest polluter." It was the second time Du Pont had received this demerit from CEP. This reputation weighs heavily in Wilmington. In talking about Du Pont's hope for the future, Woolard, according to John Himes, once made this comment to a leadership conference: "Someday I'm going to be able to walk, as I do, around this world and sit down in any meeting, whether it's a group of employees, a group of customers, a financial community, a group from GreenPeace, and I'm going to ask them the question, 'Give me the top five companies in the world that you most respect,' and Du Pont's going to be in that."

Main employment centers: Du Pont is the largest employer in Delaware with a payroll exceeding 20,000. Another 75,000 work in more than 150 plants and offices across the country. More than 30,000 work for Du Pont outside the U.S.

Headquarters: E. I. du Pont de Nemours and Company
1007 Market St.
Wilmington, DE 19898
(302) 774-1000

A. G. Edwards

A.G.Edwards

A. G. Edwards trades stock for more than 1 million investors. It is the largest brokerage firm not headquartered in New York City. Employees: 9,446.

★★★★ Pay/Benefits
★★★★ Opportunities
★★★★ Job Security
★★★★ Pride in Work/Company
★★★ Openness/Fairness
★★★★ Camaraderie/Friendliness

BIGGEST PLUS: Wall Street without the rat race.
BIGGEST MINUS: No fat Wall Street bonuses.

On the last Friday of every month, A. G. Edwards employees throughout the country huddle around their "squawk boxes," as their desk speakerphones are called. Ben Edwards, chairman and great-grandson of the founder, delivers a brief report on how things are going in the company and then opens the line to questions. In February 1991 a stockbroker in one of A. G. Edwards's 434 branch offices asked: "I am curious about Mr. Edwards's 40,000-share AGE sale." Translated into English, the broker wanted to know why Ben Edwards had recently sold a large block of company stock, worth about $800,000.

Without missing a beat, Edwards said he appreciated the question. He then explained that he has never sold any A. G. Edwards stock to make another investment. He added: "I have become a nutty collector of antiques, and I had a chance to buy a whole collection . . . so I sold some stock and, of course, as usual, looked foolish because the stock proceeded to go up eight points right after I sold. [So some people] can have a good hee-haw at me for my poor timing. But that is why I needed the money."

A homey atmosphere attracts people to A. G. Edwards. Vice-president Doug Dressel, with the company since 1974, noted that "Ben Edwards often says that our most important asset is the people who work here, and that gives you that feeling that this is a place where you can have a home if that is what you are looking for."

Mary Vahlkamp, an administrative secretary, told us that she left her job at Edwards but then returned: "The reason I came back was because of the family atmosphere. You can go down through the hall and maybe not know somebody but someone is going to say 'Hi' and smile or say 'Good morning' or 'How are you?' whether you know them or not. My husband started working here a year ago. He had always worked in a factory before and was amazed when he came home after his first day. He said, 'All these people were talking to me and I don't even know them.' And I said, 'That's A. G. Edwards.'" Vahlkamp works in the St. Louis headquarters. But most of Edwards's employees are found in the branches, where stockbrokers keep in touch with their customers, mostly small investors.

The company has an explicit goal of encouraging "full and open two-way communication" where "upward flow of information is just as necessary as the more customary downward flow. . . . It is also important that the information coming from the top be as complete and as candid as possible."

As part of this effort, Edwards visits at least 50 branches a year. He told us: "It is all too easy to sit around in these fancy meeting rooms and pontificate with each other and think that we have so much experience that we know everything, and lose total touch with reality. I call headquarters 'fantasyland,' our branches are the real world. That is why I think we have to get out there frequently or we lose touch."

It's not easy to keep in touch because the branch offices are spread through 48 states. Most are in relatively unknown towns like Storm Lake, Iowa, Carefree, Arizona, Cherry Creek, Colorado, and Natchitoches, Louisiana. In 1992 offices were added in Sunset Hills, Missouri, Tryon, North Carolina, and Modesto, California. A. G. Edwards itself reflects the values of small-town America, even though it is the seventh biggest brokerage house in the country in terms of employees. (The top two are Merrill Lynch and Shearson Lehman Brothers.) A. G. Edwards's own stock trades on the New York Stock Exchange.

It is clear that the firm marches to a different drummer. You need look no further than the firm's "corporate model," an eight-page document formulated in the late 1960s, not long after Edwards took over the firm from his father. The most notable feature of the document is the downplaying of profits. Ben Edwards said that instead of putting profit "in our corporate objectives, we put in 'having fun.' That sounds so silly for a publicly held company, but we were serious about it. We thought this is a neat business, it is an interesting business, so we are doing something wrong if there are long faces around here. . . . We concluded that you really couldn't enjoy what you were doing unless you like the people you worked with. So then the question was how do you like people? We talked about common interests and tastes and whatnot, but the bottom line was that you couldn't like people unless you trusted them and respected them."

Edwards doesn't mean that the firm ignores making money, but he sees it as a matter of focus. "I think material reward and happiness are similar in that you don't find either when you seek them. They come as by-products of doing something well, of caring for other people, and we want to care for our customers. Our lives are fulfilled and we made more money than we ever dreamed we would make, just by trying to do our jobs well." Or, as Edwards told the *Trenton Times:* "Profit was no longer the purpose of the machine, but the oil to keep it running. Our profit margins widened as soon as we stopped focusing on it."

Another way Edwards distinguishes itself from most Wall Street firms is the lack of a star system, where top performers are singled out and rewarded with huge bonuses. According to corporate vice-president Greg Hutchings, it is a "feeling of team playing and cooperation that develops the loyalty to A. G. Edwards. Unlike other firms in the business we do not have a star system. Here it is always putting the team first and the client first. As a result you are rewarded for working with other departments and being a team player, unlike other firms where everyone is out for themselves."

Teamwork is taught to managers in a rigorous six-day course called the Managerial Grid, which was also initiated in the late 1960s. At the conclusion, the group critiques itself and the company as a whole. Ben Edwards himself has attended every Managerial Grid critique since then. In 1990 the firm added a shorter version of the training process called GridWorks for nonsupervisory employees.

A. G. Edwards has also changed its compensation system to reward teamwork. Previously, top managers received bonuses based on an "override" of the earnings of those below them. Now all management bonuses are tied to company profits. By all accounts, Edwards's compensation system (virtually unique in the industry) encourages everyone to pull together to enlarge the size of the pie rather than competing with each other for a larger piece of it. No one need fear that those at the top are skimming off astronomical bonuses for themselves. In 1991 Ben Edwards took home $800,000 in salary and bonuses—a small sum when compared with, for instance, Merrill Lynch chairman's $8.5 million that year. But Edwards still told the *New York Times:* "I think I'm overpaid, too."

Stockbrokers, the customers' representatives, do well here. They make up about half of Edwards's work force, the highest ratio in the industry. And

Edwards's brokers keep 44 percent of their commissions (a higher rate than many others in the industry). The average Edwards broker made more than $76,000 in 1991.

It's not only brokers who make out well. The firm has a generous profit-sharing plan. All eligible employees receive 2 percent of earnings regardless of whether they contribute, and the company matches dollar for dollar employees' contributions up to 3 percent of earnings. In addition, Edwards makes an annual discretionary contribution that is tied to the firm's profitability. Over the past three years Edwards has chipped in a total of $107 million to the plan. If you were earning $20,000 in 1978, the year the current profit-sharing plan started, and if, heaven forbid, you had remained at that salary through 1991, the profit-sharing account would have grown to $73,350, of which you had contributed only $4,492.

All Edwards employees may buy stock in the firm at 85 percent of the market price. It would have been a good investment. Every dollar invested in Edwards stock when the company went public in 1971 was worth $33 at the start of 1992.

Money aside, employees here appreciate job security. Dick Clever, a stock trader in St. Louis, said: "We went through good markets and bad markets, and when the market got tough and business was really slow and company earnings were down, we were told that we didn't have to worry about layoffs—which at that time were sweeping the nation. We were told that you don't have to worry about that, that Edwards would stick with you, and times will change and it will get better." Vice-president of institutional sales Chuck Kaiser, who previously worked for Goldman Sachs, added: "This is probably the most cyclical business there is, and for us to feel that—and I think everybody feels it—that they have such job security at a firm that is in this business is really amazing."

Indeed, during the 1980s A. G. Edwards grew steadily from 2,400 to more than 7,400. After the October 1987 stock market crash, when other brokerage houses laid off thousands (a drop of about 15 percent industry-wide), A. G. Edwards's employment grew by almost 20 percent.

People tend to stick around here a long time, too. One reason is a promotion-from-within policy. Karen Middleton, here since 1984, explained: "It seems like even if you are in another department, if you express an interest in a different area, nine times out of 10 you are given a shot or a chance to prove yourself." Middleton started as a systems department programmer and moved into the bond department to replace a woman on maternity leave. When the woman came back, Middleton stayed in the bond department, became a trading assistant and a licensed trader.

At whatever level, employees have direct access to top managers. In addition to frequent meetings (called managerial panels), executives maintain an open-door policy. Some make it a rule not to screen their phone calls. While we were interviewing him in his office, with its view of the St. Louis skyline and Gateway Arch, Edwards was interrupted by a phone call. We asked whether it was a customer or an employee. He told us it was an antique dealer. "I'm a mark and my dealers call all the time," he said. Then, pointing to the collection of antique china in his office, he added: "As you can see, my wife says it is like a china shop that has never sold anything. She won't let me bring any more into the house."

Main employment centers: Edwards has more than 400 offices in 48 states. Twenty-five percent of the work force is in St. Louis and the rest are in offices scattered throughout 48 states.

Headquarters: A. G. Edwards, Inc.
One North Jefferson
St. Louis, MO 63103
(314) 289-3000

Erie Insurance

ERIE INSURANCE GROUP

Erie is the 15th largest auto insurer. They also issue property, casualty, and life insurance policies and have a total of 2 million policies in force. Employees: 2,700.

★★★ Pay/Benefits
★★★★ Opportunities
★★★★★ Job Security
★★★★★ Pride in Work/Company
★★★★ Openness/Fairness
★★★★ Camaraderie/Friendliness

BIGGEST PLUS: Stimulating jobs in a boring industry.
BIGGEST MINUS: Erie, Pa., gets more snow than Buffalo, N.Y.

In a recent survey, 97 percent of Erie's employees said they were "proud" to be working here. That is a remarkable statistic for any company. But it is especially notable in the insurance field, where the work is often tedious and the industry itself is often vilified for high rates and poor service.

But Erie isn't your run-of-the-mill insurance company. It consistently ranks near the top in *Consumer Reports* appraisals of insurance companies. Their reputation is so good that they rely solely on word of mouth to get new customers. They do no advertising. And you need only visit their head-quarters in downtown Erie, Pennsylvania, a few blocks from Lake Erie, to get another idea of why employees are proud to work here. Most employees work in a new building, opened in 1983, with a four-story atrium, light-filled offices, and quiet areas for reading and conversation. Employees can get a hot lunch in the cafeteria for $1.75 and sit at tables on a huge patio when the weather is nice.

The chairman's office is easy to find. It's on the ground floor of the adjacent colonial-style building that opened in 1956, 31 years after the company was founded. Because the chairman's door is always open, they've installed a door knocker on the *inside* of the door. It's one way they empha-size their open-door policy. Employees are always free to take their concerns directly to the head of the company.

Tom Hagen, Erie's chairman, has other ways of keeping in close contact with employees. He meets regularly with employees in the home office in groups of about 25 to 40 people, and he meets with all of Erie's agents each year by going to each of Erie's 18 branch offices. He explained: "We have a whirlwind blitz in the spring and the fall, and I cover all of them in the course of a year." Top managers also keep in touch with employee concerns through a written Pipeline program. Any employee can fill out a Pipeline form with a suggestion, complaint, opinion, or question and get a response from the appropriate top manager within two weeks. In 1991 employees sent 394 Pipelines. Hagen says: "We don't want to have an unhappy ship."

From talking with employees, it appears he has little to worry about. Ten-year employee Toni Wright, who worked previously at a local bank for three years, said: "The working conditions at the bank compared to here are like night and day. There is no comparison. You are really treated human here. In the last 10 years this company has grown very fast, so you would think that as it grows it would become a lot less personal, more like cattle-in, cattle-out type of thing. But they don't lose the family feeling. I have nobody working here who is my own family, but we are all more or less friends. You say hi a couple hundred times a day."

When we asked Wright what she liked most about working at Erie, she replied: "Your opinions are respected. Some people are more open than others, but if you have something to say, this is one of the only companies where you can go to the chairman of the board and ask to talk to him and he will let you."

Another plus is a free flow of information, according to Gwen White, who works in underwriting: "At Erie they foster and emphasize communication going both ways. When decisions are being made on a particular policy or change in procedure, you get information from all sources and different levels. Though you may disagree with the decision, at least you understand why the decision was made."

Erie's distinctive work environment can be traced to founder H. O. Hirt, who ran the company for 51 years. Like many entrepreneurs, he ran a tight ship. "He had his own sense of what was right and what was wrong," Hagen recalls. He controlled the temperatures in the building and "authorized the quality of the toilet paper. You had to come and ask him for a new ballpoint pen and he would get them out of the back room. Same with staplers. And he thought there was a certain way you had to use a stapler and you were in trouble if you stapled indiscriminately."

At the same time, H. O. Hirt had very high ideals. He opposed World War I as a religious pacifist and consistently voted for Socialist Party presidential candidate Norman Thomas. He preached the Golden Rule as the method for dealing with employees and customers. And there was a touch of paternalism in the founder's relations with employees. "The old man always referred to it as the Erie family and that is something that has always been a part of us," explained Hagen. "We had a tragic situation a few weeks ago where one of our commercial underwriters had a daughter seriously impaired in an accident to the point where she's semi-comatose. She had to go up to the Mayo Clinic for an operation and her benefits are nearly exhausted. The only way they could get her up there was with an air ambulance and it's not covered under our medical plan except for a small amount. I authorized us to pay that because the woman's father is a valued employee here. We have a lot of rules, procedures, and policies, but still sometimes you have to put yourself in their shoes and make some decisions that are exceptions to those things. That is what I am here for, that is my job. We want to take care of our own to the extent that we possibly can."

It's also family here in a literal sense. Hagen, for instance, is H. O. Hirt's son-in-law, and Hagen's predecessor was Bill Hirt, H.O.'s son. Many other Erie employees are related to one another. Hagen told us proudly of one family with 10 different members in three different generations working there now: "Thank God for nepotism. We believe in it, we like hiring family members. We try to keep them working for separate managers, though."

Job security adds to the sense of family. You don't kick somebody out of a family. Mary Nelson, a word processor, says: "No one has ever been laid off here. This is important when you are looking for a job, and so many places you hear about layoffs. But here they do find a position for you rather than laying people off."

Toni Wright, who helps write computer programs, added: "In the 10 years I have worked here, I have seen departments come and go because of automation and restructuring. But when they phase out departments, I have never seen them say, ' 'Bye, you are out of a job.' They have always found a place for you."

The same survey that revealed employees' pride in Erie also showed that 94 percent of Erie workers said they like the work they are doing. When we asked employees to explain this extremely high score, they talked about how the company makes a point of giving them a lot of responsibility for their work.

Rick Bengel, employee communications supervisor, said: "You have more autonomy here. If you have an idea and talk to a few people and it sounds good to them, it doesn't take a whole lot to get that ball rolling."

Gary Veshecco, assistant vice-president and claims counselor, contrasted Erie with his previous experiences as a lawyer: "The work is far more challenging. I have been given responsibility for cases far sooner than I would have been elsewhere, and the dollar amounts from a lawyer's point of view were staggering. There were millions of dollars that you were handling. In my area we are given a very free hand. Management doesn't manage everything you do."

As a promotion-from-within company, Erie emphasizes training and education. According to Marilyn Kubeja, a manager of clerical services: "We have a lot of things to offer as far as education. You can go in and take whatever you feel comfortable with. I started out as a clerk and then became a secretary and then up to a supervisor position."

On top of all this, Erie pays well. Their compensation and benefits package is second to none in the area. Ten-year employee Mary Nelson summed it up: "The reason I wanted to be at Erie is that everyone is so proud to work at Erie Insurance—the benefits, the courses you can take for advancement, the caring, the family feeling."

Types of jobs: Office and clerical—44 percent; professionals—32 percent; officials and managers—13 percent; technicians—6 percent; service workers—2 percent; crafts, operatives, and laborers—3 percent.

Main employment centers: The home office is located in Erie, Pennsylvania, and 17 field offices are sprinkled throughout Pennsylvania (Allentown, Bethlehem, Harrisburg, Johnstown, Philadelphia, Pittsburgh), Ohio (Canton, Columbus), Indiana (Fort Wayne, Indianapolis), Maryland (Hagerstown, La Vale, Silver Spring), Virginia (Richmond, Roanoke), North Carolina (Raleigh), and West Virginia (Parkersburg).

Headquarters: Erie Insurance Company
100 Erie Insurance Plaza
Erie, PA 16530
(814) 870-2000

Federal Express

Federal Express invented overnight parcel delivery. U.S. employees: 77,700.

★★★★ Pay/Benefits
★★★★ Opportunities
★★★★★ Job Security
★★★★ Pride in Work/Company
★★★★★ Openness/Fairness
★★★★ Camaraderie/Friendliness

BIGGEST PLUS: You probably won't get zapped.
BIGGEST MINUS: You may not be an overnight success.

Forrest King couldn't believe the scene. Dozens of Federal Express employees were cheering as he and his wife stepped out of the chartered Boeing 747 airplane. King had come to Memphis with other Flying Tiger employees, whose company had recently been bought by Federal Express, to see if he wanted to relocate. The welcome, complete with a red carpet and a welcoming committee that included the mayor of Memphis and FedEx's CEO, was King's introduction to this unusual company.

According to King: "It seems to me that when another company takes you over, they are not necessarily obligated to give you a job in the first place. But everyone—and it was communicated in a memo and later in video—was offered a job." King contrasted this experience with what had happened at Flying Tiger earlier: "Tigers bought Seaboard World Airlines in 1980. I remember people saying that they were promised things by the Flying Tigers that never materialized. But here, everything that Fred Smith said that he was going to do, he did it."

It's hard to talk with employees about Federal Express without hearing about CEO Fred Smith. An American business legend, he created the overnight delivery industry when he founded FedEx in 1971. The basic idea is simple. Couriers pick up packages and deliver them to the airport, where they are flown to a central hub. At the hub they are sorted and flown to the closest city, where couriers deliver them to their final destination. FedEx delivers nearly 1.5 million parcels a day, using its fleet of 32,800 vans and trucks and 415 aircraft. The nerve center of this system is the Memphis SuperHub, where more than 5,500 employees work a four-hour shift in the middle of the night to sort the 750,000 parcels that arrive and depart every night on some 80 jets and 20 turboprops. (Another 1,300 workers at the SuperHub sort approximately 180,000 parcels during the day.)

We met Joseph Smith at the SuperHub. Like many other hub workers, Smith was a student at Memphis State, working on a master's in music. Hub workers average $9 an hour for a guaranteed 17½-hour workweek, though most work more. Smith loved the nighttime work: "It's a great place. It's one giant team out here. Everybody goes out of their way to help everybody else, and to do everything we can to make sure the packages are gotten out in time. Also, it's great pay. You don't find anything else like that here in Memphis, except at UPS [United Parcel Service]. My roommate used to work for them, and he came here because he said they're like slave drivers there." Smith added that he hopes to take a management training course at FedEx.

From the outset, CEO Fred Smith intended to create more than a new way of delivering business packages. He also intended to create a model workplace. Using ideas garnered from looking at IBM, Delta Air Lines, and other enlightened employers, Smith put in place a whole series of progressive personnel practices. This "people first" philosophy can be summed up by one of FedEx's slogans—"People, Service, Profit," or P-S-P. The P-S-P philosophy is described in the *Manager's Guide*: "Take care of our people; they, in turn, will deliver the impeccable service demanded by our customers who will reward us with the profitability necessary to secure our future. People-Service-Profit, these three words are the very foundation of Federal Express."

FedEx quickly gained a reputation as one of the best employers in the Memphis area. Everett Meadow joined Federal Express in 1980: "Somewhere in the Bible it says that God will give you the desires of your heart. Well, this was one of the desires of my heart to work for Federal Express, and I think this is common in Memphis. There is a lot of pride in working for this company. You can go places, and you almost want to keep it secret that you work for Federal Express, and especially if you are a manager!

Because they hand you a résumé and ask, 'Can you get me on?' " Meadow started in an entry-level position and now works in data network support. He was taking advantage of the tuition reimbursement program to study telecommunications at a local college. He believes that Federal Express is "a company that rolls out the red carpet to you and says, 'Be all that you can be.' "

FedEx relies on its extensive in-house training program to help people achieve their potential. Approximately 7,000 customer service agents and 24,000 couriers (they're never called drivers here) have been trained through these programs.

Another cornerstone of P-S-P is promotion from within. Those interested in management can go through the Leadership Evaluation and Awareness Process, or LEAP. And every new first-line supervisor is brought to Memphis for a week-long training program to learn the basics of P-S-P. Eighty-five percent of nonentry-level positions are filled from within.

According to sort systems manager Ahmad Jaffrey: "It is a Federal Express policy that the manager works for employees. The employee doesn't work for the manager. I don't want authority. I want a job to get done. I don't care who does the job as long as it's done. That's what I tell them. I don't care how you do it, just do it."

Managing at FedEx offers one unusual challenge—a grievance procedure that involves a trial by the employee's peers. It's called the Guaranteed Fair Treatment process, or GFT, and is part of the fabric of the company. Like typical union grievance procedures, GFT provides opportunities for an employee who feels he or she has been treated unfairly to appeal a manager's decision. But FedEx's GFT process has several distinctive features. The CEO and two other top officers of the company personally hear appeals that have worked their way through the system. They do so almost every Tuesday morning in the Memphis headquarters. And if they feel the case has merit, it is then heard by a panel of five, three of whom are picked by the employee. So Federal Express is one of the few companies where employees can get a trial by their peers.

The GFT process is not as threatening to managers as it might sound. When we interviewed managers at Federal Express headquarters in Memphis, we asked how many had had their decisions challenged through the GFT process, and all the managers raised their hands. According to flight administration manager Sam Davis: "Any manager that has never been through the GFT process either hasn't been a manager very long, or he's not managing very many people, or his job isn't very complicated. I know the crew force uses the GFT vehicle quite frequently. The GFT process is a good flush-out. It's a good vehicle for the employee as well as the manager, because if the employee never GFTs the manager, how would you know how you are managing? Can anybody read the P&P [policy and procedures manual] and interpret it correctly every single time?"

We heard a particularly dramatic example of GFT in action while we were in Memphis. A courier told us she had been fired for a technical violation of company policy. She filed a GFT, went through the entire process, and eventually won. She was given back pay for the several months she was out of work. But that was not the end of the story. When she returned to work, she said her manager started doing "everything he could to make life uncomfortable." So she filed another GFT, claiming harassment. As a result, she not only kept her job but her manager was relieved of any supervisory responsibility. She said: "I feel much more secure knowing that if I have been treated unfairly, no matter what the circumstances, that there is a way to get to Mr. Smith [the CEO] and say, 'Would you please look at this and give me your opinion?'"

Another significant People-Service-Profit policy is the Survey Feedback Action. Many companies conduct annual employee surveys. But what distinguishes Federal Express's survey is the fact that the managers sit down with their work groups to discuss them. The process begins with a 26-question survey which employees fill out. The questionnaires are analyzed, and summarized results are given to each group. Work group leaders then convene feedback sessions to present the results to employees and talk about ways to improve on areas that scored low in the survey. The employee groups themselves come up with solutions and monitor their own progress.

FedEx has been one of the leaders in flextime. In some areas of the company, employees do this on their own. Judy Marshall, a senior customer service agent, said: "The Swap is a policy where you just swap a day for somebody else's day. You take their hours, and they take your hours. Giveaways are where I can get somebody else to work for me, a part-timer, they work for me and I just give them the extra hours, and I'm short that many hours."

Pilot Patricia Ahneman told us: "This is the only airline that lets you work as much or as little as you desire. The other ones have pay caps, where you work X amount of hours, and if you want to trade, it's based on seniority. Here, if I get to it first, it's my trip. I can swap with other pilots." Ahneman is one of 99 female pilots. Approximately 4.5 percent of FedEx's pilots are women—reportedly the highest in the airline industry.

This kind of freedom is reflected in a willingness to take risks. Debbie Newport, Memphis ground operations manager, said: "At Federal, you're not afraid to try new things. Each day presents something new. You can try just about anything. I manage couriers in Memphis. Not too long ago we asked them to come up with ideas for increasing productivity on the sort line in the morning, and they came up with a plan. We realigned all the vans, and they did about a 20 percent productivity increase almost overnight, just by sitting together in a small group and talking about it. I don't have any fear that if I try something that doesn't work, there will be repercussions. There have been a few things that didn't work. We just didn't do them the next day."

One reason employees are willing to take risks is that the company has maintained its commitment to avoid layoffs. According to Fred Smith: "It's just good business to have a no-layoff policy because if now I introduce a megatracker or something like that, you are not going to be afraid that it's going to cost you your job. If we were to go out to the hub and introduce a robot out there, for instance, with our no-layoff program we can talk to the employees about where we are going to put them. The robot doesn't become a threat to them."

When the company's Zapmail program was shut down in 1986, all 1,300 of the employees who had worked in that department had first priority in internal job posting applications. Those employees who could not find positions with equivalent salaries could take lower-level jobs and retain their previous salary for up to 18 months, or until they found another higher-salary job. Everett Meadow, a 12-year employee, worked in Zapmail, and he told us: "Most people came out of telecommunications and most of them found a job back in telecommunications."

In addition to the no-layoff policy, there is also no probationary program for new employees. The philosophy statement explains: "One of the primary issues on which new and current managers are trained is the elevation of human dignity. In keeping with this, and to reinforce the relationship of mutual trust and respect with our employees, there is no trial or probationary period at Federal Express."

The airline industry lost $6.5 billion from 1990 to 1992 and laid off more than 50,000 employees while FedEx maintained their no-layoff policy. FedEx uses other methods to cut costs. One is to cut executive salaries. In 1991 Fred Smith told us that top executives here "felt for some time that the people who needed to take it in the chin first are the management, particularly senior management. So if you look at my compensation over the past two years, it will actually be down 50 percent. We think that needs to be done before you go to an employee and say, 'You're not going to get your merit increase at the same rate.' The top people should bleed first."

Whether Federal Express can maintain this policy remains to be seen. In May 1992 Federal Express discontinued much of its service within Europe and reduced its European work force from 9,200 to 2,600. No U.S. personnel were involved in the reductions. FedEx received praise in Europe from the *London Sunday Times*, among others, for the way in which they went about the layoffs. For example, FedEx put full-page ads in several newspapers urging other employers to hire former FedEx workers. In Belgium alone 80 companies responded to the ad with a total of 600 job offers. In the United States, FedEx faces increased competition from fax machines, the U.S. Postal Service, and United Parcel Service. But FedEx people stick together in hard times. Debbie Newport, the ground operations manager, said: "It seems like the tougher the times get around Federal Express, the higher spirits get."

Types of jobs: Couriers and handlers—56 percent; central support services —18 percent; air operations—8 percent; information systems—5 percent; administration—4 percent; pilots—3 percent; mechanics—3 percent; customer service—3 percent.

Main employment centers: 20,000 FedEx employees work in Memphis. There are also regional mini-hubs in Indianapolis, Indiana; Oakland, California; and Newark, New Jersey.

Headquarters: Federal Express Corporation
2005 Corporate Ave.
Memphis, TN 38132
901-369-3600

COMPANIES WHERE YOU CAN GET CHILD CARE AT YOUR WORK SITE

Baptist Hospital of Miami
BE&K
Ben & Jerry's Homemade
Beth Israel Hospital Boston
Fel-Pro
Johnson & Johnson
Merck
Patagonia
Quad/Graphics
SAS Institute
Syntex
UNUM
Wegmans

Fel-Pro

Fel-Pro is one of the world's largest makers of gaskets for automobiles and industrial uses. They also make sealants, adhesives, lubricants, and epoxies. U.S. employees: 1,700.

★ ★ ★ ★ ★   Pay/Benefits
   ★ ★ ★   Opportunities
★ ★ ★ ★ ★   Job Security
  ★ ★ ★ ★   Pride in Work/Company
★ ★ ★ ★ ★   Openness/Fairness
★ ★ ★ ★ ★   Camaraderie/Friendliness

BIGGEST PLUS: Your kids will thank you.
BIGGEST MINUS: If you don't have a relative here, you might feel like an outsider.

One way to judge a workplace is to look at what the company provides for the children of its employees. From that viewpoint, Fel-Pro may well qualify as the best employer in the land.

Benefits start at birth for Fel-Pro kids. Literally. On the day a child is born (or is adopted), the company sends the mother flowers, gives the baby a pair of inscribed leather baby shoes, and enters a $1,000 savings bond in the baby's name, payable on the child's 21st birthday. When Fel-Pro kids turn two, they are eligible to attend the professionally staffed Fel-Pro day-care center, located in a separate building adjacent to the company's plant just north of Chicago. An old railroad caboose sits in the playground. After Fel-Pro kids start school, the company will send professionally trained caregivers to the home to take care of them if they get sick (at a cost to employees of only $16 a day). If a child is having difficulty in school, the company provides testing and individual tutoring (at an employee cost of $7 an hour). When they graduate from high school, the company sends them a $100 check. College? Fel-Pro offers them individual counseling in selecting their college, then the company provides all Fel-Pro kids attending college $3,000 a year (for four years) to help defray tuition costs.

For many Fel-Pro kids, summer is the best time of all. The summer day camp is held at the company's own 220-acre Triple R recreation area (the Rs stand for rest, relaxation, and recreation). On summer mornings, yellow school buses wait at the factory to drive them 40 miles to Triple R Camp, with its staff of trained counselors, an Olympic-size swimming pool, arts and crafts classes, and other activities. (In 1991 five buses took 296 kids to Triple R every day.) What about summer jobs? Fel-Pro hires employees' kids to work at the plant. In fact, virtually all temporary summer replacement jobs (usually about 150 positions) are filled by children of employees, called "future gasketeers" by other employees.

Employees talk about Fel-Pro as a big family. Lita Ignacio came to the United States from the Philippines 20 years ago and started working here in 1975 (about half of Fel-Pro's employees are minorities). She said: "I feel like I belong to a family here. They treat us like their family." She points to the day-care center, where two of her children went. "By having day care, it gives us confidence that our little ones are in good hands." Her children also went to the summer camp. "I have the feeling that the management is always thinking of what they can give us more."

There are other reasons why Fel-Pro workers talk about the company as family. Many employees are second- and third-generation. Bob O'Keefe, vice-president of industrial relations, who has been with the company since 1946, is a good example. His three sons, one daughter, one cousin, and one son-in-law also work for the firm; his three daughters and one daughter-in-law worked there during college; and he has one grandchild in the day-care center. In fact, over half of all people who work at Fel-Pro are related to someone else in the company. And there are 109 Fel-Pro married couples. Even those who are not blood-related are considered kin, as Fel-Pro's top corporate goal is "to promote a feeling that we are truly a corporate family," according to the employee handbook.

The company started in 1918 when Hugo Herz and his son-in-law, Albert Mecklenburger, began making felt gaskets and washers for Ford Model T cars, under the name of Felt Products Manufacturing Company. Within a few years they were also making cork and paper gaskets as well as oil seals for automobiles. The firm is still 100 percent owned and controlled by the founding families. Mecklenburger's own sons-in-law, Lewis Weinberg and Elliot Lehman, serve as cochairmen emeriti. Mecklenburger's grandsons (Dave Weinberg and Ken Lehman) are cochairmen, as is Paul Lehman, a copresident. The other copresident is Dennis Kessler, who is married to another of Mecklenburger's grandchildren, Barbara Kessler. Paul Lehman told us that many of the employee policies can be traced to his grandfather, "a modest, unassuming man who was known to be generous and compassionate."

Fel-Pro's employees work in an air-conditioned 780,000-square-foot manufacturing and office complex in Skokie. Visitors immediately notice a 15-foot-high steel sculpture that depicts people holding huge gaskets. The piece was made by the firm's resident sculptor, Ted Gall, who uses scrap metal and pieces of gaskets to create arresting sculptural works placed throughout the headquarters. The cafeteria, for instance, hosts a large copper sculpture portraying the history of Fel-Pro.

One of the central institutions here is the Employee Forum, which has met monthly since 1952. Each department elects its representative to the forum, chaired by one of the two company presidents. Any issue, except compensation, is fair game. The first part of each meeting is devoted to reporting on what was done about the issues raised in the previous meeting. As Jeff Aull, a customer service representative, explained: "The forum is our voice." John Kula, a sales engineer, added: "I know everything is going to be addressed. The answer may still be no, but I know it's going to go through the system." There's a saying at Fel-Pro that the worst question you can have is the one you never ask.

According to president Paul Lehman, "The concept is that if you give people an opportunity to air the things they are concerned with and you take care of them, then problems stay in their proper perspective." Another advantage, Lehman said, is that "employees keep making suggestions because they know that somebody's going to listen."

In a forum meeting 20 years ago, employees asked to have the plant air-conditioned, and the company agreed (at a cost of about $1 million). When the issue of recycling was raised recently, a CAT, or corrective action team, composed of both management and employees, was formed to explore ways to improve the company's recycling efforts. Lehman said that the process is more collaborative today than in the past: "We are trying to make it more of a partnership instead of the old way of 'employee proposes, management disposes.' The new twist on it now is that it's not enough just to make suggestions, we all have to solve the problems confronting us."

Dick Johnston, director of corporate quality, contrasted Fel-Pro with his previous employers: "There's more listening that goes on around here, more consideration of the needs and point of view of people both within and outside the company. That was being done here long before it was recognized to be in vogue in other places." He found it remarkable how much access people had to top management. "If you come from another organization, it's a culture shock because there's a trust element here. It takes a while to believe it." Because people have so much direct access to top management, Johnston felt "it's not an easy place to supervise, particularly at the beginning level and the middle levels. You have to develop a thick skin." In the long run, he thinks it is worth it, since "it makes for more open communications, more understanding on the part of everyone as to what's going on and what the real problems are."

Fel-Pro has no executive cafeterias or washrooms or special parking slots. Top executives eat in the company cafeteria with other employees and appear to be on a first-name basis with a large percentage of the work force. They are frequently seen in the offices and on the plant floor kibitzing with employees. The top four officers share one secretary. Executives are expected to write their own speeches and memos, answer their own calls, and open their own mail.

John Barry, codirector of scrap production, recalled that his first boss told him that "the forum is the most important meeting we have each month within the organization. It takes top priority." This surprised Barry, who had previously worked for seven years as a supervisor at an LTV steel mill. "There was no trust between the supervisors and hourly people at LTV. The distrust was promoted in fact, with separate lunchrooms and different-colored hard hats. Coming here, there's not even a separate parking space for the owner, for crying out loud."

Besides the benefits for employees' children, Fel-Pro offers everyone a mind-boggling array of unusual perks: an extra day's pay on your birthday, on the anniversary date of your employment at Fel-Pro, and on June 1 (extra vacation money); a free lunch in the company cafeteria on your birthday; a $200 check in case of a death in the family (including siblings, parents, and parents-in-law); a $100 wedding check; a $1,000 check on retirement; free income tax preparation; your own mini-farm (a 20-foot-square plot of land at Triple R Camp with water and gardening tools); elder-care consulting and referral; eye care (a free eye exam and pair of eyeglasses every year); two free changes of work clothes annually; a generous profit-sharing plan; group auto insurance; a fully equipped and professionally staffed physical fitness center in the factory; and special holiday gifts:

- Valentine's Day—a pound of Fannie May chocolates
- Easter—a canned ham (or a kosher turkey)
- Mother's Day—a potted plant (given to everyone, mother or not)
- Father's Day—belt buckles, ties, photo albums, etc. (again, no need to be a father)
- Thanksgiving—a can of pistachio nuts
- Christmas—a turkey and a free Christmas dinner in the cafeteria

Some outsiders may consider all these goodies paternalism. Fel-Pro has no unions and has never experienced a work stoppage. And employees proudly point to their willingness to put out extra effort for the company when called upon. But none of the employees we talked with felt they had been bought off by the benefits. Susan Schmid worked summers for Fel-Pro while attending the University of Illinois with the help of the company's scholarship assistance. Her father worked in the maintenance department, and she also has a brother-in-law with the company. Schmid insisted that she does not feel "manipulated" by the extensive benefits package: "It's a two-way street. It's a give-and-take situation. They're flexible, and so you're flexible. You give more naturally, not because you feel obligated to." Lita Ignacio adds: "You feel that they care for you, so you have to care for them, too."

Copresident Paul Lehman bridles at the depiction of Fel-Pro as paternalistic: "Paternalism connotes to me a real big-brother, big-sister idea." Instead, he called Fel-Pro's style a partnership, where "everybody has to participate to be the best company we can be." He points out that Fel-Pro has been profitable every year of its history and that the firm has had to fight to become the leading gasket maker in the United States. He characterized the ample benefits as a form of sharing the wealth with those who've helped to create it.

Jackie Kassouff, a manager in the cell manufacturing department, explained that although people worked hard at Fel-Pro, there was no pressure, unlike her previous experience in the software industry. With software companies, she said, "We prided ourselves on the number of red-eyes we would take per month and bragged about our 80-hour weeks. That is definitely not the case here. At one point soon after I got here, my boss sat me down and told me point-blank, 'You are working too many hours. We value you too much. You are getting burned out. Stop it. You can take no work home this weekend.' And they were serious."

According to Kassouff, there is "a holistic kind of feeling here about people. We do have demands and we have to pay attention to those, but we are people, too, and you have to pay attention to your personal life and your family." She summed up the attitudes of many employees: "You feel like a real human being here when you come to work every day. And that is invaluable to me."

Types of jobs: Production—65 percent; technology and engineering—13 percent; sales and marketing—12 percent; administration—10 percent.

Main employment center: Skokie, Illinois.

Headquarters: Fel-Pro Incorporated
7450 N. McCormick Blvd.
P.O. Box 1103
Skokie, IL 60076
(312) 761-4500.

First Federal Bank of California

FIRST FEDERAL
SAVINGS BANK OF CALIFORNIA

First Federal Bank is a savings and loan that ranks 13th in California and 32nd nationally, based on assets. Employees: 560.

★ ★ ★   Pay/Benefits
★ ★ ★ ★   Opportunities
★ ★ ★ ★ ★ Job Security
★ ★ ★ ★ ★ Pride in Work/Company
★ ★ ★   Openness/Fairness
★ ★ ★ ★ ★ Camaraderie/Friendliness

BIGGEST PLUS: Women and minorities can bank on this place.
BIGGEST MINUS: You've got to deposit long hours.

Women have typically filled the majority of positions in banks—and most of them could always be found in the very bottom tier of the company. Not so at First Federal Bank. Fully two-thirds of its managers are women, including 18 of the 28 vice-presidents and two of the five top officers—president Babette Heimbuch and chief loan officer Sheryl Balthazar. What's more, nearly a third of its managers are from minority groups, including Jackie Kittaka, the vice-president of human relations. Kittaka started her career with FirstFed as an entry-level payroll clerk. Forty-one percent of the officers at First Federal started in entry-level positions.

Headquartered in a high rise a few blocks from the beach in Santa Monica, First Federal has distinguished itself as a workplace in a number of other ways. In an industry known for low wages, FirstFed's average annual salary in 1991 was $40,000. FirstFed also boasts one of the lowest turnover rates in banking. The typical bank's turnover rate among tellers, for instance, is about 60 percent; at FirstFed it's less than 20 percent.

One other distinction: First Federal's chairman and CEO, Bill Mortensen, knows virtually everybody by first name. Penny Resnick started at FirstFed as a temporary worker. "My very first day here," she told us, "I was sitting up here on the 12th floor at the desk when some man walked by me and said, 'Good morning, Penny. How are you?' And I said, 'Fine, thanks.' He walked away and I looked at the receptionist, and I said, 'Who was that?' And she turned back to me and said, 'That was the CEO.' And I thought, 'The CEO took the time to find out a temporary's first name? That must be a wonderful man to work for!' Here I am seven years later and he is a wonderful man to work for. This company is a wonderful place to work."

This seeming informality, ironically, is a formal policy. On the first page of "A Personal Guide to Success at First Federal," it is written: "At First Federal, we operate on a first-name basis. We go about our work in a business-like way, but we feel that work should be enjoyable and that we can all be friendly and cheerful while we are accomplishing the tasks which are assigned to us. We believe that EVERYONE in our organization is important and that each activity is as important as another."

Mortensen explained the policy: "I try to be on first-name basis with everybody. There is nothing that makes you feel worse than to have been at a place for a certain period of time and people don't know your name. We all love to hear somebody call us. And if the person looks at you and they can't remember who you are, it's very deflating. In some ways I think management has an ability to deflate more often than they have an ability to motivate. I don't know how much you can really motivate, but I do know you can demotivate. We assume people want to do a good job, work hard, be proud of where they work and be proud of their own work."

Mortensen, grandson of First Federal's founder, started working here as a teller in 1955, fresh out of the University of Southern California. At that time there were only 11 other employees at one office in Santa Monica. They now have more than two dozen branches throughout the Los Angeles Basin.

First Federal's growth has been gradual and decidedly unspectacular. In the 1980s, while many S&Ls looked for quick profits by investing in junk bonds, FirstFed focused almost exclusively on providing mortgage loans on single-family homes and apartment buildings—the original mandate of the savings and loan industry. Mortensen told us that at the time he thought investing in junk bonds was "a smart idea for those people who understood it, but I didn't understand it." Since one of his rules was not to invest in something he didn't understand, First Federal didn't invest in junk bonds. "It turns out they didn't understand [junk bonds] very much better than I did," he said. Many of the decade's high-flying S&Ls have since gone belly-up, and a quarter of California's thrifts were still losing money in late 1991.

Meanwhile, First Federal has thrived. It logged record profits between 1987 and 1991, and its stock has appreciated 10 times from the time it went public in 1983 to mid-1992. That same year *Forbes* ranked First Federal first among all financial institutions and S&Ls in the United States in terms of assets per employee and second in terms of sales and profits per employee. At the end of 1991, FirstFed had $3 billion out in loans.

FirstFed's chairman has been careful to share the bank's success with all employees. Mortensen said that several years ago he became concerned that tellers were not paid enough: "I was reading a book on sin, which was pointing out that it was as much a sin to steal something as to hire somebody at a wage that was not a livable wage, that is, if the employer could afford to pay a livable wage. It seemed to me that we were doing so well in terms of earnings and all of us with our bonuses, that we should make sure that we paid at least a livable wage [to the tellers]. So [in 1989] we made our minimum wage $15,000 [up from $12,500]." And then the bank started a STAR training program, which pays bonuses for completing various modules in the program. As a result, in less than a year, tellers could be earning more than $20,000. In addition to the STAR training program for tellers, First Federal has similar programs for loan agents and for those in operations.

On top of salaries, employees receive a bonus of an average of 30 shares of company stock after one year. Employees with two to four years of service receive a cash bonus of 25 percent of their monthly base salary; four to six years get 50 percent; seven to nine years get 75 percent; and those with more than 10 years get a full month's salary. In addition, on their five-year anniversary, employees get a choice of gifts from a catalog (bracelets, rings, clocks, pen sets), plus $250 in company stock. At their 10-year anniversary, they get $500 in company stock and an additional $250 in stock for each five-year increment. These shares of stock are given outright in addition to shares put into ESOP accounts by the company. First Federal created an ESOP (employee stock-ownership plan) in 1984. Employees now own about 10 percent of the company. Mortensen's reasoning was, "Actually having the stock come into your hands is more real than getting a notice that the ESOP shares have gone up. It's good to know that all the people in the company are stockholders."

Owning stock is important to employees, too. Brenda Battey said: "It shows me that senior management is not interested in keeping all of the compensation and good profitability of the company to themselves. They want to share it with other people."

The various incentive and stock bonus programs are not the only reasons why employees like FirstFed. They cite the bank's open atmosphere. Assistant vice-president Mary Scipioni, who has been working at FirstFed since

1990, said: "At FirstFed you can express your opinion at any time and you don't feel like it's going nowhere."

Like many others we interviewed, George Turner considered FirstFed to be like a family where people genuinely care about each other. Turner, who worked in the general services department, said: "It's like your family where you can speak your mind. If you don't like the way something is going on, you can express your opinions. If you see some improvement can be made in a given area, you are welcome and encouraged to speak your mind. So, you are at ease to do your job, speak your mind, exchange ideas, without anybody feeling threatened."

Encouraging constructive dissent is actually company policy. One of the bank's 12 operating principles is, "We operate as a team that understands the value of constructive dissent. We encourage new ideas and individualism." Constructive dissent is encouraged in letters to their *Prime Interest* monthly newsletter. A recent letter asked: "How is the quarterly bonus calculated? Is it based on salary? It seems to us that it is being used as a tool to reward a few and punish others. The people who make more money in the Dept. receive a higher bonus, the little people . . . well . . . very little. Is that fair?" The company responded by explaining that each department head selects the criteria for incentive bonuses in their own department: "It is important to keep in mind that incentive programs are in place to reward exceptional performance and productivity."

As far as Mortensen is concerned: "I think that whenever there is 100 percent unanimity you are generally going in a wrong direction. There are always points to be adjusted."

Main employment centers: 242 work at the corporate headquarters in Santa Monica. Other employees work in the 28 branches throughout southern California. An additional 74 work on commission as loan consultants, drumming up potential loan customers.

Headquarters: First Federal Bank of California
401 Wilshire Blvd.
Santa Monica, CA 90401
(310) 319-6000

H. B. Fuller

≡ H.B. Fuller Company

Fuller is a leading maker of adhesives, sealants, and coatings. U.S. employees: 1,950.

★ ★ ★	Pay/Benefits
★ ★	Opportunities
★ ★ ★ ★ ★	Job Security
★ ★ ★ ★	Pride in Work/Company
★ ★ ★	Openness/Fairness
★ ★ ★	Camaraderie/Friendliness

BIGGEST PLUS: They stick with you in tough times.
BIGGEST MINUS: You might get stuck in a rut.

Not every company announces to employees that profits aren't everything.

H. B. Fuller, a manufacturer of adhesives, sealants, and coatings (the glue that holds books together, the gum on the back of envelopes, the sealer on Kellogg's Corn Flakes packages, the adhesive in Pampers), did precisely that in the winter of 1990 in the first issue of a new employee publication, *Fuller World*. Bill Belknap, Fuller's public relations director, assured his readers that "at Fuller profits are a byproduct of success. . . . By the Fuller standard, to truly succeed we must do more than just make money." And Belknap went on to explain what "more" meant: be fair to customers, treat employees with respect and dignity, deliver good returns to investors, and make significant contributions to "our communities."

This message was especially striking because it came on the heels of two years of declining profits. During the late 1980s and early 1990s many companies in similar straits reacted by slashing their work forces, thereby earning the plaudits of Wall Street security analysts. But that's not the

Fuller way. The company, which was 100 years old in 1987, has never laid off employees. Even when plants have been closed, employees were offered a chance to relocate to another Fuller plant, and those employees who chose not to relocate were helped to find other jobs. In fact, Fuller has an official policy that rules out layoffs unless the company loses money for the year, which has never happened. In the event of a work stoppage, employees are still guaranteed at least 32 hours of work a week. If there's not enough to do in the plant, employees will be paid to do community work.

Jerry Scott, one of 30 vice-presidents (all of them male), said that since 1982 Fuller has consolidated 30 plants into 20. "The first one was the toughest one," he told us, "because Fuller had not done many of those, and so we were neophytes in how you do that. But we knew what our culture was and we were willing to find jobs for people. We gave them six months' notice and began posting all jobs throughout the U.S. that were available. They were moved with much the same benefits as we would move any professional. You were paid a bonus to move, which was 120 percent of a month's salary." Scott reported that after closing a Dallas plant that employed 17 people, two were relocated to other Fuller plants and the company then helped the others find local jobs. "We found jobs for every one of them," he said proudly. In one case, after employees found new jobs at a lower pay scale, Fuller agreed to supplement their wages until they reached their old level.

At Fuller you also don't have to worry about losing your job to a robot. The company promises all employees that if their job becomes obsolete, Fuller will retrain them in a new technology. Like many companies, Fuller will reimburse employees for outside educational costs, including tuition, fees, and textbooks, but it goes one step further: any employee who completes courses resulting in a college degree gets a bonus of $2,000.

Working in a glue factory is not especially glamorous, but H. B. Fuller makes up for it with policies that make employees feel valued. Since 1979 these policies have been meticulously spelled out in a statement, "H. B. Fuller's Responsibility to Its Employees." So it's all there in black and white, going for 17 dense pages. One plank, for example, states that it's the company's responsibility "to involve employees in the understanding of job performance objectives, not only for individual jobs, but for the employee as part of the performance team. This will be accomplished through quarterly department meetings, where managers and employees review Company and department objectives."

The bottom line for anyone working in the chemical industry has to be: how safe is it to work here? At Fuller, it's very safe. The company boasts one of the best records in the chemical industry. Since 1987, Fuller has cut work-related injuries and illnesses in half—and that was on top of an even more dramatic decline between 1979 and 1987. The accident records for the entire U.S. adhesives industry would seem to indicate that you are more than twice as likely to be injured at another plant than at one operated by Fuller. Fuller has a rule: at any meeting of more than five employees, a minimum of five minutes must be devoted to safety. In June 1991, after Fuller's Linear Products Division in Vancouver, Washington, had achieved a safety record by going 400,000 hours without a lost-time accident, vice-president Lars Carlson hosted a lunch for all 75 employees and gave each one a cordless telephone as a reward. Every plant that goes more than 100,000 hours without a lost-time accident gets this kind of recognition.

Jim Metts, who came here from Texas Instruments in 1984 to become the top human resources officer, told us that Fuller is a company that allows "any of us to be whatever we can be. They let you do that, they encourage it and they challenge it." Dave Quade, vice-president of the Foster Products Division (insulation materials), said joining Fuller and "seeing the belief in people and having people involved in decisions, it was like coming to heaven." Quade was formerly a construction worker, and he said it took him three years at Fuller to make as much in one year as he used to make in six months, "but I felt it was worth it." Not that Fuller is a low payer. The company's strategy, Metts told us, "is to pay above the competition," especially in the lower ranks. Fuller's lowest-paid job in St. Paul is a service worker—the starting pay in 1991 was $6.84 an hour, or $1,200 a month. Factory workers begin at $19,000 a year. Midlevel production workers make $36,800. Professionals start at $22,000 a year.

From the conversations we had at Fuller, it seemed clear that the company trusts its employees. Dick Johnson, vice-president of corporate relations, told us: "I'm an alcoholic and I was a vice-president running a division 15 years ago. I had to get treatment. I came back, and the job was there and there were no severe repercussions. People are not penalized here for mistakes."

Gary Olson, a manufacturing systems manager who joined Fuller in 1988 after having worked for a clutch of Minnesota firms (Economics Labs, Toro, Watkins, and Price Waterhouse), said that before Fuller, he didn't think he had ever been in a job where the pressure to perform was coming not from the top, but from himself. "It is a lot friendlier place than I have ever been in," he said. "The public accounting firms are not friendly places to be. It's different here. People like to say that they are from H. B. Fuller. I have been from places that I really didn't want to admit that I was from."

Another reason why people are proud to work here is a strong community involvement effort that goes on wherever Fuller has a plant. Most American companies allocate 1 percent of pretax profits or less to philanthropy. Since 1976 Fuller has made it a point to contribute 5 percent of its pretax profits to support community activities (and befitting its international reach, more than half of that giving now happens outside the United States). During the 1980s this program has meant grants averaging $650,000 a year.

Equally impressive is the way this policy is carried out. Each of Fuller's 34 plant locations in the United States has a community affairs council. More than 165 employees serve on these councils, and they decide who is to get the money. Another 28 councils operate in Canada, Latin America, Europe, and Japan. Fuller encourages people to be involved. It allows employees to take up to 12 hours off each quarter for work in a community organization or project. This is paid time. In 1991 the CACs organized and carried out more than 175 service projects involving some 1,200 employees, family members, and friends.

The company's social consciousness can be traced to Elmer L. Andersen, who joined Fuller in 1934 as advertising manager, bought the company in 1941, and presided over a growth that saw sales zoom from $275,000 in 1941 to $10 million in 1960, when Andersen, running on the Republican ticket, was elected governor of Minnesota. Andersen returned to the company three years later as chairman of the board, a position he still held in 1992, at age 82. Andersen sold Fuller stock to the public for the first time in 1968, but he continues to exercise control of the company with holdings amounting to nearly 25 percent of all the votes. (Before being elected to the U.S. Senate in 1978, Dave Durenberger was Fuller's legal counsel.)

Andersen's son, Tony, who became president in 1971, at age 35, pioneered Fuller's international expansion, and remains chief executive officer today. Andersen tries to be visible in the company. Twice a year he makes himself available to everyone through the "President's Hot Line." Anybody can call him on those days on a toll-free number to complain or make suggestions or just shoot the breeze. In recent years Andersen has fielded about 30 calls on those days. In 1989 they included a 30-year employee apprehensive about his pending retirement, a plant employee dissatisfied with his management, a Colombian employee who wanted Andersen to know that things weren't as bad there as the media made them out to be, and a nonsmoker who urged that nonsmoking employees be rewarded with extra vacation days (it's not known how Andersen, a cigarette smoker, handled this suggestion).

Lack of pretension is one of Fuller's hallmarks. There's nothing fancy about their offices. The corporate headquarters in St. Paul adjoins a glue factory, where Cathy Brown, a zoologist, was running a two-shift team of 28 persons (only three of them women) when we visited in 1991. Since then Brown has become a telemarketing sales representative.

Fuller has a profit-sharing plan that is less generous than many we have looked at. It's also unusual in that the payout is linked to personal performance as well as company performance. Employees have five possible ratings, from unsatisfactory to outstanding. Anyone with an unsatisfactory rating is ineligible for profit sharing. But it seems that the only way an employee can get as much as 10 percent of pay in profit sharing is for two things to happen: he or she has to get an outstanding rating and Fuller has to net more than 5 percent on its sales, something it certainly hasn't done at any time during the past dozen years. The net profit margin in 1991 was 3.2 percent, which would bring a payout of 7 percent for top raters and 2.5 percent for employees with a next-to-last rating (marginal). However, the company does have a 401(k) savings plan in which it matches, dollar for dollar, employee savings up to 3 percent of pay. In 1991 CEO Tony Andersen earned $712,615.

Other benefits are stronger. Fuller still gives employees the day off on their birthdays, pays $100 toward any health club membership, $100 toward an annual physical exam, and up to $1,500 to cover adoption costs. New mothers can take a six-week unpaid leave. There are also generous rewards for veteran employees. Beginning with your 10th anniversary with the company, you receive an extra two weeks vacation plus $800 in cash (after taxes) to spend on that vacation—you get that same bonus every fifth year thereafter.

The final plus at H. B. Fuller is a strong environmental protection program that has enabled the company to escape any serious infraction of government regulations—and there are not many chemical companies that can make that claim. Fuller has environmental programs going throughout the world so that it can state flatly that "the preservation of natural resources and a sincere respect for the environment are woven into the very fabric" of the company. Fuller recycles waste water from production processes, tries to recycle solid materials, and packages its products in returnable and reusable containers. A glittering example of Fuller's concern is the research laboratory the company opened in 1985. The lab, in North St. Paul, is surrounded by the 50-acre Willow Lake Nature Preserve, which functions as a wildlife sanctuary and nesting area for migratory fowl. And the 100,000-square-foot laboratory is heated and cooled by a heat-pump system that eschews the use of fossil fuels. To the question "Why do this?," Fuller answered: "It's the right thing to do."

Types of jobs: Production and warehouse workers—24 percent; managers—19 percent; professionals—19 percent; clerical—14 percent; sales—12 percent; craft workers—8 percent; technicians—4 percent.

Main employment centers: More than 700 people work in the Twin Cities. The next biggest concentration is in Chicago, where 220 are employed. Another 1,000 work at small facilities in 22 states. More than 3,600 are employed overseas.

Headquarters: H. B. Fuller Company
2400 Energy Park Dr.
St. Paul, MN 55108
(612) 645-3401

General Mills

G General Mills, Inc

General Mills is a leader in cereals, dessert products, main-meal mixes, speciality side dishes, fruit snacks, and baking mixes. General Mills's Red Lobster restaurant is the leading U.S. dinner-house chain. U.S. employees: 111,500.

★ ★ ★ ★ Pay/Benefits
★ ★ ★ ★ Opportunities
★ ★ ★ Job Security
★ ★ ★ ★ Pride in Work/Company
★ ★ ★ Openness/Fairness
★ ★ ★ Camaraderie/Friendliness

BIGGEST PLUS: A company of champions.
BIGGEST MINUS: But the restaurants wouldn't win a gold medal.

There's mythic power in this company. Wheaties—"the Breakfast of Champions"—has been endorsed by great athletes from Babe Ruth to Michael Jordan. Cheerios, the best-selling cereal in the country, is over 50 years old. Betty Crocker recently passed her 70th birthday. Gold Medal flour goes back to 1880. You join up here, and you're buying into a piece of Americana.

General Mills is headquartered in the Golden Valley area of western Minneapolis, occupying 150 landscaped and sculpture-dotted acres which hold three modern, connected buildings. An artfully covered walkway snakes through the huge parking lot so that you don't freeze as you make your way from the car to the office during the cold Minnesota winters. And if your car freezes sitting out there, not to worry. Someone will come around to jump-start it. The MGO (Minneapolis General Office) has a bunch of amenities: car-washing service, dry cleaner's, barbershop, library and stores that rent videos, process film, and sell snacks. And as of 1991, there's a gleaming new fitness center available to employees—and their spouses—free of charge. One mile down the road is the James Ford Bell Technical Center, which has its own fitness center. General Mills is a benevolent employer.

Suzanne Fuller-Terrill remembers driving past the MGO shortly after her family moved to the Twin Cities from Ohio. "We were living in Maple Grove," she told us, "and as we passed General Mills, I told my dad, 'Bet they're going to hire me. Just watch.'" They did, 12 years ago. Fuller-Terrill had gone to high school at night while she worked full-time during the day, and she explained that "the reason I chose General Mills is because they would pay for my school. I had to work, so the fact that they would pay for night school was really important to me. I have had nine different jobs here." While working during the day, she took evening courses in accounting and communications. At one point, she thought she would rather go to school during the day and work at night, and so she left to work at the post office. "I was gone for a day," she said, "and I called my boss and said, 'Can I come back? I can't stand this.' He said: 'Come on back.'" When we saw Fuller-Terrill in 1991, she was an assistant marketing director on the Betty Crocker catalog. "I started here when I was 18," she said, "and I feel like it is part of my family."

Fuller-Terrill's experience in moving around to different jobs is typical. Because the company has so many old, well-established brands, an outsider might think that work here is boring: just sit back and count the money. But that's not the case. The atmosphere is electric—in fact, it borders on hyper. The packaged food business is highly competitive, and General Mills looks for people who want to shake things up. H. Brewster Atwater III, who joined the company in 1958 and marked his 10th year as CEO in 1992, has set a goal of tripling sales during the 1990s, and to that end he implores employees to be risk-takers. Speaking to the troops in 1991, Atwater stressed that it was the obligation of each employee to "put your ideas on the line, challenge the status quo, and adapt to change."

You might wonder what it means to be a risk-taker in this business. Well, here are some examples. Christi Strauss, who has an M.B.A. from the Amos Tuck School at Dartmouth, was marketing director for children's cereals in 1991 at age 30. She scored two great coups: Kix, a 55-year-old brand, had a sales boost of 30 percent after sugar was put on the coating of the corn puffs instead of in the batter; and boxes of Lucky Charms began to move more briskly after Strauss tossed in a new marshmallow bit, a green tree.

She then got 350,000 kids (or their parents) to rip off the box top and send for a free seedling. Risk-taking here means taking a chance with your number one brand by bringing out two new varieties of Cheerios—Honey Nut (1979) and Apple Cinnamon (1988)—and trying the same ploy now with Wheaties. The first variation of the Wheaties brand is Wheaties Honey Gold, and the marketing director for this new product is Maria Morgan, who is just out of the Harvard Business School (1990). She chose General Mills, she said, because "I wanted to hit the ground running." If this kind of trailblazing doesn't inspire you, General Mills may not be the place for you.

Much of the excitement here derives from being a winner. General Mills's Big G cereals have been taking market share away from Kellogg. Pop Secret popcorn has overtaken Orville Redenbacher, and Betty Crocker's Nature Valley granola bars and Helper lines (hamburger, tuna, chicken) have racked up big sales gains in the 1990s. Those were satisfying wins to the people who work here. In addition to fat bonuses, many of these young managers had their pictures run in the annual report.

General Mills attracts these young tigers by promising them early responsibility. In that respect, it's similar to Procter & Gamble, whose Duncan Hines brand confronts Betty Crocker in the marketplace. Both companies recruit heavily at the nation's most prestigious business schools. They are also similar in that after giving people hands-on training, they find that they may have trained some of them for other companies. Bob Paulson, a lawyer who's manager of strategic planning and development, pointed out to us that the general counsels at Pillsbury, Ralston Purina, and Tonka are all out of General Mills, as is the treasurer at Ralston. "We get raided a lot because there are a lot of good people here," he said. One way General Mills differs from P&G is a preference for oral communication. Procter has a longtime reverence for the succinct, one-page memo. Vice-chairman Arthur Schulze, with General Mills since 1963, told us: "Although any major project will have something in writing, we prefer to do business on a face-to-face basis." Jim Riesterer, Betty Crocker marketing manager, said: "It is amazing when you go to lunch how many impromptu meetings there are, people just meeting in the hallways. A lot of the meetings are three and four minutes long and then they're off to lunch. That is how you get stuff done."

They stress speed here. "Quick" is a word you hear frequently. Marketing whizzes are being told not to research everything to death. CEO Bruce Atwater gave this analogy: "If I had taken a vote on whether we ought to get out of various businesses we got out of in the 1980s, I suspect the vote would have been the opposite of what we actually did. You have to go out and do it if you think you're right." In other words, go with your gut. The businesses General Mills jettisoned in the 1980s included toys (Parker Brothers, Kenner), clothing (Ship 'n Shore, Izod/Lacoste), jewelry (Monet), and stores (Eddie Bauer, Wallpapers To Go). Employees at Parker Brothers and Eddie Bauer did not have their benefits reduced under the new owners because General Mills managed to persuade the buyers to continue them.

General Mills has now hunkered down to two core areas—making food and feeding people in restaurants. Their two major restaurant chains are Red Lobster and Olive Garden. In mid-1992 the company *owned* (General Mills does not franchise) and operated 960 restaurants in the United States. More than 80 percent of the people employed by General Mills work in the restaurants, and the company has introduced strong benefits programs in a business that normally doesn't have them. The benefits are not as rich as those available to the packaged foods work force, but they include medical insurance, vacations, and retirement and profit-sharing plans. Turnover at the Red Lobsters runs about 95 percent a year, considered good in an industry where people change as fast as the menus. The restaurant division, run out of Orlando, Florida, has also mounted recognition programs. Olive Garden salutes the top 20 servers in its chain every year, bringing them to the national sales meeting of general managers and awarding each of them five shares of General Mills stock. In 1992 they expanded the program to high-performing employees from all areas of the restaurant, including dishwashers, chefs, and bus people. They also promote from within. One third of the restaurant managers have come from the hourly ranks.

General Mills has been on a bureaucracy-busting drive. Schulze told us that the company has cut out "at least" two layers of management. Nancy Matthews, a sales and promotion director in the cereal division, said: "We are a lot faster now. You can go into your boss and say, 'I have half an idea, I'm not sure where it's going to take me, but I'm going to go with it.' Before, you would have your knees knocking together if you dared bring up something you hadn't thought through."

Empowerment has also reached the factory level in the form of self-directed work teams. At the cereal plant in Lodi, California, workers run the line on the night shift without any managers present. At the company's biggest plant, in Cedar Rapids, Iowa, where 685 people work, there are only three levels of management. The most efficient operation in Cedar Rapids is the layer-cake line, which now runs without supervisors. The trade magazine *Prepared Foods* visited the plant in 1991, reporting how the cake line workers "rotate regularly between five assignments, from processing through packaging. Together, team members make all decisions relating to production." Bill Mowery, plant manager at Cedar Rapids, has been with General Mills for 25 years and he is only the third manager the plant has had since it opened in 1970. Mowery was one of 1,194 General Mills employees with more than 25 years of service in 1992. There are 334 people with more than 35 years.

Participative management has also been installed at General Mills's new

$100-million plant at Covington, Georgia, 30 miles outside of Atlanta. It is so high-tech that it only needs 100 employees. The plant manager is Pat McNulty, an industrial engineer who joined General Mills in 1974 after graduating from Western Michigan University. Prior to Covington, he filled eight different production management jobs, including supervision of the Yoplait yogurt line.

Since 1987 General Mills has bumped up sales by 50 percent while profits have more than doubled. Employees have shared in these gains through high pay scales—a sweeper in the headquarters begins at $15.90 per hour, an M.B.A. marketing manager can hire in at $54,000 a year—and new incentive programs that shower stock and cash awards on people. The programs are especially rich for senior managers (some 2,000 managers now receive stock options, double the number of a few years ago), but they also reach lower levels. A performance incentive plan delivers an annual cash bonus of up to 7 percent of annual pay, based on how well employees have scored on their individual performance ratings. A savings plan enables employees at all levels to save up to 15 percent of their pay before taxes—and on the first 5 percent, General Mills matches each $1 of savings with 50 cents in stock; then, at the end of the year, if the company reaches its profit goals, it can match the other 50 percent. In 1990, 1991, and 1992 the match was 100 percent. So if your salary was $50,000 a year and you saved $2,500 a year, General Mills would have matched those savings with $2,500 worth of stock. Every year. Over those three years General Mills stock doubled in price on the New York Stock Exchange. The company reports that 90 percent of employees with three years' service are now stockholders, and they own 7 percent of the total. Of course it's skewed to the top: the directors and officers—about 40 people—own 4 percent, leaving 3 percent for the remaining 100,000.

One source of pride here is an outstanding record of support for nonprofit organizations and social service groups. In 1991 General Mills gave 2.9 percent of pretax profits—more than $20 million—to charitable activities. That's triple the level prevailing at most big companies.

Women and minorities also do better at General Mills than at comparable companies. Minorities represent 26 percent of all employees, 11 percent of officials and managers, and 4 percent of senior management. *Black Enterprise* rates them among the 25 best companies in the nation for blacks. About half the work force here is female, and women now hold a third of the marketing manager positions, which can be a route to the top. Of the General Mills people making more than $100,000 a year, 9 percent are women. Of those making above $50,000 a year, 17 percent are women. And more than 1,000 developmentally disabled people work in Red Lobster restaurants.

Types of jobs: Service (restaurants)—83 percent; manufacturing—6 percent; management—6 percent; professional—3 percent; clerical—2 percent.

Main employment centers: About 3,000 people work at the headquarters and at the research and development center (the James Ford Bell Technical Center) in Minneapolis. There are plants in Lodi and Carson, California; Chicago; Toledo, Ohio; Buffalo, New York; Cedar Rapids, Iowa; Covington, Georgia; Addison, Texas; and Reed City, Michigan. 92,000 people work in the restaurants.

Headquarters: General Mills, Inc.
P.O. Box 1113
Minneapolis, MN 55440
(612) 540-2311

Goldman Sachs

Goldman Sachs is one of the world's leading investment bankers. U.S. employees: 4,900.

★ ★ ★ ★ ★ Pay/Benefits
★ ★ ★ Opportunities
★ ★ ★ Job Security
★ ★ ★ ★ Pride in Work/Company
★ ★ ★ Openness/Fairness
★ ★ ★ ★ Camaraderie/Friendliness

BIGGEST PLUS: You can make sacks of gold.
BIGGEST MINUS: You may not have time to enjoy it.

Goldman Sachs, a demigod of Wall Street, raises huge amounts of money for corporations—and governments. They also buy and sell massive blocks of shares on the New York Stock Exchange and the other major exchanges around the world. But this is not a place you call up to buy 100 shares of Coca-Cola. They don't handle small investors. One hundred thousand shares? Well, now you're talking. They execute for big institutional investors like pension funds and insurance companies. They also advise companies on mergers and acquisitions. Big ones. But they would just as soon not help a company planning a hostile acquisition. Their relationships with some clients—Ford, General Electric, Goodyear Tire, Sears, Roebuck—go back decades. Torrents of money sluice through this investment banking house. Every day. In various forms and various currencies. They deal in virtually every type of financial instrument you can think of—stocks, bonds, Treasury notes, commodity positions, real estate, options.

The crumbs from these transactions that end up in Goldman's coffers form a very rich loaf. The firm's profits for 1991 were estimated by analysts at $900 million, or a mind-boggling $134,000 per employee. Goldman Sachs is the last of the big investment bankers still organized as a partnership—and all the partners are millionaires. Of course not everyone makes partner. In 1992 Goldman had 142 partners (up from 80 in 1984). However, even lower-level people here make out better than their counterparts at other Wall Street houses because Goldman makes a point of paying higher salaries—and on top of that, they ladle out fat year-end bonuses. The bonuses depend, of course, on how well the firm has done, but Goldman Sachs rarely misses. The average payout, in the second half of the 1980s, was 22 percent. In 1991 it was 25 percent. So if you were a support staff worker earning $400 a week, close to the lowest wage doled out here, Goldman presented you with a check for $5,200 at the end of the year. And on top of that, Goldman people participate in a profit-sharing plan (the firm's contribution, historically, has been 15 percent of salary). In addition, there's a separate pension plan.

There is more to working at Goldman Sachs than stuffing your wallet with money. It's an investment banking house with a long history, having been founded by a German Jewish immigrant, Marcus Goldman, in 1869, and it lives by a set of business principles that it takes seriously and that has served it well. Given the scandals that engulfed Wall Street in the 1980s, it may seem odd for a securities firm to talk about integrity, but Goldman Sachs does—and most observers believe it has a right to. It was embarrassed in 1989 when a senior stock trader, Robert Freeman, pleaded guilty to insider trading charges, but that seemed to be an exception that proved the rule. As a firm, Goldman followed its own path during the 1980s, not pushing at the edges to do lucrative financial deals. It thereby escaped the opprobium that cloaked so many competitors.

It wasn't just its reputation that emerged largely unscathed from the 1980s. Its business was stronger than ever.

After the 1991 upheavals at Salomon Brothers, following disclosure of its rigging of Treasury note auctions, *The Wall Street Journal* anointed Goldman Sachs as "the strongest, most prestigious securities firm on Wall Street." The *Journal* interviewed a former president of the American Stock Exchange, Kenneth Leibler, who said: "What Goldman has always nurtured is an image of integrity, which in times like this comes back to benefit them."

That Goldman's insistence on "high ethical standards" is more than window dressing became clear to us in interviews with associates who work in municipal finance, helping cities raise money through tax-free bond offerings. Tom Flato, who joined Goldman in 1990, said: "After you are here for any length of time, you realize that there is a set of values from top to bottom, norms that are shared here." Lois M. Perelson-Gross, with the firm since 1987, confirmed that Goldman has "a value system that is espoused and in fact followed at all levels." Matt Roggenburg, an alumnus of the Coopers & Lybrand accounting firm, said Goldman people "really believe that we hold ourselves to a higher standard than other firms in the way we deal with our clients. When we do a transaction, we leave a little money on the table. As a general rule, we don't try to get the last nickel because we want clients to feel that we have done a good job for them."

If you hear it once, you hear it 100 times at Goldman: this is not a place for superegos. "We stress teamwork in everything we do" is one of the guiding business principles. This teamwork extends to the top of the firm, where two lawyers, Robert E. Rubin and Stephen Friedman, lead Goldman as cochairmen of the management committee, reviving a tradition that was introduced in 1976, when the chairman's job was shared by John Weinberg and John Whitehead. Rubin and Friedman work out of modest, adjoining offices on the 22nd floor of the 85 Broad Street building that sits on grounds where the original Dutch City Hall was located. The 30-story building, a few blocks from the New York Stock Exchange, is 100 percent occupied by Goldman. Rubin and Friedman, in the Goldman mold, are soft-spoken and self-effacing. They both joined the firm in 1966. Neither has a name that would command instant recognition, not even in financial circles. But their pay is not modest. In 1992 *The Wall Street Journal* estimated that Rubin and Friedman each earned more than $15 million in 1991.

Aside from being part of the culture here, teamwork has become more crucial because of the complexity of the financial products being sold today —and Friedman believes that this has given Goldman "a big edge." In 1991, for example, Goldman put together in Europe a labyrinthian transaction for three clients—the Province of Ontario, the Inter-American Development Bank, and Finnish Export Credit Ltd. As Friedman explained to us: "If you look at the description of some of the products we serve up, they are complicated. The diagram of who has to work together looks like the wiring system for an atomic submarine. You cannot mandate that structurally, you cannot say, 'You will work with him.' You have to have people who are willing to subordinate their own immediate desires to what they perceive to be the greater good of the organization."

Friedman added that Goldman prides itself on having a diversity of people in its ranks. "We do not have a cookie-cutter mold of personalities," he said. "We don't have dress codes, we don't have 'Where did your father's father go to school?'—we have absolute disinterest in these kinds of things. My definition of high morale isn't everyone always walking around happy, it's identification with the aims of the organization. And I think we have that."

Gary Zwerling, a partner who came to Goldman from Chase Manhattan Bank in 1978, said: "Titles are a lot less important here than they were at the bank. You can be very successful here without having any title. At a bank, typically, you get a new title every two years, and it becomes very important in the way you progress. Reporting lines are very formal. Here everybody feels that they in some sense report to everybody else, even people who are on the same level. There is accountability in all different directions."

The number of people working for Goldman Sachs nearly doubled between 1984 and 1987, with the big growth coming in overseas offices. But the firm made a conscious decision then to run very lean. And over the next three years, through a combination of attrition and layoffs, total head count was reduced from 7,400 to 6,600, a cost reduction that Rubin credits for helping Goldman register record profits in 1990 and 1991. In 1991, even as it was raking in unprecedented profits, it decided to reduce staff again, letting go some 75 professionals. According to Rubin, however, "50 of the 75 would have been let go no matter what the times were; it was basically performance related."

Goldman goes to unusual pains to find people who will fit into their culture. It recruits at all the top-level graduate business schools, hiring M.B.A.'s after putting them through a grueling series of interviews—as many as 20. "We will find out the real person by the time we are done," said Roggenburg. The M.B.A. graduates start off at $50,000 a year—that's just the base salary. After one year these associates, as they are known here, are making at least $80,000 a year.

Some recently hired associates gave us insights as to why they came to Goldman. One said that in interviewing at a myriad of different firms, he asked at each place: "If you could be with any other firm, who would you be with?" The answer came back "Goldman" each time—"and so I thought this is the place I would like to be." Allen Sinsheimer, who graduated from the business school at Northwestern, said: "Salomon didn't treat me well and the guys were so aggressive. I liked Lehman but there were nine people at Goldman doing the same job as 15 at Lehman." Warren Daniels, Jr., who came here in 1989, told us: "If you are not smart, you will have a problem at Goldman."

Goldman has been dogged for years by criticism that it discriminated against blacks and women. Of its 142 partners in 1992, only four were female, none was black. In 1991 the firm was defending itself against two sex discrimination cases brought by women who had been fired. In one of them, Rita Reid, a former vice-president who had worked on mergers and acquisitions, said that in 1989 she was given a bonus of $375,000, about five times her base salary, but was passed over for partnership. In 1989 a partner resigned after being accused of sexual harassment.

The work at Goldman is intense—and the hours are still long, although there might be some slackening in the pace since the heyday of mergers and acquisitions in the 1980s. Employee relations director Jeff Sanderson told us: "You have to be prepared to work when you hit the office in the morning. You can't let down. This is a real demanding organization. It demands excellence all of the time. You make sacrifices; everyone has to make adjustments between their personal lives and their business lives." Carol Anderson, a sales associate in fixed-income securities, told us: "It seems to me at Goldman that the higher people get, the harder they work. If you look at the senior partners, they kill themselves." Jim Denaut, a municipal finance associate, described the work at Goldman as "always new and exciting, but my mom thinks I'm crazy when she calls and I am here constantly late at night."

The intensity probably explains why partners at Goldman often retire by age 50. Of course, as a partner they can afford to. In 1991 Geoffrey T. Boisi, who was regarded as the number three executive at Goldman, retired at age 44 after 21 years with the firm. In an interview with *The Wall Street Journal*, Boisi said: "I am married to my wife one more year than I have been married to Goldman Sachs. I found that Goldman has been getting more time-share than my family." *Journal* reporter Michael Sincolfi said that after joining Goldman as a summer intern in 1970, Boisi worked 18 hours a day and made partner when he was 31 years old.

Still, changes are beginning to soften this workaholic culture. Working parents are being offered reduced schedules so that they can spend more time with their families. In the San Francisco office, an annual family day in June brings 80 kids into Goldman to spend some time where Daddy or Mommy works. And in mid-1992 Goldman announced to employees that before the year's end it would open a drop-in child-care center in the lobby of 85 Broad Street to serve as a backup when employees' normal child-care arrangements are not available. The center will accommodate 30 children.

"If we are mindful of ways to help fulfill family responsibilities, we believe it will strengthen our people and our firm," said cochairs Rubin and Friedman.

Types of jobs: Sales—10 percent; traders—7 percent; investment bankers —7 percent; other professionals—22 percent; support—53 percent.

Main employment centers: 4,200 work in New York City, another 700 in 10 U.S. offices, and 1,800 (up from 400 in 1985) in 13 offices outside the United States, including 1,100 in London.

Headquarters: Goldman, Sachs & Co.
85 Broad St.
New York, NY 10004
(212) 902-1000

W. L. Gore & Associates

W. L. Gore makes Gore-tex, a synthetic material that is used in camping equipment, among many other uses. U.S. employees: 3,216.

★ ★ ★ ★ Pay/Benefits
★ ★ ★ ★ ★ Opportunities
★ ★ ★ ★ Job Security
★ ★ ★ ★ Pride in Work/Company
★ ★ ★ ★ Openness/Fairness
★ ★ ★ ★ Camaraderie/Friendliness

BIGGEST PLUS: You can make your own path.
BIGGEST MINUS: You might get lost.

One of the most delightful experiences we had in doing the first edition of *The 100 Best Companies to Work for in America* was interviewing Bill Gore. Gore started his career as a research chemist who worked on a task force at Du Pont looking for uses for polytetrafluoroethylene, or PTFE, more commonly known as Teflon. Working in his basement one night, Gore discovered that PTFE could be used to insulate electrical cable wires. Du Pont was not interested in pursuing Bill's invention, so in 1958 he and his wife, Vieve, started their own company, located in Newark, Delaware, a short drive from Du Pont's Wilmington headquarters.

What made Bill Gore fun to talk with was that he was more than a successful entrepreneur. He was a philosopher who had developed an original theory about how to run organizations—a theory he called "the lattice organization." We spent an engaging afternoon with him philosophizing about what makes for good and bad places to work and hearing his war stories of trying to implement his theory.

Sadly, Bill Gore passed away in 1986, but his spirit lives on today in his company. We found discussions in late 1990 with Gore associates (they're never called employees here) to be as stimulating as our earlier talk with Bill Gore. And we found that the company had thrived during the 1980s, growing at an annual clip of 20 percent to sales of $600 million in 1990 and more than 5,000 employees at 40 plants worldwide. U.S. plants are clustered around Newark, Delaware, and Flagstaff, Arizona. Despite this growth, it still adheres to one of Bill Gore's principles—plants should not be larger than 200 people because beyond that size you cease to be able to know everybody, and bureaucracy becomes inevitable.

Small plant size is only one element in Bill Gore's lattice philosophy. In Gore plants there are no titles, no set chain of command, no authoritarian bosses, and no rules. Associates can write whatever they want on their business cards. When outsiders ask Tom Fairchild what his title is, he responds: "I don't know. What do you want it to be?" Because there are no titles, the hierarchy is ambiguous. To Fairchild, who came here in 1985, the lack of titles and chain of command is only common sense: "Why go to someone with a title when you can go to someone with an answer?"

John Shaw, who has been with Gore since 1983, explained how the system works: "I know I can depend on certain people for technical information and guidance because we have a relationship or bond. It really isn't that much different than any other company, it's just not a formal bond. One thing here is that there is not a lot of pretense. We cut the crap out and get right to business. We don't worry about what you say to who, we just get the job done."

Gore's unique system has gotten the job done over the years. Researchers say that the freedom they have has helped them come up with a variety of applications of the Teflon-like material. In 1969 Bob Gore, Bill Gore's son, found a way to stretch PTFE into fabric, which he patented as "Gore-tex."

The pores in Gore-tex are big enough to let perspiration evaporate through, yet small enough to keep raindrops out. Gore-tex has made quite a splash in the outdoor clothing industry, but Gore also uses PTFE in many other capacities: space suits, artificial arteries and ligaments, air and water filters. In its 35 years Gore has turned out about 400 patents and currently makes hundreds of different products.

Associates claim that their unusual lattice management philosophy has fostered this growth. In this system, associates who have answers gain followers, and therefore become leaders. Bill Gore calls it "natural leadership defined by followership." Associates who have an idea for a project find others to join them. Although the project originator, hence leader, may have set objectives, the joiners can impact the original ideas. Leaders do not give orders, they secure commitment from each individual. According to Bill Gore: "No man can commit for another. All commitments are self-commitments. Authoritarians cannot impose commitments, only commands. The difference in response is enormous." And the response has been huge. In a recent survey, about half of the Gore associates answered "yes" to the question "Do you consider yourself to be a leader in your plant?"

With so many leaders, who is responsible for evaluating individual associates? Gore devised a system of sponsorship. Sponsors keep track of an individual's activities and act as advocates in compensation discussions. According to Bill Gore, a sponsor "will be knowledgeable about the activities, well-being, progress, accomplishments, personal problems, and ambitions of the person he sponsors." Associates we met described sponsors as "coaches" and "mentors." According to one: "They're not your boss, they are there to help you succeed."

Many people thrive in Gore's lattice structure. Lois Mabon, who worked at Westinghouse before coming here in 1989, said at Westinghouse "you had your little mold. Everybody comes in and works for so many months in a certain area and then gets promoted to another area, whether you want to go there or not." When she entered Gore as an engineer, Mabon's working group, an all-male group of electrical technicians, was leaderless and directionless. At the encouragement of her sponsor, Mabon became the group leader after only six months. The group of technicians later confided that they were hesitant at first when they thought that a "girl was going to be in charge," but have since overcome their prejudice. And according to Mabon: "We are a great team, and we do work together as a team."

When Joe Tanner started his career at Du Pont he was an aspiring researcher. But since Tanner didn't have a Ph.D., he was told he had no future there. Tanner heard about Gore's philosophy and knew immediately that this was the company for him. "When I got here I heard, 'You are what you are and you do what you do and if you do something good we'll pay you more money.' It was exactly what I was looking for. I swallowed it hook, line, and sinker." At Gore he was not held back by lack of credentials. In fact, Tanner has worked in all of the divisions at some point in time, including research. He says: "You're not put in a box, you're not categorized. If you want to do technical work and marketing work you can. As long as you are working on something that is making a contribution, you're not stymied. You set your own course."

The lattice organization is definitely not for everyone, however. Some people will not take Gore job offers because they are too ambiguous. Others who do accept the offers find the atmosphere here a little too unstructured. According to Aubrey Saunders, who has been at Gore since 1982: "It takes a lot of personal stamina to be successful here. You don't have structured charts, you don't have rules and regulations that you can fall back on. You've got to bring a lot of yourself to be successful here." It takes initiative to get projects going at Gore. Saunders told us that in his first two years, he was frustrated: "I could not understand why all the good ideas I had weren't happening. It was my own fault."

Associates are expected to find their own niches. Joe Tanner, currently working in marketing, told us about a former Du Pont employee in sales and marketing who was frustrated by the lack of structure. The marketing associate told Joe, "At Du Pont it is easy: you get a reassignment, you get a title, you know exactly who you are, you know exactly what is expected of you, everybody around you knows who you are, they know what position you have been put in, so it is really easy to make a change." Tanner went on to describe the difference: "At Gore it doesn't work that way. It is like, 'Why don't you go over there and see if you can't help out?' And then it is up to the individual to carve it out."

Although compensation is based on contribution instead of the number of hours you spend at the office, Gore associates find themselves putting in a lot of time. Bob Henn, who joined the firm in 1978, told us: "Very seldom do I put in an eight-hour day. It's more like nine, 10, or 11." The associates we talked with all insisted that the extra time they put in was by choice. Debbie Broadbent, who has been with Gore since 1984, thinks that "everybody has a feeling that even the smallest thing I contribute, contributes to our stock. That is what keeps people happy and wanting to put in these long hours." We did, however, find other associates who said they were not penalized for putting in a standard 40-hour workweek.

Gore qualifies as a good workplace for strictly practical reasons. The personal freedom extends to a flexible benefits program, and Gore's benefits rank 23 percent higher than comparable companies, according to a Hewitt Associates study.

One of Gore's biggest benefits is associate ownership. The firm is 75 percent owned by associates. The ASOP (associate stock-ownership plan) has helped many associates build up quite a nest egg for retirement. Sally

Gore, wife of president Bob Gore and head of the company's human resources team, knows one machinist who after 25 years of service retired a millionaire. One manager told us: "There have been times where people have made more money in the ASOP than they have in their W2."

The Lattice Organization

The closest thing Gore has to rules are the four governing principles. For the lattice organization to be successful, each associate agrees to:

1. Try to be fair. Sincerely strive to be fair with each other, our suppliers, our customers, and all persons with whom we carry out transactions.
2. Allow, help, and encourage his associates to grow in knowledge, skill, scope of responsibility, and range of activities.
3. Make his own commitments—and keep them.
4. Consult with his associates before taking actions that might be "below the waterline" and cause serious damage to the enterprise.

Associate Bob Henn thinks that there is a fifth principle: maintain ambiguity. He told us: "We worship ambiguity. Anytime that people try to put structure that is two-dimensional in nature and that can be reproduced in ink on a page, we love to stir like crazy and reintroduce ambiguity regardless of the accuracy or inaccuracy of that black and white reflection. You can't reduce an environment, a community, a culture to a definition. As soon as you allow for that definition it becomes fewer dimensions than reality."

Having an associate-owned company is just what Bill Gore envisioned. His spirit survives partly because old-timers continue to tell stories about how he related to the people here. Joe Tanner recalled that one of Gore's endearing traits was trust in people. He would let people make mistakes because he knew they'd grow from them. Besides, Gore reasoned, "maybe it's not a mistake. Maybe it's an invention."

When Gore-tex was still on the drawing boards, Tanner and a group of engineers wasted $1,000 worth of material. "We were just standing there with long faces and Bill Gore walks up and says, 'What's wrong, guys?' and we said, 'Well, we just put $1,000 of scrap on the floor.' And he said, 'Try it again tomorrow. I know you can do it.' And he walked away." And sure enough, they did it.

Older associates emulate Bill Gore's example in hopes of preserving the culture. Chief financial officer Shanti Mehta, who started here in 1970, remembers: "Bill Gore never called me into his office. He always came to my desk, sat on my desk, and talked to me as if he had all the time in the world. He was a real spring from which love flowed throughout the organization. And the culture was nourished that way. After his death, the responsibility of doing this has fallen squarely on the shoulders of all of us . . . and it is very important we do that." Shanti has started mimicking Bill Gore's practice of going to associates' desks, sitting on them, and chatting with the people. He told us: "I did that four or five times and my adrenaline just started flowing and I was a new man."

Mehta sees the maintenance of the lattice organization as his most important mission now: "It doesn't matter whether we become a $2-billion company or a $5-billion company if we keep our plants small and we continue this kind of relationship."

Main employment centers: Gore has facilities worldwide, including plants in Maryland, Delaware, Arizona, and Texas.

Headquarters: W. L. Gore & Associates, Inc.
555 Paper Mill Rd.
P.O. Box 9329
Newark, DE 19714
(302) 738-4880

YOUNGEST COMPANIES

Compaq Computer (1982)
Lotus Development (1982)
Great Plains Software (1981)
Ben & Jerry's Homemade (1978)
SAS Institute (1976)
Microsoft (1975)
Chaparral Steel (1975)
Tandem (1974)
Cray Research (1972)
Valassis Communications (1972)
Federal Express (1971)
Southwest Airlines (1971)
Quad/Graphics (1970)

Great Plains Software

 **GREAT PLAINS SOFTWARE**

Great Plains Software makes computer software programs to help small businesses with their accounting. Employees: 367.

★ ★ ★ Pay/Benefits
★ ★ ★ ★ Opportunities
★ ★ ★ ★ Job Security
★ ★ ★ ★ Pride in Work/Company
★ ★ ★ ★ ★ Openness/Fairness
★ ★ ★ ★ ★ Camaraderie/Friendliness

BIGGEST PLUS: A high-tech home on the plains.
BIGGEST MINUS: You have to *love* northern exposure.

Great Plains Software wins the award for the most original response to our initial inquiry for information. They replied by sending us an oversize scrapbook, 85 pages long, full of photos, essays, pins, stickers, videos, and a T-shirt. It weighed 56 pounds and was two feet wide, three feet long, and six inches thick. The cover title: "The 100 Best Reasons Why Great Plains Software Is the Best Company to Work for in America—and the Universe!" Assuming that we would probably not make a trek to North Dakota to visit, they gave us an 800 number and told us we could interview anyone at the company.

Intrigued, we decided to make a special trip to North Dakota to see this unusual place for ourselves. It was well worth the effort. Great Plains's home office can be found on the outskirts of downtown Fargo in a nondescript two-story office building located between a cornfield and a bingo parlor (various forms of gambling are legal in the state). You need go no farther than the reception area to observe the firm's people orientation.

The walls surrounding the receptionist display the "People Showcases," with photos of everyone who works for the company, listed by first name.

The showcase reveals that most of the people who work for Great Plains are young—average age 30. Most of the employees come from nearby, a circumstance demonstrated graphically on a huge map hung on a wall outside the human resources offices. The map shows each employee's hometown with a pin and a flag with his or her name attached. About 80 percent come from North Dakota (75 different towns) or Minnesota. Great Plains sends a press release to the local newspaper for every new employee.

One of the pins sticks into Arthur, North Dakota, about 20 miles from Fargo. It's the hometown of Doug Burgum, the firm's young president (age 36 in 1992). Burgum calls himself "the prototypical employee—grew up in a small town, with a farming background."

We first met Burgum when he was on a business trip to Silicon Valley. At the time, he showed up at our office in jeans and sneakers (with a Great Plains logo), with his long hair tied in a ponytail. When we saw him in Fargo a year later, he'd cut off the ponytail but was still wearing jeans and sneakers. His office has a six-foot-high basketball net and some small balls lying on the floor. Burgum plays in the company's intramural basketball league. He also plays in the firm's intramural softball and volleyball leagues. The only team he hasn't played on is the bowling team.

Once you engage Burgum in conversation, however, he no longer appears to be merely one of the boys. He has an M.B.A. from Stanford's business school, where he met his best friend, Scott McNealy, founder and CEO of Sun Microsystems. Burgum spent several years in Chicago with the prestigious management consulting firm McKinsey & Co. before deciding to go back to North Dakota in 1982 and try his hand at running his own business. He picked a computer store in Fargo that was selling a software package to help small businesses keep track of their financial records. He saw potential in the product (there are 19 million small businesses in the United States) and bought the store and the product with help from his family in 1984. (The Burgum family now owns about 90 percent of the company; his mother, Katherine, in her late 70s, continues to show up at the office.)

Based on his Stanford and McKinsey background, Burgum realized that to survive he needed something more distinctive than a good accounting software program. He felt that his edge would be customer support. So Great Plains made it easy for customers to call an 800 number and get quick and knowledgable responses. Customer support is still the backbone of the company, accounting for about 100 employees. Burgum's strategy is working. Great Plains ranks second in terms of revenues in small business accounting packages. Since 1983 their sales have grown an average of 37 percent a year. In 1991 they took in an estimated $24 million in revenues.

The walls surrounding the cubicles where the people answer the 800-

number calls are lined with plaques of the various awards they've won and letters from satisfied customers. (Employees get bonuses for receiving complimentary letters from customers.) They call it Letter Lane. One small-business customer was so happy with the service he'd received that he bought a customer support representative tickets for a Bears football game and flew him to Chicago.

Customer support is also a good place to start in the company if you're interested in advancement. Several of the firm's officers started answering the 800-number phones, as did many of the company's marketing and sales people. Entry-level customer service agents start at between $16,000 and $28,000 a year depending on experience. Great Plains's average turnover rate is less than 7 percent a year—extremely low for the software industry.

Getting a job here is no small task, as Great Plains is very picky about whom they hire. Employees talk about a rigorous hiring process involving at least a half dozen interviews and often several return visits for follow-up interviews. One of the executives is notorious for asking prospective employees questions like "What do you want on your tombstone?" and "Who is your hero?"

Once hired, all new employees have lunch with Doug Burgum. Denise Johnson, who works in marketing, attended a new-employees luncheon in November 1989. She recalled: "I thought it was very unusual for the president of a company to ask questions and actually want to know about me— my hometown and my life. It made me feel like I was really part of the team." Sales account executive Brent Pieterick, who had his lunch in September 1987, added: "As a new employee, I thought it was really exciting to go out to lunch and sit right next to the president of the company. I wasn't intimidated, and I was so impressed that Doug understood what it was like to grow up in a small town."

This kind of personal touch has built a sense of family here. Kevin Montplaisir, an applications development systems analyst, explained: "Everybody is your friend, they're not just your coworker. And the projects, they're team efforts, they're not something where, if something goes wrong, you lay the blame on somebody, or point the finger."

The camaraderie extends to other aspects of life. According to Spider Johnk, a creative marketing director: "There's a real blur between the time that people are working and the time that they're socializing."

In many start-up companies, this blurring between one's social and business lives can result in a high level of burnout. This can be especially true when most of the employees are young and eager. From talking with employees at many companies, we heard stories of young employees who worked long hours, then socialized with coworkers late into the night. But we did not find this to be the case at Great Plains. The company seems to have a genuine concern about encouraging life-style balance.

Jay Richardson, a marketing writer, offered this perspective on life at

Great Plains: "In a small, growing company, it takes an extra effort. But I have a family. I have a child and a wife, and my wife works. She makes lots of money, twice as much money as I do, so I'm very concerned about making sure that her pathway is very smooth. I take care of getting my son ready for school in the morning, I generally cook the meals, and I do the cleaning, and I have other responsibilities around the home that in a traditional-society American family may have been relegated to the female. Consequently I don't have the opportunity to work 60, 70, 80 hours a week. But my creativity, or my ability to empathize with the customer, is something that's valued at Great Plains, even though I may not be able to put in the gigantic hours that some of the people do. I'm not a pariah here. People don't ask me what's wrong or whether I'm going to pick up the ball sometime soon here, or anything like that. So I'm sort of living proof that somebody can make it six years at Great Plains working essentially 40-hour weeks."

Great Plains considers the balance between work and home so important that they bend over backward to be flexible about personal problems. When Cecil Bordages had to move to Texas to take care of his ailing mother, Great Plains created a new position for him so he could stay with the company. When Lynne Stockstad's husband moved to Iowa City to go to chiropractic school, she was able to keep her position as product marketing manager and work out of her new home. As she tells the story: "They said, 'Do you really feel you can do a product marketing manager job from your home and do you think you can do it justice?' And I said yes. And they trusted me and let me do it. So not only was my husband achieving his dream, becoming a chiropractor, but Great Plains was allowing me to achieve my career, too."

Other employees have taken advantage of Great Plains's "voluntary time off" policy. The demand for accounting falls off after tax time. So the company has made it easy for employees to take time off without pay while retaining benefits and insurance. Steve Osvold, a technical editor, studied French for six weeks in Quebec City; Mara Trygstad, a senior systems analyst, spent long weekends with her father, a cancer patient; and Kara Stelter, technical writer, took over her family's dairy farm for a week, so her parents could take vacation.

Lori Laub, who started answering the 800-line phones and is now vice-president of customer assistance, told us about the help she got when a Red River flood in 1991 threatened her house: "I got some sandbags, and I ordered some sand, and asked a couple people here if maybe they would want to come up and help me. And I was thinking maybe I'd get lucky if I got a dozen people. The first night, I got about 50 people from Great Plains, and the second night there were about 60 people out there. We put in about 3,500 sandbags, and it did save the house, preventing the water from reaching the home. It was the most incredible experience. The people who lived around me were floored by the fact that these people were out there. When I told them they were all people I worked with, they couldn't believe it. They were trying to get friends, family, and acquaintances to come help them, and here was this army of people out there. At the end of the second evening, here's this water, it's lapping up against the sandbags, and part of me knew that I should be afraid and nervous about it, and part of me just felt so taken care of by my extended family."

Main employment centers: There are 312 employees at Great Plains headquarters in Fargo and about 55 sales and customer service representatives in offices around the country.

Headquarters: Great Plains Software, Inc.
1701 SW 38th St.
Fargo, ND 58103
(701) 281-0550

COMPANIES WITH SIGNIFICANT EMPLOYEE OWNERSHIP

Acipco
Avis
Federal Express
W. L. Gore & Associates
Hallmark Cards
Lowe's
J. C. Penney
Polaroid
Procter & Gamble
Publix Super Markets
Springfield ReManufacturing
TDIndustries

Hallmark Cards

Hallmark is the world's largest greeting card company. They also make photo albums, calendars, candles, ornaments, crayons and other art supplies, mugs, party supplies, stuffed toys, ribbons, stickers, and stationery. Employees: 13,200.

★ ★ ★ ★ ★   Pay/Benefits
  ★ ★ ★ ★   Opportunities
★ ★ ★ ★ ★   Job Security
★ ★ ★ ★ ★   Pride in Work/Company
    ★ ★ ★   Openness/Fairness
★ ★ ★ ★ ★   Camaraderie/Friendliness

BIGGEST PLUS: They care enough to make employees owners.
BIGGEST MINUS: You can't forget to send your mother a card.

With all the changes that have racked corporate America in the past decade, it's reassuring to visit a company that seems to have changed little over that period of time. Hallmark Cards is one of those rare companies.

Not that Hallmark has stood still since we visited them in the early 1980s. In 1986 they elected a new chief executive, Irv Hockaday, the first non-Hall to run the company since its founding in 1910. And they bought a bunch of businesses, including Binney & Smith (the Crayola people), Univision (a Spanish-language TV network they later sold), and several cable TV systems. But Hallmark has such a strong culture that it seems that the more things change, the more they stay the same.

Much of this culture stems from the unpretentious and mild-mannered Hall family members who continue to hold about two-thirds of Hallmark's stock. Donald Hall, son of founder Joyce Hall, stepped down as CEO in

1986, but he remained chairman and is actively involved in the company. He still lunches in the Crown Room, the company cafeteria at headquarters in downtown Kansas City. (There are no executive dining rooms at Hallmark.) Like his father, Hall still drives an American car (a Buick) to work. (One change: Hall, a longtime smoker, can no longer indulge his habit in the office, as Hallmark's facilities became smoke-free in July 1990.) Hall still frequently attends 25th anniversary celebrations.

Twenty-fifth anniversary celebrations remain a big deal here. An employee can invite all of his or her friends throughout the company to share the anniversary cake and coffee. And there are plenty of these celebrations, as people tend to stay at Hallmark for a long time. Once a year the quarter-century club members are invited to a big dinner party in their honor. Nearly a quarter of the firm's work force—2,668 members—were invited to the 1992 banquet.

Hallmarkers cite many reasons for staying a long time. For one, Hallmark offers some of the best benefits of any major company in the land. The centerpiece is an employee profit-sharing and ownership plan established in 1956. In recent years profit sharing has amounted to about 10 percent of an employee's pay and is invested in company stock and other securities. Through the profit-sharing trust, employees now own a third of Hallmark's stock, worth $1.3 billion in 1992. This plan can translate into big bucks for individual employees. An employee who started in 1979 and was making $29,000 in 1992 would have about $80,000 in his or her profit-sharing account by 1992. A number of employees have left the firm with more than $500,000 in their accounts. And this is in addition to what employees receive through Hallmark's separate retirement plan. Every year employees receive an updated report on the current and projected value of their account, with beautiful greeting-card-like booklets replete with family photos.

Many Hallmarkers also see great benefits from living in the Kansas City area, where about half of the greeting card employees work. Senior telephone sales representative Rick Barron said Kansas City attracted him to Hallmark: "The fountains, the trees, the parks, the shopping centers, it's just a very relaxed city."

A family-run business itself, Hallmark has also long been a leader in work/family issues. They offer an unpaid six-month maternity or paternity leave and reimburse employees up to $5,000 for the cost of an adoption. (Only three U.S. companies—Hallmark, Syntex, and Colgate-Palmolive—offer an adoption aid up to $5,000.) They have a referral program to help employees find care for young and old dependents, training for care-givers, support groups, a series of noontime seminars on subjects dealing with old and young dependents. Hallmark has teamed up with several Kansas City hospitals to offer employees care for sick children. The first day of care is free and every day thereafter costs $1.50 to $2.00 an hour. During school holidays, parents can drop off their children at headquarters, where they can participate in various activities. In 1990 Hallmark appointed a manager of work and family services, Marilyn King.

Senior programmer analyst Doug Eck came to Hallmark from Arthur Young, a Big Six accounting firm, in 1989. He told us: "A lot of companies seem to pay lip service to family. Hallmark seemed to be the only one that followed up with actions." Rick Barron, who joined Hallmark from Marion Merrell Dow, agrees: "With Hallmark I don't feel like they are trying to push a family atmosphere. I think they just do it in their actions, and that is a big difference."

Hallmark is one of the few major companies in the United States that has yet to lay off employees. When we interviewed here in the early 1980s, 600 employees had been shuffled around to other jobs because there was not enough production work to keep them busy. Some had their salaries paid while they did community service work, such as weatherizing homes of residents in a low-income neighborhood. Hallmark has continued this practice, although officials insist that they have a "no-layoff history" rather than a "no-layoff policy." It seems to be a distinction without a difference. When we asked CEO Hockaday to explain the difference, he said: "Through all kinds of economic cycles and market cycles, we have found ways to keep people; maybe by retraining them, maybe by sending them out in the community to do community service without a loss of benefits. We have yet to find a situation where we have had to deviate from that practice. Do we anticipate that we will ever have to deviate from it? No. Is it conceivable that we might have to deviate from it someday? Yes, but only conceivable. I don't think it is likely."

Hallmark still has the world's largest creative staff with 700 artists and writers. Every year Hallmark artists create 18,000 card designs under the Hallmark and Ambassador brands. They are distributed in 20 languages in 100 different countries. To inspire their creative staff, Hallmark brings in visiting artists and writers like movie director Robert Benton (*Places in the Heart*), actress Betty White, anthropologist Mary Catherine Bateson (daughter of Margaret Mead and Gregory Bateson), sociologist and author Betty Friedan, and *New Yorker* cartoonist Gahan Wilson. They also send writers and artists to places as far away as Paris, London, and Bologna, Italy, as well as to the Southwest and the Pacific Northwest on research trips. What the artist's life in Kansas City lacks in cultural stimulation, it makes up for in collegiality. Artist Bob Kolar explains: "In my department, everybody is sort of thrown into the same boat and many people hired into design are from all over the country or all over the world. We are all approximately the same age and the same stages of life and it is like a graduate school almost. There is so much learning going on and sharing of what you are doing in your job, and friendships happen quite easily. So yes, it becomes family."

Hallmark has changed in one important respect. It is much more open.

This picturesque community was created at the turn of the century by Milton S. Hershey, a remarkable visionary whose legacy of combining good works with shrewd business practices survives in the company that bears his name. If you come to work here, you'll be working for a firm that mixes old-fashioned virtues with those of a thoroughly modern corporation that ranks first in U.S. candy sales (with such favorites as Hershey's, Reese's, Kit Kat, and Whatchamacallit) and second in pasta (Ronzoni, San Giorgio, and American Beauty).

From the outset, Milton Hershey sought to create a distinctive company, so the community where his workers were to live was to be more than the typical company town. He believed "that there is more to life than just work, that beauty, nature and wholesome leisure-time activities are essential ingredients to a full life." So he built an elaborate Romanesque community center (where Hershey employees today can use a big fitness center and swimming pool free of charge), two theaters, a museum of American life, a sports arena (where the Hershey Bears professional hockey team plays), five golf courses (the "golf capital of Pennsylvania"), and Hershey Park (which today has 1.8 million visitors a year). According to an article in *Business World* in 1903, his town had "no provision for a police department, nor for a jail. Here there will be no unhappiness, then why any crime?"

The centerpiece of Hershey was and is the Milton Hershey School, located across town from the corporate headquarters. When Sharon Lambly was shown the school, she was also being shown the company's largest stockholder. The school, through the Hershey Trust Company, controls 77 percent of the voting shares. So the dividends of this company go directly to educate, clothe, feed, and care for 1,150 students who have been orphaned or were born to dysfunctional and broken homes.

Hershey employees are well aware that their efforts benefit the orphanage. Glen Fair, who makes Kit Kats in the Reese plant, told us: "Something important to me is talk about values and things we feel good about doing. I think the history of the company and the contribution to the community makes me proud to be part of the company."

Employees from other corporations notice such differences almost immediately. Carl Wong worked at Pillsbury before being hired by Hershey to be senior manager of product development. He said: "Hershey in general is a little more laid-back, somewhat conservative in their attitude to the business. When I first came here, I tried to move things a lot quicker, and people seemed a little hesitant to move so quickly."

According to Wong: "One of the biggest differences was accessibility, especially to the boss's boss and his boss. I think I saw the CEO at Pillsbury a couple of times and those times were in the elevator. Here at Hershey, over a year, it has been a minimum of a half a dozen times. Not on a formal basis, say he is in the building or we may have a presentation."

Research scientist Jim Pfeifer said that this sense of informality pervades the company: "Everyone is on a first-name basis, so you don't have this seniority or superiority complex. If you need help, you don't have a problem going to someone and asking a question."

This down-home atmosphere is even more pronounced in the plants, where many workers are related. Roxanne Howard, who wraps Hershey's candy, explains that "my mother, father, my grandmother and grandfather worked here. I have uncles and aunts here, and my son works at Chocolate World. In fact, I didn't get called to work here. My father went in and said my daughter needs a job and they said tell her to come in. So I got hired right away."

Though we heard a lot about Hershey's "traditions" and what a conservative place the company is, we also learned that in recent years Hershey has been making changes to keep pace in an increasingly competitive business environment. Architect of much of this change is chairman and CEO Richard Zimmerman. We interviewed Zimmerman in his office in Milton Hershey's former mansion, which is surrounded by a golf course, a short walk from the company's main chocolate factory. To encourage more risktaking, Zimmerman instituted an award called the Exalted Order of the Extended Neck. He explained: "I wanted to reward people who were willing to buck the system, a little entrepreneurship, a little willingness to stand the heat for an idea they really believe in." Nominees are identified by department vice-presidents, and Zimmerman presents the awards. A maintenance worker was a recent award winner for figuring out a way to perform midweek cleaning on a piece of machinery without a loss of running time.

When he became CEO in 1985, Zimmerman said he was "convinced that we were wasting people's minds inside the corporation. We were getting their bodies and we were asking them to do rote things. Every time a machine broke down we called a mechanic, even though the people on the line knew how to repair it. I kept thinking we're wasting minds and creativity. Over the past years I think we have been tapping into persons' minds and capabilities much better than we ever had before."

To tap minds, Hershey launched a Quality Through Excellence program, similar to many quality programs established across the country in the past few years to encourage teamwork and worker participation. But unlike some firms, which have jumped on the quality bandwagon because it is the latest corporate fad, Hershey has done so with a concern not to disturb the underlying Hershey culture, according to Marcella Davidson, the Reese plant manager. "With Hershey they make a real strong effort to do the right thing for the right reasons to get people involved." She explained that they investigated a variety of employee involvement programs and incorporated them slowly, "maybe slower than some people would have wanted. But Hershey's deliberateness is what makes you trust what they are doing.

They go to extremes to make people feel comfortable with what is going on."

The QTE program has been accompanied by a variety of new communications vehicles, especially regular meetings where employees have the ability to ask plant managers or department heads questions. According to chocolate paste processor Donald Hainly: "As far as communications from our area, I think they are great. It has improved from years ago; way back they wouldn't tell you nothing. Right now, if they are putting in a new [production] line, a lot of times they will come and ask for suggestions, instead of putting it in and then making all the changes after it is in there."

Another big plus here is that the firm promotes from within. Job openings are posted throughout the company, and it is common for people to move into the supervisory ranks from hourly positions.

Hershey also offers training programs for those who want to improve their skills. Research scientist Jim Pfeifer said: "I am able to choose training in-house and out-of-house that helps me achieve my goals. They went so far with those of us at the Tech Center as to offer a satellite course from the Penn State main campus so we can get our food science degrees and maybe go on from there for Ph.D.'s if we decide to do so."

Hershey's cross-training enables employees to move between divisions. Candy wrapper Roxanne Howard explained: "The cross-training allows people from the plants to go see if they want to work in the office or do quality assurance for like a six-month period, and if you don't like it you have the option to go back."

Through such programs, Hershey may have pierced the paternalistic culture, where father knows best and makes all the decisions for you, that permeated the company for many years. Yet the distinctive links to the Milton Hershey legacy attract people to this unusual corporation. One benefit Milton Hershey would certainly approve of is that the company will give dependent children of deceased employees up to $4,000 per year for college.

Nutrition and food safety manager Fran Seligson summed it up: "I value the standard of ethics here at Hershey. I interact a lot with our trade associations in Washington. I always feel good that I can go there and take a position which is the high road. Now, some people may think it is conservative, but I feel good knowing I can take the high-road position on issues."

Types of jobs: Production workers—54 percent; officials and managers—10 percent; sales—8 percent; office and clerical—7 percent; professionals—7 percent; service workers—3 percent; technicians—2 percent.

Main employment centers: There are almost 7,000 Hershey employees in Hershey, Pennsylvania. The chocolate division also has 662 employees in

Reading, Pennsylvania; 496 in Naugatuck, Connecticut; 789 in Oakdale, California; 484 in Stuarts Draft, Virginia; 425 in Lancaster, Pennsylvania; 303 in Hazleton, Pennsylvania; and 41 in Farmington, New Mexico. In the pasta division there are 287 employees in Lebanon, Pennsylvania; 224 in Long Island City, New York; 139 in Fresno, California; 133 in Omaha, Nebraska; 125 in Louisville, Kentucky; and 66 in Kansas City, Kansas.

Headquarters: Hershey Foods Corporation
100 Crystal A Dr.
Hershey, PA 17033
(717) 534-4000

Hewitt Associates

Hewitt Associates

Hewitt Associates designs compensation and benefit programs for companies, ranking as the fourth largest consultant in this field. U.S. employees: 2,800.

★ ★ ★ ★ Pay/Benefits
★ ★ ★ Opportunities
★ ★ ★ ★ ★ Job Security
★ ★ ★ ★ Pride in Work/Company
★ ★ ★ ★ Openness/Fairness
★ ★ ★ ★ Camaraderie/Friendliness

BIGGEST PLUS: They wrote the book on benefits.
BIGGEST MINUS: It's not a 9-to-5 place.

When Christine Seltz, public relations associate at Hewitt, learned that we were doing a new edition of this book, she tapped into the company's interactive computer network to invite anyone who was interested to spend "no more than five minutes" reporting what came to mind about working here. Back came, within 24 hours, 199 responses—and they were extraordinary.

Al Schlachtmeyer, who has been with Hewitt since 1969, wrote: "I've got a big love affair going with this organization, so forgive me if I get gushy. I'm in a firm where, when the chief executive asked a group of new people what surprised them the most, the answer was that 'we didn't talk or behave any differently to lower-level people.' I'm with a firm who sends an employee to Germany to help another employee who's in the hospital because of a motorcycle accident that occurred while he was on vacation."

Vernon Valentine said: "I joined the firm about six months ago as a writer/consultant in New Jersey. I was surprised at the level of detail that had gone into preparation for my arrival. The secretary had ordered all the supplies I would need—not just paper and pens but schedule books and a wall calendar. One of the more experienced writers left a 'welcome' note on my desk, along with a 'survival kit' (with a candy bar and nerf ball) . . . and *everybody* came by my office to personally welcome me to the 'team.' For the first two weeks or so, somebody made a point to stop by and ask me to lunch—every day. Perhaps the most surprising, my name had been automatically added to the office softball roster—the folks who interviewed me had really listened."

Kim Naffziger, who works in flexible benefits administration, wrote: "I remember the time I came to Hewitt for my initial interview. It was pouring outside! When it was time for me to leave, the receptionist asked me if I needed to borrow an umbrella. I couldn't believe it."

Eddie Smith, a compensation specialist who moved in 1992 to a Hewitt division in Scottsdale, Arizona, commented on the open communications, saying: "Because the firm tells everyone what is going on and will answer, literally, any question honestly and openly, a high level of trust develops in the firm. People don't have to spend time tuning in to the rumor mill, they simply ask."

Steve Peterson, with Hewitt since 1985, wrote: "Last fall my three-year-old son had open-heart surgery, my wife was confined to bed with a high-risk pregnancy, and our daughter was born prematurely. Even though I handled a heavy client load, Hewitt arranged for me to work part-time for three months, continued my benefits, and installed a computer at home so I could be with my family as much as possible. At first, I was nervous about how this might affect my career. But the attitude here is that family comes first."

Sue Kachnovitz, a receptionist at the Woodlands Center office outside Houston, said that when the company celebrated its 50th anniversary in 1990, the company hired two temps so that she could participate in the festivities. "It made me feel very good to know even the little people are remembered," she said.

These feelings were confirmed in the interviews we had at Hewitt with more than two dozen employees. Bob Bernsee, an actuary who has been with Hewitt since 1974, told us: "I kind of put people in camps of givers and takers; I think everybody has a little bit of each—and we hire people who are more givers."

Hewitt crafts compensation and benefits packages for large corporations. Its first client, in 1941, was Parker Pen (still a client), for whom it created pension and profit-sharing plans. At one point or another, Hewitt has worked for 75 percent of the Fortune 500 companies. It pioneered the introduction of flexible benefits. We first heard about Hewitt from a secretary who wrote us a letter saying that "I have never felt or been treated differently than even a partner."

Donna Dempsey, a secretary-administrator who joined Hewitt in 1981, contrasted for us life here as opposed to work at her previous company, Trans Union: "It used to bother me tremendously that the executives were all 'Mr. So and So,' and you were 'Donna.' It used to bother me even more when you walked down the hall in the morning to say good morning to the executives and they wouldn't answer you. It was like you weren't even there. The first day I started here, I was working at my desk and Pete came up and said, 'Oh, you're Janet's new secretary. Hi, I'm Pete.' He went in, talked to Janet, and left. And I turned and said, 'Who was that?' That was the CEO. This is a little different atmosphere. People treat you like you make a contribution."

The warmth and openness that characterize Hewitt have remained in place in the face of tremendous growth, which often brings with it mindless bureaucracy. Hewitt expanded from 1,050 people and $75 million in revenues in 1982 to 3,400 people and $320 million in 1991. In 1985 the company had 28 offices, mainly in the United States. Today it has 60 offices in 20 countries.

Hewitt, in 1992, still called its people "associates" rather than "employees." It still had no titles. The only gradation is partnership. There are no vice-presidents or directors or senior or junior consultants. And every day at its headquarters, it still serves a free lunch.

Suzanne Kenney, who works in the communications department, told us that when she interviewed at Hewitt in 1981, "I walked away saying, 'Either this is the best place in the world or these people are very strange and they're a bunch of wimps.' Because they're all sitting around saying, 'I'll be nice to you if you're nice to me.' And to see that it actually happens with the kind of pressures we have is a real triumph, I think." One of the favorite acronyms at Hewitt, referring to the kind of candidate they look for, is SWANs—"people who are Smart, willing to Work hard, are Ambitious, and Nice."

Virtually nothing at Hewitt is secret. As a private partnership, it's not required to disclose any information. But it does. Peter Friedes, who was

CEO when we saw him in 1991, said that if any associate wants to come in and look at the books, he or she is free to do that. In 1991 Hewitt had 205 partners—and the average compensation of partners for the year was $205,000. More and more women have been making partner. In 1990 nine of the 19 new partners were women, and in 1991 six of the 24 new partners were women. Hewitt had 47 female partners coming into 1992, roughly 20 percent of the total. It takes, on average, seven to 12 years to make partner. And unlike accounting firms, where if you don't make partner, it's sayonara, Hewitt makes it clear that there are opportunities here for professionals who don't ever become partners. The perks often reserved for upper-level people don't exist here. Lew Rhoades, who works in the mailroom, said he once delivered a package to "Pete" (the CEO) "and I expected to see a big old desk and real lavish decorations. Just a table, a regular table like you'd see in a high school lunchroom. It's definitely not the type of office you see, like, on *Dynasty*."

Hewitt functions, in effect, as an extension of the client's staff. As a result, it puts a premium on teamwork, on cooperating to meet the needs of a client. Judy Whinfrey, an account manager who has been here since 1971, told us: "There's a lot of humility here, regardless of the level, and the recognition that we're all a bundle of flaws and that we rely on one another to support each other. I feel that we're trying to support one another to make sure that our strengths are there and our weaknesses are buttressed. So we can't fail."

It's not always up and up, even in the consulting business, and 1991 was a crunch year for Hewitt. Pete Friedes laid out the problem in a series of frank, detailed memos, asking everyone to pitch in with cost-saving ideas. Austerity measures—such as eliminating the company picnic, cutting down on flowers in the office, moving Federal Express delivery from 10:30 A.M. to 3:00 P.M.—were instituted. People were told to expect lower—or no—pay raises, with the burden falling mostly on senior associates. The whole point of this exercise was to avoid laying off anyone, something Hewitt had never done in its 50-year history, and it worked. Expenses were cut by $15 million a year—and no one had to be laid off. One associate offered to pay $1 for lunch. That suggestion was rejected.

One new recruit who appreciated this attitude was Jack Bruner, who works in health care benefits. He joined Hewitt in early 1991 from a competitor, Towers Perrin, which had just laid off 10 percent of its staff. He said that some Towers Perrin people were told they were being fired by messages left on their telephone. "I resigned three days before that announcement came out," added Bruner. "Towers is still a very profitable organization, and that didn't have to happen, just like it didn't happen here. Fifty years went down the tubes because the first time an economic challenge came up, people decided to panic and put on the brakes. The true test of companies comes when the industry is having more difficult times. The first three or four months I was here, I saw a memo from Pete Friedes every month that described what challenges we faced, how we were reacting to them, how we were dealing with them. When people don't know what's going on, there's an assumption it's worse than it is. People here knew exactly what was going on and what we were trying to do to react to it. I don't think everyone agreed with everything that was done, but there was a good overall spirit of cooperation."

We once received a letter from an ex-Hewitt associate who complained about the long hours people were forced to work. It's not a charge that Hewitt people even try to refute. They do work long hours here to meet client demands. John Anderson, who puts together compensation packages for top executives, told us: "We're open about that in the interview process. This is a place where you work and you have fun at the same time that you work." Computer whiz Tom Schmitz, who works in total benefits administration, added: "I tell every candidate that I expect 50 hours a week. It's not that you aren't going to give some flexibility for life-style changes, particularly when someone's beginning a family, it's just that, you know, if somebody only wants to work 40 hours a week, this probably isn't the right place for them."

You would expect benefits to be good here—and they are. It's a very rich cargo of goodies, including profit sharing, 75 percent reimbursement of tuition fees, and a flexible benefits plan that has a wide range of options. For example, you can earn a wellness credit of $50 for being a nonsmoker, another $50 for taking a cholesterol test (you don't have to pass it), and still another $50 for promising to wear a seat belt. You get an extra 15 days of vacation on your 15th, 20th, and 25th anniversaries. Hewitt also has one of the best work/family programs in the country, allowing associates to take up to two years of unpaid leave after the birth of a child (with benefits remaining intact and a job back guaranteed), giving adoption aid up to $2,500, and reimbursing parents for extra child-care expenses caused by out-of-town travel or overtime. Hewitt also maintains a "mothers' room" equipped with breast pumps for nursing mothers.

In late 1991, after 22 years at the helm, Pete Friedes stepped down as chief executive, replaced by Dale Gifford, an actuary who came to Hewitt in 1972 after graduating from the University of Wisconsin. He is only the third chief executive in Hewitt's history. Friedes was preceded by the founder, Edward Shields Hewitt. Friedes, who was only 49, had been battling asthma for many years. He announced his retirement to the staff via "Profs," Hewitt's electronic mail (he used to spend two hours a day on this system "talking" to associates). The second part of this message read as follows:

"On a personal note, I had a very hard time writing this Profs note—it reads so 'businesslike,' yet it is obviously emotional and very important personally. It seems to call for some reflection on the past and future, yet I'm still going to be here for a couple of years, and I'll have many future opportunities to speak with you.

"On the health issue, I don't know how much or how little to say—many of you have not known I've been ill and yet some of you have seen me wheeze, cough and try to catch my breath after the slightest exertion. I've been to many doctors and several clinics (including the Mayo Clinic). I've had many hospitalizations and operations. I've recently tried acupuncture. But the only approach that's partially worked has been increasing doses of medicines that, taken over a long period of time, are debilitating and life shortening. So, the phrase 'my health must become my priority' now comes to mean that I need to slow down dramatically in order to reduce the stressors that exacerbate my illness.

"It's impossible for a note like this not to raise questions. I really urge you to ask them—give me or your managers the opportunity to share more thoughts than can be covered in a memo.

"Thanks.

"Pete."

Types of jobs: Customer service—73 percent; systems development—9 percent; marketing—2 percent; administration—16 percent.

Main employment centers: Some 1,600 associates work at the campuslike glen in Lincolnshire, outside of Chicago. Another 900 are based in centers in Rowayton, Connecticut; Santa Ana and Walnut Creek, California; Woodlands and Irving, Texas; Atlanta, Georgia; Bedminster, New Jersey; Cleveland, Ohio; and Waltham, Massachusetts. The other 300 work in small offices scattered throughout the country, and 650 work overseas.

Headquarters: Hewitt Associates
100 Half Day Rd.
Lincolnshire, IL 60069
(312) 295-5000

COMPANIES WHERE YOU CAN GET A FREE LUNCH

Hewitt Associates
J. P. Morgan
Northwestern Mutual Life

Hewlett-Packard

HEWLETT PACKARD

Hewlett-Packard makes computer equipment and electronic measuring devices. U.S. employees: 56,000.

★★★★★ Pay/Benefits
★★★ Opportunities
★★★★ Job Security
★★★★ Pride in Work/Company
★★★★ Openness/Fairness
★★★ Camaraderie/Friendliness

BIGGEST PLUS: The most respected firm in Silicon Valley.
BIGGEST MINUS: Size may be their undoing.

Turn the clock back to 1980 and ask: "Which computer company should I be working for?" If you chose H-P, you had little to regret. It emerged from the decade as a stronger company, employing more than twice as many people as it had at the start, and it never had to resort to the massive downsizing that went on at Digital Equipment, IBM, and other leading companies in the industry. Just surviving in the computer industry is an accomplishment. H-P did more than survive. It came through the flak with its reputation as a company that's both smart and humane intact.

Headquartered 30 miles south of San Francisco in sunny Palo Alto, hard by the Stanford University campus, H-P is the godfather of Silicon Valley. It has spawned dozens of offshoots, including Tandem, Apple, 3Com, Sydis, and Silicon Graphics. H-P's policies and practices have been widely emulated. They abolished time clocks. They invented flextime. They introduced "management by wandering around." They invented the Friday night beer bust. They set aside vacation retreats for employees. They treated employees to free coffee and doughnuts every day. They offered one of the richest pay and benefits packages in American industry. Most of all, they created an environment where the individual employee was valued and not hassled.

During the 1980s Hewlett-Packard grew explosively as the logic of their business propelled them into the computer industry, a much more competitive arena than their traditional stamping grounds of electronic measurement. While the number of employees more than doubled, from 42,000 to 92,000, and sales increased by 138 percent to reach $13.2 billion in 1990, H-P found it increasingly difficult to convert those sales dollars into profit dollars. There were other changes, too. In 1988 overseas sales passed those inside the United States. The 1980s also marked the gradual withdrawal of cofounders William Hewlett and David Packard from the business they started in 1939 in a Palo Alto garage that is now a designated California landmark.

With all these changes, is Hewlett-Packard still the same easygoing, innovative, informal company that we found in earlier visits? Not quite. The old values remain in place—they are codified in a document called "The H-P Way"—but alongside them have come new ones emphasizing flexibility and the need for constant change. During the late 1980s and early 1990s hundreds of H-P employees were "redeployed," some into jobs and/or locations they didn't like. Thousands more accepted enhanced early retirement or voluntary severance packages. There were long periods of hiring freezes. It was a wrenching time, a new experience at a company that had previously attached so much importance to job security that it was known as a no-layoff company. It raised fears that the culture was changing.

We saw and heard that fear in interviews conducted with two dozen H-P people. They understood that the company is changing. At the same time, they didn't believe that H-P would discard its long traditions of trust, fairness, and respect for people. They just saw it as a difficult time. Jackie Sellers, who joined H-P in 1972 and now works as executive assistant to the general manager of the system support division, does feel that "some of the caring has been lost." Another veteran, Jim Herbst, who joined H-P in Chicago in 1972, echoes that sentiment: "The family atmosphere has changed," he said. "Some of the closeness is gone." Johnny Ratcliff, a 25-year veteran of H-P Labs, remembers how it was in the old days: "You worked more as a team. We had more of a warm feeling about people."

Despite these comments, H-P people believe that the company clings to the old values. They agree with Chuck Quanz, a 30-year veteran, who said: "I don't like a lot of the changes, but I'm still glad I work here." We went around a room filled with H-P employees and heard such comments as: "I can't imagine working anywhere else." "Other places don't develop you." "We have the feeling that H-P is going to take care of us."

H-P people are intensely aware of their reputation as a "nice company."

As a result, we heard such comments as: "H-P tries to bend over too far sometimes." "We don't throw our weight around in the marketplace." "We pamper poor performers."

H-P is getting tougher by phasing in a new performance rating system. Previously, employees were rated excellent, very good, good, and acceptable. Now their performances are being ranked numerically, 4 down to 1, with 1 meaning "action needed." It's similar to the new rating system adopted by IBM, now a direct competitor of H-P. One H-P manager, Chuck Bonza at the Avondale, Pennsylvania, division, said the new system will help "employees improve and managers become better managers." Ian Ross, manager of the printed-circuit assembly plant in Rohnert Park, California, said: "H-P has been described as being 'terminally nice' to its employees. Now managers will have to deal with tough evaluation situations head-on, but that's part of our responsibility as managers."

Size is often a killer. Laura Chynoweth, who works in personnel at the San Jose plant, joined H-P in 1980, and she's happy with the company, but she also has something to measure it against. Her father worked at H-P for 17 years "and he tried everything to get me to work here, and I didn't want to do it. I did finally come into H-P three years before he retired. He retired early, and one of the reasons he did was that he was so frustrated with the politics that came along as the company grew. I remember the good old days—the H-P picnics and the teamwork—and he loved all that."

Old-timers also miss the visible presence of the cofounders. John Young, who was CEO from 1978 until his retirement in 1992, didn't get around as much as his predecessors, nor did he have their charisma. Young was succeeded by Lewis E. Platt, a 26-year H-P veteran who had headed up the computer systems business and who's known as a good communicator. He said right away that there's not going to be "any change in the culture of the company." It's a culture that has served the company well. The computer industry is notorious for people bad-mouthing competitors and companies they used to work for. But H-P is rarely a target of such criticism. Yes, they are faulted sometimes for being slow to react or being late with products or being too bureaucratic. But the fact is, nearly everybody likes Hewlett-Packard or respects it as a highly competent company and a place where people get a chance to do their best work. And no one knocks them for abusing employees.

Perhaps no issue is more of a lightning rod than job security. In our original edition, we said flatly: "One of the unwritten policies at H-P is never to lay off people." The company now circles that sentence with the comment "untrue." In short, H-P doesn't want to be known as a company with a no-layoff policy. Yet, in one of our first interviews with employees, a veteran H-P employee said: "One thing unique about this company, we've never had a layoff."

In fact, H-P has never resorted to a general layoff to reduce the work force. For various business reasons—discontinuing a line, absorbing another company, relocating a manufacturing unit, slumping sales of a product—it will designate people's jobs as "excess," starting with the most recently hired employees. If you find yourself in the excess category, it means you have 90 days to find another job within H-P, during which time you have no other assignment to distract you. If you don't find one, you then move from excess to "direct placement," which means your manager is now responsible for finding you an H-P job—in any part of the country. If you are then offered a job within the same area (30-mile commute) and turn it down, you have the option of taking a severance package of one week's pay for every year of service, with a minimum of two months' pay. If you are offered a job outside your present location and turn it down, you then have the option of a severance package of two weeks' pay for every year of service, with a minimum of four months. It's not exactly a "you're-out-of-here-by-5:00-P.M." policy. In 1989 and 1990 some 2,500 H-Pers had their jobs declared excess. Eighty-five percent of them are still with H-P.

Excessing is not a downsizing tool, it's a redeployment tool. To downsize, H-P has used various lures to get people to leave. In 1991 they offered such attractive leave packages that they got many more takers than they expected. A long-term H-P employee—say, someone 55 years old with 24 years of service—was offered regular retirement plus a year's salary. H-P thought 2,000 people of the 13,000 employees who received the offer might accept. Instead, 3,000 employees, representing 5 percent of H-P's domestic work force, came forward to say, "I'm out of here." In late 1992 they offered another incentive package to take 2,700 more people (2,000 in the U.S.) out of the work force. Those accepting the offer received six months' pay plus one-half month's pay for every year of service, up to a maximum of one year.

With size comes bureaucracy, and H-P conceded in 1991 that things had gotten out of hand when it found that the personnel function had grown to the point where there was one personnel professional in the company for every 53 employees. In other words: 1,735 personnel professionals. H-P has a goal to reduce this ratio to 1-to-75 by 1993.

H-P remains a place where people laugh and are not afraid to speak their minds. We saw that in the interviews we conducted and in the letters written to the sprightly company magazine, *Measure*. In 1990 the magazine reported on how H-P was handling the redeployment of more than 1,000 employees into different jobs. That prompted a retort from Eric Hill, who works at the H-P plant in Roseville, California: "You did not mention the human-suffering angle to this story. There were families that were broken up and forced to relocate with great hardship, careers that were sidelined or terminated, demotions, people working in jobs they didn't enjoy, friendships ruined by the job competition, and some people forced to leave H-P early or against their will. I would hope that in the future you will research the whole story and include the impact to everyone concerned." A year later, *Measure* carried a story, "No Room for Dinosaurs," in which editor Jay Coleman singled out "change" as the new way of life at H-P. This raised hackles in Germany where a 17-year H-P employee, Ray Layton, commented: "I can easily think of five important officers who have left the company in the past year because they were not able to accept the changes forced upon them. They certainly demonstrated how to cope with change, but in no way were they being dinosaurs. Even at lower levels, the loss of experience and expertise is going to cost Hewlett-Packard dearly."

H-P doesn't pay as aggressively as newer companies like Apple Computer and Sun Microsystems, but its wage scales are in the upper end of the industry, and its benefits are tough to beat. These include 100 percent payment of your health insurance premium, cash and deferred profit-sharing plans, a stock-purchase program (buy H-P stock at a 15 percent discount) and a 401(k) plan in which an employee can sock away up to 12 percent of pay every year, with H-P matching every $3 of your savings with $1 of its own. Assume you're an employee who joined H-P in 1980 and received a 5 percent pay increase every year to reach a salary level of $35,000 by 1990. If you had participated to the fullest extent in all these programs, by 1990 you would have accumulated a nest egg of $89,110. Not bad for 10 years—and it wasn't the best 10 years of H-P's life.

Types of jobs: Engineers and computer scientists account for 27 percent of H-P's work force. H-P recruits 1,500 to 1,800 college students a year, 70 percent of them having technical degrees.

Main employment centers: San Francisco Bay Area, 20,000. Colorado, 6,000. Here's the complete lineup of U.S. manufacturing sites: California: Cupertino, Palo Alto, Rohnert Park, Roseville, San Diego, San Jose, Santa Clara, Santa Rosa, Sunnyvale; Colorado: Colorado Springs, Fort Collins, Greeley, Loveland; Idaho: Boise; Massachusetts: Andover, Waltham; New Hampshire: Exeter; New Jersey: Rockaway; Oregon: Corvallis, McMinnville; Pennsylvania: Avondale; Puerto Rico: Aguadilla; Washington: Everett, Spokane, Vancouver. Some 34,000 people work outside the United States, where H-P has 20 plants in 16 countries.

Headquarters: Hewlett-Packard Company
             3000 Hanover St.
             Palo Alto, CA 94304
             (415) 857-1501

Honda of America Manufacturing

HONDA

Honda makes more cars in America than any other foreign automaker and is the largest private employer in central Ohio. U.S. employees: 10,200.

★ ★ ★ ★ Pay/Benefits
★ ★ ★ ★ Opportunities
★ ★ ★ ★ Job Security
★ ★ ★ Pride in Work/Company
★ ★ ★ ★ Openness/Fairness
★ ★ ★ Camaraderie/Friendliness

BIGGEST PLUS: You make cars that are exported to Japan.
BIGGEST MINUS: You have to wear white.

Homer Dunlap took a lot of flak when he told his friends he was going to work at Honda: "It wasn't socially acceptable to work at Honda. You could sit in a restaurant and hear Grandma and Grandpa talking about the Japanese over there in Marysville, saying, 'I wouldn't work for them for 50 grand.'" That was in 1979. Dunlap was one of the first Americans Honda hired when they started making motorcycles in a plant in Marysville, Ohio, about 45 miles northwest of Columbus. He recalls how they "struggled back then to build ten little dirt bikes a day." But Honda—and Homer Dunlap—persevered. Three years later the company started making autos in Marysville and by 1989 had opened the neighboring Anna engine plant and another car plant in nearby East Liberty. Now Dunlap, a team leader in the motorcycle plant, feels "a tremendous amount of pride" when he tells people where he works, and the main question people ask is whether there are any openings.

Honda, long considered a maverick in Japan, was the first Japanese automaker to assemble cars in the United States. They employ the most American workers, over 10,000 in 1992 with Honda of America Manufacturing and nearly 4,000 more with American Honda Motor Co., the U.S. sales and marketing arm of the Japanese company. Their commitment to the United States—they have invested more than $2 billion in Ohio—has paid off. Honda is the most successful Japanese car maker in America. Consider the following facts:

• For three years in a row, 1989–91, the Honda Accord was the best-selling car model in America.

• Honda ranks third in car sales in the United States (behind only GM and Ford but ahead of Chrysler) and sells about 38 percent more cars in North America than in Japan, where it ranks a poor fourth after Toyota, Nissan, and Mitsubishi.

• Honda makes more cars in the United States than any other foreign automaker, about a half million cars a year, including nearly 15,000 that they *exported* in 1991 from the United States to Japan—nearly three times more than the cars exported to Japan by General Motors. (They also exported over 27,000 Ohio-made cars to 16 other countries.)

Exporting cars to Japan adds to the sense of pride for Honda's workers in Ohio. They are also proud of their nearly spotless factories, where everyone is required to wear white overalls, including the executives. Wearing of the company-issued green and white baseball hat with a Honda logo is optional, and a wide variety of hats can be spotted in the plants. *Production* magazine describes the engine plant in Anna (a few miles from Marysville) in these terms: "It could be a factory by Disney, something of an industrial Epcot Center. What you don't find are oil, cutting fluids and coolant on the floor . . . [or] the dirty air and the overall disorderliness that exists in many plants. It's a fact of industrial life, almost as inevitable as the law of gravity, but the Honda philosophy seems to be that it just doesn't make sense."

Honda introduces its distinctive philosophy, called the Honda Way, to new associates and their family members at an orientation session led by the president of Honda of America (HAM), Hiroyuki Yoshino. After Yoshino and the vice-president of human relations, Don English, finish their presentations and answer questions, each new associate introduces himself or herself and their guests, and the executives personally welcome each one to the Honda family. Yoshino is one of 320 Japanese associates working in America, most of them assigned to the R&D centers in Marysville and Torrance, California.

Education is a key part of the Honda Way. A training facility offers over 300 different classes, most of them taught by Honda employees. Outside instructors teach courses in engineering, English, and Japanese. Every year production associates spend an average of 35 hours in the classroom. Honda also sends associates to Japan for training in Honda manufacturing. In 1990, 400 team leaders went to Japan for four weeks. Every year about 15 welders and 50 assembly workers go to Honda's Japanese plants. Since 1979 Honda of America has sent more than 3,200 associates to Japan for training.

Honda emphasizes training because it promotes from within. Corporate communications manager Roger Lambert told us: "All but one of the managers in the Marysville auto plant started from the line, so there's quite a bit of opportunity for growth and development and promotion."

Like other Japanese manufacturers, Honda promotes an egalitarian atmosphere. There are no reserved parking spaces or executive dining rooms. Managers and engineers spend their days on the production floor because the Honda Way teaches managers that they must get close to problems to solve them. Desks of managers, engineers, and production staff are located in plain sight on the production floor, while plant managers' offices are just outside the doorways to the shop floor.

The accessibility of managers and executives makes communication easy, according to production associate Johnna Haughn: "In other places I had a fear of some of my bosses. But that's not the way it is here at Honda, it's all teamwork. Management will dig right in there with you and help solve problems. They're not going to stand back and tell you what to do."

Honda's team atmosphere encourages employees to feel involved in their work. Donnie McGhee started as a production worker and is now associate relations manager at the Anna engine plant. He explained: "It was mind-boggling for me to come here and see the amount of involvement of the general associate in problems and situations that before I viewed only as management-type issues. There is sharing of responsibility. There is the manager, but right alongside that manager you'll find a general associate. They're both out there, getting their hands dirty, problem-solving. Often it's difficult to make that separation between who is the manager and who is the general associate. There is not the divisiveness in this company that I experienced for 15 years at General Motors."

Perry Payne, who works in the associate development center, previously worked as a manager for General Motors before coming to the Marysville auto plant in 1984. "I had to make one hell of an adjustment [from GM]," he said. "I was used to that power where you did not allow the employee to get involved. It's shared information here. Initially, I felt like I was losing control."

Associates play a role in scheduling overtime and vacations. Marysville auto plant assistant manager John Aler explained: "If we're going to run overtime, we'll have meetings where the plant manager will sit down with associates and ask for their input. If they don't want to, we don't do it, because the majority rules." Aler said that when the plant manager tried to schedule overtime on a Saturday when Ohio State was to play the University of Michigan in football, workers raised a "ruckus" and they rescheduled the overtime.

A specific technique of employee involvement at Honda is the Voluntary Involvement Program, or VIP. This program has four components: NH-Circles (quality circles), a suggestion program, quality awards, and safety awards. NH-Circles are made up of five to 10 associates who work together to suggest improvements or solve problems. They have instituted programs such as recycling, which earns the plant more than $2 million a year. The suggestion program at Honda has a unique twist: employees implement their own suggestions. When three associates asked administration manager Don English if associates could purchase stock at a discount through payroll deduction, he got them together with a group of associates and the legal staff. The group visited other companies, interviewed employees, and implemented the program in 1990.

Participating in the VIP program earns points, ranging from 10 to 50, toward prizes. Associates who earn 700 points get the Silver Award: a check for $800. Those who attain 2,500 points win the Gold Award: a Honda Civic LX sedan. Finally, the coveted Honda Award goes to those who earn 5,000 points. It brings a Honda Accord LX sedan plus a vacation package: two weeks off with pay, airline tickets for two to anywhere in the world, and two weeks' spending money. By 1992, 13 associates had won the Gold Award, and two the Honda Award. The associate who gets the most points in a given year also receives the Champion Award: a free round-trip air ticket to anywhere in the United States or free use of a Honda Accord for six months. In addition, the top 100 point holders are honored at a special banquet every year and get their names engraved on a plaque displayed at the plant.

In the mid-1980s the United Auto Workers tried vainly to unionize employees here. One reason for the failure was that Honda's pay and benefits are comparable—and, in some ways, superior—to those offered at unionized plants. The starting pay in 1992 was $12 an hour for production workers, rising to $15.25 after 18 months. In addition to excellent health insurance and retirement plans, Honda distributes a profit-sharing check once a year. In 1991 the average check distributed was $1,601. In 1990 the check was $1,712, a year in which Ford gave a profit-sharing check of $1,025, General Motors $50, and Chrysler zip. Honda workers also get an attendance bonus—as much as $160 every month. They can also buy Honda cars or motorcycles at a discount, and have their cars serviced at the company's service center at discounted rates. Managers qualify for a lease-car program.

Honda offers a grievance procedure comparable to if not better than union procedures. If the company wants to terminate someone, the associate has a right to pick six peers to sit on a review panel with one senior manager. This panel decides the associate's fate by majority vote. The process has been part of the company since the company began in 1979.

The Honda Way

- Proceed always with ambition and youthfulness.
- Respect sound theory, develop fresh ideas and make the most effective use of time.
- Enjoy your work, and always brighten your working atmosphere.
- Strive constantly for a harmonious flow of work.
- Be ever mindful of the value of research and endeavor.

Honda's workers also appreciate a commitment to job security. They don't have an iron-clad no-layoff policy, but Honda has avoided layoffs. In 1991, when the plant was turning out Accords faster than dealers could sell them, rather than idle the plant and put workers on furlough, they kept production up and stored 2,000 excess cars on a parking lot. Not only did they keep associates on the payroll, they made their jobs easier by slowing the line down: instead of producing 96 cars an hour, they made 93. They also avoided layoffs in 1992 when they announced that they would produce some 27,800 fewer Accords than they had previously planned. Associates with spare time were given more technical training.

Types of jobs: Production—77 percent; other—23 percent.

Main employment centers: Honda has an automobile plant and a motorcycle plant in Marysville, Ohio, an engine plant in nearby Anna, and another automobile plant in East Liberty, Ohio. They also have research facilities in Torrance, California, where American Honda Motor Co., the sales and marketing division of the Japanese company, is headquartered.

Headquarters: Honda of America Manufacturing, Inc.
Honda Pkwy.
Marysville, OH 43040
(513) 642-5000

IBM

IBM

International Business Machines is the world's leading maker of computers. U.S. employees: 186,000.

★ ★ ★ ★ ★ Pay/Benefits
★ ★ ★ ★ Opportunities
★ ★ ★ ★ Job Security
★ ★ ★ Pride in Work/Company
★ ★ ★ ★ Openness/Fairness
★ ★ ★ Camaraderie/Friendliness

BIGGEST PLUS: Golden benefits.
BIGGEST MINUS: They're feeling blue.

Nobody goes through life unscathed by setbacks of one kind or another. Not even IBM. The leader of the computer industry reduced its worldwide work force by 85,000 between 1985 and 1992, including 45,000 in the United States. That was no fun. It was one of the most massive restructurings ever undertaken by an American company. But the good news—for the people working here and those who would like to—is that even with these cutbacks, IBM remains a superlative place to work.

Victor Nusbaum joined IBM in 1960 at what was once the IBM company town of Endicott, New York, and he's now a program manager at the disk drive plant in San Jose, California. He looked back for us and said: "IBM is a different company today than it was when I started. The first 20 years or so it was a very wealthy company and we could pretty nearly do everything that we wanted to. The personnel practices haven't changed very much. Respect for the individual is still there and it's very strong. But I think it's down a little bit, I think the priority is more: get the product out the door and be profitable—very serious business objectives. And what was at one time very absolutely top-of-the-heap—people—is probably a little lower in priority now. But I think we're still probably higher than most other companies."

The pluses of working at IBM are easy to enumerate. This is still one of the largest and most powerful companies in the world, a symbol of the computer-driven, postindustrial era of information processing. You don't have to explain to your friends where you work. IBM is, after General Motors, the largest manufacturing employer in the United States. So many people want to work here that every year IBM gets to look at 1 million applications for employment. IBM is also one of the oldest American corporations. Founded in 1911, it was a leading player in the U.S. economy before most of the companies nipping at its heels today were even born. As a result, when you sign up here, you tap into a strong tradition whose hallmarks have been respect for the dignity and rights of every employee, great training programs, fair treatment, and top-of-the-scale benefits. Many companies in the computer industry won't make it to the 21st century. Somehow you get the feeling that IBM will.

For more than 50 years IBM has practiced "full employment," promising that once you were hired here, you would not be laid off for economy reasons—a downturn in sales or the closing of a plant, for examples. It earned IBM the sobriquet of a "no-layoff company." In the middle of 1992, even after the big reductions in head count, and more downsizing in the wings, the company insisted that this policy was still in force, that they had never really laid anyone off. Outsiders doubted this claim. In October 1991 the *San Jose Mercury News* ran the headline "IBM Breaks from Jobs-for-Life Policy." And many insiders were feeling uneasy. Anne Hill, a communications specialist at the San Jose plant, told us: "I've been with the company for less than three years and when I came here I wanted to retire with IBM. Now I really question that. I'm not saying I couldn't have a job. But doing what I want to do? Maybe not." And IBM vet Nusbaum said: "There is uncertainty as to how long the company will be able to maintain its old employment policy. I feel that uncertainty."

A sure sign that the no-layoff policy might soon be up for grabs appeared in a 1991 interview with *Fortune*. CEO John F. Akers said: "We'll see more people leave IBM this year than ever before in history. We have been, I think, not sufficiently demanding of ourselves regarding those folks who aren't doing the job. We have had a very low level of separations for poor performance. That level will go up—must go up." Akers was referring to a new performance appraisal system in which employees are being rated on a scale of 1 to 4. One out of every 10 IBMers will automatically fall in the lowest grade—and they will be targeted for improvement or pushed to leave the company. IBM doesn't like to use the terms "fire" or "dismissal." They talk about MIA—"management-initiated attrition."

We encountered a number of people, from headhunters to the CEO of Intel, who derided IBM for pretending to have a no-layoff policy when, in fact, it pulls on a number of levers to nudge people out of the company. But the truth is, IBM has not moved against its employees the way other companies have, surgically removing them in abrupt, involuntary excisions. Jim Dumanowski, a Silicon Valley environmental engineer who has been with IBM for 11 years, explained: "When you go through it [a layoff at another company], you're basically told you will not have a job. 'See you later, you're on your own' is one thing. But they handle it totally differently here." And they do. IBM has never closed a plant without offering employees a chance to transfer to another facility. During the 1985–92 restructuring, while thousands left the company, 90,000 employees were retrained and 35,000 redeployed. In 1991 *The Wall Street Journal* said that IBM "has moved so many people into new jobs, often in new locations, that two years ago a book on IBM's personnel practices described the IBM restructuring as the biggest movement of people since the troops came home after World War II."

Big Blue, as IBM is called, has used various lures—enhanced early-retirement packages, enriched severance payouts—to induce people to leave. The carrots varied but were among the most generous offered by any U.S. company. Sue Cook, an ex-IBMer who is now human resources vice-president at Tandem Computers, told us about the downsizing at Boca Raton, Florida, where IBM's first personal computer was developed. To consolidate manufacturing, IBM reduced the employee population at Boca Raton from 11,000 to 5,500. "We offered people two times their annual salary plus a lump sum of $25,000," she said. "That's a lot of money. You have to be crazy not to take it."

During the 1980s, as the balance of power shifted from big mainframes to small personal computers, IBM found itself besieged from all sides—by new hardware companies (Apple, Compaq, Sun Microsystems), old hardware companies (Hewlett-Packard, AT&T), and a software giant, Microsoft, whose initial lease on life had come from IBM. According to the *New York Times*, IBM's share of the computer market slid from 30 percent in 1986 to 21 percent in 1991. Each percentage point represented $3 billion in sales. That was the hostile world IBM found itself in as it drastically reduced employee population. The bad news culminated in 1991 with the registering of the first loss in its 80-year history. However, even as it regrouped, IBM did not—as many other companies did—cut back benefits. On the contrary, benefits were strengthened with the addition of long-term-care insurance and a supplemental contribution to the retirement program that will make it possible for IBMers to retire after 30 years (they needn't wait until they're 65) with a pension equal to 85 percent of their final pay. So IBM continues to offer an array of benefits that few companies can match.

Indeed, in the late 1980s IBM quickly assumed a leadership position in programs designed to help employees balance a career with family needs. Working parents here may now take a three-year leave of absence. Company-paid benefits remain intact for the entire three years, and there's an absolute guarantee of a job at the end of the leave. IBM also introduced new flexible work schedules such as working 20 to 30 hours a week for six months or taking up to two hours for a meal break during the workday to tend to personal business. The company also put up $25 million to be invested over five years to expand the number, and improve the quality, of child-care and elder-care facilities in communities where IBM employees work and live. IBM has been a catalyst in getting other companies to address child-care needs. Among its own employees, 52,000 have used the child-care referral service and 25,000 the elder-care referral service.

Always sensitive to the needs of employees, IBM mounted these new work/family programs to respond to changes in the makeup of its employee population. In 1981 the company employed 49,800 women, or 24 percent of its U.S. work force; 10 years later there were 55,100 female IBMers, representing 30 percent of U.S. workers. Women have been percolating into the management ranks, too. In 1992 they accounted for 22 percent of managers (up from 10 percent in 1981), 15 percent of senior management (up from 3 percent), and 11 percent of executive management (up from 1 percent). IBM has two of the highest-ranking women in American business in vice-presidents Lucie J. Fjeldstad and Ellen M. Hancock. As general manager of networking systems, Hancock supervises a force of 10,000 people.

The minority population at IBM has also expanded, from 1,250 in 1962 to more than 34,000 in 1992—and minorities represent 13 percent of IBM management. During the 1980s 22 percent of the people hired by the company were minorities.

To come to IBM today is to arrive at a company in the midst of "a remarkable transformation"—those are its own words. The company is trying to decimate bureaucracy by splitting itself up into a federation of companies. It has reorganized itself into 14 different units—and each of those units may have a dozen different businesses. To tie people more closely to their business units, in 1992 IBM introduced a variable pay program that will add bonuses up to 3 percent of salary, based on the performance of your unit. IBM is also trying to move from slow to rapid response to customer needs. It's willing to bid non-IBM products to customers. It's forging alliances with other companies, notably Apple. And it's hiring more people from other companies.

When companies make these kinds of cataclysmic changes, they sometimes cry, "Nothing is sacred," meaning that anything can be dismantled. But IBM is a company with a great sense of tradition, and they have been careful to tell their employees that they are not about to abandon the qualities that have made it a place where people come to learn, advance their careers, and contribute to society. Senior vice-president of personnel Walt Burdick emphasized that IBM wants to continue to be "the employer of choice," and he said the company will do whatever it has to do "to be the most attractive employer there is." He said IBM recruits now at more than 400 colleges and is clearly hiring many young people, even as older ones leave. And what is the IBM type? He defined it this way: "What we want are people who have a record of achievement. Most of the time that's academic achievement, sometimes it's other achievement. But if you have a record of achievement, you're an IBM type."

IBM prides itself on doing things well—and one thing it has been doing in this transformation is letting its employees know what's happening. They have been bombarded with information. In an IBM first, CEO John Akers put himself on the line on April 16, 1992, with eight employees sitting around a table in a one-hour question-and-answer session that was fed live by TV hookup to IBM sites so that employees around the country could ask questions.

We didn't meet anybody at IBM who didn't realize that the company was in crisis. Executive secretary Connie Bonnell put it well: "I think that no matter where you look on the globe—a government, a country, a company—there's a tremendous amount of change going on. And I think we're all trying to face up to this change. Whatever contributions we can make, it's just going to help us get through it that much quicker. IBM is not unique in this changing process. We just happen to be part of that and part of the times."

The feeling you still see at IBM is pride. We interviewed manufacturing manager David Hoffman in a roomful of employees at the disk drive plant in San Jose. He said: "There is some feeling, I know, within probably everybody in this room of the pride that we have. The company we work for brings it out. You want to do your best because you want to protect what you have here. That's my experience of how people who work for me feel. They take a lot of pride, and it means something. We've spent too much of our lives here for it not to be."

Types of jobs: Professional (legal, accounting, auditing, engineers, scientists, etc.)—44 percent; technicians—13 percent; managers—13 percent; sales and marketing—12 percent; office and clerical—10 percent; craft workers—5 percent; production—3 percent.

Main employment centers: IBM has four major production facilities in the state of New York: East Fish Kill (10,500), Endicott (8,200), Kingston (5,100), and Poughkeepsie (8,800). There are more manufacturing facilities in Raleigh, North Carolina (11,400), Rochester, Minnesota (7,600), Austin, Texas (7,500), San Jose, California (7,300), Burlington, Vermont (6,500), and Charlotte, North Carolina (4,100). They also have sales and service offices throughout the United States.

Headquarters: International Business Machines Corporation
Old Orchard Rd.
Armonk, NY 10504
(914) 765-1900

Inland Steel

 Inland Steel Industries

Inland Steel is the sixth largest steel producer in the United States. Employees: 20,000.

★ ★ ★ ★   Pay/Benefits
★ ★ ★   Opportunities
★   Job Security
★ ★ ★   Pride in Work/Company
★ ★ ★ ★   Openness/Fairness
★ ★ ★   Camaraderie/Friendliness

BIGGEST PLUS: A steel company with a heart of gold.
BIGGEST MINUS: Steel is not as strong as it used to be.

"It's the prettiest rhinoceros." That's one way to look at Inland Steel. Dave Byrne, director of management development at Inland's headquarters in Chicago, told us he used to recruit candidates by describing the company that way. Making steel is a tough, dirty business—and Inland is no exception. But this company stands out as a cut above the other players in an industry long marked by high regard for blast furnaces and low regard for the people who tended them. Inland, celebrating its 100th birthday in 1993, has a record of progressive actions down through those years. It was the first steel company to go to an eight-hour day, start a pension plan, and adopt nondiscriminatory hiring policies.

Personnel director Bill Lowry, an African-American, told us why he came to Inland 30 years ago: "I don't think any of us joined Inland to become wealthy. In terms of being able to do the kinds of things that you feel you can do, want to do, and with the kind of people that you want to do it with —those are the things that I think are the most important. One of the reasons that caused me to join is that I looked at Inland as having a conscience. I like to consider myself part of it."

We interviewed Lowry in 1991 on the 19th floor of the Inland Steel building in Chicago's Loop overlooking the Chagall mosaic in the First National Bank plaza. It's 25 miles, and a world away, from the grimy, smoky Indiana Harbor steel mill that's the source of Inland's fortunes—and misfortunes. We had interviewed at the mill earlier in the day, and the contrast between the two locales was striking. It was upbeat in downtown Chicago, downbeat in East Chicago, Indiana, where the mill sits on 1,900 acres alongside Lake Michigan. It's the largest steel mill in the country, and it was, until recently, the only mill that Inland operated.

In the late 1980s, Inland made a pact with the enemy, joining with Japan's largest steelmaker, Nippon Steel, to build two side-by-side high-tech cold-rolling steel mills at New Carlisle, Indiana, 55 miles south of the Indiana Harbor Works. Sitting in the middle of cornfields in northwest Indiana, they look more like pharmaceutical or computer laboratories than steel mills. Although the joint ventures were expected to reach, in 1993, an annual capacity of 1.9 million tons of coated steel, the total employee force is only 500, most of them recruited from the Indiana Harbor Works. By prior agreement, they are represented by the United Steelworkers of America.

Inland is up-front about its game plan. It's counting on these two new plants to make it the leading U.S. producer of sheet steel. That would help to shift a considerable chunk of Inland's annual shipments from low-value, commodity-type steel to high-value products like sheets and bars. A corollary of this strategy is that Inland will be needing fewer people to work in its mills. Its future is at New Carlisle, not East Chicago.

That will not come as a surprise to the embattled steelworkers at Indiana Harbor, whose ranks have been ravaged since 1979, when employment stood about 25,000. With the latest cutbacks, announced at the start of 1992, employment is heading toward the 10,000 level. That's not out of line with the rest of the steel industry. An industry that once employed more than half a million people now employs fewer than 200,000. More than 400 mills closed during the 1980s. Inland has been under severe pressure. From 1982 through 1985, it recorded losses of $450 million. In 1991 the company posted the biggest loss in its history: $275 million.

We saw the frustration at Indiana Harbor. Inland has not been hiring hourly workers for more than 10 years. And since those who left had been the last ones hired, this means that you don't encounter too many people with fewer than 10 or 12 years of service. The aging of the work force has implications for safety. Older workers, not as nimble as they once were, are more prone to accidents. "We don't have the young kids in here anymore to take care of us like we used to," said Danny Lyman, a mechanic who works in mobile maintenance. "Now they are starting to take more care of their people. If you are inexperienced, you get safety orientations in a much more detailed scope."

Lyman comes from an Inland Steel family, as do many workers at the mill. His father and one uncle still work here, and he has a brother and sister at the joint venture. Kathy Hilbrich, a staff representative with 15 years here, followed her father into the mill—and her brother works here, too. Maria Lopez, who's now a secretary at the Loop headquarters, started working at the mill as a file clerk in 1974. Her father, sister, and brother-in-law worked here. Having grown up in East Chicago, she said: "The place to work was Inland. If you lived in the Harbor, you didn't even have to ask, 'Where do you work?' The answer was, 'At Inland.'"

Scott Vliek, an instrument technician, joined Inland in 1987 (there were murmurs of surprise in the room that anyone had been hired so recently) after spending five years as an ironworker. "I decided that I didn't want to be an ironworker for 40 years," he said. "I have one crooked finger. They usually have 10 or 12 crooked fingers." Prior to that, he worked at the nearby Youngstown mill (now part of LTV), and he recalled that people there "always held Inland up as an example. If you saw something bad about the way things were done, there was always somebody who would say, 'Oh, they wouldn't allow that over at Inland.' When I did get here and worked at the electric furnace, it was a lot better as far as maintenance, shop cleanliness, organization of the shop floor than what I had been familiar with at Youngstown."

Old hands miss the good times when the mill was going full blast. Flo Balser, a clerk who came here in 1970, told us: "My whole family was working here. Way back, it used to be family-oriented. Now it is not that way anymore. Before it used to be enjoyable coming to work. Now it seems like everybody is so scared that they are going to lose their jobs, their attitudes have changed. It is almost cutthroat to try and keep your job." Bill Miller, a mechanic with 13 years of service, has been worried about losing his job. He told us that at one point when the mill was rife with rumors of impending layoffs, he came down with the hives. "I never had them before," he said. "My back swelled up like I was stung by 1,000 bees."

All through this trying period steelworker wages, bargained for by the United Steelworkers, have remained high, compared to other industries. In 1991 the wages and benefits at the mill averaged $25 an hour. The mill workers we talked to were, for the most part, not angry with Inland. Most seemed to understand the company's situation. But it didn't make them any happier.

Inland is trying to introduce employee involvement programs at Indiana Harbor, although Lynn Williams, president of the United Steelworkers, told us that he sensed "an ambivalence in management about sharing power with workers." It was clear from our interviews that the mill hands appreciate the new training programs, even though they have been late in coming. A visible example of this effort is Job Link 2000, a rudimentary schoolhouse on the property. A joint venture of Inland and the union, it opened in 1990 and has concentrated on remedial education, lifting workers with fifth-grade levels in math, reading, and comprehension to eighth-, ninth-, and 10th-grade levels. There's also an English-as-a-second-language course. More than 700 employees have volunteered to attend classes there —on their own time. Leander Gilliam, an hourly laborer at a basic oxygen furnace, who signed on here in 1964, told us: "There is now a lot of emphasis in my department on retraining people. It might be a case of closing the barn door after the horses are already out of there. When they first began to reorganize and restructure, they should have realized that they had to do something with people who had a lot of time. It was a matter of Inland not tapping what they already had."

Traveling to Inland headquarters in downtown Chicago, we were feeling rather depressed. Chopping a work force from 25,000 to 10,000 is not fun. But it was clear that Inland had been caught in a vise. It was part of an old order that was dying. We were cheered by our conversation with Robert J. Darnall, who was then president of Inland Steel Industries and would become chief executive officer a year later. He was sensitive to the pain experienced by the workers. After joining Inland in 1962 (Darnall has a B.A. from DePauw, a civil engineering degree from Columbia, and an M.B.A. from the University of Chicago), he was posted to the Indiana Harbor Works, where he spent 19 years, rising to general manager of the mill. Like Bill Lowry, he emphasized Inland's long-standing commitment to ethical conduct. "You have to *stand* for something," he said in a recent talk that is now passed out to every new recruit. "You have to take ethics and values out of the corporate policy manuals, out of the realm of philosophy. You have to *breathe life into them* by applying those values to the issues—tough issues—that affect the company, its communities, and its people." And Darnall insisted Inland had done exactly that in its agonizing downsizing, "developing a severance and employee assistance program that went far beyond the norm" and cutting executive salaries by 20 percent. He told us that when Inland took out 1,000 salaried employees in the 1985–86 period, "I probably got 50 letters from people who were leaving. I didn't really count them but it was something on the order of 10 to one saying, 'Bob, I understand why the company is going through this change. I wish I were going to be a member of your new team, but I am not. Inland has been fair to me and I appreciate the years that I have had here.' I probably had 10 of those letters to one that said, 'I think I have been discriminated against. Somebody played favoritism,' and that kind of thing. There were practically no legal actions that came out of it."

Darnall sees the joint ventures with the Japanese as providing the path out of Inland's current morass. "It is structured far differently than our Indiana Harbor agreement," he said. "We do not have supervisors on the turn there. It is really a self-directed work force. I get so damned excited when I go out there and walk through that place and talk to people. I see what is possible. If we can demonstrate that 55 miles from Indiana Harbor this kind of working relationship is possible, maybe that will leverage back on the larger, older work force at Indiana Harbor and start to bring change there." Darnall emphasized that the union is a joint partner with the company. "We could have gone nonunion," he told us. "We went to Lynn Williams and said, 'Lynn, we clearly have that option, but that is not our primary thrust. The fact that we are going to invest $1 billion out here in world-class technology means that we also need a world-class working relationship with our people.'" Darnall added that Inland is making the investments in plant and people that "will continue to make us the best integrated steel producer in this country."

Even as it was moving through this wrenching period of its life, Inland was the setting for a remarkable drive to breach the white dominance in upper management. Inland, as a whole, has a diverse work force—18 percent black and 16 percent Hispanic—but as of 1987, 88.6 percent of managers and officers were white; and 95.2 percent were male. In 1987 four black employees—salespersons Tyrone Banks, Robert Hudson, Jr., and Scharlene Hurston and human resources staffer Vivan Cosey—sought out a white manager, Steven Bowsher, to deliver a message about minorities getting shortchanged on upward promotions. The discussions impelled Bowsher to go to Atlanta to sit in on a two-day race relations workshop conducted by the late Dr. Charles King and attended mostly by blacks and women. It turned out to be a transformational experience for him. Bowsher calls it "the single most important training I've been through." Returning to Chicago, he put into motion a series of steps that resulted in more than 100 Inland managers experiencing King's seminars and the formation of a new group, the Affirmative Action Focus Group. Darnall went to the Atlanta seminar with two African-American employees and reported: "It was a truly moving experience for me. I thought before that I was pretty progressive and pretty sensitive, but I did not recognize some of the behavior that I had allowed and the negative impact it had on some of the minority employees." The black employees who spurred this drive said the minority employees at Inland now feel better about the company. "The 'veil of discomfort' that previously existed for females and minorities within this company is diminishing," said Scharlene Hurston. The Inland employees were given an award in 1992 by the Business Enterprise Trust for their efforts to promote diversity in the ranks.

It may be possible for such events to unfold at U.S. Steel and Bethlehem Steel, but we doubt it. There is a culture at Inland Steel that encourages this kind of dissent. It's a complex company, with problems, but we certainly feel confident about recommending it, especially for college students interested in a manufacturing career. In 1992 Inland had 43 co-op students at the company. Beth Keeve, a compensation and benefits manager at headquarters, joined Inland in 1988 after working at Whitman chocolates and Continental Bank. "I can honestly say," she told us, "that I have never in my career worked for a corporation where I actually felt so much that I could have an impact. It is not just at my level. It is virtually at every level."

And Dave Byrne said he felt that Inland is still benefiting from a family feeling that goes back many years. "Families have changed," he told us. "Families like mine and all of ours. My kids are growing up differently from the way I did. I am sure that their kids will grow up differently. That is what is happening in corporate America, too. This is not the same company it was 25 years ago. It couldn't be. We just couldn't exist if it was, but there are vestiges of that family that are different here than they would be at some of our competitors. There are a lot of companies out there that have blown up their family orientation. I don't think that is true here."

Types of jobs: Production—62 percent; officials and managers—10 percent; office and clerical—10 percent; professionals—8 percent; sales— 5 percent; technicians—4 percent.

Main employment centers: Inland's headquarters is in Chicago. Their steel plant, research labs, and fleet operations are in East Chicago, Indiana. Two joint-venture plants are located in East Carlisle, Indiana. They also have an iron ore mining operation in Minnesota and a limestone company in Michigan.

Headquarters: Inland Steel Industries, Inc.
30 W. Monroe St.
Chicago, IL 60603
(312) 346-0300

$5,000 REIMBURSEMENT OF ADOPTION EXPENSES

Hallmark Cards
Syntex

Intel

intel®

Intel invented the microprocessor chip, the engine that drives most computers. They also make enhancement products for personal computers and supercomputers. U.S. employees: 16,870.

★★★★ Pay/Benefits
★★★★ Opportunities
★★★ Job Security
★★★★ Pride in Work/Company
★★★ Openness/Fairness
★★★ Camaraderie/Friendliness

BIGGEST PLUS: They're INTELligent.
BIGGEST MINUS: They still yell at each other a lot.

One measure of the humanity of an organization is its ability to laugh at itself. Intel, a company in the forefront of the computer revolution, passes that test with high marks. This is a company that knows its strengths and foibles. In 1988, to celebrate its 20th birthday, Intel hired Ray Bloch Productions to put on a 90-minute musical show featuring actors and actresses with Broadway credits and a script that spoofed many of the Intel idiosyncrasies—endless meetings, long hours, lack of structure, use of acronyms. It was a show in which the three principal people in Intel's history—the late Robert Noyce, Gordon Moore, and Hungarian refugee Andrew Grove—pranced onto the stage dressed in "clean room" bunny suits.

Then there's the annual April Fool's Day issue of *The iNTeLNATIONAL iNQUIReR*. A dead ringer for the supermarket tabloid, *The National Enquirer*, it has been published at Intel since 1983. In 1990 it had an "Ask Doctor Groove!" advice column: "Feeling lonely, depressed, unable to cope? Can't get along with your boss . . . Then you probably work at Intel! Each week, Doctor Groove answers your questions about life as we know it at Intel, 'A Great Place to WORK! WORK! WORK!' " (One of the goals in Intel's Mission Statement is to be "a great place to work.")

Beneath the humor, of course, is dead seriousness. Intel is on the leading technological edge of the computer industry. They make a variety of semiconductor chips, such as memory chips and embedded controllers which have a variety of uses including the electronics of newer automobile engines. They also make some of the most powerful supercomputers in the world and assemble personal computers for AT&T and Digital Equipment. But Intel is best known for a chip they invented in 1971, the microprocessor, a semiconductor that is, in effect, the brains of a computer placed on a minuscule silicon chip. When IBM started making personal computers in the early 1980s, it picked Intel's microprocessor. Intel's chips—including the popular i386 and i486—power more than 100 million IBM-style personal computers. Microprocessors account for more than half of Intel's sales and profits and are the mainstay of this company. They have held off the Japanese at the pass, and this has meant a relentless, riveting drive to score the next breakthrough.

Life at Intel is intense, just as we found it in our earlier visits, although company representatives insisted that the company has mellowed. It has sometimes been called a "Marine Corps culture." They have forged here a confrontational style of operation that tests people, including those at the top. CEO Andy Grove presides over half a dozen open forums each year. "I go somewhere," he told us, "and people fill a cafeteria. I have a microphone and overhead projector. I start by showing a few slides and then hands go up and there are questions. And I answer them. I find these open forums with employees far more stimulating, in terms of the variety and incisiveness of the questions, than meetings with security analysts." In an interview with *Compass*, Grove said: "Nothing tops the question a woman asked me during the 1986 industry downturn at our open forum in Phoenix. Sitting in the front row, she asked, 'Isn't it time for Intel to change its management?' All of a sudden I had 400 people staring at me and sitting on the edges of their seats waiting for my answer. Facing those kinds of questions has honed my managerial capabilities as well as kept me reasonably humble. Intel will always be an open company, with a strong flow of information in every direction."

The tone at Intel is set at the top by Andy Grove, whose strong card is not humility. Nor is he one to mince words. At the end of 1991, *Fortune* did one of its round-robin surveys, asking leading corporate executives what they hoped to see in the coming year. Grove's first sentence was: "In 1992, I would like to see a government that gives a shit about U.S. industry before it's too late."

In keeping with Grove's intensity, Intel has always been a no-frills place

—no cushy offices, no executive dining rooms, no reserved parking places, no corporate jets—but the ambience has mellowed a bit in recent years. Intel people who like to jog used to lobby for on-site showers, getting this response from Grove: "As long as I'm here, there will be no showers at Intel." In 1988 he relented and Intel installed showers. And who took the first one? Andy Grove. In 1992, as Intel moved into a new six-story headquarters building named for Robert Noyce, it also opened, at its Santa Clara campus, a 7,000-square-foot, freestanding fitness center. Today, a "par course," where joggers can stop at different stations to exercise, loops around the campus. And a new split-level cafeteria with an outdoor patio was opened in December 1991, with the caterer, Marriott, under instructions to push the envelope on food. So now there are cooking demonstrations several times a week and menus featuring stir-fry vegetables, fajitas, omelets, shrimp and lobster. Loren Almeida, who supervises recreation activities in the human resources department, told us that Intel has decided that "part of making this a great place to work is to have good food."

Another change at Intel has been abolition of the late list. The company used to insist that everybody be in by 8:00 A.M. They still want you in early but the receptionist no longer marks down people who are late. According to Carlene Ellis, vice-president–human resources, Intel "lost a lot of people" who regarded this as kindergarten stuff.

Intel does not pay at the high end of the market—and this is true right up to the top. Although Intel is a much bigger company than AMD, Grove has consistently drawn a much smaller paycheck than AMD's CEO, Jerry Sanders. Intel believes in a pay-for-performance ethic. Cash bonuses are paid twice a year, skewed to how well the company does. The key relationship is pretax profits as a percentage of revenues—every 2 percent yields each employee a half-day's pay. For 1991, Intel employees received an extra 12.5 days of pay as a reward for the company earning better than 20 percent on sales.

Intel's performance review system, once described as so rigorous that it bruised employees "with verbal brutality, even ridicule," has been softened. Previously, employees were rated on a five-point scale: superior, exceeds, meets, marginally meets, and does not meet. Now it's down to three ranks: outstanding, successful, and improvement required. And the guidelines are that 15 percent will fall in the "outstanding" category, 80 percent in "successful," and 5 percent in "improvement required."

The fringe benefits at Intel are strong. There's a deferred profit-sharing plan, three weeks of vacation and personal absence time after the first year, opportunity to buy stock at a 15 percent discount, and a sabbatical—eight weeks of paid leave, in addition to regular vacation—after seven years of service. Intel pays the entire premium for medical insurance for the employee and covers 30 percent of the premium for dependents.

Intel's turnover rate in 1990 was 7 percent, the lowest in the company's history, not counting the traumatic 1985–86 period when sales stagnated, profits turned into losses, and 7,000 people were lopped from the payroll. It was not Intel's finest hour—people were notified to be "out of here" by the end of the day—and the company itself looks back on it with some regret. Today, Intel has in place what it calls a "redeployment policy" designed to "give the employee due notice, a variety of alternatives and to treat each person with dignity." Between 1989 and 1991 Intel closed plants employing 2,000 people and relocated 80 percent of them to other locations. The company runs lean these days. Although sales have tripled since 1985, total employment has declined by 3,000.

We had extensive discussions about layoffs with Andy Grove and Carlene Ellis. Ellis said: "We are really working on a continuous redeployment strategy that will allow us to avoid layoffs. And as head of HR, that is absolutely my goal. And if I can't avoid them, I've failed. To do that, we've really got to do long-range manpower planning better—and we have to have a strategy with massive retraining. We are going to do everything we can to avoid layoffs. However, if we can find no other means, we will."

Intel does regular employee surveys, and over the years they show that employees have a strong sense of pride in what they are doing. But they have also shown that a significant minority of employees sometimes feel bruised by the "constructive confrontation" sessions that are so celebrated here—this is not a place for people with thin skins. The surveys have also indicated that many employees realize that this is a culture where "it is acceptable to make more commitments than I can meet." In view of what looks like a workaholic atmosphere, how can it be a good place to work? Listen to Intel people:

Pat Lee, a marketing supervisor who has been at Intel for nine years, said: "Personally, competing and working with some of the best minds in the industry forces me to think out of my comfort zone and not become complacent. You have to run fast to keep up with the pack and, in many cases, leave the pack. If you're not comfortable in that situation, you're not going to be happy here. Some people wish for stability, not me."

Janice Wilkins, a 12-year Intel veteran who was working on the "Intel Inside" marketing campaign, told us that management people do work 50 to 60 hours a week but that they are given "a good amount of independence and autonomy" to get a job done—and when "you get it done, you feel you have made a difference." But she added that "you have to be a type of person who can work without being stroked continually for doing a good job. I like the feeling that I have been given the power and authority to get the job done. If you see a problem here, it's yours to solve it or get someone to own up to it."

We talked to Katie Woodruff in 1992 shortly before she left Intel to enter the public health school at the University of California at Berkeley. She had come to Intel after graduating from Brown in 1988 and had worked in corporate communications. She said the one downside of Intel, for her, was that it didn't provide an opportunity "to do something good for the world." But she was full of praise for the work-style. "Yes, it's absolutely workaholic, but it's also absolutely rewarding," she said. Woodruff told us that people with good ideas have no problem presenting them to senior managers, even if they are down low on the totem pole. "The politics here is incredibly low," she said, "compared to other places. And if you make a mistake, it won't be held against you forever. For someone who works hard and takes some risks, there are amazing growth opportunities here."

Types of jobs: Managers and professionals—50 percent; production—25 percent; technicians—15 percent; administrative—10 percent.

Main employment centers: Santa Clara, California, 3,600; Portland, Oregon, 3,000; Phoenix, Arizona, 3,000; Albuquerque, New Mexico, 1,200. Another 10,000 work overseas.

Headquarters: Intel Corp.
2200 Mission College Blvd.
Santa Clara, CA 95052
(408) 765-8080

BEST FOR PAY/BENEFITS

Leo Burnett
Fel-Pro
Goldman Sachs
Hallmark Cards
Hewlett-Packard
IBM
Merck
Procter & Gamble
Syntex
Xerox

Johnson & Johnson

Johnson & Johnson

Johnson & Johnson is the world's largest maker of health-care products. U.S. employees: 39,300.

★ ★ ★ ★　Pay/Benefits
★ ★ ★ ★　Opportunities
　★ ★ ★　Job Security
★ ★ ★ ★　Pride in Work/Company
　★ ★ ★　Openness/Fairness
　★ ★ ★　Camaraderie/Friendliness

BIGGEST PLUS: It's a healthy atmosphere.
BIGGEST MINUS: A little too antiseptic.

One of the most overworked words in the English language is "nice," but if there's any company that fits this description, it's Johnson & Johnson. J&J is a nice company filled with nice people. A little formal—and wholesome. But what else would you expect from the company that makes Band-Aids, Johnson & Johnson baby powder, Johnson & Johnson baby shampoo, and Johnson & Johnson baby oil?

If you've worked at J&J for five years and then get married, the company has this wonderful wedding present for you: an extra week's paid vacation. And if you and your spouse then have a child, you can bring the baby to work with you, dropping him or her off at the on-site child-care center. At lunchtime, you might want to visit with your child or you might opt for a workout in the on-site fitness center, perhaps under the supervision of a personal trainer.

All these amenities go with the territory here. They may not be exactly the same at every J&J unit, because the company prides itself on decentralization, allowing big and small decisions to be made locally, but the spirit and caring are central and pervasive. No one goes against this grain without getting into trouble here.

At the same time, no one should make the mistake of taking J&J for a softie. In the drug industry, they know how to knock heads with the best of them. Just ask Bristol-Myers Squibb or American Home Products, which have had to contend with the biggest product in the Johnson & Johnson medicine chest, Tylenol. And this sweet old lady is behind the aggressive drumbeating you see on television for the over-the-counter remedies Micatin (for athlete's foot) and Mylanta (for heartburn).

Inside this company, people do feel like winners. Interviews we conducted at the 15-story, I. M. Pei-designed headquarters tower in New Brunswick, New Jersey, certainly underlined the impression that J&J is a special place. We whipped around a room full of J&J people, asking questions and getting responses such as these:

"You feel more wanted here. The other company I worked for, you were there to do the job and it was just let's get it done. Here at Johnson & Johnson, I feel that I just cannot do enough for the company because they make you feel at home."

"I wish I had been here years ago. Instead of seven years, I wish I would have been here 20 years."

"I used to work at Chase Manhattan Bank. Chase's rigidity is something they take pride in. J&J's structure is formal but there's more mobility and there isn't the same kind of barriers with people."

"There's a lot of care and attention. The recognition is there that your employees are your greatest resource."

"When things are really getting to you, I think more people tend to think of bidding out to another job within the company rather than going outside."

"There are not many jobs that are open. People just don't want to leave."

The last two comments are telling. J&J entered the 1980s with sales of $4.2 billion and 72,000 employees. It's now logging $12.4 billion annually with 83,000 employees. In other words, sales just about tripled while the number of employees went up only 14 percent. That's tight management, reflected in the growth of after-tax profits from $350 million in 1979 to $1.4 billion in 1991.

So if you want to work for a superbly managed company, head straight for New Brunswick. Except that it's not New Brunswick where newcomers are likely to get their start. Johnson & Johnson is a big company, ranking 34th on the Fortune 500, but it tries not to act like one. Business is carried out by 166 different companies—and they enjoy a high degree of autonomy. Each has its own management board. Each does its own planning, marketing, and hiring. And rather than say that they work for Johnson & Johnson, people are more likely to say that they work for Ethicon in Somer-

ville, New Jersey, or Vistakon in Jacksonville, Florida, or Iolab in Claremont, California, or Ortho Pharmaceutical in Raritan, New Jersey. In a
cover story in its May 4, 1992, issue, *BusinessWeek* dubbed J&J "a big
company that works." The magazine reported that two J&J units, Janssen
Pharmaceutical and McNeill Pharmaceutical, signed a formal marketing
agreement in 1989 when McNeill salesmen helped to introduce a new Janssen antihistamine to doctors. Larry G. Pickering, president of Janssen, said:
"We have to keep reminding ourselves that we work for the same corporation." Another J&J manager, Marvin L. Woodall, president of J&J Interven-
tional Systems, told *BusinessWeek*: "I'm almost never distracted by Johnson
& Johnson management."

As decentralized as J&J is, a set of core values, expressed in a document
called "Our Credo," links the separate companies together in a family. The
document details the responsibilities of the company, in rank order, beginning with customers and employees and ending with shareholders. "Our
Credo" adds up to a prescription to do the right thing, and it's a living
document in the minds of both management and rank-and-file employees.
J&J makes a point of saying that "the most important thing we have in this
corporation is the value system we live by." Nancy Lane, who works in
government affairs and has been with J&J for more than 17 years, told us:
"Our culture is so important to us that when we acquire a new company,
they may complain about being 'Johnson & Johnsonized,' but that's because of the emphasis we put on maintaining the same environment at all
our locations. On the one hand, we have decentralization so that Ethicon
can have its own culture. On the other hand, we have the whole J&J. And
though it always sounds hokey to outside people, the basis for the whole
culture is the credo."

James E. Burke, who retired as J&J CEO in 1989, credited "Our Credo"
with helping the company to weather the Tylenol crisis of the early 1980s,
when a madman who was never apprehended laced capsules of the analge-
sic with cyanide, killing seven people. With no hesitation, Burke went on
television to accept responsibility and ordered the immediate recall of every
package of Tylenol capsules. Burke's successor, Ralph S. Larsen, has reaffirmed the importance of "Our Credo," calling it "the heart of our value
system," adding: "The only way to keep values alive is to continue to talk
about them, to study them, to live them."

An exhibit staged in 1991 at J&J's World Headquarters Gallery was an
example of how the value system lives. The exhibit displayed photographs,
paintings, sculpture, and prints celebrating the life of Paul Robeson, the
actor, singer, and political activist who was hounded by the FBI, the Justice
Department, the State Department, and congressional committees because
of his unwavering support for left-wing causes and his refusal to answer the
question "Are you, or have you ever been, a member of the Communist
Party?" Martin B. Duberman's biography, *Paul Robeson*, appeared in 1988,

12 years after Robeson's death, and it stimulated two J&J employees in the law department, Benjamin Lambert and Kathleen Augelli, to mount this exhibit. Lambert, a patent attorney, is black; Augelli, a paralegal who works on trademark protection, is white. They worked together for more than a year to collect the materials for the exhibit, which had photographs from Robeson's days as an All-American football player at Rutgers University, based across the street from Johnson & Johnson in New Brunswick.

Big companies are notorious for being slow afoot. But J&J has demonstrated that it can move fast. It did so during the Tylenol crisis, and in the late 1980s it did so again when it addressed the thorny issues surrounding work and family. Other companies had begun to offer working parents new benefits such as flexible schedules and child-care support while J&J seemed to be lagging. Then, in 1988 and 1989, J&J launched a dozen new programs, including a referral service for employees looking for child care or elder care, a one-year parental leave, financial help for employees adopting children (up to $2,000), and new flexible work schedules. Coincident with these moves, J&J did something it has virtually never done—it altered "Our Credo" to include this new responsibility: "We must be mindful of ways to help our employees fulfill their family responsibilities."

And that wasn't the end of it. In 1990 J&J opened a child-care center at headquarters, which has room for 200 children of employees. As decentralized as J&J is, it knows how to fan out programs through this corporation. In 1991 a second center was opened at Ortho in Raritan, a third was opened in 1992 at Janssen's facility in New Jersey's Hopewell Township, and a fourth was set for Fort Washington, outside of Philadelphia, to serve McNeill Consumer Products and several other J&J companies in Montgomery County. In 1991 the Families and Work Institute in New York did an exhaustive survey of the work/family programs in place at 189 companies, and it then ranked the companies based on how many strings they had to their respective bows. Johnson & Johnson took first place.

We talked to one childless employee at headquarters who noted the difference the child-care center has made: "It used to be we would get in the elevator and you would nod or kind of say hello. Now conversations start because everyone wants to know what the baby's name is. I came in in a real bad mood one day, and I wasn't quite sure why. I got in the elevator and this adorable little girl looked at me and she said, 'Hello,' and then I found myself smiling all the way to the office. I find myself feeling that way a lot."

The work/family programs joined a compensation and benefits package that puts J&J up among the leaders of American industry. In 1991, for example, 28 percent of sales—or $3.5 billion—went for employee costs, including salaries and benefits. That worked out to an average of $42,000 per person! In 1992 an entry-level secretary was being paid $22,000 a year, a beginning accountant $30,000. Women account for a little more than half

OUR CREDO

We believe our first responsibility is to the doctors, nurses and patients, to mothers and fathers and all others who use our products and services. In meeting their needs everything we do must be of high quality. We must constantly strive to reduce our costs in order to maintain reasonable prices. Customers' orders must be serviced promptly and accurately. Our suppliers and distributors must have an opportunity to make a fair profit.

We are responsible to our employees, the men and women who work with us throughout the world. Everyone must be considered as an individual. We must respect their dignity and recognize their merit. They must have a sense of security in their jobs. Compensation must be fair and adequate, and working conditions clean, orderly and safe. We must be mindful of ways to help our employees fulfill their family responsibilities. Employees must feel free to make suggestions and complaints. There must be equal opportunity for employment, development and advancement for those qualified. We must provide competent management, and their actions must be just and ethical.

We are responsible to the communities in which we live and work and to the world community as well. We must be good citizens—support good works and charities and bear our fair share of taxes. We must encourage civic improvements and better health and education. We must maintain in good order the property we are privileged to use, protecting the environment and natural resources.

Our final responsibility is to our stockholders. Business must make a sound profit. We must experiment with new ideas. Research must be carried on, innovative programs developed and mistakes paid for. New equipment must be purchased, new facilities provided and new products launched. Reserves must be created to provide for adverse times. When we operate according to these principles, the stockholders should realize a fair return.

of J&J's employees, and they now hold 28 percent of jobs classified as "officials and managers." Among the highest-paid people in the company —the top 20 percent—the female representation in 1992 was 22 percent. One out of every four J&J employees is a member of a minority group.

One of the guidelines followed here is that managers cannot look to fill a position from the outside without first seeing if it can be filled by people who, as one official told us, "have already made a commitment to the corporation. Our first obligation is to them." That's reflected in longevity records. In 1991 J&J had 1,624 people with more than 25 years of service, 507 with 30 years, 190 with 35 years, and 80 with 40 years.

Types of jobs: Production—40 percent; office and clerical—17 percent; operations—10 percent; research and development—10 percent; technicians —6 percent; marketing—5.5 percent; information services—5 percent; finance—3.5 percent; management and administration—3 percent.

Main employment centers: New Jersey is the mother lode. About 1,000 employees work in the New Brunswick area, and another 12,500 are with other companies in New Jersey, most within a 10-mile radius of New Brunswick. Other major domestic locations include Tampa, Florida; Arlington, Texas; and Claremont, California. Some 50,000 people work outside the United States.

Headquarters: Johnson & Johnson
One Johnson & Johnson Plaza
New Brunswick, NJ 08933
(908) 524-0400

SC Johnson Wax

⊖Johnson wax

SC Johnson Wax is a leading maker of household products. U.S. employees: 3,154.

★★★★ Pay/Benefits
★★★ Opportunities
★★★★★ Job Security
★★★★ Pride in Work/Company
★★★ Openness/Fairness
★★★★ Camaraderie/Friendliness

BIGGEST PLUS: They pledge job security.
BIGGEST MINUS: Stay away if you like life on the edge.

Racine, Wisconsin's fourth largest city, sits 90 miles north of Chicago on Lake Michigan, and it has always been home for Jim May, corporate public relations manager of SC Johnson Wax. May was born there in 1941 in a house on the north side of town, moved when he was three years old to a house on Main Street, and today he and his wife, Carol, also a Racine native, live on Standish Lane in the southwest part of Racine. They have seven children. A graduate of Marquette University in Milwaukee, May joined Johnson Wax in 1968. Whether coming from home or Johnson Wax's spectacular Frank Lloyd Wright-designed headquarters building on the south side of town, Jim May can easily retrace his historical steps. The two houses he grew up in as a boy, with six brothers and sisters, still stand, occupied now by other families. And all but two of his siblings still live in Racine.

Jim May's story is not atypical. Johnson Wax is filled with people who grew up in Racine and are comfortable working not too far from where they were born. That also goes for the founding family, the Johnsons, who not only still own the company but play active roles in its management. And that goes also for Richard M. Carpenter, who was elected chief executive officer of the company in 1990, becoming only the third non-Johnson family member to hold that position in more than 100 years. Carpenter was born—and grew up—in Racine. As a matter of fact, one of Jim May's sisters is married to Carpenter's nephew.

The family atmosphere that pervades this company was accented by an event in 1986 when Johnson Wax was celebrating its 100th birthday. A globe demarcating the countries of the world had been put up in front of the headquarters building in 1954. Aside from being dated, it was showing its wear—and an organizing drive among employees was initiated to replace it with a modern version that they would present as a thank-you gift to Samuel C. Johnson, who was then chief executive officer of the company founded by his great-grandfather. They wanted it to be a surprise, and so the campaign was conducted under wraps; it was called Project Mum. In the end, 95 percent of the 2,500 employees in the Racine area dug into their own pockets to contribute to Project Mum. They raised a total of $310,000, an average of $125 per person.

The globe, measuring 11 feet in diameter and made of carbon fiber, cost $210,000. The remaining $100,000 was used to install brass plates showing the names of every single employee and to establish a fund for the upkeep of the globe, which marks the worldwide locations of Johnson subsidiaries (Johnson Wax does 60 percent of its sales outside the United States). The employees were able to remove the old globe and implant the new one while Sam Johnson was out of the country on a business trip. They then put a shroud over it, which he noticed but couldn't get a proper explanation for until the annual profit-sharing meeting in December at Armstrong Park, the 147-acre recreation area in Racine that is reserved exclusively for Johnson employees. The presentation was made via a film, and after viewing it Sam Johnson immediately drove the six miles to headquarters to see this 100th birthday gift.

In an interview with us, CEO Richard Carpenter stressed how important it was to have had the continuity of four generations of Johnson family members. "They were all enlightened employers," he said. "If you go back to 1917, that is when we started profit sharing. If you go back in history and look at all the problems that management and labor had in those days, the kind of strife and difficulty that was going on then, here was this small company in Racine, Wisconsin, saying, 'We are a family. How can we help these people be more successful at their jobs?' That is where the success of the company is. Those are the beliefs that the company is founded on."

Johnson Wax is now one of the largest privately owned companies in the United States, with estimated worldwide sales of $3.5 billion, a figure that would gain it admission to the Fortune 500 at the 135th slot. Being family-owned, it sailed through the 1980s without having to worry about takeovers or leveraged buyouts. During the decade sales more than doubled through such offerings as Pledge furniture polish, Glade air fresheners, Future and Brite floor cleaners, Raid insecticides, Edge shaving gel, Halsa and Agree hair shampoos, and Curel and Soft Sense hand lotions. All of these products are turned out at Waxdale, the company's massive (2 million square feet) and spotless manufacturing facility in the western suburbs of Racine.

While it's clear that the company is a lot more than wax these days, the old name hangs on despite periodic efforts by younger people to come up with a new corporate symbol. The latest move is the name, SC Johnson Wax, with the idea that over time "Wax" will be phased out. It's yet to happen. People, especially in Racine, continue to call it Johnson Wax, and Dick Carpenter, for one, is dubious about the change ever happening. "I'm an old-timer," he told us. "Never ask an old-timer. I say never. I say that Johnson Wax is a marvelous identification, and I think it's good at least for another generation."

In 1992 Sam Johnson was still a very visible chairman of the company, and a fifth generation was waiting in the wings. The eldest of four children, S. Curtis Johnson, who has a master's degree in finance from Northwestern's Kellogg Business School, was director of worldwide business development; he was 37. The next oldest, H. Fisk Johnson, who holds two master's degrees and a doctorate in applied physics, was general manager of the Canadian company; he was 34. Helen P. Johnson-Leipold, who has a degree in psychology, worked for a Chicago ad agency before joining the company in 1985; she was director of marketing services for U.S. consumer products in 1992, and was 35. And the youngest, Winifred Marquart, 33 in 1992, lived in Virginia Beach but worked part-time for the company. This is a family that sets great store on tradition. All the children went to Cornell, as did their father, who is a great benefactor of this upstate New York college.

In making our rounds of the company, we didn't encounter anyone who resented the Johnson family's presence. Sue Helland, a marketing research director, works with Helen Johnson and reported that when she talks with her, "it is very much like talking to a friend. It is not this artificial sense of 'I am the Johnson kid.' You don't see any of that at all. She is very professional and competent."

The Johnsons are not the only family with multiple members here. Roy Villarreal, an electrician with 22 years service, related: "When I got hired, my older brother worked here. Then I got hired. Then my other brother got hired. Then the other one. Then the other one. [Now] there are five brothers and my uncle. Then my wife worked here. Her sister works here and her brother works here. My wife's brother-in-law also works here."

The family benefits provided here go back a long way. Company-paid vacations began in 1900, group life insurance (along with profit sharing) in 1917, a pension plan in 1934, and hospital insurance in 1939. A major medical plan was introduced in 1953. At Johnson Wax today, the company pays the entire premium for employee health coverage and 80 percent of the premium for dependent coverage, which works out to $23 a month for an employee with one dependent and $39 a month for an employee with two or more dependents. A prescription drug costs $5—$3 for the generic version. Another feature of this plan is that there is no lifetime maximum for health-care expenses.

This benefits package is continually enriched. In 1987 the company presented, as a centennial gift to employees, a 46,000-square-foot aquatic center whose centerpiece is an L-shaped, Olympic-size swimming pool with ample space for lap swimmers and an instruction area for children. And in 1991 the company opened a new state-of-the-art child-care center capable of handling 250 infants and toddlers and open from 6:30 A.M. to 6:00 P.M. to accommodate shift workers. Both of these facilities were placed in Armstrong Park adjacent to the recreation and fitness center, which holds a large gym, squash and handball courts, and meeting rooms.

Along with a lot of other companies in the 1980s, Johnson Wax downsized and embraced the concepts revolving around employee-directed teams. But layoffs were never an option for a company that didn't fire anyone during the Great Depression of the 1930s. Nico Meiland, a Dutchman who heads up manufacturing at Waxdale (he came from the Johnson Wax plant in the Netherlands), told us: "I went from 140 managers to 40. I also went with my hourly people from about 1,600 to 1,000, but we basically have not laid off anybody. We offered them early retirement. We offered them very, very attractive separation packages, and then we have attrition obviously." One example of the attractive separation packages was cited by Garvin Shankster, senior vice-president of human resources: "In the factory, where we had an imbalance in certain job categories, we basically offered a $20,000 check to anybody who would like to resign. We defined what the population was. It couldn't be everybody. In this particular case, it was at the factory floor. We structured it so that the newly hired could not get that. I think you had to have eight to 10 years of service, and I think we had 30-some people who took it. They used that for a variety of things. Some people decided to go into business for themselves. We had several people who went back to pursue their education."

According to Meiland, getting people to work in teams where they evaluated one another was a little wrenching, especially for older workers. "That is nice for the youngsters," he said, "but if I am in the highest-paid group and I have my seniority, working days, or if I am the chief of the line and suddenly I have team members and I am not the only guy who can make decisions, you are cutting away my power. I don't like it. I have been working 30 years to get here and now the Dutchman from Holland is telling me that is all gone and I am in a team! Hey . . . So that is a bit of a difficult process and we have to handle it carefully."

Here's how it worked, Meiland said, when Waxdale went to a seven-day production schedule: "We went to the work teams and said, 'Hey, guys, it is your decision. What we want from you—and we won't tell you how to do it—is: how do you cover seven days a week?' They all elected 12 hours a day. So now in one week they work four days, which is 48 hours. The other week they work three days, which is 36 hours. Together we have over 80 hours in two weeks, which we needed. That was their own free choice. My regular lines are only three shifts, five days a week, with eight-hour working days. The teams work seven days a week and are all 12 hours."

Ron Wolter, a corporate facilities manager, who is coming up on his 25th year at Johnson Wax, told us that "over the years we've all said, 'Can we do this?' and the response has been, 'No, it's not in the budget.' What is the budget? Finally, we gave them one and said, 'Here, you take it; you manage it.' I think that is what we have to do with our people: give them the credit they deserve. They manage the budget at home, so they can manage one here."

The biggest change market research director Sue Helland has noticed in her 11 years here is that "people used to talk about Johnson's as being a country-club atmosphere. I think it was. I think that had a lot of positives to it. But the people who were very highly motivated and were good, quality performers back then had a lot of frustration with it. There were probably times when too much mediocrity was accepted. I have seen that diminish. I have seen people working much harder and earning their money much more than they did 11 years ago. You hear people saying, 'You always will have a job here if you are a good performer.' There is much more emphasis on being a good performer and working harder for that money." That sentiment was echoed by senior information services manager Louis Sesso, who told us: "I have known the company for 40 years. My father was here and I have seen a lot of change. Sue makes a good point: it used to be lifetime employment. Once you were in, you were in. That is not the case now; you have got to work for it. I think that is good."

Waxdale was not hiring for eight or nine years during the 1980s, but when it does, applications pour in. It always helps to know someone here, because the company, when it needs to fill jobs, puts applications in the hands of current employees. Nico Meiland told us that on one occasion, when 20 jobs were open, he received 3,000 applications. In 1991 the entry-level wage at Waxdale was $8.75 an hour, moving up to $12 to $13 within two years. Profit sharing has consistently augmented pay by 12 to 13 percent every year. Joanne Brandes, senior counsel in the law department, was recruited by a headhunter from a large Milwaukee law firm where she was a partner, and she says that in the past few years pay for managers has improved to the point where executive compensation here is "extremely competitive." Some 250 to 300 top managers at Johnson Wax are now eligible for so-called phantom stock programs in which they receive certificates that model the performance of the Johnson company shares; they get cash dividends and they are able to realize appreciation in the value of the shares.

Johnson Wax enjoys a reputation as the best employer for miles and miles around. John VanderWielen, a customer service representative, told us that he always takes his company sticker off the windshield and puts it in the car ashtray "just so people don't nag me. I mean, really, sometimes you get, 'You work at Johnson's? Are they hiring? Can you help me?' It's not an everyday occurrence, but it happens. You get, 'Oh, you're rich. You work at Johnson's.' " Don Paar, a chemical process operator, added: "It's funny. You go to buy a car and they hear that you work at Johnson's and they say, 'Okay, we don't have to do a credit check.' "

Johnson Wax was one of the first American companies to move overseas, and here, too, it expanded as a family, bringing with it profit sharing and a commitment to community service. The 1980s saw spectacular examples of how the company considers all its employees, everywhere in the world, part of its family. In 1984, when the British subsidiary, its first overseas unit, was celebrating its 70th anniversary, Sam Johnson chartered a plane and flew all 480 employees to the United States because he got the sense, after touring the factory in Frimley Green outside of London, that the British hands were feeling a little alienated. The English employees spent three days in Racine and had a weekend in New York before flying home. Well, if you do it for one member of the family, you have to do it for the others, too. So, in 1987, when the Australian company marked its 70th birthday, the 230 employees there were flown to Racine for three days of commingling with U.S. employees—and spent a weekend in Los Angeles before flying home. And in 1990, when Johnson Wax–Canada had its 70th birthday, all 350 employees were brought to Racine and Washington, D.C.

Types of jobs: Production—27 percent; sales—16 percent; office—14 percent; technicians—6 percent; administration, research, information services, and marketing—37 percent.

Main employment centers: Some 2,600 work in Racine, site of the main manufacturing plant (Waxdale), a research and development center, and the administrative building that houses Frank Lloyd Wright's "Great Workroom," a designated national landmark and worth a visit by itself. Another 530 work in field offices scattered throughout the United States, and nine work in a small chemicals plant at Seaford, Delaware. Nearly 10,000 people work overseas. Johnson Wax manufactures in 27 countries, including China, Argentina, and Ukraine. At the South African plant, two-thirds of the supervisors and 10 percent of the managers are black. Sixty-four percent of all South African employees are black.

Headquarters: S.C. Johnson & Son, Inc.
1525 Howe St.
Racine, WI 53403-5011
(414) 631-2000

Kellogg

Kellogg is the world's largest cereal maker. They make more cereals, frozen waffles, toaster pastries, and frozen pies than any other company in America. U.S. employees: 6,378.

★ ★ ★ ★ Pay/Benefits
★ ★ ★ Opportunities
★ ★ ★ ★ Job Security
★ ★ ★ ★ Pride in Work/Company
★ ★ ★ Openness/Fairness
★ ★ ★ ★ Camaraderie/Friendliness

BIGGEST PLUS: Benefits are gr-r-reat!
BIGGEST MINUS: Your future depends on flakes.

Entering the world's largest cereal plant at Battle Creek, Michigan, you see a number posted. When we were there, it said 37, which represented Kellogg's percentage share of the cereal market in the United States at that time. No other plant or office that we know of displays such a figure to employees every day. They might show the stock price or number of units produced or other indices, not market share. But to Kellogg—and to the people who work here—market share is crucial. A one-point swing, for example, means a gain—or loss—of $40 million in annual revenues to Kellogg. And what it comes down to, in the end, is jobs. The Kellogg plant runs three shifts a day, turning out more than 25 different cereals. There would be no need to maintain that furious pace if breakfast eaters started to buy fewer boxes of Kellogg's Corn Flakes, Rice Krispies, Frosted Flakes, Special K, Nutri-Grain, and other Kellogg brands.

Cereal market share is especially important to Kellogg because unlike its two major competitors, General Mills and General Foods, it lives and dies by cereal. It does make some other food products—Mrs. Smith's frozen pies, Eggo waffles, Pop-Tarts—but more than 80 percent of its $6 billion in sales comes from· those cereal boxes. So if you work for Kellogg, you're going to eat your bowl of cereal in the morning and you're going to be hoping that other people do, too.

Kellogg makes cereal in other places—Memphis; Omaha; Lancaster, Pennsylvania; and San Leandro, California—but the ethos of this company comes from Battle Creek, a farmland city of 50,000 in south-central Michigan, 40 miles southwest of the state capital, Lansing. Kellogg was born here, dry cereal was invented here, and more than half of the company's U.S. employees are based here. In this setting, Kellogg, as one of the largest employers in that part of Michigan, carries a fair amount of clout. The company determined in the early 1980s that if Battle Creek was going to rehabilitate itself, it needed to merge with Battle Creek Township so that the more affluent suburbanites could not wall themselves (and their taxes) off from the needs of the increasingly poor and growing black population of the city proper. Kellogg laid down an ultimatum. If the voters didn't approve a merger, the company would look elsewhere for a headquarters site. The merger was approved, and in the mid-1980s Kellogg put up a gleaming new headquarters complex in bedraggled downtown Battle Creek.

On October 18 and 19, 1986, Kellogg held an open house to show off its new home to local citizens, and more than 7,000 people trooped through the red brick building, oohing and ahing over the lavish use of wood, the hanging tapestries and Amish quilts, the on-site fitness center and test kitchens, outdoor patios and the soaring, glass-enclosed atrium that has trees, a fountain, and escalators to all the floors. One of the visitors was Bob Edmond, who works in Battle Creek for General Foods, which also makes cereal here. (GF was founded by C. W. Post, who was a patient at the Seventh-Day Adventist sanitarium where the Kellogg brothers—John Harvey and William Keith—made the first batch of corn flakes in 1894.) Edmond said: "I've been in our corporate headquarters [at White Plains, New York], which was built two or three years ago, and yours is warmer. It fits the Battle Creek agricultural image."

Battle Creek looks like a town that needs help. Aside from Kellogg, it doesn't seem to have a lot of energy. And it's somewhat isolated. Commercial airlines no longer service Battle Creek, so you need to go to Kalamazoo, 20 miles to the west, to catch a plane. William E. LaMothe, who retired in 1991 after 12 years as chief executive officer, told us that's why it was a godsend to have a corporate jet. Otherwise, say on a trip to Europe, where

Kellogg has a big chunk of its business, it would have taken him many hours to wend his way back to Battle Creek on commercial airliners. In its recruitment literature, Kellogg tries to put the best face on its location by pointing out that Detroit and Chicago are "accessible" via two- or three-hour car drives. In 1992 Kellogg was recruiting at 43 colleges, including Stanford, Tuskegee, Babson, Kansas State, and Purdue (no Ivy League schools).

For those who prefer small-town living, Battle Creek—and Kellogg—fill the bill. Employees praise Battle Creek as a good place to bring up children, although one conceded that "if you're looking for excitement, this may not be it." Recruiter Annette Zalner said she has been able to pry people out of New York by talking about "children, family, and the excellent school system." However, if the candidate is single, she talks about Kalamazoo, home of Western Michigan University. Sally Anderson, who joined Kellogg in 1988, returning to work after raising a family, lives in a small town near Lansing and said: "It's nice to be able to work for a Fortune 500 company and drive 45 minutes to get to work without seeing another car for 600 feet. You are more likely to be hit by a deer than a car."

If you come here, you will find a strong family feeling that spans generations. People tend to join Kellogg and stay for life. Many are related to one another. Husband and wife teams make up about 10 percent of the factory work force in Battle Creek. When you pass your 25th anniversary with the company, you are automatically enrolled in the Kellogg 25-Year Club, which in 1991 counted 4,700 members, of whom 3,500 were retirees.

People stay for incredibly long periods. Jim Cox, a project engineer at the Battle Creek plant, retired in 1986 after 47 years of service. Not only that, he went more than 35 years without taking a sick day. His record was topped in 1991 by Marguerite Liva, who retired from the packing line at the Battle Creek plant after 55 years of service. Liva was originally hired at 35 cents an hour and told, "One mistake and you're out." She followed in her mother's footsteps, who retired in 1959 after 39 years of service. Her brother spent 44 years at Kellogg and her sister 18 years. Each year *The Kellogg News* prints the names of retirees, and the list always seems to run to more than 200. It's commonplace to see employees who have put in 30, 35, 40, and 45 years. And it's not just Battle Creek that has longtimers. The other Kellogg plants, including the ones overseas, also have people who have spent decades on the job.

Kellogg has one unique benefit for retirees—a trust fund to help those who encounter financial problems. Since it was set up in 1944, the fund has paid out more than $10 million to retirees in need of help. In 1991 the fund disbursed $1.2 million to 143 retirees. Kellogg also has one of the most generous holiday allowances we have come across—14 paid holidays a year, including Martin Luther King Day, Columbus Day, the day before

Christmas, and two special days that are selected every year (in 1992 they were the Mondays after Easter and July 4).

You can work your way right to the top here. Bill LaMothe started with Kellogg in 1950 as a route salesman in Brooklyn. He was succeeded by Canadian-born Arnold G. Langbo, who also began his Kellogg career as a salesman, starting out in Vancouver in 1956. Both LaMothe and Langbo had international experience, and this area is increasingly seen as the route to the top here. While you don't see many foreign nationals in Battle Creek and while Kellogg looks like the quintessential American company, the company now derives nearly half its revenues outside the United States. And well over half the people who work for Kellogg are outside the U.S. They are trying to convert everyone in the world to dry cereals. In 1992 they were building new plants in Latvia and India.

Kellogg's soft culture doesn't tolerate abrasive types. That's what Horst W. Schroeder discovered in 1989. A German national, Schroeder had joined Kellogg in Bremen in 1970, worked his way up to head of European operations, and then moved to Battle Creek, where a passion for work and a steel-trap mind propelled him up the ranks. At the start of 1989, he became president and heir apparent to LaMothe. But Schroeder rubbed Kellogg people the wrong way. He had an imperious manner that didn't fit in too smoothly here. Employees we met told us how Schroeder would administer tongue-lashings in meetings. In September 1989, while Schroeder was flying on Kellogg's Falcon 50 jet from Ontario to Chicago, LaMothe called the pilot and told him to land the plane in Battle Creek. The Kellogg CEO met the plane, took Schroeder into an airport conference room, and fired him. They're still making jokes about it here, with employees warning colleagues about having any meetings at the airport.

Kellogg is old-fashioned enough to have a harmonious relationship with a labor union. When we visited, plant manager Bob Martin and union business agent Richard Feld seemed to be buddy-buddy. The American Federation of Grain Millers has represented Kellogg workers since 1937, and they do so at every single cereal plant in the United States. Since 1981 the Kellogg cereal boxes have been carrying the union label. Straight-time wages at the Battle Creek plant average $18.29 an hour—and the average worker there earned $43,337 in 1990. The company has had union cooperation in the addition of Building 100 to the Battle Creek complex. This is a high-tech addition that relies heavily on computers to drive the production. Kellogg has trained workers for these jobs. One other reason for the management-labor harmony is that Kellogg has never had a permanent layoff of factory employees.

In 1990, though, Kellogg became the stern father when it laid off 7.5 percent of its white-collar staff (160 people). Since it was the first layoff in the company's history, it was a traumatic event. The blow was cushioned by a vigorous outplacement effort and an exit package that typically gave departees 12 weeks' pay and one week's pay for every year of service. During this period, officers took a 50 percent cut in bonuses—and there were reductions all the way down the line, to 10 percent for clerical people. Someone looking at Kellogg's 1989 financial results may have wondered: why the layoffs? In that year, the company earned $470 million after taxes on sales of $4.6 billion. That beats the pants off most companies. But those earnings were down 2 percent from the previous year, and in Kellogg's universe, that's unacceptable. The company has long been the leader in the food industry in sales and profits *per* employee, and it never wants to jeopardize that position. Kellogg increased its profits to $502 million in 1990 and to $606 million in 1991. In 1991 it increased the cash dividend to stockholders for the 35th consecutive year.

Along with an obsession for making money for shareholders, the biggest one of which is the Kellogg Foundation (it holds 34 percent of the stock), Kellogg is a very security-conscious firm. It stopped running plant tours in 1986 because it found that competitors were sending spies to Battle Creek to take the tour. Visitors to its offices are required to wear badges, and the company maintains a "clean-desk policy," mandating that employees keep confidential information "out of view or face down when not in immediate use." You'd never know the main product here is corn flakes.

Types of jobs: Officials and managers—12 percent; professionals—14 percent; office and clerical—7 percent; production—67 percent.

Main employment centers: Battle Creek, Michigan, houses 2,400 production employees and 1,400 administrative and sales personnel. There are also manufacturing locations in Lancaster (500 employees) and Muncy (200), Pennsylvania; Omaha, Nebraska (750); Memphis, Tennessee (700); and San Leandro, California (400); as well as in London and Rexdale, Ontario, and in 15 countries overseas. 10,000 people are employed outside the United States.

Headquarters: Kellogg Company
P.O. Box 3599
Battle Creek, MI 49016
(616) 961-2000

Knight-Ridder

Knight-Ridder is the third largest newspaper chain in the United States, publishing the *Miami Herald, Detroit Free Press, Philadelphia Inquirer, San Jose Mercury News*, and 25 smaller ones. Employees: 18,000.

★★★★	Pay/Benefits
★★★	Opportunities
★★★	Job Security
★★★★	Pride in Work/Company
★★★	Openness/Fairness
★★★	Camaraderie/Friendliness

BIGGEST PLUS: It's a big chain.
BIGGEST MINUS: But you might wind up at the weakest link.

Disasters often bring out the best in people—and organizations. Hurricane Andrew certainly brought out the best in Knight-Ridder and its flagship newspaper the *Miami Herald*. Residents throughout hard-hit southern Dade County were amazed to see carriers the morning of August 25, 1992, the day after the storm, delivering the *Herald* even though roads were blocked and no services had been restored. And for the crucial weeks after the hurricane, the paper served as Miami's main community bulletin board.

Behind the scenes, the *Herald* and its parent company Knight-Ridder (headquartered in the *Miami Herald* building) went to great lengths for their own employees, many of whose lives were also devastated by the storm. They rented a block of hotel rooms for employees whose homes were destroyed, distributed massive quantities of food and water, offered $5,000 loans secured only by a signature, and distributed dozens of boxes' worth of miscellaneous supplies donated by employees from throughout the Knight-Ridder chain. About 50 *Herald* employees from the finance department were so moved by the company's actions that they wrote: "During these recent events, Knight-Ridder and the *Miami Herald* have displayed an incredible degree of caring that could never be found in an institution which *only* cares for its 'bottom line' . . . We feel privileged to work for a company like OURS."

Much of Knight-Ridder's identity is wrapped up in being one of journalism's class acts. Over the years, Knight-Ridder newspapers have won 59 Pulitzer Prizes, more than any other newspaper chain. And they talk about their role in society in language that reminds you of a high school civics class. In the 1990 annual report to shareholders they say: "We know that ours is not just another business, but one that requires special fidelity to the principles of American democracy. We promise to be faithful to those principles, mindful of our responsibilities under the First Amendment to the Constitution of the United States."

Knight-Ridder's chairman, Jim Batten, put it succinctly when we interviewed him in the corporate office in Miami: "The belief that first-class newspapering is a wonderful business strategy as well as a wonderful public service strategy animates us every bit as much today as it did when Jack Knight was riding high in the 1950s."

Batten was referring to one of the chain's founders, who, along with his brother Jim, inherited the *Akron Beacon Journal* from their father. They began building their chain when they bought the *Miami Herald* in 1937. Other papers followed, including the *Detroit Free Press* and the *Philadelphia Inquirer*. In 1974 they merged with the Ridder newspaper chain, which owned the *San Jose Mercury News* among others. (In Charles Whited's 1988 book *Knight*, about the life of John S. Knight, his newspapers were portrayed as cherishing tough investigative journalism, while the Ridder newspaper operations "prospered more from shrewd business operations than quality journalism.")

The collection has much in common with other newspaper chains like Gannett and Times Mirror, but Knight-Ridder people bristle at the use of the word "chain." When we interviewed a group of Knight-Ridder and *Miami Herald* managers, *Miami Herald* publisher Dave Lawrence, Jr., said: "Jack Knight would turn over in his grave if he knew that word was being used. We always felt that we were somehow different from the 'chains.' "

One of the primary ways Knight-Ridder has distinguished itself from other media companies has been its reputation for a more open, less political work environment. According to David Hunke, advertising director for the *Miami Herald*: "We don't keep secrets very well around here, which is kind of our own joke. It is impossible to keep secrets, largely because of the issue of integrity. You can't imagine somebody at the very top of this corporation telling you something that wasn't true. We trust just about every-body with all information unless they give us some reason to think other-wise." Hunke says this philosophy is very different from his previous employer, where "you determined who needed to know. And it was under-stood that usually not everybody needed to know. It's an inverted pyramid here, I think. As an employee you are trusted with information. Many supervisors don't have a great deal of anxiety about having subordinates who perhaps know more than they do."

Over the years Knight-Ridder has developed a number of methods for sharing information. One is the management coffee break, which is held regularly between top managers and small groups of rank-and-file workers. Cash and debt management director Melanie McNab says that in the cof-fee break meetings "they listen to anything you have to say. In our level, we have complained about supervisors. What the management does after that is get together and discuss it. They try to solve whatever problems you have. They meet with the managers and with you separately to discuss what you think is wrong." She related how the secretaries were dissatisfied with the lack of advancement opportunities. After this concern was aired in coffee break meetings, "they revised the certified professional secretaries program. They advanced someone in-house to train us and do an examina-tion to be certified secretaries."

The sharing of information discourages the office politicking that plagues many media companies. Carol Weber, director of customer satis-faction, explained: "I used to hear stories, before I was hired, about politics in the newsroom where there were some really hard-charging editors, all wanting to make their place in the world, or where people were trying to aggrandize themselves at somebody else's expense. I didn't find it here, however. There is such a team atmosphere at Knight-Ridder. There are so many team approaches to problem-solving that it tends to knock down some of the barriers that promote politicking. I think we still have some barriers to knock down, but we're working on it."

Fabiola Santiago, managing editor of the Spanish edition of the *Miami Herald*, agreed: "There is no need for politics because so much attention is paid to individual growth and challenging people individually, see-ing what each person wants. In a big corporation, you would think that is lost. That is often lost in other big newspapers. Here, we operate a major newspaper almost the same way that other people run a small paper."

At the *Miami Herald*, people talk about it being like a "family." Eleanor Tubbs, a long-term clerk in the advertising department, described part of what working at the *Herald* is like for her: "I bake all the cakes for the birthdays and supply candy for everybody [in my department]. Whenever it is anybody's birthday we always have a cake and a gift and take time out to sing 'Happy Birthday.' " Other employees told us that this practice goes on in other departments, "even on deadline days."

Former corporate relations director Jean Thompson said she worked at the *Miami Herald* for 10 years before leaving. But she decided to come back and accept a job with Knight-Ridder, which is housed in the same building, for 16 more years: "I would say that it is the people who drew me back. I had grown so close to people at the *Herald* when I worked there. It was not only the benefits, but the people themselves. At the *Herald* we had bowling, softball, picnics, and everything you could think of because everybody considers it a family."

Not all the Knight-Ridder papers have the same kind of family environment. In fact, a few have had difficult labor relations over the years. For instance, there were six strikes between 1978 and 1988 at the *Philadelphia Inquirer* and its sister publication, the *Philadelphia Daily News.*

Vice-president of operations Jay Harris said: "I think the local companies are different, and they should be. They are managed locally and they are a reflection of and part of, at best a distinction of, their community. The *American News* in Aberdeen [South Dakota] probably should not be like the *Boca Raton News.* The *Miami Herald* does and probably should have a culture that is different from the *Mercury* in San Jose. It seems to me that what binds them together is a set of values which are distinctly Knight-Ridder values. The sense of values is related to our role and responsibility in each community."

Knight-Ridder has long been an industry leader in training. The Knight-Ridder Institute for Training (KRIT), founded in 1968, is the only in-house newspaper training school in the United States that is certified for college course credit. Approximately 750 employees a year from various Knight-Ridder publications come to Miami for seminars ranging from new newspaper production techniques to team development to newsroom management.

Knight-Ridder has also tried to get more women and minorities into executive positions. They lag behind Gannett in this area but are much better than most American firms. Of the 24 corporate officers, four are women and four are minority.

One of the minority officers is vice-president and controller Tally Liu. He said, "I was the first Asian or minority CFO [chief financial officer] in all of the newspaper industry. There are 1,600 to 1,700 newspapers. Twelve years later, I am still the only one."

Knight-Ridder is not immune to the challenges facing other newspaper companies. *The Wall Street Journal* put the problem well in a 1990 article about Knight-Ridder: "In pre-video 1950, with many adults reading two papers, the household penetration of newspapers was 150 percent. By 1980, only seven out of ten adults were reading newspapers, forcing many publications to close or join with local rivals to survive. Today, only six out of ten adults read a daily paper."

Knight-Ridder has responded by launching several electronic information services and hopes to have nearly a quarter of their sales from business information services by the mid-1990s. Meanwhile, they have had to confront the problem of shrinking revenues in newspapers, particularly during the recession of the early 1990s. On this score, Knight-Ridder seems genuinely committed to providing job security.

According to Eustace Clarke, who loads rolls of newsprint onto the presses: "Firing and laying off are dirty words for the *Herald*. They always look for another place to put you. They will put you somewhere and move you around. It is really hard to be fired."

They did, however, have limited layoffs at the *Miami Herald* in January 1991. Only a handful actually left the company, as most of the people whose positions were eliminated found other jobs at the paper. The company conducted outplacement services for those who did leave.

The same kind of process occurred throughout Knight-Ridder. Customer satisfaction director Carol Weber said, "I think one reason cutbacks have been less traumatic for us than for a lot of other companies is the way we go about it. First of all, being open and honest with people in letting them know what is coming and why makes it easier. Number two, those cuts start at the top. When our cost-cutting and belt-tightening started, it started right up here on the sixth floor with all officers' salaries being frozen for 18 months and anybody under officers having salaries frozen for 15 months. We went through and cut every budget up here. We communicated all of this. We had management coffee break meetings up here. Dave Lawrence had a series of meetings down at the *Herald*. At our other papers, the publishers did the same things so that people would understand and know that we were all in the same boat. This way folks wouldn't be looking around saying, 'Look what is being done to me while the fat cats are still up there getting everything that is coming to them.' That speaks to our values. Although we are not perfect, I have never seen a place that tried as hard to be caring about its employees and the effect the changes would have on them."

Types of jobs: Production—26 percent; administration—23 percent; news and editorial—21 percent; circulation—19 percent; advertising—11 percent.

Main employment centers: Knight-Ridder has 4,800 employees in Detroit; 3,000 in Philadelphia; 2,900 in Miami; 2,000 in San Jose, California; 1,100 in Charlotte, North Carolina; 1,000 in New York City; 1,000 in St. Paul, Minnesota; 900 in Columbia, South Carolina; 700 in Long Beach, California; and 600 in Akron, Ohio.

Headquarters: Knight-Ridder, Inc.
One Herald Plaza
Miami, FL 33123
(305) 376-3800

Lands' End

Lands' End sells high-quality clothing, sheets, towels, and soft luggage through mail-order catalogs. U.S. employees: 2,400 plus as many as 4,150 temporary.

★★★ Pay/Benefits
★★★ Opportunities
★★★ Job Security
★★★★ Pride in Work/Company
★★★ Openness/Fairness
★★★★★ Camaraderie/Friendliness
BIGGEST PLUS: Warm hearts.
BIGGEST MINUS: Cold winters.

Some people at Lands' End milk cows before coming in to work. Betty Bussan is one. She and her husband have a dairy farm near Dodgeville, Wisconsin (population 3,458), and she came to work here in 1985 to make some extra money. She was already working at another part-time job when she began answering phones at Lands' End, but she said the benefits were so good here that she quit her other job. She is now a training specialist. Phyllis Toay, who hems pants, also lives on a dairy farm but doesn't milk cows anymore because of a ruptured disk caused by a steer kicking her. Margaret Dunbar, manager of the customer service department at Lands' End, also lives on a farm.

Dunbar was one of the first people hired by Gary Comer when he moved his mail-order catalog business here from Chicago in 1978. For the next dozen years Lands' End continued to keep its advertising and marketing staffs (the people who write and design its catalogs) in Chicago, but in 1990 they, too, made the 150-mile trek to Dodgeville. It's a major step to move from a big city to the boondocks, but two-thirds of the 90 people employed in Chicago opted to stay with Lands' End. Because of the influx of people, Dodgeville has had to upgrade its infrastructure—now it has two traffic lights instead of one.

Lands' End became one of the major catalog sellers of high-quality, traditional clothing (turtlenecks, dress shirts, twill trousers, sweaters, and the like) during the 1980s on the strengths of careful design, friendly and prompt service, and an absolute, iron-clad guarantee to refund the money spent on any item that the customer found wanting, for whatever reason.

A lot of that friendly service derived from folksy, homespun handling by the Wisconsin operators who answer the 800-number calls that pour into Lands' End day and night (the phone lines are open 24 hours a day). While we were there, we listened to an operator dealing with customer calls and were amazed at the patience, good humor, and empathy with which these calls were handled. Some customers just want to talk or tell you their problems, and if you call Lands' End, you can do that with an operator who is not going to cut you off abruptly. Mary Garvey, who started as an operator in 1982, recalls talking to a Montana customer holed up by a raging snowstorm who called, talked at length, and ended up ordering 14 shirts for her husband. "She had already told me that they couldn't get anywhere, do anything, and so, you know, she was just chatting because the weather was bad. I was sure she'd send all those shirts back."

Operators, who receive 80 hours of training before getting on the phones, sign on here for $5.50 an hour. They're not on commission. The average hourly wage at Lands' End is between $7.50 and $8.00 an hour. The phones are answered in three places—at Dodgeville; Cross Plains, a small town 30 miles away, near Madison; and Reedsburg, which is 50 miles to the north in a popular Wisconsin resort area known as The Dells.

Of course, one downside of this location is an absence of diversity. Lands' End looks like an all-white enclave. Nilda Thym, one of the managers we met, whose family runs one of the two main restaurants in Dodgeville, told us: "I like raising my two children in a small community where they know everybody and everybody knows them. But at the same time I know they're missing out in talking and playing with children of different ethnic groups. So we try to do different things to help them learn to understand people with different backgrounds. We are the awkward ones because my children speak Spanish. And they don't want to do it now because they think their friends are going to call them geeks."

Except for soft luggage, which it manufactures in plants at West Union and Elkader, Iowa, Lands' End, like other catalog sellers, doesn't make anything. All the product comes from outside suppliers, more than 350 of them, but Lands' End people play active roles in the design, development, and testing of all the items in the catalog. Marketing, packing, and shipping are all done out of Dodgeville. Lands' End has a sophisticated distribution center that prides itself on shipping product within 24 hours of a customer's order. The company put more than 100 million catalogs into the mail during 1991. Each catalog features a story about a Lands' End employee. Past catalogs have included photos of a customer service representative with one of her dairy cows and a quality assurance employee dressed in the Civil War uniform he wears for battle reenactments.

Eighty-five percent of the telephone operators are women, and the work is highly seasonal, with the pre-Christmas weeks being the peak time. Of the 6,600 people who worked for Lands' End during 1991, only 1,400 were full-timers. Another 1,000 were regular part-timers, and another 4,200 were temporary employees.

Working in a mail-order house can be drudgery, but Lands' End has succeeded in creating a feeling of teamwork and family. Movement and flexibility are encouraged here. Instead of posting jobs that are open, it uses a program called job enrollment that enables people to get training in an area other than their own even before there's an opening. Betty Bussan explained how it works: "You can sign up for any other department. If you have an interest in seeing what packing's all about, then you can fill out a job enrollment, and after a certain period of time, you get to go over there for maybe a two- or four-week period. And if it works out for you, and if it works out for the department, then you may transfer there." Bussan got her job with the training department through job enrollment. In 1989, of 618 nonsalaried positions that were filled, 617 were taken by job enrollees.

Connie Hampton, an ex-farmer, started here in 1987. "I started out as a packer," she said. "Then I trained new employees. Then I went as a group assistant, helping out with the work flow during our busy times. Then I was very fortunate to become a lead in the returns department. And I got offered the lead job down in packing. The nice thing is, you can move around to different departments." Now Hampton leads the hemming department.

There's a camaraderie here based on the shared background as farm folks. From time to time, people bring in home-baked cakes and vegetables grown on their farms. And when a snowstorm hits, they really pull together. A four-wheel-drive truck will pick people up at certain points, but sometimes employees are snowed in and can't leave the office—and they talk about those experiences as some of the best they've had here.

Richard Anderson, who succeeded Comer as CEO in 1989, summed up the Lands' End philosophy this way: "I think the first principle of the company, the foundation, is to create an environment for our people in which they are all treated as we would like ourselves treated. So it is not really a company where you'll see too many people stand on titles or things like that. People talk to each other. People will say, 'Hi, Dick,' to me. I can't remember all their names anymore, there are so many of them. We felt that the better they felt, the better the benefit systems, the better they were taken care of, the better we were all going to prosper. And we felt that if our people felt good, this would come out over the phone. It's kind of simple but that's about the truth of it."

As nice as the Wisconsin farmers are, they didn't have the management expertise Lands' End needed when sales quadrupled between 1984 and 1991. So while the foot soldiers were hired locally, the generals were imported. William T. End came from the Maine catalog operator, L. L. Bean, in January 1991, and a year later he became president and chief operating officer, putting him in line to succeed the 62-year-old Anderson as CEO. Other top executives have come from such firms as Burdine's, Sears, Jos. A. Bank Clothiers, The Limited, Maas Brothers/Jordan Marsh, Strawbridge & Clothier, and Young & Rubicam (the alma mater of Gary Comer).

These executives don't milk cows before coming to work. In fact, most of them don't live in or near Dodgeville. They commute from the more sophisticated city of Madison 35 miles away. Madison is the state capital and home of the University of Wisconsin. Once they do move to Wisconsin, they become converts. Anita Iodice, product manager for linens and sheets, told us: "I worked for a lot of retail companies, like Federated and Associated Dry Goods. And so I'm used to environments where they really use people and then just kind of throw them out. At Lands' End, I look around and see people doing jobs that they thoroughly enjoy doing. And if by some chance they get into a situation where it doesn't work for them, we as a company are committed to the people that work for us and we find a way to make it right for that person."

As the company became bigger, Comer and Anderson made a greater effort to keep in touch with employees by meeting regularly with them. Anderson now lunches with about seven lower-level people every other week. "These are the packers, the inseamers, the monogrammers, the salespeople, the service people," he explained. "Not bosses, not leads, not supervisors, but the people on the line. I hold it in the founders' room, which is a room that Gary and I built for ourselves to have special lunches with people. But the reason for those lunches was to say, 'Look, we're probably doing an excellent job with 95 percent of our customers, but is it possible that with 5 percent of them, there's something we're not doing? You guys are out there putting the stuff in the boxes every day. You sense things going on.' That kind of a dialogue is an example of what we try to do so that people feel free at all times to tell us what's bothering them."

Gary Comer, a copywriter and Olympic-class ocean sailor, started Lands' End in 1963 to sell equipment for sailboats. The misplaced apostrophe in the name—it should be Land's End—resulted from a typo in the first mailing piece; Comer said he couldn't afford to rerun the job and so the name stuck. Later he began including a small clothing section in the catalog, and the response was so good that by 1977 he stopped selling winches, barometers, and sailbags to concentrate on garments. In 1986 Lands' End sold stock to the public, and its shares now trade on the New York Stock Exchange. Comer, in early 1992, still owned 56 percent of the shares, a stake with a market value of $350 million. Anderson held nearly 5 percent of the shares. Top executives—but not rank-and-file employees—are awarded stock options. All employees participate in a profit-sharing plan whose payout is geared to the performance of the company. The maximum payout, 16 percent of pay, happens when Lands' End earns 16 percent on sales—a level never yet reached.

Lands' End has a spectacular activity center, thanks to Gary Comer's generosity. The 80,000-square-foot center includes a 25-meter swimming pool, a whirlpool, a gymnasium, an exercise equipment room, a darkroom for nonathletic photographers, a glass-walled indoor track, and an outdoor area for picnics, walking trails, and tennis courts. A questionnaire was sent to employees soliciting their opinions on what the center should have. A pool was not in the original plans but was quickly added when it came up high on the employee wish lists. The cost of the center, about $9 million, was borne entirely by Comer as a gift to employees. On one end of the pool the names of 1,300 employees are hand-lettered on tiles, with the inscription reading: "These are the names of the people whose daily work and good spirit at Lands' End have made this building possible. It is dedicated to them and to their continued good health."

Types of jobs: Well over half the people who work for Lands' End are telephone operators.

Main employment centers: Of the 2,400 full-timers, 85 percent work in Dodgeville; telephone operators answer the 800 number in Dodgeville and two other Wisconsin towns, Cross Plains and Reedsburg; 425 work in 13 outlet stores in Wisconsin, Illinois, and Iowa; 140 assemble soft luggage in West Union and Elkader, Iowa.

Headquarters: Lands' End
Dodgeville, WI 53595
(608) 935-9341

Lincoln Electric

LINCOLN ELECTRIC

Lincoln is the world's largest manufacturer of arc welding products. They also make industrial motors. U.S. employees: 2,668.

★ ★ ★ ★   Pay/Benefits
★ ★ ★   Opportunities
★ ★ ★ ★ ★   Job Security
★ ★ ★ ★   Pride in Work/Company
★ ★ ★ ★ ★   Openness/Fairness
★ ★ ★   Camaraderie/Friendliness

BIGGEST PLUS: Electrifying bonuses.
BIGGEST MINUS: No sick pay.

The first Friday of December is the biggest day of the year at Lincoln Electric. The workers crowd into the company's spartan cafeteria, where their annual bonus checks are distributed. These checks can be whoppers, as the annual bonus typically equals a worker's entire income for the year. A production worker who earns $20,000 a year may well receive a bonus of $20,000. (The actual *average* in 1990 was $21,000.)

Joe Sirko has worked on Lincoln's production lines since 1951. He explained what it's like when they hand out the bonus checks: "It's like a dream to make good money all year and then get it all again in one lump at the end of the year. You could spend all of your paycheck if you want, and still you get money at the end. I've been totally happy for 40 years."

Lincoln's factory, on the east side of Cleveland, sits just off a major interstate highway (I-90) from where you can see dozens of shuttered mills and plants, reminders of why the region is known as the Rust Belt. By contrast, Lincoln is alive and well. The parking lot was packed the day we visited. The factory itself is huge—1.7 million square feet (36 acres, one-half mile long) under one roof. The administrative and marketing offices are located in a two-story, windowless building located in the center of the plant facility. Both the offices and the plant are reached by walking through a long tunnel. The company motto is etched in large stainless-steel letters across the entrance to the tunnel: "THE ACTUAL IS LIMITED, THE POSSIBLE IS IMMENSE."

We went directly to the office of chairman and CEO George Willis, only the fifth man to lead the company in Lincoln's nearly 100-year history. Willis's office, like others in the firm's cramped "executive suite," defines the notion of austerity. No potted plants, original artwork, or fancy electronic gadgets here. A big globe of the world was the only item that could pass for decoration.

A chemical engineer, Willis first learned of the company when he heard James Lincoln speak at the Harvard Business School in the 1940s. Lincoln was then running the company founded in 1895 by his older brother John, who had developed the company's main product, the electric arc welding machine. Today, Lincoln makes more than half of all electric arc welding machines (priced from $150 to $14,000) in the United States. They are used by industrial firms for soldering. While John Lincoln may have been a technical genius, his brother James was a managerial genius who preached an unusual gospel for his era combining beliefs in "People, Christian Ethics, Principles, Simplicity, Competition, and The Customer."

Intrigued by Lincoln's managerial concepts, Willis joined the company in 1947 after getting his M.B.A. From talking with him, you get the idea that little has changed in the basic policies since that time. Now in his 70s, Willis looks trim and athletic. He was once an Olympic fencing champion and outfenced college-age men until he gave up the sport a few years ago.

Willis talked proudly of how Lincoln's distinctive system helps generate an average of 200 to 300 suggestions per month, about 50 of which are implemented: "We probably have more innovative ideas coming from our people than any other company that I know of. I think it's because we reward people for what they contribute. By reward, I mean that they get the recognition that they have done the job in a meaningful way. The reward will also come in increased responsibility or in a change of job. Finally, the reward will come at the end of the year with the bonuses. This all adds to where over the years people have built up a basic trust that management is going to be fair in dividing the profit of the company among those who have produced it." (We saw Willis on our visit to Lincoln in 1991. In mid-1992 he retired after 45 years with the company. His successor is another Harvard M.B.A., Donald Hastings.)

Because of the sums involved, everyone pays a lot of attention to how the annual bonus is calculated. Briefly, workers are rated in four areas: production; cooperation and ideas; supervision required; and quality. Except for the quality area, employees compete directly with others in their work groups. No worker gets a higher bonus without someone else in the group getting a lower one. Workers lose points for virtually any absence, including job-related accidents or illness. One of the few exceptions is a week off without penalty for a death in the family.

Don't come to work for Lincoln if you're looking for special benefits like child care, flextime, or tuition reimbursement. You get holidays with unpaid time off, vacations must be taken during the plant shutdowns in August and December, and health-care benefits premiums are deducted from the annual bonus.

But Lincoln may have the best retirement plan in the land. An employee like Sirko, who has worked here for 40 years, receives an annuity enabling him to retire at *full pay*. And one of the best features of the plan is that you don't have to retire to get it. If you continue to work beyond age 65, as Sirko and others do, you get your regular pay plus bonus *and* the "pension." It's like having your cake and eating it too.

People come to Lincoln to work and work hard. According to Richard Sabo, the CEO's assistant: "It's nice to have fun on the job, and I have a very, very enjoyable job. But you can earn a very, very good income and then have fun off the job. That is how many of our employees see it."

Yet, there is little evidence that people burn out at Lincoln from overwork. We talked about this issue with factory worker Kathleen Hoenigman (about 2.5 percent of Lincoln's work force is female), who has been here since 1977. She said: "You can't burn yourself out. That's the way you lose out. If you come in here and really work too hard all day, you're not pacing yourself. If they don't know how to pace themselves, they will get hurt, and those are the people who end up with sore backs."

Our conversations with other Lincoln workers revealed little concern with overwork despite the competitive, no-nonsense environment. This was confirmed during our tour of the plant. Lincoln's workers give the impression of being in control of their destinies. They seem to understand exactly where they stand, how their effort impacts their pay and their careers. And, partly because they all own stock in the company (30 percent is owned by employees, most of the rest by Lincoln family members), they also give the impression of working for themselves.

Lincoln's workers also know that they aren't going to work themselves out of a job. The company has a no-layoff policy. Every year since 1952, the company has guaranteed that anyone who has worked here more than three years (previously two years) will be given at least 30 hours of work a week. In return, the workers have to agree to be shifted to whatever job is needed, even if it means working at a lower piecework rate or hourly wage.

Workers find this guarantee reassuring. According to factory worker Ken Litman: "It's a tough world. Every day you read and hear about layoffs at some other company. I've been here 26 years. When I worked for Fisher

Body, I got laid off. It was the same over at Chevrolet. They call you back, and you get laid off again. That's the difference between working here and those places. The last 26 years I could be thankful that my paycheck was coming in."

So Lincoln's competitive, incentive system has not fostered a cutthroat, dog-eat-dog environment, but rather one where people seem to be working harmoniously. According to some studies, Lincoln's workers are three times more productive than workers at comparable plants. Interestingly, the idea for the bonus system came from the employees themselves. They requested a pay raise in 1933, but the Depression made it impossible for the company to give them one. So the workers suggested that if they could help make Lincoln Electric more profitable, couldn't the company share the proceeds with them? Management agreed and implemented the incentive system still in effect.

Lincoln also offers employees a variety of ways to complain about unfair treatment. The central vehicle is the advisory board, first established in 1914. Composed of 27 representatives elected by fellow workers, the advisory board meets twice a month with the CEO and the president. From all accounts, nothing is too small to be discussed. Production worker Sirko explained: "You tell them everything you want to tell them. It's just like if you had a union, but you tell it to top management, the chairman and the president. They listen to everything and they check it out until it's solved, whatever it is. No matter what the problem is, you go to the representative in your department [who is elected every year]. The minutes are published, and they post it on the board. The minutes from the last meeting are on the board now."

Lincoln's supervisors also like the advisory board. Ted Sutyak, who has been here since 1956, said that he thinks the board "keeps it like a family, not like a union environment." Supervisor Ed Birch agreed, saying that it means there is always an "ongoing dialogue" within the company about issues of concern.

Since Birch joined the company in 1965, he recently passed the 25-year mark with Lincoln. He received a Rolex watch and saw his name inscribed on a bronze plaque near the entrance to the plant and offices as one of some 1,101 workers who belong to the Quarter Century Club. Their names are removed when they leave the company unless they reach the 50-year mark, when their names are permanently inscribed. Thirty employees have achieved that distinction. Turnover is negligible, hovering around 3 percent a year, mostly through retirements.

The plaque makes no distinction between managers and nonmanagers, typical of a company that resists executive perks. During our visit we were accompanied by Richard Sabo, a former high school football coach and guidance counselor who joined Lincoln in 1965 after he learned that several of his former players were making more money working here than he was. Sabo started at the bottom and rose to become special assistant to the CEO. When he took us to the cafeteria, he pointed to two tables in the middle of the room. "That's our executive dining room," he exclaimed.

Types of jobs: Production—40 percent; office and sales—30 percent; other —30 percent.

Main employment centers: 2,450 employees work in Cleveland, Ohio. The other 250 work in sales offices and distribution centers throughout the United States.

Headquarters: Lincoln Electric Company
22801 St. Claire Ave.
Cleveland, OH 44117
(216) 481-8100

Los Angeles Dodgers

The Los Angeles Dodgers own one professional major-league baseball club and nine minor-league teams. U.S. employees: 1,100.

★ ★ ★ ★ ★   Pay/Benefits
★ ★ ★   Opportunities
★ ★ ★   Job Security
★ ★ ★ ★   Pride in Work/Company
★ ★ ★   Openness/Fairness
★ ★ ★ ★   Camaraderie/Friendliness

BIGGEST PLUS: Treats employees like all-stars.
BIGGEST MINUS: Some seasons are very long.

In 1988, when the Los Angeles Dodgers won the National League pennant and squared off against the Oakland A's in the World Series, the nonuniformed employees of the Dodgers flew to Oakland to see the away games, courtesy of club owner Peter O'Malley. And when the Dodgers beat the A's to win the series, O'Malley decided to treat all the front-office employees *and* their spouses (no live-ins) to a five-day vacation in Rome. Everything— airfare, hotel, sight-seeing tours—was on the house, and O'Malley threw in 300,000 lire (about $215) of spending money for each family.

Juanita Landry, who had just joined the office staff as a secretary that year, was still shaking her head over this largesse three years later. "I couldn't believe it," she said to us. "I thought, 'Wow, did I die and go to heaven or what?' It was really great, and I'm still enjoying it. It's a real fun place to work. Nice people to work with, great organization."

Cynics might say that the Dodgers, the winningest team in the National League (they have won 21 pennants and six world championships), could easily afford to reward its employees in this manner. But other clubs don't do it, even when they finish on top. And this was not a onetime gesture. Dodger employees went on company-sponsored trips to Hawaii in 1983, Vero Beach, Florida (the team's spring training site), in 1984, and St. Louis in 1985 to watch the Dodgers play—and lose to—the St. Louis Cardinals three times in a row in the league championship series.

Brooklynites will never forgive the team for leaving New York in 1958 to become the Los Angeles Dodgers (when they entered the National League in 1890, they were called the Trolley Dodgers because of the maze of streetcar tracks in the borough of Brooklyn). But it was more than a ball club that moved. More than half the employees, including ticket takers, secretaries, and grounds crew, made the move, and the family feeling that was in place in Brooklyn continued in Los Angeles. Much of that feeling derives from a continuity of family ownership. The O'Malley family has owned the Dodgers since 1951. Peter O'Malley's father, Walter, headed the club for 20 years. And Peter took over as president in 1970. It's the oldest family-owned and -operated team in baseball. O'Malley is unique among baseball owners in another important respect: the only business he has is baseball— and he pays attention to it. He's in his office every day, usually before most employees arrive, and he leaves late.

O'Malley rarely goes down on the field but he is a visible leader inside the company. He meets with employees quarterly, always leaving time for questions. Manager Tommy Lasorda said to us: "Walk up on the fifth floor where the offices are, his door is always open. If you want to see him, you can just walk right in there and he'll motion for you to come in. I don't think you see that in a lot of corporations. I don't think you can walk up to the president of General Motors and see him; you'd have to make 15 phone calls. He treats everybody with the same feeling, the same appreciation, the same love. I don't care what your position is in this organization, Peter O'Malley is always there if you have any problems."

Lasorda is not known for understatement, but in this case it was not difficult to find corroboration for the uniqueness of the Los Angeles Dodgers. Talks with employees from all ranks—ball players, ushers, secretaries, management—bore out what he was saying. Financial vice-president Bob Graziano, who used to audit the club's books when he was at the Arthur Young accounting firm, was asked if there was any difference between the Dodgers and other baseball teams. He replied: "Seems like the only thing that's similar is the fact that we play baseball and sell hot dogs." Mailroom clerk George Barajas said: "They treat you like a human being here, not like a number." And catcher Gary Carter, a Los Angeles native who played for the New York Mets, Montreal Expos, and San Francisco Giants before coming to the Dodgers in 1991, said: "Some ball clubs are a little bit more family-oriented than others. And some are more first-class in the way they take care of families and things like that. I've been in all these organizations and I'd have to rate the Dodgers right up there at the top because of the way they take care of family."

The Dodgers were the first major-league team to have a profit-sharing plan for employees—it began in 1961. They have a human resources director (not a common title among ball clubs), Irene Tanji, who started as a secretary in 1959. She told us that when the Dodgers were recently considering the addition of an employee assistance program, she checked with some other teams, and most of them didn't know what she was talking about. The Dodgers started an EAP program, which provides confidential counseling for personal problems, in 1991. The Dodgers pay 100 percent of the health insurance premium for employees—and for their dependents as well. Full-time employees receive four tickets for every game; part-timers get two tickets.

The Dodgers set great store on tradition. In 1990, when they celebrated their 100th anniversary, they dressed all their ushers, already known as the best-dressed ushers in baseball (with their blue jackets, neckties, and straw hats), in uniforms that were replicas of the ones worn in 1890—and they got to keep these uniforms after the season was over. One of the latest traditions, introduced by Peter O'Malley in the 1980s, is the Häagen-Dazs cart. Whenever the Dodgers are in first place and increase their lead over the second-place team, a cart of Häagen-Dazs ice cream is wheeled out the next afternoon for the office staff to scoop. The women who work there say: "When we gain, we gain." The cart was nowhere to be seen in 1992 when the Dodgers, stuck in last place, were having their worst season since 1905.

Going to visit a ball club, you might expect to find a hang-loose atmosphere. That's not the Los Angeles Dodgers. This is a buttoned-up place where people dress in business attire and observe regular office hours. It was not until 1991 that they introduced a casual day—you can now wear jeans on Fridays. Communications vice-president Tommy Hawkins, who was a broadcaster and NBA basketball player before joining the Dodgers in 1987, said to us: "From a player standpoint—and I was a player representative and union negotiator with the Lakers—this is the most structured and most corporate of any sports franchise that I have ever seen. It's a sport and it's also a business. I like to say to my people that there are two games going on, and I think you can see this as we sit here today: there's a game being played on the field and there's a game that is played concurrently right here in the front office."

Hawkins was alluding to the physical layout of the Dodger offices on the club level of Dodger Stadium, between the loge boxes and reserved seats. Hawkins and other managers have offices with windows that look out onto the field. When the curtains are drawn, you are in an office. When they are opened—and we were there for a day game—the whole ball field is spread out before you. Some support staffers also have views that face the field. One of the perks of working here is the ambience of one of the most beautiful stadiums in the major leagues. The Dodgers own it and they keep it spotless. There are no columns to obstruct views. Seats are color-coded to correspond to terraced parking levels. It's a pristine park: the Dodgers leave $1 million a year on the table to keep the park billboard-free. They sell 27,000 season tickets. They could sell more but O'Malley refuses because he does not want to squeeze out the average fan. During the 1985 season, a baseball fanatic, Bob Wood, traveled to every park in the major leagues and then did a book, *Dodger Dogs to Fenway Franks*, that rated each one. Dodger Stadium finished in first place, ranking low only (and rightfully) in food service. "If King Arthur owned a baseball team, this is where they'd have played," decided Wood.

The loyalty of the staff is reflected in tenure. Tommy Lasorda joined the Dodger organization in 1949 and became manager in 1976. He succeeded Walter Alston, who had been the skipper for 23 years. (Most club owners, confronted with the dismal record of the Dodgers in 1992, would have fired the manager in midseason, but the Dodgers don't operate that way.) Since 1950 the Dodgers have had only three minor-league directors, three scouting directors, and three player personnel directors. Four of the current vice-presidents rose through the office ranks and have been with the club from 23 to 31 seasons. There's even long tenure in the broadcasting booth. Vin Scully, who began broadcasting for Brooklyn in 1950, was still the voice of the Dodgers in 1992. With him in the booth were Ross Porter, starting his 16th year, ex-Dodger pitching star Don Drysdale, beginning his fifth year, and Jaime Jarrin, doing the Spanish-language broadcast for the 19th year.

This longevity in the office contrasts sharply with what has happened on the field since the advent of the free-agent system, enabling players to move from team to team. Of the 25 players who were on the roster when we interviewed here in 1983 just before a game with the Montreal Expos, only one—iron-man catcher Mike Scioscia—was still with the team when we reinterviewed in 1991 just before a game with the San Diego Padres. The Dodger player payroll going into 1992 was the highest in the majors, $41 million, an average of $1.6 million per player. But the amazing part of this story is that the Dodgers, more than most clubs, have been able to maintain a mystique that players buy into, even if they are only going to be there a short while.

Some of it, to be sure, is Lasorda hype. He's always talking about the Dodgers being the greatest organization in the world, and he tries to instill that feeling in his troops. The day we were there, he yelled at his players to tell us how it is. Darryl Strawberry, a recent import from the New York Mets, responded dutifully: "We bleed Dodger blue. We eat it, we sleep it, we drink it, we think Dodger blue. It couldn't be no better. Best team I ever played for." And Brett Butler, a recent recruit from the San Francisco Giants, said: "Being an opposing player and watching Tommy the way he's been, I always thought that was an act. It's not. It's the one thing that surprised me. It is absolute, honest, to the core, L.A. Dodgers. When you come over here, something about being on this team, just the pride of wearing this uniform, something about it changes you, and you say, 'I just want to be part of it.'"

No one can say that the Dodgers don't work at maintaining that pride. For example, they keep track of every person who has ever played for the Dodgers, and the media guide they issue to reporters covering the team lists in alphabetical order every man who has ever worn a Dodger uniform —all 1,200 of them. In 1983 they launched a quarterly publication, *Alumni News*, that they send to every alumnus of the team who has retired from the game. *Alumni News* is filled with nostalgia and news about retirees. In 1990 they asked some of the alumni to say something about the 100th anniversary. Tony Cuccinello, one of the star infielders of the 1930s, said: "The Dodgers will live forever, whether they are the Brooklyn Dodgers, Los Angeles Dodgers, or whatever Dodgers." And Don Newcome, the big right-handed pitcher who now works for the Dodgers in community relations, along with Roy Campanella, said: "Greatest organization in baseball for all these years and still are."

One comment that stuck with us came from a security guard at Dodger Stadium, Tony Frumento, a former police officer who runs an Italian food market that his father had. He said: "You know, being in business for myself and then coming to work here part-time has given me a different outlook. I mean, at my own place I'm the owner or the boss or whatever. And what I have learned here, from how management works, has really helped me in my business, because I try to treat my employees like I'm being treated here, trying to show some kind of personal feeling towards them. It's meant a lot to me. To give you an example, I can remember

Walter O'Malley coming in one day and it was in the beginning of the season and it was kind of cold. And he walked up to me and says, 'Tony, come here a minute.' And I said, 'Yes, Walt?' And he says, 'I want you to go inside and get a jacket because I don't want you to catch cold.' "

Types of jobs: Stadium operations (ushers, ticket takers, groundskeepers) —550; players (including minor leagues)—250; Los Angeles office staff— 100 (145 during season); managers, coaches, trainers, scouts, clubhouse attendants, batboys—155.

Main employment centers: Los Angeles and Vero Beach, Florida (Dodgertown). Minor-league clubs are in Albuquerque, New Mexico; San Antonio, Texas; Bakersfield, California; Yakima, Washington; Great Falls, Montana; Vero Beach and Kissimmee, Florida; and Santo Domingo and Moca in the Dominican Republic.

Headquarters: Los Angeles Dodgers
1000 Elysian Park Ave.
Los Angeles, CA 90012-1199
(213) 224-1500

MOST BEAUTIFUL CORPORATE HEADQUARTERS

Cummins Engine
John Deere
Erie Insurance
SC Johnson Wax
Los Angeles Dodgers
Merck
Northwestern Mutual Life
Reader's Digest
Weyerhaeuser

Lotus Development

🔲 Lotus

Lotus Development, home of the 1-2-3 spreadsheet program, is a major developer of computer software. U.S. employees: 2,780.

★★★★ Pay/Benefits
★★★ Opportunities
★★★ Job Security
★★★★ Pride in Work/Company
★★★ Openness/Fairness
★★★★ Camaraderie/Friendliness

BIGGEST PLUS: They're enlightened.
BIGGEST MINUS: You may not make out as well as the CEO.

It's not every company that has as one of its operating principles the dictum "Have fun." Lotus Development, a major developer of computer software, does. "Have fun" is one of 11 principles designated as "guidelines for interaction between all employees."

The enigmatic Jim Manzi, who succeeded founder Mitch Kapor as chief executive of Lotus in 1986, told us that when he interviews candidates for jobs here, he looks for people who can "laugh aloud. People who like to muffle their laughter, that says something about them. This is a big test of mine." One manager told us: "No manager sits around in this company with a stone face. How you laugh is how you manage." And another chimed in: "I think what you notice here from the time you start is a lot of laughter. There are days when I think to myself, 'Did I stop laughing today?' "

Just in case you need something funny to relieve a dreary day, you can dive into the joke data base lodged in Notes, the Lotus interactive computer network. That's not all you'll find on Notes. It has hundreds of data bases, including one for parents. One employee told us that when her baby was having teething problems, she tapped into it and asked for help. Back came 100 responses. Other Loti—this is what Lotus people call themselves —have used Notes to rent apartments, sell cars, find a recipe for an exotic dish, or discuss *Star Trek*. Notes, a software package that enables teams of people to work on a computer network, is the product Manzi identified in 1992 as "the future of the company"; that is, he hopes that it will end Lotus's dependence on its 1-2-3 spreadsheet program.

It's not all fun and games here. Developing software to drive computers can be very intense work. Lotus officially has a 35-hour workweek, but the computer software business doesn't fit into an orderly schedule. Russ Campanello, head of human resources, told us: "The truth absolutely is that this is not a 35-hour week. We are a young company and a young industry with young people. And all that energy comes together to drive a pace that is a little frenetic."

The tension at Lotus revolves around the nature of software development. It's absorbing work, and while some employees question whether it has to be so all-consuming, it's a difficult pattern to change. George Gilbert, an associate product manager on Notes, told us that when he joined Lotus in 1988, "what blew me away was not only how bright everyone was but how people here were generally captivated by the stuff they were working on. It was not like a job, it was like an adventure." However, we talked to one program developer who agreed that "you do get caught up in your work, especially since we are working on teams," but she questioned whether "work has to be this way." She said that Lotus was, in effect, telling its people: "Give us your soul."

To relieve the tension, Lotus has generous time-off benefits. Employees get 12 paid holidays a year (including your birthday), three weeks vacation after one year, and a four-week sabbatical after six years. But that doesn't stop Loti from being addicted to their work. One manager told us: "I may work 60 hours a week, and I know officially it is 35 hours a week, but I leave here at the end of the day feeling energized. I am amazed at the number of people I know who tolerate their jobs and do it because they have to earn a living. I am here because I want to be here." Reed Sturtevant, senior product development manager for graphics products, said: "There is this strange paradox here. People like to come in and work even though it is killing their personal life. And yet we sort of enjoy doing it, with people going from one high-pressure project to another. There is kind of a macho —that is not the right word—thing about how much you can work. I think that is less at a premium now so much as quick-wittedness. [Today] you can do your job better and still have a rational life outside of Lotus. But don't get me wrong, this is never going to be the post office."

Manzi is also a workaholic: "I work real, real long hours, which is not to be prescriptive to anybody else, and fundamentally there is no corporate prescription. It is an individual decision. My decision is that I get here very early so that I can get home at night religiously at 6:30 to have two hours with my kids. And if necessary I come in at 5:00 in the morning to do that."

One way to get a handle on Lotus is to compare it with the software industry leader, Microsoft. They are both driven by the same demons who make the relentless demand: come up with new programs to enhance the power and versatility of the computer—or someone else will. Lotus on the East Coast, Microsoft on the West Coast. But the defining difference goes back to their origins. Whereas Microsoft was founded by computer nerds, Lotus has countercultural roots. Former disc jockey Mitch Kapor practiced transcendental meditation before starting Lotus in 1982 when he was 32 years old. He named his company Lotus because it represents, in the Hindu philosophy, the state of perfect enlightenment. Kapor departed with all his millions in 1986 but he left behind a social consciousness that remains part of Lotus—and doesn't exist at Microsoft. In 1989 the Lotus in-house newsletter carried reminiscences by 13 employees who had been present at the "peace and love" Woodstock music festival of 1969.

At the Microsoft campus in Redmond, Washington, the faces are nearly all white. Lotus is 11 percent minority, and in January 1991 the top 20 people in the company went off on a retreat for three days to discuss the single topic of diversity at Lotus, not a meeting that Bill Gates is likely to convene at Microsoft.

At its headquarters complex in Cambridge, Lotus has a spectacular child-care center that it operates itself, subsidizing the rates for low-income employees and paying teacher salaries that are considerably above market rates. Lotus was the first corporate sponsor of the AIDS Walk in Boston, and in 1991 it became the first large company in the United States to offer health insurance and other benefits to partners of gay employees. This was not a move copied by Microsoft. An estimated 10 percent of Lotus's employees are homosexual.

Jim Manzi was certainly not at Woodstock. Prior to coming to Lotus, he worked at the management consulting firm McKinsey & Co., where his client was Lotus, and he wrote for William Buckley's conservative opinion weekly, the *National Review*. In a 1991 interview with Rich Karlgaard, editor in chief of *Upside*, Manzi recalled that the two people responsible for him coming to Lotus were Kapor and the then head of human resources, Janet Axelrod, who describes herself as a "socialist." It's safe to say that I learned something from them, and they from me." Asked by Karlgaard if he was still a political conservative, Manzi replied: "My basic beliefs are. I have a pathological dislike of being told what to do."

The average age at Lotus is creeping up—it was 34 in 1991, up from 29 five years ago (and three years older than the average at Microsoft). The average wage at Lotus is $52,000 a year, not counting a very rich benefits package. The goal here is to retire people with a pension amounting to 85 to 90 percent of their final salary. Lotus now gives stock options to 1,100 employees, compared with the handful of people who receive them at most American corporations. Manzi's stock-option awards, however, have eclipsed what's given to everyone else. Thanks to stock options awarded shortly after he took the helm in 1986, Manzi became one of the highest-compensated executives in American business. According to calculations done by *Forbes*, Manzi's total pay for the five years 1987 through 1991 was $51.6 million, making him seventh on the roster of best-paid CEOs. Manzi owns 3.6 percent of Lotus's stock.

Given the egalitarian values espoused by Lotus, was there resentment in the ranks at the huge stock awards to Manzi? We put that question to Russ Campanello, who said: "There was outside of the building." He was quickly contradicted by a Lotus veteran, Marilyn Considine, director of employee communications, who said: "I think, to be honest, there was some inside the company as well." To which Campanello replied: "You think so? I didn't. It is amazing once you get this type of job, how little you begin hearing."

Openness is prized at Lotus. All employees at headquarters gather in a hotel ballroom for a quarterly meeting where Manzi takes questions—and other sites around the world are teleconferenced into the session. Sales manager Anita Harris, an eight-year employee, said: "The good news at Lotus is that if you disagree with something you can voice that. You may not get exactly what you want, but an ear is open to hear what you would like." Associate product manager George Gilbert described the Lotus environment as "half think tank, half university, but still the playing field of competition."

Employees we met also expressed pride in Lotus's strong philanthropy program. It has a number of distinctive features such as a democratically elected philanthropy committee that decides where the money goes. The number one priority of Lotus giving has been to combat racism. (It was the funder that made possible the TV documentary "Eyes on the Prize.") And Lotus believes in sticking its neck out to support programs that are not funded by established foundations. One employee told us of asking a member of the philanthropy committee why Lotus didn't give money to National Public Radio. Back came the answer: "Because everybody else does."

Lotus's reputation as a socially minded company is well known. After they had their first layoffs at the end of 1991, letting 400 people go, the news was greeted with joy on Wall Street, where David Readerman, an analyst with Lehman Brothers, chortled: "It signaled that they were ready to focus on operating margins, not some Cambridge form of socialism." Of the 400 people who left the payroll, some 150 were contractors or temporary employees. It was a painful experience for Lotus, and they softened the layoffs with an extraordinarily generous program, giving severance of eight weeks of full pay plus one week for every six months of service, as well as all accrued vacation and sabbatical pay. In addition, each displaced employee had access to the services of an outplacement firm for as long as it took to find a new job.

In 1992 Lotus was moving its manufacturing plant, where it duplicates disks and packages them, from Cambridge to North Reading—and every effort was being made to retain all 650 employees, including 153 mentally handicapped people who work on the final assembly line. To help with the commute, Lotus pays the full cost of a rail transit ticket from Cambridge to Reading. And a shuttle bus will run all day long to pick up people at the station and bring them to the plant 12 minutes away.

Lotus receives 20,000 job applications a year, and many of the people it hires come from other companies. Many also come in as referrals from present employees. An employee receives a $1,000 bonus for recommending a candidate who is hired; the bonus is paid after the candidate has been with Lotus for three months. Program manager Elaine Giangregorio told us: "My sister works for Jim Manzi, my husband works in telecommunications." Another employee added: "I know people who have five of their family members here. I have one friend that I referred. I was referred by a friend. He turns out to have referred four people. Talk about community."

Types of jobs: Sales and marketing—36 percent; software development—34 percent; manufacturing and distribution—14 percent; finance and administration—12 percent; consulting—4 percent.

Main employment center: Cambridge, Massachusetts.

Headquarters: Lotus Development Corp.
55 Cambridge Pkwy.
Cambridge, MA 02142
(617) 577-8500

COMPANIES WHERE YOU HAVE A SWIMMING POOL

Hershey Foods
SC Johnson Wax
Lands' End
Methodist Hospital
Nissan Motor Manufacturing
Odetics
Springs
Tandem

Lowe's

======

LOWE'S
Companies Inc.

Lowe's is the second largest building supplies/home center retailer in the United States with 304 stores located mostly in the Southeast. Employees: 23,362.

★ ★ ★ Pay/Benefits
★ ★ ★ ★ Opportunities
★ ★ ★ ★ Job Security
★ ★ ★ Pride in Work/Company
★ ★ ★ Openness/Fairness
★ ★ ★ ★ Camaraderie/Friendliness

BIGGEST PLUS: You can build a great nest egg here with the tools they give you.
BIGGEST MINUS: Your nest egg is only as sturdy as the stock market.

Instead of cutting a ribbon when they open a new store, Lowe's officials saw a two-by-four in half. Lowe's has sawed a lot of two-by-fours since we last visited them in the early 1980s, opening over 100 new stores to give them more than 300 by 1992. Lowe's also plans to open 60 new warehouse stores in 1993. And they sawed through two-by-fours at more than three dozen openings above the Mason-Dixon Line, extending their presence outside the South. The number of employees nearly tripled during this period, as most of their new stores are much larger than the older ones. Lowe's needs larger stores because they have expanded beyond the professional builder market to include home improvement items for do-it-yourselfers and appliances such as TVs and VCRs.

Larger stores with a different focus have brought changes, but Lowe's retained many of the down-home features found in our earlier visit. They're

still headquartered in North Wilkesboro (population 3,260) in the Pied-
mont Mountains of North Carolina, where you can buy homemade Appalachian woodcrafts and quilts at roadside stands along the highway leading
into town. Employees still receive a turkey for Thanksgiving, a ham at
Christmas, and a free lunch on their birthday. They have grown so much in
recent years that instead of an annual picnic and pig roast, headquarters
employees now spend a summer day at the Carowinds amusement park
near Charlotte.

And despite the expansion, many employees still consider Lowe's a family. Gary Holbrook, who works in a distribution center, told us: "Lowe's is
more like a family than they are a place to work. It just seems like I'm going
home, instead of going to work. Everybody is so close to each other. If
you've got a problem, they're right there to help, anytime."

The family atmosphere extends to relationships with top executives.
Data specialist Gretchen Heunemann explained: "You can interact with
upper management. I have no problem talking to Mr. Herring [CEO Leonard Herring], who I see pretty much every day. They don't make you feel
like you're lower than they are." Jesse Miles, who works in plumbing at the
store in Wilkes County, compared Lowe's to his previous employer: "Mr.
Herring, our president, walked through one day, and just stopped and
shook my hand. You would think that these people would walk through
with a cold shoulder, but they have the time to stop and say, 'Hey, how is it
going? Are you enjoying yourself?' At the company I worked for in Moores-
ville, the president would walk through, and he would never speak to you.
He would only talk to his right-hand people."

Not only do top people make themselves accessible, but Lowe's has been
making an effort to acquaint the headquarters staff with what goes on in
the stores. In 1990 Lowe's began sending vice-presidents and managers to
work in Lowe's stores for a week. The next year other headquarters employees also joined the program, checking into a motel and working different
shifts at a local store to learn about life on the front lines. Over 250 have
participated in the program since 1990. They are expected to spend one
week in the stores every two years.

Many of the people who work at Lowe's do so with their relatives. Secretary Pat Anderson's family is an example: "My dad, my two brothers and
two sisters, and both of my children worked for Lowe's. So there are eight
of us from one family that have worked at Lowe's. And since both of my
children have worked at Lowe's, it is a household word." There are so many
relatives at Lowe's that the company newsletter, *Lowedown*, featured an
article on the subject. In that article Jeff Osborne, whose mother, uncle,
and brother-in-law work for Lowe's, said: "I always knew I'd come to work
for Lowe's. It was such a big part of my life growing up that I always
planned on working here."

As in many retail companies, employees work long and hard. The manager of the Muscle Shoals, Alabama, store, Tommy Bee, whose two brothers also work for Lowe's, told *Lowedown:* "You have to have an understanding wife and children to make it at Lowe's." One thing that makes the long hours easier is the camaraderie among employees. Store manufacturing vice-president Larry Stone told us: "I just think it's a joy to get up and come to work every day. Working 10-hour days or 12-hour days, it doesn't bother you. You're paid to work 40 hours, and I would say for most managers, 45 to 50 is probably the norm. And they don't mind it, because they see us moving forward. And they're making a contribution. And enjoy doing it."

Because of continuing growth, Lowe's is a place where hard work pays off. Jan Lambert's career history is typical. She started as a salesperson in 1983, was promoted to assistant retail manager and then to retail manager. After that, her career went from operations manager to store manager. Today, she is an area manager. Lambert told us: "They have given me the opportunity, and the best thing about it is that I have been able to feel some self-satisfaction. I set a goal, and with the help of the team, I achieved it."

Entry-level store employees receive a card listing the seven steps they need to take to become a customer service manager. It takes most employees fewer than four years to complete the steps, during which time their salary will have doubled. Another program enables employees to receive cash awards from $50 to $100 and small prizes like T-shirts for providing exceptional customer service. Managers from the first level of store supervisors to general managers who oversee a number of stores have an unusual incentive program through which they receive a gold ring by meeting their budgets. The first year the manager receives a gold ring and has a diamond added each subsequent year until the ring holds as many as 18 diamonds.

Lowe's also pays employees for good suggestions. Secretary Gretchen Heunemann told us: "I keep getting money, and I'm thrilled to death. I suggest tiny things that I think of when something ticks me off. I'll write it down and send it in, and I've gotten $25, $50, and $75 for my ideas." In 1991 ideas ranged from establishing a human resources hot line to a new method to record customers' credit card payments.

Lowe's store managers can also enter contests for selling certain items. In 1992 there were 30 contests. The winner of the "Siding for Salmon" contest won a three-and-a-half-day fishing trip to Canada for selling more aluminum siding than any other store manager. The "Annual Roofing Products Sale" contest winner went on a cruise to Alaska. The contest with the biggest prize has never been won—yet. Held every year at a store managers' meeting in Charlotte, the "Big Bucks Beach Blast" has multiple prizes and drawings. Any golfer who makes a hole in one wins $50,000 and another $50,000 to be split among his or her employees.

Employees do not have to compete for what many consider the biggest prize Lowe's offers: the employee stock-ownership plan (ESOP). Every year the company buys back stock and deposits it into employee accounts. The amount of the contribution is a percentage of salary that varies depending on profits (Lowe's has averaged a 14 percent contribution since 1978). The ESOP is the employees' retirement nest egg. They can keep their stock after retirement or sell it back to Lowe's. In 1992 the ESOP trust owned about a quarter of the company's stock.

Before 1986, the cash dividends on the stock were automatically reinvested in employees' accounts. Since 1986, employees have been paid their quarterly dividends directly. In 1991 Lowe's paid $3.6 million to the 7,300 employees who were vested in the plan (it takes seven years to qualify). The average payout was $486. Human resources director Ed Spears explained the philosophy behind the change of policy: "We felt that this would be tangible evidence to people that they really had an asset there that was earning something, without having to wait 15 or 20 or 30 years to see the evidence of it."

The evidence of the assets after 20 or 30 years of working here is certainly impressive. An employee hired as a management trainee in 1962 retired in 1992 as a midlevel manager with $750,000 in his ESOP account. According to human resources director Ed Spears: "We've had upper-middle managers retiring with high six-figure balances. We had one person who was a senior executive, who retired with more than seven figures."

Ferrel Bryan, whose son Melvin also works for Lowe's, spent 20 years in the Sparta warehouse and retired in 1970 with enough money to buy a 179-acre farm and cattle. Bryan told *Lowedown* that when he first heard founder Carl Buchan's promise, "If you work for me, I'll make you rich," he was incredulous: "We didn't believe in this 'profit-sharing' plan for a long time. But when one of our own gang [a delivery driver in Bryan's warehouse] retired rich, we all sat up and took notice. . . . Lowe's has meant a lot to me. I don't know where our family would have been if it had not been for Lowe's."

Ownership also gives employees a sense of control. Riff Footland, director of store systems, said: "I'm very high on the stock ownership of this company. It's not only just from a wealth-building aspect, but it also means that you're in control of your destiny. I really believe that I'm the owner of this company."

Because of their stock ownership, employees are extremely interested in what happens on the New York Stock Exchange. Warehouse employee Tom Wyatt told us, "We announce the stock price at noon and after the market closes at 4:00. And when the closing price is announced there's this sudden power surge, with everybody turning on their calculators to figure out how much money they'd made. You could walk up and down the hall, and you could hear the calculator buttons going *click click click click click*." Of course, that's on an up day. Other times they're figuring how much they lost.

Types of jobs: Customer service—30 percent; distribution center associates—30 percent; finance—11 percent; merchandising—9 percent; management and supervisors—7 percent; information services—7 percent; sales and store operations—3 percent; advertising—2 percent; real estate—1 percent.

Main employment centers: Lowe's stores are located in the southeastern United States. They have 71 stores in North Carolina, 34 in Virginia, 27 in Tennessee, 23 in South Carolina, 22 in Georgia, 19 in Florida, 18 in Kentucky, 15 in West Virginia, 14 in Alabama, 13 in Louisiana, nine in Maryland, eight in Texas, seven in Mississippi, Arkansas, and Pennsylvania, five in Ohio, four in Indiana, three in Delaware, and one in Missouri and Illinois.

Headquarters: Lowe's Companies, Inc.
Box 1111
North Wilkesboro, NC 28656
(919) 651-4000

BEST FOR OPPORTUNITIES

Dayton Hudson
Microsoft
Motorola
Nordstrom
J. C. Penney
Publix Super Markets
Rosenbluth International
Southwest Airlines
USAA
Wal-Mart

Lyondell Petrochemical

Lyondell Petrochemical makes gasoline, motor oil, heating oil, and jet fuel at the 10th largest oil refinery in the country. It also runs a petrochemical complex that makes building-block chemicals used in a wide variety of products, including plastics, paint, clothing, medicines, trash bags, tires, rubbing alcohol, and carpets. Employees: 2,250.

★★★★★ Pay/Benefits
★★★ Opportunities
★★★★ Job Security
★★★★ Pride in Work/Company
★★★★ Openness/Fairness
★★★★ Camaraderie/Friendliness

BIGGEST PLUS: High-octane communications.
BIGGEST MINUS: Low-octane opportunities.

Lyondell is one of the most dramatic business turnarounds of the past decade. The story began in 1985 when Atlantic Richfield (ARCO) decided to create a new division called Lyondell Petrochemical out of its two biggest losers—a huge oil refinery located adjacent to the Houston Ship Channel and a petrochemical plant in nearby Channelview. Almost everyone expected that Lyondell, operating on its own, would fail, since the operations had been losing $200 million a year. But, by its second year, Lyondell was profitable. And in the next five years Lyondell earned *$1.6 billion* after taxes. Among Fortune 500 companies, it was the most productive company in the United States in 1989 and 1990 (in terms of profits per employee). In 1992 *Fortune* wrote that "Lyondell has set new performance standards for its industry."

In strictly business terms, Lyondell is a success story with few parallels in American business history. But it's also a terrific workplace story—as Lyondell has become a great place to work. Indeed, much of Lyondell's business success can be traced to the dramatic change in the relationship between workers and management.

The principal architect of Lyondell's transformation has been Bob Gower, a Ph.D. biochemist. He was ARCO's senior vice-president of planning in the early 1980s when the big oil company was trying to decide what to do with what are now the Lyondell facilities. One option was to sell off the plants. But Gower persuaded ARCO's management into setting up a separate entity, with himself at the helm. At first Lyondell, although it was free to operate independently, was still legally a division of ARCO. But in 1989 it was cut loose when half the stock was sold to the public (ARCO retained 49.9 percent). From the start, though, Lyondell was calling its own shots. The refinery, for example, was no longer required to buy crude oil from ARCO—it could wheel and deal for the lowest price it could get. And it was under no obligation to sell the gasoline that came out of the refinery to ARCO. In short, Lyondell was expected to sink or swim on its own.

When we interviewed him in 1991, Gower told us that he didn't have a clear strategy at first: "Our goal was to still be in business by the end of 1985. It wasn't much more sophisticated than that." The key was changing the attitudes of employees. Gower said: "We felt the best way to do that was to get people really fired up and enthused and give them responsibility."

Giving workers more responsibility was out of the question in the beginning. There was too much bureaucracy caused by too many managers. According to Gower: "My belief is that most large companies are overmanaged and this one was severely overmanaged. When you are overmanaged, that doesn't allow the people doing the work to actually do their jobs. They are inhibited." Fortunately for Gower, ARCO offered generous early-retirement packages in 1985 and 1986. About 1,000 people out of 3,500 left the Lyondell division—all voluntarily. Most of them were managers or professional-level workers.

Allen Reynolds, a worker at Channelview, noticed the change almost immediately: "When Gower took over as president, he made a formal statement that they would remove some levels of supervision and that they would put authority and responsibility down to the level where people were actually doing the work. He followed through with that, and it has happened."

Reynolds monitors a control board in the petrochemical plant, and he pointed out that before Gower took over, "chain of command was the key phrase. You didn't do anything until you were told to do it. It was crazy because you knew already what you needed to do. But that's the way it was." Reynolds thinks the process is controlled much better today: "Now we just react to what is going on. We do it. If the supervisor happens to walk by, we may mention, 'Hey, I just changed so and so.' But that is not even necessary. He may ask later on, 'I noticed that the feed was changed today.' " Leticia Ligsay, a Channelview lab technician, said she likes Lyondell's new style, "because we have the freedom to think. And it is fun."

We met Reynolds and Ligsay at the Channelview petrochemical plant. This plant receives petroleum by-products through a 16-mile pipeline from the oil refinery in Houston and converts them into petrochemicals—ethylene, propylene, butadine, benzene, toulene, and methanol—that are sold to various chemical companies that turn them into a variety of products. According to *Fortune*, Lyondell's business success has largely come from its "unparalleled flexibility." The Houston oil refinery, for instance, is the only refinery in the world that can process any form of crude oil, and the Channelview plant can quickly change its processes to vary the types of petrochemicals it produces. In 1992 Lyondell became the first oil company to begin making gasoline from used motor oil, to the applause of many environmentalists. That same year Lyondell introduced a re-refined brand of motor oil called Enviroil.

Lyondell's flexibility stems from the new work culture that has enabled employees to take more control over their jobs and implement innovations. We heard about a new willingness to take risks not only from the blue-collar Channelview workers but also from employees at Lyondell's headquarters 20 miles away in a skyscraper in downtown Houston. Dominic Ching, an evaluations analyst, contrasted the great difference with the ARCO culture: "Before we became Lyondell, there was a lot of finger pointing." People worried about taking risks because they feared becoming politically isolated. "Now we feel like, 'We didn't make it work this time, let's try it again. Let's try something else. Let's find someone else that can help us to solve the problem.' So we are not avoiding problems as we used to. We get more work done, and more problems solved."

Soon after taking over, Gower initiated what has become one of Lyondell's key institutions, the Gower Hour—a monthly meeting with all employees at each of the company's four major locations. He explained his reasoning: "The typical way to change the culture of a company is you talk to the first level and maybe get them on board and then hope they go talk to the next level, and within five or six years, maybe in some distorted fashion it would work down to the bottom level. What I do instead is to talk it through with my officer group, and then I immediately go out and tell all the employees what we are going to do. That makes it move fast." Employees who can't come to the monthly meetings can watch it on videotape.

Gower also began meeting with smaller groups of employees over lunch twice a month. These are brown-bag lunches, not fancy ones. Gower has observed that the higher the quality of food, the less open people will be in meetings: "If you take them to a fancy hotel, you won't learn anything."

As with the Gower Hour, Lyondell's president concludes each meeting with a question-and-answer period. Every question is answered either on the spot or in a follow-up letter. Employees have other ways to get their questions answered. There is a "Dial Info" system, enabling them to call the human relations department and ask any question about company policies. Answers are printed in a monthly publication called *Straight Scoop*.

This free flow of information helped Lyondell's management gain a reputation for credibility. As Channelview worker Leticia Ligsay told us: "Since [Gower] became president he has always been honest to us. Upfront. People trust him. Even when the picture is not good, he will tell us."

Lyondell has also implemented a wide variety of recognition programs. One is the EPIC (efficiency, productivity, innovation, creativity) Award, which salutes employees for noteworthy performance and ideas that improve profitability. Employees nominated for this award by other employees get $100 gift certificates and are considered for the $2,500 EPIC Award. In 1991, 150 employees received $100 certificates and 25 won $2,500. In 1991 Lyondell distributed $366,125 in monetary awards.

Other awards include the Award of Merit, Quality Recognition Award, Technical Achievement Award, Achieving Total Quality ring, Award of Distinction, and Award of Excellence. There is also the President's Club to honor outstanding employee performance in sales and marketing. And Volunteer Awards for contributions to the community. There is even a Perfect Attendance Award.

Employees like the recognition. Senior secretary Cindy Jackson said: "It makes you feel good that somebody notices that you are doing something." And Byron Lewis, a Channelview lab technician who once played for the Pittsburgh Steelers, said: "You will be recognized for doing a quality job here. The reason why we are successful is because we are now pulling together as a team. We are not individuals looking to make our own way."

Lyondell is as team-crazy as it is award-crazy. There are multifunctional Business Teams, QITs (Quality Improvement Teams), TAPS (Team Approach to Problem Solving), QBTs (Quality Breakthrough Teams), Production Resource Teams, Quality Improvement Audit Teams.

Planning vice-president Debbie Starnes explained: "Teamwork is very important here. People who go out and try to be a Lone Ranger and make themselves look good at the expense of everybody else or at the expense of getting a job done, it just doesn't work here."

The same point is made by Gerald Sherman, who works at Channelview: "We live by consensus, as in any true democracy. I may agree or disagree with any of the people in here and they may disagree with me, but I support them in any decision that we make as a team." Sherman works on a team that is trying to redesign the way work is done at the refinery. The team is composed of operations employees, support people, technical staff, and one manager who "sponsors" the team and gives advice and guidance.

Because of all the teams and the relative absence of management positions, Lyondell is not an easy place to move ahead quickly. Dominic Ching calls it a problem of "plateauing." He said Lyondell is "good for the beginner but not so good for the people who are already here for a long time." He has been encouraged, however, that the company has recognized the issue and has been willing to engage in an "open discussion" about it. One solution has been to cross-train people in different specialties so they can move around and keep from feeling stagnant.

Even for those who plateau, however, Lyondell makes sure they are well taken care of financially. According to Dick Park, vice-president of human resources, Lyondell is in the 90th percentile in terms of pay and in the top quartile of the high-paying oil industry in terms of benefits. Their premier benefit is a savings and capital-accumulation plan. If an employee puts aside 5 percent in the plan, the company will not only match the 5 percent but add another 3 percent. Park calls it "the Cadillac in the industry."

Lyondell also has a profit-sharing plan, which is paid out in cash. For Channelview workers, who make an average of about $32,000 a year, this has meant an extra $2,000 or so a year in four of five recent years. And when Lyondell is doing extremely well, they've even kicked in bonuses of $500 and $1,000 in midyear as a way of saying thanks for helping turn around what was once considered a loser.

Types of jobs: Production and maintenance—54 percent; manufacturing management—12 percent; clerical and technical—9 percent; sales and marketing—7 percent; administration—7 percent.

Main employment centers: Houston is home to both the headquarters and the oil refinery. Chemical plants are located in Channelview and Pasadena, Texas.

Headquarters: Lyondell Petrochemical Company
One Houston Center
1221 McKinney St.
P.O. Box 3646
Houston, TX 77253
(713) 652-7200

THE 100 BEST BY INDUSTRY

Airlines & Travel

Avis
Delta Air Lines
Federal Express
Rosenbluth International
Southwest Airlines

Automotive

Apogee Enterprises
Cooper Tire
Cummins Engine
John Deere
Donnelly
Fel-Pro
Honda of America
  Manufacturing
Nissan Motor Manufacturing
Springfield ReManufacturing

Banking & Finance

A. G. Edwards
First Federal Bank of California
Goldman Sachs
J. P. Morgan

Media & Entertainment

Leo Burnett
Hallmark Cards
Knight-Ridder
Quad/Graphics
Reader's Digest

Computers & Chips

Advanced Micro Devices
Compaq Computer
Cray Research
Hewlett-Packard
IBM
Intel

Motorola
Tandem

Construction & Engineering

Apogee
Armstrong
BE&K
TDIndustries
Weyerhaeuser

Drugs & Cosmetics

Johnson & Johnson
Mary Kay Cosmetics
Merck
Procter & Gamble
Syntex

Food & Beverage

Anheuser-Busch
Ben & Jerry's Homemade
General Mills
Hershey Foods
Kellogg
McCormick
Procter & Gamble
J. M. Smucker

Forest Products

Weyerhaeuser

Glass

Apogee
Corning
Donnelly

Hospitals

Baptist Hospital of Miami
Beth Israel Hospital Boston
Methodist Hospital

Industrial & Farm Equipment Products

John Deere
Corning
W. L. Gore & Associates
Lincoln Electric
3M
Moog
Tennant

Household Products

Armstrong
Corning
Johnson & Johnson
SC Johnson Wax
3M
Procter & Gamble
Springs

Insurance

Erie Insurance
Northwestern Mutual Life
UNUM
USAA

Legal & Consulting

Hewitt Associates
Morrison & Foerster

Medical Equipment

W. L. Gore & Associates
Hewlett-Packard
Johnson & Johnson
Marquette Electronics
3M
Physio-Control

Office Equipment

Haworth
Herman Miller
3M
Pitney Bowes

Steelcase
Xerox

Printing

Quad/Graphics
Valassis Communications

Oil & Chemical

Du Pont
H. B. Fuller
W. L. Gore & Associates
Lyondell Petrochemical
3M

Retail

Dayton Hudson
General Mills
Lands' End
Lowe's
Nordstrom
Patagonia
J. C. Penney
Publix Super Markets
REI
Wal-Mart
Wegmans

Scientific & Precision Equipment

Hewlett-Packard
Odetics
Polaroid
Xerox

Software

Great Plains Software
Lotus Development
Microsoft
SAS Institute

Sports

Los Angeles Dodgers

Steel & Iron

Acipco
Chaparral Steel
Worthington Industries
Inland Steel

Textiles & Apparel

Du Pont
W. L. Gore & Associates
Lands' End
Patagonia
Springs

Trucking

Federal Express
Preston Trucking
Viking Freight System

Utilities

Alagasco
U S West

Marquette Electronics

Marquette Electronics makes medical equipment, including electrocardiographic and patient monitoring machines. U.S. employees: 1,402.

★ ★ ★	Pay/Benefits
★ ★ ★ ★	Opportunities
★ ★ ★ ★ ★	Job Security
★ ★ ★	Pride in Work/Company
★ ★ ★	Openness/Fairness
★ ★ ★ ★	Camaraderie/Friendliness

BIGGEST PLUS: They don't monitor their workers.
BIGGEST MINUS: The physical plant needs a checkup.

Nobody has a big office at this medical electronics company, not even Michael J. Cudahy, the cofounder and president, who occupies a cluttered, 12-by-16-foot cubicle at one corner of a rambling, 300,000-square-foot building on Milwaukee's northwest side. A one-story, unprepossessing structure, the building holds the corporate headquarters and factory of Marquette Electronics. At another end of the building, next to the assembly plant for diagnostic equipment, is the KIDS department, a hallway bordered on each side with four brightly colored rooms where 140 children of employees, from six-week-old infants to six-year-olds (more than half under the age of one), were being cared for in 1992. In the middle of the complex is Le Bistro, a cafeteria which serves Milwaukee-type fare like hot Sicilian subs and grilled turkey and Swiss-cheese sandwiches, has a dance floor and the distinction of being perhaps the only on-site corporate restaurant (outside of France) where employees can have wine and beer with their lunch. Asked once why he secured a license to serve alcoholic beverages, Cudahy said: "It's just another example of how we trust our workers."

The small office for the top gun, the child-care center, and trust for employees are all hallmarks of Marquette. It opened its child-care center in 1984, the first company in Wisconsin to have an on-site center. Marquette was founded in 1965 by Cudahy and Warren B. Cozzens with only a hazy idea of what they would do. An early product was an electric piano. Their breakthrough came with the development of an electrocardiographic system for Northwestern University's medical school. Marquette pioneered with computer-driven equipment enabling hospitals to do a better job of collecting, storing, and diagnosing the results of electrocardiograms, used to identify potential and actual heart damage and disease. In addition to electrocardiographic equipment, Marquette now makes patient monitoring devices (a business it acquired from General Electric), defibrillators to get the heart pumping again, and gas analysis products for anesthesiologists. Virtually all their products are for use in critical-care situations. Sales zoomed from $32 million in 1982 to $233 million in 1992.

It's difficult to separate Marquette from Cudahy, a hands-on, tieless, charismatic leader who welcomes employees to the company with a promise of freedom from "petty rules" and an invitation to come see him whenever they wish (see box). A scion of the Cudahy meat-packing family, Mike Cudahy enjoys playing the maverick. He never went to college, and he is proud of the fact that Marquette has no organizational charts.

Cudahy told us that the reason Marquette has a strong people orientation is that "I didn't go to school to learn how to run a company. I think that what you learn in school is how to build hierarchy, how to do it like people have done it for many years. And I really didn't do any of that. I started with one employee. And when you have one employee, you either treat him right or he leaves. So being a little bit stupid, I got it through my thick head that it was a good idea to be reasonable to the guy. Then I got another fellow, then a third guy, who was finally the professional engineer that came on the scene, thank God. And he was kind of temperamental, so I had to treat him right or he would leave. And it just grew from that. I never had this idea that by hierarchy or structural rules of management, you could control people. For instance, somebody was just taking some doctors on a tour this morning and one of them said, 'You don't have any time clocks?' I said, 'No, because peer pressure takes care of that.' It's not that we don't care what time people come to work, it's just that if you have a team and they're building a product and they're all on profit sharing, if Maybelle shows up late all the time, the other three say, 'Maybelle, you've got to stop showing up late or we won't get our products out.' "

The people who work here do feel they are trusted, especially in comparison to previous places where they may have worked. Percy Dandridge, a plant technician with 13 years of service, assured us that "there's a lot of freedom. They put you on your honor. They assign you a task, and nobody stands looking over your shoulder." Michele Hoch, an electrical engineer, joined Marquette in 1989, coming from one of Milwaukee's largest employers, Briggs & Stratton, the world's largest maker of air-cooled gasoline engines. She said the difference between the two companies is "like night and day. There's just a ton of things. But the biggest difference, I think, is the trust. They trust you here to do your job. They expect a lot but that's kind of neat, too: to have a lot of interesting work, things that you like to do. It's real flexible. I've found that if you have a forte in a particular area, you can work in that area. Everyone is pretty flexible about it. And they allow you to make decisions. At Briggs, to make a decision on anything you had to have meetings, tons and tons of meetings with tons and tons of people. You'd have to have a meeting to decide if you were going to make a decision to make a decision. It was just incredible and it would take months for the tiniest little thing to happen. There were so many layers of management you had to go through to get a decision made. Here you're given a job and they trust you to do it and do it right and to make the best decision."

Trusting people also works out better for the company, according to Chris Nemacheck, quality assurance inspector. He explained that "the more freedom we give technicians and the more regulations we pull away, the better the quality gets. Because you're allowing those people to start doing their job better. In other words, we've said, 'We're putting this in your hands now. I'm not going to watch over your shoulder and make sure you did a good job. You're going to have to do it yourself.' And you start seeing them do a better job. Because they care about what they're doing; they're not robots anymore." Linda Tellier, who manages Marquette's in-house travel department, said: "I keep reading these articles lately, I guess the new word is 'empowerment.' That's been going on at Marquette for a very long time. These companies are saying, 'Empower your employees to make decisions.' Well, we've been doing that for years."

Sandy Grindey, a secretary whose husband also works at Marquette, likes the flexibility she has here. "If we have to be longer at lunchtime," she said, "or if we have to be late in the morning, the work will get done. It may mean you don't leave at 5:00 some days, but you don't think about that—you do what's necessary." Dandridge told us that "at the other places I worked, the bell rang at 7:00 in the morning and you started work. Four hours later the bell rang and you took a break. The bell rang and you would come back to work. The bell rang at the end of the day and you'd go home. Here you don't have that. If you want to take a cup of coffee or stop and chat with one of your friends, you don't have anybody cracking that whip saying, 'Hey, get back to work.' If you've got to make a phone call, you can do that. It's a big difference."

Cudahy has mixed feelings about the growth of Marquette. "I hate to see the company get big," he said. "I remember very distinctly when there were about 11 or 12 people, and we used to go down to Louie Wren's bar on Friday night and get a little loaded and sort of unwind and tell each other our problems. It was a wonderful thing. For a long time I knew everybody by their first and last names, and their wives' names and their kids' names. I startle people by how many I know. But sometimes I startle myself with how few I know. And I hate that." Because it is difficult for everyone to know everyone, the company has a "family album" —pictures and names of all employees—displayed on the wall outside Le Bistro.

There's still plenty of socializing at Marquette. Employees and their families turn out in force for the annual summer picnic, an all-day affair usually held at Lake Denon, 10 miles southwest of Milwaukee. Employees sing in a chorus, others play in a jazz band. And there are celebrations at the office, regular and impromptu. Ian Rowlandson, engineering manager of the diagnostics division, disclosed that his department parties every Friday night—and Sandy Grindey reported that the week before our visit, the diagnostics division had introduced two new products "and they celebrated from 4:00 to 10:00. We had a big pig roast." This *is* Milwaukee. Dave Perren, a technical support manager who has been here 11 years, then chimed in and, looking at personnel director Gordon Petersen, said: "I don't know if Gordy knows this but I'm from the service division and we've always had a beer tapper in our department for all these years. A keg. And we still have one here. It's more of a ritual. At 4:00 you're free to have one, and once in a while someone will tap one here or there." This *is* Milwaukee.

Virtually all the big companies we visited now test employees for presence of drugs. Not Marquette. One of its customers is Du Pont, which not only tests its employees but asks that suppliers or companies sending service people to Du Pont premises do likewise. Marquette told Du Pont it did not intend to test its employees—and the giant chemical company did not make an issue of it.

Marquette has never had a layoff and has offered to reassign employees when a facility was closed or relocated. In 1991, when the gas analysis division relocated from St. Louis to Milwaukee, 10 people made the move, too. And between 1988 and 1990, when the service and supplies division relocated to Jupiter, Florida, 20 miles north of Palm Beach, 58 Milwaukee employees jumped at the chance to escape the cold climate. The other 120 employees in the division were all offered jobs in Milwaukee. In designing the Jupiter facility, Marquette allocated space for a child-care center, and in 1992 employees had 40 of their children enrolled in this on-site center.

Introduction to the Employee Handbook
of Marquette Electronics:

A NOTE FROM THE PRESIDENT

From the time we're old enough to go to school we're taught that play is fun and work is not; that we must tolerate this unpleasantness to enjoy the pleasures of life.

I never did believe that work had to be drudgery. I never felt that people should do things they're not good at or don't like to do just to make a living.

I'm convinced that a company like ours can be operated in such a way as to create an atmosphere for maximum productivity and creativity. I'm convinced that pleasant surroundings, good working conditions, and the lack of petty rules and regulations will bring about the greatest rewards for employee and company alike.

So Marquette tries hard to provide an atmosphere of this kind. You can see it everywhere in our new building. There are no time clocks because we assume you're honest. When you want to call home you don't have to use a pay phone; there are phones everywhere for local calls. We don't tell you what to wear, we just want you to do a good job. If you're unsuited for what you're doing, we will try to get you into something you're good at.

We strive to avoid hierarchy and organizational charts although, obviously, there has to be some chain of command. But if you want to talk to me or any other "boss" feel free to do so. Communication is a byword we'd like very much to preserve.

I think you'll enjoy working at Marquette.

Sincerely,

MICHAEL J. CUDAHY

Entry-level assemblers in the factory were starting here at $6.30 an hour in 1992, engineers at $31,500. This pay could be supplemented in three different ways: profit sharing, a savings plan in which the company matches 25 cents on the dollar the first $2,000 saved by an employee, and an employee stock-ownership plan (ESOP). Marquette's ESOP was established in 1974, with shares accumulating in each employee's account through company contribution of 5 percent of pretax profits. Employees don't have to put up any money of their own for the shares. Those shares now have a market value because Marquette went public in the fall of 1991, selling 15 percent of the company to outsiders—and the stock now trades on the over-the-counter market. The ESOP owns 20 percent of the shares, worth roughly $50 million in mid-1992.

Cudahy retained control of the company but he wasn't altogether happy about selling shares to the public. He called it "the lesser of two evils," made necessary by the need to establish a market value for the stock. Only a year earlier Marquette's 1990–91 annual report had carried a Mike Cudahy coda in which he blasted the "sell out syndrome." He disclosed then that he was contacted every week about selling the company, and he asserted that he was going to set a course for the next 10 years "so that we let the young, talented, capable guys in our company become major stock-holders. And the stock will come from us . . . the oldtimers who must step back and have faith that someone else can carry on the work we're doing to advance the science of electrocardiography." Going public doesn't invalidate that plan. After the public offering in November 1991, more than half the stock was held by 13 directors and officers. Cudahy himself still owned 37.6 percent of the shares.

Cudahy told us that he wasn't going to let Wall Street narrow his vision to short-term results. "I'm just going to do it the way I have been doing it," he said, "and if they don't like it, they can lump it."

Of course there's some evidence that Cudahy's philosophy has paid off. In 1990 the *Milwaukee Sentinel* reported that after a nurse from a Los Angeles hospital had toured Marquette's plant and saw the child-care center, she said: "Anyone who cares this much for their employees deserves our order."

Types of jobs: Manufacturing—30 percent; sales and marketing—25 percent; service—19 percent; engineering—14 percent; administrative support —11 percent.

Main employment centers: 860 employees work in Milwaukee, 235 in Jupiter, Florida. Some 300 are scattered throughout the United States in sales or service offices.

Headquarters: Marquette Electronics
8200 W. Tower Ave.
Milwaukee, WI 53223
(414) 355-5000

Mary Kay Cosmetics

═══════════════════════

✿ MARY KAY

Mary Kay sells and packages their own brand of cosmetics through independent beauty consultants. Employees: 1,600. Beauty consultants: 220,000.

★ ★ ★   Pay/Benefits
★ ★ ★   Opportunities
★ ★ ★ ★   Job Security
★ ★ ★ ★   Pride in Work/Company
★ ★ ★   Openness/Fairness
★ ★ ★ ★   Camaraderie/Friendliness

BIGGEST PLUS: Gifts make up their foundation.
BIGGEST MINUS: You have to paint on a smile.

Dennis Boykin will never forget his first two weeks at Mary Kay, where he works on the cosmetics production line. He received a free calculator (given to all plant employees for no lost-time accidents in the previous month), a birthday card (signed by Mary Kay herself), and a Thanksgiving turkey. Boykin told us he was "flabbergasted," having never worked at a company that bestowed gifts for anything.

This barrage of presents is not unusual for Mary Kay. The company runs on a high-octane mixture of recognition and rewards. Founder and chief inspiration/cheerleader Mary Kay Ash wouldn't have it any other way. As she told us when we met her in her Dallas office: "Every single person you meet has a sign around his or her neck that says, 'Make me feel important.' If you can do that, you'll be a success not only in business but in life too.

God didn't have time to make a nobody. Everybody is a somebody in my book."

Mary Kay herself spends a lot of time trying to make her employees feel important. The night before we interviewed her, she had been up late signing 400 birthday cards. The cards offered a free lunch for two at the company restaurant (a full lunch here can usually be had for less than $3) or free movie tickets. Ash sends employees gifts on other occasions, too. For a new child, she sends a little silver bank shaped like a duck. For newly-weds, a silver bowl. Every employee gets a turkey on the Monday before Thanksgiving, because Mary Kay knows it takes a full three days for a frozen turkey to thaw properly. On every anniversary of hire, employees receive a card personally signed by Mary Kay. Employees also receive a $100 U.S. savings bond after every five years of service. Ten-year veterans are profiled in *Heartline*, the company newsletter, and honored in a special ceremony in Mary Kay's office. She tries to make employees feel important even when there's no special occasion by providing fresh flowers and white tablecloths in the cafeteria, and perfume and makeup in the rest rooms. The reason for all this? According to Ash, "Appreciation is the oil that makes things run."

Such little touches are a big part of working here because Mary Kay Ash sees recognition as part of her company's mission. Ash felt underappreciated for the 25 years she spent in previous jobs with door-to-door sales organizations. At one company, where Ash worked as a sales consultant, she attended a conference where a woman was awarded an alligator-skin purse for reaching a sales goal. Ash coveted that purse. She worked so hard the next year she earned a sales award. But this time the award had changed. It was a flounder light for night fishing. Ash told *Savvy* magazine: "I made up my mind right then that if I ever ran a company, one thing I would never do was give someone a fish light."

Mary Kay sells cosmetics through an army of 220,000 beauty consultants, who invite customers to shows in their homes. Since they get paid a percentage of their sales rather than a salary, beauty consultants are considered independent contractors rather than employees. Sales directors, who usually oversee about 40 individual consultants, make an average of $48,000 a year. The 71 national sales directors make even more—their average commission in 1990 was $169,000. In fact, Mary Kay boasts about having more women earning over $50,000 a year than any other company in America. As of 1991, 47 women had earned over $1 million selling Mary Kay products.

For the sales force, the Mary Kay Seminar marks the high point of the year. Held every summer at the Dallas Convention Center, the three-day seminar attracts thousands of beauty consultants from across the country. The seminars resemble beauty pageants, only women are rewarded for their sales prowess rather than how they look in a swimsuit. Top sellers are marched onto the stage, where they are crowned with diamond tiaras and draped in mink coats or given a set of gold keys to their very own pink Cadillac—a Mary Kay trademark.

Most beauty consultants work part-time, and 70 percent of them have other jobs. Turnover, 40 percent a year, is high but considerably lower than at many of Mary Kay's competitors. Avon, for instance, has a turnover rate of between 100 and 150 percent, according to *BusinessWeek*. Turnover among Mary Kay employees—the people at headquarters, in the distribution centers and factory—is less than 10 percent.

Virtually all the beauty consultants are women, but most of the managers in the company founded by Mary Kay Ash have been men. Richard R. Rogers, Mary Kay's son, is chairman, and former Tupperware sales executive Richard C. Bartlett is president. However, women have been moving up. In 1992 they held 39 percent of the managerial jobs, including the positions of executive vice-president–sales (Barbara Beasley), senior vice-president–marketing (Curran Dandurand), chief scientific officer (Myra Barker), controller (Sharon Drobeck), and senior vice-president–human resources (Amy DiGeso).

When we first interviewed here, in 1983, Mary Kay Cosmetics was a publicly held company, with a listing on the New York Stock Exchange. Anyone could buy its shares. That's no longer possible because in 1985 Ash and other top managers took the company private by buying out the public shareholders. As a result, Mary Kay no longer has to report sales and profits, but the company told us that since reverting to private ownership sales have nearly doubled, reaching $520 million in 1991. Retail sales, meaning the dollars taken in by beauty consultants, exceeded $1 billion.

Mary Kay Ash still sets the style and the tone of this place. Her office, designed to make people feel comfortable during meetings, features pale pink chairs and a pale pink crescent couch, an Edward Fields custom-designed floral-print carpet, a brass peacock, and a breakfront displaying a collection of porcelains including Cybis figures, Boehm flowers and Lalique birds (many of them gifts from her late husband, Mel). Mary Kay's personal powder room has 14-karat-gold-plate fixtures.

Her upbeat personality also still informs the day-to-day culture of the company. A sign outside her office describes her department as the "Department of Sunshine and Rainbows." Ash told us: "Such thinking permeates the whole company. It's not phony and they all know that. If you look in the mirror, and I don't care how bad you're feeling, and you say, 'You are terrific, you are wonderful' and so forth, it sort of helps you feel better about yourself."

Ash practices her philosophy everywhere she goes, including the elevator. Ash met product marketing employee Debby Hennebury in the elevator one day and asked her how she was doing. When Hennebury responded "Fine," Mary Kay scolded her. Hennebury recalled: "She said, 'Don't say that. You're not fine, you're great.' Now when she sees me and asks how I'm doing, I've gotten into the habit of saying 'Great' every time. It's catching. I was surprised that kind of attitude could be transferred through the whole company. People look at you and think, 'If you're great, maybe I can be, too.' "

The upbeat atmosphere translates into a friendly workplace. Cheryl Halpern, a supervisor in product marketing, told us: "People are smiling all the time here. People are having fun, not every minute of the day, but I can't think of a day that goes by that we don't laugh about something at some point. You're never afraid to interject a joke in a meeting to lighten it up."

The company also makes a conscious attempt to reduce the distinctions between the management and other employees. Sheila Cooper, who has worked in the legal department for three years, said: "One of the things that struck me when I came here was how friendly people were. There aren't levels. You can talk to anybody. Everybody goes by their first names." Kim La Rue, who spent her first eight years with Mary Kay in manufacturing and is now a supervisor in the Southwest distribution center, added: "From the day I came here I always felt like I could talk to anybody in the building."

In recent years the company has been making stronger efforts to involve lower-level employees in decision-making. To get a feel for what factory employees are doing and thinking, managers now spend one day a year working on production lines. President Dick Bartlett also started the Creative Action Team program in 1988. This involves groups of employees working together on projects. CAT teams—more than 60 of them have been formed—helped launch Mary Kay cosmetics in Japan and developed a savings plan for sales directors. In 1992 a CAT was working on the 30th anniversary celebration planned for 1993. Tina Lynch, who works as a supervisor in the Southwest distribution center, told us: "They listen to you in the CATs. You can make a point and nothing gets thrown out. Everything is weighed. It may be a crazy idea or it may be a time-consuming idea, but they really do listen."

When Jenny Cheek grew tired of her overflowing newspapers at home, she asked her boss if they could start a recycling program. She formed a CAT team that instituted companywide recycling. Mary Kay was one of the first companies in Dallas to start a recycling program, and they also founded the Corporate Recycling Council in Dallas.

Recent employee surveys show that less than 60 percent of the work force feel they are paid fairly. The company told us that in 1992 general secretaries were earning $23,000, production line assemblers $16,800. Mary Kay pays an annual Christmas bonus that ranges from $25 up to $500, depending on length of service. Profit-sharing contributions augmented salaries by 15 percent in 1990 and 1991. According to the company, one woman who hired on as an assembler in 1967, earning $1.70 an hour, retired in 1991, when she was making $11.70 an hour, with $158,000 in her profit-sharing account.

Types of jobs: Distribution—37 percent; manufacturing and research—35 percent; administration—12 percent; sales and marketing—10 percent.

Main employment centers: Mary Kay's employees work in Dallas, or in distribution centers in Los Angeles, Atlanta, Chicago, and Piscataway, New Jersey. The 220,000 beauty consultants who sell Mary Kay products work in every state in America and 15 other countries.

Headquarters: Mary Kay Cosmetics, Inc.
8787 Stemmons Freeway
Dallas, TX 75247
(214) 630-8787

McCormick

McCORMICK

McCormick is the world's biggest maker of spices. U.S. employees: 6,274.

★ ★ ★ Pay/Benefits
★ ★ ★ Opportunities
★ ★ ★ ★ Job Security
★ ★ ★ ★ Pride in Work/Company
★ ★ ★ Openness/Fairness
★ ★ ★ ★ Camaraderie/Friendliness

BIGGEST PLUS: Well-seasoned employee involvement.
BIGGEST MINUS: Limited career menu.

Ellie Newman still remembers the sign on the wall of the personnel office when she applied for a job in McCormick's Baltimore spice plant more than 20 years ago. The sign read: "We pledge faith not fear." When Newman started her job filling spice jars, she quickly saw that the sign meant she didn't have to punch a time clock. Newman explained to us: "They honor that we are going to be here on time. They just take your word for it."

Not requiring assembly-line workers to punch a time clock was unusual in the late 1960s when Newman started working for McCormick. It was unprecedented in the 1930s when Charles P. McCormick abolished time clocks. The founder's nephew took over the company from his tyrannical uncle Willoughby McCormick, who founded the company to manufacture root beer and fruit syrups. Although the company had expanded to making spices, it was losing money when "C.P.," as he was known, took control. C.P.'s approach was, to say the least, unconventional. Besides abolishing time clocks, he cut workers' hours from 56 per week to 45, increased wages by 10 percent, and started involving employees in decision-making through Multiple Management boards. McCormick also became one of the first companies to offer medical and life insurance and profit sharing. C.P. also gave every employee a turkey at Thanksgiving, a free lunch on their birthday, and a week's holiday with pay between Christmas and New Year's Day (traditions followed to this day). McCormick's radical changes worked. Just one year after he took over, McCormick was profitable again, and it has been ever since. In 1949 C.P. McCormick put down his business philosophy in a book titled *The Power to the People*. It's still handed out to every new employee.

Duke Dugent joined McCormick in 1942 and remembers C.P. well. According to Dugent, C.P. remembered everybody's first name: "He was right down-to-earth. He had a lot of love for his people, he just really believed in people. He backed his people 100 percent. All the executives were the same way no matter who they were or where they went. If they were down in the plant they would come up and talk to you for a few minutes. They were always friendly. You got to know them by their first name and they got to know you by your first name."

McCormick has grown a great deal since C.P.'s day, but it retains much of his spirit. The company now accounts for about 40 percent of the spices sold in grocery stores and supermarkets (under the McCormick label in the East and the Schilling label in the West). McCormick also sells flavorings directly to 80 of the top 100 U.S. food manufacturers and to restaurant chains like McDonald's. Reflecting on C.P.'s legacy, McCormick's current chief executive, Bailey Thomas, said: "There were people who thought he was a communist because these principles were unheard-of. Turning over your business to the employees to run was considered a rather radical concept. In some respects I think he probably pioneered a lot of the systems that are really coming into play in the '80s and '90s."

Thomas cited employee involvement as an example. The Multiple Management boards C.P. McCormick instituted are still in place today. The 12 MM boards act like junior boards of directors, working on solutions to nuts-and-bolts problems and hashing over new ideas. The boards expedite company business and serve as training grounds for middle managers. Being involved with issues and ideas outside of their functional areas gives middle managers experience to help them move up the ranks. Hunt Valley plant materials manager Katie Carolan told us about an MM board she served on that evaluated coupon redemption houses. The board discovered that Mc-Cormick could save money by going to a different clearinghouse. As a result, the clearinghouse they were using cut its prices.

In recent years, McCormick has extended employee involvement to include lower-level workers through the Total Quality program (TQ). Through TQ, decision-making has been pushed to the lowest level, and employees themselves hold more responsibility over their jobs than before. Every month production teams meet with their managers for creative problem-solving sessions during which employees can share ideas or gripes and address plant problems. Bailey Thomas told us: "I've attended meetings where people have stood up and said, 'For the first time in 30 years I'm really happy to come to work because I really feel like I'm making a contribution. I feel like I'm now part of the team.' These are plant employees who are saying this. It's made people feel more important, like they have control over their destiny."

Total Quality has enabled employee teams to draw up their own budgets and make other decisions that affect their jobs. Dry-seasoning-mix department team leader Gregg Black explained: "All the responsibilities for the business are brought down to my level and even to the people who work for me. It's kind of like we're entrepreneurs running our business. It's our own little cookie shop and we can control the waste and we can control how much time we spend working on a certain project."

The day we visited the plant in Hunt Valley, a Baltimore suburb, workers were filling spice bottles with vanilla and allspice. Employees told us that what makes McCormick a good place to work extends beyond specific programs like the Multiple Management boards or TQ. The informality and people orientation that Dugent described in C.P.'s era still prevail. Human resources vice-president Karen Weatherholtz, who joined McCormick in 1977, from a bank, told us: "From my first day one of the things I noticed in McCormick was that as people walked through the hall they always looked at you and smiled and said hello—even to people they didn't know."

William Smith, a lab technician, said: "It really has a family atmosphere. When I first started working here I didn't believe it, but then I found that was just the way it is. It's contagious. I found myself the other day with a dustpan and broom sweeping out the floor in front of my laboratory and I never would have done that at another company."

Since C.P.'s day, McCormick has shared profits with each family member. At the end of the year McCormick hands out the employee dividend, a bonus of at least 4 percent of an employee's salary. When McCormick does especially well, management has been known to increase the bonus. In 1989, McCormick's centennial year, employees received a 6 percent bonus. Seventy percent of the employees own stock through a stock-purchase plan.

Another tradition is Charity Day, or C Day. C.P. McCormick held the first C Day in 1941 for employees who wanted to donate money to the community but couldn't afford to. He opened the plant on a Saturday and told employees that if they chose to come in to work, McCormick would donate double their daily wage to a charity of their choice. On C Day 1990, $769,000 was raised for charity groups.

Types of jobs: Managers and supervisors—25 percent; skilled craft—23 percent; laborers—13 percent; office and clerical—11 percent; sales—9 percent; technicians—4 percent; maintenance—2 percent.

Main employment centers: 1,900 work in Hunt Valley, Maryland. The spices and flavorings division also employs 1,200 people in Salinas and Gilroy (their only unionized plant), California. They also have a spice plant in Bedford, Virginia. McCormick's packaging plants are located in Anaheim and Oxnard, California; Cranbury and Freehold, New Jersey; and Easthampton, Massachusetts. An additional 1,447 employees work overseas.

Headquarters: McCormick & Company, Inc.
11350 McCormick Rd.
Hunt Valley, MD 21031
(410) 771-7301

Merck

Merck is the world's largest maker of prescription drugs. U.S. employees: 19,000.

★ ★ ★ ★ ★   Pay/Benefits
★ ★ ★   Opportunities
★ ★ ★ ★   Job Security
★ ★ ★ ★ ★   Pride in Work/Company
★ ★ ★ ★   Openness/Fairness
★ ★ ★   Camaraderie/Friendliness

BIGGEST PLUS: It has the right prescription.
BIGGEST MINUS: You have to follow directions.

You would have had to be proud to work for Merck during the 1980s and early 1990s as the company introduced drug after drug to combat life-threatening ailments: Mevacor and Zocor for lowering cholesterol; Vasotec and Prinivil for high blood pressure and heart failure; Pepcid and Prilosec for ulcers; Noroxin for urinary tract infections; M-M-R II vaccine for measles, mumps, and rubella; Proscar for enlarged prostate glands. Merck ranks as both the U.S. and world leader in prescription drugs.

People we talked to at Merck did express pride at working for a company that makes disease killers. One employee told us: "It makes you feel good to work for a company that is manufacturing medicine." Another said: "Here we make drugs and there's no room for error." Sara Peterson, an inventory control clerk at Merck's plant at West Point, just outside of Philadelphia, was featured in a company publication after reaching her 25th anniversary with the company in 1991. She said: "Saving lives and helping sick people is always something special."

There are other reasons for being proud to work at Merck. The company is a tiger about the safety of their products. Numerous drug companies, some of them leading players in the industry, have popped up in newspapers and on *60 Minutes* in connection with charges that the pharmaceuticals they released had horrifying side effects. Not Merck. It has never been accused, as many competitors have, of carrying out shoddy research. One manufacturing employee we interviewed, Diana L. Cooksey, recalled working previously in the petrochemical industry where "a number of times we said quality was number one and we were pushing for that, but there were other times when people were asked to look the other way. Here that would never fly. I have never been asked to look the other way for anything. In fact, people are always questioning back and forth. I have never heard of quality being compromised here."

Merck has also been more sensitive than many other companies to consumer complaints about the high cost of drugs. In 1990 the company announced that it would keep price increases down to or below the change in the Consumer Price Index. It was the first pharmaceutical maker to adopt that policy. For many years it has been donating drugs for needy and indigent patients. In 1991 Merck's chief executive, Dr. P. Roy Vagelos, a physician and research scientist, wrote a letter to *Science* magazine asserting that the drug industry "must set responsible prices, must keep prices down, and must help improve access to important medicines."

In 1991, when Congressman Pete Stark (D-Calif.) introduced legislation designed to curb high drug prices, he called Merck "the outstanding bright spot in the otherwise dismal picture of greed that marks this industry."

Dr. Vagelos, who grew up in Merck's headquarters town, Rahway, New Jersey, where his family had a luncheonette, works out in the company's fitness center and eats lunch in the company cafeteria. It was his decision, in 1987, to give away Mectizan, the drug developed by Merck to cure river blindness, a parasitic disease common in rural villages throughout Africa. The decision earned Merck wide praise, including an award in 1991 from the Business Enterprise Trust, a new nonprofit group formed to recognize "acts of courage, integrity and social vision in business." The Children's Inn on the campus of the National Institutes of Health houses children with rare diseases who are undergoing experimental treatment at the NIH. It was built with $3.7 million of Merck money.

Of course, cynics might say that Merck, as one of the most profitable companies on the face of the earth (in 1991 only three U.S. companies made more money than Merck), could easily afford this kind of largesse. But that misses the point. Other companies make a lot of money and don't act the way Merck does. The culture here is steeped in acts of benevolence. The company made streptomycin available to all comers during the 1940s, and in 1986 it sold, for a pittance, a vaccine-manufacturing technology to help the Chinese prevent liver cancer, the second largest cause of death among adult males in China. Merck is guided by a philosophy once expressed by George W. Merck, the last member of the Merck family to head the company. Merck, who died in 1957, said: "Medicine is for the patients. It is not for the profits. The profits follow, and if we have remembered that, they have never failed to appear. The better we have remembered it, the larger they have been." The profits have certainly cascaded like an avalanche. In the last half of the 1980s, Merck's after-tax earnings more than tripled, and the company entered 1992 with 19 drugs each selling more than $100 million a year, a feat never before achieved in the drug industry.

Employees have shared in those profits through a wage and benefits package acknowledged to be the richest in the drug industry. Professionals —a biologist, a management trainee—start here at $30,000 a year. Entry-level secretaries or technicians begin at $18,000. The pay is supplemented by a savings plan under which Merck contributes $1 for every $2 an employee saves, up to 5 percent of pay. Premiums for medical and dental insurance for the employee *and all dependents* are 100 percent paid by Merck. In 1991 Merck spent $2.1 billion on salaries, wages, and benefits, which works out to an incredible average of $57,000 per employee. Bernard D. Yanacek, a finisher in Merck's pharmaceutical packaging plant at West Point, Pennsylvania, reached his 25th anniversary with the company in 1991, and when he was asked what he remembered most about the year 1966, he said: "My paycheck was twice what I made at my last place of employment."

One of the rare labor disputes in Merck's history occurred in 1984, when 4,000 unionized employees went out on strike for five months over company demands for a temporary wage freeze and more flexible work rules. The strike was settled largely on Merck's terms, and all the employees returned to work. In 1990 union steward Bob Huxford told us that while there were day-to-day problems, the Oil, Chemical and Atomic Workers, which represents 840 employees at Rahway, were now on good terms with the company. They had just signed a new contract calling for wage boosts of up to 5 percent, and the union was delighted with the job security prevailing at Merck. There have been no layoffs at Merck since the 1960s.

To cut employees in on the super-profits being logged, Merck has rolled out new programs. In the late 1980s they instituted a stock-option plan for researchers, keying the awards to such milestones as filing an application with the Food and Drug Administration for approval of a new drug. Then, in 1991, when the company was celebrating its 100th birthday, Merck became one of the select few American companies to offer stock options to all employees. The effect was to open for rank-and-file employees the road that top executives of American companies have taken to accumulate large stashes of cash. Between 1985 and 1990, Merck's stock price appreciated 34 percent a year. If it rises 20 percent a year during the 1990s, then an individual Merck employee exercising the option on 100 shares would make about $55,000. Huxford, who works as a chauffeur, told *USA Today* reporter Gary Strauss: "It's a terrific deal for us and a nice gesture on the company's part, and it's a no-lose situation."

Merck's virtues have not gone unheralded. Indeed, the company has won so many awards—best company for blacks, for women, for working mothers, for salespersons, to name just a handful—that they might have to put up a separate building to hold them. In 1992, for the sixth year in a row, Merck came out on top in the annual *Fortune* poll of business executives to determine the most admired company in the United States. Merck's reflex action on winning this award has been to thank its employees. One year it ran the names of employees in local newspaper ads. In 1992 it decided to donate, on behalf of employees, $1 million for two mobile medical units that will bring medical care to families in disadvantaged areas.

One by-product of this reputation is a flood of applications for employment. More than 150,000 flow into Merck every year. Merck hired more than 700 university graduates in 1991—44 percent were women and 21 percent were minorities.

It's easy to overemphasize the money and benefits that accrue to people here. But equally attractive are a collegial atmosphere that you might expect at a company spending $1 billion a year on research (Dr. Dennis Schmatz, a research scientist, told us that "Merck is the closest thing you're going to get to academic research in industry") and a warmth engendered by years of working together to deliver products that have made a difference in health care. Other employees we talked to cited the training programs (Merck spends $40,000 in a one-year training program for each sales representative), the ability to bring complaints, the openness, and the zeal with which the company solicits opinions from the work force—and then acts on them. The employee communications vehicles are also superb. Merck publishes a slew of publications for employees, including a daily news bulletin at headquarters, and they rank among the best in corporate America. Hardly anyone ever leaves here. Turnover runs at 6.9 percent a year, a figure that includes retirements and deaths.

Thoroughness and concern for employees are Merck hallmarks. In the fall of 1992 the company was moving 1,900 employees to its new headquarters at Whitehouse Station, 30 miles west of its historic campus at Rahway. They began briefing employees about this move in 1989, offering a wide array of relocation help, including a guaranteed sales price at appraised value for homes that had to be sold, assistance for first-time home buyers to keep their down payments as low as 10 percent of the purchase price, payment of the interest cost on a car loan for employees needing to buy an automobile, and "grossing up" all relocation allowances so that any extra tax liabilities would be borne by the company, not the employee.

Merck's new headquarters in New Jersey's Readington Township is a 900,000-square-foot hexagon designed by architect Kevin Roche. It includes a child-care center with slots for 130 children (a new child-care center was also being built at the same time at Rahway), a spacious cafeteria that features a series of semiprivate dining rooms and a take-home service, a 2,500-square-foot convenience store, and a two-tier underground garage designed so that you will never have to walk more than 50 yards to the nearest elevator. During the winter months, ramps to the garage will be heated to prevent icing. The hexagon sits in a wooden glen, with every window having a vista of greenery. The 460-acre site was formerly farm fields and woods, and every effort was made to preserve the natural landscape. The reason for putting the garage underground was to save cutting down 20 acres of woods for an ugly blacktop. Ann Raver, who writes a gardening column for the *New York Times*, described how landscape designers Edmund Hollander and Maryanne Connelly visited the site after being hired by Merck and "wandered beneath American beech trees, white oak, red maple, red cedar, hawthorne, dogwood, shadblow, wild pear, sassafras, black walnut and black gum." They had the idea, "Why not try to save this?" And so, Raver reported, they suggested to Merck that the old trees be transplanted instead of being bulldozed. Merck executives were, at first, incredulous but then, Raver reported, "let themselves be persuaded." Ergo, some 1,300 trees were moved to a nursery and then replanted, at an estimated cost of $1 million.

Types of jobs: Manufacturing—41 percent; research—23 percent; administration—19 percent; sales and marketing—12 percent; engineering—5 percent.

Main employment centers: Whitehouse Station, New Jersey, 2,000; Rahway, New Jersey, 2,000; West Point, Pennsylvania, 4,000. Merck does half its business overseas, where 20,000 are employed.

Headquarters: Merck & Co., Inc.
P.O. Box 100
Whitehouse Station, NJ 08889
(908) 423-1000

Methodist Hospital

===

Methodist

Methodist Hospital is the largest private, nonprofit hospital in the United States. Employees: 7,000.

★★★ Pay/Benefits
★★★ Opportunities
★★★★ Job Security
★★★★ Pride in Work/Company
★★★ Openness/Fairness
★★★ Camaraderie/Friendliness

BIGGEST PLUS: Medical miracles happen every day.
BIGGEST MINUS: Pay is not miraculous.

How would you like to work for the best? Employees at Methodist believe they are doing just that by working for the largest private, nonprofit hospital in the land. Home to famous heart surgeon Dr. Michael DeBakey, Methodist is one of the world's premier hospitals. Its state-of-the-art facilities attract some 35,000 patients every year from all 50 states and more than 80 countries.

Being associated with such an institution has a big impact on the people working there. Senior physical therapist Louise Chalupa explained: "We see things that most people wouldn't see, working with patients that have just the most unique situations in the world, and it's exciting. People come here from all over the world. So we get the worst of the worst. And we work miracles. I love it."

Head nurse Donna Hahus added other reasons. She started in 1966 as a staff nurse and worked her way up through the ranks: "I've always worked with people that I respected, quality coworkers at all levels. When you say you're an employee of Methodist Hospital, people are impressed, either in the community or other health professionals. Several months ago someone from another medical center came to my office about a matter pertaining to a professional organization. She'd never been inside the hospital, and when she got to my office she said, 'Wow, I would be so proud to work here.' It was just the appearance of the place, the attitude of the people that she ran into in getting to my office."

Patient administration secretary Mary Gentempo also cited the hospital's appearance: "I'm proud of the facilities here. So many times I've seen people come in from out of state or even from around the country and they always comment on the beauty of the hospital. They say, 'We've never seen anything like this. When we first walked in, we thought it was a hotel.' "

It's easy to see why. Located in Houston's Texas Medical Center complex, Methodist sits across the street from an upscale Marriott hotel. But you could easily mistake Methodist's entrance for the Marriott's. Incoming patients and their families can have a valet park their cars while white-jacketed bellhops put their luggage on brass baggage carts. (There is a "No tips" sign on the marble-covered reception desk.) The lobby looks even more lush than the Marriott's, furnished with a beautiful fountain, a tropical garden, and antique chairs.

Methodist has distinctive facilities for employees, too. The employee fitness center has a swimming pool, racquetball courts, an indoor track, and weight-lifting equipment. In addition to aerobic classes, it offers courses in stress management, smoking cessation, and diet. The director of the center is Cletus Clark, who won a gold medal at the 1991 Pan American Games in the 110-meter high hurdles. He credits the hospital for his being able to pursue track and advance in his career at the hospital.

Clark said: "When I came out of college, I had a strong athletic background, running track, and I wanted to train for the Olympics. It was hard to find an employer who was going to give me a job and allow me time off to train, go to Europe, and things like that, in order to participate. But Methodist has been doing it for the past six years now. They're really interested in what a person can do for the hospital, not so much, 'Are you here eight to 10 hours a day doing this, this, and this?' "

You don't have to be a gold medalist to get flexible hours. Louise Chalupa related: "I've been a part-time worker here for 15 years, but my situation has changed over those years, from having just little teeny-weeny kids to teenagers, working in the evenings, taking just four hours a day, working three days a week eight hours a day. Now I'm working four days a week and have one day off. So it's very flexible."

Methodist also goes out of its way to meet special needs for leaves of absence. Nurse Diana Cruzan told us: "Leaves are not hard to get here. If you want one, for whatever reason, you've got it. Because they want to keep you and they want you back." Methodist has not had a single layoff in its 65-year history.

Overseeing Methodist these days is Larry Mathis, who became the hospital's president and CEO in 1983. One of his first actions was to institute twice-yearly all-employee meetings, which are held at the Marriott. He also holds monthly breakfast meetings with randomly selected groups of non-management employees and quarterly meetings with managers. He meets every new employee during receptions in his office. Mammograph operator Alicia Salazar said that at the large employee meetings "if you have a problem in a particular area, Mr. Mathis will hear you out. He's not defensive. He likes to hear what you have to say."

This attitude of being listened to is new, according to Cruzan, who has been with Methodist for 20 years: "I've seen lots of changes. I've seen Larry Mathis change this particular hospital from a good-ole-boy, physician-oriented, 'let's please the entrepreneurs and benefactors' kind of place. I've seen the hospital change their focus to the employees and patients."

The hospital has close ties to the Methodist Church, considered, in fact, an extension of the Texas Conference of the United Methodist Church. Its 48-person board of trustees includes eight Methodist ministers, a bishop, and 24 representatives from Methodist church districts. Phil Robinson, senior vice-president of diagnostic and therapeutic services, said: "I don't want to sound corny but the healing ministry is an important part of what we do. It's kind of nice to walk in the front door and have a chapel there." The chapel is nonsectarian, however, and there are more than a dozen chaplains of different faiths, including a full-time rabbi and a Muslim cleric as well as clergy from various Christian denominations.

Methodist tries to pay at the top of the market for jobs that are in great demand such as nursing and to be "above the midpoint" for most other positions, according to vice-president of human resources Bill Fugazzi. He pointed out that it is one of the few hospitals in the country (and the only one in Houston) that have an employee bonus program based on tenure with the hospital. The average bonus in 1991 was $309.

Pay is not, however, the main attraction, as only half of the employees feel that their pay is fair compared with other local workplaces. A higher percentage gave a better rating to Methodist's benefits package. One of the more popular benefits is a subsidized child-care center with provisions for children when they are sick.

The child-care center staff pitched in during hurricane season in 1990 and 1991, taking care of employees' kids. Nurse Diana Cruzan explained: "In the last year or two we've had the threat of a couple of big ones. And the hospital's philosophy is, 'We would like to have you here. If you feel that you can't come, we understand, but if you can, bring your kids.' I could put my dog in the kennel and put him in the garage if I wanted to. They took the gymnasium over in the Scurlock Towers and made a big day-care center for 24 hours out of it. And they brought TVs and movies and they had little exercise classes for the children and they all had their little coolers and their backpacks and there were bedrolls and everything. It made a fun time out of something that could have been a real crisis."

Types of jobs: Professional and administrative—21 percent; direct care-giver—19 percent; support staff—34 percent; other—26 percent.

Main employment center: Houston.

Headquarters: The Methodist Hospital
6565 Fannin St.
Houston, TX 77030
(713) 790-3354

Microsoft

Microsoft is the world's largest independent developer of software for computers. U.S. employees: 7,500.

★ ★ ★ ★   Pay/Benefits
★ ★ ★ ★ ★   Opportunities
★ ★ ★   Job Security
★ ★ ★ ★   Pride in Work/Company
★ ★ ★   Openness/Fairness
★ ★ ★   Camaraderie/Friendliness

BIGGEST PLUS: Macro paychecks.
BIGGEST MINUS: Micro leisure time.

Looking for high energy? Come to Microsoft. It's like being plugged into a high-voltage power line.

Looking for challenges? Come to Microsoft. All they want to do is crush their opponents and acquire a 100 percent market share in computer software.

Looking for money? Come to Microsoft. By one estimate, one out of every five persons working here in 1992 was a millionaire.

Be prepared to work long hours. The lights are always on in the evenings at the 250-acre Redmond campus outside Seattle where new software programs are being developed to enhance the capabilities of computers. And if you come in on weekends, you won't be alone. In fact, it might be a good idea to pick up a pizza on your way to the office. These guys are always hungry.

In many ways, Microsoft seems to be an extension of college life. Scruffy youngsters in jeans sit in offices eating a cheeseburger and a Coke while they stare at a computer screen. Practical jokes are always being played on people. Espresso bars stay open 12 hours a day. Floor hockey is being played in open areas. There are chess tournaments. Outdoors, people are shooting hoops or juggling or playing Ultimate Frisbee. A team of software developers will crash for weeks to complete a project, and then—maybe in the middle of an afternoon—someone will get up and say, "Let's go to the movies," and they'll all pile out of the office and head for a nearby theater. No one pays too much attention to the clock. Everyone is intensely engaged in Microsoft's mission, which is to be *the* intelligence that powers computers. And so far, with DOS, Word, Windows, and Excel, to name four of their most popular products, they have gone a long way toward dominating the software industry, so much so that they are regarded with suspicion, envy, and hatred by competitors and—sometimes—customers.

The sense that Microsoft is a "Joe College" kind of place is reinforced by the comments made to us when we visited and by the way the company positions itself when it recruits on college campuses. One recruiting booklet quoted former summer intern Will Kennedy: "The work environment is what persuaded me to come back to Microsoft for a second summer as a development intern. Sure, I looked elsewhere, but no other company would let me wear shorts and play golf in the halls." Another techie described Microsoft this way: "I like to think it's like playing with one of those erector sets we had as kids: you have everything you need to create just about anything, and all the control to decide exactly what to build." One manager told us: "Since everyone is the same age, it's hard to distinguish when work stops and play starts. It's a bunch of people in their 20s having fun. This is our family." The average age at Microsoft is 31. Another manager, Sue Boeschen, said: "There's a sense of fun here. Pranks are not discouraged. We put sod on the floor of Jay's office not too long ago with a sprinkler system and lawn mowers. This would not be condoned in most companies because we stole it from the gardener's shed. This kind of thing goes on a lot. It's not that the company encourages misbehavior, but there is a sense of fun, a sense of playfulness, that really balances the intensity of the work."

Corporate communications editor Sarah Hersack summed it up for us: "It's a graduate school that stays forever."

It's not IBM, the company that gave Microsoft its lease on life by making DOS the operating system in its first personal computer, but there's a lot of contempt here for IBM—and, for that matter, for virtually every other company in the computer industry. Chris Peters, who was general manager of the Word business unit when we visited here in 1991, told us: "I worked at IBM for a summer, and the difference between here and IBM was that they had a group of 30 people—five were not working at all, 20 were pretending to work, and five were doing the job. At Microsoft, we have three and those three people will be very busy. This place is an incredible amount of fun. I love this place. You can do anything you want if you're good. You can do nothing if you're bad."

The ringmaster of this circus is, of course, William H. Gates III, the Seattle native who dropped out of Harvard when he was 19 to start this enterprise with his high school crony, Paul Allen. A computer nerd who also happens to like running a business, Bill Gates reigns over Microsoft like a god or Svengali or tyrant, depending on whose perspective he's being viewed from. Gates is like no other leader, even in the quirky computer software field. Although he was 37 years old in 1992, he still looked like a precocious teenager, usually dressed in his trademark sweater and intent on the matter at hand: Microsoft's prowess. He is intensely competitive, abrasive in his handling of people, but admired for his technical wizardry. Jay Blumenthal, director of program management, told us: "One of the things that characterizes Microsoft is insecurity. People never believe that they've got the best product. It's always the fear that somebody is going to come up with a better product. Bill is at the top and he always wants it to be better and everybody has picked that up through the years."

Sue Boeschen, who joined Microsoft in 1983, said: "This concept of Bill as the visionary is a real important factor here. He really is the corporate culture hero, particularly for those who are in development. They've come to work for the person that they regard as the best in the industry. I think he is intelligent by historical standards. I think he could be as smart as Einstein or Michelangelo or any of them. I'm not kidding. He's the kind of person who comes around every hundred or 200 years. If you have a meeting with him, you'll be totally amazed. It feels good to work for someone like that, someone you can really admire. There's nothing he doesn't know. I've seen him go from meeting with you to meeting with me and it's about completely different details and he seems to know them all."

Robert X. Cringely, who writes a gossip column for the industry trade paper, *Info World,* has another view. In his book *Accidental Empires* he said that Microsoft is "like any successful cult," utilizing "sacrifice and penance and the idea that the deity is perfect." Cringely added: "Each level, from Gates on down, screams at the next, goading and humiliating them. And while you can work any eighty hours per week that you want, dress any way that you like, you can't talk back in a meeting when your boss says you are shit in front of all your co-workers. It just isn't done. When Bill Gates says that he could do in a weekend what you've failed to do in a week or a month, he's lying, but you don't know better and just go back to try harder."

Taking potshots at Bill Gates is *de rigueur* in the fratricidal computer industry, but we didn't sense any resentment of Chairman Bill when we visited here. He's not loved either, but he's widely admired, and he was wildly cheered in October 1991 when he came riding into Seattle's Kingdome for an all-employee meeting on a Harley-Davidson bike, flanked by nine leather-clad bikers on Harleys, the loudspeakers blaring "Leader of the Pack." Nor did it escape anyone's attention that Gates was preceded into the arena by a vehicle carrying the legend "OS/2," which is the IBM software that competes against Microsoft's Windows. The vehicle was an Edsel. It's the kind of fun and games they love at Microsoft.

Two features of work here were cited as big pluses by employees we met. One is the absence of the dead hand of tradition, meaning you won't be impeded by regulations and can make your own path here. The other is the sense that you are at the center of the world, at least as far as computer technology goes—and, in the opinion of many who work here, what other world is there? Here's a sampling of comments we heard:

"I don't think that there is any company around that you can come in right out of college and have the responsibility that I was given."

"We are not held up by dumb rules that somebody invented that doesn't have anything to do with what we're doing."

"There is very little dead wood here. People just care passionately about what they're doing. I think that's because we've done a pretty good job of putting them into small teams and empowering those teams. They feel like they own the product. It's a world of difference from the more hierarchal organization where decisions are filtered down from the top."

"If you've got ideas and want to pursue something, you're not stymied by the bureaucracy or past history."

John Prumatico, Microsoft's director of human resources, was in one of our group interviews, and he summed up the culture this way: "This organization isn't one that's built on control mechanisms. Your job isn't defined for you. You've got a basic assignment and you can kind of elbow your way in there and hammer out your job definition. In personnel, it's worrisome sometimes. I have to work overtime to fight off those feelings of people doing work outside their job titles. But it doesn't bother them, it doesn't bother senior management, and I've got to get over it. People just get so enthused about what they're doing."

It can make for a certain amount of chaos. Everything is always being reorganized—even at the top. In 1983, when the company was tiny, Gates hired away James C. Towne from Tektronix to serve as president. Known around Microsoft as "the suit" because he wore a coat and tie, Towne lasted less than a year. "He was sort of random," Gates told *Fortune*. Then he hired away Jon Shirley from Tandy as president. Shirley retired in 1990, and Gates replaced him with Michael R. Hallman, whom he hired away from Boeing, Seattle's largest employer. At 48, Hallman was one of Boeing's youngest executives. At Microsoft, he was nearly twice the average age. In early 1992 Hallman was fired, replaced by a troika of Microsoft veterans. No one blinked. Bill Gates was still there.

WHERE THE JOBS ARE

Worldwide Employment at Microsoft

1987	1988	1989	1990	1991	1992
1,867	2,793	4,037	5,635	8,226	11,500

The employee population at Microsoft has been doubling every two years, but it's not easy to get hired here. Every year they recruit at more than 140 campuses, look at 120,000 résumés, and interview 7,400 candidates. Your chances are better if they have hired someone from your school in previous years because they always ask those people, "Who else is good there?" You may also have to answer oddball questions like: "Why are manhole covers round?" "How many gas stations are there in the U.S.?" or "Why do vending machines and jukeboxes have both letters and numbers?" If Bill Gates is interested in someone, he will pursue him to the ends of the earth. In his book, Cringely reported that "one year Microsoft got in trouble with the government in India for hiring nearly every computer science graduate in the country and moving them all to Redmond." According to *BusinessWeek*, Gates pursued James Allchin, former technical officer at Banyan Systems, for a year before landing him. Allchin took a 35 percent pay cut, explaining that Gates convinced him "of one thing. If you want to change the world—and being the silly kind of guy I am, I do—I would have a bigger impact at Microsoft."

People who do come to Microsoft find that the pay is lower than it is at such places as Apple and Hewlett-Packard. But the big lure has been the option to buy stock. Microsoft first sold stock to the public in 1986, and it has escalated in price by 25 times since then. Gates has given out stock options freely, especially to software developers. By one estimate, half the people who work here have options, which gives them the right to buy Microsoft stock at a set price, usually the price it was selling for when the option was granted. The options can run for 18 months to four years, and you don't have to pay for the stock until you exercise your option. Ergo, if the stock price has risen since the option grant—and it always has so far— you're home free with an instant profit. A Wall Street analyst, Michael Kwatinetz, did a study which showed that by 1992, at least 3,400 of the 11,000 people who work for Microsoft had become millionaires by virtue of their stockholdings. The biggest beneficiary is, of course, Bill Gates, whose 32 percent holding in Microsoft gave him, in mid-1992, a net worth of about $7 billion, making him the richest American. In mid-1992 Microsoft's market value was greater than that of 3M, Ford Motor Company, Atlantic Richfield, or Eastman Kodak.

Main employment center: Redmond, Washington.

Headquarters: Microsoft Corporation
One Microsoft Way
Redmond, WA 98052
(206) 882-8080

Herman Miller

⊔ **herman miller**

Herman Miller is a leading designer and maker of modern office furniture. U.S. employees: 5,600.

★ ★ ★ Pay/Benefits
★ ★ ★ Opportunities
★ ★ ★ ★ Job Security
★ ★ ★ ★ Pride in Work/Company
★ ★ ★ ★ Openness/Fairness
★ ★ ★ Camaraderie/Friendliness

BIGGEST PLUS: They've dethroned hierarchy.
BIGGEST MINUS: Executives have been playing musical chairs.

When J. Kermit Campbell became chief executive officer of Herman Miller on April 13, 1992, he made a vow to meet every one of the company's 5,500 employees. As a new kid on the block—he came here from Dow Corning—Campbell felt it was important to make this special effort. He was succeeding Richard H. Ruch, who had spent 36 years with Herman Miller. And before Ruch became CEO in 1988, the company had always been headed by members of the founding family, the De Prees, who had intertwined an innovative office furniture business with a culture whose hallmarks are worker participation, sharing of the gains, and gentleness. It's a culture that has become celebrated by people seeking new and better ways of working. In his book *Leadership Is an Art*, which he wrote in the 1980s during his final years as CEO, Max De Pree said: "My goal for Herman Miller is that when people both inside the company and outside the company look at all of us not as a corporation but as a group of people working intimately within a covenantal relationship, they'll say, 'Those folks are a gift to the spirit.'"

It's no wonder as he took on this mantle that Kermit Campbell felt the need to introduce himself.

When we caught up with him three and a half months after he took over, Campbell was one week shy of fulfilling his pledge. He had been to Asia and Europe, and he had visited all the U.S. plants and distribution centers except one. In the following week he met and shook hands with employees at a distribution center in Dayton, New Jersey. And that was the last stop on his schedule. Mission accomplished.

The remarkable aspect of this exercise in communications is that these were all one-on-one meetings. Campbell didn't want to summon employees to group meetings. He wanted to look each one in the eye. And he wanted to do it at times convenient to them. So he walked through offices and factories to meet people at their workstations. The headquarters plant at Zeeland, Michigan, works three shifts, and he woke up early to be there at 6:00 A.M. to greet employees coming off the overnight turn.

In getting out to see everyone who works for Herman Miller, Campbell was delivering a message that had two parts seemingly contradictory. One was that he had no intention of dismantling the people orientation of this company. In our interview with him, he described the Herman Miller culture as "wonderful." The second part, though, was a determination to change practices that may have caused the Herman Miller engine to stall during the late 1980s and early 1990s after two decades of spectacular growth.

Herman Miller, more than any other company, is responsible for the crisp, clean, flexible lines of offices and homes in America. Its name is synonymous with modernity in furniture, symbolized by the Eames chair and the "open office" environment. The *Minneapolis Tribune* once credited the company with having "done more to revolutionize the way Americans live, what they sit on, what kind of space they work in, and how their functional surroundings look like than any other design group. The reason is the company's incorruptible honesty of design and its ability to inspire some of this country's greatest designers." That vision was blessed with commercial success. Sales leaped from $250 million in 1980 to $800 million in 1988. It's easy to be benevolent when the dollars roll in this way.

But the company proved not to be immune to the recession of the late 1980s and early 1990s when its customers—and potential customers—downsized their white-collar ranks, laid off thousands of employees, and postponed or canceled plans to buy new furniture. Herman Miller's sales stagnated, profits nose-dived, and 70 people left voluntarily under an early retirement program. It was a period marked by uncertainty and lack of focus, compounded by the rise of hierarchy in a company committed to work teams. To dispel the malaise, Herman Miller went outside to find a new leader. As the company grew, hierarchical structures had grown up, despite a commitment to work teams.

Kermit Campbell therefore arrived here with a mandate to introduce flexibility. One hears a litany of words these days at Herman Miller: "structureless," "relational," "borderless," "cross-functional," "the networked organization." It's the gobbledygook of organizational development. The ultimate goal is to give people at all levels more freedom, to enable them, as Michele Hunt, vice-president for quality and people development, explained to us, "to come together around a task," not a hierarchy, and "to take ownership of what they do." Campbell told us that one of his first moves, to facilitate this transition, was to cut out layers of management. So he now has 15 people reporting directly to him, instead of seven. He described his mission as one of "liberating the human spirit," and he reported that it "had taken the company by wildfire."

It bears repeating that Campbell wants to bring about this change within the context of the unique Herman Miller culture. The qualities we originally found admirable here remain in place. They serve as magnets for candidates, with unsolicited résumés pouring in here at the rate of 75 a day. Diana Bunse, a fabric supervisor at the Zeeland plant, told us: "I had never heard of Herman Miller and somebody kept telling me that there was this wonderful company in western Michigan that was the only company, when it came down to a question of profit versus people, that would have to think about it." Scott Turik, a financial analyst who previously worked for General Motors, said the recruiter who landed him here in 1989 came to him with the news, "Boy, have I got a company for you."

Herman Miller articulates its values. Over and over. In fact, some people may find it a little preachy. Bill Manifold, organizational development manager, pointed out to us: "We are pretty up-front about the human element of the organization but we don't pretend to be perfect. In a human organization you're going to have differences and inefficiencies as well as strengths. It's okay to be a human being here. In fact, it's not okay if you're not. And we discovered that as many folks as there are who succeed in Herman Miller, there are also folks who don't assimilate well and choose to go someplace else. So it isn't like you've died and gone to heaven, but it's clearly a human organization."

Herman Miller values are not just window dressing. They have worked their way into practices. Participative management has recently become a fad in American business, but it's old hat to Herman Miller, which adopted a Scanlon Plan in 1950. Scanlon is a gain-sharing plan whereby employees work together in teams, set goals to cut costs and/or improve productivity —and then share in the savings achieved by the company. All employees here are stockholders in the company through a profit-sharing plan. Herman Miller stock can also be bought at a 15 percent discount. In coming to Herman Miller, Campbell knew his compensation was governed by a policy that restricts the CEO from making more than 20 times the average paycheck. That average, in 1991, was $28,000, which meant that the then CEO, Ruch, could earn no more than $560,000 in salary and bonus. In fact, he made $490,000. Campbell told us he was quite comfortable with this formula.

Other companies have vice-presidents for human resources or personnel directors. Herman Miller has a vice-president for people. The first holder of this position was Michele Hunt, who is one of the 15 people reporting to Campbell—and she now works out of Chicago. The current vice-president for people is Craig Schrotenboer, a 20-year veteran of Herman Miller.

Environmental programs are very strong here. They recycle everything, and the company has long followed the 25-25-50 rule with respect to any properties it has. This means that 25 percent of the area is allocated to pavement, 25 percent to buildings, and 50 percent to open space. The power for the headquarters site is generated entirely from burned waste. At the 1990 annual meeting, shareholders were all given seedlings to plant. Herman Miller has even taken the risk of tinkering with its signature Eames chair out of concern for endangered rain forests. The chair was originally designed with rosewood, which comes from tropical rain forests. In 1990, in an effort to prevent these forests from being depleted, Herman Miller substituted cherry and walnut for the rosewood. We interviewed one employee who said, "I go camping and you see a lot of trash. At least you know it's not the fault of the place you work for. They're doing something about it."

Employees we met feel good about working at Herman Miller, even with all the frustrations that have come in recent years of no growth. It's a company with a warm, personal feeling to it, although there's also a touch of moral rectitude stemming from its birth and location in western Michigan, which was settled by members of the Reformed Church in America. The De Prees were members of this church, and if you go down the roster of Herman Miller employees you will see many Dutch names. Western Michigan is an enclave dotted with farms and more churches than shopping malls. The work ethic is strong. And those feelings carry over to the Herman Miller company. Alcoholic beverages are never served at a Herman Miller function. Smoking has been banned here since 1987. Large meetings often begin with a prayer. And all the meals at Herman Miller are supplied by a hospitality services staff made up of local people, all of them Herman Miller employees. We read in the November 1991 issue of the company newspaper, *Connections*, how the hospitality services people, most of them women, fed shareholders at the 1991 annual meeting, held at the Midwest Distribution Center in nearby Holland. A staff of 31 put together 900 beef kabobs in less than three hours, cooked all the desserts at the historic Marigold Lodge which the company maintains on Lake Macatawa, and then served 750 people in 10 minutes. Reporting on this feat, the company paper noted that the cost of the meal was about $9.50 a person, $15 less than an outside caterer would have charged.

We asked about life at Herman Miller during our interview sessions and received answers like these:

"The founder of the company realized that if your workers aren't happy, you're not going to get the kind of production and quality that you would like."

"People like living here. Driving home, you don't get run off the road by a bunch of crazy people."

"We have what we call our strolling choir at Christmastime. They get on a little tugger train and ride all through the plant caroling. And it's gotten to the point that so many people want to do that, they're going to have to break it up into two choirs."

Kermit Campbell hails from Kansas and came to the attention of Max De Pree through his service on the board of trustees of Hope College, a western Michigan school established by Reformed Church members in 1866. De Pree graduated from Hope and also serves on the board of trustees. Max De Pree's father, D. J. Pree, the founder of the company, died in 1990 at the age of 99. He had spent his entire life in Zeeland. In 1923, with financial backing from his father-in-law, he bought the Star Furniture company. And then he renamed the company after his father-in-law.

Types of jobs: office employees—54 percent; production—36 percent; management—10 percent.

Main employment centers: 2,800 people work in the western Michigan communities of Zeeland, Holland, Grandville, and Spring Lake, where the company has its headquarters, manufacturing facilities, and Midwest distribution center. Another 2,800 work in plants (Roswell, Georgia; Grand Prairie, Texas; Rocklin, California), distribution centers, and sales offices/showrooms in the rest of the country. More than 400 work overseas.

Headquarters: Herman Miller, Inc.
8500 Byron Rd.
Zeeland, MI 49464
(616) 772-3300

3M

3M

3M (Minnesota Mining & Manufacturing) makes 60,000 different products —adhesives, tapes, surgical dressings, drugs, sponges, orthopedic implants —that stretch over four fields: industrial and electronic, information and imaging, life sciences, commercial and consumer. U.S. employees: 49,400.

★ ★ ★ ★ Pay/Benefits
★ ★ ★ ★ ★ Opportunities
★ ★ ★ ★ Job Security
★ ★ ★ ★ Pride in Work/Company
★ ★ ★ Openness/Fairness
★ ★ ★ Camaraderie/Friendliness

BIGGEST PLUS: They'll stick with your good ideas.
BIGGEST MINUS: Lots of red tape.

Every company likes to talk about its success stories—and 3M has plenty of them. But here's a company that also likes to tell about its failures, not so much to celebrate them as to encourage people to keep trying out ideas. So they're not averse to recalling that the company was founded in 1902 to mine a very hard mineral, corundum, on the northwest bank of Lake Superior, midway between Silver Bay and Duluth, only to discover that the area had no corundum deposits. Another favorite story is about Francis Okie, an inventor who worked here in the early 1920s when the main product was sandpaper. He suggested, seriously, that 3M market sandpaper to compete with the razor blade, the idea being that men could sand the hair off their face without any fear of nicking themselves. Undaunted by the failure of his idea to catch on (he continued to sand the hair off his face), Okie went on to develop a waterproof sandpaper that turned into 3M's first sales blockbuster.

3M, as they prefer to be known rather than by their legal name, Minnesota Mining & Manufacturing, is a self-contained world, with its own principles, practices, and customs. When we visited 3M Center in St. Paul, we felt that we had entered a city within a city. The 425-acre headquarters campus constitutes, by itself, a fairly large town, what with 12,000 people working in 25 interconnected buildings. The center has its own dining rooms, parking lots, stores, post office, and other conveniences. The corridors are so long that we saw some employees doing their speed-walking on breaks. 3M Center even has its own newspaper, *Stemwinder*, a weekly tabloid that can run to as long as 36 pages. It turns a profit on paid ads from local merchants, but employees are allowed to place 10-word want ads free of charge. The paper also runs news of 3M Club activities, and there's plenty going on here. At the last count, more than 60 clubs or activity groups were functioning, among them an orchestra, male chorus, women's chorus, Afro-American Society, various hunting and fishing clubs, Toastmasters, and groups devoted to such pursuits as stamps, sports cars, scuba diving, windsurfing, running, table tennis, and tai chi. Some of these activities take place at Tartan Park, a 483-acre recreation area located seven miles east of 3M Center and reserved exclusively for the use of 3M employees. Membership in the 3M Club costs $12 a year.

3Mers continue to invent today, encouraged by a companywide policy that allows employees to devote 15 percent of their time to projects of their own choosing. It's called bootlegging. One of the great bootleg successes of the 1980s was the Post-it notepad, which was developed by researcher Art Fry after he became frustrated at bookmarks falling out of his hymnal during church services. Post-it sales are now estimated at more than $300 million a year—and it's a classic example of how 3M develops products by adding new wrinkles to old technologies. (The adhesive in Post-its had been around for decades.) At 3M, one product frequently leads to another and someone is always thinking of new uses for an old product. Their best-known product is Scotch transparent tape, whose annual sales are estimated at $750 million. In 1990, when Scotch tape was 60 years old, the company newspaper ran an article detailing 60 different uses for it, everything from removing dog hairs to covering the cracks in the shells of fertilized pigeon eggs.

3M has other ways to stimulate thinking about new products. The company maintains guidelines that demand that 25 percent of sales in every division be derived from products developed during the past five years. With sales now over $13 billion, that means a slew of new formulations every year. Still another spur is the Genesis Program, adopted in 1983, which enables 3Mers to submit proposals for a project requiring considerable funding and having the potential to become a significant new business. A Genesis grant can be as much as $50,000. Twenty-three are awarded each year.

Headhunters—people retained by corporations to recruit top executives—have a very hard time with this company. They can't pry managers out of here. They also can't place managers here. This is a company, like Procter & Gamble, that trains its own people and moves them up. They rarely hire anyone from the outside for an upper-level position. But unlike P&G, hardly anyone leaves here to go to another company where the ascent to the top might be quicker. 3Mers are in it for the long haul. In 1992 some 5,000 of them had been with the company for more than 25 years.

Allen F. Jacobson, a chemical engineer who was born in Omaha and joined 3M in 1947 right after his graduation from Iowa State University, rose through the tape business to become CEO in 1986. He retired five years later and turned the reins over to another 3M "lifer" and another chemical engineer, Livio D. DeSimone, who joined 3M in 1957 right after his graduation from McGill University in Canada.

For a big company, 3M functions with an amazing lack of bureaucracy. When we saw Jacobson at 3M Center shortly before he retired, he explained how they do it: "We are so diverse as a company that you can't make all the decisions on the 14th and 13th floors of this building. So we have built a culture that puts a lot of responsibility on the people closest to the job, closest to the technology, and closest to the customer." Jacobson credited William McKnight, the spiritual father of the company, with introducing a way of managing that relied on people to make their own decisions. McKnight joined 3M as a bookkeeper in 1907 and was still serving on the board of directors in 1976, when he died at age 90. According to Jacobson, McKnight laid down this 3M principle years ago: "The mistakes that people will make are of much less importance than the mistake that management makes if it tells them exactly how to do a job." Today's 3M, Jacobson pointed out, is "pretty tough in setting goals, but we don't tell them exactly how to do the job." Of course that's not the way outsiders sometimes perceive the company. When we interviewed at General Mills, managers there told us that bureaucracy was rampant at 3M.

3M's trust in its employees has yielded a happy bunch of self-motivated people. Employee transportation manager Tim Hoffmann told us: "The idea of not having to ask permission goes throughout this corporation. I can't ever remember going to a boss and asking, 'Can I do this?' I have many times gone to one of my managers and said, 'Let's do this,' and he has jumped right up and said, 'Great, go ahead.' " Technical director Judith Benham, with 3M for more than 15 years, added: "One of my very first supervisors said, 'Don't ask permission, Judy, ask forgiveness. And you really only need to ask forgiveness if you've done something seriously wrong.' Even if you make a mistake, we'd rather have you take the initiative. Management wants to give employees at every level a long rope and see what they do with it." Senior research engineer Michael Griffin said: "In many cases you often have more independence than you know what to do with." And Evelyn Songco, a manufacturing operations manager, related: "I was talking to one of my colleagues the other week, and he said, 'Another day is another adventure at 3M.' You look at it as an adventure because no one is dictating the work we do, it's by choice. If you fail, you don't get punished for that. At least you're doing something."

The chance to experiment is not restricted to technical people or managers. Joanne Englund, a senior secretary with the health-care group, told us that she has always been able to find "challenging" jobs. "If we find ways of doing things better, we're given the charge to do that," she said.

3M's homespun philosophy is often expressed in maxims. One is: "The product belongs to the division, but the technology belongs to 3M." This means that the technology that spawns products should be shared by everyone. Once a year 3M holds a technical forum where all the divisions showcase their latest products. Dr. Ernest Duwell, who has been with 3M for more than 35 years and holds the highest technical title in the company, corporate scientist, said: "When you go there, you are really surprised. It's amazing to those of us who are inside the company to see what the other divisions are doing." Another well-known 3M saying is: "Make a little, sell a little." This expresses the basic approach the company uses in entering a new field or a new country. It means: start small, learn how the business works, then expand.

Another way to foster a small-company feeling is by keeping units in the field small and putting them in small towns. 3M has 88 U.S. plants in 40 states, and only two of them have more than 1,000 employees. The typical 3M factory has 400 employees. You'll find 3M plants in places like Wahpeton, North Dakota; Cynthia, Kentucky; Belle Mead, New Jersey; and Prairie du Chien, Wisconsin. Its largest U.S. plant is in Hutchinson, Kansas, population 8,000.

3M's work force today numbers about the same as it did in 1985, although the proportion working overseas has increased. The company did not lop off a lot of people, thereby disappointing Wall Street security analysts who looked to head-count reduction as a good way for the company to cut expenses. Christopher Wheeler, senior vice-president for human resources, who began his career with 3M in London, explained that the company's approach has been to reassign people instead of getting rid of them when their jobs disappear. "Since the mid-'80s," he said, "we have reassigned something like 3,000 employees. There were no large-scale layoffs or terminations in this company." And he added: "We are blessed by the fact that our businesses are so diverse that you can grow here and have a range of experiences that in other companies would involve leaving the company."

As to what kind of people would not fit in here, Alan Jacobson gave us this pithy advice: "There are three things that I think are real obstacles to personal success in this company. The first is having a big ego because this is a team. The same for the person who is political. I think within 3M there is always office politics; you can't get vaccinated against it. But I think it's about as low a level here as you will find. The other thing is somebody who is turfy: their job or their department is their own turf. To make a business like ours work, you have to be able to cross boundaries. We encourage it. Some people are good at it, some aren't."

Getting hired by 3M is not easy, as the competition is fierce. A technical background helps. The company hired 341 college graduates in 1991. Once you are hired, extensive training and educational programs are available. 3M's 1992 "Catalog of Development Opportunities" ran to 115 pages and included everything from workshops in managing total quality to a Dale Carnegie course. 3M has a strong commitment to research. More than 7,500 scientists, engineers, and inventors work in research laboratories—and about 1,000 of them have Ph.D. degrees. 3M has a separate career track for scientists who want to stay in the lab and not become managers.

Once 3Mers are hired, opportunities abound. According to Richard Stoebe, market development manager: "I think 3M hires and promotes people, not résumés. You don't need a degree from MIT plus a Harvard M.B.A., plus 10 years of executive management experience in your field. I think we put a lot of faith in people versus the résumé."

Barbara Lother, international operations office manager and a 27-year 3Mer, agreed: "I can attest to that because when I came into the company, I was a clerk without a degree. I have worked on my education while at 3M and have received excellent support because they are paying for the education, and I've made several moves from the day I was a clerk until a few years ago when I became a manager. During that whole time I did not have a lot of credentials behind me except past good job performance and other skills. I have come up through the ranks and I have been supported all the way."

Main employment centers: 23,000 employees work in Minnesota, 12,000 of them at the St. Paul world headquarters. There are some 4,000 in southern California and 1,600 in Austin, Texas, where six of 3M's 45 divisions have their administrative offices. There are 83 plants in 39 states. 39,000 people work outside the United States in 57 countries.

Headquarters: Minnesota Mining & Manufacturing Company
3M Center
St. Paul, MN 55144-1000
(612) 733-1110

THE 100 BEST BY LOCATION

(NOTE: This lists only the states in which these companies are headquartered. Most of them have offices, plants, or stores in many other states. Some have facilities in nearly every state.)

ALABAMA: Acipco, Alagasco, BE&K

ARKANSAS: Wal-Mart

CALIFORNIA: Advanced Micro Devices, First Federal Bank of California, Hewlett-Packard, Intel, Los Angeles Dodgers, Morrison & Foerster, Odetics, Patagonia, Syntex, Tandem, Viking Freight System

COLORADO: U S West

CONNECTICUT: Pitney Bowes, Xerox

DELAWARE: Du Pont, W. L. Gore & Associates

FLORIDA: Baptist Hospital of Miami, Knight-Ridder, Publix Super Markets

GEORGIA: Delta Air Lines

ILLINOIS: Leo Burnett, John Deere, Fel-Pro, Hewitt Associates, Inland Steel, Motorola

INDIANA: Cummins Engine

MAINE: UNUM

MARYLAND: McCormick, Preston Trucking

MASSACHUSETTS: Beth Israel Hospital Boston, Lotus Development, Polaroid

MICHIGAN: Donnelly, Haworth, Herman Miller, Kellogg, Steelcase, Valassis Communications

MINNESOTA: Apogee Enterprises, Cray Research, Dayton Hudson, General Mills, H. B. Fuller, 3M, Tennant

MISSOURI: Anheuser-Busch, A. G. Edwards, Hallmark Cards, Springfield ReManufacturing

NEW JERSEY: Johnson & Johnson, Merck

NEW YORK: Avis, Corning, Goldman Sachs, IBM, Moog, J. P. Morgan, Reader's Digest, Wegmans

NORTH CAROLINA: Lowe's, SAS Institute

NORTH DAKOTA: Great Plains Software

OHIO: Cooper Tire, Honda of America Manufacturing, Lincoln Electric, Procter & Gamble, J. M. Smucker, Worthington Industries

PENNSYLVANIA: Armstrong, Erie Insurance, Hershey Foods, Rosenbluth International

SOUTH CAROLINA: Springs

TENNESSEE: Federal Express, Nissan Motor Manufacturing

TEXAS: Chaparral Steel, Compaq Computer, Lyondell Petrochemical, Mary Kay Cosmetics, Methodist Hospital, J. C. Penney, Southwest Airlines, TDIndustries, USAA

VERMONT: Ben & Jerry's Homemade

WASHINGTON: Microsoft, Nordstrom, Physio-Control, REI, Weyerhaeuser

WISCONSIN: SC Johnson Wax, Lands' End, Marquette Electronics, Northwestern Mutual Life, Quad/Graphics

Moog

================================

MOOG

Moog (rhymes with vogue) makes electrohydraulic valves and other items for the military and the aerospace industry. They also make machine tools. U.S. employees: 2,200.

★ ★ ★ ★   Pay/Benefits
★ ★   Opportunities
★ ★   Job Security
★ ★ ★   Pride in Work/Company
★ ★ ★ ★   Openness/Fairness
★ ★ ★ ★ ★   Camaraderie/Friendliness

BIGGEST PLUS: You're guaranteed a window.
BIGGEST MINUS: But not a job.

Moog does much of their business with the military, but you wouldn't know it by visiting their plants in upstate New York. There are no picture ID tags for employees, no fences, no "no trespassing" signs. Even the CEO leaves his keys in his car in the parking lot. You might think this sounds a bit dangerous, but nothing more valuable than a house plant, a rug, or a VCR has ever been stolen, unless you count the time one employee got mad and threw two propellant valves for an MX missile into a nearby field. They cost $4,000 apiece.

Moog employees aren't often mad, however. Quite the contrary. The lack of overt security illustrates a relationship of mutual trust and respect. As CEO Bob Brady explained to us: "You can't say this is an organization based on the premise of mutual trust and confidence and then turn around and say, 'I'm going to check your badge as you walk in and out.' It just wouldn't work."

Moog's unusual employee philosophy and culture can be traced to founder Bill Moog, who invented the electrohydraulic servovalve which has been the company's mainstay since its inception in 1951. He designed it to control the movements of guided missiles. He also found a market for this device in military aircraft. It is also used on many commercial airplanes, such as the Boeing 747. It was not until 1958 that Moog developed servovalve applications for industrial customers. Since then they have been used in a variety of nonmilitary systems, such as controlling the movements of the scenery for the Paris Opera. But until recently Moog relied on its military contracts for more than half of its business. For years this was a booming market, as Moog servovalves became standard equipment on virtually all missiles and military aircraft.

Reliance on the military became a liability when the arms race cooled off and resulted in two major cutbacks. In 1988 Moog laid off 280 people. In 1992 Moog suffered its worst reversal when Washington canceled or severely cut programs that use Moog's valves, including the B-2 bomber, the F-15 fighter, and the MX, Midgetman, and Maverick missiles. Moog responded by closing down its factory in Clearwater, Florida, two of its plants in upstate New York, and laying off 429 workers (24 percent of its work force) and demoting another 322. John Pagliaccio was demoted from group manager to supervisor of product support, with a correspondingly large salary cut. A 36-year Moog veteran, Pagliaccio told us he was not pleased with his involuntary demotion, but he didn't know what else the company could have done considering that "$70 million was taken out from under us." He felt the company had been very "sensitive" and "did everything with as much compassion as possible," including setting up a job search center for those who'd been laid off. Pagliaccio insisted that Moog remains a "good place to work" and that "mutual trust and confidence is still here."

Founder Bill Moog would be pleased to hear Pagliaccio's remarks, as he set up his company to run on the basis of mutual trust. He had no time clocks and no security guards. In the early days, Moog couldn't afford to pay anyone a regular wage. Instead, employees had a cash box. Executive vice-president Joe Green explained the company's first compensation system: "People put money in and took out money on the basis of what was going on in their life."

Although the company has become considerably more structured, trust is still present. Newcomers notice the difference. According to machine shop supervisor Gene Garnett, "In other companies you learned how to survive, and you just stayed out of your boss's way. Here I'm encouraged to be myself." Garnett came to Moog in 1986 from Westinghouse, where he said most employees kept a "butcher book" detailing the operation of their machines. The information in these books was kept secret from other employees, who were often suspected of trying to steal your job. In fact, Garnett's training supervisor at Westinghouse warned him never to write anything down, so that he could remain indispensable. When he left

Westinghouse Garnett destroyed all of his documented information. The contrast at Moog could not have been greater. Garnett said: "It took me a little while to adjust. At Westinghouse [where he was a supervisor], I would tell somebody, 'You get your butt over there and you stay there until I tell you to move.' But the language is different at Moog, people respect each other."

Employees can also voice their ideas and concerns at quarterly meetings where top executives meet with groups of 50 to 200 workers. After giving a brief business report, executives open the meeting to questions. Employees can ask the questions on the spot, or, if they prefer anonymity, they can write them down on 3-by-5 cards. Every question is answered. Complaints range from dissatisfaction with a current supervisor to safety hazards and the temperature of the water in the toilets. Ron Benczkowski, a project engineer, assured us that even "if the complaints are trivial, the company does not take them trivially, they address them." And Moog responds quickly. When an employee complained about getting his papers wet on the counter of the men's bathroom, shelves were installed the next day.

Management is also socially accessible. Technical coordinator Ray Cummins, who worked here from 1955 to 1992, calls his company "a big family." Top executives are on a first-name basis with production workers and will stop and talk to them as they walk through the plant. Eighteen-year employee Lenny Baker remembers sitting next to Bill Moog at one of his first company picnics: "We struck up a conversation and I called him Mr. Moog out of respect. But he scolded me and said, 'Don't call me Mr. Moog, you call me Bill.' "

Dave Gromek, who came here in 1979, added, "Moog is the kind of place that you like to work. There are people in the organization who know you by your name, you know your employees by name, what their jobs are and what their responsibilities are. There is a sense of camaraderie at Moog." According to Chet Sadowski, an engineering supervisor: "We are all treated the same, people just have different jobs."

Visitors notice the unique architecture of Moog buildings. Managers' offices have no doors, and the walls are made of glass so employees can see whether their manager is in. One plant is a circular building, designed so that employees can look outside while they are working. Dave Gromek, an assembly and test supervisor, explained: "You want to feel comfortable at work, and part of that is knowing what's happening outside around you. Where else do you find a manufacturing area where at least 270 degrees of it is surrounded by windows?"

In the same Moog building, the parking area encircles the building so people have to walk through various parts of the plant on their way to their own station. This was done intentionally. In most plants, workers see only their own part of the process. But CEO Bob Brady said that at Moog, the workers get a sense of the whole, almost by osmosis, since they can see into other production areas as they pass by them on their way to their own jobs. Much of the factory work here involves tooling different parts of servovalves to very precise specifications. So the overall cleanliness of the plant is especially notable since machine shops typically are dirty and grimy.

Moog also makes it easy for people to move between departments. Sylvia Wright moved from a secretarial position to a higher-paying job in assembly. Before she came to Moog in 1978, Wright had never been interested in manufacturing, but she was impressed by the cleanliness and comfortable atmosphere. She applied for a job in the assembly and test area. Once she got the job, Moog provided classes in technical reading and math, in addition to the regular job training. Wright now does orientation and training for the assembly area and the company is paying for her work toward a bachelor's degree. Moog provides extensive in-house training programs, and 100 percent tuition reimbursement for outside education.

Moog prizes relaxation. If your manager approves, there are an unlimited number of unpaid personal days an employee can take off. On her second day of work Anne Everts's four-year-old child had an abscessed tooth. Her supervisor gave her time off without question. That summer she needed to take more time off because two of her children were hospitalized. Again, there was no problem taking off personal time. Now she is a shipping and receiving supervisor and appreciates her freedom: "I, as a supervisor, allow my people the opportunity to take care of the family things that interfere with their life at work. And that is very important. Because they have given me so much, I am more than willing to give back. It's not an overtime issue."

In addition to offering employees personal days, sick leave, and vacation days, Moog gives all employees five additional days of vacation on their fifth anniversary of hire. For their 10-year anniversary, employees are awarded seven weeks of vacation in addition to the three weeks of vacation they normally get. This offer is then repeated every subsequent five-year anniversary. If an employee doesn't want to take the time, he or she can request the cash equivalent.

But Moog is not quite as relaxed as it used to be. Joe Green told us that in the past "there was a notion that Moog was a sort of laissez-faire country club. We had this exciting product, but internally speaking, you were supposed to come to this place and really enjoy the hell out of it. There weren't any real norms or codes of conduct or performance criteria. The company was supposed to always make you feel good."

Today, life at Moog is more rigorous because of the tougher business environment. Employees still have faith in the culture, however. Roger Schultz, a section supervisor in shipping and receiving, told us that even without Bill Moog at the helm, "that initial philosophy that he tried to promote—mutual trust and respect for the people you work with—I think that has carried over the years even though he is no longer a part of the company."

After all, Moog's philosophy is not just a passing whim. Joe Green explains, "We have never gravitated toward the fads of the time . . . We have a highly skilled work force and you don't fool them with fads. They are well-read people and they know what's going on. People have to be involved, committed, understand and believe, or it's all a big waste of effort."

Main employment centers: East Aurora, Elma, and Orchard Park (all suburbs of Buffalo, New York).

Headquarters: Moog Inc.
East Aurora, NY 14052
(716) 652-2000

J. P. Morgan

JPMorgan

J. P. Morgan is the third largest bank in the United States, based on assets and deposits. U.S. employees: 8,175.

★ ★ ★ ★ ★   Pay/Benefits
★ ★ ★ ★   Opportunities
★ ★ ★   Job Security
★ ★ ★ ★   Pride in Work/Company
★ ★   Openness/Fairness
★ ★ ★   Camaraderie/Friendliness

BIGGEST PLUS: Gentility reigns here.
BIGGEST MINUS: You need $5 million to open a checking account.

Morgan remains the class act in American banking. It's a mark of prestige to work here, and the money isn't bad either. Morgan paid salaries totaling $690 million in 1991. That worked out to an average of $51,300 per employee. And that's just the salary component. Bonuses, insurance, profit sharing, stock awards, and other employee benefits mounted up to another $753 million, an average of $55,985 per person. Of course that's a mythical "average." Bonuses and stock incentive programs are largely reserved for the top people in the company. Stock options, for example, go to 750 officers. In 1991 the top five officers of Morgan received total compensation ranging from $1.4 million to $2.1 million. Lower-level people get some goodies, too, although not on that grand scale. In 1990 the profit-sharing payout was 13 percent of salary, and in 1991 it was the highest ever paid by Morgan—17 percent. Morgan was one of the first banks in the country to have a profit-sharing plan. It's a tradition that goes back to their legendary leader, J. Pierpont Morgan, who died in 1913. In his will he left one year's salary to every employee of the company.

Money washes over this place the way water goes over Niagara Falls. In 1990 Morgan took in $10.4 billion for the financial legerdemain that it executes. That's considerably less than the $38.3 billion Citicorp logged that year, but Citicorp had 93,000 people on its payroll while Morgan's total employment, worldwide, was 13,000. In 1990 Morgan earned $75,202 in profits for each employee on the payroll. That's a ratio no other bank comes close to matching.

Morgan doesn't need a lot of people because it's a wholesale bank, not a retail bank. There are no ATM machines outside the offices of its banking subsidiary, Morgan Guaranty Trust. Morgan provides financial services to corporations, financial institutions, governments, and wealthy individuals. It lends them money, raises money for them, and takes care of their investments. It also buys and sells—trades—currencies and bonds for its own account.

Strictly speaking, J. P. Morgan is no longer just a bank. It will also arrange mergers or help a company take over another company, and in 1990 it became the first bank since passage of the Glass-Steagall Act in 1933 to be allowed to sell stock to the American public. It's therefore an investment bank as well as a commercial bank.

Morgan Guaranty does have checking accounts, but they are not available for the asking. To open one, you need to have $5 million. That's the smallest amount of money that Morgan feels comfortable handling. This means that most Morgan people don't get one of the perks that usually come with bank employment: a checking account free of charges. However, for officers, Morgan does arrange for free checking at the Bank of New York. One perk the 7,000 Morgan people in New York continue to get is a free lunch every day. There are two cafeterias, sans cash registers, two floors below the lobby of its new headquarters building—and on the 47th floor there are private dining rooms for senior officers and guests. No alcohol is served in the private dining rooms and the service is elegant. At the end of lunch, in a throwback to another era, waiters and waitresses offer cigars. The free lunch program costs Morgan $8 million a year.

Prejudices die hard. When you make your first visit to J. P. Morgan, because of its reputation as the cathedral of capitalism, you expect to find a snooty, effete bunch of Ivy Leaguers who look down their noses at the hoi polloi. But that's simply not the case. Morgan is not a place for backslappers, but it's an environment where people work together in teams and care for one another. It's a comfortable place characterized by good manners and understatement. And it's a place where secretaries are treated with respect and given opportunities to move up. Dennis Weatherstone, who became chief executive in 1990, began his banking career when he was 16 as a clerk in the London office of Guaranty Trust, which merged with J. P. Morgan in 1959.

Herbert Hefke, managing director and head of human resources, slayed the Ivy League myth for us right away: "I grew up in Queens, went to Jamaica High School and City College, and I am having a reasonably successful career here. There are people here who, like myself, never went to Ivy League schools who are equally successful. There are a number of Ivy League people who are successful, too. It is a heterogeneous population." Morgan is not an all-white enclave either. One out of four U.S. employees is a minority, but the ratio declines with rank. Nearly half the clerical staff and service workers are minorities while only 9 percent of officials and managers are nonwhite. Women make up 52 percent of the total and between 35 and 40 percent of the officers.

Laura Miner, who worked at Morgan between 1982 and 1991, overseeing such amenities as furnishings and artwork, described the company as "gentle." She recalled that when she first arrived there and asked for help to open a window, "seven people stood up."

Two key terms Morgan people use over and over again are "relationship banking," which means the bank fosters long-term ties with clients instead of looking for one-shot deals, and "teamwork," which means there's no room here for superegos. In 1990, in an interview with a Japanese journalist, chairman Dennis Weatherstone stressed that Morgan looks for people "who have pride and modesty."

Morgan trains its own people, expects them to stay for the long haul, and virtually never hires people away from other firms. It now runs five professional training programs (Corporate Finance, Global Markets, Global Technology and Operations, Audit and Financial Management, and Management Services), which vary in length from four to 16 weeks and are attended by some 350 recruits annually. An M.B.A. degree is by no means a requirement, although usually half of the Corporate Finance trainees have one. Morgan does not look askance at B.A.'s in history.

Once out of training, a recruit joins a team whose members have different roles—one might be a corporate finance specialist, another an industry analyst, another a client contact person. He or she is given responsibility early on. And exposure. To solve a problem for a client, a Morgan staffer, even a junior one, has the run of the place, free to go to anyone for help. Kelly Bodnar, who came to Morgan with a civil engineering degree from Princeton, said: "Teamwork was one of the selling points that most impressed me during my interviews. If I was skeptical after the informational session, I was completely convinced after being here a day." She added that teamwork "is what sets Morgan's culture apart from others I have looked at. It creates an atmosphere more like a family." Bodnar left Morgan in 1992 to enter the Stanford Business School. Perry Bartol, a Colgate graduate who joined Morgan in 1988, told us that "there is nothing more important to teamwork than understanding people's roles. When you have specific roles in a project, people don't step on each other's toes or try to usurp roles from other people." An associate in corporate finance was quoted in the company newspaper, *Morgan News*, as follows: "Everyone wants to succeed, but we don't have to beat one another or compete against one another to do so."

According to Hefke, Morgan encourages movement in the ranks. He told us that "the propensity is for us to ask people to move before they ask themselves. You can come in here and start out in a particular business, and you will have the opportunity to change assignments either within that business or within a location, change location, or change businesses." This is true, he added, for secretaries as well. Morgan has about 1,000 people in the secretarial ranks—and they, too, get training before starting in a job. They are actually called secretaries only on the bottom two levels; they then move up to "staff assistants" and "executive assistants." Along the way, they have a chance to improve their skills through classes at Morgan or through outside courses. "My former secretary," related Hefke, "went to school at night and went through the training program and is now a vice-president in our operational products area. I can't think offhand of any managing directors who are former secretaries but it is certainly in the realm of possibility."

The secretaries we talked to were happy to be ensconced at Morgan. Kelly Palmer, who came here in 1984 after graduating from State University of New York at Farmingdale, said: "The best thing about being interviewed at Morgan is that you didn't have to go home for a couple of weeks and wait to hear. They told you right there as soon as you were done with testing." She feels that in her time "the role of the secretary has changed to be more of an assistant to your manager than just doing filing or clerical work or typing. I think you are more valued now, which is very uplifting. I have seen my friends at other companies change jobs four or five times while I have been here."

Nivia Soto, a Katherine Gibbs graduate who came to Morgan in 1986 after working at Shearson and Prime Time Entertainment, said: "It is very good compared to other companies because you are promoted on your own, you don't have to be promoted with your officer." Stephanie Feldman, a legal assistant, came to Morgan in 1988 directly from high school and likes it so much that she commutes to work from Stony Brook, Long Island, two hours away. When we saw her in 1991, Feldman had just been promoted to a new job in the legal department and was a little flustered because now she had an assistant herself and wasn't sure how to handle that. "It is hard for me to give her things to do," she said. "It is a big adjustment. They are giving me a chance to prove myself, to see what I can do."

Maureen Brennan, who helps to train secretaries, has been in and out of Morgan. She says they will always rehire you if your work was satisfactory. "A lot of people call this place 'Mother Morgan,' " she said. "You can come back whenever you want. They will always feed you." Brennan first joined Morgan in 1985 from Merrill Lynch, which she said she left because "they were laying off 1,000 people, they didn't have a bonus, they didn't have profit sharing, they didn't have free lunch, and they didn't have tuition reimbursement."

With nearly half its business outside the United States, Morgan is a very cosmopolitan place, and if you are in the professional ranks, the chances of an overseas assignment are good. Some 500 Morgan people are now working outside their home countries. In the New York office, 9 percent of the employees are foreign nationals—and at the senior vice-president/managing director level, the ratio is 30 percent. Of the five top officers in 1992, three were born outside the United States: chairman Dennis Weatherstone (Britain), vice-chairman Kurt Viermetz (Germany), and vice-chairman Roberto Mendoza (Cuba).

Morgan's big challenge today is to preserve its culture as it moves into the Wall Street deal-making business that was all the rage in the 1980s. This has already had the effect of pushing up incentive bonuses, although Morgan executives still do not come close to the compensation made by their counterparts at investment banking houses like Morgan Stanley, Salomon Brothers, Goldman Sachs, and Bear Stearns. Morgan has tried to import some of its values into this transactional business. It has run ads saying: "We don't do deals to generate fees. If a transaction isn't in a client's interest, we'll recommend against it." Morgan has also earned the contempt of other investment banking houses by charging less for its financial advisory services than others do.

In 1990 Morgan moved 4,000 people into a 47-story skyscraper at 60 Wall Street, just down the street from its historic office at 23 Wall, where it had been for 75 years. The 23 Wall Street office, across the street from the New York Stock Exchange, will remain in the family.

Of course, with all this modernity, there are some Morgan touches. Weatherstone and the other top officers elected not to have their offices at the top of the building, where there are commanding views of New York City, but on the 20th floor so that they could be at the very heart of the company. And as the Morgan people prepared to relocate to the new building, they were reassured that the lobby of 60 Wall would have a reception center where, "in the Morgan tradition, each visitor will be treated cordially and given personal attention. The greatest care will be taken to ensure that your guests will arrive at your office without delay."

Main employment centers: 3,900 people work at 60 Wall Street and another 3,200 work in other offices in New York City. Morgan has offices in eight other U.S. and Canadian cities, where an additional 1,150 people work; 5,290 are employed in offices in Europe, Latin America, and Asia.

Headquarters: J. P. Morgan & Co., Inc.
60 Wall St.
New York, NY 10260
(212) 483-2323

Morrison & Foerster

MORRISON & FOERSTER

Morrison & Foerster practices law for corporate clients and is the ninth largest law firm in the country. Employees: 1,609.

★★★★ Pay/Benefits
★★★★ Opportunities
★★★★ Job Security
★★★ Pride in Work/Company
★★★★ Openness/Fairness
★★★★ Camaraderie/Friendliness

BIGGEST PLUS: Best law firm for nonlawyers.
BIGGEST MINUS: Guilty of reneging on the 35-hour week.

Morrison & Foerster doesn't fit the conventional image of a law firm. It's not stuffy or hierarchical, it's not a workaholic's paradise, and it's not focused narrowly on making potfuls of money. Instead, it has a sense of humor and an egalitarian streak that you would never expect to find in a prestigious law firm. And MoFo, the nickname by which it goes, is prestigious, serving a number of blue-chip corporations. It's the largest law firm in San Francisco, and nationally it ranks ninth in terms of the number of lawyers on staff—638 in early 1992. MoFo's 1991 revenues were $217 million.

At most law firms, the demarcation between lawyers and staff is sharp. At MoFo, new partners receive a handbook which tells them: "We care about our legal assistant and staff employees. Partners are judged by their partners on how they treat people who cannot necessarily advance their careers. We do not tolerate abuse of our employees by partners, no matter how senior or how 'important.' "

They practice what they preach here. Most of the benefits, for example, are uniform, the same for secretaries and partners. There are no separate dining rooms or washrooms for partners. In 1986, when they moved into a skyscraper in the heart of San Francisco's financial district, the corner offices became conference rooms instead of sumptuous offices for senior partners. Everyone, right up to chairman Carl Leonard, is on a first-name basis with everyone else. And according to Penelope Douglas, human resources director who came here via Wells Fargo Bank and Ernst & Young (she calls MoFo "100 times better as a place to work"), when MoFo people congregate for drinks at the Mandarin Hotel bar on the ground floor at the end of the day, there's a good mix of lawyers and staff people.

Carl Leonard pointed out to us that treating the support staff well is not just some "nice California granola kind of warm fuzzy thing," but makes economic sense: "It doesn't matter how great a brief you've written, if you are dependent on a messenger and at 5:00 or 5:30 that messenger says, 'I've done my job and I don't have to do this,' that great brief never gets there on time. This is hardheaded economics, running a law firm. And if these people feel like they are part of a team and treated with respect, they will outperform their counterparts in other places who aren't treated that way."

It may be hard economics but it also reflects a warm heart. And MoFo values glue people together here. Lynn Azevedo, a litigation secretary, said: "I think that our salaries are above what some of the other larger firms are paying, but in addition to that, it is the way they treat you as people. I came here from a very large firm, and if a secretary there, for instance, didn't care for the people she was working for—attorneys, legal assistants, or whatever—she had no say in the matter. You were just let go. Here that never happens. You can talk to your floor supervisor, you can talk to your attorneys about it. I have been in situations where that has come up and everybody listens."

Robin Rouda, who works in recruiting, said the firm makes it "very clear" to law students who work as summer interns that "our staff is like gold to us and are not to be treated any less preciously. In fact, anyone who is found to be speaking down to somebody or mistreating them verbally, or in any other way, is really out on their ear. We just will not tolerate it." Janice Sperow, an associate (law firm lingo for a lawyer who has not yet made partner), added this confirmation: "We have had people who have all the credentials, top of their class from Harvard Law School, they're on the law review, they have clerked for so and so, they have done all the right things and then they came here as interns and acted like a jerk to their secretary— fetch me this, fetch me that, run my personal errand—and they did not get an offer to come back here."

Lawyers just out of law school start here at salaries that ranged in 1992 from $67,000 in San Francisco to $83,000 in New York, competitive with the entry-level pay at other prestigious corporate law firms. But MoFo always makes it clear to law students that the firm "takes pride in measuring 'success' in more than just financial terms." It emphasizes "enjoyment of a meaningful home life," and it insists on devoting many hours to *pro bono* work on behalf of groups and people who can't afford to hire lawyers. Law firms make their money by billing their time to clients. At many of the biggest firms in the country, a lawyer is expected to bill 2,300 to 2,400 hours a year (or more than 46 hours a week). MoFo's guideline is 1,800 billable hours a year (about 36 hours a week)—and that includes *pro bono* time. In effect, the partners, out of consideration to family life, have made a decision to give up some profits.

As the recession impacted law firm revenues in the 1989–92 period, many big firms laid off people. MoFo did not. During hard times many law firms will admit fewer associates to partnership. MoFo does not apply an economic test to this decision. It's made strictly on merit. When an associate is ready to be moved up, he or she is promoted. In 1991, when MoFo billed 5 percent fewer hours than the previous year, it admitted 20 new partners, up from 17 in 1990. This practice has two consequences. MoFo partners tend to be younger than partners at other firms—in 1992 the average age was 41. And the older partners, by admitting new partners, reduce, in the short term, their potential income because the profits are shared among more people. Of course, it's not exactly a hand-to-mouth existence here. Between 1984 and 1990 the salaries of associates went up from $38,000 to $65,000, and average earnings of partners doubled.

Not many law firms in the country can boast of the diversity MoFo has. Of the 233 partners at the start of 1992, 47 were women and 12 were minorities. Of the 20 new partners named in 1991, nine were women—and two were working part-time. Women are managing partners of three offices, including the biggest one, San Francisco. And the executive director of the San Francisco office—an important law firm position that is 99 percent held by men—is also female: Nancy Siegel.

The MoFo people we talked to were clearly pleased with being able to be themselves in this work environment. Cecile Javier, a Filipino accounting clerk, said: "The first time I came here, everyone was so friendly, smiling at you. I thought it would be stuffy, elitist, or that they would ignore you because you are a minority. But no. I never felt anything like that, never felt that they talked about me because I am different from them." Penelope Douglas told us: "I find that this is a tremendously responsive place for people to be themselves. In both the banking profession and the accounting profession, as a woman in a management group full of men I always found myself trying to mold myself to a style that would allow me to kind of survive. I have a real ridiculous sense of humor and I am sort of casual and I like to use my brain and all these things work for me here. I can be myself. I have a number of women colleagues and I really enjoy the friendship of women here as well as men."

Portia Moore is another MoFo person who told us that she appreciated being able to be herself here, "with my big mouth and everything." Moore is typical of the diversity that MoFo looks for. A black who grew up in humble circumstances in Seattle, she became a registered nurse before going to law school at the University of Michigan. She is now managing partner of MoFo's Seattle office.

MoFo has a strong commitment to public interest law. In 1990 *American Lawyer* recognized them for having the largest *pro bono* program among all law firms in the country. In that year, MoFo contributed 74,240 hours of time to *pro bono* work, an average of 114 hours per attorney, with a billable time value of more than $11 million. They have represented AIDS sufferers, illegal aliens, and the homeless, but their major priority in recent years has been helping children trapped in poverty. Law students who interview with MoFo are always told that they are expected to buy into the value of public service.

One candidate who certainly did is Arturo Gonzales, the eleventh child of Mexican immigrants, who grew up in Roseville, California, and decided he wanted to become a lawyer in 1978 after sitting through three trials in which an older brother, Santiago, was accused of killing his wife's lover. The trials ended in two hung juries and a mistrial—and in 1981 Arturo went off to Harvard Law School. In Arturo's final year in law school, Santiago was tried again, and this time he was convicted. As he entered prison, his brother Arturo came out of Harvard Law School and accepted an offer from Morrison & Foerster. When we asked him why he took the MoFo offer, Gonzales replied: "That's pretty easy. Because of their commitment to *pro bono* service. I knew that at MoFo I would be able to contribute to people who cannot afford legal services. For the past six years the firm has allowed me to do that—over 200 hours every year." In 1991 Gonzales was the lead attorney in a nationally publicized suit that succeeded in forcing the state of California to keep the predominantly black public schools of Richmond open even though the district had run out of money because of mismanagement. Six months later, a little more than six years after joining the firm, Gonzales was elected a partner—at age 31.

In the summer of 1991, just before one of our visits to the firm, MoFo made a move that struck some people as completely out of character. It increased the work hours for support staff. Secretaries, clerks, and other nonsupervisory employees had been on a 35-hour week—they now had to work 37.5 hours; managers on the support staff had their workweek increased from 35 to 40 hours. The firm explained that the change was dictated by client complaints about high fees and the need to become more efficient so that layoffs could be avoided.

At other firms, there might have been muffled dissent. At MoFo, it was something else. Support staffers organized a protest by having everyone come to work wearing black. We interviewed at MoFo shortly after this event and found very few employees who were still exercised over the extension of hours. Most seemed to understand the firm's reasons, and they were especially pleased that it had been communicated in typical MoFo fashion at a "town hall" meeting where management was on hand to face the music. Still, legal secretary Ronnie Marshall told us that in her 15 years here this was "the first callous thing I have seen this firm do."

They do seem to have fun here. Marshall said: "One of the things that I enjoy the most about working at MoFo is that when they party, they party. And everyone is invited." Associates have weekly Thursday night get-togethers, and the legal assistants have one every month. Another staffer said: "We have Friday afternoon get-togethers celebrating something. There is always an excuse to have a party." And one manager said: "In this office we have what we call stairwell parties. I don't know why they are called that unless because sometimes the bar is under the stairwell." Every year MoFo has a new T-shirt. The firm newsletter prints a drawing of a blank T-shirt, with everyone invited to fill it in with their own design and colors. The design that gets the most votes becomes the T-shirt of the year, and everyone gets one. A wall on the third floor of the MoFo offices displays all the T-shirts, year by year.

MoFo's dedication to support-staff people has roots in its history, but everyone agrees that the modern flag bearer of this value was Joe Terraciano, who was managing partner during the firm's meteoric growth during the 1980s. Terraciano, who may have been the first openly gay partner of a major law firm, died of AIDS in the fall of 1989. In a memo to the staff, the firm said: "We would be remiss if we did not say something about Joe's feelings towards those of you who are not lawyers. Put simply, he respected and loved you best. He cared deeply and personally about you and your families. Most of all, he admired your patience and resiliency over the years in dealing with the idiosyncrasies of the lawyers." In his memory, the firm established the Joseph E. Terraciano scholarships, two of which are now being awarded annually to children of MoFo employees who are *not* lawyers to help fund their college education. The scholarships are $8,000 a year through graduation. The initial winners were all children of secretaries or clerks.

Types of jobs: Attorneys—36 percent; legal secretaries—22 percent; legal assistants—11 percent; marketing—7 percent; office services—6 percent; word processing—5 percent; information systems—4 percent; accounting —4 percent; human resources—3 percent; management and administration—2 percent.

Main employment centers: There are 723 employees who work at the main office in San Francisco. The other 886 employees work out of offices in Los Angeles, Sacramento, Orange County, Walnut Creek, and Palo Alto,

California, as well as in Denver, New York, Seattle, and Washington, D.C. There are also offices in London, Brussels, Hong Kong, and Tokyo.

Headquarters: Morrison & Foerster
345 California St.
San Francisco, CA 94104
(415) 677-7000

BEST FOR WOMEN

BE&K
Ben & Jerry's Homemade
Federal Express
First Federal Bank of California
Mary Kay Cosmetics
Morrison & Foerster
Nordstrom
Patagonia
Pitney Bowes
Xerox

Motorola

Motorola is one of the world's leading makers of electronic equipment such as two-way radios, pagers, cellular phones, and semiconductors. U.S. employees: 60,000.

★★★ Pay/Benefits
★★★★★ Opportunities
★★★★ Job Security
★★★★ Pride in Work/Company
★★★★ Openness/Fairness
★★★★ Camaraderie/Friendliness

BIGGEST PLUS: A chance to get rid of your defects.
BIGGEST MINUS: Nobody's perfect.

Almost everywhere we interviewed in America, companies were either putting in—or talking about putting in—new quality programs. But when it comes to efforts on this front, Motorola is off the charts. It has been working at it longer than most companies—and it has the results to show for it. We were amazed when we went to lunch at the Food Works café at Motorola headquarters in Schaumburg, a northwest suburb of Chicago, and found a spacious, attractive restaurant with Corning dishes and stainless-steel flatware that didn't have a tinny feel to it. When we expressed surprise at these accoutrements, Motorolan Bobbi Gutman, a recent transplant from Digital Equipment ("They're like kids in a sandbox there, no structure"), said: "Why not? If we're going to be a Six Sigma company, we're not stopping at the doors of the cafeteria."

Six Sigma is the name of Motorola's companywide quality program to drive defects down to virtually zero. Sigma, the 18th letter of the Greek alphabet, refers to a statistical measurement of defect. In 1986 Motorola set a goal of reaching Six Sigma—3.4 defective parts per million or well-nigh perfect—by 1992. In 1988 Motorola became the first company to win the prestigious Malcolm Baldrige National Quality Award. At the start of 1992, the company reported that it was at 5.4 Sigma. In 1993 it will be eligible to apply again for a Baldrige Award, and it will do so. Not just apply —it expects to win again. It wants to become the first company to win two Baldriges.

It's exciting to work at a company with such out-of-sight goals, especially since Motorola hasn't imposed them from the top as a ukase but has instead involved people all the way down the line. We saw that excitement when we were standing in the middle of a work team at the cellular phone plant in Arlington Heights, seven miles north of corporate headquarters. Here was a multicultural group of workers, including women and blacks, and they were clearly enjoying the flexibility and freedom of a no-time-clock environment that tapped their brains, their sense of responsibility to deliver for the customer, and even their sense of humor. The guru of this plant, a diminutive vice-president, Rick Chandler, explained to us that the whole point of work at Motorola is to get rid of managers and let workers manage. "I don't have managers," he said. "My workers are my managers. They manage my business, whether it's purchasing or production. So I have 1,000 managers. I have more managers than anybody else I ever met in my life. I've got about 45 leaders. I don't have many of those. This is a manager-run business. They determine when and how they should have a team, who goes in and who goes out."

Enthusiasm of this kind is rampant at Motorola. It's a revved-up place, with everyone seemingly enrolled in the crusade for quality. The company has printed up wallet-size plastic cards in 11 languages, spelling out its dedication to "total customer satisfaction," and it has issued them to every single employee around the world, suggesting that they carry them around "to remind yourself and others of the important statement we have made to our customers." And Motorola doesn't just push its employees, it leans on suppliers. It notified IBM and some 10,000 other companies that sell to Motorola that it expected them to apply for a Baldrige Award or produce a timetable as to when they will apply—or else lose their Motorola business. In 1989 supplier Charles Gonsior of St. Paul Metalcraft told *Fortune:* "If we can supply Motorola, we can supply God."

The head cheerleader of this crusade is CEO George Fisher, who came to Motorola from Bell Labs in 1976 and who's as accessible as a leader can be in a company of 100,000 employees around the globe. Bobbi Gutman observed: "I have never heard anyone, from the janitor to a secretary, call him other than George. He floats around. Everybody knows him." Fisher and the other top two Motorola officers—Gary L. Tooker, president, and Christopher B. Galvin, senior executive vice-president—spend a lot of time on the road. According to executive vice-president Dave Hickie, the trio will also take time to have two-hour "rap sessions" with groups of 20 to 25 low- to mid-level employees. They were expected to do between six and 10 of these in 1992. Hickie said to us: "I'm not the greatest supporter, frankly, of corporate jets because they are very expensive. But look at what they do with those! They will be in Phoenix for a meeting. They'll fly to Albuquerque for an employee dinner. They'll come back to Chicago that night. They'll be at a breakfast the next morning. If they are not visible, I don't know who is."

When companies talk about quality, they are usually referring to products coming out of a factory. Motorola has extended its crusade to every corner of the company. Patent lawyers reduced the time for filing for new patents from six months (and sometimes a year or more) to a few weeks. The accounting department reduced the time for closing the books from 14 days to four days—and was looking to cut it to two days in 1992. Software manager Marsha Burks told us that in her area, reducing defects means measuring minutes of uptime. "We have to reduce our minutes of outage on the system," she said. Food Works director Richard Ysmael, a veteran of 23 years with Motorola, runs an operation that encompasses 26 restaurants in Illinois, Texas, Florida, and Arizona, employs 440 people (all Motorolans), and feeds more than 40,000 Motorolans every day. His customers are the employees, and while he's not entirely certain that statistical measurements can be applied to food service, he figures that Food Works has hit the 5.5 Sigma level. He arrived at that calculation by tallying up the number of complaints received on the comment cards available in the cafés against the number of meals served.

Although Motorola is a big company, it still has a family feeling, a reflection of its heritage. Paul Galvin, who founded the company on Chicago's near west side in 1928, was a feisty, hardworking, no-nonsense, paternalistic employer who gave his workers bonuses during the 1930s, urged them to buy stock, and set up, in 1947, a profit-sharing plan into which he pumped 20 percent of pretax profits. Chicago has always been a labor union stronghold but Motorola was never organized. After Paul Galvin died in 1959, the mantle passed to his son, Robert Galvin, a Notre Dame graduate who took Motorola out of TV set making, steered it into the wizardry of computer electronics, and initiated the quality drive that now consumes the company. He held the CEO's post until 1986 and remains active in the important post of chairman of the executive committee. He's the company's largest shareholder, owning 3.5 percent of the stock, and his son, Christopher, who was 41 in 1992, is one of the three members of the office of chief executive. So there's continuity with the past here.

Motorola is an authentic hero of American technology, having made the transition from a maker of car radios to a world leader in high-tech electronics. It's one of the largest U.S. manufacturers of semiconductors, the brainpower in computers. And no one in the world produces more two-way radio sets, pagers, cellular car phones, and modems. Motorola chips sit inside every Sony camcorder, Apple Macintosh computer, Canon 35mm camera, and most of the cars produced by Chrysler, Ford, and General Motors. Motorola has a major presence in the high-tech alleys of Phoenix and Austin, but there's a corny Chicago flavor to the company. Irene Short, a nurse in the health services department, told us: "Motorola has quite a few long-service employees, and I think there is a great deal of pride associated with Motorola. There is also a Motorola culture. It is not, 'I work for Motorola.' It's 'I am a Motorolan.' "

One institution that goes back to Paul Galvin's day is the Service Club for employees who have worked at Motorola for 10 years or more. It continues today as an important part of Motorola culture—and it's linked to a promise of job security. Dave Hickie recalled for us the dark days of 1975 when Motorola was reducing its payroll by 30 percent: "Bob [Galvin] would not let them take out any Service Club people. And if you had been taken out and he found out, he called up and said, 'Hire them back.' And they were hired back. The lesson has stuck." Motorola's recruiting booklet puts it this way: "Employees with 10 or more years of service cannot be released without the explicit concurrence of the Chairman of the Board." And that's a policy promulgated worldwide. Of the 100,000 Motorola employees, about 40,000 are Service Club members. Motorola has not had any large-scale layoffs in recent years.

Motorola does not throw people out of work because of new technology. On the contrary, it retrains employees—and this commitment has led to one of the most impressive education and training components in American business. Classes are held everywhere at Motorola—on site, off site, and in a new entity called Motorola University. It's a law here that every employee take at least five days of training every year. Motorola U. is more than an in-house training center. It's an engine for education which offers a wide range of skill classes (46,500 people took courses in 1991), serves suppliers as well as Motorolans, and works closely with schools, from nearby grade schools to graduate business schools, in developing curricula. More than 1,200 people at Motorola are involved in education and training, some 300 of them full-time. Motorola became this learning and teaching organization during the 1980s after it reached the appalling conclusion that half of its 25,000 manufacturing and support people in the United States could not meet seventh-grade standards in English and math. William Wiggenhorn, president of Motorola U., explained in a 1990 article in the *Harvard Business Review* that the company's policy is that everybody has a right to retraining and that people have a right to a job even if they fail the training. "But," he added, "if people refused the training, then we said we'd dismiss them. In fact, we had refusals from 18 employees with long service, and we dismissed all but one. That sent another strong message."

Personnel vice-president Bruce Mueller conceded that Motorola may not be "a place for everybody. Some people don't want to become part of a family or a part of a goal or a drive." People who do come here can expect to work hard, even without time clocks. Wiggenhorn explained that employees "must accept our definition of work and the workweek: the time it takes to ship perfect products to the customer. That can mean a workweek of 50 or even 60 hours, but we need people willing to work against quality and output instead of a time clock." Software quality assurance manager Frank Gray told us: "I love coming to work every day. I put in 11½-hour days, no problem. It's because I am having fun doing what I am doing." We asked one manager, Tom Tischhausere, what happened to lazy people at Motorola. He replied: "Their peers will kill them. They will get run over."

Types of jobs: Production—47 percent; engineering—28 percent; clerical —9 percent; sales and marketing—7 percent; administration—4 percent; finance—3 percent; human resources—1 percent.

Main employment centers: Schaumburg, outside of Chicago, is home to the headquarters staff, Motorola University, the Land Mobile sector (two-way radios), and a new museum that's worth the visit: it's a hands-on exhibition tracing the history of electronics (and Motorola). Admission is free. Manufacturing sites include Arlington Heights (cellular phones) and Northbrook (automotive electronic systems), Illinois; Phoenix (semiconductors) and Scottsdale (missile guidance), Arizona; Albuquerque, New Mexico, and Boynton Beach, Florida (pagers and telepoint systems); Mansfield, Massachusetts, and Huntsville, Alabama (network management systems and modems).

Headquarters: Motorola, Inc.
1303 E. Algonquin Rd.
Schaumburg, IL 60196
(705) 576-5000

Nissan Motor Manufacturing

Nissan's Tennessee plant turned out 450,000 cars and trucks in 1991. They make pickup trucks, passenger cars, engines, and other auto parts. Employees: 6,000.

★★★★ Pay/Benefits
★★★★ Opportunities
★★★★ Job Security
★★★ Pride in Work/Company
★★★★ Openness/Fairness
★★★ Camaraderie/Friendliness

BIGGEST PLUS: You can make your car and drive it, too.
BIGGEST MINUS: But it won't have a union label.

When we last visited Nissan's plant near the rural central Tennessee town of Smyrna in 1983, it had just started assembling vehicles in the United States. Construction was going on all around, executives were working out of trailers, and the production lines inside the plant were moving slowly because they were still getting kinks out of the system. At the time, they were producing light pickup trucks.

A lot has happened since then. Two years after our visit, they started making passenger cars (Sentras). Four years later the 1 millionth vehicle—a Nissan truck—rolled off the assembly lines. It was given to a local resident chosen by lottery. In 1992 the plant was expanded to 4.6 million square feet, making it the largest auto manufacturing facility under one roof in the

United States, employing more than 5,000 workers. And the United Auto Workers conducted a highly publicized unionizing drive at Smyrna. By a two-to-one margin, the UAW lost the election in 1989 and has apparently abandoned efforts to unionize Nissan.

When we visited Smyrna in mid-1991, we found a company very similar to the one we had praised in our earlier edition, but much bigger and more mature. Nissan is still the only Japanese automaker whose U.S. manufacturing subsidiary is run by Americans. The first president, Marvin Runyon, moved on to run the Tennessee Valley Authority and is now head of the U.S. Postal Service. He was succeeded by Jerry Benefield, who came to Nissan with Runyon from Ford Motor in 1980.

Benefield made a big point with us about Americans running the place: "Nissan is the only Japanese company that I know of that's truly American-managed. We have no Japanese with any line authority in this company whatsoever. I do have a Japanese board of directors. I'm a member, but the other members are Japanese. I think it's a significant statement in trust. I think it says a lot to our employees and to the middle managers of this company. It says, 'You, too, can become president. You're not limited to middle management. You can move all the way to the top of this company if you do a good job.' "

Other Nissan workers we met also felt that way. Bill Caruthers, manager of the plant's paint area, said: "The Japanese influence is quite a bit different here than what I hear about at Honda and Mazda. They are Japanese-operated. Not only owned, but operated. But we're American-operated, Japanese-owned. The Japanese influence here is heavy, but the Japanese presence is very minimal. There are about four or five Japanese technical advisors at Smyrna."

In keeping with the Japanese style, Nissan makes no distinction between the shirts worn by managers and other employees. Benefield has his name inscribed on his blue shirt, in just the same way any assembly-line worker does. There is an American touch, however. Although employees are given blue work shirts and work pants, they are *not* required to wear them; 10 percent wear their own shirts to work. (All employees at Honda's plants in Ohio, by contrast, must wear white overalls.) Benefield and other top managers eat in the employee cafeteria, and there are no reserved parking spots. There are also no time clocks. Benefield explains: "If management doesn't punch time cards, then technicians shouldn't have to punch time cards."

Benefield and other executives also communicate directly with employees. After the union drive in 1989, for example, Benefield told us: "As soon as the vote was over, I went on television, and I asked all of our employees to respect that decision. I asked the people who were on the company side not to gloat, not to tease or chastise the people who were on the union side, and I asked the people on the union side to please continue to be good team members and let's don't have any animosity whatsoever from either side, and we didn't."

That wasn't the first time employees saw Benefield on the internal TV station, Nissan News Network (NNN). Benefield delivers a news update on the 120 monitors located around the plant every quarter. NNN also keeps employees updated daily, showing current production figures, quality grades, progress on the company's success-sharing bonus, and the cafeteria menu. Benefield also meets with employees in person. Executives, including Benefield, have lunch with groups of 20 employees every week. Benefield says: "We try not to have any secrets from them, we try to tell them what our costs are, and how we're doing, and how we're performing to our budgets."

Nissan's open communications goes hand in hand with the Japanese-style teamwork that's expected on the plant floor. Teams meet for seven minutes every morning before they start working. There are also weekly meetings of groups working on production method improvement. These groups, called Involvement Through Teamwork (ITT) teams, are made up of day-shift and night-shift technicians, their managers, a process engineer, manufacturing engineer, and industrial engineer. They meet for two-day stretches to work on production problems. Another program is Involvement Circles, where a group of technicians picks a project from a list of suggestions. They meet once a week for as long as the project takes and present their solution to management. More than 30 Involvement Circles meet every week. These teams have come up with 225 ideas that have been implemented at the plant, including the installation of robots to get seat units into car frames and putting in props to help employees lift heavy car hoods.

This kind of open environment made the UAW's battle an uphill one. What may have made it insurmountable was Nissan's pay and benefits package, which is comparable to those of unionized auto plants at GM, Ford, and Chrysler. Smyrna workers make an average of $14.41 an hour, slightly less than UAW members elsewhere, but substantially above the average local manufacturing wage of $9.64 an hour. In addition, Nissan workers get two kinds of bonuses. The first is guaranteed and is based on the hours worked and the quality produced. It usually amounts to $1.55 an hour and is distributed twice a year. The company calls the second bonus "success sharing." It's handed out twice a year if Nissan reaches profit and quality targets. In 1991 Nissan employees received an average of $448 as a success-sharing bonus.

Nissan also offers a leased-vehicle benefit that no other automaker, U.S. or Japanese, offers. The company pays for registration, maintenance, and insurance. Employees have a monthly lease fee, which varies according to the kind of car they choose. A four-door automatic Sentra GXE leases for $263; a Sentra E model for $179; a 300ZX 2+2 for $666 per month. Body and frame technician Elaine Dawson told us: "I live 45 miles south of here so the lease-car program is very good for me because I don't have to purchase a car and put a lot of miles on it. It's an excellent program if you live out of town. Also, I have a 17-year-old daughter, and we tried to put her on our other insurance, and it was going to cost so much. But with the lease-car program, all you have to do is put your child through the safety class for one day, and they're automatically on the insurance, with no extra charge. So, what better program can you get, if you've got teenagers?"

Another perk is terrific recreation facilities. The plant itself has Ping-Pong tables, basketball and volleyball courts. A nearby fitness center includes aerobics classes, a picnic center, baseball fields, racquetball courts, tennis courts, a track, playgrounds, a driving range with three greens, and two swimming pools. The recreation center was the site for the 1991 annual picnic. In 1990 the company held their annual picnic at Opryland in Nashville, about 25 miles from Smyrna.

One other plus that comes from working for a Japanese-owned company: By mid-1992, 1,095 Nissan workers had made 3,385 trips to Japan. Beverly Bogle, who manages a vehicle assembly section area, went to Japan in 1990 for three weeks. She emphasized that the object of such trips is to learn Japanese automaking techniques, not Japanese management philosophy: "Their culture is entirely different from ours. Our technicians out here talk among themselves, play radios on the line. Their technicians, while they're working on the line, they never talk to each other or anything like that. When they take a break, everybody takes a break together, and they talk to each other then. But when they go back to work they don't talk. It's just different there than it is here. You never saw anyone there leave the line for any reason, to go to the rest room or anything. They work from break to lunch or whatever, they never leave the line, they're just there working."

Types of jobs: Manufacturing—82 percent; quality—7 percent; engineering—5 percent; finance and information systems—3 percent; purchasing—2 percent; human resources and legal—1 percent.

Main employment centers: Smyrna, Tennessee. In 1992 Nissan began construction on an engine manufacturing facility in Decherd, Tennessee; production is expected to begin there in 1996.

Headquarters: Nissan Motor Manufacturing Corporation U.S.A.
983 Nissan Drive
Smyrna, TN 37167
(615) 459-1400

Nordstrom

═══════════════════════

NORDSTROM

Nordstrom sells upscale, fashionable clothes and shoes in 73 stores. U.S. employees: 35,000.

★ ★ ★ ★	Pay/Benefits
★ ★ ★ ★	Opportunities
★ ★ ★	Job Security
★ ★ ★	Pride in Work/Company
★ ★ ★	Openness/Fairness
★ ★ ★	Camaraderie/Friendliness

BIGGEST PLUS: Employees get a lot of credit.
BIGGEST MINUS: You'll wear out your soles getting it.

Nordstrom came roaring out of the Pacific Northwest in the 1980s, and before the decade was over it reigned as the largest specialty store chain in the United States, eclipsing the old leader, Saks Fifth Avenue. When we first interviewed here in 1983, Nordstrom had 36 stores and 9,000 employees. In 1992 it had 75 stores and 35,000 employees. This expansion has created great opportunities for Nordstrom employees, called "Nordies." In 1988, when the company opened its first store on the East Coast, in Tysons Corner, Virginia, several hundred Nordies moved cross-country, at their own expense, eager for a shot at the management jobs opening up there. Women have found that their paths to management slots are not blocked here. Of the 74 store managers, 53 are women. Of the top 23 officers, six are women. Nordstrom has therefore broken the traditional pattern of retail industry employment where women typically represent two-thirds of the employees and a minuscule part of management. As for the very top of the company, that's reserved for Nordstrom family members, who own 39 percent of the stock. And up to now, no female member of the clan has chosen to pursue a career in the business.

"Specialty store" is one of those opaque industry terms, but if you have been in a Nordstrom, you know what it's about. Valet parking. A concierge. Pianos. Espresso bars. Marble and polished wood. Diaper-changing tables (in both men's and women's bathrooms). Wide aisles. An upscale, high-fashion store that sells primarily clothes. And shoes. Lots and lots of shoes. Nordstrom was founded in 1901 as a Seattle shoe store, and it's proud of that heritage. The company's hallmark is customer service, a holdover from the shoe business. As it likes to point out, "Selling shoes is the epitome of one-to-one service—nowhere else will you find a salesperson on his or her knees in an effort to please the customer."

Pampering the customer is at the core of Nordstrom. You don't wander in one of their stores for very long without being approached by a salesperson. Nordies tend to be young, enthusiastic, competitive overachievers, and they love to regale you with their personal stories of heroic service on behalf of the customer. Jim Wilds, who sells men's clothes in the mother store in downtown Seattle, told us that the understanding here is that "you will never be faulted for erring on the side of the customer." And he recounted how he once delivered a suit to the hotel of an out-of-town customer who didn't have time to get to the store. Wilds emphasized that he wanted to provide this kind of service; no one was telling him to do it. "If somebody had told me to do it," he said, "I would have resented it."

That gets to another core value here: empowerment of the salesperson to do what he or she thinks is necessary to please the customer. A shopper will rarely find a Nordstrom salesperson saying, "I have to check this with my supervisor." Decisions are made on the spot. Returns are accepted without question, even sometimes when the salesperson knows the item was not bought at Nordstrom. Kathleen Sargent, another men's clothing salesperson, said that she once bought a coat at Nordstrom and found out when she got home that it had an I. Magnin label. It was simply a customer return that had been slipped into stock.

Nordstrom doesn't have any trouble acting in this manner. John Rockwood, who sells women's shoes in Seattle, told us that in the summer of 1990 "we were selling a cheap shoe [cheap at Nordstrom meant it was selling at $38] but didn't have a customer's size. She saw it in the Neiman Marcus catalog for $5 more than what we were selling it for, and they had her size. She had them hold it and called us and said, 'I want this shoe.' She wanted me to buy it from Neiman Marcus and sell it at our price. It didn't make any sense, we lost money on it. Except that this customer wanted us to do it. I charged it on my American Express card. The company reimbursed me and the lady came in and picked it up. I hated this woman for making me do it but she came in and spent an additional $500 with me."

A similar story surfaced in the *San Francisco Chronicle* in the summer of 1992, reporting on the goings-on at the Valley Fair mall in San Jose. The Nordstrom store there had been selling Cole-Hahn Dunbars, a flat-soled women's shoe, for $154.90 a pair. At the other end of the mall, Macy's was selling the same shoe for $99.90. A platoon of Nordies, each clutching a $100 bill, descended on the Macy's store, bought out the entire stock, and placed them on sale at Nordstrom for $99.90.

Nordstrom has created an army of high-spirited, entrepreneurial-minded employees who live and die by the sales they ring up. Nordstrom pays better than other stores. In 1990, when they entered the New York metropolitan market with a store in the Garden State Plaza mall in Paramus, New Jersey, they offered entry-level wages of $9.50 an hour, $2 to $3 above the going rate. Nordstrom salespersons earn an average of $2,000 a month, also well above the usual pay in department stores. And because salespersons are on commission, there are always stories of people, usually in the shoe department, who are hauling down $80,000 and $100,000 a year.

Nordies are encouraged to set goals for themselves. And those who exceed these goals by a considerable margin receive the Pacesetter Award, which brings a certificate, a new business card that says "Pacesetter" on it, and—for you and a guest—a lavish evening of dining, dancing, and entertainment. In addition, for the following year Pacesetters enjoy a 33 percent discount on all Nordstrom merchandise (the standard employee discount is 20 percent). Since the Pacesetters Club was started in 1970, 1,645 employees have been admitted.

The downsides of this sales zealotry are high turnover among new hires (management people rarely leave) and a stressful atmosphere. Many people thrive in it and become intense Nordstrom loyalists. But it's not for everyone. As *Wall Street Journal* columnist Tim W. Ferguson put it in 1991: "Nordstrom attracts and rewards a special type of employee, and the rest of us should punch in elsewhere."

As Nordstrom broke sales record after sales record in the 1980s, it also became the center of a controversy over whether it was exploiting its workers by not paying them for extra services to customers such as personal deliveries and the thank-you notes that the company is famous for. These charges were raised by the United Food and Commercial Workers, a union that had represented Nordstrom employees in Seattle since 1931, and were ventilated in a front-page *Wall Street Journal* story and a Morley Safer report on the CBS show *60 Minutes*. Nordstrom loyalists responded by holding pep rallies to support the company. And in several cities, employees chipped in to buy ads to say they loved Nordstrom. We aired the issue in a focus interview we had in early 1991 with 10 Nordstrom employees in Seattle. There was not much support for the union position in that room, but one longtime salesperson, Caryman Komm, reported that she had seen people work overtime without getting paid and that the company had recently changed its policies and now did pay employees for the time they spent attending after-hours meetings and work parties.

Komm said she remembers being told by her manager that "I'd like 10 thank-you notes before you go home and if you have to make them up, that's fine with me." Others in the room said she should not have put up with that. Shoe salesman John Rockwood said: "I don't think a manager has any right to demand that. We had one manager who did demand that and we told him that it wasn't going to happen that way and if he didn't like it, he could go manage somewhere else. The demand was dropped within a week." David Ackerman, who sells men's active wear and has been at Nordstrom seven years, said: "If people were bullied into doing things, that's really not my fault. I would say no to something I didn't feel good about. I would go talk to Mr. John Nordstrom, because he is very approachable. That's my experience here."

SHORTEST EMPLOYEE HANDBOOK IN THE U.S.

The following is the Nordstrom employee handbook, in its entirety:

WELCOME TO NORDSTROM

We're glad to have you with our Company.
Our number one goal is to provide outstanding customer service.
Set both your personal and professional goals high.
We have great confidence in your ability to achieve them.
Nordstrom Rules:
Rule #1: Use your good judgment in all situations.
There will be no additional rules.
Please feel free to ask your department manager, store manager or division general manager any question at any time.

The sense that you can make your own way and call your own shots animates many of the people who work for Nordstrom. As Noel Martin, a 10-year sales veteran, put it: "I think one of the neat things here is that you're running your own business. Each person has a book, a list of customers. They call their customers about sales. There's an excitement, an entrepreneurship. You can make as much money as they will allow. A lot of times you're making decisions, and it's up to you how you want to handle that situation. You have that latitude. Nothing is set in concrete."

In the summer of 1991, employees at the five Seattle stores voted overwhelmingly to decertify the union as their bargaining agent. The vote was

1,022 to 407. The company was gratified. It had strongly lobbied employees to turn down the union. Joe Peterson, a former Nordstrom shoe salesman who heads the union local, attributed the defeat to the high turnover at the company. He told *The Wall Street Journal*'s Francine Schwadel: "Over 50 percent of the employees have been there less than two and one-half years." Seattle has always been a strong union city—a stronghold of the Wobblies and the hometown of legendary Teamster leader Dave Beck— and the Nordstrom shoe store was a union shop from its very earliest days. The Nordstroms always believed they knew what was best for employees, and now, for the first time in this century, they don't have to run it by the union.

Is there a place here for people who don't want to sell? Bridget Mayfield, a black woman who works in customer service, thinks so. She told us her story: "I'm in customer service because I can't hack sales. I've had managers approach me and try to get me to work in their departments. Before I came to Nordstrom, I worked at the Bon [Bon Marché], selling a black cosmetic line in Northgate. You might see 10 black people walking through the mall. So it was impossible for me to make my draw and that was a very bad experience for me. I came to Nordstrom and was a rover and that was lots of fun, getting around to the different departments. And I thought I was going to work in the Gallery. I tried it for two weeks and then said, 'I don't want to do this. Twenty years of working in the Gallery with all those sharks down there is not the place to be.' So I finally got into customer service, and I love it because I love the company. I'm going to stay here. If I ever did go out on the sales floor, it would be my goal to get into management real quick so I wouldn't have to compete with the rest of the people."

The Nordstroms have always run this place with a minimum of hierarchy, and they are trying to maintain this collegiality even with the tremendous expansion. During the 1980s the top management consisted of a group called "the five"—Bruce A., John N., and James F. Nordstrom, grandsons of the founder; John A. McMillan, a cousin-in-law; and a close family friend, Robert Bender. The Nordstroms used to rotate the title of president. They were known throughout the company as "Mr. Bruce," "Mr. John," and "Mr. Jim"—and they answered their own phones. In 1990 they did a little tinkering with this "structure." The three Nordstrom brothers and McMillan now all have the same title, cochairman. Bender is vice-chairman. And four nonfamily members, all of whom came up through the ranks, now share the title of copresident. Right behind them is the fourth generation of Nordstroms. Seven members are working their way up the ranks. The oldest is Blake W. Nordstrom, who was 31 years old in 1992 and general manager of the stores in the state of Washington. James A. Nordstrom, 30, was general manager of the northern California stores in 1992.

Main employment centers: In 1992 Nordstrom had 73 stores in 11 states: Washington, California, Oregon, Utah, Arizona, Alaska, Virginia, Maryland, New Jersey, Illinois, and Minnesota. More than 1,400 people worked in the corporate offices in Seattle, and another 5,000 were employed in stores in the state of Washington. The biggest concentration of people was in southern California, where more than 10,000 are employed. Another 6,700 work in northern California. Coming up soon: Indiana, Colorado, and New York.

Headquarters: Nordstrom
1501 Fifth Ave.
Seattle, WA 98101
(206) 628-2111

Northwestern Mutual Life

Northwestern Mutual Life®

Northwestern Mutual Life Insurance Company is the nation's ninth largest insurance company in terms of assets and second in terms of the number of policyholders. U.S. employees: 3,011.

★★★ Pay/Benefits
★★★★ Opportunities
★★★★★ Job Security
★★★★ Pride in Work/Company
★★★★ Openness/Fairness
★★★★ Camaraderie/Friendliness

BIGGEST PLUS: A free lunch here—and it's a good one.
BIGGEST MINUS: The paperwork might give you indigestion.

In an age of layoffs, here's a company with a no-layoff policy.

In an age of turmoil and hanky-panky in financial services, here's a financial giant that's serene and the soul of rectitude.

In an age of job-hopping, here's a company where people come to spend the rest of their working life.

Northwestern Mutual Life Insurance, known as NML or "The Quiet Company," provides life insurance to more than 2 million people across the country but has a presence largely limited to its headquarters city, Milwaukee, where virtually all its employees work. Its policies are sold by more than 7,000 independent agents who are so strongly linked to the company that they are considered extensions of the NML family. They are the only agents authorized to sell NML policies.

In Milwaukee, everyone knows NML's ornate, eight-story, Corinthian-columned building one block from Lake Michigan. It has been a city landmark since it went up in 1913. If you're from out of town, you might mistake it for a museum. The South Building, as it's called, is no longer large enough to house all the NML people. In 1978 the East Building, a 16-story modern office tower sheathed in granite and solar bronze glass, went up alongside the original building, and in 1990 the NML complex was augmented by the North Building, an 18-story steel and concrete structure that houses the company's data processing operations, a fitness center, and an airy, comfortable employee restaurant.

The restaurant is a knockout, from both the visual and culinary standpoints. It can seat more than 600 people at one time on three different levels, with many tables having views of the outside plaza. The restaurant is a clone of the one that continues to operate in the South Building, and the remarkable feature of both eating places is that lunch is on the house. The menus list calories instead of prices. A number of NML employees told us that they make lunch their main meal of the day. The NML chefs, all employees of the company, feed about 2,500 people a day, including some 70 managers and their guests in private dining rooms on the eighth floor of the South Building. The free lunch costs NML more than $3 million a year.

The company believes it's worth it to preserve the family feeling and traditional values that mark NML as a unique insurance company. They are very big on tradition here. The free lunch, for example, has been a perk since 1915. Harry Glowacki, a manager in policyowner services, told us: "What makes it so great is that the family I came into 31 years ago is still the family today. And although we have changed the way we do things and we do things a heck of a lot faster and our products and procedures are a heck of a lot more complex because of the computer age, we still are family. We come pretty darn close to knowing everybody because of all the offshoot organizations we have here. We socialize quite a bit with each other. Our managing group does, and we have a men's club, a women's club, we have our trail runners, all these things that we get together at—

our quarter-century club, which I am a proud member of. It gets our retirees and some 250 active employees who hired with the company over 25 years together at least three times a year."

Retirees—there were 595 of them in 1992—do remain part of the NML family. Six times a year they receive a 12-page magazine, *New Life News*, and for the past 36 years they have gathered for an annual summer outing at the Lake Lawn Lodge in Delavan, 50 miles southwest of Milwaukee. Those who don't drive are bused from NML's headquarters to the lodge, where they partake of a banquet, miniature golf, shuffleboard, cards, and bingo.

The family feeling was much in evidence on a summer's day in 1991—August 25—when 6,000 employees and their family members trooped through the NML complex in celebration of the new North Building. Along the way they were entertained by musicians and downed 5,500 boxes of popcorn, 10,000 cookies, and 6,500 ice cream sundaes. Although it was a Sunday, NML executives, including CEO Don Schuenke, remained in their offices to greet visitors. We saw Schuenke a month later, and he was still glowing from the experience. He said he stayed in his office from noon to a little after 5:00 P.M., and when he went to lock the door, people were still coming through.

Public confidence in financial institutions nose-dived in the 1980s because of scandals in the savings and loan industry and loan problems at banks and some insurance companies, including major operators such as Mutual Benefit Life and Equitable Life. NML was an island of strength in that storm. The company doubled in size during the last half of the 1980s, so that today it's collecting more than $8 billion a year in premiums and investment income. NML sticks to its knitting. While it offers disability insurance and annuities, it focuses primarily on life insurance for individuals. It doesn't insure cars or homes.

Even though NML was in fine shape, Schuenke decided, because of the turmoil in the industry, that he wanted to meet face-to-face with every employee in the company in 1991. Two years before, he had presided over an all-company meeting at Milwaukee's Performing Arts Center, answering presubmitted questions. This time he wanted to get closer and so he went department by department at the home office. The largest meeting was 300 people, the smallest 25. The sessions ran for about an hour, with 40 to 45 minutes reserved for questions.

Schuenke said: "I started off by telling them that I had read a lot about problems in the insurance industry. The industry is not in trouble. Some insurance companies are. We are not one of them."

Employees we met had positive reactions to the meetings, ranging from "I was told to be patient to wait for my parking spot—it could be a few more years" to "They asked him some pretty tough questions—how he saw the work force in the future and how committed Northwestern was to community service."

Relations are good between the company and the Office and Professional Employees International Union, which represents most of the nonmanagement staff. The union organized NML workers during the 1930s.

NML is one of a handful of companies in America that say proudly they have a no-layoff policy, and Schuenke made a point of reaffirming that policy in his chats with employees. Noting all the companies that have resorted to layoffs and downsizing, he told employees: "We are not doing that. We have never done it and we don't anticipate doing it."

Hardly anyone ever leaves NML (turnover—including retirements—runs at a remarkably low 4.5 percent a year), and one reason is a strong commitment to continuous retraining and education. James W. Ehrenstrom, the senior vice-president in charge of human resources, pointed out to us that "we have a policy that says, in effect, that if your job is eliminated through no fault of your own—through changes in technology, for example—you will not be terminated, you will not be laid off, and we won't reduce your pay or your job grade." You can search American business for a long time before finding a similar policy.

Ehrenstrom recalled that he was "sitting around a table one time with my peers, and they all wanted to talk about problems they were having with downsizing. And one of them turned to me and said, 'How do you guys do it? You are not laying anybody off.' And I said, 'Well, we are doing well but we also try to stay lean in the first place.' " Anyone who looks at the NML profile can see that. In the mid-1980s they had 2,300 employees; today, they have 3,000; meanwhile, the amount of life insurance in force more than doubled. In industry surveys, NML consistently comes out in first place as the lowest-cost insurance company.

Of course a no-layoff policy is no boon if the company is a boring place to work. That doesn't seem to be the case at NML. Lynda Taylor, a senior programmer in information services, told us she took a job with NML in 1990 because of "the training they offer, the tuition reimbursement, the in-house classes. With computer programming, the job is very similar no matter where you go, but I didn't want to be working in a place that looked like a warehouse. And I interviewed with some places where you looked like you were working in a warehouse. I wanted to feel good when I came in to work every day and enjoy my surroundings. And enjoy the people I was working with."

Eve Vitale, a manager in field financial services who has been with NML since 1978, said: "It kind of makes me a little nervous the way quality is used as a trendy, cool kind of thing to do. Northwestern was into quality before quality was the cool thing to do. And it's just demonstrated in every aspect of life here as an employee."

Claims analyst Beverly Krawczyk, who has been here since 1976, said: "I came from a bank and I worked there two years. It wasn't family at all. This company is pure family. It is a very elite company to work for. Very classy. I enjoy it. My sister also works here and she was responsible for my getting a job here."

One unusual perk available to all employees is the ability to take salary increases in one lump sum at the beginning of the year.

NML is organized as a mutual company, as are some other big insurance companies like Prudential, Metropolitan, and John Hancock. This means that the policyholders own the company. In practice, it's often a legal fiction, with management running the company the way they want to. At Northwestern, they take responsibility to policyholders very seriously, tracing it back to a mission statement crafted in 1888. This statement said, in part: "The ambition of the Northwestern has been less to be large than to be safe; its aim is to rank first in benefits to policyowners rather than first in size."

It was surprising to see how many employees buy into this mission. Gloria Venski, a policy benefits manager, told us: "Policyowners own the company, and we always keep them in the forefront. They are the reason we are here. We have to do things for them. We are not working for a person or a corporation. Every time a policyowner calls me on the phone, that is your contact with somebody out there that is very important to this company. And you don't lose sight of that here."

Employees feel good about working for a company that espouses and practices fairness. Jean Maier, a director of policyowner services who joined NML in 1979, used to work in claims investigation and she told us that before she accepted that job, she sat down with her boss and said: " 'I can't do this job unless I know I can do the right thing. I can't take some old lady's policy away from her or not give her money if I think it's not honorable.' And my boss said to me, 'You will never have to do that.' And I have never been put in that position. I never had that separation of my personal morals from what the company was." Sally Ostergaard, a manager of legal support services who has been with NML since 1965, seconded that viewpoint: "I don't think I have ever been asked to do anything in this company that was in conflict with my own value system."

Seventy percent of the work force at NML is female, but it's only in recent years that they have been penetrating upper echelons. Of NML's 27 executive officers—the top tier in the company—four are women. They are Deborah Beck, vice-president–new business; Madonna M. Hostetter, vice-president–underwriting services and standards; Barbara F. Piehler, vice-president–corporate services; and Martha M. Valerio, vice-president–policy benefits.

Types of jobs: Insurance—38 percent; corporate/staff—24 percent; information systems—16 percent; marketing—10 percent; investment—9 percent; financial—3 percent.

Main employment center: Milwaukee.

Headquarters: Northwestern Mutual Life Insurance Company
720 E. Wisconsin Ave.
Milwaukee, WI 53202
(414) 271-1444

Odetics

Odetics

Odetics makes robots, video security systems, time-lapse recorders, video-cassette carts used by TV stations, precision timers, and 80 percent of the recorders used in spacecraft. Employees: 586.

★ ★ ★   Pay/Benefits
★ ★ ★   Opportunities
★ ★ ★   Job Security
★ ★ ★   Pride in Work/Company
★ ★ ★ ★   Openness/Fairness
★ ★ ★ ★ ★   Camaraderie/Friendliness

BIGGEST PLUS: You won't be treated like a robot.
BIGGEST MINUS: You might work as long as one.

"The wackiest place to work in the United States." That's what *Industry Week* once called Odetics. A tour of the headquarters—located across the street from Disneyland—offers plenty of reasons. The conference room houses a model of the Challenger space shuttle made out of Budweiser beer cans. An engineer's office has a hanging wooden flying dinosaur with a four-foot wingspan and a model of a Federal Express plane in its jaws. The corporate conference room displays a collection of whimsical masks made by local artists.

These clues would tip off anyone that Odetics is not your usual corporation. In talking to people you hear about the differences. There's a Fun Committee, whose raison d'être is to think of offbeat activities. One year they dubbed Valentine's Day as Carrot Day. Committee chairman Keith Brush, an associate relations manager, said: "We didn't think it was appropriate to deliver valentines to your coworkers because husbands and wives would get upset. We thought that carrots would be funny. So for 25 cents, you could buy a bunch of carrots and have them delivered to anybody here at the company with a card. I think we ended up delivering about 500 bunches of carrots."

Another Fun Committee activity: A '50s day featuring a sock hop that started at 6:00 in the morning, a telephone booth stuffing contest (16 people won), a Hula-Hoop contest, bubble gum blowing, and '50s music played on the lawn during lunch. To support company athletes participating in a corporate Olympics contest in Anaheim, the Fun Committee sponsored a pep rally led by three cheerleader squads (one of which was made up of the company's board of directors).

A high point of the year is Halloween. One year they had a Halloween party with prizes to be given for the best costumes. But you never know what to expect here. Three people were called out of the audience and dressed as pumpkins. Then all the company's officers—also dressed as pumpkins—suddenly appeared singing a song and got the three new "pumpkins" to join them in a dance. At the end of this routine, the chairman informed the three new pumpkins that they were being made company officers. The pumpkin dance was their induction ceremony.

Employees appreciate Odetics's unusual style. Electronic assembler Donna Pichette remarked: "I have worked for several companies, and without a doubt this is the most fun place. The main reason for leaving my last job was because I was tired of working with unhappy people. I wanted to go somewhere where it was pleasant, where there was more besides punching a clock, coming in and working eight hours and then leaving again. There are just so many things going on here. And the atmosphere is almost like family. People you don't know, they say hello."

Joel Slutzky, the white-bearded cofounder and CEO, explained his unusual philosophy: "We feel that if it's not fun to get up in the morning and go to work, then it doesn't matter what the P&L [profit-and-loss statement] looks like. You've missed something. Life isn't that long that you can overlook the social aspect of the company as well. And, in fact, we've found that there is a tight linkage between how you feel about the company and how you are going to do as far as growth and profitability and things like that."

Another example of the Odetics style is the cafeteria. Slutzky said the company recently "took over management of the cafeteria, and it really has improved. We said to the cook, the same cook, 'We want you to be experimental, we want you to try new things, have some failures, but make it interesting.' And he asked, 'What about ingredients? I was capped in the type of ingredients from the profit motivation.' We said, 'Why don't you take the caps off and we'll see how that works out?' It's not going to kill the company to do that. An interesting thing happened. The cafeteria improved and activity in the cafeteria went up. I don't know how much more we're paying for these ingredients, but there is no doubt that we're doing better on the cafeteria than the people to whom we were leasing out because the attitude changed."

Chief technical officer Kevin Daly calls the Odetics style "structured spontaneity," explaining: "We have adopted a posture of not institutionalizing anything. If something is a success, we don't want it to go on in perpetuity. There is a point in the success cycle that you say, 'Let's quit right now.' And I always get the response 'How come we're not doing that again? That was great.' And I come up with the same answer each time: 'Let's remember it as being great because there is a point where if it persists, it becomes the obligatory company picnic or that sort of thing, and it carries a life of its own.' In a sense our way is more challenging because it means that you can't rest on your success."

Odetics likes constant change for some hardheaded business reasons. Most of what it makes today did not exist when we visited Odetics in the early 1980s when their main product was digital tape recorders for space vehicles. (Every space shuttle carries at least five Odetics recorders, each costing from $400,000 to $3 million.) Today, space recorders constitute only about a third of their business. A few weeks after our 1983 visit, Odetics introduced a six-legged walking robot called the Odex I, which has since been inducted into the Smithsonian Institution's permanent collection, as it was the first commercial model of countless science-fiction writers' fantasies. (During a demonstration Odex I lifted a small pickup truck and carried it across the room.) In 1991 the French Atomic Power Commission bought an Odex III to perform dangerous maintenance tasks. Odetics's entry into the world of robotics led to a "cart machine" now used by TV studios to automatically play commercials and short news items. At a cost of about $375,000 a pop, Odetics cart machines are now used by NBC Network News and some 24-hour all-news TV stations, among more than 100 other stations all over the world. Odetics engineers have also created time-lapse recorders used in ATMs that can record 30 full days of transactions on one regular VCR tape. (You may not realize that every time you visit an ATM, you are being recorded, possibly by a video recorder made by Odetics.)

Of course, innovation and creativity require risk-taking. And Odetics's unusual style seems to encourage people to take risks. According to Joe Orzech, an engineering technician: "They allow you enough freedom to make mistakes and there is not a lot of supervision. They will allow you to do the job as you see fit."

Having fun also seems to make it easy for people to work together as a team. Marti Cassell-Fix, a software engineer, explained: "Everyone works very hard and everyone is very team-oriented. They do their own part, but they support everyone else. If we're working on a deadline or a program, as soon as one person gets their work done, they will go and help the next person to get theirs done."

Odetics has a variety of communications vehicles to encourage a sense of belonging. A bimonthly newsletter, *The Family Tree*, is not your typical employee newsletter. According to Holly Barnett, manager of public relations, "Good news and bad news are given equal time in the newsletter and other communication forums—company fluff is avoided in an effort to foster trust." Odetics also conducts an annual associates survey. Every year they use a fresh set of questions, and Slutzky responds to each signed survey individually. One of the more important forums is the town meeting. According to Slutzky: "We have town hall meetings when there is something important that we're about to institute."

Another forum is the C-cubed meeting (which stands for "control change through communication"), often held over lunch. Slutzky said: "We'll invite a random group of employees to a C-cubed meeting and say, 'Here is what we're thinking of doing. It may not affect anybody in this room, or it may affect somebody in this room, but we want to get your feedback before we implement it.'"

Mark Bastani, an engineering manager, says: "I haven't seen anything, any decision, that does not involve every level of associate. They bring up questions and they get input from everybody."

Some employees feel there is too much openness. Payroll clerk Heather Bullock told us: "I think they are too open. They don't have many restrictions for associates. We bend over backwards in payroll. When there is a vacation request or something like that, associates are given a check at the drop of a hat. And it puts a lot more work on us."

For some employees one downside is the long hours. (Employees who come in on Saturdays get a free lunch.) Controls engineer Susan Boltinghouse said: "A lot of people I work with put in quite long hours. It's working on interesting stuff, so that helps a bit. In my division there is a fair amount of peer pressure to do that; it has never come from management, but when your peers are working particularly hard, you kind of feel like you had better do that as well." Software engineer Marti Cassell-Fix added: "People put in a lot, and some of us don't get paid for our overtime. There is that peer pressure to work, but you always want to, you enjoy what you're doing."

One explanation for the long hours came from program management vice-president Margaret Lamb. (Lamb was one of the three who were turned into pumpkins when they were made officers.) She says: "There are two key phrases that inspire us to be here when we're not scheduled to be here. One is that we are a 'team player,' so if the ball is in my court when I get ready to go home, I am going to stay and finish it so I can hand it to the next player. The other thing is that we're 'task-oriented' instead of clock-oriented. I don't care what the clock says. If it needs to be done today, it's going to get done today before I go home."

Still, Odetics doesn't appear to be a burnout place. One reason may be that Odetics is generous with time off. In addition to regular vacation time, everyone gets a week off with pay between Christmas and New Year's. Professional and managerial associates (all nonhourly workers) also can get an extra week off with pay every year. Everyone also qualifies for a four-week, paid sabbatical every seven years. As could be expected, Odetics has an unusual way to celebrate service anniversaries. On your 10th anniversary with the company, you get a check for $250 for a "night on the town."

Turnover is low (about 10 percent, which is about half the rate in comparable high-tech companies in Orange County). And they put a lot of emphasis on health and fitness. The company has a full gym, a swimming pool, basketball and volleyball courts, and a full-time trainer. There are also aquaerobics, a bowling league, walking clubs, and running clubs. There is also "Friday night beat-the-traffic basketball." Slutzky plays whenever he can. In an effort to reduce auto use, the company reimburses associates for all or part of the costs for walking shoes or biking gear used to commute to work. The company also sponsors programs in stress management, acupressure, and hatha-yoga.

Types of jobs: Professionals—43 percent; technicians—19 percent; clerical —17 percent; production—17 percent; service—3 percent; sales—1 percent.

Main employment center: Anaheim, California.

Headquarters: Odetics
                  1515 S. Manchester Ave.
                  Anaheim, CA 92802
                  (714) 774-5000

Patagonia

patagonia®

Patagonia makes high-quality sports and outdoor equipment and clothing.
Employees: 425.

★ ★ ★   Pay/Benefits
★ ★ ★ ★   Opportunities
★ ★   Job Security
★ ★ ★ ★   Pride in Work/Company
★ ★ ★ ★   Openness/Fairness
★ ★ ★ ★   Camaraderie/Friendliness

BIGGEST PLUS: You can surf at lunch.
BIGGEST MINUS: Your job might go out with the tide.

Megan Montgomery discovered that Patagonia was a different sort of company during her first week on the job: "A woman walked into a meeting and breast-fed her baby. She gave this great presentation. Everyone agreed with her point, and there was a baby sitting right there. It was so normal and healthy and natural that it just fit."

Welcome to Patagonia, one of the nation's most free-spirited companies. A brief tour of their headquarters in southern California offers numerous unusual sights. Adjacent to the entrance, you see children playing in the playground of the on-site day care. Twenty staff members supervise 80 children, from preschool and kindergarten to an after-school Kids' Club (to age 14).

From the reception area you walk through a cafeteria to reach other offices on the first floor. The cafeteria serves health foods, desserts without sugar, and a wide range of herbal teas. Most any time of day, one or more small groups of employees can be seen holding meetings there. The cafeteria is used because no Patagonia employees, including top executives, have private offices. So conferences must be held either in the cafeteria or in one of the handful of conference rooms scattered throughout the building.

Patagonia has one of the most relaxed dress codes in the country. Throughout the day employees can be seen walking through the building in jogging or exercise outfits. If you visit the rest rooms, you will notice that many have showers and lockers. Where else could you go to work barefoot? If you look out behind the building, you will see the company's sand volleyball court, which is used several hours daily.

From the beginning Yvon Chouinard, Patagonia's founder, has focused on making top-of-the-line gear aimed at serious mountain climbers and outdoor types. In 1957, frustrated by the poor quality of climbing equipment available on the market, Chouinard invested $100 to buy an anvil and a book about blacksmithery. He started making his own equipment in his parents' backyard in Burbank, about 50 miles from the current Patagonia headquarters in Ventura. He sold his homemade climbing gear for $1.50 from the trunk of his car or out of his backpack while on climbing expeditions. Before long Chouinard was making outdoor clothing as well, and a growing business was born.

Chouinard says he likes to hire people who, like himself, are users of the company's products, because "pride in our company comes from knowing we make the best products, and that comes from using them." So over the years Patagonia has hired many expert kayakers, skiers, fishermen, and climbers. Emily Boyes, a merchandiser, feels this is an important part of why she likes it there: "I know I feel very much aligned with what this company embraces. For instance, if I go out hiking in the Sierras and I talk to other climbers, I feel really proud to say that I work for Patagonia."

It doesn't make sense to hire a collection of mountaineers and surfers and then keep them cooped up indoors. Most Patagonia employees are on salary, giving them the flexibility to pursue their sports. During our visit, Bill Logan, a dealer service representative, was planning to take off a half-day to go rafting, and a whole day to go skiing. Logan's schedule was not unusual. Chouinard once outlined company policy in a speech to employees entitled "Let My People Go Surfing" in these terms: "You are allowed to take time off, whether it's two hours or two weeks, as long as your work gets done and as long as it doesn't screw up the others from doing their work." It's not unusual for employees to go surfing at lunch, as the ocean is less than a mile away from their headquarters.

Taking longer periods of time off is also encouraged. Chouinard himself works only about half the year, spending the rest of the time on extended expeditions to places like the Patagonia mountains of South America, Antarctica, Costa Rica, Siberia, Alaska, and Africa. Many employees in the Bozeman, Montana, distribution office take two or three months off a year to lead climbing trips or work as river guides. Two San Francisco store managers, who are also avid rock climbers, worked out a job-sharing arrangement trading off three-month shifts. Some employees in the Ventura headquarters also alternate working full-time for three months with taking three months off to pursue their outdoor activities.

The relaxed free-wheeling atmosphere may be what is most noticeable to a casual visitor. But Patagoniacs (as they call themselves) work hard, too. The same people who leave at 3:00 in the afternoon to go surfing are back at the office until 9:00 at night to finish their work. Megan Montgomery, public affairs director, thinks the dedication is linked to the fact that "there are a lot of really good athletes here, and that takes a lot of self-discipline. That same self-discipline applies to their work responsibilities." Hal Arneson, a promotions director, explains: "If you are going to play, you have to work accordingly to make up for the time of play. So a lot of us end up on the surface being very casual and playing very hard, but you have to work very hard, too. A funny sort of workaholism exists here." Bill Kulczycki, vice-president of marketing, has this explanation: "It's almost a paranoia that if you don't work hard enough you won't get to play. And none of us want to sacrifice playing."

Patagonia also attracts people because of its environmental activism. It has donated money to Planned Parenthood, Earth First!, the Rainforest Action Network, Greenpeace, and, of course, the Surfrider Foundation. Patagonia also donates food and gear to environmental research scientists and activists, Special Olympic athletes, Native American orphanages, and needy families in the United States and Central America. Kevin Sweeney, former director of public relations, explained their process: "One of our criteria is: would IBM give to them? Would Exxon? Would Mobil? If yes, well, then let them, and we will give to somebody else." Patagonia even joined several other companies (including Ben & Jerry's) in taking out an ad opposing U.S. military intervention to oust Iraq from Kuwait shortly before the Persian Gulf War in 1991. One Patagonia customer presumably did not appreciate the gesture. George Bush was featured on the cover of *People* and in a *Sports Illustrated* article wearing a Patagonia jacket.

Company guru Chouinard relishes controversy. He told us he thinks the reason most businesses are unwilling to take such stands is that they are afraid of alienating potential customers. Chouinard doesn't consider the entire population prospective customers: "I look at 250 million people in America, and I say 125 million of them are full of shit and they're doing everything wrong. They are leading this country down a suicide path and they are destroying the place. I don't want those people to buy my stuff, I don't want to sell anything to those people. I want to piss off 50 percent of the people in America, and the other 50 percent are going to be absolute, rabid, loyal customers. That is enough for me. I really believe that if you're not making enemies you're not trying hard enough."

Chouinard says he gets about 20 letters a day from people complaining about the charities he donates to. But he insists he also gets 20 letters a day from people praising his gumption. Sweeney thinks many people respect the company's bravado: "People are so tired of background noise and the same crap out there all the time. Everything sounds like a government spokesperson. When somebody speaks with clarity, people listen. And they respect you for saying it, even if they don't agree with you. So we can get away with supporting controversial groups like Earth First! and Planned Parenthood. We call it courage points."

Patagonia's employees love the strong political stances and the almost anticorporate tone of the place. Many employees find their way to Patagonia from organizations like Outward Bound or other nonprofit organizations. Others, like Bob McDougall, a world-class kayaker and product line director for paddling, never had regular jobs before coming to Patagonia. McDougall told us: "I wouldn't have ever taken this job if the company didn't stand for something beyond just business for sales and profits. I think for most of us it's really important that the company is trying to do the right thing most of the time and trying to show better ways to do business."

But, like other corporations, Patagonia has to contend with economic realities. In mid-1991 they found themselves mired in the recession and laid off 120 employees—the first layoff in their history. The company was generous with those laid off—10 days' notice, a minimum of four weeks' severance pay plus one week of pay for every year of service.

Patagonia's problems brought forth criticism from *Inc.*, one of the business publications that had praised it several years earlier. Analyzing the "disaster" that culminated in the layoffs, *Inc.* senior writer Edward O. Welles cataloged numerous problems with Chouinard's "cult of personality" style, including his frequent absences, "vacillation between an elitist and a populist approach to clothing," "mercurial shifts in thinking," and efforts "to forge his company into a tool for social change." Welles summed up his indictment: "Yvon Chouinard touts his company as a model for the future, when, in fact, its time may already have passed."

In their own defense, Patagonia's executives acknowledge that they had grown too rapidly, but deny that the recent cutbacks represent a "disaster." CEO Kris McDivitt told us she was most bothered by the *Inc.* article's "assumption that because we have chosen to run this company differently, people are suspect of its capacity for success." She pointed out that Patagonia has made a profit every year for 20 years, including 1991, a track record that no other company in their industry can match. She added: "I think people do respect us for showing continuity in our beliefs about environmental issues, social issues, and at the same time in being the company that develops the most innovative, high-quality products."

Patagonia has earned a lot of respect over the years for opportunities it has provided women. Patagonia's U.S. work force is 65 percent female, and 61 percent of managers are women, including CEO McDivitt, who started as a part-time shipper in 1972. The percentage has gone down since the early days of Patagonia, when the company had 45 employees, 40 of whom were women. Some women don't see the firm as being particularly feminist. Kathy Larramendy, research and design director, told us: "It's a company of smart people, not necessarily smart men or smart women."

Types of jobs: Customer service—34 percent; administration—33 percent; production—17 percent; distribution—16 percent.

Main employment centers: More than 300 work in Ventura, located between Santa Barbara and Los Angeles. Another 40 Patagoniacs work in the distribution center at Bozeman, Montana, and 85 work overseas.

Headquarters: Patagonia, Inc.
259 West Santa Clara St.
Ventura, CA 93001
(805) 643-8616

BEST TRAINING PROGRAMS

Federal Express
General Mills
Haworth
IBM
J. P. Morgan
Motorola
J. C. Penney
Procter & Gamble
Quad/Graphics
Rosenbluth International

J. C. Penney

JCPenney

J. C. Penney is the fourth largest general merchandise retailer in the nation.
U.S. employees: 185,000.

★★★ Pay/Benefits
★★★★ Opportunities
★★★ Job Security
★★★★ Pride in Work/Company
★★★ Openness/Fairness
★★★★ Camaraderie/Friendliness

BIGGEST PLUS: The Golden Rule is stitched into their fabric.
BIGGEST MINUS: The pattern hasn't changed since 1902.

On Thanksgiving Day in 1991, with the country gripped in a stubborn
recession, President George Bush decided that he needed to do something
to stimulate the economy. So on the next morning, November 29, the
traditional start of the Christmas shopping season, he tried to set an example for his fellow Americans. He went shopping at the J. C. Penney store in
Frederick, Maryland, where he bought socks and a child's Houston Oilers
sweat suit. Tim Farrell, the salesman who sold the sweat suit to the president, told the local newspaper: "There won't be a customer I can't handle
now."

The choice of Penney was a natural. It has been part of the fabric of
America for virtually the entire 20th century. The founder was James Cash
Penney, a remarkable merchant who valued his employees so much that he
never called them employees. They were always associates—a practice later
copied by a number of other companies, including Wal-Mart, which was
founded by a former J. C. Penney associate, Sam Walton. Penney opened
his first store in 1902 in the mining town of Kemmerer, Wyoming. He

called it the Golden Rule Store because he believed in treating customers as he himself would like to be treated. In 1992, when the company celebrated its 90th birthday, it returned to Kemmerer to hold its annual meeting in the local high school there. Five hundred stockholders trekked to the southwest corner of Wyoming to attend the meeting. Kemmerer still has a J. C. Penney store.

An old-fashioned, down-home feeling permeates J. C. Penney. Associates stay for a long time. And they tell their relatives to come to work here, too. Nepotism seems to be the official policy. William R. Howell, who became chief executive officer in 1983 and was still in that post in 1992, is the son of a onetime Penney store manager. Robert Gill, who retired as vice-chairman in 1992, is also the son of a former Penney executive—and his two children work at Penney's. Donald V. Seibert, whom Howell succeeded, told the top managers of the company in 1983: "We're very proud of our two-generation and three-generation Penney families. We emphasize our family relationships more than other companies I observe. We see one another socially. We like each other."

At Dallas headquarters, we met Lillian Krysak, who works in the catalog department and has been with Penney's since 1972. She said: "I love the company. I like the people. I think there is a certain type of person who works for Penney's. It's a homey feeling." You can catch that feeling in flipping through the pages of *JC Penney Today*, the bimonthly company newspaper, although you risk being drowned in a tidal wave of heart-tugging stories. One issue in 1992 told how Michael Adams, a part-timer in the Shawnee, Oklahoma, store, went out of his way to help a family find comfortable clothes for their son, who was dying of cancer. Another issue in 1991 reprinted a column written by Glenn Scott for the *Modesto Bee* in California. It told the story of Lanette Davis, a 21-year-old clerk in Penney's Modesto store, who had helped a family get a burial outfit for a baby who had been stillborn three months before term.

At another California store, in Chula Vista, Maxine Storm was saluted in 1992 on her 75th birthday. Storm works in the cash room and has been with the store since it opened in 1963. Virginia Cooper retired from the Ashtabula, Ohio, store in 1991 after 44 years of service. She said that she originally took the job only to buy Christmas gifts for her two sons. (Associates get a 15 percent discount on store purchases.) Now she has 11 grandchildren and 17 great-grandchildren.

In Dallas, Kathleen Holliday, a catalog department manager, told us: "I can remember the first month I was with the Penney company, my boss said to me, 'This is a big company, it's the biggest company I've ever worked for.' I said, 'This is not a big company, this is a small town.' You interact that way. The elevator banks are like Main Street. It's like the small towns I have lived in."

J. C. Penney is big, with 1,283 stores at the end of 1991, plus 530 drugstores operating under the Thrift and Treasury names. It's the only retailer with a presence in all 50 states plus the District of Columbia and Puerto Rico. With 1991 sales of $17.2 billion, including $3 billion in catalog sales, it is, not counting food stores, the fourth largest retail operation in the country after Wal-Mart, K mart, and Sears, Roebuck. And with 185,000 employees, it's one of the 10 largest employers in the United States.

Size, however, did not keep it from shifting gears during the 1980s when many of the nation's biggest department stores ran into severe problems. Penney's spent more than $1 billion to modernize its stores, which anchor malls across the country. It stopped selling hard goods like appliances, TV sets, and sporting equipment, and it gave up feeding customers in restaurants or processing their film or servicing their cars. Instead, it greatly expanded its clothing departments, especially for women. Today, clothing accounts for nearly three-quarters of total sales. And, in a very big move for J. C. Penney, it began stocking national brands like Levi's, Haggar, Palm Beach, Vanity Fair, Van Heusen, and Henry Grethel. The company has a very clear fix on who its customers are, identifying them as middle-income and upper-middle-income families. And J. C. Penney, in its own words, seeks to be "their national department store."

While they didn't change their values in the 1980s, the J. C. Penney Company did change their headquarters address. In 1988, after 74 years in New York City, the company moved to Dallas, taking with them 1,200 managers. Left behind were another 1,200 managers who didn't want to move to Texas plus 1,200 nonmanagement associates who were not offered the generous relocation terms made available to managers. Penney said the move was dictated by both economic and strategic considerations. It would save them money—an estimated $60 to $70 million a year, the company said—and also put them in closer touch with their regional centers and stores. In Texas, the company leased space in three different buildings while it was putting up a gleaming new headquarters complex in Plano, a northern suburb of Dallas.

Associates began moving into the new headquarters in 1992. It's a far cry from the 45-story skyscraper Penney's used to occupy on the Avenue of the Americas across the street from the New York Hilton. Set on 122 acres in Legacy Corporate Park, the company's new home is low-rise rather than high-rise. It has only three floors, which stretch the length of five football fields. The plan was to make it a "walking building" to stimulate interaction among associates. The building itself takes up only 20 percent of the land bought by Penney's. On the outside are hiking and biking trails that connect with other parts of the office park, a six-acre lake, and 4,000 indigenous American shade and ornamental trees and shrubs. The inside of the building houses a 3,500-square-foot fitness center, a three-tiered restaurant, a medical clinic, and a child-care center that can accommodate 130 infants and toddlers.

All the Penney associates were expected to be in their new environment by January 1993.

Associates we met in Dallas praised the company for the relocation help. Marian Algarotti, who works in corporate personnel, and her husband, Lou, who works in the catalog department, were a little fearful about the move from New York to Dallas. "I had lived in the place where I was for 35 years," she said, "and I had never really traveled or anything. They gave us the opportunity to come down for a look-see two or three times. They gave us the option of either Lou flying home to be with us on the weekends or myself going down to be with him here. Once I was here, I really liked it. With the relocation I couldn't have asked for anything better as far as the moving itself, packing us up and getting us here."

Donna Nall, another personnel associate, said that during the relocation Penney's organized an orientation program for the transferees, taking them on sight-seeing trips in the Dallas area and briefing them on cultural events. That worked so well that the headquarters office now has an activity center to carry out this function on a permanent basis, publishing a monthly newsletter, sponsoring trips, and offering discount tickets to performances. Dallas has a new symphony hall, and in 1990 Penney's bought out the house for its associates on two nights. It's not Broadway, but there it is.

The new headquarters, in keeping with a long Penney tradition, has a management development center that represents a consolidation of four regional training centers. As a promote-from-within company, Penney's does extensive in-house training. Most of its senior managers have never worked for another company. In 1991 more than 5,700 management associates attended training sessions at headquarters. Thousands more went through the training sessions held in stores. A large J. C. Penney store will have as many as 200 training programs during the year. Penney hires between 600 and 800 management trainees a year. They train for 26 weeks, rotating among all departments in the store. While it recruits at 200 colleges, it has drawn heavily in recent years from the University of Florida, Texas A&M, Brigham Young, Howard University, Indiana University, Southwest Texas State, and the California State University system.

Cheryl Hall, who works in merchandising at Dallas headquarters, told us that in the three years she has been with the company, she has received three promotions, the last one into management. Even though she knew nothing about marketing, she was hired as a marketing retail assistant and received "great training." From there she went into visual organizing and now, as a manager, she's being trained in computer-aided design on the Macintosh. "When I was nonmanagement," she said, "I did not feel like an outcast. I was treated the same as a management associate. A year ago I was offered a management position and I turned it down because it involved numbers and that wasn't my career path. They didn't look down on me on that." Sylvia Deadwyler, who works in administrative services, told us that she was also able to move up to a supervisory position within three years of coming in as a secretary. Trained as a librarian, she had reentered the work force after taking time out "to be the traditional homemaker, involved in a lot of charity work and volunteer programs." Deadwyler was able to take a workshop in supervisory skills. "There is ongoing training here," she said. Tim Voss, a manager in the catalog department, told us: "About the time I'm getting bored with something at Penney's I've had the opportunity to move on. I appreciate my managers taking the time to ask me what my long-term career path is. And not just asking but listening and helping me to improve or advance along that goal."

Unless you are in the top brackets, pay is not great at Penney's. If you divide the 1991 payroll dollars by the number of W-2 forms issued, you arrive at an average of $11,800. Even taking into account that many of these went to part-timers and people who worked short stints and then left the company and to associates who retired early in the year, that's not a munificent wage. Meanwhile, CEO Howell earned $1.5 million in 1990 and $1.2 million in 1991. He also owned stock and options worth about $14 million in mid-1992. Four other Penney officers earned between $347,000 and $800,000 in 1991. There are various incentive pay plans in place for management associates, one covering as many as 3,000 managers. Everyone is covered by a pension plan, and all associates are eligible to participate in a savings plan in which the company matches an employee's pretax contributions up to 6 percent of pay. The match, in company stock, depends on profits. In 1991 it was a 64 percent match. Thanks to these matching contributions in stock, two employee trusts own 24 percent of all J. C. Penney stock.

As is the case with all retailers, Penney's relies heavily on part-timers. To be eligible for full benefits, an associate must work at least 25 hours a week for three months—and 106,000 of the company's 185,000 associates do that. Having a large number of part-timers enables Penney to offer job security to regular associates. In tough times, the part-timers are the first to go.

Penney's is one of the few companies which report publicly on the progress of minorities and women. At the start of 1992, 17.2 percent of all associates were minority group members, up from 15.2 percent in 1987, and minorities made up 11 percent of the broad group called "officials, managers, and professionals." Eighty percent of Penney's associates are female, and while the table shows that they now hold 45.3 percent of positions among officials, managers, and professionals, when they reach the top tier they find themselves surrounded by a sea of white males. Of the 58 officers listed in the 1991 annual report, only two are women: merchandising vice-president Marilee J. Cumming and assistant secretary Margaret R.

Johnson. This lineup may change in the future. Of Penney's 496 management trainees in 1991, 21 percent were minorities and 68 percent female.

Types of jobs: Sales—51 percent; office and clerical—17 percent; technicians and craft workers—14 percent; officials and managers—11 percent; laborers and service workers—7 percent.

Main employment centers: Most of the people who work for Penney's are in the stores located in all 50 states, the District of Columbia, and Puerto Rico. 4,000 work at headquarters in Plano, Texas. 2,200 work in Puerto Rico.

Headquarters: J. C. Penney Company, Inc.
6501 Legacy Dr.
Plano, TX 75024
(214) 431-1000

Physio-Control

PHYSIO CONTROL

Physio-Control makes defibrillators and other cardiac-care products. U.S. employees: 918.

★ ★ ★   Pay/Benefits
★ ★ ★   Opportunities
★ ★ ★ ★ ★   Job Security
★ ★ ★ ★   Pride in Work/Company
★ ★ ★   Openness/Fairness
★ ★ ★ ★   Camaraderie/Friendliness

BIGGEST PLUS: A four-day workweek may be your lifesaver.
BIGGEST MINUS: Lilly, not Physio, has ultimate control.

One of the topics of conversation here is how people who come out from Eli Lilly in Indianapolis to work at Physio-Control don't want to go back. The reason they come out is that Lilly, a 116-year-old manufacturer of prescription drugs, owns Physio-Control, a company started in 1955 to make defibrillators, a lifesaving device that gives an electrical jolt to hearts in cardiac arrest, thereby helping to restore the heart to its normal rhythm. In contrast to Lilly's urban setting in Indianapolis, Physio occupies a bucolic, 26-acre campus on high-tech row in Redmond, an eastern suburb of Seattle; you reach it by crossing one of two floating bridges that span Lake Washington. When we visited Physio in 1983, we were impressed that this Pacific Northwest company had been able to preserve its feisty, egalitarian culture even within the corporate embrace of a conservative, midwestern company like Lilly.

However, much of that culture had to do with someone who is no longer here: W. Hunter Simpson, an ebullient, charismatic, chain-smoking ex-IBMer who joined Physio in 1966 when it was a research laboratory with four employees. Simpson not only built up Physio to $100 million in sales and 1,100 "team members" (he refused to use the term "employee") but was responsible for an environment featuring a four-day workweek, profit sharing, subsidized bus service, adoption aid, and jobs for developmentally disabled persons. Under Hunter Simpson, Physio had no time clocks, everyone was on a first-name basis, and people were not laid off. And those practices stayed in place after he sold the company to Eli Lilly in 1980.

Simpson left Physio-Control at the end of 1985, saying: "Twenty years in the same job is long enough." He was succeeded by Gilbert W. Anderson, a Seattle native who joined Physio in 1976 after 20 years with two industrial manufacturers. His style was much more restrained than Simpson's. In 1991 Anderson retired and was replaced by an outsider, Richard Martin, who came north to Redmond from Angleton, Texas, where he had been president of Intermedics, a maker of cardiac pacemakers. A Ph.D. electrical engineer who became interested in biomedicine when he was at Duke, Martin told us in early 1992 that he has no intention of changing the culture here. Like his predecessors, he still makes a point of meeting every new person hired, writes to team members on their anniversaries, and presides at the quarterly kickoff rallies that punctuate life at Physio. Colleagues describe him as "down-to-earth" and "a square shooter."

At the same time, it's clear that a new era has begun here. During the Hunter Simpson regime, Physio's sales spiraled upward as the defibrillator became standard equipment on emergency ambulances. The Lifepak model made in Redmond found its way into hospitals all over the world. The second half of the 1980s was different. Parts of the market were saturated, and Physio faced more competition. Also, in Martin's view, the company had become "too comfortable with success," with the result that "there was a lack of intensity." He sees his job at Physio as one of preserving all that's good about the culture established here but generating more enthusiasm. And that mission is linked to a strategy of making new defibrillators that can be used by rescuers with less training than, say, paramedics on an ambulance. For example, the Lifepak 300 system introduced in 1991 was designed for easy operation by such first responders as fire fighters and police officers. Indeed, Martin looks forward to a day when defibs will be as common as fire extinguishers. Aside from doing wonders for Physio's sales, such a development would help save the lives of heart attack victims and prevent brain damage.

The team members we talked to at Physio conceded that the departure of Hunter Simpson was a blow—training administrator Rick Karnofski said the company went through "a mourning"—but they all backed up Murray Lorance, a nine-year team member who said: "I think his [Hunter Simpson's] spirit still lives here." Inventory control manager Gary Sheneman added: "I think all his values, the integrity of the individual, the reward and recognition, it's all embodied in the company. He left an indelible impression on me. His memory and his values are clear today in our actions. The open-door policy is still there."

Physio's work force has been reduced about 15 percent since the mid-1980s while sales have increased 40 percent to about $140 million. However, no one was laid off. The reduction came mostly from attrition. A third of the team members have been here for more than 10 years, two-thirds for more than five years. So this is a work force thoroughly indoctrinated with Physio values. They certainly don't have the sense that Eli Lilly dictates what goes on here, even though in 1992 the director of human resources, Alice Oliver, and the legal counsel, Christie Fields, were both Indianapolis transplants. Dave Shelton, director of national sales, said: "You won't see Lilly plastered on any of the stationery or any of the brochures. They allow us to operate independently and we think they recognize that we have something good here." Quality assurance engineer John Gaffney added: "I don't feel any outside influence from Lilly." Karnofski, who joined Physio in the early 1980s, believes "it's a real good marriage. It's almost a pat on the back to both companies because Lilly funded our research and development, strengthened our benefit package, but then a lot of things that were really critical to Physio, like the four-day workweek, that really set us apart from other companies, they have left intact. It's refreshing to see a company that purchased another company say that we purchased you because we believe in what you're doing and you're doing something right so we're not going to change it." Gil Anderson, before he retired, told us: "The day we signed the deal we were standing in front of the building and I said to the head Lilly person, 'Do you want to put your flag up there?' and he said no. I think that's the game plan they've run since day one."

Teamwork has always been enshrined at Physio, coupled with a work-style that allows people to think and act for themselves. Connie R. Kanter, who holds an M.B.A. from the University of Chicago Business School and who worked at Arthur Anderson and Hewlett-Packard before coming here in 1989, was recently promoted to chief financial officer at Physio. She told us that when she recruits for Physio at business schools, "teamwork is probably the thing I talk to people about most. I really don't care about their grades; it's a matter of how they work with other people and how they achieve results." Recruiters don't have to beat the bushes too hard. Physio gets more than 1,000 résumés a month.

According to product manager Paula Lank: "I think the best thing about working at Physio-Control to me are the people. I moved from domestic marketing to international marketing, and I had to interact with a lot of different departments to get my job done and support the sales of our products around the world. And it makes me really appreciate working here when I can talk to someone who is just as eager to get the job done as I am. Throughout your life you interact with lots of different folks and they're not always cooperative. I think there is some level of politicking in all companies, but I would say it's at a minimum here." When Gary Sheneman was asked what kind of person would not fit in at Physio, he responded, "Somebody that spells team *m-e*." It's a standard procedure at Physio for senior managers to spend a week on the assembly line learning how the products are put together. Technical support supervisor Tom Clemson told us that "it's not uncommon to see the vice-president down on the production floor soldering parts together."

Informality is another hallmark of Physio's work-style. Karnofski said: "The thing that first struck me when I got here was that everyone was on a first-name basis. I came from the insurance industry, which was very regimented and structured. It just threw me off guard completely that you could actually run a company on this informal basis but still get the job done and get the respect of the people. That really broke my idea of the corporate environment."

Telecommunications supervisor Cathy Coulter said: "Team members have a lot of respect for one another and when you're working with somebody, you don't necessarily see their managerial hat or their whatever-level hat, you just see what they are contributing to whatever process you're trying to complete. I find it really refreshing to go up to a group of people who I need help from and not have to worry if I have to talk to their supervisor or their manager. I just talk to them, they're the people who know. Physio is really strong on enforcing that in people and saying that you are the ones who do the work, you are really the experts. That's really what performance excellence is all about."

Tom Clemson, a supervisor in technical support, said: "What makes

Physio fun is change itself and how it evolves. It evolves almost from the bottom up. Everyone gets involved and that's what makes it so exciting. That's why I'm here—because of that capability of taking something from the ground up and running with it." Lorna MacKenzie, who joined Physio in 1989, added: "I think the thing I like most about the company is that they really encourage you to go ahead and take the initiative to work on your own. I'm actually just a process assembler. But they're really good about letting you run your own line, learn everything yourself so you can actually run your line without your supervisor. For me, that's been a new experience."

Physio's four-day workweek was instituted after a group of production technicians suggested the idea to Hunter Simpson in 1971, and it's still in place today. Manufacturing employees work 10 hours a day four days a week. Roland Rice, a 14-year team member, said: "The main thing that keeps me here is the four-day workweek. I've got a degree in Bible literature and was a youth pastor before I came here. We lived in Alaska and had no time to ourselves. I worked a full-time job during the day, and then in the evenings it was the kids from church and on weekends it was the kids from church. Coming here I went to a four-day workweek and it was like being a preacher again. Working 10 hours a day I'd just be beat when I went home. That lasted for about a month and then, with Fridays off and no preaching, it was nice."

There has always been a lot of hoopla at Physio, and that continues. Hunter Simpson, a rabid fan of the University of Washington, used to get the school's marching band to come to the quarterly kickoff meetings. Team members are still entertained by live performers at these rallies, and the fourth-quarter meeting still begins with a pancake breakfast served to team members by senior managers. A Team Club stages an annual picnic, a year-end party, and various outings.

Physio team members have an unusual benefit—a free checking account at the Key Bank of Puget Sound, where the company banks. Express buses still make the 30-minute trip from downtown Seattle to Physio every morning, and return in the evening. Physio pays half the fare for team members.

Dick Martin appears to appreciate this culture, and he gets high marks from Physio stalwarts. Hunter Simpson himself told us that Martin "is the right person for the company at this time." Connie Kanter said he has brought "new energy" to Physio. Martin wants team members to focus on the "opportunities" the company has, and he also wants them to get rid of what he called the "entitlement mentality." He told us a story to illustrate his point. Seattle is a hotbed of coffee addicts, and the Physio cafeteria used to have a coffee cart that dispensed espresso, cappuccino, and latte until the operator decided he could do better somewhere else. After appeals from deprived team members, Martin okayed the purchase of an elaborate coffee maker that can, with a lot of hissing, dispense the steamed milk needed for lattes. The machine set Physio back $14,000, and Martin said he made a point of telling the team members precisely what it cost. "No one had told them that kind of information before," he said.

Types of jobs: Manufacturing—41 percent; sales and service—30 percent; research and development—16 percent; administration—10 percent; marketing—3 percent.

Main employment centers: Redmond, Washington, is home to 750 team members. Another 200 work in sales offices in the United States and overseas. Sales offices are located in Irvine, California; Arlington, Texas; Crystal Lake, Illinois; Cordova, Tennessee; Rowayton, Connecticut; Cherry Hill, New Jersey; Manassas, Virginia; Birmingham, Alabama; and Columbus, Ohio.

Headquarters: Physio-Control Corp.
11811 Willows Rd. NE
P.O. Box 97006
Redmond, WA 98073
(206) 867-4000

Pitney Bowes

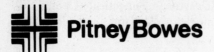

Pitney Bowes is the world's largest maker of postage meters and mailing systems, and also supplies dictaphones, facsimile machines, copiers, and Monarch price markers that leave those obscure bar codes on packages you buy in supermarkets and drugstores. U.S. employees: 24,350.

★★★★ Pay/Benefits
★★★ Opportunities
★★★★ Job Security
★★★ Pride in Work/Company
★★★★★ Openness/Fairness
★★★★ Camaraderie/Friendliness

BIGGEST PLUS: People are handled with care.
BIGGEST MINUS: Your check is in the mail.

People who believe one company is the same as any other haven't visited Pitney Bowes, the king of the postage meter business and longtime resident of Stamford, Connecticut, on Long Island Sound. It deliberately placed its new headquarters building on the "wrong" side of the railroad tracks so as not to abandon a working-class section for the sterile corporate high-rise zone in downtown Stamford. "For us, it's the right side," said George B. Harvey, chairman, president, and CEO of Pitney Bowes.

They do do things differently here, to wit:

• When you reach age 50, you're eligible for an annual $300 reimbursement of educational costs you might incur in preparing for retirement. Your spouse is eligible for this benefit, too. And no one's pushing: Pitney Bowes does not have a compulsory retirement age.

• Since 1985 the company has had in place a 35-15 policy *mandating* that women make up at least 35 percent and minorities at least 15 percent of all new hires and promotions. As a result, women now make up 36 percent of the employee population and 24 percent of the management, compared to 34 percent and 20 percent in 1985; and minorities now represent 23 percent of the work force and 11.5 percent of management, compared to 17 percent and 7 percent in 1985.

• Headquarters employees have a choice of two dining rooms, a cafeteria where you push your tray through the line and a sit-down restaurant, the Atrium Cafe, where you order from a menu and are served. For this latter indulgence, you pay 50 percent more.

• During the summer months there's dining on an outdoor patio, and on Wednesdays a chef will grill hamburgers, chicken, and hot dogs to order. The restaurant is operated by Pitney Bowes itself, so you're being served by fellow employees. The menu always features "Healthy Heart" selections, and the calorie and sodium contents of all items are noted.

• Since 1987 Pitney Bowes has had a corporate ombudsman, David Nassef, who is available, on a confidential basis, to any employee who feels he or she has been unfairly treated. He also serves as enforcer of the values statement adopted by the company in 1988. Nassef came to Pitney Bowes in 1973 from the city of Stamford, where he was assistant manpower director.

Behind these benign policies and practices is a patent-protected business that gives Pitney Bowes a virtual monopoly on postage meters. While the company makes other products these days—fax machines, copiers, dictating machines, price-marking equipment—mailing systems account for more than half its sales. The U.S. Postal Service derives more than $17 billion a year, or 44 percent of its annual revenues, from the 1.2 million meters that dispense stamps in corporate mailrooms and post offices—and Pitney Bowes's share of that meter business is estimated at close to 90 percent. In a penetrating look at this business in 1991, *Wall Street Journal* reporter Johnnie L. Roberts found that Pitney Bowes and the Postal Service are entwined in a symbiotic relationship based on technology that the company is reluctant to share. And the result is to freeze out competitors. Interviewed by Roberts, CEO Harvey said: "Our customers choose to come to us. Should we say, 'No, we don't want you to come to us—go see someone else'?"

Founded in 1920 by inventor Arthur Pitney and salesman Walter Bowes, the company used to have a strong family feeling. When it was smaller, many employees were related. Today, it has more of a corporate feeling (the carpeting in the executive wing is palpably thicker than it is on the rest of the floor), but the company has retained institutions that encourage employees to speak their minds freely. Still in place are the annual jobholders' meetings, started in 1947, where employees get a shot at asking senior managers any questions they want, and the Council of Personnel Relations, which consists of a series of management-employee committees—they start at the bottom and work their way up to the top—that hear and resolve grievances. Employees elect representatives to sit on these councils, which hold open monthly meetings.

Questions asked at the jobholders' meetings cover a wide range of issues. Internal audit manager Harrish Dua said some "ask about global strategies of the company" while others complain about "too much oil in the salad bar and stuff like that." To encourage sharp questions, Pitney Bowes awards a $50 savings bond for the best query asked at a meeting.

CEO Harvey, who started here as an accountant in 1957, told us that the point of these practices is to preserve a culture where "employees can stand up and challenge management and feel good about doing that." And he added: "I've seen managers that come to Pitney Bowes from outside and have a tough time with that. I believe that people are the company. If you've got good people and allow them to be creative, then you're going to win. And if you're any good as a manager, you can allow that to take place. Employees will throw out managers if they feel that they don't allow them to contribute and have a certain amount of freedom in doing their job. A dictator is not going to make it around here."

Pitney Bowes pledges to provide a work environment "marked by trust, integrity, fairness, and diversity." This means the company is likely to be continually tested. One such test came in the early 1980s when Pitney Bowes regeared its postal meters, moving from mechanical parts to electronic signals. Faced with a similar need, NCR closed down its Dayton, Ohio, cash register production facilities and moved to low-cost plants in the South. Pitney Bowes took a different route: it chose to retrain its Stamford work force and keep the production there. "We liked the talent that we saw here," explained Harvey. "People here are not lazy. They're hardworking and smart. They just need to be trained." Harvey confessed that it wasn't a decision that could be absolutely justified as cost-effective. His thinking, he said, ran as follows:

"I like to see people with the desire to do things, to make themselves different, to learn. When you see that desire out there, that means a lot. How do you measure that in terms of dollars and cents? Some things you can feel. I think that's what makes the difference in companies. Sometimes you feel things that you can't prove. There's no book out there that tells you what to do. You just feel it's right sometimes to do those things. And this is one of those things that I just sort of felt was right to do: to stay here, to take this money and train these people and give them a chance to show that they really want to do this, and in Fairfield County. People think I'm nuts."

Loyalty was tested in 1989 when Pitney Bowes had one of its rare reductions in work force, cutting their worldwide payroll by 1,500 people. The decision was announced to all employees at a company meeting. And a strong effort was made to get people to volunteer to leave by offering inducements. The Pitney Bowes package was: leave with 75 percent of your annual pay or two weeks for every year of service, whichever is greater. During the four-week window 1,000 employees accepted the offer. There were no terminations.

Employees we met were generally satisfied with the way the company handled the downsizing, although program analyst Nieves Acosta, a 30-year employee, said it was a new experience and "made it a little insecure for people." Jackie Booker said that part of the leave package included an option for people to return to the company after three years away, although they would not have their previous seniority. "A lot of them now call and say, 'I have a few more months to wait, I am coming back.'"

Harvey also noted that Pitney Bowes has a displaced-persons program, which assigns people whose jobs have disappeared to a pool. Managers have to consider people from this pool first before hiring from the outside. People in the pool must be prepared to take the jobs that are offered them. "It may not be the same job, but I believe working is important, and there comes a time in your life when you have to do something different. It doesn't mean it's forever. But you ought to be prepared to take another job, become a security guard, whatever it might be," said Harvey, who earned $1.1 million in 1991.

Benefits at Pitney Bowes include an on-site fitness center (used by 16 percent of employees in the Stamford area), quarterly profit-sharing checks that in 1991 supplemented salaries in the mailing systems unit 3.8 percent, and a retirement plan geared to provide a pension equal to 70 percent of final pay for employees who have put in 35 years. However, the best benefit may be the opportunity to grow. Al Negron said: "I came in as a purchasing manager and today I am the manager of the supplier management group at shipping and weighing systems, which is a concept I created. That's one of the benefits of being with a company like Pitney-Bowes: you have the ability to take a couple of ideas, put them together, and create your own operation." Eugenia Bakes, manager of office support services, who has put in 28 years at Pitney, said she started as a clerk typist in the transcribing department and is still in that department, although she has been able to switch from full-time to part-time and back to full-time, and has become a proofreader, supervisor, and manager.

Anthony Dileo, an operating mechanic, came to Pitney in 1985. "I really got here through family," he reported. "My uncle has been here for 35 years, my father for 20, and my sister for 10. Where else could I go? I came when this building was being built, and so I saw the construction. I was only 19 when I got here, and I saw a lot of room for advancement. I took an air-conditioning class at night, they financed that for me. That was definitely a big help because I could not afford to go to school. They are very good with that. That is one of the big reasons why I stayed here. There is definitely room to move."

Types of jobs: Office and clerical—25 percent; skilled craft—23 percent; sales—20 percent; management—12 percent; production—9 percent; professionals—8 percent; technicians—2 percent.

Main employment centers: Pitney Bowes has 6,000 employees in Fairfield County, Connecticut, 1,200 employees in Dayton, Ohio, and 750 in Melbourne, Florida. 5,500 people work overseas.

Headquarters: Pitney Bowes, Incorporated
Stamford, CT 06926
(203) 356-5000

Polaroid

==================

Polaroid.

Polaroid, the inventor of instant photography, makes cameras, film, and new electronic imaging devices. U.S. employees: 8,099.

★★★★ Pay/Benefits
★★★ Opportunities
★★ Job Security
★★★ Pride in Work/Company
★★★★★ Openness/Fairness
★★★★ Camaraderie/Friendliness

BIGGEST PLUS: You can develop your own picture here.
BIGGEST MINUS: The future is not in focus.

Never underestimate the power of tradition. Polaroid continues to be a good place to work, even though it continues to shrink as a workplace, because the spirit and ideas of Edwin H. Land have taken root here. Land, who founded Polaroid in 1937, died on March 1, 1991, just as the company was preparing its annual report for 1990. There was time to insert a black-and-white photograph of the founder on page 3 along with an excerpt from his letter to shareholders in 1980. There he asserted that "industry should be the intersection of science and art," adding: "The second great product of industry should be the fully rewarding working life for every person."

The concept that it is the obligation of companies to provide a nurturing workplace for *every* employee is at the heart of Polaroid. It was enshrined in a statement of personnel policy adopted in 1967. This policy declared that Polaroid has "two basic products"—one, "products that are genuinely unique and useful," and two, "a worthwhile working life for each member of the Company." The policy statement added: "These two products are inseparable."

A cynic might add: "Easier said than done." Polaroid wrestled with the implications of this philosophy all through the 1980s as it sought to develop new, meaningful products in the wake of the declining popularity of instant photography. In 1978 Polaroid sold 9.4 million instant cameras. In 1989 it sold 3 million. That slump had a horrendous effect on employment. In 1979 the company had nearly 21,000 employees worldwide. At the end of 1983 it had 14,500, including 10,000 in the United States. At the end of 1991 it had 12,000, including 8,000 in the United States. In short, employment has been nearly halved. And the company has given up its insistence on unique products. In 1989 it began making conventional photographic film.

However, we still like Polaroid because it did not compromise its values during this difficult period. And that's important to employees. They cited it a number of times during our interviews in March 1991. Those who are left enjoy working here. Paul Henry, an evaluation technician who joined the company in 1966, told us: "I have not had one day here that I have regretted." Barbara Waterman, manager of affirmative action administration, described Polaroid as a "company where your opinion is respected." She related how, after she was hired as a clerk in 1967, she barged into the office of Tom Wyman, who was then president, and berated him about racism in the company. "I thought I would be fired," she said. Instead, he talked with her for 25 minutes and finally told her that she should be doing something about this situation at Polaroid. That's when she was assigned to affirmative action, where she is still trying, as she put it, "to get my 40 acres and a mule."

Polaroid was the first major U.S. company to withdraw from South Africa (in 1970), and blacks are well represented here, in the total work force (14 percent) and in management ranks (5 percent). We met one of them, John Jenkins, director of human resources in the manufacturing department, who said that Polaroid still wants "to be known as an employer of choice." He described the company in such terms as "caring," "participative," "intimate," and "open." Jenkins has been with Polaroid since 1972. "We grew up together," he said, talking about the people here.

We also talked with Harry Johnson, manager of corporate communications, who was so stunned by the April 29, 1992, verdict that acquitted four white Los Angeles police officers in the Rodney King beating trial that he took the morning off to write a poem, "Damn you, America!" It said, in part:

> Yes, I try to believe—God knows, I try to believe
> that America works nearly all the time
> for nearly all the people.

But, don't ask me to believe today.
Today, I believe something different.
Today, I believe that America lies.
Today, I am disappointed. Shocked. Angry. Enraged.
Today, I am a skeptic. A cynic. An unbeliever.
Today, I am not an American.
Today, I am a black man.

One stanza of the poem was printed in *The Wall Street Journal,* bringing Johnson a torrent of calls and letters from all over the country. He also read his poem on National Public Radio's "All Things Considered" program. "It provoked me finally at age 55," he said, "to admit to being a poet. I did so reluctantly because the poet's discipline is rigorous. It's his or her mandate to tell the truth in culture, where telling the truth brings harsh consequences and requires youthful innocence or wisdom of age."

It's surprising to see such thoughts expressed inside a major U.S. corporation, but it's less surprising because it's Polaroid.

Polaroid's values helped it during the 1980s—first, when thousands of people left the company, and second, when it was confronted with a takeover attempt. The company offered generous severance packages to induce people to leave. For example: one month's pay for every two years of service up to a maximum of one year's salary. Joseph Oldfield, vice-president–manufacturing, told us that the package was so good that 200 companies inquired about it and 60 employees took Polaroid to court for not letting them take advantage of it.

In 1988 Roy Disney's Shamrock Holdings announced that it planned to take over Polaroid by buying up all the shares. To foil that bid, Polaroid set up an employee stock-ownership plan, allocating 14 percent of the company's shares to the ESOP. The company has continued to allocate shares to the ESOP so that by 1992, this employee trust owned 20 percent of Polaroid. Unlike many ESOPs, where management gets to vote the shares, each Polaroid employee has voting rights on his or her shares. That was an important consideration in the Delaware court's ruling on Shamrock's bid for the company. Judge Carolyn Berger said that since employees held the voting rights, the ESOP was not a scheme to protect the management. Disney could have continued with his bid, and it would have been up to each Polaroid employee to decide whether he or she wanted to sell. Clearly, they did not. Polaroid's unionlike employee committee backed the ESOP.

This employee committee was another hallmark of the Land era. Launched in 1952, it was, in effect, town hall democracy inside Polaroid. Employees elected representatives to the committee, which then represented all employees—hourly and salaried—to management. But in 1992 the committee was forced to disband after the Department of Labor, interpreting the National Labor Relations Board Act, ruled that it constituted an illegal internal labor union. Under the NLRB Act, a company management is not permitted to financially support such an activity. So, after 40 years, it was shut down, and in 1992 Polaroid was working to set up alternative mechanisms to provide the voice employees used to have through this committee. One of the first steps was the formation of a 30-person employee committee to examine wages and benefits.

As it entered the 1990s, Polaroid was trying out new programs in the workplace. The company was putting employees through a Total Quality ownership program, and it was using a new compensation system to reward employees for learning new skills. The changes were designed to promote more flexibility. Another experiment involved the managerless factory. Three Polaroid factories—one in Mexico and two in the suburbs of Boston where Polaroid has most of its factories—are now being run by teams instead of a plant manager. Other long-standing Polaroid benefits remain in effect—profit sharing and subsidies for child care that reimburse low-income families up to 80 percent of the cost. Polaroid has the oldest child-care subsidy program in American business. It was adopted in 1971.

The very values we appreciate in Polaroid are the very ones often fingered by Wall Street analysts as reasons for the company's malaise. Thus, in 1988, *BusinessWeek* decreed that it was incumbent on Polaroid to "remake itself —instantly." The magazine depicted Polaroid as stodgy, lazy, complacent, and too dependent on the old Land traditions. It complained, too, that Polaroid "maintained expensive, paternalistic policies," and it cited a Boston University professor, Fred K. Foulkes, who said: "There comes a point where they cannot afford their culture." It was more of the same in 1991 when the *New York Times* reported on Polaroid's push into new fields such as a computerized system for producing medical images in seconds, a digital scanner to enter pictures into computers, and a printer that makes instant snapshots from a computer screen—and then couldn't resist the observation that company executives now talk about reforming a "company where Mr. Land's spirit still lingers."

We think that one of the reasons Polaroid is a strong company is that this spirit does linger. I. MacAllister Booth, a Polaroid veteran who became chief executive officer in 1986, said it well in responding to the *Business-Week* comments in 1988: "These values aren't soft and mushy. They're hard, and tough, and fair."

As Barbara Waterman found out shortly after she came to Polaroid, dissent is accepted here. Owen Gaffney, the senior vice-president who has headed up human resources since 1988 and who has been with the company for 30 years, once pointed out that at Polaroid "it is not only okay to be critical of things that you don't feel are right, but you are not really living up to your obligations as a member unless you speak up." Gaffney made this comment at a 1991 conference in the context of a discussion about executive pay. He pointed out to his colleagues that the anger in the

ranks at the high salaries received by executives is "like a time bomb click-
ing away in the American workplace." At Polaroid, said Gaffney, employees
are saying: "It isn't right that I'm making $30,000 and someone else at
Polaroid who I see every day and is a regular person, who wears pants and
eats lunch in the cafeteria, it's not right that he makes $250,000."

Gaffney reported that Polaroid is making progress in changing a culture
that was weighted down with we/they attitudes and arrogance by people at
the top. But he conceded that it's tough to change established practices. As
an example, he cited the attempt to do away with the reserved parking lot
at Polaroid's headquarters in Cambridge, where 19 spaces are set aside for
officers of the company. "There are five or six officers who will not park in
this lot," he said. "They believe it sends the wrong signal—and that includes the president, who parks up the street in the regular parking lot.
There are other officers whose position on the subject is 'I'll be happy to
give up my space, just show me how that enhances shareholder value.'
Others have said, 'I've worked for the company for 28 years. After the 25th
year I got a private parking space and now you're trying to take it away from
me.' I've had people come up to me and say, 'Gaffney, you're going to
screw up the system. I've been working for this corporation for 15 years and
someday I'm going to be an officer, and by the time I get there, it won't be
worthwhile the way you're doing away with the few privileges that were
available to corporate officers.' "

A year later, the officers' lot was still there. Gaffney thinks the new group
of managers coming up feel differently. He predicts that "it's going to take
three or four retirements—and the lot is going to go away."

Polaroid still faces considerable business challenges. But it clearly has in
place a system that values the people who pass through here. It will be up
to newer people to find the products of the future. One of these people is
Dr. James Ionson, who signed on in 1991 as director of research. He was
formerly a senior executive in the "Star Wars" research effort launched by
the Reagan administration.

Types of jobs: Manufacturing—56 percent; marketing, sales—18 percent;
research, engineering—16 percent; support services—10 percent.

Main employment center: Cambridge, Massachusetts.

Headquarters: Polaroid Corporation
549 Technology Sq.
Cambridge, MA 02139
(617) 577-2000

Preston Trucking

Preston Trucking hauls freight throughout the Northeast and Midwest, from Virginia to Maine and St. Louis. Employees: 5,613.

★ ★ ★   Pay/Benefits
★ ★ ★   Opportunities
★ ★ ★   Job Security
★ ★ ★ ★   Pride in Work/Company
★ ★ ★ ★   Openness/Fairness
★ ★ ★ ★   Camaraderie/Friendliness

BIGGEST PLUS: Your ideas get mileage.
BIGGEST MINUS: The business has had tough brakes.

Six clerical workers in Preston Trucking's home office were delighted when their departmental phone bill arrived in the mail in early 1991. They discovered that their efforts to save money had paid off—to the tune of $300 worth of savings on the month's bill. Such events don't go unnoticed here. Each person made a poster. The first sign said "We," the second said "saved," the next, "$300," and so on. Then they all donned trench coats, party hats, and sunglasses, and proceeded to snake-dance through every department in the building while tooting party horns.

Preston is one of the few trucking companies in America that have something to toot about. They survived the brutal battles that raged in the trucking industry after it was deregulated in 1980. Of their 67 direct competitors in 1980, only 16 were left in 1990. Preston also grew, employing nearly 50 percent more people by the decade's end.

Preston's workers can also toot their horns about the way in which this company managed its survival. Rather than increasing pressure on the work force, chairman Will Potter and other executives created an entirely new relationship, one based on partnership. It was a revolutionary concept in trucking. Most truckers, including Preston, have a long legacy of adversarial relations with their workers, most of whom belong to the Teamsters or International Longshoremen's Association. Preston decided to teach their supervisors to manage according to a philosophy of, as they put it, "pats on the back rather than kicks in the butt." They also began to involve workers in decision-making about their jobs. "The person doing the job knows how best to do it" became the unofficial company slogan and was plastered on company literature and posters.

By the early 1990s Preston, headquartered in a town of the same name on Maryland's picturesque eastern shore, was a desirable place to work. Maintenance manager Howard Bradshaw told us: "Twenty years ago, you came to work, you did what you were told, and you didn't question it. If you didn't like it you could go someplace else. I worked over in maintenance, and you had to have authorization to do anything. You didn't do anything on your own. 'Mr. Foreman, this light bulb is out. May I fix it?' He'd say: 'Yes, you may.' Now people know what is expected of them. It makes it a whole lot simpler. I'm the coordinator of the shop and I have people working on their own from the start of the day to the end of the day. Some days I never even get to see them."

Employees, now called associates, are involved in day-to-day decision-making with their supervisors, now called coordinators. William Joyner, who has been driving for Preston since 1978, explained: "I think drivers have more to say about what goes on as far as how things are loaded and how things are done in general. It wasn't like that in the beginning. Thirteen years ago we had a lot of grievances."

Associates throughout the company participate in a far-reaching suggestion system that brought in 4,412 ideas in 1988, averaging $300 in savings apiece. In 1991, 7,882 suggestions were generated, and 74 percent of them were implemented. Each suggestion is printed in the newsletter. Suggestions included everything from repainting the lines in the parking lots, to putting a rubber mat in front of the ice machine to keep people from slipping, to purchasing rechargeable batteries for pagers. They even have a toll-free phone number for drivers to call with suggestions when they're out on the road.

Associates are rewarded for their ideas. Recognition ranges from reserved parking spaces, to Preston jackets, to pizza parties. Celebration, like the horn-tooting clerical workers described earlier, has became a way of life here. Lyn Hollingsworth, at Preston for eight years, told us: "We celebrate things to death around here. If somebody does a good job we celebrate and reinforce it. And that reinforcement is passed along. In the collections department, when our percentage of outstanding bills goes to a certain level, the whole team will dress casual and bring something in to eat for lunch."

Middle managers are also more deeply involved in decision-making today. In 1991 company president Bill Terrell and senior vice-president of customer service John Hiltz didn't attend the annual business planning session so that other officers could. Former accounting manager Lois Karpinski explained: "Previously, the officers locked themselves in a room somewhere and put together the plan. Then they came back and said, 'This is our plan.' Now they're including more department heads and managers to create more of a roll-up rather than a bring-it-down plan." Preston's vice-president of quality, Pat Walsh, said: "I think that was the best business plan they've had since I've been with Preston."

The new involvement gives middle managers a sense of pride. Larry Callahan, director of customer billing information, told us: "One of the things that has always made me feel good about working at Preston is being involved in terms of the direction the company was going to take."

These changes have reduced conflicts between labor and management. The number of grievances per 100 associates decreased 32 percent between 1978 and 1988. Since management has put greater trust in the associates, they have reciprocated with increased flexibility. Hiltz explained: "Local-level Teamsters have given us flexibility to do some things operationally that we wouldn't otherwise be able to do. In Detroit, a union leader introduced me to a couple people from other carriers, and he raved about the things that Preston does with their people. He stated quite frankly, 'That's why I give them all the flexibility. They treat their people with dignity and respect, and so as far as I'm concerned they can do whatever they want to do.'"

Better communications has helped, too. In addition to regular employee meetings, Preston issues a quarterly magazine which heralds births, deaths, and marriages, lists suggestions and tells readers how they were implemented, and includes photos of celebrations. For drivers who may miss meetings, Preston makes audiocassette tapes which include music and general-interest stories in addition to company news and interviews. LeRoy Washington, a 26-year driver/salesman in the Washington, D.C., terminal, told us: "If the company is doing badly, they publish it and everybody knows it."

The 1990s may present even more difficult challenges to Preston and other truckers. Many of them, including Preston, lost money during the recession years of 1990 and 1991. In 1990 Preston Corporation, the holding company that owns Preston Trucking, was forced to shut down two of its trucking lines, Pioneer and Reeves, putting 1,000 people out of work. (No Preston Trucking employees were affected.) But there is every indication that Preston will stick to the course that helped them survive the last decade and create what some workers call a family. According to cost analyst Jim Lafemenia: "It is a tough industry to make a good buck in, and a lot of trucking companies have gone under and folded. But when the good times are there, the company shares it with everybody. When it's not been there, everybody has to share a little bit of the burden."

Types of jobs: Pick-up and delivery drivers—48 percent; long-haul drivers —12 percent; managers and supervisors—13 percent; office and clerical— 13 percent; dock workers—6 percent; maintenance—6 percent; other—2 percent.

Main employment centers: Preston has terminals in 19 Mid-Atlantic and northeastern states: Pennsylvania (1,420 employees), Maryland (769), Ohio (559), Indiana (544), New Jersey (467), Illinois (435), New York (398), Virginia (253), Michigan (194), Massachusetts (124), Connecticut (93), Delaware (71), Washington, D.C. (62), Kentucky (57), Missouri (50), Wisconsin (40), Rhode Island (39), New Hampshire (20), and Maine (18).

Headquarters: Preston Trucking Company, Inc.
151 Easton Blvd.
Preston, MD 21655
(410) 673-7151

BEST FOR MINORITIES

Beth Israel Hospital Boston
Cummins Engine
Federal Express
Fel-Pro
IBM
Inland Steel
Los Angeles Dodgers
Pitney Bowes
Polaroid
Xerox

Procter & Gamble

 THE PROCTER & GAMBLE COMPANY

Procter & Gamble dominates the soap and detergent industry, makes many other household and personal-care products, and ranks perennially as one of the largest advertisers in the world. U.S. employees: 48,800.

★ ★ ★ ★ ★ Pay/Benefits
★ ★ ★ ★ Opportunities
★ ★ ★ ★ Job Security
★ ★ ★ Pride in Work/Company
★ ★ ★ Openness/Fairness
★ ★ ★ Camaraderie/Friendliness

BIGGEST PLUS: You'll cheer for the bounty of training.
BIGGEST MINUS: They safeguard information.

Cheryl McKettrick graduated from the engineering school at Michigan State University and had two interviews at Procter & Gamble before deciding to come here in 1985. The factor that swayed her the most was the promise that she would get a chance to have a responsible position early on. She began as a team manager in P&G's oldest plant, the Ivorydale factory outside of Cincinnati, where Crisco is produced, and six years later she was managing the packing department at this unionized factory, having meanwhile acquired a master's degree from MSU.

There are many stories like McKettrick's at P&G. This is a company that gives people hands-on experience early in their careers, with the promise that if they do well, they'll move up. P&G does not hire people away from other companies. It prefers to train and promote its own. John Smale, who stepped down as chairman and CEO at the end of 1989, started as an assistant brand manager in 1952 when he was 25 years old. Edwin L. Artzt, who succeeded him, began in the advertising department in 1953 when he was 23 years old. Cheryl McKettrick is an example of how women are finally moving up the ranks here. In 1991 P&G elected the first female vice-presidents in the company's history—five of them (out of 121).

P&G recruits at more than 150 colleges and universities in the United States, hiring about 1,000 entry-level managers a year. And it hires another 2,000 abroad. P&G favors bright people who have been active outside of academic work. In the company's own words, it looks for "people who make things happen." Competition to get into P&G is tough. One good way is to work as a summer intern. P&G hires about 800 interns every year, most of them college juniors and first-year M.B.A. students. The interns appear to like what they see. Companies that have summer intern programs for M.B.A. students find, on average, that 25 percent of them accept jobs there; at P&G, 75 percent of the interns end up returning.

Recruits, when they sign on, may feel they have joined an institution rather than a company. Founded in 1837 as a soap and candle maker, Procter & Gamble predates 99 percent of the business corporations in the United States. Tradition weighs heavily here. P&G tends to be set in its ways. Conservative business attire is the uniform. But a company that sells millions of items to consumers all over the world every day can't afford to be inflexible or stodgy. It's a place obsessed with winning. If a P&G brand does not hold down first place in its market, it's close to the top. Most products were developed in-house, but during the 1980s the company went on an acquisition binge that brought in a slew of new brands. Someone once did a pantry check of American homes and found that 95 percent had at least one Procter & Gamble product. You're a customer of P&G if you use any of these brands they developed in-house: Tide, Cheer, Crest, Pampers, Folgers, Dash, Charmin, Bounty, Citrus Hill, Duncan Hines, Pringles, Secret, Pert Plus, Jif, Camay, Safeguard, Scope, Comet, Cascade. You're also a P&G customer if you use any of these brands acquired since 1985: Oil of Olay, Max Factor, Old Spice, Hawaiian Punch, Vicks, Metamucil, Cover Girl, Noxzema, Nyquil, or Pepto-Bismol.

As you might surmise from that lineup, advertising is a key activity here. P&G has long been one of the largest advertisers in the world, spending well over $1 billion annually to register its sales messages. This is one of the few companies where the ad department can be a route to the top. But don't assume that it's just advertising that sells these products. One of Procter & Gamble's hallmarks is paying close attention to the product itself. P&G scientists work hard to develop products with physical properties that differentiate them from those of competitors—Tide, Crest, Charmin, and Pampers are four classic examples. In the 1980s one of P&G's big success stories was the transformation of a moribund hair shampoo brand, Pert, into the field's top seller under the name Pert Plus. This feat was accomplished after P&G chemists figured out a way to blend a conditioner with a detergent and have the conditioner (silicone polymers) stick to your hair while the detergent (with the dirt) is rinsed away. If that kind of adventure doesn't excite you, this may not be the company for you.

Rumblings that P&G was becoming nastier and more bottom-line-oriented began to surface after Artzt was named the new CEO at the annual meeting in late 1989. Known for his aggressiveness and brusque manner, he began pushing people to execute more quickly, focus globally, and think frequently about killing the competition. *Fortune* likened him to the late football coach Vince Lombardi ("Winning is the only result that matters"). *BusinessWeek* headlined: "No More Mr. Nice Guy at P&G." We talked about the recent changes with John Pepper, the president of P&G, who conceded that "there has been a stronger bottom-line orientation," but he added that "it certainly hasn't been profit for profit and be damned on other factors. I don't think we've changed the fundamental things of respect for people and consumers."

The suspicion that P&G is changing, for the worse, was reinforced by a flap in 1991 that involved the police search of 803,000 Cincinnati area telephone lines to determine whether an employee was leaking information to *The Wall Street Journal*. This fishing expedition brought down on P&G's head the wrath of civil libertarians, First Amendment lawyers, civic leaders in Cincinnati, newspaper publishers and editors, columnists, and employees. The incident ended with Artzt writing a letter to employees apologizing for the action, calling it "an error of judgment" that "created a problem that was larger than the one we were trying to solve."

We visited P&G a week after Artzt ate this humble pie and found that employees were embarrassed by their company's spying on them but felt that it "was an aberration, a onetime thing." Dave Phillips, a black engineer who has worked for P&G for 30 years, helping to put up detergent and food plants all over the world, said: "I can't tell you how much I've been razzed about this particular *faux pas* at social functions and so forth, because it's so rare that you catch Procter on the wrong side of the coin." Another employee added: "In the end they did the right thing. Mr. Artzt wrote us a letter saying, 'If this has embarrassed you, I'm sorry. We may have erred in doing it. Our intentions were pure.' So I think it goes back to our values: they responded to people feeling badly and being embarrassed by it. The way it was brought to closure was very consistent with the character of the company. We'll let Ed make a mistake because he lets us make mistakes and we're not fired."

Ed Artzt is unlikely to dismantle a tradition that is built into the woodwork here—and into the policies and practices of P&G companies across the world. It's easy to make fun of Procter & Gamble for being an uptight organization, closed to outsiders, but few people can fault its performance as a supplier of high-quality consumer goods or its long record as a company that does right by its employees and the communities where its plants and offices are located. Those principles have not been breached. Even in the profit-driven days of the late 1980s and early 1990s, when other companies were laying off people in droves, P&G was closing plants and asking workers if they wanted to transfer to another location. In 1991, when P&G closed its soap plant on Staten Island in New York City, the company offered to transfer employees to other locations. Excluding those who opted for retirement, 60 percent of the employees accepted the offer and transferred to other Procter plants. P&G does not want to be known as a "no-layoff company," but its latest mission statement contains an implied promise: "We recognize the vital importance of continuing employment."

Procter & Gamble recognized more than 100 years ago that "the company's interests and those of its employees are inseparable." Many actions flowed from this conviction. Its profit-sharing plan, adopted in 1887, is the oldest in continuous operation in American industry. In 1903 it began helping employees acquire stock by matching every $1 they put up with $3 of its own. It became, in 1915, one of the first companies in the nation to offer employees health, disability, and life insurance plans. Three years later it introduced the eight-hour workday. In 1933 it implemented a five-day workweek. All were pioneering efforts, setting P&G apart from its corporate brethren.

Today, P&G continues to be a pacesetter in employee benefits, trying always to stay ahead of the pack. They offer 12 paid holidays a year, plus two personal days; four-week vacations after 10 years, five weeks after 15 years; a choice of medical insurance plans, including a high-deductible one ($550 per person a year, $1,100 for a family) for which it pays the entire premium; prescription drugs at $5 a pop; 100 percent payment of dental insurance premiums; long-term-care insurance for employees and their dependents; adoption aid (up to $2,000); a free $12,500 life insurance policy to all employees who retire after 25 years of service. A recent study by the employee benefits consultant, Towers Perrin, ranked P&G number one in the value of its benefits program, compared to the plans at 21 other big companies, including IBM, Merck, Philip Morris, Xerox, and Johnson & Johnson.

The jewel in this galaxy of benefits is P&G's profit-sharing plan. Instead of a pension plan, P&G relies on profit sharing to provide retirement benefits to employees—and it has worked superbly because company contributions have been invested in P&G stock. The initial contribution, after one year of service, is 5 percent of salary. It then increases every year to the point where, after 20 years, the annual contribution approaches 23 percent of salary. John Smale gave a striking dollars-and-cents example of what this has meant to employees in his address to shareholders at the 1988 annual meeting. He said that the average employee who was retiring that year, after 40 years of service, could take their profit-sharing proceeds and buy an annuity that would give them 150 percent of their final pay for the rest of their lives. "Or," he added, "they can hold the stock, simply receive the dividends, and together with Social Security, have income equal to about 80 percent of their final pay—and again, they still have the stock."

Employees own 25 percent of P&G's stock.

Types of jobs: Production—30 percent; management—18 percent; office and clerical—13 percent; sales—11 percent; skilled crafts—10 percent; professionals—7 percent; technicians—7 percent; laborers—3 percent; service —1 percent.

Main employment centers: Cincinnati, 14,150; another 34,000 at 57 plants and offices in 25 states. Nearly 55,000 people work outside the United States.

Headquarters: Procter & Gamble Company
One Procter & Gamble Plaza
Cincinnati, OH 45202
(513) 562-1100

Publix Super Markets

Publix is Florida's largest supermarket chain with 395 stores. Employees: 68,000.

★ ★ ★ ★ Pay/Benefits
★ ★ ★ ★ ★ Opportunities
★ ★ ★ ★ Job Security
★ ★ ★ ★ ★ Pride in Work/Company
★ ★ ★ ★ Openness/Fairness
★ ★ ★ ★ ★ Camaraderie/Friendliness

BIGGEST PLUS: Your career is in the bag.
BIGGEST MINUS: No time to bake in the Florida sun.

When we visited Publix's huge warehouse in North Miami, we ate in the cafeteria, where lunch is free. Behind the food line was a large sign declaring: "Publix—where working is a pleasure." On the wall in the eating area was this statement: "Publix will be a little better place to work—or not quite as good—because of you."

If working is indeed a pleasure at Publix—and a lot of employees enthusiastically proclaim that it is—much of the credit must go to the author of that statement, founder George Jenkins, whose portrait rests on yet another wall. Jenkins believed that top managers should spend time in the field, visiting stores, meeting hourly employees (called associates here). Jenkins used to do that himself. He shook so many hands that when Publix issued its annual yearbook saluting employees with five, 10, 15, and more years of service, in virtually every photograph the associate is shown shaking hands with George Jenkins in his outlandish green and orange sport jacket emblazoned with dozens of Publix logos. At store openings, Jenkins would often pitch in and help, pushing a broom or greeting customers, whatever was needed.

Jenkins is no longer actively involved in the business, having suffered a disabling stroke in 1989, but his spirit lives on. Publix's top managers are extremely visible. They visit stores, and every October, during Associate Appreciation Month, executives travel to every store to walk the aisles and shake hands with workers.

Another Jenkins principle deeply ingrained here is promotion from within. Stock clerk Jose Tomas explained: "A lot of college students, even M.B.A.'s, come up to me and ask about Publix. I tell them, 'You've got to start from the bottom. You've got to be a bag boy.' That doesn't go over very well with some of the management students, but for those of us who have been here for many years, it's great. I started as a bag boy, then went to produce, and now I'm doing management training."

Why would someone who is a college graduate be willing to start as a bag boy? For one thing, Publix offers great opportunities to advance. The chain has nearly doubled in size in the last decade, all by expanding within the state of Florida. In 1991 they opened their first store in Georgia and plan to expand in that state as well. For another thing, Publix has never laid off anyone in its 60-year-plus history. That's an extraordinary feat in the Florida supermarket industry, where numerous chains have been buried. Office cashier Connie Granato said: "When people are telling you about losing their jobs or having their benefits cut, it's a really good feeling to work for a company that has not changed in this time of economic woes."

And for another thing, Publix pays well, better than any of its competitors. Cashiers make up to 32 percent more than counterparts at their closest competitor, Winn-Dixie. Meat manager Bill Young told us: "As far as income goes, we are number one in pay of all the chain stores. Everybody knows that Publix has the best benefits, and we continue to get more."

For associates who work their way up to store manager, the rewards are even greater. In 1991 managers were making a base salary of $44,700 a year plus a bonus based on the profits of their store. Some managers can double their salary with the bonus. In 1990 two store managers made more than $100,000.

Store managers are not the only ones who share in the profits. Every full-time store employee does, too. All associates also get a bonus of up to four weeks' pay at Christmastime, based on their length of service.

Getting ahead here has its price—long hours, the bane of the supermarket industry. We talked to Pete Newsome, vice-president of the Miami division before he retired in 1992 after 50 years with Publix. He said: "It is all hard work, either physically or emotionally. Basically, that is our philosophy on people: we pay them more and we expect more from them."

Several employees confirmed Newsome's observation. Diane Godoy, who manages the meat department in the Hammocks store, told us: "Management puts in a lot of hours, but also there are days when we can go home early. I put in about 55 or 56 hours a week, and then there are weeks when things are going great where I will only put in 45." Store manager Bob Pendelton, who started working for Publix in 1978 at age 14, said: "I know we work 15-hour days quite often, but every day there is something to do, especially in the grocery business."

But associates don't equate long hours with drudgery. On the contrary. There's an amazing *esprit de corps* at Publix, related to a strong family feeling. Mike Armstrong, meat cutter at the Miami Lakes store, said: "Publix is real family. At individual stores, when you come in with a bad mood people lift you up."

Family means more here than at most companies that use the term. Many associates are related. People here even defend nepotism. Public relations manager Bob McDermott told us: "Nepotism scares most companies, but it is the heartbeat of our company. You have cashiers with husbands that are truck drivers, you have executives whose wives are office cashiers. It is all through the ranks, and they are proud of it. It is a good comfort zone because we know who we are working with." McDermott's wife has worked for the company in the past, and his son is second assistant to the manager in an Orlando Publix.

Nepotism starts at the top. Since Jenkins's stroke, leadership has passed to the second generation of the family. George Jenkins's son, Howard, became chairman and CEO. Four other relatives of the founder sit on the board.

This tight-knit family atmosphere has created some problems. Truck driver Ronnie Romero, who started working for Publix in 1980, said: "About 15 years ago or more, this used to be a very hard company to get into because there were so many families. Everybody was related to somebody." The old-boy network meant it was tough for minorities and women to get into management. Publix has been working on that problem in recent years. They now make special efforts to encourage female and minority associates to take management training. Among other efforts, Publix appointed black store manager Lee Brunson to the new post of director of minority affairs in 1992 to encourage blacks to seek management careers at Publix.

Betty McCray, who was promoted to foreperson in the North Miami produce warehouse in 1989, told us: "I was a little skeptical about taking the position, me being a black woman. But my department head, Bob Borges, reassured me. He changed my career objectives by showing me that I can be a pioneer. I am the first female foreperson at the warehouse."

Publix makes a big production of store openings. For years they held a banquet the night before a store opened, with the chain's top brass flying in from Lakeland to spur on the new associates. The next morning the top executives would pitch in to get the store ready for the customers. At a store opening in Jacksonville in 1985, we saw George Jenkins helping set up displays in the produce area and president Mark Hollis pushing a broom. That kind of camaraderie is deeply ingrained at Publix.

Although they still continue the tradition of top executives helping to open a new store, they have eliminated the banquet in favor of Family Night. They now ask associates to invite their family and friends to a pep rally inside the store the night before. Pete Newsome described some typical scenes from a Family Night: "You will see some of the teenagers bringing their mom and dad and showing them 'my store.' We try to give them a sense of ownership in their job so they feel like 'Hey, this is my store.' You will hear at these openings a bag boy calling it 'my store,' a cashier calling it 'my store,' a manager calling it 'my store,' the district manager calling it 'my store.' Hell, Mark Hollis will even be calling it his store. George Jenkins even calls it his store."

Everyone at Publix has a right to call it "my store" since they are all owners. One of the principal legacies of George Jenkins is employee ownership. When he opened his first store in Winter Haven, Florida, in 1930, he gave employees pay raises so that they could buy stock. Today, employees own 82 percent of the company through direct purchase, 11 percent through a profit-sharing plan, and 7 percent through an ESOP trust.

Associates act like owners, too. Miami Shores store manager Isaac Coen explained: "I like the power that Publix gives me as far as letting me run my store. They have their guidelines, but they don't tell me what to do. They let me do what I feel needs to be done."

Employee ownership has translated into a rich benefit for Publix people. There are stories of cashiers who worked for 30 years and retired with a quarter of a million dollars. Managers can accumulate even more. Miami division personnel director Don Cameron cited his own experience: "I started at 19, as a bag boy, and if I work until the year 2000, when I am 57, and if things continue the way they have been going, I will retire with an excess of $1 million in my retirement fund plus the stock I have bought."

So employees have plenty of reason to stay here until they retire. And they do. The turnover among part-timers is 86 percent, but this figure is low compared to 125 percent at rival Winn-Dixie. Turnover among full-timers is 9 percent, very low for the retail industry.

For many people, working at Publix is more than a job, it's a way of life. Associates have a tremendous amount of pride in their company. They wear their pink and teal uniforms all over town. Connie Granato, who started here in 1974, became a store manager at Coral Springs and stepped down to office cashier in 1992 so that she could spend more time with her family, told us: "At times when you are working in the store you feel like you are cheering for your football team. When your store does good or the company does good, you are just really proud of them and you are rooting for them."

Main employment centers: Publix had 395 stores in Florida and one in Georgia in mid-1992. Its largest division, with 27,800 associates, is the Lakeland division. Forty percent are part-timers.

Headquarters: Publix Super Markets, Inc.
1936 George Jenkins Blvd.
Lakeland, FL 33801
(813) 688-1188

Quad/Graphics

QUAD/GRAPHICS

Quad/Graphics is the 9th largest printer in the United States in number of employees. U.S. employees: 5,300.

★ ★ ★ Pay/Benefits
★ ★ ★ ★ Opportunities
★ ★ ★ Job Security
★ ★ ★ ★ Pride in Work/Company
★ ★ ★ ★ Openness/Fairness
★ ★ ★ ★ ★ Camaraderie/Friendliness

BIGGEST PLUS: You can print your own ticket here.
BIGGEST MINUS: You have to be the right type.

One way they measure progress here is by toting up party statistics. In 1981, when this printing company was 10 years old, the annual picnic at Wisconsin's Pine Lake drew 600 people (employees, relatives, and friends) who feasted on 60 pounds of baked beans and an uncounted number of Italian sausages. In 1989, 2,400 people from headquarters and the three Wisconsin plants held summer festivals at Fond du Lac County Park and Amman's Beach in Muskego, and together they consumed 956 pounds of baked beans, 2,900 Italian sausages, 2,200 hot dogs, 43 tanks of soda, 39 half-barrels of beer, eight cases of wine coolers, and 500 steamed clams. In 1991, when Quad/Graphics was celebrating its 20th anniversary, the summer picnic was staged in the heart of Wisconsin farmland at the company's newest plant site in Hartford; this time more than 7,000 revelers indulged in a host of outdoor activities (miniature golf, a petting zoo, children's gunnysack races, horseshoe pitching, bocci ball, basketball, volleyball, pony rides, hayrides, softball) and consumed 18,000 Italian sausages, 510 pounds of fried onions and green peppers, 4,300 hot dogs, 9,500 ears of corn, one ton of baked beans, 130 half-barrels of beer, 755 gallons of soda, and 3,000 cups of juice.

They take partying seriously at Quad/Graphics, and not just at the Wisconsin plants near headquarters. The Saratoga Springs plant in upstate New York, which was built from scratch and opened in 1985, stages its own summer bash, and the Thomaston, Georgia, plant, acquired in 1989, hosts a family picnic where employees bring the trimmings: in 1991, each Thomaston employee was asked to bring enough food to serve 12 people (those whose last names began with A–C were assigned snacks, D–I salads, J–N fruit, O–S raw veggies, and T–Z desserts).

The idea of managers entertaining the staff is enshrined at Quad/Graphics. Management has been putting on musical revues for the troops at every Quad holiday party since 1981. Founder Harry V. "Larry" Quadracci is fond of telling employees: "You perform for us throughout the year. This is our opportunity to perform for you." Fun is also enshrined here. One year Quadracci made his entrance to the party riding on an elephant. In his "president's letter" to employees in 1984, he said: "Clowns are a perfect symbol of Quad/Graphics philosophy of management, because, unlike so many others, they are not wedded to conventional wisdom. They retain their childlike ability to be surprised, and the flexibility to adapt to, or even thrive on, change."

When they're not partying, Quad/Graphics people are operating the most unusual company in the printing industry. Like other printers that use high-speed presses to turn out magazines, Quad/Graphics runs its plants 24 hours a day, seven days a week, but here there are only two shifts a day, each 12 hours. So operators rotate three-day and four-day weeks. Like other printers, Quad/Graphics needs to have people on hand and on time, but Quad/Graphics has no time clocks—workers are trusted to show up and fill out their own time cards. Unlike many other big printers, Quad/Graphics has never been unionized, and there are no rigid lines here between management and workers. Quad/Graphics likes to describe itself as "a company without walls." One manager told us: "I remember when Larry named more people to be vice-presidents because [accountant] Arthur Andersen told him we didn't have enough vice-presidents for the number of employees and the sales we had." Quad/Graphics still doesn't have executive or senior vice-presidents. The company has 12 officers: Larry, president; his father, Harry R. Quadracci, chairman; a treasurer; a secretary; and eight vice-presidents, one of whom is Tom Quadracci, VP–manufacturing, who is Larry's brother.

Quad/Graphics uses highly automated equipment, but there is an extraordinary emphasis on training and education here. "No one is ever done learning at Quad/Graphics" is one of their shibboleths. Courses conducted by Quad/Graphics people cover all phases of printing, and in 1990 three out of every four employees attended at least one. Customers are welcome to sit in on these classes, too. Ray Minturn, a manager in the finishing department at the Sussex plant, told us that "there is no way we could have grown at the rate we have without the training." Pewaukee plant manager Steve DeBoth added: "All of us for the most part started out with absolutely next to nothing in terms of education and ability in this industry. At Quad/Graphics I think that we can say that those of us who are specialists in what we do are the best specialists in the industry, period." According to information systems manager Pam Nettesheim, the company philosophy is to work yourself out of your job. She said: "If you can say I will work myself out of this job, then I don't have to worry about politics, I don't have to worry about insecurity, I can grow with other people. People from other companies say, 'Oh, my God. I would never do that. If I lose my job, where will I go?' I say, 'Where else is there to go in your company?' 'No place.' I say, 'You are in the wrong company!' "

In his 1989 book, *Doing Business Boldly: The Art of Taking Risks*, Daniel M. Kehrer devoted a chapter to Quad/Graphics, pointing out: "Elsewhere, it might take someone 8 to 10 years to become a first pressman, the person in charge of the press and the five-member crew it takes to run it. Even then, he'd still be an hourly wage earner. Quad has compressed that time to three to five years. Its first pressmen have been as young as 22 years old. They become salaried managers with a say in all areas that affect their press."

In 1991 the starting wage at Quad/Graphics was $6.50 an hour. Turnover among new hires runs 25 percent, as many soon discover that work at Quad is demanding and you are expected to make your own way. Jeanne Kuelthau, corporate secretary and director of employee services, who has been here from the start, emphasized that "you don't come here for entry-level pay, you come here for a career." She said that after four years "our first pressmen, with their salary and bonus, make more money than first pressmen in union printing shops." Those who do stay for the career have access to a wide array of benefits. Every Quad/Graphics location has a fitness center—and most of them offer massages (including head and neck ones at your desk).

The Sussex plant, 18 miles west of Milwaukee, has a big child-care center, capable of handling 165 children, and there's a smaller center at the

Lomira plant, 45 miles northwest of Milwaukee. Employees who adopt a child can be reimbursed for costs up to $4,000. The pay at Quad/Graphics is augmented 15 percent by a combination of two plans: profit sharing that allocates stock to each employee's account and a savings program in which the company now matches every dollar saved by an employee with 30 cents of its own, up to 6 percent of pay. One of the newest benefits, for people at the Sussex and Pewaukee plants, is a company medical clinic that was opened in 1991. Offering primary care to employees *and their families*, the clinic, by mid-1992, was seeing more than 100 patients a day. It has nine physicians, two pharmacists, a staff of medical technologists and nurses. Employees who use the clinic reduce their medical costs to zero. Drugs can be bought there at a 75 percent discount.

To say that there's a family feeling at Quad/Graphics is somewhat of an understatement. In 1991, 2,640 employees, a little more than half, had relatives working here. There were 137 husband and wife teams, 568 brothers, 184 sisters, 599 cousins, 546 in-laws, and three grandparents. The average age of the work force was 29. There were only 600 people over the age of 40. In 1991 Jerry Kreuzer retired from the company after having been there from the start. He left behind at Quad/Graphics two sons and three sons-in-law.

People at Quad/Graphics trust one another. Managers still gather for an annual two-day conference, now called Quad University instead of Spring Fling, leaving nonmanagement personnel to run the presses. One employee pointed out to us that to work at Quad, "you've got to trust everybody who you're working with to do their job so that things get done." Another added: "You need to be a team player. If you try to do something single-handedly you are going to die here."

Allied to this feeling of trust is the Quadracci admonition that people need to be left free to do their best, without a lot of pesky rules or fear that they will be punished if they make mistakes. The Quadracci theories have never been set down in stone, and they are expressed differently at different times, but they add up to a compelling vision. In a talk at the 1987 year-end party (where he played the saxophone and danced to "Victory, Victory"), Quadracci said: "As individuals, you've got to think big. But as a company, we've got to think small. 'We're getting to be a big company, so let's get organized.' No. We're getting to be a big company, let's not get organized. Let's get disorganized. Think small." According to another story told by Kehrer: "In 1973, when the company started adding presses, he refused to put anyone in charge of the pressroom. 'Just as each lawyer is a partner and runs his own part of the business,' he recalls, 'I said each pressman is going to run [his] own press.' Other managers objected. 'You can't do that,' said one. 'Why not?' asked Quadracci. 'Because you'll fragment management' was the answer. 'I think that sounds like a good idea,' said Quadracci. 'Let's fragment management.'"

Another story frequently told here is about the time Quad/Graphics decided that its trucks, after delivering their magazines and catalogs, should carry cargo on the return trip. According to the account in the trade magazine *LithoWeek*, Quadracci "handed each driver a key to one of the trucks. From now on, he said, they were all owner-operators, partners in a new division called Duplainville Transport, and it was their duty to make the trucks profitable on return trips. The drivers asked what kind of loads they should take and he shrugged. 'How should I know? I don't know anything about driving an 18-wheeler. I'm not going to carry your loads.' This principle has been called 'management by walking away.' "

It sounds chaotic, but it's not. If you have visited a Quad plant or office, you will see that these are well-organized places. People know what they have to do. They have pleasant surroundings in which to do it. And they do it with a lot of smiles on their faces because they are not browbeaten. The company itself once described its way of doing business as follows: "Have fun. Make money. Don't do business with anyone you don't like." Employees are not forgotten people here. Every year the company produces a yearbook that, in addition to recounting the major events of the past year, carries a photograph of *every single* employee throughout the company, showing his or her date of hire, place of residence, and name of husband or wife.

Every company has its little rituals. At Quad/Graphics, it involves extensive use of the prefix "Quad." In full swing here are: Quad/Cuisine, which runs the cafeterias (and sells take-home fare to employees and is one of the nation's few company cafeterias with a liquor license); Quad/Education, the training component; Quad/Med, in-house medical services; Quad/Galleries, which has wonderful art up on the walls; Quad/Temps, a part-time, on-call employee pool; Quad/Travel, an in-house travel agency which will book personal trips for employees; Quad/Text, which provides typographic services; Quad/Care, the child-care centers; Quad/Pop, the free popcorn that's always available; Quad/Gardens, which does all the landscaping and tree planting for all properties, including the 40-acre Camp/Quad nature preserve, and also maintains three baseball diamonds, two volleyball courts, a basketball court, and an archery range.

It's a rich environment, and one directly in line with the vision Larry Quadracci had when he started this company in 1971. A lawyer, he had been working for a big Milwaukee printer, W. A. Krueger, where his father also worked, and he was mired in an adversarial relationship with the unions representing employees. "It doesn't have to be this way," he said to himself, and so he raised the money to start a new printing company that would be, as he put it, "run by employees for employees."

Quad/Graphics has been a success beyond anyone's dreams, probably even Quadracci's. It's now printing 100 million magazines a month, among them *Newsweek, Time, Journal of the American Medical Association, Play-*

boy, *Black Enterprise, Utne Reader,* and *Milwaukee Magazine* (which it owns). When we first visited Quad/Graphics in 1983, it had only 800 employees. In 1992 more than 5,000 people worked for the company.

Types of jobs: Production—50 percent; pre-press production—12 percent; mailing and distribution—9 percent; plant services—7 percent; information systems—7 percent; sales and marketing—6 percent; Quad/Tech—6 percent; Quad/Temps—3 percent.

Main employment centers: Wisconsin (plants at Sussex, Pewaukee, Hartford, and Lomira) has more than 4,000 employees; 800 are at the Saratoga Springs plant in New York; 400 at Thomaston, Georgia; 35 at Anaheim, California.

Headquarters: Quad/Graphics, Inc.
Duplainville Rd.
Pewaukee, WI 53072
(414) 246-9200

Reader's Digest

Reader's Digest Association publishes the world's most widely read magazine and is the second largest book publisher in the world. U.S. employees: 2,850.

★★★★ Pay/Benefits
★★★ Opportunities
★★★ Job Security
★★★★★ Pride in Work/Company
★★★ Openness/Fairness
★★★★ Camaraderie/Friendliness

BIGGEST PLUS: Benefits are easy to digest.
BIGGEST MINUS: They've condensed their work force.

Shortly after he took over the Reader's Digest Association in 1984, George Grune unlocked the company's boardroom and announced that the room was now open to employees. It was a symbolic act, indicating that under Grune's leadership the Reader's Digest was going to be different from the genteel, paternalistic place we described in our last edition. True to his word, Grune has shaken up the culture here.

To get an idea of the culture we're talking about, consider the boardroom Grune opened up. It has artworks that any museum in the world would covet—paintings by Renoir, Degas (*Dancers*), Cézanne, Manet, Matisse, Monet (*Water Lilies*), and a sculpture by Picasso. The boardroom is not unique. Reader's Digest's headquarters in Pleasantville, 40 miles north of New York City, houses some 3,000 works of art. The main building is topped with a Georgian tower with four sculptures of the mythical winged horse Pegasus, the Digest's corporate logo. It sits on 127 acres of well-manicured lawns. (The fall day we were there, workers were vacuuming up the leaves that had fallen the night before.) You have the sense of entering a quiet museum rather than a busy magazine office as you spot two Modigliani paintings in the art-lined main hallway. In the library, you see two famous Van Gogh paintings. Chagall's *The Three Candles* hangs above the desk of the editor in chief of *Reader's Digest*, the flagship magazine of this global media empire.

The editor's office used to be occupied by founder DeWitt Wallace, who, along with his wife, Lila Acheson Wallace, launched *Reader's Digest* in 1922 with condensed articles from other publications. It has become the world's most widely read magazine, selling 28 million copies each month in 17 languages and 41 different editions. Since its humble origins beneath a Greenwich Village speakeasy, the company has become a major book publisher (20 million copies of its Condensed Books in 10 languages are sold annually), CD and record distributor (5 million music collections), and home video seller (1.7 million). And they publish a handful of other magazines: *American Health, The Family Handyman, Moneywise, New Choices for the Best Years,* and *Travel Holiday*.

The Wallaces, both children of ministers, had a clearly defined formula for their "Little Magazine," as *Reader's Digest* was originally subtitled. Articles were to be short, readable, and uplifting. (The late Norman Cousins, onetime editor of the *Saturday Review*, called *Reader's Digest* "the best-edited magazine in America.") Subjects were picked to inspire or entertain. Ken Gordon, international group president, told us that the *Digest's* mission then and now is to show "the power of the individual to make a difference." The Wallaces didn't accept advertising in the U.S. edition until 1955, and even then they didn't allow any ads for cigarettes, liquor, drugs, or other products they found distasteful.

The Wallaces also had a clear sense of the kind of workplace they wanted. It started as a mom-and-pop operation, and the childless Wallaces always considered employees to be part of their family. Employees still tell stories of how the Wallaces would take care of employees who had met with misfortunes. And they showered their employees with unusual benefits, like a turkey at Thanksgiving, Fridays off in May, four weeks vacation after only one year on the job, and buses that brought employees to and from work at a cost of $3 a week.

This cozy workplace no longer exists here. The Wallaces both died in their 90s in the early 1980s (DeWitt in 1981, Lila in 1984). George Grune, a former ad salesman who joined the Digest in 1960, has his eye riveted on the bottom line. In a few short years, he turned Reader's Digest on its head. He eliminated the Thanksgiving turkeys and several other distinctive Digest benefits. He laid off several hundred workers. Especially hard hit were the blue- and pink-collar departments, such as subscription fulfillment. Reader's Digest continues to hire for more professional positions, however. When we visited in late 1991, there were 100 openings.

Another Grune change was to sell Reader's Digest stock to the public for the first time in February 1990 (although the Wallace foundations continue to hold 78 percent of the voting shares). In doing so he pocketed $5 million in cash and another $6 million in stock, while paying himself about $1 million a year to boot. He might argue that he is worth every penny, as Reader's Digest has been an unqualified business success. The firm's sales and profits have soared, and Grune has been the subject of several fawning articles in the business press.

Some employees question whether the drastic changes of the Grune era have destroyed too much of the Wallace culture. Chris Madera, test processing supervisor, said: "Even though we're a tightly knit company, I don't think we feel that we are a family-run company anymore. I think we're more on the corporate level and the competitive level. There is more professionalism in the company, a lot of expectations in all areas, always being aware of cost expenditures. It's no longer family like it was when the Wallaces were alive." Administrative assistant Natasha Cherney added: "I think that kind of personal, paternalistic caring has changed radically. I think there used to be an intimacy here that is now waning. It's not gone, but it's waning."

In Grune's defense it should be noted that Reader's Digest has not eliminated all of the Wallace-era perks. Employees may no longer get frozen Thanksgiving turkeys, but they do get $10 grocery store coupons enabling them to buy a turkey or an equivalent item. The Digest bus system has been eliminated, but employees can now come to work by van pool. Employees now work Fridays in May, but they've received four more holidays per year that they can take whenever they wish. And new employees get three weeks vacation after six months on the job, but after one year's service they can take a fourth week without pay.

Though Digesters (as employees call themselves) feel that times have changed, many prefer the new Digest. Naomi Marrow, director of training and development, said: "In the old days, you would walk down the hall and see people with their head down. People were operating in very routine, unchanging tasks. Their jobs were unidimensional. They were uninformed about where we were going. There was an enormous amount of benevolence, but information was maintained in a few hands and people really didn't have a sense of control over what was happening. Now people are much more certain of where they are, what's happening, where they fit in, and what the value of it is. When you walk down the hall, there's a much more upbeat, quicker pace. People seem to be more alive about what they're doing."

Human resources assistant Irene Honse, who has been with the company for 19 years, agreed: "The buses, the turkeys, all that stuff was very nice.

Now there is less of that, but I think there's more attention paid to consistency and fairness. Like any company, it's not perfect, but if I feel like it, I can at least stir the dust a little with a complaint, and I think that's more important."

Also important are the benefits. Digesters share in the company's profits. In 1991 the company contributed stock worth 15 percent of an employee's annual salary to his or her profit-sharing account (though employees of some of the newly acquired magazines are not eligible). Employees can also buy stock at a discount, and about 44 percent have done so. Digest stock has been a great investment as shares more than doubled in value, from $20 a share in 1990 to $50 a share in mid-1992. Employees receive a free *Reader's Digest* subscription and two books each year. And Digesters benefit from the Wallaces' giving to the arts. Employees receive reimbursement for half the ticket price to any Lincoln Center performance and free admission to museums, galleries, botanical gardens, and historical sites in the tri-state New York metropolitan area and colonial Williamsburg, Virginia. The annual Family Fun Day attended by Digesters and their families is another perk that employees rave about. Past Fun Days have included performances by the New York Philharmonic and the New York City Opera at the company headquarters, trips to Central Park and the Bronx Zoo, and a day at the Playland amusement park. For Family Fun Day 1992 Digesters attended a New York Yankee game.

At one end of the Digest estate in Pleasantville is a community garden with individual plots for the employees. If you come by on Saturdays, you'll see the Digesters tending their vegetable gardens. The employee garden program was started in 1975, and in 1992, 37 Digesters were part-time farmers. In addition to providing the land, the Digest plows, fertilizes, and puts on a winter cover. There is now a fee of $20 to use the plots.

CEO Grune and other top Reader's Digest executives did not spend enough time in face-to-face communications with the troops at the outset of their revolution from within, according to some Digesters. They began to rectify this problem when Grune conducted the first town hall meeting in 1988 at the Pleasantville headquarters auditorium. Grune and his senior managers head these meetings, which are held on an as-needed basis, and typically involve a presentation (the first one was about going public) and question-and-answer session. The meetings are broadcast from the 400-seat Pleasantville auditorium and shown on big-screen TVs throughout the headquarters and to Digesters in the New York City office. In 1987 George Grune began having breakfast meetings with groups of employees from a variety of divisions each month. He hopes to eventually meet with all the employees. The idea for the breakfast meetings came from a 1986 employee survey.

Regardless of how they feel about the changes, Digesters generally agree that it's still a good place to work, and there remains a great sense of pride about their company. Naomi Marrow said: "People hold very, very high personal standards. You almost want to tell people to lighten up. They work very, very hard. They care deeply about what they do. That's been a value and an ethic in this company from the beginning. They take their work quite personally and they feel as if they're putting their personal stamp on it."

Types of jobs: Administrative services, production, customer service—33 percent; marketing and sales—32 percent; information systems—14 percent; editorial—14 percent; corporate staff—7 percent.

Main employment centers: 2,300 people work at the world headquarters in Pleasantville, New York. Another 200 people work in New York City. Nearly 5,000 work overseas.

Headquarters: The Reader's Digest Association, Inc.
Reader's Digest Rd.
Pleasantville, NY 10570
(914) 769-7000

REI

REI sells outdoor gear and clothing through 34 stores and a mail-order catalog. Employees: 3,200.

★★ Pay/Benefits
★★★★ Opportunities
★★★★ Job Security
★★★★ Pride in Work/Company
★★ Openness/Fairness
★★★★★ Camaraderie/Friendliness

BIGGEST PLUS: They'll help you scale a mountain.
BIGGEST MINUS: You'll spend your whole pay check getting there.

In 1990 Keith Seydlitz, a security officer at REI's mother store in Seattle, was part of an American team that tried to reach the summit of K2, the Himalayan mountain between China and Pakistan that is 28,250 feet high —the second highest peak in the world. They got as far as 23,600 feet before being turned back by 100-mile-an-hour winds. Meanwhile, Rick Ray, a salesman in the Seattle store, was climbing in Nepal, and in Alaska Norma Jean Saunders, who works in the Anchorage store, became the first woman to successfully scale Mount McKinley alone, doing it in 12 days. At the same time, five REI employees (Ben Johns, Veronica Johns, Mike Cannon, Matt Colonius, and Kirk Grantham) from three stores (Bellevue, Berkeley, and Sacramento) and the headquarters staff participated in the Markleeville Death Ride, a notoriously difficult 12-hour bike ride through the mountains of northern California that covers 142 miles over five passes, going up as high as 15,000 feet.

For REI, these activities constituted business as usual. Recreational

Equipment Inc. was founded by mountain climbers, and while its stores and catalogs now carry, to the disgust of old-timers, such items as flannel bathrobes, raspberry truffles, and Timberland sandals, the company still defines itself as "the premier supplier of equipment for the serious outdoor adventurer"—and it continues to attract people who are outdoor enthusiasts. "REI employees are hired for their product expertise, knowledge of outdoor sports and dedication to customer service," states a company handout. Among their employees, in addition to mountain climbers, are ski racers and ski instructors, rock climbers, bike racers, topflight runners, kayakers, triathletes, trekkers, and regular backpackers. We're not sure this is actionable, but REI may discriminate against couch potatoes.

Employees clearly get a kick out of being in this milieu. Miller Myers, training coordinator at REI's headquarters in Kent, just south of Seattle, told us: "I came here in '74 because I wanted to hang out with outdoor people who were doing the same sports I was doing. People do things together here both at work and play. Sometimes it's hard to distinguish between the two."

REI people have a special bond with their customers. Jerry Watt, a merchandise buyer, said: "Our customers are part of our conscious culture. I introduced a little wood block game for Christmas. They're called gravity blocks. And on the label it says, 'made with exotic hard wood.' I had to come up with a list of each wood used to show that it wasn't a threatened or endangered species of wood."

Retail director Debra Whitted, who opened stores for REI in San Diego and College Park, Maryland, said: "You get a wall of Christmas cards from customers. They send you pictures when they're married. Sometimes they'll be backpacking somewhere on their honeymoon and they'll send us pictures with their equipment. These are people we have a relationship with."

Of course one reason for this close relationship is that REI is owned by its customers, literally. It's organized as a consumer cooperative along lines of the Rochdale Plan, formulated in England in the 19th century. This means one member, one vote. It also means that most of the profits are returned at the end of the year to the customer-owners as a rebate on purchases they have made. You can become a member of REI by paying a onetime fee of $10. Anyone can shop in an REI store, but you don't get the patronage dividend unless you're a member.

The two strands of outdoor sports and communality are roped together in REI, forming their heritage. From 1970 to 1979, the company was headed by Jim Whittaker, the first American climber to reach the summit of Mount Everest. Before Whittaker, REI was headed by its founder, Lloyd Anderson, who climbed to 450 peaks, 19 of them first ascents. His wife, Mary, who also worked at REI, scaled 64 peaks.

Anderson, along with 22 other mountain climbers, formed REI in Seattle in 1938. Their aim was not to make money but to enable members to get climbing gear like pitons and ice axes at reasonable prices. Anyone could join for $1. REI's start as a co-op devolved from the tenor of the times and geography. The country was still gripped by the Depression, millions were jobless, and Seattle was a hotbed of radicalism.

Many co-ops have been founded on a wave of idealism, and they usually foundered on the same wave. REI has survived—even prospered—by not letting politics get in the way of sound business practices. Never once has it failed to pay a patronage dividend to members. In 1991, when many stores in the country were having problems, it rolled up sales of $258 million, on which it earned almost $25 million. And of those profits, about $15 million was distributed to 960,000 members in the form of an 11 percent rebate on the purchases they made during the year. Arguments have raged as to whether REI is a business that happens to be structured like a co-op or a cooperative that is run like a business. Whatever, it is indisputably the largest consumer co-op in the nation. And it's on a roll. When we placed REI on this roster in 1985, it had 11 stores and 1,000 employees. In 1992 it had 34 stores and 2,900 employees.

This growth has meant new opportunities for REI managers, since the company usually promotes from within. In 1991 REI filled 79 percent of management positions internally. Five of REI's eight vice-presidents began as hourly employees. All of REI's 34 store managers have come from inside the company. In 1984, when we interviewed Arlene Hiuga, she was—at 31 —manager of the Berkeley store; now she manages the Bellevue store outside Seattle. Kevin Washington, who was then assistant store manager in Berkeley, now manages the San Dimas store in southern California. David Towe, who joined REI in 1988 as a part-time salesman in the Federal Way store near headquarters, now manages the San Diego store. And Kim Ufford, who also came to REI in 1988, in the Denver store, opened the Cary, North Carolina, store in 1992.

Wally Smith, who joined REI as a part-timer in 1965 when he was 17 years old, became a full-timer after graduating from the University of Washington in 1971. He opened REI's first branch store—in Berkeley, California—in 1975, and in 1983 he became CEO. He pointed out to us that from its inception REI has focused on the product—the quality of the gear, its price, its availability—and not on "trying to fulfill some kind of political mission." However, he pointed out that "the co-op structure, from a people point of view, has a real interesting dynamic, because what you do is remove the shareholder and an element of greed. The two basic constituencies are the employee and your members. Our mission is to serve our customers and that really supports our service objective, as opposed to the mission of creating shareholder wealth."

Decisions are made here on those values. REI conducted a survey to determine the best area to put up a new distribution center to replace the one they had near headquarters. The answer, based on efficiency, was Salt Lake City. But when they considered the disruption it would cause to the people then working in the distribution center, they rejected this solution —and in 1992 they began construction of a new center in Sumner, Washington, 10 miles south of their headquarters. Sharon Deibert, director of the center, said REI could have saved over $1 million the first year by going to Salt Lake but decided against it because of "our commitment to our long-term employees. We have three employees at the center with more than 20 years."

Not many people at REI have 20 years of experience. The work force is young—average age is 31—and 70 percent are part-timers, many of them working while attending school. The wages, while not munificent, are in line with the pay at other retailers. In 1992, in the Berkeley store, REI was paying part-time stock clerks $5.80 an hour, $6 in sales. Full-timers were getting $7 an hour. A supervisor began at $25,000. In Seattle, entry-level salespeople and cashiers were making between $5.80 and $8.70 per hour, those with experience, between $7.38 and $11.07 an hour. Secretaries at REI headquarters earn between $9.05 and $13.57 an hour. REI's annual turnover runs at 37 percent, but it's obviously heavier among the part-timers. Those who stay on and join the salaried ranks can fashion a satisfactory career for themselves. Some 130 managers at REI draw incentive bonuses in addition to salary, and this can put them well over the $50,000-a-year mark. REI may be a co-op but that doesn't mean it's open about salary levels. The money made by the top people in the company, including CEO Smith, is not disclosed.

REI has a strong cadre of loyalists. Deibert, who came to the company in 1972, said: "I started as a part-time wrapper, which is the lowest-paying job in this company. I was making $2.10 an hour. I had very little other job experience, but people believed in me. They gave me the opportunity to take classes and continued to promote me to where I am today. I'm the mom now doing it for the new people." Debra Whitted said: "I didn't come to work for REI because I thought I was going to become a millionaire. One reason I'm here is because of the values REI has. They're very much aligned with mine. This might sound a little hokey, but my mom brought me up by the Golden Rule. And it's important for me to be able to treat people in a certain way. At REI I can treat people with respect and get respect back. We don't want to get ourselves into the position that we're selling for the dollar, the number, the bottom line. This is mountain-climbing merchandise we're selling and it's real important for people to get the right equipment for what they're doing."

Benefits at REI include a retirement and profit-sharing plan that has consistently paid out 20 percent of compensation annually, a flexible benefits program, vacation time beginning at 11 days after one year, escalating to 16 days after three years and 21 days after nine years, a turkey at Christmas, the day off on your birthday, and—important for this group—discounts up to 30 percent on REI merchandise. One employee told us: "We spend most of our money here. We get a discount, but it just helps you spend more." Part-timers who work 1,000 hours in a calendar year are eligible for the profit-sharing plan. To tap into the full range of benefits, they have to be employed here for about a year and a half (1,500 hours) and work an average of 20 hours a week. Another benefit unique to REI is a challenge grant to help you achieve a personal goal in some outdoor activity. The company will support that effort with equipment and small cash awards. In 1990, for example, REI had a challenge grant budget of $14,000, which helped to support some 50 employees in such pursuits as a volcano climb in Mexico, a Pacific West Coast bike tour, a Black Hills triathalon, and kayaking in Alaska's Inside Passage.

Rick Ray had one of these grants for his trek in Nepal in 1990, and he told us that one of the fun events of that trip was stopping for a rest on a long trail and "seeing a couple of REI Marrakesh packs go by. This is a pack we sell." We were told a similar story by Ron Lee, who became manager of the Berkeley store in 1987 after managing the outpost in Tucson. He went hiking in Nepal in 1991, and while he was in a Buddhist temple, a woman approached him to say: "Don't you remember me? You sold me my water filter in the Berkeley store."

Training coordinator Miller Myers had a similar story: "You're sitting in a remote region of Alaska and someone paddles up in their kayak. You strike up a conversation. They find out you work for REI, and you spend some time talking about product and how they shop at REI stores. They ask you for advice. I've sat on mountain peaks and had the same thing happen. I don't think Nordstrom employees have that kind of fun."

Types of jobs: Retail—76 percent; distribution—9 percent; mail order—4 percent; information systems—3 percent; merchandising—2 percent; marketing—1 percent; public affairs—1 percent; facilities—1 percent; research —1 percent; finance—1 percent; human resources—1 percent.

Main employment centers: About 1,000 people work in the Seattle area, including 320 at headquarters in the Kent Valley south of the city, 430 in the distribution center at Sumner, even farther south, and 201 at REI's biggest and oldest store in downtown Seattle. Another 2,000 work in 34 stores in 17 states.

Headquarters: Recreational Equipment Inc.
P.O. Box 1938
Sumner, WA 98390
(206) 395-3780

Rosenbluth
International

ROSENBLUTH®

Rosenbluth is the nation's fourth largest travel agency. Employees: 3,000.

★★★★ Pay/Benefits
★★★★★ Opportunities
★★★★★ Job Security
★★★★ Pride in Work/Company
★★★ Openness/Fairness
★★★★★ Camaraderie/Friendliness

BIGGEST PLUS: You can book your own destination.
BIGGEST MINUS: The itinerary may wear you out.

Rosenbluth International may be the only company in America that uses a salmon as its mascot. Salmons appear on the internal newsletter, banners, name tags, pins, stickers, stationery, and mugs. Rosenbluth even sends a stuffed salmon doll to clients. Why the salmon? Because the salmon likes to buck the tide.

Inspirer of the salmon motif and chief tide bucker is CEO Hal Rosenbluth, who turned 40 in 1992. He likes to do things differently. One year, instead of using an employee survey, Rosenbluth sent out crayons and paper to 100 associates (never employees here), asking them to express what they felt about the company. He now repeats the exercise four or five times a year because he is so pleased with the results: "It elicits feelings that aren't going to come out in a survey," he explained to us. He once asked a group of senior managers to write down the names of every green vegetable they could think of to demonstrate that nobody knows all the answers to everything. He told a reporter from *Inc.* about his unusual method of interviewing potential executives: "I play basketball with them. . . . I like to see who's passing the ball, who's hogging it, who's taking shots they shouldn't." One candidate for a vice-president position even found himself and his wife invited to go on vacation with Rosenbluth and his wife.

Hal Rosenbluth's maverick style has paid off. Hal's great-grandfather Marcus started the enterprise in 1892 in an ethnic Philadelphia neighborhood to book steamship tickets for his neighbors to bring their European relatives to the United States. After World War II, the agency moved downtown to book trips for vacationers. In 1975, just before Hal Rosenbluth joined the family firm as a gofer, it was still a local operation with about 60 employees and only a handful of corporate clients. Since then Rosenbluth Travel has vaulted into the big time. By 1992 it ranked fourth among the nation's travel agencies (after American Express, Carlson Travel Network, and Thomas Cook), with annual sales of $1.5 billion and more than 3,000 associates at 582 sites in 396 cities. But it's not surprising if you've never heard of Rosenbluth, since 95 percent of its business comes from some 1,500 corporate clients, including Du Pont, Merck, Chevron, Eastman Kodak, Scott Paper, and General Electric.

Some of Rosenbluth's business success can be traced to technology— they've long been a leader in computer automation of travel reservations. And they've made what others consider brilliant tactical moves—like being the first firm to develop its own back office (accounting and client reporting system) that is independent of the reservations system maintained by airlines. Having their own back office makes it easier for Rosenbluth to offer corporate clients detailed reports on how they are spending their travel money. But some travel industry observers insist that Rosenbluth wins through superior customer service delivered by highly motivated people. Mike Field wrote in *Travel Weekly* that Rosenbluth people are "so relentlessly upbeat that it's hard not to wonder whether it's all simply too good to be true; whether there aren't some serious service problems just waiting to be discovered. Perhaps there are, but most industry insiders, when asked to comment on Rosenbluth's growth and market position, give the company excellent marks for delivery of services."

If this were the typical contemporary business story, we'd now hear that Rosenbluth delivers "excellent" service because he puts the customer first. But that's not the Rosenbluth story. Ever the salmon, Hal Rosenbluth wrote a book called *The Customer Comes Second.* The obvious question is: who comes first? The company's associates come first, Rosenbluth told us when we interviewed him at the agency's executive offices on the 51st floor of a downtown Philadelphia skyscraper. "We don't believe that the customer can come first unless our people come first. If our people don't come first, then they're not free to focus on our clients; they're worrying about other kinds of things." So clients who are repeatedly rude to associates may find themselves asked to find another travel agency. Hal explained in *Inc.*: "Usually these are companies that mistreat their own people, so they mistreat ours over the phone. I think it's terrible to ask one of our associates to talk with someone who's rude to them every fifteen minutes."

Rosenbluth came to his customer-comes-second philosophy in an unusual way. After working his way up from gofer to divisional vice-president, he demoted himself to reservations agent. In an article he wrote for the *Harvard Business Review*, Rosenbluth recalled: "One day in 1978, I wandered into the area where a group of about eighteen reservations agents did our business travel . . . I stood and watched for a while, then sat down in an empty chair and picked up a phone to help out. I stayed all day and came back the next. I loved it. In fact, in that room I fell in love with the company—or at least with the corporate travel agents and the way they worked together. There were no political squabbles. They worked hard, they worked hard with each other, they were a thousand miles from the petty backbiting I'd seen in other departments [of the company]." From his experience in the trenches Hal realized that supported, friendly workers are the keys to success.

As could be expected, there are no slave-driving bosses here. Supervisors (called leaders) defy conventional stereotypes. "I never feel like I manage anybody," said Terri Hafer. " 'Manage' sounds like you're controlling the actions. Sometimes I feel like a leader and sometimes like a supporter of people and their ideas."

Rosenbluth's ambience comes partly from unusual hiring practices. When Hafer applied for an administrative position, she failed her typing test. Her interviewer said: "Your typing skills are not good, but I'm afraid that if we let you go I won't find someone as nice as you are, with a great attitude like you have. So we're going to work on your typing skills together." Hafer went home and practiced typing for two weeks, came back in, passed her test, and was hired. She is now an area director.

According to Rosenbluth: "Our company is made up of friends. We didn't hire friends, we just became that way." Rosenbluth does take personality into account in choosing a new employee. He said: "Nice is mandatory." He has never had a secretary who could type, but they have all been friendly. When Pam DiPretore decided to join the company three years ago, she lacked experience and technical skills. When she told her interviewer about these deficiencies, the interviewer responded: "It's not technical skills we're looking for, it's nice people. We can train people to do anything technical, but we can't make them nice." DiPretore was hired as a reservationist, worked in training, and is now a national account manager.

New associates—from entry-level clerical workers to new vice-presidents —are inculcated with the Rosenbluth culture from their first day on the job. No matter where they are hired, they are brought to Philadelphia for

two days of orientation at the firm's training center in Essington, a Philadelphia suburb. Orientation groups not only hear the Rosenbluth philosophy, they get exposed to it firsthand. They role-play skits to illustrate bad
service—like a flight attendant allowing an obviously drunk passenger to
board a plane. They play games like "whisper down the lane" and
blindman's buff. They finger-paint. The climax comes when the group (no
more than 14) climbs into the Rosenbluth van and goes to the corporate
headquarters, where CEO Hal serves them high tea in expensive china (to
demonstrate quality service) and then spends as much as an hour informally chatting with them.

The orientation is not their last visit to Philadelphia. To reinvigorate
associates with the Rosenbluth culture, the company invites all associates
to Philadelphia every other summer for a "Live the Spirit" weekend featuring seminars and entertainment. We attended the "Live the Spirit V"
weekend in July 1992 that coincided with Rosenbluth's 100th anniversary.
The Saturday afternoon celebration in Philadelphia's Civic Center marked
the high point of the weekend. Hal made his entrance by dancing down the
middle aisle dressed in a salmon costume while playing a saxophone with
the song "He's a Rebel" blaring through loudspeakers. When he hopped
onto the stage, whipped off his salmon head, and asked, "Is this any way to
run a travel company?", the 2,600 laughing and cheering associates and
several hundred clients roared back "Yes!" Rosenbluth's top officers concluded the celebration with RTV (their version of MTV), dressed as various
rock stars while lip-synching their music. Hal's brother and executive vice-
president Lee was at the drums as Phil Collins. Other vice-presidents did
creditable renditions as Madonna, Tina Turner, Bob Marley, Bruce Spring-
steen, Rod Stewart, and others. The last act was Hal, as Michael Jackson.

Among the associates attending "Live the Spirit" were some 130 from
Linton, North Dakota, where Rosenbluth has a major data processing and
customer service center. Most were farm wives; some had never been out of
the state; we talked with one who had never before flown on an airplane.
Why Rosenbluth picked Linton tells a lot about the company. In 1988
Rosenbluth needed another data processing center. One evening Hal saw a
news story describing the terrible drought in the Midwest and how so many
farms were being foreclosed. He believed that as a company, Rosenbluth
could do something to help, so the next day he called the Commerce
Department and found out that North Dakota was the hardest hit state.
He then contacted officials in Bismarck and learned that Linton was the
most severely affected county. Within a matter of months, Rosenbluth was
taking applications for jobs in Linton. The center now employs 180 full-
time associates, and Rosenbluth has built a $1.5 million conference and
retreat center nearby called the Rivery.

"Live the Spirit" is followed in August by Associate Appreciation Month,
when offices have special events like "Hawaiian Shirt Gonzo Friday,"

"RosenJeopardy," "Hoagie Day," and "Salmon-chanted Evening" (a formal party). In 1989 Hal, dressed as an English beefeater, greeted associates at the door of the Philadelphia operations building and invited them to a tea party replete with scones, clotted cream, and jam.

Another unique feature of life at Rosenbluth is the Associate of the Day program, which began in 1990. Any associate can spend a day following around another associate, of any rank, to see what his or her job is like. Often associates take advantage of this program to see whether they would like to apply for a job in a different department. But many also want to see what it's like to be one of the top officers, in which case the company will pick up the expenses for out-of-towners to come to Philadelphia. By 1992, 56 associates had spent the day with Hal Rosenbluth.

This company doesn't substitute fun and games for low pay, however. Rosenbluth associates are compensated well—typically making 20 percent above the travel industry average. Nancy Costanzo told us that when she came for an interview, she asked for a salary slightly better than what she'd been receiving at a small mom-and-pop agency. Her interviewer responded by picking up a calculator, punching in a few numbers, and coming up with a higher offer. When we asked Cecily Carel, director of human resources, about the incident, she said: "We shouldn't exploit somebody because they're saying less is okay. That's not appropriate."

Working here offers one of the best vacation and travel benefit packages in the land. Travel agents often receive free trips courtesy of airlines, hotels, and others in the travel industry who want agents to promote their products. In keeping with their egalitarian principles, Rosenbluth pools all such perks and offers them to all associates (not just the reservations agents). Associates are then apportioned these familiarization or "fam" trips according to seniority. These trips are often to exotic locales both within the United States and overseas. Associates with one to three years get a five-day fam trip, plus $100 spending money. Those with four to seven years get eight days plus $200; eight to 11 years, 12 days plus $300; and over 11 years, 15 days plus $400. These fam trips are in addition to regular vacation time. So, for instance, someone with 11 years seniority at Rosenbluth would qualify for four weeks of paid vacation plus another 15 days of fam time. In honor of Rosenbluth's centennial celebration in 1992, Lufthansa offered all Rosenbluth associates a special offer of a $100 round-trip ticket to Germany. You could take your spouse for another $100.

In 1991 Rosenbluth initiated a new pay program for reservations specialists called "pay for quality." Associates receive a monthly bonus based on the number of error-free reservations. The average pay for reservations agents immediately rose 32 percent, and some started making more than their supervisors. The agency said the program was a financial success, as costs dropped 4 percent because of fewer errors and lower employee turnover. The turnover rate at Rosenbluth is 12 percent. The industry averages between 30 and 50 percent.

Rosenbluth's low turnover can also be attributed to the opportunities opened up by rapid growth and extensive training programs. Rosenbluth operates 10 training centers throughout the country in addition to mobile training teams who conduct seminars at branch locations. The company also has a weekly job posting system.

The travel business is traditionally cyclical, and the early 1990s were especially unforgiving. The combination of the Persian Gulf War and the ongoing U.S. recession resulted in huge layoffs throughout the travel industry. But not at Rosenbluth. Instead of resorting to layoffs, they instituted a wage freeze in early 1991. It lasted seven months for nonmanagerial employees and nine months for managers. Scores of associates helped the company out by taking voluntary time off without pay and submitting over 400 cost-saving ideas through "Operation Brainstorm." To reassure employees that they would not resort to layoffs, Hal Rosenbluth sent every associate a memo in January 1991. It said: "The obvious and simple thing to do would be to follow the course that our competition has chosen and reduce staff, since 50 percent of all costs are in payroll. But let's face it—that's not the action a salmon would take!"

Main employment centers: 700 work in the Philadelphia area, 200 in Linton, North Dakota, and the rest in 582 offices in 48 states. There are also offices in London and Tokyo.

Headquarters: Rosenbluth International
                 One Liberty Place
                 1650 Market St.
                 Suite 5100
                 Philadelphia, PA 19103
                 (215) 981-1700

SAS Institute

SAS®

SAS Institute, the world's 10th largest independent computer software company, provides products to help companies manage data. U.S. employees: 1,711.

★★★★ Pay/Benefits
★★★ Opportunities
★★★★ Job Security
★★★★ Pride in Work/Company
★★★ Openness/Fairness
★★★★ Camaraderie/Friendliness

BIGGEST PLUS: Software and child care.
BIGGEST MINUS: May be more family than you want.

This is not a company many people are likely to have heard of. It doesn't sell anything to individual consumers. It's not listed on any stock exchange. Even its name, SAS Institute, strikes a noncommercial note, suggesting a school or nonprofit organization. But SAS—they like to be called *sass*—is fairly well known in the Raleigh-Durham area. A lot of people there will say, "SAS? Oh, that's the day-care company." Here's a company that has become identified with a spectacular benefit that it provides for employees.

It wasn't that big a deal in 1981 when SAS first confronted the issue of child care for employees. The company was then five years old and employed a total of 60 persons. SAS wanted to retain its people, and so it decided to open an on-site center for children of employees. The initial enrollment was six children. The question arose as to how much parents would pay for this care. Dr. James H. Goodnight (he holds a Ph.D. in statistics), cofounder of SAS and chief executive officer from the company's inception, decided that SAS would pick up the *entire* cost.

The 1980s turned out to be heady times for SAS, a developer of computer software that enables a company to access, manage, analyze, and present data more effectively, no matter which hardware it's using. Revenues went up every year without fail. (As of October 1, 1991, the SAS system was installed at 22,288 sites.) Every year 200 new employees were hired. And these people, mostly young, were starting families and having children. This population growth didn't phase Jim Goodnight. To keep pace, SAS kept expanding the child-care facilities on the parklike, 100-acre campus that SAS occupies in Cary, just south of the Raleigh-Durham airport. Today, two of the 13 buildings at the site are dedicated exclusively to child care—one for infants and toddlers, the other for preschoolers. In early 1992, 289 children of SAS parents were enrolled—and yes, the company was still picking up the tab. Parents pay only for the children's lunches and snacks ($1 to $2 a day, deducted from paychecks). This North Carolina company, with revenues of $280 million in 1991, operates the largest corporate child-care center in the nation. And it's also the only one we know of that's free of charge to parents.

Visitors to SAS are impressed with the spaciousness and cheeriness of the two child-care centers. Care-givers, 88 percent of them certified or trained Montessori teachers, are smiling and helpful. The spaces are light, airy, and generous in size: 24,000 square feet in the infant and toddler center, 16,000 square feet in the preschool facility. The infant and toddler center has 10 classrooms for infants. It also has a nursery room, lounges, and conference rooms. Parents who drive up in the morning to drop off their children bring their cars under a portico—to keep the children from getting wet if it's raining. There are 97 married couples at SAS.

Most companies offering child care hire an outside contractor to provide the service, but that's not the SAS way. The 80 people who were working at the two centers in 1992 were all employees of SAS and therefore eligible for benefits. And the same holds for everyone else you encounter on the SAS campus: the people who prepare and serve the meals at Pennies, the company's prize-winning cafeteria, the groundskeepers who do the landscaping and tend to the six-acre lake in the middle of the complex, even the security guards—they're all SAS employees. Dr. Goodnight has created a family environment here, one where people feel connected to one another. Keith Leister, an associate development tester who served 11 years in the Air Force before joining SAS in 1989 and whose wife also works for the company, says he gets gardening advice from the maintenance people. Elly Sato, a project manager with seven years' service, says that because of the security guards, she has no fear of checking in at any time of the night or early morning to finish a task. Miranda Drake, a marketing assistant and single mother, sings the praises of the care-givers at the child-care center for the attention they gave to her little boy, who was hyperactive because of an attention disorder. "Those teachers are more than teachers," she said.

Pennies, the cafeteria that for three years running received the Best in Triangle Award from the *Raleigh Spectator*, is an attractive, two-level eating place where a pianist plays during lunch. Pennies serves 1,000 meals a day, and the menu is not the usual company cafeteria fare. The day we visited, it featured tomato soup with fresh basil, white wine, and onions (90 cents); chicken marinated in orange and grapefruit juices, ginger, garlic, and soy sauce ($2); a baked potato with a topping of broccoli, carrots, cauliflower, and zucchini in a Dijon sauce ($1); six different vegetables, including a "peppy artichoke casserole" (60 cents); various sandwiches; and an array of desserts which included a raspberry crème brûlée (90 cents) and Snickerdoodle cookies (35 cents). The calories and fat content of each item are specified on the daily printed menu. Employees can sign up for leftovers to take home.

The cash registers run on SAS software—they take no money but record the employee's identification number; the cost is deducted from paychecks. This computer-driven system also enables the cafeteria to get a fix on the popularity of different dishes. At the end of every month, the cafeteria is the setting for a company party—everyone's invited. Other homey traditions have grown up at SAS. When you show up at your building on Mondays, there are baskets of fruit, free for everyone; on Wednesdays, it's M&Ms, and Fridays, croissants and Danish.

Unlike some companies, where amenities begin and stop at headquarters, SAS exports the culture. It has seven field offices in the United States and Canada, including one opened in New York in 1992, and parent-employees in those places are eligible for the same benefits received by the people in Cary. The number of children enrolled at the child-care centers at headquarters represents about 15 percent of the employee population there; ergo, in Austin, Texas, where 100 people are working for SAS, 15 child-care slots are available to those employees at local centers, with SAS picking up the entire cost.

Everything at SAS is state-of-the-art, but the quality that makes the company special is the thoughtfulness behind the benefits. For example, working in tandem here are a health-care center and recreation and fitness center, each with its own building on the SAS campus. The health center has 11 full-time employees, including three family nurse practitioners. It offers consultations, physical exams, emergency care, and a host of wellness programs to employees and their dependents at no charge. More than 5,000 patient visits were recorded in 1989. (Naturally, the medical records are maintained with SAS software.) Opened in 1985, the fitness center has nine employees, five full-time, four part-time. It occupies a 26,000-square-foot building that houses three racquetball courts, two basketball courts, a weight training room, an exercise room, locker rooms, steam rooms, pool table, and juice bar. On the outside are three tennis courts (with lights), a softball field, a two-mile running trail, and numerous walking trails. There's also boating on the campus lake. In addition to entering teams in the Raleigh Parks and Recreation leagues (SAS has a crack running team), the fitness center supports a host of intramural leagues on the campus—in the 1991–92 year nine volleyball teams and eight two-on-two basketball teams were in action. Many companies charge a fee for use of the on-site fitness center. At SAS, it's free to employees and their adult dependents (no one under age 18 can use the center regularly). There are other SAS touches. Users of the fitness center get a laundry bag: clothes are returned to your locker within 24 hours; if you use the center more than once a day, you can get two laundry bags; there's no charge for this service. You can buy SAS shorts and a T-shirt for $15; when they are worn out, they are replaced free of charge. It's no wonder that 75 percent of SAS employees have used this fitness center.

For SAS, it all makes business sense. Healthy employees make better employees. Absenteeism is low and productivity high. And it ties in with the company's health insurance plan, which is self-funded. In our travels, we found that because of soaring health costs, most companies have been forced in recent years to make employees bear a greater portion of the insurance premium. Not SAS, where its plan has been enhanced without adding to the employee cost. An employee pays nothing for his or her medical insurance; family dependents are covered for $90 a month; and there's still first-dollar coverage. The people who started SAS—mostly statistics professors out of North Carolina State University—still own all the stock in the company. Employees therefore cannot have a sense of ownership from being stockholders, but there's a profit-sharing plan that has paid out 15 percent of salary for 15 consecutive years.

Job satisfaction is high at SAS because the work is interesting and people have a sense that if they have an idea, the company will back them. The pockets that have grown up at SAS—the child-care centers, the fitness center, the restaurant—were allowed to grow under their own steam. A good example of how this works is the growth of their video department, which was started in the early 1980s to produce films, tapes, and tutorials to help customers understand and master the SAS software systems. But SAS gives people a lot of latitude—and as the video people developed their skills, they became interested in serving markets beyond the SAS base: for example, advertising agencies that need studios to produce their commercials. The video gang was allowed to pursue that path. As a result, in 1992 a new building was opened on the SAS campus to house the video department. In 1991 the video department, which employed 17 persons, did 160 projects, 70 to 75 percent of them for SAS internal uses. In the new building, SAS expects to be doing half of its video work for outside customers such as ad agencies, corporations, and independent producers. The SAS video center is the largest facility of its kind between Washington, D.C., and Atlanta.

The computer software industry has an annual turnover rate of 25 percent. At SAS, it's 7 percent. People just don't leave here. And many that do, return. Turnover is even unusually low in the child-care centers. In 1990 only one care-giver left. But the tie that binds most of all is the sense that the product you are working on—software to help people manage their businesses—is making a difference and that you, too, have a chance to influence that business. It was best expressed to us by Paul Bachteal, a sales and marketing representative for the Ohio Valley region. SAS salespersons do work on an incentive program, meaning that the more sales they make, the more money in their pockets, but Bachteal, who worked previously for Burroughs, said: "We care about our customers. That's the challenge. We don't have the attitude: what's in it for me?"

Types of jobs: Professionals—57 percent; management—18 percent; office and clerical—15 percent; facilities—6 percent; technicians—4 percent.

Main employment centers: 1,531 work at the Cary headquarters. Another 180 work out of eight field offices (Austin, Texas; Irvine, California; Chicago; Washington, D.C.; New York City; Kansas; Seattle; and Toronto). 650 work overseas.

Headquarters: SAS Institute, Inc.
SAS Campus Dr.
Cary, NC 27513
(919) 677-8000

J. M. Smucker

Smucker's makes more jams, jellies, preserves, ice cream toppings, and fruit syrups than anybody else in the United States. U.S. employees: 1,900.

★★★ Pay/Benefits
★★★ Opportunities
★★★★ Job Security
★★★★ Pride in Work/Company
★★★★ Openness/Fairness
★★★★ Camaraderie/Friendliness

BIGGEST PLUS: They've preserved a sweet environment.
BIGGEST MINUS: The path to the top is jammed.

"With a name like Smucker's, it's got to be good." This is one company where the advertising slogan applies as much to the workplace as to the product.

Just ask Bob McGuire, who has worked in the firm's big jelly and jam plant in Orrville since 1975. "If people ask you where you work and you tell them Smucker's, their eyes kind of light up and they get a big smile on their face and say, 'Oh, I hear that's a good place to work, man. You're so lucky.'"

Or you could ask the head of the Teamsters unit at the Orrville plant, Robert Johns. When we interviewed Johns in the summer of 1991, he said: "I was elected president of the union a few months ago, so for me to sit here and say it's a great place to work, you know it is." Johns operates a machine that recovers flavors which have evaporated in the jam-making process. He told us: "It really is an honor to represent the union against them because they are very easy to work with and it is just a pleasure. They do really care about their people."

Headquartered 60 miles south of Cleveland in a small town surrounded by lush farmland, Smucker's seems like a throwback to a different era. Company headquarters is located on Strawberry Lane, a block from the modest house formerly occupied by founder Jerome M. Smucker, whose first product was apple butter. According to company lore, the apple butter was made from the trees originally planted in the area by the legendary Johnny Appleseed. Many residents of the town and surrounding communities are Amish or Mennonites, and they make up a large part of Smucker's local work force. In fact, the company founder, a strict Mennonite himself, changed the family name from "Smoker" to "Smucker" because he was against cigarette smoking. Today, Smucker's refuses to allow its ads to be shown on TV programs with sex or violence.

Smucker's is, however, a very modern corporation despite the small-town charm of Orrville. More than a third of all jams and jellies spread on toast every morning come from Smucker's. The clean and efficient Orrville plant churns out more jam and jelly than any other plant in the world—400 different items, totaling 1 million pounds of jam a day. To keep up with demand, Smucker's has opened plants in five other states. It has also expanded to Australia and Britain, and it has acquired Knudsen's, a California juice squeezer. Between 1982 and 1992, profits tripled while the price of the company's shares, traded on the New York Stock Exchange, escalated by 10 times.

However, Smucker's is not about to become another faceless, multinational corporation. Not if the Smucker family has any say in it—and they do, since they remain in firm control through their ownership stake. Paul Smucker, grandson of the founder, became chief executive officer in 1970, and he still held that post in 1992 at age 75, along with the title "chairman of the executive committee." His sons, Tim and Richard, were chairman and president respectively. And two of Tim's children work in the plant.

Employees at all levels call the Smuckers by their first names, and Paul's two sons are often referred to as the "Smucker boys," even though they are in their 40s. Dave Thomas recalled: "When I first came here [in 1980], I found it real strange because I was used to calling elders and people with more responsibility 'Mr.' Since then I really can't think of too many times when I heard Paul, Tim, or Richard called 'Mr. Smucker,' except by people who don't work here."

This informality reflects the accessibility of top management. Deb Mizer, a filter operator, explained what happened when she became frustrated by the waste generated by a new machine and went to Paul Smucker to talk about the problem: "It's not unusual at all for people to go right to Paul Smucker. You might be a little bit nervous, thinking you're going over somebody's head and may feel the effects of it later on. But you don't get into trouble. The door is open."

Twice a year, top managers meet with all employees at every major facility in the company. Johns believes the meetings are "one of the best things that ever happened here because every employee has the chance to get their hands on the president of the factory and make a complaint." He told us that pay day is now on Thursdays instead of Fridays because one female worker complained to the Smucker boys that "the breads are fresher and everything is not picked over" on Thursdays. "They listened to it," said Johns, a little flabbergasted himself. "I couldn't believe she even said it."

Smucker's is very selective in hiring, even for entry-level positions. Employment development manager Tim Miller said candidates are interviewed not only by managers but by people they will be working with. Andy Traicoff, a marketing manager, added: "If there is anybody in that process, anywhere in this chain, if they have any uncomfortableness about that person at all, that's it. We don't try to lobby against each other. The few times we have ever deviated on that it has come back that the person didn't quite fit in."

Once you are on board, especially in the professional and managerial ranks, you can expect a lot of career opportunities. Industrial product development manager Mary Kay Stephenson, who came here out of college, reported that she has had six jobs in eight years: "I started out in quality control, then into production as a production supervisor, then to personnel as a recruiting manager, and then in product development, and have had three different jobs in that area."

Working at Smucker's offers more than a fast track. There are a handful of unusual benefits, like the Christmas bonus check of 2 percent of your annual salary along with a turkey and a specially designed holiday plate. More important, there is a sense of belonging and caring. Packaging helper Alicia McDonald told what happened when she had a house fire in 1987 and "lost everything we had. Of course, the people at work collected up for me, you know, gave me clothes and money and whatnot. But as an extra gift of thoughtfulness, Tim Smucker gave me an extra check on the side. They really are concerned and six or seven months later they're still saying, 'Do you need anything?' "

McDonald's words echo an explanation of the corporate philosophy related in the company's history book, *With a Name Like* . . . In it, an unnamed vice-president is quoted as saying that Paul Smucker's way of managing "totally reversed any management theory I ever heard of. The manager works for his staff. The higher your promotion, the more people you have to serve . . . help them get their job done. You see it in the next generation of Smuckers, too. Their approach to their staff is 'What do you need?' Under Paul's system if you're trying something new, it's O.K. to make mistakes. He's got that in the budget."

Paul Smucker says that this philosophy can be traced right back to his grandfather, J. M. Smucker. He noted that in one of the rooms in his grandfather's home was a quote on the wall from the Bible: "Be not deceived; God is not mocked: for whatsoever a man soweth, that shall he also reap." Paul Smucker says: "I can hear Grandfather telling me, and also Dad, that he interpreted that Bible verse as saying that if you put something good in your product, you will get good results. If you live a good life, you are going to have good results. It was so simple. That has carried through."

Types of jobs: Production workers—45 percent; management—18 percent; office and clerical—12 percent; skilled crafts—11 percent; service—8 percent; professionals—3 percent; technicians—2 percent; sales—1 percent.

Main employment centers: Orrville, Ohio; Salinas, California; Memphis, Tennessee; Ripon, Wisconsin; New Bethlehem, Pennsylvania; Chico, California.

Headquarters: The J. M. Smucker Company
Strawberry Lane
Orrville, OH 44667
(216) 682-0015

Southwest Airlines

Southwest, the seventh largest airline in the United States, flies to 34 cities in California and 14 southwestern and midwestern states (as far east as Cleveland). Employees: 9,500.

★★★★ Pay/Benefits
★★★★★ Opportunities
★★★★ Job Security
★★★★ Pride in Work/Company
★★★★ Openness/Fairness
★★★★★ Camaraderie/Friendliness

BIGGEST PLUS: It's a blast to work here.
BIGGEST MINUS: You may work your tail off.

Flight attendant Matt McCauley likes to have a good time at work. On one flight he played "The Eyes of Texas" on his harmonica over the loud-speaker after touchdown and sang the cautions about remaining seated until the crew brought the aircraft to a stop at the terminal. A customer reported that McCauley received "three ovations" from the passengers, adding, "There would have been a 'standing' [ovation] except that the seat-belt sign was on!"

McCauley would have had no difficulty with two of the questions South-west asks prospective employees: "Tell me how you recently used your sense of humor in a work environment. Tell me how you have used humor to defuse a difficult situation." Those who can't answer these questions satisfactorily are automatically disqualified. That may make Southwest Air-lines the only U.S. company that actually requires a sense of humor.

Hiring people who enjoy the lighter side of life is part of what makes

Southwest a fun place to work. Mary Mortenson, a former Texas Instruments employee, said: "We take what we do seriously, but we know how to have a good time doing it." Frank Stockton, a nine-year Southwest employee, said: "Everybody here, they're really upbeat and they're always happy. They want to come to work. They get here early and they have smiles on their faces."

You grasp some of the flavor of life at Southwest by seeing how employees dress. Most airlines require employees who deal with the public to be dressed in businesslike uniforms. Not Southwest. Flight attendants and ticket agents typically dress in casual outfits, like golf shirts, shorts, and sneakers. Southwest has run recruiting ads that point up this facet of work life: "Work at a place where wearing pants is optional, not to mention high-heeled shoes, ties, and panty hose. . . . Which not only makes Southwest Airlines people look a little more hip, but feel a lot more comfortable. . . . We're always looking for people who take their jobs seriously, but not necessarily themselves."

Behind-the-scenes employees share in Southwest's laid-back culture. Libby Sartain, who handles compensation and benefits in the airline's People Department, worked at four other companies before she came to Southwest. At two of them, she said, "I've actually had my boss call me in and say, 'You laugh too loud in the hall and that's unprofessional.' It took me a long time to unlearn some aspects of my personality that I've had to keep under guard. Now I can laugh in the hall as much as I want to. I think that's the neatest thing about Southwest Airlines. They allow each person to really be themselves."

It's clear where Southwest's distinctive culture comes from. If you come to work here, you'll be working for one of the zaniest characters ever to run a major corporation in America. Herb Kelleher, CEO and cofounder of the airline, comes across as almost a caricature of the hard-driving, fun-loving Irishman. He loves to party and drink (little figurines of wild turkeys adorn his cluttered office in honor of his favorite drink), and he loves to smoke (he smoked most of a pack of Barclays during our one-hour interview). He has been known to sing "Tea for Two" while wearing bloomers and a bonnet at a company picnic (featuring a chili cook-off) in front of 4,000 employees. He regularly helps flight attendants serve drinks and peanuts when he flies. One Easter, he walked a plane's aisle clad in an Easter bunny outfit, and one St. Patrick's Day he dressed as a leprechaun. When Southwest started a new route to Sacramento, Kelleher sang a rap song at a press conference with two people in Teenage Mutant Ninja Turtles costumes and two others dressed as tomatoes.

Kelleher is also fond of playing pranks. The *Texas Monthly* reported one that occurred soon after Southwest decided to promote vacations to Sea World. They painted one of their planes to look like Sea World's killer whale and christened the airplane *Shamu One*. Reporter Jan Jarboe wrote that Kelleher received a telephone call from Bob Crandall, president of American Airlines, congratulating him for the clever marketing tactic: " 'Just one question,' asked Crandall. 'What are you going to do with all the whale shit?' In a nanosecond Kelleher replied, 'I'm going to turn it into chocolate mousse and spoon-feed it to Yankees from Rhode Island.' The following Monday, Crandall, a Yankee from Rhode Island, received a large tub filled with chocolate mousse with a Shamu spoon stuck poetically in the center."

It's not all fun and games at Southwest. They run an airline that has acquired a good reputation from both investors and "Customers" (they always capitalize the c in "customers"). In 1991 they had the fewest consumer complaints of any major airline, nosing out Delta, the longtime leader. And Southwest has been profitable every year since 1972, including 1991, when it was the *only* major airline in the black. And while other airlines were laying off or cutting back, Southwest was hiring at a clip of 200 new employees a month in 1992. In the company's 1991 annual report Kelleher attributed the firm's success to its business strategy and "because our people have the hearts of lions, the strength of elephants, and the determination of water buffalos."

Part of Southwest's appeal has been bargain fares and no-frills service. But they don't offer low fares at the expense of employee paychecks. Almost 90 percent of Southwest's employees are unionized, and pay is comparable to that of other carriers in the relatively high-paying airline industry. What's more, Southwest was the first carrier to offer a profit-sharing plan to employees (it started in 1973). Some early participants in the plan have become millionaires.

Southwest also puts a lot of money into training. Its University for People, located in a terminal building at Dallas's Love Field, not far from the corporate headquarters, runs quarterly leadership training programs that are required for all supervisors and managers, and customer-care programs run by line-level employees. For example, flight attendants teach other flight attendants. Pilots get customer-care training, too—a very rare practice in the airline industry.

Training is emphasized in part because Southwest promotes from within. The airline fills roughly 80 percent of higher-level jobs through internal promotion.

We heard numerous stories of people who moved up from low-level positions. Fourteen-year employee Ruth Ann Lassiter's was one of the more impressive. "I started here as a secretary in ground operations," she said. "At that time there were five staff members. After I had been here for about three years I went into the vice-president and told him how I thought we could form a position I could do that would make the company money. He listened to me and he gave me that position. That was in 1981. I went from a secretary to an analyst. From there I went to a managerial position on the staff, from there to director and then to regional director. You can set your goals with this company and you can realize those goals. There are no limits."

Lassiter should have added that there are no limits so long as you're willing to work extremely hard. By some standards, Southwest has a workaholic culture. Chuck Martin, director of maintenance, said: "In my interviewing process I say that when we hire an individual at Southwest, 'We always work understaffed. The reason is that we have a no-layoff policy and when we hire you we like to feel like this is the last job that you'll ever have to have. So with that understanding you have to realize that when you come to work for us, you're going to have to work a little harder.' "

It's not absolutely necessary to bury yourself in work. Ticket agent Mitzie James points out that "the company will let you trade days with another employee so that you can be off as many days as you need to be." The same is true for many other positions, including flight attendant.

But there is peer pressure to work harder. When Kevin L. Freiburg was doing research for a doctoral dissertation on Southwest, he asked flight control director Dale Foster what enabled Southwest dispatchers to work 50 to 80 flights a day compared to United's average of 20 or 30 flights. Foster responded: "Just the pride of it. . . . It's just something that's been ingrained and those of us who have come from another airline have said, 'Wow, I didn't know you could do this much.' It's something that is expected of you and you don't want to sit back and be embarrassed by not doing it."

Like everything else, workaholism starts at the top. When we asked Kelleher about his hours, he said he typically works 14-hour days, seven days a week. But he insisted that the long hours were not a problem because "it's fun. If your vocation is also your avocation you don't burn out because it's like being on vacation every day. There is a lot of talk in America about being a workaholic and so forth and so on. Well, if you enjoy it, it's not stressful."

A lot of people at Southwest share Kelleher's view. Mitzie James, who started here at age 18, said: "It's not just a job, it's an extracurricular activity or a hobby, because there is always something else you can do that involves someone from Southwest Airlines. If you want to play softball, basketball, there are charity benefit games. You can travel to the chili cook-off, to the Christmas party, to the Halloween celebration here at the general office. There is always something going on." Perhaps because of all this extracurricular activity, there are over 300 married couples at Southwest Airlines.

Like many others, James calls Southwest a family. Like many American families, Southwest has its family photos adorning the homestead. When Southwest built a new corporate headquarters several years ago, every art company in Dallas offered to decorate the hallways and reception areas.

But Southwest bought no art, and instead put up hundreds of employees' pictures on the walls, many of them taken at a seemingly constant round of parties.

The Southwest family talks a lot about love. Some of it seems hokey to an outsider, such as their employee magazine being called *Luv Lines* (with the dot over the *i* in the shape of a heart). During their 20th anniversary in 1991, the company's slogan, appearing on stationery and in ads, was "20 Years of Loving You." Their New York Stock Exchange ticker symbol is LUV. And Southwest's flight attendants serve "love potions" (drinks) and "love bites" (peanuts).

There seems to be a genuine sense of affection among employees, toward each other and their larger-than-life CEO. As Chuck Martin says: "Herb Kelleher is Southwest Airlines. We all love him."

The feeling is mutual. Kelleher told CBS's *60 Minutes:* "It's very simple. I love them. They kid me, they're irreverent toward me. They're a joy to be with. It's a kind of reciprocation there. They know that I love them and I'm proud of them."

One way Kelleher demonstrates his love is through his uncanny knack for remembering employee names. When we were interviewing a group of employees in Dallas, Sandy Poole said she had been working at Southwest as a flight attendant for three months before she happened to meet Kelleher. He introduced himself to her and they talked for only a few minutes. Six months after that encounter, "I was walking down the hall of the headquarters and he said, 'Hi, Sandy Poole. How's the new job?' And that is just so flabbergasting. And you do feel important, it really makes a difference." When we asked the group whether Sandy's story was unusual, virtually everyone in the room came forth with a similar tale. Since then we have taken several Southwest flights. Virtually all the employees we talked with report that Kelleher does indeed remember them by name even if they had only met him once before.

They're big on poems at Southwest. One issue of *Luv Lines* was full of poems by employees telling why they love working there. Tammy Schaffer, a reservations center manager, wrote a poem especially for us explaining her feelings about the company:

> Southwest Airlines is the place to be.
> A lot of hard work, but it's worth it to me.
> To Herb "his" people are number one.
> He gives US the credit and lets us have fun.
> We're 8,000 strong on the ground and in the air.
> When one has a problem, we're all there to share.
> Our customers are our biggest asset.
> When we make them happy then we have no regret.
> The events of the year are carefully planned.

From Chili Cook-offs starring Duck Soup Band.
Halloween is quite a sight . . .
Throughout the system it's really a fright!!
At this time NO ONE is sane.
Count Dracula might be flying the plane.
The very best part of the year
Is when Herb brings us his message of cheer.
He visits his troops everywhere
And lets us know how much he does care.
Why do I work for Southwest?
Because it's superb!!!
"I don't want to grow up."
That's why I work for Herb.

Types of jobs: Reservations—20 percent; flight attendants—19 percent; ramp agents—11 percent; customer service—10 percent; managers and supervisors—9 percent; operations—5 percent; skilled crafts—4 percent; office and clerical—3 percent; provisioning and skycaps—3 percent; other—16 percent.

Main employment centers: Most Southwest employees are stationed in Dallas, Houston, or Phoenix. There are 40 other smaller offices, located mainly in the southwestern United States.

Headquarters: Southwest Airlines Co.
P.O. Box 36611
Love Field
Dallas, TX 75235-1611
(214) 904-4000

WHERE FUN IS A WAY OF LIFE

Ben & Jerry's Homemade
Great Plains Software
Odetics
Quad/Graphics
Rosenbluth International
Southwest Airlines

Springfield ReManufacturing

Springfield ReManufacturing remanufactures motors for companies like Sears, Chrysler, General Motors, and J. I. Case. Employees: 690.

    ★ ★ ★   Pay/Benefits
   ★ ★ ★ ★   Opportunities
   ★ ★ ★ ★   Job Security
   ★ ★ ★ ★   Pride in Work/Company
★ ★ ★ ★ ★   Openness/Fairness
    ★ ★ ★   Camaraderie/Friendliness

BIGGEST PLUS: You can be a big fish.
BIGGEST MINUS: But it's a small pond.

Every Wednesday afternoon, a group of 40 to 50 Springfield ReManufacturing employees sit around a table in a small conference room to play a game. To an outsider, the game doesn't look like much fun. Most of the time is spent with individuals shouting out numbers and everyone else busily writing down those figures on sheets of paper. But the participants seem to be enjoying themselves as they are constantly joking.

SRC calls this "the Great Game of Business." The participants are representatives from different parts of the company. The representatives are shouting out the income and expense numbers for the week from their departments. They will report the week's company-wide results to other workers in their departments after the meeting. Employees here are quite interested in these results, as they have been taught the meaning of such terms as income statements, balance sheets, cash flow, equity, and retained earnings. Strategic planning director Dave LaHay explained: "We don't keep secrets. Normally, financial information is closely held—here it is just the opposite. We get each person to understand the financial statement so they understand why we make the decisions we do."

This may sound a little odd when you realize that we're not talking here about a Wall Street bank but a small manufacturing company nestled in the Ozark Mountains of southern Missouri. Their three Missouri plants are pretty grimy, as their main business is remanufacturing car and truck engines. They buy worn-out engines and engine components like oil pumps, water pumps, and fuel injection pumps, take them apart, fix them to work like new, and sell them to auto, truck, and farm equipment manufacturers like General Motors, Chrysler, Sears, Mercedes-Benz, Navistar, and J. I. Case.

By any of the typical business tests, SRC has played the game extremely well since 1983. That year, International Harvester agreed to sell its failing Springfield plant to factory manager Jack Stack and a dozen other employees rather than close it down. Stack, now president and CEO, said the reason they decided to buy the failing factory was quite simple: "We bought the company because we didn't want to lay anybody off, and we were scared to death of not getting jobs ourselves. The reality of the situation was that we bought our jobs." Since then SRC has grown from 119 employees to 690 in 1992. The company went from losing $60,000 in its first year to profits of $1.3 million (on sales of $65 million) in 1992, and the value of its stock has multiplied 180 times. The value is determined by an outside appraiser. Employees own 30 percent of SRC's stock through an employee stock-ownership plan (ESOP). The rest is owned by Stack and the other top managers. So this appreciation has meant that an hourly worker who has been with the company since the original buyout now has shares worth about $35,000, about what a home costs in Springfield. Jack Stack explained: "The stock, the equity of the company, is the product at the end of the rainbow, it's their treasure."

Giving employees a stake in the company has been crucial to SRC's success, according to Stack. But he doesn't think that an ESOP alone is enough. Stack told us: "All companies play the same game. We all have to determine the same sets of numbers. It's just that so few people know the numbers in most companies. The message the CEO gives to the investors at the end of the year or quarter is impersonal and has basically nothing to do with all the things that the workers did. Nobody understands those financial statements. And then people come in and talk about trying to create job security. The only measurement of job security is in the balance sheet. We teach our employees that job security is an equity ratio. And if you get that ratio, you are more secure. When you can create stories with numbers and you can animate them, the whole thing makes sense."

SRC educates everyone on the rules of the game of business. Cindy Jacobs, who works on fuel injections, explained: "They are training us on financial statements right now and they're hard to understand. They show us the sales and profits, what they ship, they go through every item. Every week you sit down with your supervisor and he gives you the numbers. You can see how your own work affects the statement. It is interesting. At first I was not interested and did not think it was beneficial to us. But as you learn about it, it becomes more beneficial. How is it beneficial? If you are not working up to standard, it's going to show up on that paper."

SRC employees use the financial data in their daily work. Ken Hedgepeth, who works in automotive production, said that at SRC "you track your labor daily, you know what your overhead absorption is at the weekly staff meeting. With my prior company [Pro Bass Shop, a boat manufacturer], about every quarter they would come down and say, 'You lost $200,000 this last quarter.' You don't actually know where it was lost. Here you have a total view of everything that is going on and it is updated."

And when employees realize where money is being lost, they can save it. Productivity rose 30 percent within the two years after the ESOP buyout. Engine disassembler Freeman Tracy has saved the company $2 million with 88 different suggestions since the ESOP buyout. Tracy told *Inc.* magazine that before the buyout, "I wasn't in a thinking mood. But now you know you're helping yourself as well as the company." And he has helped himself. Since SRC pays employees up to $500 per idea, Tracy had collected $10,000 by 1992. His most profitable idea was for salvaging fuel injection pump heads, saving SRC $1 million in one year. Engine assembler Charles Albright explained why associates are willing to pitch in: "The thing that motivates me is that if I feel that the company is looking out for me, then I am going to do my part as far as looking out for them. And that is the bottom line for me."

Education doesn't stop with learning how to read balance sheets. SRC expects its workers to spend at least 100 hours a year in classes. They sponsor classes from seventh-grade reading and mathematics to statistical process control at all their plant sites. They also expect employees to continue their education and offer full tuition refunds to employees who do. The company boasts that the average employee has furthered his/her education by two years since being hired by SRC.

Continual learning has many payoffs at SRC, as over 90 percent of supervisory positions are filled from within. Jobs are posted in the cafeteria and employees get first dibs on new positions. Virtually all supervisors have come from the ranks. Denise Bredfeldt, who started working at SRC in 1975 as a production worker, told us that after she became supervisor of the hydraulics department, she saw that SRC was not making a good profit there and should get rid of it. She explained: "I got rid of the product I was working on and got rid of my job. The agreement that Jack [Stack] and I had was a gentleman's agreement that I would go back and obtain my degree. I did that through the tuition refund program and the company paid for it. I got my degree in business administration and economics." She is now an engineer in the research and development department.

SRC has another unusual way to promote from within. Ambitious employees can ask SRC to help them launch their own businesses. SRC started this spin-off program in 1989 and had funded five new companies by 1992. SRC funds 80 percent of new ventures and offers the new business owners the option of acquiring the SRC shares so that they can own their company. Eric Paulson started Engine Plus in 1990 to supply SRC with oil coolers to remanufacture engines. He got backing of $60,000 from SRC. The first year, Engines Plus did $300,000 in sales to SRC alone. By 1991 the company had three more product lines (including remanufactured engines), two factories, and sales of $3.5 million. In 1992 SRC still owned 72 percent of Engines Plus. Other businesses bankrolled by SRC include Megavolt, a company that remanufactures starters, alternators, and generators; Avatar, which makes water pumps; Newstream Enterprises, which assembles and packages various motor vehicle components; and the Great Game of Business, a management consulting and training company.

Those who stick with SRC talk as if they do run their own businesses. Bus Bryant, supervisor of service engineering, said that SRC is very different from the old owner, International Harvester: "You always had to wait for Chicago to do this or that. Now you do it yourself or go up to the guys and make a decision. It is refreshing because you can see the results of your action, whether negative or positive, right away." Scheduler Mike Campbell agreed: "The top managers are not breathing down your neck if mistakes occur. Everyone pulls together real well."

While SRC pays its worker-owners a little below the going manufacturing wage in Missouri, employees end up far ahead of other factory workers when the quarterly bonus kicks in. Every year SRC sets profit and bonus targets. If the company reaches those goals, employees can be rewarded with up to 13 percent of their compensation as a bonus. Pat Brigance points out: "If we show a profit, that goes into our pocket as our bonus. That makes people work harder to get a bigger bonus."

Playing the game of business is not the only thing that makes SRC a good place to work. It is located in the middle of one of America's favorite vacation destinations. One of the many attractions of the Ozark Mountains is great fishing lakes, where many employees like to hook bass. They do that every year at a company-sponsored fishing tournament. The fishing is so great here that the company spreads the tournament out over the entire season (March through October), holding one leg of the tournament each month at seven different area lakes. At this event, people draw fishing partners from a hat. Bus Bryant said this means that "Jack Stack may pick a guy from one of the lowest-paid hourly jobs in the plant. You are not out lobbying to get a better job or transfer. You are out to fish and have a good time." In 1991 Stack and his partner, product engineer Al Fabbri, placed second in one leg of the fishing tournament. They caught almost seven and a half pounds of fish.

SRC also involves its employees in other sports events. Stack, whose father played professional baseball, loves to play golf. Every year the company holds a golf tournament with no distinction between managers and employees.

While some observers of the American business scene consider SRC to be a harbinger of the future, Stack sees things in a more down-to-earth way: "We are trying to get a bunch of people through life. We are not trying to change the world. We work together, we play together, we win together."

Types of jobs: Production—76 percent; supervisors and administration—21 percent; sales—3 percent.

Main employment centers: There are SRC plants in Springfield, Willow Springs, and Marshfield, Missouri.

Headquarters: Springfield ReManufacturing Corp.
P.O. Box 2024
Springfield, MO 65801
(417) 862-3501

Springs

Springs is one of the world's largest producers of sheets, towels, tablecloths, draperies, and other home furnishings under such labels as Springmaid, Bali, Andre Richard, and Wamsutta. U.S. employees: 20,000.

★ ★ ★	Pay/Benefits
★ ★ ★ ★	Opportunities
★ ★ ★ ★	Job Security
★ ★ ★ ★	Pride in Work/Company
★ ★ ★	Openness/Fairness
★ ★ ★ ★	Camaraderie/Friendliness

BIGGEST PLUS: They haven't thrown in the towel on U.S. workers.
BIGGEST MINUS: Paternalism spreads.

For many of us, a big southern textile mill conjures up scenes from the 1979 Academy Award-winning movie *Norma Rae*, a contemporary drama of a union-organizing drive. The textile mill depicted in that movie was dirty, hot, and noisy, with managers who were equally unpleasant. The Hollywood moviemakers had clearly not done their research at Springs, whose mills are scattered throughout South Carolina and other southern states. Not only are these mills air-conditioned and extremely clean, but relations between workers and managers are more like a big, happy family than a breeding ground for class conflict.

We interviewed a group of hourly Springs associates (they don't use the word "employee" here) from several mills in South Carolina. Twenty-three-year employee Mattie Goodman, a training instructor at the Elliott mill, told us: "Both my children worked for Springs out of high school. Springs has really been good to us. Everybody in my family has grown up with

Springs. I have nine brothers and sisters and at one time or another we have all worked at Springs."

Springs encourages promotion from within. Plant manager Judy Wertz started as a secretary in 1973, was promoted to accountant, and then took manufacturing training. After working at four different plants, she was promoted to operations manager to coordinate the activities of those plants. Wertz now manages 600 associates who work in the two-year-old H. W. Close plant, located in Fort Lawn, South Carolina. Every week associates at Wertz's plant make 32,000 comforters and 50,000 other accessories like bed ruffles and fancy pillowcases.

Wertz's career path is only one route to the top. The other route, used by the college graduates Springs recruits every year, is through the production management program (PMP). Carl Boyd, accessory department supervisor at the Elliott plant, described the program: "It takes from six months to a year. You work with a supervisor and learn how to do the paperwork. Then you get an opportunity to work in the plants on every line and individual job, getting hands-on experience. By actually running the hourly associates' job for some time, you gain more respect from employees when you get on the floor as a supervisor."

We gained another view of Springs by visiting the Elliott plant in Fort Lawn, one of Spring's 14 "grey" mills (where basic textile fibers are woven into cloth). When we were there in the summer of 1991, the lobby displayed homemade crafts made by 50 of the 270 associates. The crafts fair was organized entirely by the hourly force and included large wooden carvings of Native Americans, colorful quilts, and dolls. A first-place ribbon was pinned on a cross-stitch hanging of a rural scene of a wooden shack with a Coca-Cola sign; it had been sewn by Johnsie Moore, a weaving machine operator.

The Elliott plant is highly automated, with relatively few workers on the floor (especially when compared with the crowded working conditions in scenes from *Norma Rae*). When we asked whether the mill used to have more workers, we learned that indeed about 50 more were there until new machinery was added 10 years ago. What happened to the 50 workers? None was laid off. They were given new jobs at other Springs mills. What happened at the Elliott plant was typical. Springs has avoided the layoffs that have plagued most of the American textile industry, which has been severely hurt by foreign imports.

We get even more of a feel for the company by interviewing three managers at the Elliott plant, which was named for Colonel Elliott Springs, president from 1931 to 1959. Delbert Sellers, superintendent of the weaving department and cloth room, started working second shift at the plant as a learner while still in high school in 1963. His father and all eight of his brothers and sisters have worked for Springs.

Seller's immediate boss was mill manager Jack Caroway, who, unlike most Springs managers, came here in 1981 from Burlington Industries, a huge textile maker headquartered in North Carolina. According to Caroway: "There is as much difference between Burlington and Springs as daylight and dark. I worked for Burlington for 19 years, and they weren't as people-oriented as Springs is. I was approached by Springs in 1981. We discussed pay and fringe benefits and I couldn't believe they were that far ahead of Burlington Industries. Burlington never praised you or said 'good job,' they always wanted more. I have not run into that in my 11 years at Springs. Springs is like a big happy family; they give us freedom and trust us to run our job. They don't breathe down your neck."

We heard a third perspective from personnel manager George Dobson, who has been with Springs since 1956. When he first started, Elliott Springs, known simply as "the Colonel," was in charge. Dobson reminisced about him: "He was a car buff and he would bring the cars that he purchased to the foundry. He bought a Cadillac, in 1955 or '56, with a brushed stainless-steel trunk, and the first thing we did was take the emblems out of the hubcaps and put on a decal of the Springs girl that says 'protect your assets.' we also put on the Springmaid girl as a hood ornament." The Colonel's Springmaid-girl advertising campaign helped to catapult Springs from 13th to first place among sheet makers, a position it still holds today. These ads featured drawings of scantily clad women with a heavy dose of sexual double entendre. They were risqué enough to cause magazines like *Life* and *The Saturday Evening Post* to refuse to run them.

Springmaid-girl posters still grace the walls of corporate headquarters, as do drawings by Grace Drayton, the artist noted for her cherubic children in Campbell soup ads. When the headquarters was built, the Colonel insisted the windows be set like those in the zeppelin dirigible, at a 45-degree angle. His office has an even more unusual feature: a conference table rises from the floor at the push of a button. When he ended meetings, the Colonel would press the button and executives would have to scurry from their seats to keep from being bruised by the table descending into the floor.

With all his eccentricities, Colonel Elliott Springs was a people-oriented leader. He established pioneering benefits such as a cafeteria that serves low-cost hot meals, a medical clinic, health and life insurance, and a vacation bonus. The profit-sharing plan instituted in 1953 was the first one of its kind in the textile industry.

Another Elliott Springs legacy is employee parks. The 102-acre Spring Park in Lancaster, South Carolina, has an Olympic-size swimming pool, miniature and full-size golf courses, a skating rink, and horseback riding facilities. The sports complex in Fort Mill has an indoor pool, gymnasium, racquetball and tennis courts, softball and soccer fields, a golf course, and playgrounds. Springs also built a golf course near the Chester, South Carolina, plant. Any associate can use these facilities without charge. They can also rent rooms at Springmaid Beach near Myrtle Beach, South Carolina, for $34 a night or travel to Springmaid Mountain, near Spruce Pine, North Carolina, where they can stay for $28 a night.

Springs's corporate headquarters is located in Fort Mill, South Carolina, about a half-hour drive from Charlotte, North Carolina. Despite the proximity to major urban centers, Fort Mill (population 4,162) is clearly in the Deep South. A Confederate Park, with three statues of Confederate soldiers and a Civil War cannon, sits in the middle of town. On the outskirts is the huge PTL resort where Jim and Tammy Faye Bakker used to broadcast their evangelical Christian TV show before Bakker's indictment and conviction for fraud.

Overseeing Springs is Walter Elisha, the first non-Springs family member to run the company since its founding more than 100 years ago. In early 1992 Elisha unveiled a statue of a woman holding a piece of cloth on the grounds of the headquarters. The statue depicted "quality," one of the seven values called Springs of Achievement. The other values are creativity, education, personal and family well-being, respect for history, and planning for the future.

The Springs of Achievement values resulted from Elisha's and other top managers' reflections about the company as it approached its centennial celebration in 1987. In the 1980s Springs had made a series of acquisitions, the largest involving Wamsutta, a textile company nearly as large as Springs. Elisha told us that when he looked at the company in the mid-'80s he asked himself: "How do you carry through all these things that we say are Springs? How do you transport these values into organizations of people who have their own history?" They then defined the values that made Springs successful.

When he introduced the Springs of Achievement, Elisha did not give managers specific instructions for applying those seven concepts to work life at their plants or offices. Instead, he let managers decide which ones best fit their needs and interests. While the marketing department might choose a Springs of Achievement project that focused on customer service, a plant might choose one that involved community service.

The campaign has had a big effect. James Bullman, a frame operator in a spinning and finishing plant in Rock Hill, South Carolina, explained in *The Springs Bulletin*: "When I first came to work at the bleachery, I had a supervisor who referred to workers as 'hands.' In my mind, I envisioned myself as a disembodied hand. The thing that Springs of Achievement has done is all of a sudden Springs realizes the production worker is more than just a 'hand.' He has arms and legs and a body and, more importantly, he has a brain. And he can think and has ideas."

Yarn spinner Rebecca Leak from the Close plant agreed with Bullman. She told us: "They care more now, they respect the associates and their feelings. They realized that we know more about the job because we are on it eight hours a day." Associates also have more control over their jobs. In

1992 five Springs plants used self-managed teams where groups of associates elect a coworker to handle scheduling and ordering of supplies.

Springs of Achievement also helped open communication channels between management and associates. Packing clerk John Deese said: "It is more open, people are not afraid to talk to management."

The company has been more specific in issuing directions for its new no-smoking policy. As of April 1, 1992, all Springs offices were to be entirely smoke-free—no exceptions. The company newsletter described the new policy and included stories of those who had quit with the help of company-sponsored stop-smoking programs. But, as a testament to Springs's respect for individuality, the newsletter also included comments from employees who were not happy with the ban or did not intend to quit (though they won't smoke on the job). Credit manager Nick Yoder tried the smoking-cessation program, but decided he did not want to quit the habit. He told *The Springs Bulletin:* "For about two weeks, I was horrible. I wasn't a pleasant person. Now I leave every day for lunch so I can have a cigarette. That's about all we can do. I have thought about quitting, but I can't honestly tell myself that I want to." Shortly after he made that comment, Yoder left the company.

Types of jobs: Production—85 percent; sales and administration—15 percent.

Main employment centers: Springs is the largest industrial employer in South Carolina with 24 mills. Their other 16 plants are located in North Carolina, Georgia, Alabama, Tennessee, Pennsylvania, Wisconsin, Nevada, and California. Springs has sales offices in more than 30 cities throughout the United States including New York City, where 300 employees work at the Springs building on the Avenue of the Americas.

Headquarters: Springs Industries, Inc.
205 N. White St.
Fort Mill, SC 29715
(803) 547-3738

Steelcase

═══════════════════

Steelcase

Steelcase is the world's largest maker of office furniture. U.S. employees: 14,000.

★★★★ Pay/Benefits
★★★ Opportunities
★★★ Job Security
★★★★ Pride in Work/Company
★★ Openness/Fairness
★★★ Camaraderie/Friendliness

BIGGEST PLUS: Bonuses will leave you sitting pretty.
BIGGEST MINUS: Managers get softer seats.

If you work for a Fortune 500 company, you probably know Steelcase. You may be using a Steelcase desk, sitting on a Steelcase chair, or stuffing folders into a Steelcase filing cabinet. If you live in Grand Rapids, Michigan, you're also a sure bet to know Steelcase. It's not only the largest employer in this western Michigan city, it's also known as the employer of choice, the one that's on the top of every job hunter's list. In the country at large, Steelcase does not have much visibility, despite sales of nearly $2 billion a year. You'll never see its shares cross the Dow Jones ticker because Steelcase is still privately owned. Some 100 descendants of the families who founded the company in 1912 own all the shares.

Although Steelcase employees have no chance to own stock, they have a sense of ownership because the company, when it's profitable, pays out profit-sharing bonuses quarterly as well as at the end of the year. These bonuses, combined with extra pay based on piece rates (the more you turn out, the higher you pay), can easily bump up your salary by more than 50 percent. In 1991 the entry-level factory wage was $9.71 an hour but the average W-2 slip for hourly employees was $38,000. And that was a recession year for Steelcase and the furniture industry. On top of that, Steelcase has a deferred profit-sharing program that serves as a retirement plan for employees. Between 1943 and 1991, the company kicked in 15 percent of an employee's pay to this plan in every year except two. An hourly employee who retired from the company in 1992 at age 65 with 30 years of service and a final pay of $50,000 would have been able to buy an annuity giving him an annual income of $21,600.

The pay and benefits were certainly cited to us by employees we met here at the end of 1990.

Ted Tomaszewski, a factory hand who joined Steelcase in 1973, told us: "I've always considered myself an owner of the company through their profit-sharing plan. The better we work, the harder we work, the more they sell, the more profits, and then they share them at the end of the year. My wife has never worked. We have four children, and I need the money. That's why I came to Steelcase."

Dick Beirschbach came to work at Steelcase in 1965 and left after six years "because I hated punching that time clock." He went to work at a local store but decided to return because of the bonuses and benefits he was missing out on at Steelcase. He says: "After five years of being out of here, the people that I had worked with were so much farther ahead as far as retirement and benefits and profit sharing. And so I have been back here about 14 years." Beirschbach is now a supervisor at Steelcase's new 788,000-square-foot Context plant, where we interviewed employees in a conference room that had a picture window opening on the plant floor. "We're trying to think from a team-building standpoint," said plant manager John Gruizenga. The window, he says, is "an attempt to link our technical support side directly with our craftsmen. We want the people working on the plant floor to relate to the front office as their office, not just 'the office.' "

The Context plant opened in 1990, a year after the opening of another spectacular workplace, the Steelcase Corporate Development Center, a seven-story, pyramid-shaped structure that sits in the middle of a restored prairie in rural Gaines Township, six miles southeast of the corporate headquarters in Grand Rapids. This is home to 675 designers, engineers, and others involved in new product development, and it has a variety of features designed to stimulate creativity, to wit: 14 specially designed, one-person think tanks; 589 bronze-tinted windows; 28 skylights; a 71-foot, kinetic, stainless-steel sculpture suspended like a pendulum from the cone of the pyramid, endlessly sweeping a seven-foot-wide disk over a reflecting pool; a central atrium through which all employees must pass, coming in or going home, the idea being to encourage a "town hall" interaction. This 575,000-square-foot building costs nothing to heat, even in the middle of winter, thanks to seven 50,000-gallon thermoslike bottles buried outside: they capture heat from the building's computers and recirculate it through 40 miles of piping.

In addition to providing these nifty work environments, Steelcase has recently joined other U.S. companies in embracing "world-class manufacturing" and "employee involvement," which it defines as "making maximum use of the skills, knowledge, and potential of every employee." As a result, work teams are in vogue here. Some 700 have been formed in the nine Steelcase plants that dot the Grand Rapids area. Each team has seven to 10 members, and they meet weekly. "For the first time," a manager told us, "people feel that they have a say in what's going on in this company. For a long time we just said, 'Do it our way or hit the highway.' Now they've got something they can participate in."

Kevin Koopman, who has spent 20 years at Steelcase, said: "Once you give the people that power, it's just amazing to see what they can do," and he cited the example of a work team he supervises at the file plant: "They set their own hours. If they get their work done by noon on Friday, they go. This week they decided they had to work 10 hours on two days. I didn't know anything about it. I come in here in the morning, and here's my work cell working 10 hours today. They have their schedule and they know what they have to get out. Some of them really like to get out early on certain days, and so they work accordingly. People told me, 'If you let them determine their own hours, they're going to bail out on you.' What I find is that it's just the opposite. They stay a little bit longer to make sure they are where they should be. We haven't missed a schedule in a year."

Job security was a legendary Steelcase benefit until the recession of 1991 came along—and even then the company tried to hold the fort. Furniture is a cyclical business. When a company is going through hard times, the easiest decision is to postpone buying new desks and chairs. Steelcase began feeling the pinch in 1990 when we first interviewed here, but employees reassured us that "if it gets slow, we'll cut back but we won't lay off." Frank Merlotti, who was then president, said in response to a question about possible layoffs that this "is not a solution we're looking at."

This resolve withered in 1991 when sales plunged 13 percent. At first Steelcase resorted to a companywide freeze on pay raises, a 5 percent cut in salaries of the top 25 executives, and voluntary paid leaves of absence (some 250 hourly employees took eight weeks off at reduced pay—$250 a week). But those measures were not enough. By the end of 1991, Steelcase had fired 300 white-collar employees and laid off 930 hourly workers. In previous layoffs—1970, 1975, and 1983—Steelcase had recalled all hourly employees to work within six months. This time it took a little longer, but by the summer of 1992, invitations to return to work had gone out to all of the laid-off employees.

The layoffs affected newer employees, those hired since 1988, and Steelcase tried to cushion the blow for them by offering outplacement help, including a letter of recommendation written by president Rob Pew to prospective employers in Grand Rapids. Employees on layoff had their health insurance continued for three months, and Steelcase extended this coverage another 90 days for employees who signed up for 20 hours a month of volunteer service with a nonprofit agency affiliated with the United Way.

"This process is really painful for all of us," said Pew.

What helped to carry Steelcase through this difficult period was a tradition of caring for their people, reflected in the extraordinary number of longtimers (they have more than 640 employees who have worked here for more than 25 years). This has always been a family-oriented company, in a quite literal sense. We interviewed one third-generation Steelcaser who reported that he had 15 relatives working here, including four brothers-in-law and four sisters-in-law. Steelcase people who have been here for 15 years have a right to "sponsor" a person as a new employee. And when the company does hire, it fills 80 percent of new jobs from the sponsorship list before going outside to community agencies.

The work ethic that's so much a part of western Michigan is reflected in the large numbers of employees who rack up perfect attendance records. In 1991, of the 6,718 hourly employees in Grand Rapids, 23 percent or 1,549 received perfect attendance awards, which range from $25 dollars for one year to $200 for five or more years. Of this group, 374 had perfect attendance for five or more years, and 33 had gone 10 or more years without missing a day, including Henry Stedman, an assembler in the Context plant (25 years), forklift operator Gary Kubizna (22 years), and Garry Vincent, a team supervisor in the Systems III furniture plant (17 years). Stedman, Kubizna, and Vincent may be shooting for the incredible record set by Dick Woodwyk, who retired in 1991 after working for 41 years in Steelcase's chair plant, never having missed a single day. Woodwyk was born—and still lives—in Hudsonville, a community 10 miles southeast of Grand Rapids settled by immigrants from the Netherlands. He credited his endurance to eating one or two apples a day, never drinking and never smoking.

Lloyd Fitch, Jr., and his brothers used to farm the land that now holds some Steelcase properties. They grew hay and corn. How he got to Steelcase was described in the company newsletter, Case Line: "Lloyd and Evelyn, his high school sweetheart, had this deal: First they would graduate from high school, then Lloyd would serve a two-year Naval tour in the Atlantic, then would find a job, and then he and Evelyn could get married. Well, while Lloyd served on the USS Newport, Evelyn started working at Steelcase, in cost accounting. And when Lloyd returned to Grand Rapids, Evelyn had a Steelcase job interview already scheduled for him." That was

27 years ago. Lloyd and Evelyn are married and now have three daughters. He's the auditor at the computer furniture plant.

Les Clark, manager of the Systems I plant, who has put in more than 40 years with Steelcase and has three daughters working here, told us: "There are some companies around that will not hire relatives because of the potential problems it might cause. We have found it to be a strength. It's been that way since the start of the company. There are grandfathers and fathers and grandsons and granddaughters who have worked here."

During the 1980s Steelcase pioneered new benefits. They adopted a cafeteria benefits plan, set up a department to match parents with appropriate family child-care providers, promoted the idea of job sharing, where two employees share one job, and implemented an adoption aid benefit that will reimburse costs up to $3,000. They also mounted wellness programs run out of their elaborate, 25,000-square-foot fitness center, which costs families $420 a year to join, and they now have a 17,000-square-foot medical center staffed by two physicians, 9 nurses, and two physical therapists. If you're too tired to think about cooking dinner, you can buy meals to take home at the three cafeterias run by the food services department in Grand Rapids. And if you want a cheap vacation, there's Camp Swampy, a 1,170-acre campground on Diamond Lake 60 miles north of Grand Rapids, where there are 50 campsites, electrical hookups, canoes, and a fulltime campground biologist to conduct hikes and wildlife programs—all for the exclusive use of Steelcasers and their families. In 1992, for the first time, they imposed a charge: $6 a night.

It does make a difference here whether you are a salaried or hourly worker. The salaried folks get two weeks vacation after one year, the hourly people have to wait three years; salaried staffers are eligible for health insurance on the day they're hired, hourly workers have to wait 30 days; salaried people are told to keep personal telephone calls "to a minimum," hourly workers are directed to use pay phones for personal calls; and salaried people don't seem to be subjected to the disciplinary code applied to the hourly work force, a code that assesses penalty points for rule violations (failing to display a parking sticker on your car, unauthorized use of company phones, tardiness) and calls for terminations if you pile up a lot of them.

Types of jobs: Production—76 percent; supervisors and administration—21 percent; sales—3 percent.

Main employment centers: Grand Rapids is home to 8,300 Steelcasers, working in 10 plants, corporate headquarters, and the spiffy new development center. Another 5,700 work in plants, offices, and showrooms scattered across the country, including about 1,000 employed in Design Partnership companies that have been acquired by Steelcase. Outside the

United States, Steelcase has 6,300 employees, half of them in eight French plants.

Headquarters: Steelcase Inc.
P.O. Box 1967
Grand Rapids, MI 49501-1967
(616) 247-2710

Syntex

Syntex, the largest drug company headquartered in the West, makes two major arthritis drugs (Naprosyn and Anaprox). U.S. employees: 6,410.

★★★★★ Pay/Benefits
★★★ Opportunities
★★★ Job Security
★★★ Pride in Work/Company
★★★ Openness/Fairness
★★★★ Camaraderie/Friendliness

BIGGEST PLUS: You'll always have enough sick days.
BIGGEST MINUS: R & D needs a new Rx.

When they opened a child-care center in 1984 near its headquarters in northern California, Syntex was hailed as a pioneer in providing this benefit. But this center was *not* the company's first foray into child care. You would have had to go back to 1947 to see Syntex's first child-care center in Mexico City, where the company was founded. Syntex also provided their Mexican employees one free meal a day, a good pair of work shoes, and a company store, where employees could buy rice and beans and other essentials at cost.

Syntex's reputation as a benevolent employer started with cofounder George Rosenkranz, a Hungarian-Russian Jew who joined several other scientists in synthesizing the female hormone, progesterone, from the black, lumpy root of vines that grew wild in Mexican jungles. (The "synt" in their name comes from chemical synthesis, the "ex" from Mexico.) Syntex hit the jackpot in the 1950s and 1960s by using their compound to make birth control pills. Today Syntex makes other winners, including Naprosyn, an arthritis drug; Cardene, for hypertension; and Toradol, a potent, nonaddictive pain reliever.

By all accounts Rosenkranz was an unpretentious man with tremendous compassion for others. He helped to foster a family spirit among employees even as Syntex grew into a large multinational. When he left the firm in 1980, the company's leaders didn't want to lose his spirit. So, as Paul Freiman, Syntex's current CEO and chairman, put it: "We locked him in a room with a camera, and we interviewed him for a week. We made him suffer through that. We asked him all the questions about 'What is important to you in running a business, not the science end but the people side.' We captured that. I don't know how many hours it totaled, but we then boiled it down to a program we call 'Managing at Syntex.' It essentially describes how to deal with subordinates, bosses, peers, community work, and government. It became part of the training for all management people in our company."

Judging from interviews we conducted at their sprawling headquarters campus in Palo Alto, Rosenkranz's spirit has been kept alive. According to research laboratory supervisor Michaela Hart: "In our department, it is very much like a family. You know, if somebody gets pregnant, they have all of these parties. If you were here at Christmas, you would understand. There really is a sense of it. People don't just come here and then go home. Even at a personal level, people are very involved with each other."

Senior administrative assistant Kathy Collins offered a similar perspective: "We are very much a team organization. We try to act like a family, a happy family. You do get the feeling that management cares. Since I've been here, I have had a father die tragically after a long illness and I have had a divorce. The company has always been as accommodating as it could possibly be."

Collins works for Syva, a medical diagnostic subsidiary which, in late 1991, was moving its 800 employees from Palo Alto to a new site in San Jose, 30 miles away. How Syntex was making this move says a great deal about this company. Suzanne Yokota, new business development manager, said: "They are going to great lengths to make sure that employees understand that they are very, very valued by the company. We have things like the ability to relocate if the drive is going to be horrendous. [Syntex offered low-interest loans for down payments on home purchases for first-time home buyers who had to relocate.] They are offering things like leased van-pools to get us there, and they are encouraging carpooling. It is really, really shocking. My husband works for the electronics industry. If that company decides to move and it is not convenient for you, tough."

Yokota also said she was impressed at how Syntex was making efforts at the San Jose site to emulate the campuslike environment of the Palo Alto facility. They are also going to provide an on-site day-care center. The company contracted with Rachel Samoff, director of the Palo Alto center, to manage the new center. She said: "We really view ourselves as a family support service, not just a place for kids. If ever a parent is uncomfortable about anything, we will fix it." Parents have a strong role in the center. They funded the playground and many of the facilities there.

The Palo Alto campus is one of the most pleasant work environments in corporate America. Among the more than 200 works of art scattered throughout the campus are a Henry Moore sculpture and a Robert Rauschenberg serigraph. An art gallery is open to the public for special exhibits, including an employee art show that Syntex has sponsored since 1975. The day we were there a group of employees were playing volleyball on the lawn during their lunch break. Club Syntex, the firm's health and fitness center, includes an on-site gym and aerobics room. The Syntex Employee Recreation Association sponsors a wide variety of activities, including skiing and hiking.

Syntex tries to pay at the top of the high-paying pharmaceutical industry, but it's no longer a place where you can take your job for granted. In late 1992 it gave notice that it would be reducing its work force and consolidating production facilities. They do offer some unusual benefits. In 1992 Syntex gave all employees options to buy 100 shares of stock. Typically stock options are offered only to top executives and can be lucrative if the company's stock rises. The option costs the employee nothing. The company shuts down for the week between Christmas and New Year's, and everyone is paid for those days. The sick pay policy is perhaps the best in the nation—182 days of full pay. We asked compensation and benefits director Pat Bennett whether people abuse this policy. She responded: "Our sick-leave utilization is actually lower than we would have predicted for a company our size. I think it would be naive to think that there hasn't been somebody out there who has gamed us on that policy, but in terms of the vast majority of our employees, they respect why we gave it to them and they do not abuse it. If you are gone beyond three days, we ask them to clear through our own medical staff here coming back on board. That is it. There are no doctor's notes."

But Syntex is no nirvana. We found dissatisfaction in the research division. Chris Henderson explained: "I cannot say that my interactions have been perfect working in research. I know a lot of great people, and I hear a lot of happy remarks from people who work with those types of people. The type of people I work for don't happen to be so congenial. Sometimes I feel that as a biologist, I don't really get any say as to what is being decided for me, like the projects that I am on. I have also noticed that a lot of people aren't happy because of this lack of communication or caring extending beyond upper management to lower management. I think upper management and CEOs have very good intentions. The thing is that middle management is making a lot of decisions. Middle management, I feel, is causing a lot of separations between the biologists and them. There is a lot of stress that has been created by people who I feel are working with their egos and who really aren't looking at what the biologists are saying."

When we asked Paul Freiman, chairman and CEO, whether he was aware of such problems, he said: "I think research more than any other area is probably the biggest challenge, primarily because the middle managers in research are bench scientists. These are guys who are wrapped up in their work. I have found that by and large in this company and in this industry, management in research is not an art that is appreciated by a good scientist. They don't look at the human side maybe as deeply as people in other parts of the company." He then described a number of approaches he is pursuing to improve the morale in the research division.

Freiman and other top managers have developed a number of vehicles over the years to keep in touch with employees. Every spring in Palo Alto they conduct all-employee meetings, where the top managers give a presentation and are interviewed by a group of employees who carry questions from other workers. According to Freiman: "We get lots of questions: some verbal, from the brave few, and a whole bunch of them written in. They are pretty tough questions. At the last meeting, we had a running dialogue about whether we could add more benefits. It's a two-way street. People have to give back to the company. It is not just, 'What is the next benefit I can get?' I opened my mouth up at that meeting and I made a few promises. I think that I have been good in keeping them. One was to get at least one woman on our board of directors. I just appointed one." Miriam Stoppord, M.D., a British author and health expert, is the new director.

In addition to the all-employee meetings, senior managers hold periodic open forums. Freiman also holds a monthly chairman's luncheon with 18 randomly selected employees. Employees can also fill out a "Speak Out" form, an anonymous written note to make suggestions or complaints known to upper management. Other managers use a variety of methods to keep in touch with the employee pulse, including meetings, brown-bag lunches, and surveys.

One area of special concern is the status of women at Syntex. The percentage of professional and managerial-level positions held by women (46.3 percent) almost equals their percentage in the work force (48.7 percent). But many women feel there is a "glass ceiling," since few females have made it into upper management.

To deal with the problem, the company set up a "glass ceiling" task force of about three dozen fast-track management women to come up with suggestions. Freiman explained what happened after they gave their first report: "The men sat and talked with each other. We said, 'Let's be honest with each other. How do we deal with women differently than we deal with men?' Guys my age are used to dealing in a different way than maybe my 28-year-old son deals with women. He has women friends. I never had a woman friend. I recognized when we talked about this that even when I evaluate a woman at the year-end evaluation, I am a lot kinder in her evaluation than I am with her peers who are males if they are doing something wrong. I hit the men right between the eyes. But if she is doing something wrong, I kind of dance around it. So it is not honest. They don't get the real feedback about what really is wrong."

Syntex has gone beyond consciousness-raising. In 1991 and 1992 the company promoted nine women and recruited another to top corporate positions, including eight vice-presidents. Kathleen Gary, vice-president of public affairs and communications, ascribes the promotions to the glass ceiling task force: "I was recruited to Syntex in 1981 as its first female corporate vice-president, but a decade later, I was still the sole female corporate officer. As a result of the task force's efforts, management was willing to recognize that we might be wasting some of our most valuable assets by not exploiting women to their fullest potential. The results speak for themselves. There never were any formal, structural impediments to women's progress at Syntex, but now we're confident that most of the informal (often subconscious) obstacles to upward mobility for women have been eliminated."

Types of jobs: Professionals—35 percent; sales—20 percent; management—19 percent; office and clerical—13 percent; technicians and support people—8 percent; service—2 percent.

Main employment centers: Palo Alto and San Jose, California.

Headquarters: Syntex Corporation
3401 Hillview Ave.
P.O. Box 10850
Palo Alto, CA 94303
(415) 855-5050

Tandem

Tandem makes "no-fault" computers for banks, airline reservations systems, stock exchanges, and other big companies. U.S. employees: 8,697.

★★★★ Pay/Benefits
★★★★ Opportunities
★★★ Job Security
★★★ Pride in Work/Company
★★★★ Openness/Fairness
★★★ Camaraderie/Friendliness

BIGGEST PLUS: Plenty of backup.
BIGGEST MINUS: Your job is not fail-safe.

Two weeks after the Democratic Party nominated him for President, Bill Clinton took his campaign to California's Silicon Valley. He stopped at Tandem Computers and talked with 200 employees in the cafeteria while being telecast via satellite to more than 9,000 employees at 100 Tandem facilities over the company's state-of-the-art private TV network (called TNN). The satellite hookup enabled Tandem employees at sites across the country to pop questions to the candidate, just as they do on the Friday of each month when Jimmy Treybig holds a one-hour, all-company meeting. TNN is one of the largest private TV networks in corporate America.

High-tech, high-speed communication of information is what this company is all about. Treybig, a former Hewlett-Packard engineer, founded Tandem in 1974 to develop computer systems that wouldn't crash, a common problem in those days. His idea was to link two central processors in tandem (hence the company's name) so that if one failed, the other would take its place. The idea was a hit among big computer users who can't afford to have their machines go off-line. Tandem became a Fortune 500 company by selling these systems (priced between $24,950 and several million dollars) to 38 stock exchanges, more than 300 banks, 400 retailers, and 30 phone companies, among others.

One feature that distinguishes Tandem from other Fortune 500 companies is a distaste for structure. We met a number of ex-IBMers when we made our own stop here in late 1991. Sue Cook, who was at IBM for 17 years before becoming Tandem's vice-president of human resources in 1988, told us: "IBM's culture is very structured. Tandem's is not. Ours is much more open and more loose. IBM's is more measurement-oriented. They are also 75 years old. We are 16. We do things more quickly."

Another refugee from IBM, customer engineer Jackie Stepek, joined Tandem in 1985, and she said: "At IBM there was not a great tolerance for ambiguous situations. Everything was well packaged before it went out. We let much more hang out here. One of the characteristics we measure people on is a tolerance for ambiguity."

Another ex-IBMer, Bill Copeland, who spent 27 years with Big Blue, described Tandem as having "a rugged individualist culture" that sometimes complicates efforts to promote teamwork.

So you shouldn't come here if you like structure or expect the perks that come from hierarchy. Tandem does not have an executive dining room, special benefits for top managers, time clocks, or organizational charts. And the only reserved parking spaces are for disabled employees. Chief operating officer Bob Marshall explained: "We are trying to be very egalitarian. If a customer has a system that is down, and a customer engineer can fix it—who is more important to the company at that point in time, that customer engineer or the president or me? It's the customer engineer. So everyone is critical. We don't try to differentiate."

Tandem has a dual-career track that allows people to rise on technical rather than managerial merit. Liz Chambers told Tandem's newsletter *Nonstop*: "When I made the decision to move out of my management position and back to my job as a software designer, the thought never entered my mind that it would be unacceptable to my peers. That's because the Tandem culture I've been exposed to says that individual contributors and managers are equally valuable. People are judged by what they contribute, how they help others, and their creative ideas, not by their job titles. I came to Tandem in 1981 to work on high-level data base products. In 1983 I became a section manager . . . [and] about a year later, I decided I wanted to become an individual contributor again."

Tandem fills 70 percent of their positions internally.

Though promotions are common, getting hired here is not easy. Tandem screens people thoroughly to make sure they fit into the culture. Candidates are interviewed by potential bosses, peers, and even by those who would be reporting to them. Ann Stobing, an administrative assistant in the public relations department, said: "I came in as an entry-level secretary. I had eight interviews. I thought, 'I am just a little person. Why me?' " People who have made it through the hiring process have an interest in who joins the team, too. They can get a $750 bonus for referring someone who is hired.

Having 10,000 people working harmoniously in a relatively structureless company could become a nightmare unless they all share a common philosophy. Not to worry. Tandem may be the only firm in America with a "Philosophy Department." It runs an all-day class for employees called Focus on Fundamentals, which includes dinner with CEO Treybig. Managers take a follow-up course from the Philosophy Department called Focus on Values. Part of this half-day class is spent playing the Tandem Values Game, in which small groups go through different case studies applying Tandem values to real-life situations.

Everyone at Tandem refers to Treybig as "Jimmy." He is one of the more accessible CEOs of a Fortune 500 company. Every week or so Treybig noshes with about a dozen employees for an hour and a half over breakfast. The breakfasts started from a suggestion made in the comment section of Tandem's biannual president's opinion survey.

In addition to the monthly satellite meeting, Treybig and other executives meet regularly with larger groups of employees at different Tandem sites for town meetings, an institution here since 1984. There they answer presubmitted questions and queries from the floor. Candace De Cou, head of the Philosophy Department, cited an example of a town meeting at Tandem's former manufacturing facility in nearby Watsonville where someone in the employee audience complained to Treybig: "We don't have a swimming pool and you guys do!" Treybig responded by having a pool built at Watsonville, a clone of the one that was installed at Cupertino headquarters in 1979. In 1992 the Watsonville plant, pool and all, was sold to another company. It was a casualty of the recession that resulted in Tandem's first major layoff. The 700 employees who left the company were given the right to exercise their stock options for the next three years. Options enable a holder to buy stock at a set price over a period of years, a valuable benefit if the stock price goes up. It is traditionally reserved for the very top people in the company. Tandem has long offered these options to all employees. Options cost employees nothing up front.

If the town meetings seem too formal, you might run into Jimmy at a Friday afternoon "beer bust," a ritual here since the company was founded (Treybig imported the idea from his days at Hewlett-Packard). Beer busts are not just a Silicon Valley phenomenon. Nonstop reports on "Beer Busts Around the World." Each office adds its own twist to the Friday celebration: bluegrass music in Austin, dim sum in Hong Kong, paper airplane contests in Louisville. As Tandem has matured, the beer busts have changed; they're not as rowdy as they used to be and some Tandem employees have suggested changing the name to "popcorn busts" to discourage drinking.

Tandem has one of the nation's most active in-house electronic mail networks, with three classes of mail. First-class mail is strictly for business; second-class, for ideas or suggestions; and "no-class" is a bulletin board with jokes and classified ads. One of the electronic mailboxes, reserved for complaints, is labeled "Pipeline." Chief operating officer Bob Marshall calls it his "bitch line"—he gets two blasts a day. Marshall described one Pipeline from an administrative assistant who complained that her new manager wasn't working very hard, and was taking credit for everything she did. "She put up with it for about a year and a half before she sent a Pipeline message," Marshall recalled. "It took us six months to figure out the truth, but he is gone. She is back to work and doing great."

When we visited Tandem in the early 1980s, we noted that one of the "golden" benefits here was a sabbatical program, introduced in 1974. Tandem still offers it. Every four years employees can take a six-week sabbatical. Everyone takes advantage of it, including Treybig, who was on his the day we were visiting. He only took four weeks off, however, spending one and a half weeks on Pinape Island in the North Pacific and the balance in the Madeira Islands off Portugal.

Tandem has added another option to the sabbatical, the "Public Service Sabbaticals." Through this program employees can extend the time of their sabbatical and even get grants. We met Dana Gilligan, who spent hers in Zimbabwe in 1989, where she did a nutrition study for Earth Watch, a nonprofit world health organization. In addition to the time off, Tandem gave her $5,000 for airfare. In 1991, 13 employees took public service sabbaticals, including Dianne Busse, who taught English to youths in Poland, and Laura Valverde, who repaired roads, dug a latrine, and renovated a building in Tanzania.

In 1991 Tandem announced a plan to build a company town near its Cupertino headquarters. While Tandem is continuing to talk with city officials about construction plans, they have purchased 115 acres on which they plan to build more office buildings, a child-care facility, a retail center, several parks, and 500 houses for Tandem employees. Employees will be able to commute from their company homes via a company-sponsored transit system.

Types of jobs: Marketing—40 percent; service—18 percent; software—18 percent; administration—9 percent; manufacturing—8 percent; engineering—6 percent.

Main employment centers: Over half of Tandem's work force is in the San Francisco Bay Area: Cupertino, Sunnyvale, and Santa Clara. Tandem also has manufacturing facilities in Boulder, Colorado, and Plano, Texas. The sales offices hold an additional 3,000 employees. The largest sales and marketing offices outside the Bay Area are in Omaha, Nebraska (482 employees), and Austin, Texas (581 employees).

Headquarters: Tandem Computers, Inc.
19333 Vallco Pkwy.
Cupertino, CA 95014
(408) 865-4500

TDIndustries

TDIndustries
An Employee Owned Company

TDIndustries ranks as one of the nation's largest installers of plumbing and air-conditioning systems. Employees: 579.

★ ★ ★   Pay/Benefits
★ ★ ★   Opportunities
★ ★ ★   Job Security
★ ★ ★ ★   Pride in Work/Company
★ ★ ★ ★ ★   Openness/Fairness
★ ★ ★ ★   Camaraderie/Friendliness

BIGGEST PLUS: Employee ownership is cool.
BIGGEST MINUS: Their business has been stopped up.

TD is one of the few companies whose CEO can be voted out of office by the employees. That's because TD is not only an employee-owned company, but employees (called partners here) have the right to vote their shares of stock—a right denied people at many other companies with a large percentage of employee ownership. Employees, former employees, and their spouses own 93 percent of TD's stock, with officers and directors holding slightly more than a quarter of total shares.

No one believes the CEO is about to be kicked out, however. Jack Lowe, Jr., has headed TD since 1980 when his father died. Jack Lowe, Sr., founded the company as Texas Distributors in 1946 to sell air conditioners made by General Electric. The postwar period was a good time to be in the air-conditioning business in Dallas. The summers were hot and tract housing subdivisions were proliferating on the surrounding prairie. Later on, TD jumped into the office-building boom, installing heating, air-conditioning, and plumbing equipment in many big commercial and industrial buildings in the Dallas area. When we visited in 1991, one division, TDMechanical, was designing and installing the air-conditioning and plumbing systems at several large projects, including the Dallas Convention Center and J. C. Penney's new corporate headquarters. TD had its own trailers at the J. C. Penney site, where its design engineers and construction workers were putting in 80 miles of heating and cooling systems. When the Dallas building boom cooled off in the late 1980s, TD branched out to major building projects in other states, although the bulk of their business is still in Texas. They installed plumbing, heating, and air-conditioning in the new Nations-Bank headquarters building in Charlotte, North Carolina. In 1992 their out-of-Texas projects included jobs in Florida (Orlando), Maryland (Baltimore), and California (Orange County).

TD continues to sell and service air-conditioning equipment in single-family houses and multi-unit apartment and condominium complexes. More than 150 TDService vans can be spotted in Dallas–Fort Worth, Houston, and San Marcos, Texas; Norcross, Georgia, and Tulsa. TD also sells air conditioners from their TDI Air Conditioning and Appliances stores in Tyler and Longview, Texas.

Jack Lowe, Sr., was one of the most progressive voices of the Dallas business community. In the mid-1970s he chaired the Dallas Alliance, a community group formed to address civil rights issues, and he authored the plan for desegregation of the Dallas public school system.

Lowe carried his sense of justice into his business. He started a profit-sharing plan during the company's first year, giving 25 percent of the profits to employees. In 1948 he began selling stock to employees. By the time he died, virtually all of the stock was in the hands of the employees, with his wife and two sons (Jack and Bob) owning less than 15 percent.

The elder Lowe also left another important legacy. Several years after founding the company, he ran across an obscure pamphlet entitled "Servant as Leader," written by an AT&T management trainer named Robert Greenleaf. Greenleaf believed managers should serve their employees rather than the other way around, and he became TD's unofficial guru, visiting the company a number of times. Even today, any TD partner who supervises at least one person must go through training in servant leadership at TD's Leadership Institute. Programming manager Jim Bivins explained: "The leadership training I went through boiled down to a couple of concepts. Honesty is way up there and so is treating people right. It's really common sense that you treat people the way you want to be treated. Another is that you do not have to sit there and look over somebody's shoulder to get them to do their job. In fact, you really shouldn't do that. Most people want to do a good job. You give them the freedom to do it and they typically will."

TD partners talk a lot about "freedom." Gary Brackett, a service technician, told us: "Around here you're basically your own boss. I do big jobs for my boss. He sends me out, I go look at the job, I bid on it, and I put it in. Half the time he doesn't even see the job or know what's involved unless I tell him. And as long as it makes money, he doesn't care."

Paul Sterling, who also drives one of the TDService vans, agreed: "In the service department you're out in the field most times by yourself. There's nobody to tell you that you got to fix a problem a certain way. Actually, you're your own boss. Sure we have people to call if we got problems or we can't figure it out, but nobody's really checking up on you to give you a hard time if maybe you didn't fix it the way they wanted you to. You have a lot of freedom here to do it the way you want to."

Once a year each TD worker meets with his or her supervisors for a "One with One" conference. At this meeting, the two negotiate an agreement detailing how the supervisor will evaluate the partner's performance during the year. At another point in the year, every worker evaluates his or her supervisor. The questionnaire opens with the following statement: "Your supervisor is interested in knowing how he/she can be more effective in helping you achieve a satisfactory and rewarding career." After completing the questionnaire the employee sits down with the supervisor and shares the responses so that the supervisor can learn how to serve the employee more effectively.

By visiting the Dallas headquarters you get a sense of how TD turns traditional workplace relationships on their head. At the entrance, a large sign proclaims: "TDIndustries: An Employee Owned Company." Inside the entrance a smaller plaque reads: "This building is dedicated to all Texas Distributors people—and we include our families. It is a symbol of commitment to each other in a partnership of the spirit—1974." (They changed their name to TDIndustries in 1981.)

Off the lobby is an oak-paneled alcove known as the oak room. Its walls are covered with large color photos of every TD partner with five or more years of service. The photos show them at their workstations and are arranged by years of service. In the office area, there are no closed doors. Every partner works in a simple cubicle, including CEO Jack Lowe, Jr.

One conference room at headquarters is the site of the Friday Forums, which have been held since 1946. Three times a month top management holds an open meeting at 7:00 A.M. where business information is shared with all partners who wish to attend. Jim Klander, a former engineering manager, went to his first Friday Forum two days after he was hired. "I was a brand-new employee," he told us, "and I found out about absolutely every dollar that was spent for everything in the company; how much money we made this year and the prospects for the new jobs we were going to get. I was just amazed that I knew anything at all about the company's financial background, because where I came from you never knew what kind of profit the company was expecting to make. I had never been in an atmosphere where you were told what was going on and what was to be expected, and then encouraged to be a part of that."

CEO Jack Lowe, Jr., also meets with smaller groups (15 to 30) to exchange information and discuss ideas at least once a month at breakfast sessions (which actually last until lunch). The supervisor's survey resulted from a suggestion made at a breakfast session. Other breakfast meeting ideas have included the addition of Memorial Day as a holiday, an employee opinion survey, and a community volunteer program.

Partners who work in the field get a lot of information, too. Senior project engineer Denny Amorella explained: "Field personnel in the other companies I was with never had any meetings. They just went to work, they were told what to do, and that was it. They didn't know anything about the company at all. Here everybody has meetings. There's a little griping that we've got too many meetings. Sometimes we overdo it. But overdoing it is better because the majority of the people like getting the information."

If employees don't get the information they're looking for in one of the many meetings, they are free to ask anyone in the company. According to TDMechanical vice-president Harold McDowell: "People have access to the senior leaders of our company. There are no doors and pretty short walls in between most of the spaces, and for those of us that are tall enough to look over them, there are no secrets around here. Everybody knows what's going on."

New partners receive four different orientations to TD—a one-day safety meeting on the first day, a session led by the CEO after 90 days, a benefits orientation after six months, and a full-day workshop, TDOpportunities, after one year.

We heard numerous stories about the opportunities here. Van Johnson, with TD since 1972, told us: "I started out in the field and got hurt, but was able to come into the office and moved right on up into project management." Laura Price started working for TD in 1982 as a customer service clerk. By 1992, as a senior project manager, she was working on the new $7-million Dallas Convention Center. Price said: "It's kind of sink or swim. But I was so eager that I did okay."

Opportunities aside, stock ownership provides a lucrative enough benefit for employees to remain with the company many years. Former general superintendent Mack Sexton left TD in 1990 after 35 years with more than $750,000 in stock. Another retired with more than $1 million. TD gives every retiring employee $100 for every year of service when they retire—payable in cash or merchandise.

TD supervisors share in the profits here through two bonus plans. Project superintendents and foremen who spend less than they bid to finish jobs share in the savings. This bonus has amounted to as much as $50,000. In addition, supervisors (and some nonsupervisory employees) get an annual bonus (up to 20 percent of base pay) based on the profitability of their division. Even with the bonuses, you're not going to get rich quick here. Senior project manager Denny Amorella told us: "People who don't like it here are the ones who come for the quick dollar because they will not find it. The money is in the long term. In the short term, you make less, but in the long term you make more."

TDINDUSTRIES PEOPLE OBJECTIVE

Each and every TD person should feel successful as a person—as a total person—with his co-workers, his family, his friends, his community, his God and with himself. Among other things, this means he must feel growth, must feel individually important—and it requires of him a high order of responsibility and self-discipline. If through oversight, or neglect, or just not caring much, we fail to do what we can to help even one person in this objective, it's really a bad failure. For this concept to be real, it must be total. There must be no one excluded.

Although they've had stock ownership for a long time, employees didn't get to vote their shares until 1976, when top management voluntarily relinquished control. Not only do they have a vote, employees have a voice in decisions via the "Oak Room Council," comprised of employees with more than five years of service (whose photos are on the wall in the headquarters). It meets whenever major issues arise. Several years ago, it rejected Jack Lowe, Jr.'s proposal for a new company logo, and in 1985 it decided the complicated issue of how to buy back shares of stock from retiring partners.

The council's biggest meeting took place in 1989, when the company was suffering from the collapse of the construction industry in Texas. For the first time in its recent history, TD lost money (about $3 million), and the company was faced with serious credit and bonding problems as its main bank, MCorp., had failed. Management came to the council and asked employees to terminate their overfunded pension plan and invest some of their money in a new ESOP plan and put the rest in a new 401(k) savings plan. Most employees agreed to do so, thereby averting a financial crisis. According to Jack Lowe, Jr.'s brother Bob: "Not a lot of places would put their own money into a sinking ship to keep it afloat, and we did that. It was an inspiring moment."

Main employment centers: Texas is home to most TD employees: 414 in Dallas, 47 in Houston, 46 in East Texas, and 26 in Austin/San Antonio.

Headquarters: TDIndustries, Inc.
P.O. Box 819060
Dallas, TX 75381
(214) 888-9500

Tennant

Tennant is the world's largest maker of industrial floor maintenance equipment, including sweepers, scrubbers, and polishers. U.S. employees: 1,200.

★ ★ ★ Pay/Benefits
★ ★ ★ ★ Opportunities
★ ★ ★ ★ Job Security
★ ★ ★ ★ Pride in Work/Company
★ ★ ★ ★ Openness/Fairness
★ ★ ★ ★ Camaraderie/Friendliness

BIGGEST PLUS: You won't get swept under the rug.
BIGGEST MINUS: You may not clean up right away.

This is the company that wrote the book on quality. Literally. In 1987 they published *Quest for Quality: How One Company Put Theory to Work*, reporting on the quality effort they started in 1979—well before it became a corporate fad.

Tennant converted to the quality cause after reports of hydraulic leaks from their floor maintenance machines. About the same time, Toyota announced it was going to make industrial floor maintenance vehicles. Tennant's managers thought if they didn't improve their products quickly, they would soon face the same competitive problem already plaguing American car and electronics manufacturers. Since then Tennant has embraced a variety of quality improvement methods, reduced defects dramatically, and shored up their dominance in the floor maintenance equipment market.

Tennant's devotion to quality is apparent throughout its main plant, adjacent to corporate headquarters in Minneapolis. Aisles have street signs with such names as Zero Defects Avenue, Error Prevention Boulevard, and Quality Street. Posters and banners exhort workers to improve quality, and there are numerous bulletin boards with statistics, bar charts, and graphs showing how well each area is doing.

Visitors are also shown many examples of quality improvement in action, such as the stockroom without a stock clerk. Workers pick up bolts, nuts, and other parts they need from open containers, and outside suppliers refill items without having to wait for the paperwork. The idea of eliminating the stock clerk position and the ancillary red tape (and expenses) came from one of the stock clerks.

Tennant is not a company of mechanical cheerleaders trying to beat the Japanese and other competitors. There is a distinctly human face to its approach, exemplified by huge paintings on the factory walls—of a loon duck, a koala bear, a Minnesota Twins baseball player, a horse and her colt, and two dinosaurs. Frank Smith, the maintenance employee responsible for the paintings, is quoted in Tennant's book as saying: "I've been working in this plant for twenty-five years and it's like a second home. If I paint something on the wall, as far as I'm concerned, it's mine. If you do a job, it belongs to you."

Walking through the company offices, you see other unusual sights. Like the koala teddy bears on desks. More properly known as Koala T. Bears, these are handed out monthly to employees, nominated by their peers, who "consistently meet their job standards and display a positive attitude." An employee committee selects the winners. A committee member, dressed in a bear costume, arrives unannounced at the winner's workstation and presents a stuffed koala bear while other committee members gather around to applaud. The Koala T. Bear Awards supplement an array of formal group and individual awards, which cost Tennant over $100,000 a year.

Another common sight on people's desks is bright yellow stickers with the word "Thataway" written on the top. Michele Dahl, who joined Tennant in 1986, explained: "I've gotten a lot of Thataways. Employees get them from other employees, from managers, from supervisors. It's just simply a little notepad where you can write to say thank you for whatever, like to thank you for doing a fantastic job. Those really mean a lot to me."

While Tennant is generous in recognizing productivity, it is downright stingy with perks associated with status. President and CEO Roger Hale, great-grandson of founder George Tennant, insists that top executives only have two perks: their names printed on letterheads and 15 reserved parking slots, which he thinks are justified because of frequent off-site meetings.

We met with Hale in the spartan company cafeteria, where he regularly eats lunch with employees. Hale said: "I have a total aversion to perks. I feel one of the curses of American executive life is the isolation that occurs. Some pretty high-powered executives don't ever come into contact with a real person, only retainers and sycophants. You drive to work in a chauffeured car and then you come into an isolated parking garage and you go up in a sealed elevator and you are greeted with somebody holding out a piece of beautiful china with coffee in it. And then you fly a corporate jet. You just never, ever talk to people who aren't being paid to make you feel good and important. I think it's a curse."

Employees appreciate Hale's egalitarian attitude. Publications manager Phil Hagberg said: "I think over the years it has made a big difference. There are not a lot of employee comments about what upper management gets or receives."

Another issue Hale feels strongly about is sexual harassment. Tennant developed a model program in 1988 to combat sexual, mental, and physical harassment, which a number of other firms have studied. Hale instituted the policy after discovering that a manager had been harassing a number of women over a period of time. The incident showed him how difficult it was for women to step forward in such cases (instead of reporting the manager, the women had just quit) and how the manager was almost always able to stonewall the charges. When Hale saw the televised Senate hearings on Clarence Thomas's Supreme Court nomination, he ordered a refresher course on the policy.

Tennant has progressive policies on other women's issues. A monthly forum called WINGS (Women Involved in Networking, Growth, and Skill-building) has been supported by the company since it began in the early 1980s. Marliss Sorlien saw a stark difference here, compared with her previous employer, where she worked for 11 years: "In that bakery, they had policies that you had women's jobs and men's jobs, and you couldn't sign for the other jobs. I am the first woman here to work in paint and grinding and probably the first woman that has ever been promoted in that area." She now is a paint supervisor and manages two areas.

One worker in Sorlien's group is disabled, as are 14 percent of Tennant's employees. Sorlien said: "I have a hearing-impaired person who works with me. The company not only tries to find close-captioned videos for section meetings, but they also give sign-language classes that people who work with hearing-impaired people can go to." Sorlien says that she has learned sign language through those classes.

Tennant pays well compared to similar manufacturers in the Twin Cities and provides several unusual benefits, including a profit-sharing program started in 1944 (that pays out up to 5 percent of an employee's annual salary) and a stock-purchase plan (with a 20 percent discount off the stock price). Tennant provides regular benefits to temporary and part-time workers. Tennant also offers several types of leaves of absence—a six-month paid leave (after 10 years and every five years after that), a parental leave (for either parent, covering adopted children as well), and a preretirement leave for up to three months. Compensation and benefits manager Barbara Clarity recalled: "We did have someone [Bill Tim] who rented a motor home and went on a trip to see if that's the way he would like to retire." It was, and he did. John Kuenzel took a sabbatical and went to his cabin and fished for a couple of months, but decided he wasn't ready to retire.

When the Minnesota Twins played in the World Series in 1991, everybody around town was scrambling for tickets. Vice-president and general counsel Janet Dolan tells what happened at Tennant: "I had friends at all the big companies and they were all talking about how, of course, the executives were going to get the World Series tickets. But Tennant did what every employee here expected. They put the tickets in a lottery, and 32 Tennant employees won. [CEO Roger Hale did not win.] What really surprised me was the absolute expectation of the employees of 'Why, what else would you do?' They just had no expectation that it would be handled any other way."

Types of jobs: Manufacturing—35 percent; sales and marketing—30 percent; customer service—15 percent; administration—12 percent; chemistry, engineering, and research—8 percent.

Main employment center: Minneapolis, Minnesota.

Headquarters: Tennant Company
701 North Lilac Dr.
P.O. Box 1452
Minneapolis, MN 55440
(612) 540-1200

COMPANIES WITH VACATION SPOTS FOR EMPLOYEES

First Federal Bank of California
Hewlett-Packard
SC Johnson Wax
Springs
Steelcase

UNUM

UNUM sells group insurance policies to employers and is the largest long-term-disability insurer in the world. Employees: 4,600.

★★ Pay/Benefits
★★★ Opportunities
★★★★★ Job Security
★★★ Pride in Work/Company
★★★★ Openness/Fairness
★★★★ Camaraderie/Friendliness

BIGGEST PLUS: You can get a third of your pay in January.
BIGGEST MINUS: You might be snowed in when you get it.

Guarding the entrance to the Portland harbor on the rock-ribbed coast of Maine is an old lighthouse, the Portland Head Light. Established by George Washington in 1791, it was the first lighthouse authorized by the U.S. government. UNUM, founded in 1848 as the Union Mutual Life Insurance Co., has been using the lighthouse as its corporate symbol for 100 years. A lighthouse strikes just the right note for an insurance company: safety in an uncertain world. That's how they want customers to feel. The people who work for UNUM also feel safe. Many insurance companies have been laying off workers. The Maine economy has been depressed. But UNUM has been on a roll. The premiums it collects from customers who buy its insurance—mostly small and medium-sized companies—spiraled from $1 billion in 1987 to $1.6 billion in 1991, an increase of 60 percent. UNUM employed 3,525 people in 1985. By 1992 it had 4,600 employees, an increase of 30 percent.

UNUM doesn't lay off people even when it shuts down businesses. Their main business is selling group insurance packages to businesses, including long-term disability and life insurance. So most of UNUM's customers are employers, though they do sell disability insurance to individuals (mostly business owners, corporate executives, and professionals). In 1988 they decided to exit the group health insurance field. Over the next two and a half years, as the business was phased out, they implemented an advanced hiring program to give employees in this division a chance to sign up with other departments. By the end of 1991, all 200 employees had been reassigned. Toward the end of 1991, UNUM decided to get out of another business: 401(k) employee savings plans. Some 100 employees were affected. By mid-1992, 78 had been placed in other jobs—and the remaining ones were also expected to be reassigned.

A big benefit of working for UNUM in Maine is Maine. It's a state of rugged beauty, immortalized in the paintings of Winslow Homer, John Marin, and Andrew Wyeth. It has both winter and summer sports, the best lobster in the world—and only 1.2 million people. Some UNUM employees have come here—or returned here—to escape urban blight. Ann Devine is one. She was trading bonds at Merrill Lynch in New York when she decided in 1984 to return to her native state and join UNUM, where she is now director of investment systems (UNUM has about $9 billion invested in bonds, mortgages, stocks). Lois Judge made the same decision. She used to live in Bangor before moving to New York, where she worked for the compensation and benefits consultant, Towers Perrin. In 1985, when she heard about an opening at UNUM, she and her husband fled Manhattan. She helps to market UNUM's bread-and-butter product, group long-term-disability insurance, commuting to the home office in Portland from Cumberland, 25 minutes away. She said she doesn't miss New York at all, "except for the ethnic diversity." Maine is 98.4 percent white. Rosemary Lavoie, who grew up in New York's Rockland County and has a degree in biochemistry, worked as a researcher in the Boston area when she and her husband decided in the late 1970s that they wanted a different quality of life—and so they packed up and moved to Maine, sans job. Thanks to a strong math background, Lavoie was hired by UNUM in 1979, started working in the actuarial department ("I had no idea what I was doing"), and eventually moved to marketing, where she now designs compensation and incentive programs for the field force.

Ed Hellenbeck, who heads up market program development, was born in Brooklyn and joined UNUM in 1973 after working for Mutual of Omaha. He reported that he has had 17 different jobs at UNUM. Hellenbeck's wife, Anne Dinsmore, also works at UNUM, in the disability benefits area. Husband and wife teams are common at UNUM. Beth Greenwood, an eight-year employee, works as a cost analyst in corporate finance while her husband, Keith, works in marketing systems. Tom Gilligan, an ex-IBMer who told us that in 12 years he had 10 different jobs, was about to be transferred to the Denver field office. Gilligan had been doing recruiting for UNUM. Asked what kind of people he looked for, he said: "Hard chargers, not geniuses." Gilligan's wife, Anne, had been working for UNUM in Portland, but in Denver she reverted to a full-time homemaker. The Gilligans have three children.

Of course there are downeasters here, too. Kathi Breton grew up in Lewiston and joined UNUM right after high school in 1976. She began as a clerk typist and is now a legal secretary. Despite all the paperwork, she calls UNUM "a great place to work." Five years after she started here, her husband, Scott, who had been working in a small office supply company, also joined UNUM; he's a purchasing agent. Dick and Priscilla Badgley were another UNUM couple. They came up to Maine to retire. Priscilla signed on with UNUM in 1980 as a benefits specialist ("No one here has ever made me feel old," she said), and Dick came aboard in 1983, working in technical support.

Both Badgleys went out for the UNUM track team—she ran and he threw the shot put and discus—and Dick retired from UNUM in the summer of 1992, at age 62, after participating in the national corporate track and field championships at Santa Barbara, California. He was happy to take advantage of a special UNUM benefit: he received half pay for 20 weeks to help him adjust to retirement.

Being part of the UNUM track team is nothing to sneer at. Organized in 1985 as part of a Wellpower program, the team has put UNUM on the map. Some 60 employees turn out every year to train and compete for UNUM in regional and national meets. Their efforts culminated in 1990 when a sprint relay team made up of Sam Kane (corporate accounting), Valerie Langmaid (facility planning), Scott Davidson (long-term disability benefits), Malcolm Harris (corporate information services), and Andrew Whittaker (group customer service) finished first with a time of 3:32.6 to give UNUM the national title in its division (companies with fewer than 10,000 employees) at the U.S. Corporate Athletic Association's meet in Boulder, Colorado. UNUM became a two-time national winner in 1991.

The victories must have pleased James F. Orr III, the CEO of UNUM, who was a sub-four-minute miler at Villanova University in the 1960s. Orr, trim, low-key, and disciplined, gets credit—on Wall Street, in financial publications, and from the people who work at UNUM—for the company's spectacular performance during the last half of the 1980s and early 1990s. He has a Wall Street background, came to UNUM in 1986 from Connecticut Bank & Trust, and became CEO in September 1987. It was his task to usher in a new era for UNUM as a stockholder-owned company. Union Mutual Life Insurance Co. was converted from a mutual company, where policyholders are the owners, to a stock company in 1986. That was the year the UNUM name came into use, and the company's shares were listed on the New York Stock Exchange.

Orr has succeeded in energizing UNUM. This is now a gung-ho place where people work very hard and are focused on the goals of the company. In 1988 UNUM adopted a "Vision and Values" statement that served as a rallying cry for such principles as "acting with integrity," "treating each other as we would like to be treated," "building long-term relationships with our customers," and "building an environment which encourages open communication, participation, honesty and candor." Orr set the tone at the top, meeting frequently with employees to get them to buy into this mission statement. We watched him one afternoon sit for two hours at a rectangular table in UNUM's training center and patiently answer questions put to him by two dozen managers. If anything, he was more critical than the employees clustered around him, saying the company wasn't doing enough to develop people. "We're doing a lousy job of empowerment," he said.

Insurance companies have always been long on award programs—and UNUM has its share of them: Employee of the Month, Rookie of the Year, Gold Medalist, Million Dollar Club, to name just four. But the conversion to a stock company enabled UNUM to implement incentive plans that tie people directly to the fortunes—or misfortunes—of UNUM. Employees, especially those in the upper ranks, have an abiding interest in the earnings-per-share figure posted after the year is over because annual bonuses are skewed to those results. Most employees participate in a "success-sharing plan" that has in recent years supplemented salary from 5 to 14 percent because UNUM has consistently exceeded its earnings target. Officers and other managers participate in an Annual Incentive Award where the payouts are much bigger—as much as 40 percent can be added to their salaries. In 1992 the management crew pocketed $8 million in bonus payments while the peons collected a total of $10 million. UNUM pays above-average salaries, especially for Maine. In 1992 clerks were starting at $15,000 to $17,000 a year, professionals (programmers, management trainees) $27,500. And the company has rich benefits, including long-term-care insurance (one of its products) and a 401(k) savings plan in which every pretax dollar you save up to 4 percent of pay is matched, dollar for dollar, by UNUM. Jim Orr's pay in 1991 was $1 million, 66 times what he pays entry-level clerks.

A new award program introduced by Orr in 1989—the Chairman's Award—gets a lot of attention at UNUM. Designed to recognize people whose efforts and accomplishments "have gone beyond the ordinary," it goes to five to 10 employees each year—all below the rank of senior vice-president. Anyone can nominate a candidate in a one-page memo. A team of employees narrows the field to about 25—and Jim Orr then selects the winners. There were eight winners in 1991, four men and four women, ranging in rank from a graphic arts specialist to department heads. Each award winner receives $5,000 in UNUM stock, a $2,500 travel certificate, a

Mont Blanc pen and pencil set, and a Portland Head Light lithograph. On top of that, they and their guests are honored at a banquet hosted by Orr, the board of directors, senior management, and their immediate supervisors.

UNUM has one other unusual benefit, although some people consider it a mixed blessing. In January, if you so choose, you can elect to take 30 percent of your salary for the coming year in one lump sum. Merchants in Portland, where UNUM is a major employer, do what they can to snare this bonanza. And how many employees opt to do this? Two out of every three. In 1991 UNUM anted up $16.8 million for this payment.

UNUM was a caring employer in the pre-Orr days before it went onto the New York Stock Exchange. In 1979 it opened an on-site child-care center—the first in Maine and one of the first in New England. Rosemary Lavoie, who had two children in the center in 1992 (plus another who has graduated), calls it, understandably, "the best benefit." Every morning when she leaves her home in Kennebunk, she packs her two children—a three-and-a-half-year-old and an eight-monther—in the car, drives the 25 minutes to UNUM, drops her kids off at the center, and doesn't see them until the end of the day. In 1992, 68 children of employees were being cared for in the low-slung brick building behind UNUM's home office in South Portland. Rates at the center, which is operated by an outside provider, range from $92 (preschoolers) to $135 (infants) a week, but UNUM subsidizes the cost for parents making under $35,000 a year. The maximum subsidy is $40 a week. This subsidy is also available to parents using an off-site provider.

UNUM was one of the first insurance companies in the nation, in 1985, to ban smoking in all its buildings. That marked the start of a Wellpower program that culminated in 1990 with the opening of a 10,000-square-foot fitness center, which has three full-time employees and one part-timer to oversee a wide variety of programs, including 32 aerobics classes a week, five-minute stretch breaks conducted in office areas, intramural sports such as volleyball, softball, basketball, and bowling, individualized exercise regimens, and, of course, the track team. (Parents who come out for track can bring their kids—there's a baby-sitting service.) The center's monthly fee is $17, and more than 750 UNUM people use it. To encourage participation, Wellpower reimburses employees half of the membership fee if they attend 85 percent of any class or program.

Types of jobs: Insurance operations—43 percent; sales and marketing—24 percent; administration—21 percent; customer service—12 percent.

Main employment centers: About 3,300 employees work at the home office in Portland, Maine. The other 1,300 work in sales offices throughout the United States.

Headquarters: UNUM Corporation
2211 Congress St.
Portland, ME 04122
(207) 770-2211

USAA

USAA

USAA is the fifth largest auto insurer and the sixth largest home insurer in the nation, selling only to current and former military officers. U.S. employees: 14,840.

★★★★ Pay/Benefits
★★★★★ Opportunities
★★★★★ Job Security
★★★★ Pride in Work/Company
★★★★ Openness/Fairness
★★★★★ Camaraderie/Friendliness

BIGGEST PLUS: A big place with a small feel.
BIGGEST MINUS: Only ex-generals make it to the top.

Many people know that the Pentagon is the largest government office building in the world. But would you have guessed that the largest private office building is USAA's headquarters in San Antonio, Texas? Even though USAA is one of the largest auto and home insurers in the country, it is relatively unknown. But if you work at the Pentagon, there is a good chance you've heard of USAA, since more than 95 percent of all military officers have USAA policies. USAA sells insurance only to military officers, both those on active duty and retirees. The company was started in 1922 by Major William H. Garrison, a West Point graduate, and 25 army officers because of problems in getting their personal cars insured as they moved from one military post to another.

Working for USAA, however, has little in common with working for the military, even though all the CEOs in its 70-year history have been retired military officers—as are most of the current top executives. There's an open and friendly feel to USAA that permeates its massive headquarters (5 million square feet, one-third of a mile in length), where more than 9,000 employees work. Special projects director Donna Wildey, who came to USAA from Arthur Young, a Big Six accounting firm, said she experienced "culture shock" from the size of the place and the way she was treated. She described Arthur Young as a "machine" where "there was very little focus on the individual and very little support for the employee. They use people as long as they can, then they get new people in." But at USAA, she said, "they keep telling me that I'm important in various ways—through benefits and all the different kinds of communications. And my boss is just there all the time. For a place this size, it's remarkable to me that you feel like you're part of a family."

It's quite a large family, of course. But USAA's massive headquarters (which has its own zip code) has all the comforts of home—and then some. With numerous lounge areas and plenty of windows, the interior has a light, airy feeling. The building has won numerous architectural awards and blends into a hilly 286-acre site 12 miles northwest of downtown San Antonio. Many employees think that the facility is the biggest plus about the company. For starters, there are five employee cafeterias, one with white tablecloths and waiter or waitress service and others with three-story windows and views of the city. Employees can order dinners and home-made pies to take home or shop the company store, which is the size of a small supermarket. Within the complex are two walk-in medical clinics with a staff of a dozen nurses. And then there are two physical fitness centers (with exercise equipment, whirlpool baths, saunas, and steam rooms). Employees who use the fitness centers are provided with clothing —a light blue shirt and dark blue shorts.

After business hours USAA's campus turns into a sports paradise, as 2,500 USAA employees play in at least one intramural sport. USAA's outdoor facilities include a five-mile walking/jogging trail and Parcourse, a golf driving range, softball field, soccer field, two outdoor basketball courts, six tennis courts—most of which are lit for evening playing. The fields are in terrific shape, according to Mary Migl, an account analyst in the life sales department: "My husband is a baseball coach at the university, and he says that we have the best baseball field this side of Texas." There are also a number of picnic pavilions and children's playgrounds for use by employee groups or their families on weekends or evenings. There's even a fishing lake.

USAA's concern about a good work environment extends to employees' workstations as well. Service representative Mary Jane Garza said: "That's one of the things that amazes me the most—they want the work area to be as comfortable as possible for you. To give you an example, last year my area tested out chairs. We went through about ten different chairs before they decided on one of them."

USAA wasn't always a great place to work. When Robert McDermott, a retired Air Force brigadier general, took over as CEO in 1968, the company had a 42 percent a year turnover rate (worse than average for the insurance industry), and the average employee stayed with the company a little over 11 months. Today turnover is in the 6 percent range, and a very high percentage of the employees see themselves making a career here. McDermott (called "Mac D" by employees) set out to change the environment with what he calls a "high-tech, high-touch" strategy. By making large investments in computers and telecommunications, McDermott told us he wanted USAA to be "more efficient and also more convenient for the customer to do business."

At the same time, McDermott realized that "it's useless if you don't train people and motivate them to use the technological advances to serve the customer better." He initiated seminars "so people in the company would not feel that they were merely like workers on an assembly line, to let people know they were part of a very intricate pattern of delivering good service to customers." He then made efforts to broaden people's jobs. When he started, each auto insurance application went through 55 separate steps—one person would spend all day opening envelopes, another stapling pieces of paper, still another removing staples, and so on.

Broadening jobs so people would do a variety of tasks required training, lots and lots of training. McDermott explains his philosophy in scriptural terms: "The Golden Rule can only be lived if in fact you first love yourself and then love your neighbor. Love yourself means discover yourself, develop your talents, and so on. So our job in management or in any supervisory role is to help others discover themselves and develop themselves." Today, you can see posters on walls with USAA's "Two Golden Rules." They are: "1. Treat each and every person the way you would like to be treated. 2. Treat each and every employee the way USAA expects [you] to treat the member [customer]."

Training is still one of the hallmarks of life here. In 1990 USAA employed 159 full-time trainers and spent nearly $19 million on career training. (The $19 million represents 2.7 percent of their sales and is nearly double the industry average spent on training, according to *Fortune*.) Evelyn Wilhelm, an auto claims manager, was studying for certification as an insurance underwriter (CPCU). Not only was the company paying for her courses, she said, but "once I complete it, I'll get my bonus [of $1,750]. Then I'll also get a one-week paid vacation for myself and my spouse." The week's vacation is to the site of the convention where the CPCU certificates are awarded. One year the convention was held in Hawaii.

Training is not restricted to insurance-related courses. USAA also puts a lot of money—over $1.35 million a year—into tuition reimbursement so employees can get degrees. Some 1,800 employees are enrolled in one of the 110 college courses sponsored by six area colleges, held in classrooms at USAA's headquarters.

USAA puts so much emphasis on training and education because it expects to promote people from within. Jai Jeter, who works in the accounts payable department, explained: "Right now I'm going for my accounting degree. I know beyond a doubt that once I get my degree, the ladder is open for me. I feel the sky is the limit here. The only person who will stop me will be me. If that means I have to get more education, that's up to me to decide."

Promotions are common at USAA. According to McDermott, about 45 percent are promoted every year, and half change jobs. Much of this movement comes through USAA's ubiquitous job posting system. Job openings are posted on bulletin boards located throughout the headquarters, and employees can complete applications and put them in collection boxes. Women have done well at USAA, holding 43 percent of the managerial positions.

The company is also flexible about working hours. Most of the office staff works nine and a half hours, four days a week. Mary Migl said: "To me, that's probably the greatest benefit because I have 52 Fridays a year off. I can do all my errands and running around on my day off instead of Saturday and Sunday."

The company is less flexible when it comes to dress. USAA's dress code prohibits jeans, shorts, and sandals in the building. The prohibition extends to weekends. But USAA seems to be very accommodating about personal problems. According to health underwriter Joe Hubb: "There is an atmosphere here that people care. There is concern. It is sort of a family atmosphere. If there is sickness, illness, or death in the family, people go the extra mile to get in touch with you to find out what they can do to assist. USAA as a whole does something, too, when people have tragedies, like someone who recently had their house burn down. USAA contributed clothing, food, money."

USAA has never resorted to layoffs. That does not mean jobs haven't been eliminated. According to McDermott: "I took out 800 to 900 jobs the first year, but that was all right because people hated working here anyway. With the huge attrition rate we had at the time, I didn't actually have to lay anybody off. The jobs were enriched. The people that stayed in the company were happy." Since that time, USAA has been changing almost continuously. Units are dissolved, business lines are started or eliminated, but the company helps the affected employees to find new positions in other areas.

The personnel department has a staff of a dozen or so counselors who can help employees find new positions. These counselors perform other important functions as well. The counseling program was started in 1978 to facilitate communication. According to human resources vice-president Bill Tracey, the program was put in place after they had "some rumblings of union activity here. For a company as paternalistic as we were back then and probably still are, it really hurt that any employee would feel that we weren't putting their best interest first." Although the union effort was "relatively insignificant," he says the management went through "a lot of soul-searching" to see if they were doing a good job of "listening to employees." He says that they discovered that "employees did not have good ways to vent and come forward with their ideas—to be heard outside the normal chain of command. So if you weren't getting along with your supervisor, you couldn't just go to your supervisor for help." So one of the major functions of the counselors is to provide a vehicle to mediate supervisor-employee disputes.

Employees have other ways to vent their frustrations. The company has an ombudsman who will investigate any complaint brought forward and bring it to the attention of General McDermott if it appears warranted. And there's a "Speak Out" program, with forms located throughout the facility, that employees use to voice complaints of any sort about policies. Answers to some questions are published in a company newsletter.

David Lindley, an applications systems manager, summed up why he likes working at USAA. He worked here for three years after graduating from college, then went to Columbia University's business school to get an M.B.A. After earning his degree, Lindley says, "I probably interviewed with 30 or 40 companies and the more of them that I researched and interviewed with, I realized that I started out at the best place all along. I got four or five offers for a lot more money with companies up in the Northeast, but there were just so many great things at USAA that I decided to return."

Lindley has been very happy with his decision: "Soon after I came back, I met my wife here at one of the company events."

Types of jobs: Claims—31 percent; sales and service—25 percent; information services—12 percent; facilities—8 percent; accounting—7 percent; human resources—4 percent; underwriting—3 percent; miscellaneous—10 percent.

Main employment centers: 9,500 employees are located at the main office in San Antonio. Another 1,223 are in Tampa, Florida; 1,106 in Sacramento, California; 588 in Colorado Springs, Colorado; 568 in Norfolk, Virginia; 385

in Tulsa, Oklahoma; 360 in Reston, Virginia; and 179 in Seattle, Washington.

Headquarters: United Services Automobile Association
USAA Building
San Antonio, TX 78288
(800) 531-8100

U S West

USWEST®

U S West is a communications company whose main arm provides telephone service to more than 25 million residential and business customers in 14 western and midwestern states. Employees: 65,000.

★ ★ ★ Pay/Benefits
★ ★ ★ Opportunities
★ ★ Job Security
★ ★ ★ Pride in Work/Company
★ ★ ★ ★ Openness/Fairness
★ ★ ★ Camaraderie/Friendliness

BIGGEST PLUS: You can speak your mind.
BIGGEST MINUS: They may disconnect you.

Created in 1984 by the breakup of American Telephone & Telegraph, U S West is the best of the seven so-called Baby Bells, from the standpoint of providing a workplace where people don't get mangled in the telephone wires.

U S West is the new name for companies that used to operate under the names Mountain Bell, Northwestern Bell, and Pacific Northwest Bell. By the measures of revenues and employees, it ranks fifth among the Baby

Bells, but its territory is the largest, stretching from Canada to Mexico and from the Pacific Ocean to Minnesota. And of all the Baby Bells, U S West has been, from the start, the most aggressive in cutting its ties to Ma Bell, even to the point of risking confusion in the marketplace by expunging "Bell" from all the names that it uses. The late William McGowan, founder of MCI and an expert on AT&T culture, once said that all the Baby Bells retained their pre-divestiture mentality "except for U S West."

The transition has not been easy, and we sensed a tension in the employee ranks when we visited in 1991. There were certainly strong testimonials to the new environment. Becky Longest, a customer service representative for U S West Direct, publisher of the white and yellow pages in the company's 14-state territory, said: "I think the company is more focused on employees now. They seem very concerned about helping their employees grow and setting goals and getting to where they want to go, whereas several years ago, there was management and then there was everybody else." And Linda Tate, another customer service rep, added: "The difference is like night and day. It's not so restricted. You're free to do more. You're able to take more risk. You can make your own decisions."

But other employees had mixed feelings about the changes, much of it revolving around the issue of job security. Like the other regional phone companies, U S West has been in a downsizing mode since it became an independent company. From 70,000 employees in the mid-1980s, it slimmed down to 65,000 by 1992. Since they were also hiring during those years, this means that many more than 5,000 people exited the company. It was traumatic for longtime Ma Bell people, who had grown up in a company where employees were assured of a job until retirement. Bill Nelson, a manager who retired in the spring of 1992 after 29 years of service, told us six months earlier that despite all the talk about open communication, he believes some people are afraid to speak up for fear that they might lose their jobs in the next cutback. "I'm sure it's something that will go away when people get more comfortable," he said, "but right now it is there." Shari Revier, an engineering specialist, agreed with him, reporting that older people still talk about the security they used to have with Ma Bell. Now, she said, "employees feel a little insecure." But she quickly added that she recognizes the company had to change to become more competitive, and that today she believes "they are utilizing employees more to their fullest potential, whereas before you could get stuck someplace for a long time."

There's no question that the divorce from AT&T was painful to many longtime employees. Jo Pigg, a clerk whose service with the company began in 1949 (she worked for seven years, left to raise a family, and returned in 1979), said: "I cried the day they changed the name." And Phil Henry, manager of Denver field operations, who started with Mountain Bell as a lineman in Phoenix in 1968, said: "On December 31st, 1983, it was sort of emotional. I was terribly upset. But since then, I have to admit, this has been better, a more enjoyable company to work for. As a manager, we've had more ability to make decisions, run our own operations, and take some risks."

Richard McCormick, who became CEO at the start of 1991, talked to us about the downsizing: "We've tried everything imaginable: voluntary early retirements, relocation, attrition—and there's probably more coming in the future. I don't know the answer. We've instituted procedures—transfers, enhanced leaves, training in other skills. We've tried every idea. And we're communicating, meeting with the CWA [Communications Workers of America], meeting with employees. We have done it in a humane fashion, treating people the way we would like to be treated. And my sense is that we have been more caring than other companies, particularly the other phone companies."

We talked with McCormick in late 1991, and he reported that the previous week he did "a Phil Donahue-type show" in the Seattle Civic Auditorium attended by 1,000 employees at which he sat in the middle, answering questions. He told us that he had recently conducted similar "general unstructured meetings" attended by 200 in Colorado, 200 in Denver, 300 in New Mexico, and 400 in Nebraska. According to McCormick, each group voiced different concerns: "Seattle is worried about lack of resources, New Mexico worried about pluralism, Omaha worried about loss of jobs to Denver." A 30-year veteran of the phone wars, McCormick said: "I think I have a good radar screen for the pain resulting from a changing culture." The U S West CEO told us about a lunch he had with a nonmanager engineer in a Denver shop who complained about the company moving too quickly and not communicating. "He was dead right," said McCormick. "His supervisor had never met with his group. There's no reason why every director [those supervising 300 to 400 people] can't get before his people two or three times a year."

U S West's determination to be a good communicator has resulted in unusually frank discussions of downsizing in the company's twice-a-month newspaper, U S West Today. One issue in early 1992 focused on people who had been forced to leave the company. Betty Zube, who had worked for U S West Financial Services, said she was still angry, 18 months later, at how she was told that her job was being phased out: by a letter in her mailbox. She has since found another job but she told the U S West Today reporter, Angela Brooks, that she would probably be willing to work for U S West again because "it's a good company with good employees." And then she had this piece of advice: "The company, though, needs to be more in tune with employees than the bottom line, because employees *are* the bottom line."

Other recent issues of this paper carried letters to the editor with harsh criticisms of the company, illustrating how U S West has fostered an independence of spirit that feeds on information and encourages people to speak up. A letter from John Hutchins of U S West Communications in Seattle declared that the company, while successful financially, "is emotionally unwell" and "it's time we got rid of the middle-management M.B.A.'s and business school whiz kids who've brought our company to this state." And we saw another issue in which a letter writer criticized Tom Bouchard, U S West's new human resources director, for talking in one breath about the need "to do away with the sense of entitlement that's crept into this company" but saying in the next breath, when he was questioned about the high pay drawn by top U S West executives, that "I'm satisfied our executives are paid competitively, according to industry data." Eli Walls, from Salem, Oregon, said Bouchard seemed to forget about the need to offer higher pay "at *all* levels of the business to attract and retain the best people."

You will, however, find little criticism of the company on diversity issues. Workshops on racism and sexism have been conducted throughout the company, and the words have been backed by some muscle. Even suppliers find out quickly that U S West's tolerance for racist or sexist jokes is zero. The company fired its advertising agency, Fallon McElligott Rice of Minneapolis, for responding to criticism of its ads as being too macho with comments and illustrations that the agency thought were funny but that the people at U S West found smacked of racism and sexism. Minorities (more than half are Hispanic) make up 15 percent of the employee population—and they hold 13 percent of managerial and 11 percent of executive jobs. Fifty-five percent of U S West employees are female, and they are well represented in management—49 percent of all managers and 29 percent of executives. Darlene Siedschlaw, who began working for Mountain Bell as a part-time operator in Wolf Point, Montana, in 1951, heads up this pluralism effort at U S West, and she told us that the company's attitude toward the "glass ceiling" that keeps women from penetrating the upper levels is: "We are going to take down that sucker, pane by pane." U S West has more high-ranking women than any of the other Baby Bells. At the start of 1992, for example, if you took the 650 highest-paid people in the company (the top 1 percent), 22 percent were women.

Seven different employee support groups function at U S West with official blessings from the company. They are: U S West SOMOS (for Hispanics); PAAN (Pacific Asian Network); Voice of Many Feathers (for Native Americans); EAGLE (Employee Association of Gays and Lesbians); U S West Black Alliance; U S West Veterans; and FRIENDS (for people with disabilities). While visiting the company in Denver, we lunched with representatives from three of these groups—Terrie Miyamoto (PAAN), Bill Houston (EAGLE), and Eileen Masquat (Voice of Many Feathers)—and they all praised the company for being sensitive to their needs. American Indians make up only 2 percent of the U.S. population but they are concentrated in the 14 states served by U S West, where there are 134 different tribes. In 1991 U S West came through with the largest commitment ever made by a company to the two-year community colleges that have been set up in remote American Indian villages: $2 million to 19 schools. U S West has also started to recruit at these colleges. Twelve American Indian interns were working at the company in the summer of 1992. Of the 65,000 employees at U S West, 630 are American Indians. Bill Houston of EAGLE told us that gays and lesbians at U S West now have a clear channel to management to present their concerns and demands. They have recently been pressing the company to become the largest firm in the nation to extend benefits to partners of gay employees. And what other company in the United States has had gay and lesbian employees meet regularly in a conference to network and map out an agenda? This happened at U S West in 1989, 1990, 1991, and 1992.

One of the unique initiatives at U S West is a Women of Color Accelerated Development Program. It was launched in 1988 to provide mentors and career plans for nonwhite women, who have historically occupied the very lowest rungs in the company. The impetus came from a group of Hispanic women who presented figures that showed, according to McCormick, that women of color "had a better chance of winning the jackpot from Publisher's Clearinghouse" than reaching the middle management ranks at U S West. Of the 50 women enrolled in the first class, 30 moved up at least one level within two years and 13 percent moved up two or more levels.

Phil Henry, one of the managers we interviewed, has been in and out of a number of the Bell companies, and he said that "as a white male, I have to admit that in the very beginning, I felt a little threatened. But as it's progressed in my own organization, which in the old network used to be totally white males, we've made some big strides. We have a mix of males and females and different minority groups, as well as college hires—people that are on the fast-track management program mixed with people that have come up through the company as well. They seem to all learn from each other. We have a team that works well together, with all those different backgrounds, education, work experience, gender, race. . . . Oh, another thing, we're allowed to do such things like last year I took an entire management team of 17 for three days to Colorado's Outward Bound. Now we're doing team building with other groups. Even though that was a little risky because I was spending a lot of money, we're still allowed to do things like that."

Types of jobs: Telecommunications—83 percent; directory publishing—6 percent; headquarters-financial services-international—7 percent; cellular-paging—4 percent.

Main employment centers: U S West serves 14 western and midwestern states, with the biggest concentrations of employees in Colorado (16,250), Washington (10,459), and Minnesota (7,120), and the smallest in Wyoming (735) and South Dakota (810).

Headquarters: U S West, Inc.
7800 East Orchard Rd.
Englewood, CO 80111
(303) 793-6500

Valassis
Communications

Valassis Communications is the largest printer of cents-off coupon inserts distributed with Sunday newspapers. Employees: 1,170.

★★★ Pay/Benefits
★★★★ Opportunities
★★★★ Job Security
★★★ Pride in Work/Company
★★★★ Openness/Fairness
★★★ Camaraderie/Friendliness

BIGGEST PLUS: You can redeem your mistakes.
BIGGEST MINUS: People throw away your work.

Next time you open the Sunday newspaper and an insert full of coupons falls out, this is the company you can blame. Valassis Inserts created the newspaper coupon insert business. And they remain the biggest single company in the field, delivering coupons to 53 million households in 360 Sunday newspapers.

On one level, Valassis is a conventional entrepreneurial success story. George Valassis was looking for a way to keep his new printing press busy when he first heard of the idea of coupon inserts in 1972. A natural salesman, Valassis found some big advertisers—General Mills, Procter & Gamble, General Foods—who saw the potential. (Valassis sells space to the advertisers and then buys the right to run inserts from the newspapers.) Although he lost money for a few years, Valassis turned a profit in 1976 and grew at rates in excess of 40 percent per year for the next 10 years, adding dozens and then hundreds of new employees a year. Valassis is no longer a small company. By the early 1990s, it had annual sales of $600 million, three huge printing plants, and more than a dozen sales offices across the country. In 1992 Valassis became a publicly held company, selling half of its stock to outsiders. The other half is owned by Australian media magnate Kerry Packer, who acquired Valassis in 1986.

Valassis has made a concerted effort to keep a small-company atmosphere. Much of the credit goes to Dave Brandon, who joined George Valassis's young enterprise in 1979. Brandon was lured here from his marketing job at Procter & Gamble by Larry Johnson, George Valassis's son-in-law. Johnson and Brandon had played football together at the University of Michigan.

Brandon, who turned 40 in 1992, was determined to avoid the pitfalls of working for a big corporation. "I think Procter is a great company. They were terrific to me and they are wonderful. But there were some things about being a part of a multinational, multibillion-dollar, bureaucratic, political machine that just made me believe that I'm going to be too old before I can really get to the point of making a difference. I wanted to go someplace where I can make that difference quicker." Brandon vowed to make sure other Valassis employees would have the sense that they, too, could make an impact. He explained: "We have worked really hard to stay a small company even though we're getting bigger and bigger all the time."

Valassis employees say Brandon has succeeded. We interviewed them at the corporate offices and printing plant in Livonia, a Detroit suburb. Leslie Christian, who evaluates client orders, said: "No matter what level you're at, you cannot help but feel that what you do matters. When I was a secretary, I felt like I impacted the bottom line of the company. And that is so important to me. When I moved to the next level, order processing, I worked my butt off, but I felt like what I did impacted the company. Now I have a position of more responsibility and I know I impact the company, but it's at this awesome level. They give you this responsibility, they trust you."

Greg Rivers, account service supervisor, echoed these sentiments: "I had been here less than six months when they sent me to visit a subcontracted printer. I was responsible for the printing of a couple of million pieces, making sure the codes are right, values are right, colors are right. It was a little scary at the time, but the trust and confidence that they showed in me helped me personally. Now that I'm a supervisor it helps me to remember that those things really do make a difference to the people who are working for me."

One of the central institutions at Valassis is a once-a-year Make It Happen Day for salaried employees. After a brief slide-show presentation of corporate goals for the year, employees break into smaller groups to discuss their divisional and departmental goals. Then each person sits down and writes his or her own individual goals for the year. A pressman could set a goal to learn another function in another department, such as the plate room. He might spend 40 hours during the year training in that area.

When we visited, the theme for the year was training, and we saw posters of trains on walls throughout the company. Whenever an employee completed his or her training objectives, a car with his or her name on it was added to the train. Employees tried to avoid being the caboose in their departments. In addition to the recognition, those who reached their goals —nearly all of the 452 participants in 1991—receive a gift such as a $75 dinner certificate.

Company president Brandon said that soon after he came up with the idea of Make It Happen Day, he ran across this quote: "The great frontier today is the exploration of the human potential, man's seemingly limitless ability to adapt, to grow, to invent his own destiny. There is much to learn, but we already know this: the future need not happen to us, we can make it happen." Brandon explained: "I read that quote and I thought, 'God, that's us and that's what objective-setting is all about, making things happen as opposed to waiting for things to happen or hoping things will happen.'"

Banners with the quote went up everywhere. Brandon then passed through the company with "a fistful of $10 bills" and gave one to anyone who could recite the quote from memory. He claims the employees passed with a 99 percent success rate, including a woman who stood up on her desk and recited the quote backward. She got $20.

Since its founding, Valassis has made a point of sharing profits with employees. The vehicles today are a deferred profit-sharing plan that can kick in as much as 15 percent of pay every year and a bonus program keyed to both company and individual performance. Employees who get top ratings from their supervisors can get a bonus equal to 20 percent of their annual salary. In 1991 this payout to employees totaled $5.3 million. While bonuses are paid to all employees, the incentive programs for salaried people are richer. Nearly 60 percent of Valassis's employees are hourly workers. According to Lynn Bandy, manager of corporate benefits and human resources, the bonus is given in one lump sum: "Typically, the division VP, the division director, and the employee's direct supervisor sit down with that individual and discuss what they achieved over the year as a department and as an employee in that department and then the actual check itself is presented to the employee."

Valassis has certainly showered coupons—and not the penny-ante kind—on its owner, Kerry Packer, and its top executives. Packer has already netted a profit of more than $900 million from his 1986 purchase of the company. Brandon and his old college pal, Larry Johnson, each received a bonus of $8.2 million in 1990. In 1991 another $8-million bonus went to Brandon and other top officers, with the stipulation that Brandon receive no more than 50 percent of it. Brandon now has an employment contract that guarantees him a base salary of $1.1 million a year, to be supplemented by bonuses that could reach $2.5 million a year. Four other top officers each have base salaries of $250,000 a year, with bonus possibilities of 100 percent in each year through 1994. Larry Johnson retired from the company in 1991.

But Debbie Farhat, a forms specialist, appreciates the profit-sharing dollars that trickle down to her. She told us: "The company I worked for before made lots of money, but they never shared it with the employees. At Valassis, everyone shares in the profits."

Profit sharing aside, employees insist that the personalized attention they receive keeps the small-company feel. As CEO Brandon puts it: "There are traditions that we have here that we just won't let go of." Brandon still sends employees a little personal note on the anniversary date of being hired to thank them for their work. Since he sends them to hundreds of employees a year, he says it takes him a lot of time just to dictate them.

Brandon makes an effort to personalize these messages. Joe George, an insert publishing supervisor, told us: "A friend and I started on the same day, so we have the same anniversary. And so when we got our anniversary letters, we thought we would be sneaky and compare them. So we sat down and discovered that they were completely different letters, totally specified to who we were, what he had heard about us, and what we were doing. And there was not a sentence that was the same. That is a thing that you know is genuine. You know that he took the time to sit down and write it specifically for me. He does that all year long."

The company has also maintained a tradition of top managers giving everyone a Christmas basket full of a variety of goodies. In 1991 they gave a large white picnic basket with such items as a set of four holiday mugs, a tin of cocoa, a 14-karat-gold-plated Christmas ornament, and a tin filled with chocolate-covered pretzels—a retail value of $125. They don't just restrict such gifts to employees. Mike Happy, a head press operator, says: "If someone is interviewing with the company and they're being interviewed over the Christmas period, as a courtesy they send them a Christmas basket saying, 'Thank you for interviewing with us. This is something we give to our employees. You're not with our company yet, but happy holidays.' "

Another small touch is the welcoming note. Paula Wygonik, who works in marketing, research, and development, said: "The first time I came to the company, I went to my desk and I looked and there was all this mail for me and I thought, 'I don't work here yet, what is all this mail?' " She discovered that a memo had been sent introducing her to everyone in the company. Many employees then wrote a short note on the memo and sent it back to her to express their welcome. "So people were writing me memos and sending them to me from California, New York, Livonia, even the president of the company sent me one. I'm still meeting people and I think, 'I got a letter from you.' On your first day on the job, you're so nervous and you feel uncomfortable, and it just really makes a difference and makes you feel comfortable."

The sense of appreciation doesn't just come from top management. Mary Smith, customer service representative, says her manager came into work one day "with a handful of long-stem roses and a poem that she had done herself rolled up in red paper with a ribbon and just passed one rose and this poem of appreciation to every person. It was not a special day, but it was so nice. It just gives you this nice warm feeling that you are appreciated."

Types of jobs: Manufacturing—60 percent; sales and marketing—22 percent; administration—10 percent; information systems—3 percent; administration and security—2 percent; accounting—2 percent; other—5 percent.

Main employment centers: Nearly 60 percent of employees work in Michigan. Printing plants at Livonia, Michigan; Durham, North Carolina; and Wichita, Kansas, employ 298, 174, and 195 respectively. Some 100 people work in nine sales offices.

Headquarters: Valassis Communications, Inc.
Westwood Office Park
36111 Schoolcraft Rd.
Livonia, MI 48150
(313) 591-3000

Viking Freight System

===========================

Viking inc
FREIGHT SYSTEM

Viking trucks deliver freight in eight western states, Hawaii, Alaska, Guam, and Australia. Employees: 4,200.

  ★ ★ ★   Pay/Benefits
★ ★ ★ ★   Opportunities
★ ★ ★ ★   Job Security
  ★ ★ ★   Pride in Work/Company
★ ★ ★ ★   Openness/Fairness
★ ★ ★ ★   Camaraderie/Friendliness

BIGGEST PLUS: You can start on the dock and get to the top.
BIGGEST MINUS: Roadway is in the driver's seat.

Founder Dick Bangham wanted Viking to be a different kind of company. So he decided not to celebrate service anniversaries every five years, that is, after five, 10, 15, 20 years, and so on. Instead, he made the first celebration after three years, the next after six, then 12, 18, and so on in increments of six.

That's just one way Viking is not your usual trucking company. Another indication can be found on the first page of the employee handbook. It reads: "Most people spend approximately one-third of their adult life working. Viking was founded on the idea that anything to which a person dedicates that much of his or her life should be enjoyed." Viking tries to make work life enjoyable by providing several creature comforts that are unusual in the trucking business, like trucks with AM/FM cassette radios and heated mirrors, free coffee at the terminals for drivers and dockworkers, televisions with VCRs in the off-duty rooms, free uniforms.

Some big changes have happened since the first edition of this book.

The founder left and is now semiretired on a Caribbean island, where he runs a rental car business. His brother Randy Bangham, who was with the firm from its start in 1966, has taken over as president. An even bigger change occurred in 1988 when Roadway Services, the nation's second largest trucker, bought the company. But the ownership change appears to have had little impact on Viking. Viking and Roadway were not direct competitors, as Viking is a regional carrier (average haul 1,000 pounds for 430 miles) while Roadway transports its cargo an average of 1,000 miles. Roadway did not bring in any of its executives and has stated that it intends to let Viking run its own business. In fact, in keeping with the long-established informality here, where top executives typically wear sport shirts to work, Roadway executives don't wear their neckties when they visit Viking's San Jose offices. (Viking's managers do, however, wear business suits when they visit Roadway in Akron, Ohio.)

Another aspect of Viking's culture has remained intact: promotion from within. In most trucking companies, people are hired in either white-collar or blue-collar jobs and never switch over. Executives typically started as management trainees and worked their way up. Not so at Viking. Eight of the 17 top executives started on the docks and worked as drivers. Viking has a goal of filling at least 80 percent of its openings with internal candidates. And they have reached or exceeded that goal for the last five years.

In 1991 Viking launched a mentor program to help nonmanagement employees move up the ranks. San Jose terminal manager Joe Finney explained: "Any hourly person who wants to get into management can apply to join the mentor program. We will work with them, teach them, and help them if that's an avenue that they want to pursue." In 1992, 25 people trained as mentors, 30 people had requested mentors and 21 of those had been promoted.

People also move easily between departments. Pricing specialist Steve Misch, who started on the docks, is now working in his fourth department. He said: "When I first got off the docks I went into a department that I really had no background in and Viking was more than willing to train me because they saw that I had the desire to advance. And the same thing occurred when I went into pricing from my previous position in the rate department. They saw that I had the desire and the capabilities and were more than happy to train me."

One way dockworkers advance is through the Earn While You Learn program. In this eight-week course they learn to become drivers while being paid their regular hourly wage for most of the training sessions. Once they complete the course, dockworkers are promoted to a driver's wage and receive a $250 bonus. By 1991, 46 employees had completed the program.

Viking emphasizes training and promotion from within because they want to be sure that they retain their distinctive corporate culture. In fact, before either internal or external candidates are accepted as supervisors, they come to the corporate office for a round of interviews with executives, including the vice-president of human relations and the vice-president of operations. Human relations vice-president Terry Stambaugh explained: "It gives us the feeling of comfort that this person is right for the job and fits the culture of the company and also makes the point to the person of how important we see the job as being." Managers are not the only ones who get to meet company executives. New employees from all levels are also flown to San Jose for orientation 90 days after they are hired.

Once new hires are on board, they don't have much worry about losing their jobs. In an industry still reeling from deregulation, Viking has fared well. While many large trucking companies went out of business in the 1980s, Viking thrived, growing from 890 employees in 1980 to 3,883 in 1990. They managed to avoid layoffs by giving drivers and dockworkers other assignments during cyclical downturns. Tough times did catch up with Viking in 1990, though, and they were forced to temporarily lay off 29 employees for as long as three months. According to Randy Bangham: "Better than half of them found other jobs within the company at that time. They might have to work for a different location, and instead of driving, work on the dock. But it was a way to maintain their income during that time. We tried to accommodate as many as possible."

Viking has a bonus program called the Viking Performance Earnings Plan (VPEP) which distributes a share of the profits to all employees. VPEP is related to the corporate and division profits. VPEP usually pays each employee a bonus of 5 to 7 percent of salary.

Open communications is a byword at Viking. Every terminal is equipped with "Direct Line" forms. Randy Bangham receives about three of these forms a week and responds personally to every one. Viking also has an "Easy to Do Business With" direct line for employees to call with ideas about how to improve operations. Vikings (as employees are called here) are encouraged to use the open-door policy to ask questions of top executives. Drew Betts, a computer operator, said he used it to ask why some company basketball hoops were eliminated. Betts learned that the baskets were removed because they were in a traffic lane between two buildings. A committee was formed to find alternatives in the exercise room. Sales manager Mark Jaruszewski told us: "The Viking management treats all the employees as human beings here. You just don't become a statistic or a number. Your ideas and your input are always listened to."

Vikings get a chance to tell management what they think every month when top executives travel to terminals to meet with the troops. (They go to smaller terminals every other month.) The meetings involve both a company update and a question-and-answer session. Randy Bangham said: "We can sit here in San Jose and make some great decisions about how to run the company, but the troops in the field are the ones that are seeing it day to day. And if we didn't have these scheduled monthly employee meetings, I can assure you none of us would take the time to get out in the terminals and find that information out. We'd find excuses for not being out there. Now we are forced to get in front of the people on a regular basis and listen to what they have to say. And it makes us better managers."

When executives return from the employee meetings, they are debriefed on the issues that came up and any questions they could not answer. The company responds to specific questions on electronic mail. Answers are posted at the terminals.

Employees also keep in touch through a monthly newsletter, the *Independent Times*, which goes directly to their homes. There they read about the many awards Vikings receive: Easy to Do Business With pins for employees who go above and beyond the call of duty, rings and belt buckles for service anniversaries, jackets for drivers completing 100,000 miles, and ride-along privileges for safe driving (after six months of safe driving, employees can bring a passenger with them on their route).

The newsletter also tells what Vikings do in their spare time, reporting on fishing trips and showing photos of prize catches. They also profile employees with interesting hobbies. Some examples: an employee who played in a Sacramento rock-and-roll band, another who is the Oregon state muzzle-shooting record-holder, one who hang-glides in her spare time, another who races go-carts. There have also been stories about employees who raise snails, race turtles, or pursue modeling careers.

One recent issue was dedicated to the Trucking Roadeos, a major Viking institution. Instead of riding Brahma bulls, drivers vie in events like Off-Set Alley and the Serpentine (maneuvering an 18-wheeler through a barrel course). Viking management attends the regional, state, and national roadeo competitions and provides a huge barbecue for competing associates (featuring safety director Scot Bishop's famous roadeo chili). In addition, the company awards its state champions with a free trip for two to Hawaii. Fourteen drivers won this trip in 1992. Winning the state championship also qualifies drivers to compete in the national tournament. The national champ wins a new car. The second- and third-place finishers win a trip to Europe.

Types of jobs: Drivers—50 percent; dockworkers—20 percent; administration—22 percent; mechanics—5 percent; information systems—3 percent.

Main employment centers: Viking is headquartered in San Jose and has terminals throughout the western U.S. Their largest terminals are in Los Angeles, Sacramento, Phoenix, Tucson, Las Vegas, Reno, Salt Lake City, Denver, Portland, Seattle, Spokane, and Boise, Idaho.

Headquarters: Viking Freight System, Inc.
P.O. Box 649002
San Jose, CA 95164
(408) 922-7200

Wal-Mart

WAL★MART®

Wal-Mart, the world's largest retailer, operates more than 1,800 discount stores, 250 Sam's Wholesale Clubs and 25 Supercenters (a discount store plus supermarket) in 43 states. Employees: 390,000.

★ ★ ★	Pay/Benefits
★ ★ ★ ★	Opportunities
★ ★ ★ ★	Job Security
★ ★ ★ ★	Pride in Work/Company
★ ★ ★	Openness/Fairness
★ ★ ★ ★	Camaraderie/Friendliness

BIGGEST PLUS: You can check out with a small fortune.
BIGGEST MINUS: Meanwhile you may be making six bucks an hour.

Working at Wal-Mart is like playing on a winning sports team: playing with winners is exciting, and you'll always be prodded to perform at your best, but you may find the pace exhausting.

Wal-Mart has been growing exponentially since its founding in 1962. By 1990 it had passed both Sears and K mart to become the world's largest retailer with a very simple formula: provide low-cost items with superior service. In the process, Wal-Mart created more new jobs than any other company in America. To the late Sam Walton, highly motivated employees were the key to his business strategy. In his autobiography, *Sam Walton: Made in America, My Story,* he said: "I think our story proves there's absolutely no limit to what plain, ordinary, working people can accomplish if they're given the opportunity and the encouragement to do their best."

His company has developed countless ways to give that encouragement. Sam Walton constantly visited stores and held employee meetings that many compare with pep rallies. At these meetings he invariably led them in a cheer: "Give me a 'W,' give me an 'A,' give me an 'L,' give me a squiggly, give me an 'M,' give me an 'A,' give me an 'R,' give me a 'T.' " Managers throughout the company conduct similar meetings.

You can get an idea of Wal-Mart's turned-on atmosphere from looking at the employee handbook. They call it the associates handbook. Sam Walton adopted the term "associate" rather than "employee" from his previous employer, J. C. Penney. Every page of the handbook has the same header— a smiling face and the greeting "We're glad you're here"—and footer: "Our PEOPLE make the difference." Wal-Mart associates are bombarded with the slogan "Our PEOPLE Make the Difference" wherever they work, on signs in front of warehouses, on the backs of hundreds of trailers that carry goods to the stores.

Not only are associates constantly told how important they are, they are peppered with little reminders about how Wal-Mart team members are expected to play: "Regardless of where you work, remember to SMILE." "Happy people are healthier and more successful." "Listen and learn from others and enjoy what you do." "We want you to be happy at Wal-Mart." Another reminder: "Always wear your SMILE—you're never fully dressed without your friendly 'Wal-Mart Associate' SMILE."

When we visited Wal-Mart's huge (1 million square feet) distribution center in New Braunfels, Texas, we saw more examples of these exhortations. At the front entrance, a sign read: "Smiling is the window cleaner of the mind." When we passed by later in the day, the sign had been changed to read: "Don't look down on someone unless you are helping them up." Similar homilies are plastered on every wall of the employee break room inside the New Braunfels store.

An associate in the New Braunfels store, Nancy Menard, worked for seven years at Eckerd's, a large drugstore chain, before joining Wal-Mart in 1986. Menard told us she preferred Wal-Mart's pumped-up ambience: "You just don't have the enthusiasm with your management and your associates at Eckerd's that you have at Wal-Mart. Here everyone is enthusiastic. With Eckerd's, people sort of drag in to work. But here it is different. You get to know everybody. We all get along very well."

Associates like Menard say they also get along well with their managers, who are described in the associates handbook as "coaches" rather than "bosses." The harmony between staff and managers stems partly from the egalitarian behavior expected of the managers. Managers are known to pitch in anytime extra help is needed. Distribution center manager Karl Mace, who joined Wal-Mart in 1977, encourages his managers to dress in jeans and help employees with their jobs at least once a week. Mace explained: "I think that keeps us all in touch with what they are doing, what their problems are, and how hot it is. It makes us not forget." Store manager Mark Woods told us: "You can go around the store any time of day and you will see me with a mop or a broom. I am not any better than anybody else. Management helps out whenever it is needed. We just help them for however long it takes. Whether it is working an overnight shift with them or whatever. We stay at the counter until it is 100 percent done. Then we go back to our manager duties."

Wal-Mart also places a great premium on listening to associates' concerns and complaints. Every year Wal-Mart stores hold grass-roots meetings where employees gather to share their ideas. Between the annual meetings are mini-grass-roots meetings, where representatives from each department meet with a general manager and personnel manager to voice concerns and air ideas.

Wal-Mart also believes in the open-door policy. Electronics department manager Becci Pickelman explained: "You just go through the steps of the ladder and express that there is a problem. If that doesn't work, then you go to the manager. You can go as far as you would like to go. You can pick up the phone and call Bentonville [Arkansas, headquarters] if you are not happy with what you are getting and what is going on in the store."

In addition, Wal-Mart believes in sharing information with associates. The closing price of Wal-Mart stock is broadcast every day over the intercom in stores and warehouses, and associates are kept abreast of their own stores' weekly sales and profits. Store manager Chris Seamon, who worked at Winn-Dixie, a supermarket chain in the Southeast, before coming to Wal-Mart in 1987, told us: "They just let you know more of what is going on than Winn-Dixie did. You are aware of policy changes or new programs being implemented. It's not kept a secret and all the sudden you find out from somebody else through the grapevine. It is told to you."

Top Wal-Mart managers practice face-to-face communication as well. On Monday through Thursday of every week Wal-Mart executives fly from store to store in one of 15 small planes, lead the Wal-Mart cheer, meet with groups of associates, and wander the aisles talking to their flock. Executives insist these meetings are more than morale boosters. Andy Wilson, a regional vice-president, told *Fortune* that he really listens to the workers "because all the best ideas are going to come from them." At Wal-Mart the executives see their role as serving the workers rather than the other way around. At the same time, the executives don't lead flashy lives on the road. They often sleep two in a room at moderate-priced Holiday Inns and Ramada Inns, and, according to Sam Walton's autobiography, eat at "family restaurants when we have time to eat." Executives convene at the corporate headquarters in Bentonville on Friday and Saturday to share their findings.

Stores and warehouses are also linked to the corporate headquarters via a six-channel data and TV satellite system. Wal-Mart transmits training programs, store data, and other information through this system. The satellite has sped up credit card approval to five seconds and enables the top people in Bentonville to get on the tube instantly with a message about a hot-selling product or dud. It also enables the managers to convene in Bentonville every Saturday morning and have in front of them a computer break-out of sales *for the past week*—store by store, department by department.

Though they are very high-tech, Wal-Mart maintains a down-home tone in their communications. The employee newsletter will feature stories and pictures on everything from associates who win weight-loss bets to interdepartmental tug-of-war competitions.

Because it is growing so rapidly, Wal-Mart is a land of opportunity for those seeking to get ahead. Although it's already the largest retailer, it has just begun to penetrate the far western states and it has the northeastern tier of the country before it. Sales hit $43.8 billion in 1991, but the company expects that figure to reach $100 billion by the end of the 1990s. So there will be many more openings here for store managers and assistant store managers. Assistant store managers at Wal-Mart make between $20,000 and $30,000 a year and typically move to a new store every 24 months. Store managers earn more than $100,000 a year. But the price is high. Store managers and assistant managers can work 60 hours or more a week, including time spent on the night shift. Mark Woods told us: "If everything is running smoothly, assistants work about 52 to 55 hours, and I work, as store manager, probably 60 hours. I know as a manager that if I need to work 70 hours this week to get everything done for next week, that's what I am going to do. Nobody really needs to tell us. We just do it. We work two nights a week till close. Those days we'll come in at 7:00 in the morning and get out of here at 10:00 or 11:00 at night. The other three days, you work from 7:00 to 5:00. When I first worked with the company, we used to work 90 hours a week. Every year that I have been with the company, they have reduced our hours. I like working. I am a workaholic myself."

Another downside of working for Wal-Mart: it does not offer iron-clad job security. The associates handbook tells employees: "Employment depends on performance and the Company's needs. Fluctuations in sales or workload may make it necessary to reduce the number of associates working or the number of hours each associate works in a facility." And sales or the work load have fluctuated slightly at different stores. In October 1991, for example, *The Wall Street Journal* announced that Wal-Mart was laying off as many as 1,200 associates as a "normal adjustment to market conditions."

But, as a practical matter, layoffs are not a major concern at a company that has been adding employees at the rate of tens of thousands per year.

The company also makes it easy for employees to transfer to other stores elsewhere in the country. One distribution center associate, Teresa Bruns, said: "I started out in Springfield, Missouri, and transferred to a distribution center in Iowa. Then I came down here. We are all offered the same thing. You can go anyplace, whether from store to warehouse or from any state to any state."

There is a light at the end of the tunnel of hard work at Wal-Mart, however. While Wal-Mart pays average wages, its profit-sharing and stock-ownership plans can provide a rich payoff. It made Sam Walton the richest man in America, but it has also made thousands of employees richer. Every year Wal-Mart contributes an average of 6 to 8 percent of every employee's income in stock to their profit-sharing accounts, investing about 80 percent in Wal-Mart stock. This has been one of the best investments imaginable. Between 1982 and 1992 the value of Wal-Mart's stock multiplied by 45 times, nearly tripling between 1990 and 1992 alone. This has meant a rich payoff, giving hourly associates with more than 10 years at the company profit-sharing accounts worth more than $100,000. This means associates can retire with quite a sum. Shirley Cox, for example, was earning $7.10 an hour in 1989 when she retired after 24 years at the register. She received $262,000 in retirement benefits. Associates also get a 15 percent discount on purchase of Wal-Mart stock. An associate who had used this discount to buy $2,550 worth of stock in 1981 would have had shares worth $170,000 in 1992.

Managers can accumulate even more. Distribution center manager Charlie Eddings, who joined Wal-Mart in 1982, plans to retire at age 50. He and his wife, who also works for Wal-Mart, hope to have $2.6 million on retirement if the company continues on its current course.

At the conclusion of his book, Sam Walton said that the way to revitalize the American economy is for management to forge a partnership with its workers. "But if American management is going to say to their workers that we're all in this together," added Walton, "they're going to have to stop this foolishness of paying themselves $3 million and $4 million bonuses every year and riding around in limos and corporate jets like they're so much better than everybody else.

"I'm not saying every company should necessarily be as chintzy as Wal-Mart. Everybody's not in the discount business, consumed by trying to save every possible dollar for their customers. But I wonder if a lot of these companies wouldn't do just as well if their executives lived a little more like real folks. A lot of people think it's crazy of me to fly coach whenever I go on a commercial flight, and maybe I do overdo it a little bit. But I feel like it's up to me as a leader to set an example. It's not fair for me to ride one way and ask everybody else to ride another way. The minute you do that, you start building resentment and your whole team idea begins to strain at the seams."

Main employment centers: Wal-Mart's headquarters and three distribution centers are located in Bentonville, Arkansas. There are major distribution centers in Texas, Louisiana, Mississippi, Georgia, South Carolina, and Iowa. There are Wal-Mart stores in 43 states.

Headquarters: Wal-Mart Stores, Inc.
Bentonville, AR 72716
(501) 273-4000

Wegmans

Wegmans Food Pharmacy

Wegmans runs the largest supermarket chain in upstate New York. Employees: 18,765.

★ ★ Pay/Benefits
★ ★ ★ ★ Opportunities
★ ★ ★ ★ Job Security
★ ★ ★ ★ Pride in Work/Company
★ ★ ★ Openness/Fairness
★ ★ ★ ★ Camaraderie/Friendliness

BIGGEST PLUS: If you want to move up, check it out.
BIGGEST MINUS: Get a good pair of shoes.

When we stopped by the Wegmans market in Greece, New York, a suburb of Rochester, the first thing we noted was several wheelchair shopping carts with signs reading: "For our valued customers who like a lift. Because we care."

Wegmans has a well-earned reputation for caring. Across the parking lot from the supermarket is their child development center, opened in 1990. Like their stores, the center is built with a distinctive brown brick. It employs 70 full- and part-time workers and can handle up to 300 children at a time. The *Rochester Times-Union* calls the center "the Disneyland of Day Care."

The supermarkets have a Disneyland quality, too. The Greece store offers a wokery (with take-out Chinese food), pizza shop (offering 800 different combinations, including a burrito pizza), European-style bakery (bread made from scratch), floral department, self-service yogurt stall, salad bar, pharmacy, and a huge deli with two chefs behind the counter. Even the produce department is distinctive, with fruits and vegetables displayed much like an open-air farmers' market in bushel baskets.

Employees we met ascribed the constant innovations to the openness of Wegmans management to new ideas coupled with a tremendous amount of autonomy and freedom to experiment. Rochester personnel manager Anne Peterson found the atmosphere here entirely different from Wendy's, where she had worked in human resources. She recalls that shortly after coming to Wegmans in 1985, someone mentioned they were trying to think of ways to recruit summer employees. Peterson came up with the idea of "Opportunity Week" to promote the idea of full-time employment at Wegmans. Even though she was a newcomer, her idea was immediately accepted by Danny Wegman, president of the company. At Wendy's, she said any new idea would have meant research and investigation.

All stores have a monthly employee breakfast where the manager and personnel representative meet with a dozen randomly selected employees. Often these meetings generate new ideas. At one store, cashiers mentioned how tired their feet became from all the standing. In a short time, the store manager purchased cushioned mats for them to stand on, and before long other stores copied the idea.

The chain's 35 store managers share ideas at a weekly meeting at corporate headquarters across the street from the Rochester airport. At one session a few years ago, the group was discussing problems cashiers were having with a new register system. The managers promptly agreed to work as cashiers for a four-hour shift themselves to get a better feeling for the problems.

Rich Simbari, bakery manager at the Mount Reed store in Rochester, recalled how two cashiers, one a part-timer, walked into the store manager's office and told him that they felt cashiers deserved a special recognition day considering how hard they worked. The store manager discussed it with a supervisor and then told the women that he thought it was a good idea. A few weeks later, "they put posters up all over the store in honor of Cashier Appreciation Day. They gave all the cashiers a carnation when they came onto their shift that day and gave the cashiers a free lunch on the store." Simbari said: "I feel very comfortable walking into a store manager's office and discussing an idea. It just seems like the only way to run a supermarket."

Simbari's wife also works for Wegmans at a different store, and their four-year-old son is enrolled in the child-care center. Simbari joined Wegmans in 1976 as a part-time cashier and bag boy when he was 17. He talks about the "family feel," having worked with different generations of employee families: "It's fun and exciting to watch family members grow that way. It just makes work more personal, I guess."

The family atmosphere starts at the top. Founded in 1916 by John Wegman, who sold fruits and vegetables from a horse-drawn cart, Wegmans is 90 percent owned by the founding family. Chairman Robert Wegman is the nephew of the founder, and Robert's son Danny is president.

Creating a family atmosphere was part of the motivation behind the child-care center. It's one of the most lavishly equipped centers in the country, with a full-size commercial kitchen, a full-time registered nurse, three separate playgrounds for infants and toddlers, another for preschoolers, and still another for children ages five to 12 who attend the before and after school programs. Preschoolers have a sight-and-sound area where they can make their own audio and video shows, an art area, microscopes, an indoor tree house with stuffed animals, an outdoor garden and petting zoo, and even a computer area where they can play educational games on two computers. There is also a full-day kindergarten program with a certified teacher. Construction costs of the center exceeded $3 million. Employees are offered discounted rates (based on their salaries) on the weekly fees of $140 for preschoolers and $165 for infants. In mid-1992 there were 199 children of Wegmans employees at the center.

Connie Morris-Pease, director of personnel, said: "The idea was to provide the best quality care anywhere for our employees at a reasonable cost to the employees. Our employees were not well served by the traditional child-care market because they are only open till 6:00, and our employees work all kinds of different shifts." The center is open seven days a week to employees, shoppers, and community residents. On weekdays it is open until 10:00 P.M.; on Fridays and Saturdays, till midnight. Half the spaces are reserved for drop-ins. Parents who want to run a few errands can drop their kids off at the center for $5 an hour ($4 with a Wegmans check-cashing card).

Mary Beth Stalter's four-year-old daughter, Jessica, goes to the center, and Stalter, who works in the finance department, has seen her blossom there: "It's amazing what she's learned. She hasn't been there a full year, and she recognizes all her letters. She's learned to tie her shoes, and when she comes home at night, she is always so stimulated." According to Stalter, the center's full-time chef, "Chef Gordon," has become her daughter's "new best friend."

Besides having her child at the center, Stalter took advantage of another Wegmans benefit, a scholarship program, which pays up to $2,200 a year for tuition. In 1990 more than 1,000 employees won the award. Like medical and vacation benefits, scholarships are available to part-timers. (Many retailing firms do not offer benefits to part-time employees, even though they typically make up the majority of the work force. At Wegmans, 60 percent of workers are part-timers.) Stalter started as a cashier at age 16 and went to Niagara University, graduating five years ago. She joined Wegmans full-time in the employee credit union and transferred to the finance department, where she works as a project coordinator.

The pay at Wegmans is competitive with other supermarkets. Checkout clerks start at $6.05 an hour, department managers make between $30,000 and $40,000 a year, assistant store managers make $40,000 to $50,000, and store managers make $50,000 to $80,000.

Intramural sports are big here. A huge recreation center near headquarters holds four softball fields and several volleyball courts. In the winter the center is set up for cross-country skiing and sledding, and there is an ice-skating rink with hot chocolate available. Stores form their own volleyball teams, with managers playing alongside their employees. There are 39 winter volleyball teams with 400 participants in Rochester alone, and 20 sand-volleyball teams in the summer. Every year there are playoffs with teams from Wegmans stores in Buffalo and Syracuse and other upstate New York cities.

Wegmans received a presidential Point of Light Award for their work-scholarship program. Wegmans takes "at-risk" teenagers from nearby public schools and offers them part-time jobs and tutoring. If they graduate from high school, Wegmans offers to pay up to $5,000 a year for their college tuition. At the graduation dinner, one student said: "Without the program I think I would have dropped out of school or something." She was, instead, valedictorian of her senior class. In the summer of 1992, 150 students were participating.

Main employment centers: 44 stores in upper New York state.

Headquarters: Wegmans, Inc.
1500 Brooks Ave.
P.O. Box 844
Rochester, NY 14692
(716) 328-2550

Weyerhaeuser

 Weyerhaeuser

Weyerhaeuser is one of the nation's largest owners of forestlands and ranks as one of the world leaders in the production of wood and paper products. U.S. employees: 34,715.

★ ★ ★ ★ Pay/Benefits
★ ★ ★ Opportunities
★ ★ Job Security
★ ★ ★ ★ Pride in Work/Company
★ ★ ★ Openness/Fairness
★ ★ ★ Camaraderie/Friendliness

BIGGEST PLUS: They're saps about saplings.
BIGGEST MINUS: They've been cutting jobs like trees.

A key player in the Pacific Northwest for this entire century, Weyerhaeuser is a big, complicated company that people are proud to work for. The forest products industry, involving the growing and cutting of trees and the converting of that wood into lumber, plywood, paper, and packing cartons (among other products), has a history disfigured by labor-management antagonism. Weyerhaeuser, despite its size, has generally managed to avoid such confrontation. It's not that they have never gone to the mat with unions. In 1986 they took a six-week strike by two unions representing 7,500 woodworkers in Washington and Oregon. In the end, the company got what it wanted—a lower wage rate and more flexibility in work rules—but it coupled this gain with a new profit-sharing plan and employee involvement programs. It was one of the rare times that Weyerhaeuser has had to duke it out with its workers.

The attraction of Weyerhaeuser lies deep in its roots. Founded in 1900 by Frederick Weyerhaeuser, a German immigrant who was then 65 and who had already built a successful wood business in the Midwest, the Weyerhaeuser Company works off a heritage of fair dealing. From its birth in Tacoma, Washington, right after Frederick Weyerhaeuser and 15 partners bought 900,000 acres of Pacific Northwest timberland from the Northern Pacific Railway for $6 an acre, to the present day, when it owns 5.6 million acres of forestlands in Washington, Oregon, North Carolina, Alabama, Mississippi, Oklahoma, and Arkansas, the company has earned a reputation as both a caring forester and employer. When it first put a trademark on its lumber, the name it adopted, in 1928, was 4 Square. It was the first company in the United States to look upon timber not simply as something to cut but as a crop, capable of regrowing. It began enunciating this idea in the 1930s, and in 1941 it established the nation's first tree farm. In 1943 the *Tacoma News-Tribune* described the company as operating "on standards of ethics and far-seeing vision almost strange to the world of business as we know it today."

Environmentalists may argue with Weyerhaeuser over the issue of clearcutting land but even the company's severest critics are not likely to label it as a rapacious cutter of trees and denuder of forests. The people who work here know that the company continues to exercise a strong sense of stewardship for the timberlands it owns. In the forest products industry, it's regarded as the polar opposite of hardline operators like International Paper and Georgia Pacific. An article in *Audubon* magazine once described them as "The Best of the S.O.B.'s."

So this is the place to come if you are interested in fashioning a career based on forestlands. Weyerhaeuser employs people with a wide variety of skills—foresters, loggers, engineers, paper chemists, lawyers, forklift operators, agronomists, millwrights, machinists, helicopter pilots—at a wide variety of locations across the country. On the manufacturing side alone, the company has plants—sawmills, pulp and paper mills, carton factories—in more than 100 communities. Of the 35,000 people employed by the company in the United States, 19,000 are represented by unions. The pay is good (average wage in 1991 was $39,000), and the benefits package is strong.

The tradition of caring that overlays Weyerhaeuser is not perceived by everyone as a strength. Wall Street analysts, unhappy with erratic earnings, have urged the company to adopt the "lean and mean" tactics of competitors. In 1989 *Forbes*, self-appointed watchdog for shareholders, berated George Weyerhaeuser, great-grandson of the company's founder, for being paternalistic, complaining that he "shut mills only as a last resort and reportedly brooded about it." It didn't seem to us that brooding about throwing people out of work was a cause for censure. On the other hand, it's clear he had a lot to brood about. From 1985 through 1991, the company closed more than 40 plants, divested or sold off a number of businesses, including gypsum wallboard, milk cartons, paneling, garden supplies, beauty aids and dog food, and said goodbye, in one form or another, to more than 15,000 employees. Meanwhile, Weyerhaeuser was also hiring people—19,000 from 1988 through 1991.

This was the biggest upheaval in the history of the company, and it culminated in 1991 with the retirement of George Weyerhaeuser as CEO. It was George Weyerhaeuser who was responsible, more than anyone else, for the popularization of the family name by virtue of his being kidnapped in 1935 when he was nine years old. He became chief executive in 1966 when he was 39 years old. Succeeding him in 1991 was John W. Creighton, Jr., an accountant and a lawyer who had risen through the ranks of the company's real estate and financial services businesses. He is the first person to head the company who is not a Weyerhaeuser or member of one of the other founding families. And his first act has been to repudiate the diversification of the 1980s and insist that the company is now returning to its roots: forest products.

Along with finding out that it's really a wood company, Weyerhaeuser has also joined the Total Quality crusade. Top executives, including George Weyerhaeuser and Jack Creighton, visited other companies (Motorola, Westinghouse, and Florida Power & Light), and they crafted a "Vision & Values" statement that embraces all the buzzwords: "relentless pursuit of full customer satisfaction," "empowering Weyerhaeuser people," "manufacturing excellence." Anyone who comes aboard now will therefore catch this company as it tries to re-create itself.

The architect for the people part of the equation is Steve Hill, senior vice-president–human resources, who has a degree in forestry from the University of California at Berkeley. Hill told us that in today's economic climate the mark of a good company is not a no-layoff policy but a strong program dedicated to the training and development of employees. The basic issue for Weyerhaeuser, he added, is this: "There isn't a lot of difference between our two-by-fours and Georgia's [Georgia Pacific]. It's a tough, low-margin business. So we have to be very cost-conscious. The dilemma for us is how to create a great working environment and really engage people and at the same time realize that if you're lucky, you've got a 3 percent margin in this business, and in a bad time you have negative margins."

It's easy to be lulled into a euphoric appreciation of Weyerhaeuser when you visit its lush corporate headquarters at Federal Way between Tacoma and Seattle. Nestled in a glen of Douglas fir trees, invisible from the nearby freeway, the low-slung, five-story, ivy-covered structure looks more like a luxury ski lodge than an office building. It has an ambience of warmth, openness, and quiet elegance.

It's not so pristine in the mills and factories, but no matter where you work for Weyerhaeuser, you have a sense that you're not just toiling for another lumber or paper company. We visited a box plant at Olympia, Washington, one of 42 plants where Weyerhaeuser makes packaging cartons (it's the world's third largest maker of these products). Safety supervisor Bob Thomas told us: "I've worked in sawmills for 10 years and I've worked as a laborer, a ranch hand and carpenter, I've done lots of different things. This is easily the best place I've ever worked. There is more education available here to people than anyplace I've ever been." The Olympia box plant is spotless—production supervisor Mark Riley said compared to other box plants, "this is like a hospital atmosphere"—and one wall holds a photo gallery showing pictures of the 160 people who work here.

One of the pictures is of Bob LaLonde, who started here in 1964 with an eighth-grade education and worked his way up to corrugator supervisor. "We are a family here," he said, "and have been for years. When someone retires or leaves, it's like losing one of the family. We've all certainly had our ups and downs and our arguments and likes and dislikes, but come right down to it, we'll all go down together. It's a great place to work." And for LaLonde, it's literally a family. His son, son-in-law, and two brothers work here.

Getting hired at Weyerhaeuser is not easy. In more cases than not, it's the best place in town to work. In Olympia, for example, the entry-level wage is $8.69 an hour, and it can quickly move up to $14 and $15 an hour. Turnover is virtually zero. Applicants go through extensive testing and interviews, including a drug test. Hank Duran, a maintenance supervisor at Olympia, reported: "I hired two people last year and it took me about six months because of the testing we do." At Columbus, Mississippi, where a new pulp and paper mill was opened in 1990, Weyerhaeuser looked at 3,000 applicants before hiring 275 people who work on four shifts.

Like a lot of other companies, Weyerhaeuser has jumped on the quality bandwagon and now emphasizes teamwork and self-management. "We've always been very interested in technical skills," said Hill. "What's new now is that we are very interested in the social side, how people interact with each other. A lot of this new work design is trying to figure out what it is that individuals and teams control. It's the way football teams work, it's the way the Army works. We've been in the logging business for a long time. Logging crews are very autonomous organizations. We've had five or six logging crews, with one foreman, scattered over miles. So the logging crews have been operating on their own without supervision. The processes are so dangerous that you have to have the right controls or you'll kill somebody. And all the skills are right there in that work crew."

Steve Hill told us that the impetus for Weyerhaeuser to focus on quality came from a customer, Anheuser-Busch, the nation's largest brewer. "They came to our box business," he related, "and said, 'We're taking our suppliers from fifteen to five. You rank seventh and you're off the list.' They told us that our cartons were not delivered on time and were not printed right.

We said they meet the specifications. They said, 'We don't care about that, what we care about is quality.' That started this company on a quality journey in 1982."

Doors are also beginning to open at Weyerhaeuser for women. At Olympia, scheduling supervisor Chuck Tichenor said: "When I started here 12 years ago the female employees, and there were about 10 of them, all worked in the miscellaneous labor pool. We now have female operators running gluers and other machines. Driving lift vehicles. They play major roles in the safety process. We have a relief scheduler. There are also females on the supervisory staff."

We interviewed Steve Hill in 1991 on the day he addressed a Martin Luther King, Jr., celebration event. This celebration was instigated in the 1980s by a group of employees at corporate headquarters. Hill said: "When they started, it was not a company thing, it was a volunteer group. It was first held in a room about this size [a small conference room]. I expect today we'll overflow our big assembly room upstairs [they did]. It's a big event." Hill said they decided to add Martin Luther King's birthday to their corporate holiday schedule three years ago. "I think he's a model of a leader," Hill added. "It's not just a holiday for black people, it's a holiday for all of us to think about our fundamental principles and how one changes things that aren't right." Hill says they get "a fair amount of negative feedback" because of the holiday. Some prefer their holidays in the summer. Others say that instead of celebrating King's birthday, they should hire more black people. Hill's response: "But there's more to this than being a black holiday. I think it's important for corporate headquarters to be a model, especially given the amount of southern operations we have. We do have a significant number of minorities, particularly in lower-level production jobs. We've got to get more in the management levels of the company."

During a group discussion we had at the Olympia box plant, employees told us a story about a veteran employee, Merlin Vernam, who suffered a heart attack at the plant on January 29, 1990. Three fellow employees— Carleen Blair, a volunteer fire fighter, Terry Crawford, who had been trained in CPR at the plant, and a police reservist, Scott Maynard—restarted Vernam's heart as he lay on the plant floor and kept him stable until a medical crew arrived. Vernam recovered and went back to work later in the year. For their rescue efforts, the three Weyerhaeuser employees were given the Governor's Lifesaving Award by the state of Washington. The three people who won the award had to travel across the state to Spokane to accept it at the annual Governor's Safety Convention. "And what Weyerhaeuser did," Chuck Tichenor said, "was to send the corporate jet to Olympia to take the employees to Spokane and back. That's the kind of company this is."

Types of jobs: Production—62 percent; officials and managers—12 percent; office and clerical—10 percent; professionals—7 percent; sales—5 percent; technical—3 percent.

Main employment centers: Weyerhaeuser's has more than 150 plants scattered through the country, with 14,000 employees in the Pacific Northwest (9,000 in Washington), 9,600 in the Southeast, 5,700 in the Northeast, and 5,300 in the Southwest. 4,300 work outside the United States.

Headquarters: Weyerhaeuser Company
Tacoma, WA 98477
(206) 924-2345

Worthington Industries

Worthington Industries, Inc.

Worthington processes steel for a variety of industrial uses and makes plastic products, undercarriages for subway cars, pipe fittings, and pressure cylinders (such as those used for barbecue grills). Employees: 6,600.

★ ★ ★ ★　Pay/Benefits
★ ★ ★ ★　Opportunities
★ ★ ★ ★ ★　Job Security
　★ ★ ★　Pride in Work/Company
★ ★ ★ ★　Openness/Fairness
　★ ★ ★　Camaraderie/Friendliness

BIGGEST PLUS: Employees vote in their coworkers.
BIGGEST MINUS: They may not vote for you.

One could argue that in a truly democratic workplace, workers would have the right to vote on whether to accept someone into the company. If the idea sounds farfetched, you haven't been to Worthington Industries, a steel processor headquartered in a suburb of Columbus, Ohio, and a company that has long championed forward-looking employee practices.

Most Worthington plants have councils composed of nonsupervisory employees who serve two-year terms. One of the council's important functions is to vote on whether to give regular status to temporary employees. Don Harmon, an annealing operator in the Worthington steel plant, explained how it works: "When a new person is hired in, they're told that they are going to get a 40-hour workweek, but they're here on a temporary basis. The employees vote in the people who become permanent employees: it's not done by management. We have employee councils, and after a person's put in so much time [at least three months] and has done an exceptional job, they bring their name up." A candidate must receive a majority vote to be accepted.

Technically, getting voted in means being accepted into Worthington's salary and profit-sharing plan. Regular Worthington employees are paid a salary rather than the usual hourly wage. The company sets their pay in the top 25 percent of local salaries. In addition, Worthington employees participate in a profit-sharing plan and get a stock bonus as an award for perfect attendance. Profit-sharing checks are distributed every three months and typically equal 35 to 55 percent of an employee's base pay. In 1991 the average production worker received $10,000 in profit-sharing checks. In addition to cash-profit-sharing, the company contributes to deferred profit-sharing accounts. Production employees who have participated in the plan since it began in 1970 have between $300,000 and $450,000 in their accounts.

Worthington's profit-sharing plan can be traced to the philosophy of founder John H. McConnell, who was still chairman and CEO in 1992. In 1955 McConnell, using his 1952 Oldsmobile as collateral (he used to work in an Oldsmobile axle plant), borrowed $600 to buy a load of flat-rolled steel, which he and three employees processed and sold to other companies. Today, Worthington has 10 steel-finishing plants and operates 15 other factories where it makes plastic, metal, and cast-steel parts for industrial users such as car companies and appliance manufacturers. Steel processing still accounts for 70 percent of the company's $1 billion in sales, and Worthington was able to navigate its way through the weak economy of the late 1980s and early 1990s without taking anyone out of a job. The no-layoff policy we admired in our first visit here in 1983 is intact, expressed in the company's mission statement: "We believe in the philosophy of continued employment for all Worthington people."

McConnell told us where his philosophy came from: "I worked a lot of jobs in my life and learned something on every one of them. The biggest influence came from working for Oldsmobile for two years when I was in college. Some of the practices there were to my mind terrible. You had a number of machines you had to produce in eight hours. You could do it in five. So after we finished our production, we would take our books and go up in the cafeteria and study. But the union stopped us, saying we had to spread it out over eight hours. That was a very telling thing to me. I never forgot it. It was a total waste. You had to produce that number, no more, because that would make other people look bad. I felt that if people were motivated to do more, they would do it, if they had a reason to." Frustrated with being held back, McConnell decided that he wanted everyone to benefit from higher productivity when he founded his own company.

McConnell believes that the secret lies in trust: "You have to trust the work force. If you don't, you've done an awfully bad job. There are always going to be some you never trust; there are always a few con men around that will take advantage of anything they can find. But, by and large, American workers will do a job if motivated. The work ethic is still there, and to me, it's management's job to get that out."

This trust works in a variety of ways here. Worthington does not provide coffee breaks for its workers. Instead, coffee and other hot beverages are available at all times as the company assumes "team members" can be trusted to decide for themselves when to take breaks. Workers don't punch time clocks, they fill out their own time cards. One employee told us: "There's a lot of trust in that employee to actually tell what hours he worked. There's also peer pressure. The bottom line is: they're here to do the best they can and see the results in their income. So if you have somebody cheating, they're not only cheating the company but everybody that works here."

Slitter helper Tim Ulmer added: "They'll give you some breathing room, respect your decisions, and back you up on how you would do things. They're not always there watching over your head."

McConnell believes that business should be run according to the Golden Rule. The 1990 annual report stated: "Thirty-five years ago Worthington Industries began business with a philosophy based on the Golden Rule, 'treating customers, employees, investors, and suppliers as you would like to be treated.' The people of Worthington have never lost sight of this ideal."

This philosophy is reflected in an open-door policy. Fred Sorrell, who works in quality control, explained: "As a worker on the floor, I can question management or a decision that management's made. If I want to know why, all I have to do is ask, and it's never been held against me. I feel good about that." The open-door policy hasn't always been enough to resolve differences between management and labor. In mid-1990 unionized employees at Worthington's Buckeye Castings plant went on strike for three weeks in a dispute over pension benefits. The company attributed the walkout to "poor communication between the union negotiating committee and the work force on the shop floor," pointing out that the dispute was settled on terms similar to the ones originally offered. Buckeye is one of five plants that were unionized before Worthington acquired them. At four other plants acquired by Worthington, employees who had been represented by unions voted to decertify them.

The open-door policy worked for forklift driver Susie Coulter. She said: "I am trying to get into sales. And to do that I needed to go out into the plant and get experience on the mills and the splitters. [Worthington requires its salespeople to work four to six months on every piece of equipment in the plant before peddling the products.] But at the time they didn't want to take me out of the department I was in to gain that experience. So I wrote a letter to John McConnell. He said, 'Allow her to do whatever she has to do to get qualified for the job she wants, and after that she's on her own.' Which is fair. That is the only thing I wanted. If you don't hear what you want to hear, you can take it up to the next person up and no grudge is held. You can go right up the ladder."

Coulter is one of the many employees who are climbing the corporate ladder. In fact, 95 percent of jobs are filled by internal candidates. And many of the top executives started at the bottom. Company president Donal Malenick started as a general laborer. Five of the nine vice-presidents also started in entry-level positions. According to cylinder plant supervisor Jim Knox: "The opportunity at Worthington exists unlike any other company as far as moving up through the ranks. If you set a goal, you can reach any level of management you want to."

One strong testimony to employee satisfaction here is the number of longtimers in the original business, steel-processing, which started in 1955. Of the 776 employees in these plants, not counting those that were acquired later, 346, or 44 percent, have been with Worthington for more than 15 years. Forty-seven have been with the company for more than 25 years. The average age of the entire group was 45 in 1992.

Though they might have moved up through the company, officers stay in touch with workers. President Malenick says: "It's nothing to have a guy in the plant offer Mr. McConnell a chew of tobacco, or vice versa. I've seen that happen countless times. When he is in town, John [McConnell] is on the floor talking to the people in the plant. He has never separated himself from labor. He's always kept that informal environment that makes it easier for people to work together as a group. We have never had the formal structure that I think older, more established corporations have. And it's worked very well here from day one."

Not only do management and labor work well together, they play together. Jim Knox said: "When I started here as a temporary, one of the things that I admired the most was the feeling that it was a family-oriented place. If you had a problem, you communicated about it and it was addressed. Then the very next day the same person you were complaining to or going to with a problem was out on the ball diamond playing ball with you or at the bowling alley with you. There seems to be no barrier."

While the company does not have its own bowling alley, they do have a softball diamond at the company's industrial park, which holds the three-story headquarters building and the processed steel and cylinder plants. Also in the park are a children's playground, picnic area, and pond. After hours, plant workers can fish in the company pond for bluegill and bass. One other unusual perk: a barbershop in the plant where workers can get a haircut for $3 on company time.

Types of jobs: Production—82 percent; management, administration, supervisors, information systems, and technical services—18 percent.

Main employment centers: Worthington has 25 plants in eight states: Ohio, Kentucky, South Carolina, Maryland, Michigan, Georgia, Indiana, and Oklahoma. Most of the plants employ 150 people and run two or three shifts. However, one steel plant has 600 employees, and the plastic molding plants, which run three shifts, each employ an average of 500 people.

Headquarters: Worthington Industries, Inc.
1205 Dearborn Dr.
Columbus, OH 43085
(614) 438-3210

COMPANIES WITH SABBATICALS

Advanced Micro Devices
Intel
Lotus
Moog
Tandem
Tennant

Xerox

═══════════════════════════

XEROX

Xerox makes, sells, and services copy machines, printers, fax machines, and other document processors. They also sell insurance and handle investments. U.S. employees: 56,000.

★ ★ ★ ★ ★ Pay/Benefits
★ ★ ★ ★ Opportunities
★ ★ ★ Job Security
★ ★ ★ ★ Pride in Work/Company
★ ★ ★ Openness/Fairness
★ ★ ★ Camaraderie/Friendliness

BIGGEST PLUS: The benefits are hard to duplicate.
BIGGEST MINUS: You may feel like just another copy.

Xerox is America's corporate success story of the 1980s. At the beginning of the decade, it looked like a sure loser as its once dominant grip on the photocopying market was rapidly slipping away to Japanese competitors. When we considered Xerox for our list in the early 1980s, we didn't feel it measured up. Employee morale was in the pits; employees talked of the erosion of a humane culture that had been so carefully nurtured by founder Joe Wilson. But we have no reservations about including Xerox in this edition. The company has undergone a radical transformation that has seen Xerox win back customers from the Japanese through a single-minded focus on quality, while revitalizing the people-oriented values of the Wilson era.

We visited Xerox's huge photocopy machine manufacturing plant in Webster, New York, a few miles from Rochester. According to company lore, it was here at the annual stockholders meeting in 1981 that the transformation began. Xerox had recently halted production of a notoriously unreliable new copier, the 3300, which was supposed to be its answer to the low-cost Japanese competitors. When then CEO David Kearns opened the meeting to questions, an assembly-line worker named Frank Enos stepped up to the microphone. In a booming voice, Enos told the CEO: "We all knew the 3300 was a piece of junk. We could've told you. Why didn't you ask us?" Kearns later acknowledged that he was embarrassed by the encounter with his own worker, as he didn't have a good answer.

Within a few years, Kearns did have an answer in the form of an elaborate quality training program that started with himself and other top executives. A worker at the Webster plant since 1965, Lou Marth, explained to us how the training evolved: "What made the difference with this quality program was that it was top down. It wasn't a situation where the top told the middle what to do to the bottom. It started at the very top with David Kearns. He taught his family, the people who worked for him. Then they taught those who worked for them, and it cascaded down. It took a year and a half to complete that cascading process, but that did two things: one, everybody was going through this experience; and second, we did it worldwide with all of our employees." In these quality courses employees learned everything from statistical methods and problem-solving techniques to group process. Xerox sent more than 100,000 employees through the six-day course at a cost of $125 million. Incorporating these new skills and techniques, Xerox was producing high-quality products by the end of the decade and winning back market share from the Japanese. In recognition of their achievements, the U.S. Commerce Department awarded Xerox the coveted Baldrige Quality Award in 1989. Kearns invited Frank Enos to the award ceremony in Washington.

A number of Webster employees told us how the quality process completely changed work life at Xerox. Union member Bill Bishop, an assembler and tester at the Webster plant and an employee since 1957, said: "It got to the point where relations between the union and management were so bad we were referred to as animals. People in the office would say, 'Let the animals do it. Go out on the floor with the animals.' . . . For a long time I just didn't have much trust in my management as to what they would do for me or against me. I trust them more now. It took years. I did see changes in some of management's attitudes toward the union people. And they have listened to our suggestions and we've been able to input things and get them in place where it does work. There is still a distinction between management and union, and when the pressure is on, you will see that distinction very clearly. But the working conditions I have today compared to what I had when I first came here are considerably better."

Along with increased involvement, Webster plant employees are enjoying increased freedom, as many groups now set their own schedules and work with little or no supervision. Time clocks have been eliminated. Edith Page, an assembler and tester, explained: "We are on the trust system. You know what time your schedule is. You come in and do your job. We're being treated like people who are responsible and come and do their job well and then go home."

Key to the new Xerox is teamwork. They call the smallest work units "family groups." Employee teams compete with each other to be featured in Teamwork Day, a show-and-tell fair now held every October. The event is run entirely by employees; the only management people involved are those the employees invite to speak. Twelve thousand employees, customers, and suppliers attended Teamwork Day 1991 events in Rochester, Los Angeles, and Arlington, Texas. Employees in another 67 offices watched via satellite. Members of the top teams win $500 and get to broadcast their quality story to every Xerox office in the country. In 1990 the top six quality teams included a group that diverted 6,500 tons of waste from a landfill through a recycling program, nine employees who reduced on-the-job injuries by 71 percent by introducing a stretching program, and a team that saved Xerox money by automating a box-folding process.

Teamwork Day is not the only time employees get together via satellite. Every year at the end of January, Paul Allaire, who succeeded Kearns as chairman and CEO in 1991, conducts a two-hour broadcast called "Focus," which includes answering call-in questions. "Focus" is the second step of the "communication blitz." The first is a meeting between Allaire and Xerox's top 150 managers at headquarters in Stamford, Connecticut, just before the "Focus" broadcast. The blitz continues after the broadcast as Allaire goes on the road to meet with groups of managers in about a dozen Xerox offices.

Wherever he travels, Allaire meets with small groups of rank-and-file employees for roundtable discussions. In Stamford, he often eats in the employee cafeteria, as do other corporate officers. There is no executive dining room. According to *Fortune:* "Allaire doesn't give a hoot for most CEO perks. He drives himself to work and, when he takes a ski trip, flies coach. Nor is he a workaholic. While his day typically runs from 7 A.M. to 7 P.M., he makes it a rule to work only the occasional Sunday and never on Saturday."

Employees also get a chance to see their CEO on "Ask Your CEO," which airs every quarter as part of a two-hour company news broadcast. If a question is not answered on the show, the employee is mailed a response. Another communications tool, which allows employees anonymity, is the "Comment" card program. Responses to Comment cards are printed in one of the company newsletters or magazines. As the self-styled "document company," Xerox may produce more written employee communications than any other company, with multicolored magazines, bulletins, newsletters, and memos on almost any topic imaginable. And their focus on quality shows in these publications.

Even with all of these communications tools, there are some offices in this huge corporation that appear to have missed the human aspect of the quality program. In 1991 *The Wall Street Journal* described the Cleveland sales offices run by Frank Pacetta. Although Pacetta had been successful in the four years he had managed the office, almost three-quarters of the employees had quit, transferred, or were fired. He was known for heaping praise and perks on those who bring in the sales, but woe betide those who did not measure up to his high standards. The worst sales manager of the month was recognized with a troll-like doll hung by a noose in his or her office.

Xerox has not been immune to the recession and laid off 2,500 employees and eliminated layers of management in 1992. But they haven't gutted their benefits package. According to a 1992 survey by *Money* magazine, Xerox offered one of the ten best benefits packages in America. One of its most important benefits is profit sharing, started by Joe Wilson in 1945. February 28 is profit-sharing day, when the company notifies everyone how much they'll receive. In 1991 employees received 5 percent of their base pay in profit sharing. Employees can opt to receive the entire amount in cash, buy company stock, put it into a 401(k) savings plan, or combine these options.

Since Wilson's time, Xerox has been considered one of the most socially responsible big companies. To encourage employees to get involved in their communities, Xerox has a variety of programs. Through the social service leave program, employees can get anywhere from one month to one year off with pay. Almost 400 employees have been granted this leave by a committee of their peers. Some of their projects have included: ministry at a local jail, caring for AIDS patients, providing legal aid for the poor, teaching living skills to disabled people, and counseling drug addicts. Through the Xerox Community Involvement Program (XCIP), founded in 1974, employees can get seed money from Xerox for community projects such as playground building projects, tutoring disadvantaged children, running a health awareness workshop, cleaning up a park, and raising money for a senior center. Since 1985, over 79,000 employees have participated in XCIP in over 3,580 projects in more than 150 cities. They also have a good record in minority and female hiring and advancement. As of 1992, 32 percent of employees were women and 26 percent were minorities. In top-level management, 7 percent were women and 18 percent were minorities. Thirty-two percent of employees promoted to the top ranks in 1991 were women. Barry Rand, executive vice-president of operations, is one of the highest-ranked blacks in corporate America.

Types of jobs: Officials and managers—31 percent; technicians—28 percent; office and clerical—21 percent; sales—10 percent; laborers—10 percent.

Main employment centers: There are sales and services offices in every state. Manufacturing facilities are in El Segundo, Pasadena, San Diego, and Sunnyvale, California; Canandaigua, Henrietta, and Webster, New York; and Lewisville, Texas. They have a major research and development facility in Palo Alto, California, and support offices in Rochester, New York.

Headquarters: Xerox Corporation
800 Long Ridge Rd.
Stamford, CT 06904
(203) 968-3000

Epilogue:
Why Levi Strauss
Didn't Make It

Our original list of 100 good workplaces has held up well since 1984, considering the tremendous upheaval that has beset corporate America since then. Most of them are prospering and remain superior places to work. Fifty-five are reprofiled in this book. Of course, that raises questions about the other 45.

None of the companies on our original list went out of business, although People Express probably would have crashed had Continental Airlines not taken it over in 1987. Four other companies were taken over by other firms and lost their corporate identities. (Two—Security Pacific and Rainier—ended up in the vaults of Bank of America.) Ten other firms opted out of reconsideration, advising us that they no longer qualified for our list.

After eliminating these 15 firms, we re-interviewed at the remaining 85 companies. A few of them had indeed changed for the worse, but most of them seemed to be better employers today than a decade ago and were viable candidates for this book. However, in the final analysis 30 of them failed to make the cut because they were not as strong as our new candidates. Levi Strauss is a good example.

In San Francisco, where Levi Strauss has been headquartered since its founding in 1850, the company—and the members of the founding family—have long been leaders in philanthropy. The Bay Area is dotted with cultural amenities resulting from their bequests. The company pioneered the concept of community involvement teams at all its work sites. These teams bring together employees in projects of their choosing to tackle pressing social needs in the community, with the company backing them with funding. Levi's has also been willing to stick its corporate neck out when others didn't. It has been in the forefront of companies with programs to support victims of AIDS. It has also extended benefits to gay partners of employees and unmarried heterosexual partners, and it cut off funding to the Boy Scouts of America for banning homosexuals. In 1987 the company adopted an "Aspirations Statement" that spells out its values. Levi Strauss, then, is a company with great interest in human and social concerns, and asks to be measured on its performance in these areas.

Levi's has also earned kudos for its personnel policies. In June 1992, *Money* magazine ranked it first among all companies for employee benefits. So how could a company that ranked first in a nationwide survey of employee benefits and with such a sterling reputation for corporate responsibility not make our list?

We visited a Levi's 501 jeans plant in El Paso, Texas, in August 1991. One of seven Levi's plants in El Paso, the Lomaland plant puts out 21,500 pairs of pants a day. The plant was clean and air-conditioned, a relief in the hot Texas summer. Radio music was piped in through loudspeakers and was clearly audible over the constant noise from the sewing machines. The overwhelming majority of the 550 operators and most of the 100 support staffers were Hispanic females. One exception was plant manager Daril Doran, who started as a secretary in the home office in San Francisco in 1973, became a management trainee five years later, and worked her way up the ranks to become plant manager in 1987. She is one of two Levi's female plant managers. (Levi's has 34 production and finishing plants in the United States. Its total U.S. employment is 22,750.)

In our tour of the plant, we were struck by the minute segmentation of operations. Six different sewing machine operators, each doing one simple task, were needed to sew a pocket onto the pants. And most operators did the same task, hour after hour, day after day, year after year. They were paid piece-rate at an average of $6.50 an hour—that is, they earned that rate by sewing a minimum number of garments in that time period. The plant's base wage rate was $5.64 an hour. Piece-rate standards (quotas) for most 501 pants operations were set by extensive time-and-motion studies in the early 1970s. One recent innovation: small computer terminals at each work station keep track of each operator's completion rate. We remarked to plant manager Doran that Frederick Taylor, the turn-of-the-century father of time-and-motion studies (as well as of efficiency experts and assembly lines) would have loved this plant. Doran acknowledged our implied criticism, saying, "Piece rate does not fit into our aspirations or modern management techniques." She said that she hoped to introduce group methods of pay in the future.

The hourly workers and supervisors we interviewed at the plant cited a number of positive aspects of work at Levi's. Several talked about "family," as many employees are related to each other. They appreciated the tuition reimbursement program, English as a second language classes, help in becoming naturalized citizens, and the Hispanic Leadership Association (a mentoring and networking group). And they appreciated Levi's sense of social responsibility reflected in the community involvement team. (We attended the plant's CIT meeting that afternoon.) One other nice touch employees appreciated: plant manager Doran held a weekly birthday party in her office for employees who were celebrating their birthdays that week.

But employees found it difficult to differentiate work at Levi's from work at other sewing plants. Isela Rueda, who had come to Levi's from a Farrah's plant in El Paso four years earlier, said: "It is mostly about the same except that Levi's is more modern. We are going into computers a lot, and Farrah, I guess, not yet. It is mainly the same, clean like ours. Our machinery is more modern though." She said the pay was about the same, as were the relationships with the supervisors.

The problem of stress was brought up by both the hourly employees and the supervisors, most of whom had started as sewing machine operators. Jorge Melchor, a line manager, said: "The thing I don't like is being stressed out. We are dealing with production, we have to get our numbers. I hate Tuesdays, Wednesdays, and Thursdays, but I love Fridays. When Friday comes along, we have made it one more week."

We also noted that none of the assembly-line workers or any of the supervisors was wearing Levi's. In fact, they were all wearing jeans made by Levi's competitors.

Supervisors and operators told us that they appreciated Levi's benefits, although the package is less generous than the one enjoyed by headquarters personnel. A number of the benefits that put Levis Strauss at the top of the *Money* magazine chart are simply not available at plant locations, where most of the company's employees work. The El Paso plant closes down for three weeks a year (one week in July and two weeks in December), and employees are expected to take their vacations at that time. However, they are not paid for all the time off unless they have been there at least five years. They get one week's vacation pay if they have been with the company for six months to three years, and two weeks' pay if they have three to five years of service. Employees with more than 15 years get the maximum of four weeks' annual vacation pay. On the other hand, people on the headquarters payroll receive three weeks' vacation after six months, increasing to seven weeks after 20 years. Other benefits, such as life insurance and personal leave, are also not as liberal in the plants as they are in San Francisco.

One benefit the El Paso workers like is profit-sharing, especially the $500 profit-sharing bonus checks they received in December 1989 after the company registered the most profitable year in its history ($272 million in profits on sales of $3.6 billion). But one month later, Levi's announced the closing of a 1,115-employee Dockers pant plant in San Antonio. Production was transferred to private contractors in the Dominican Republic and Costa Rica where workers are paid approximately $6 a day, roughly equal to what the San Antonio workers made in one hour. Levi's had a generous severance package for laid-off workers, including 90 days' notice and extended medical insurance benefits.

But the shutdown in San Antonio provoked the most severe criticism ever experienced by the company in a plant closing. (During the 1980s, Levi's shuttered 58 plants, laying off 10,400 people.) The San Antonio plant closure was the biggest layoff in the city's history and resulted in a class-action lawsuit, a union-sponsored boycott of Levi's products, and even a demonstration by 80 people in front of Levi's headquarters in San Francisco. Congressman Henry B. Gonzalez told the *San Antonio Light*: "When a company is so irresponsible—a company that has been making money and then willy-nilly removes a plant to get further profit based on greed and on cheaper labor costs in the Caribbean—I say you have a bad citizen for a company." Levi's responded to the firestorm by pointing out that their severance package went far beyond what was required by law. The company also donated $100,000 to local agencies and $340,000 to the city for extra services for the laid-off workers. Despite these extensive efforts and a tax-funded retraining system, 10 months after the shutdown only 14 workers had found jobs.

The workers we met in El Paso were intensely aware of the San Antonio shutdown because they realized it could happen to them. They said the company had given them no assurances that it wouldn't happen. Plant manager Doran told us that after the San Antonio shutdown, she experienced "a rash of incidents of insubordination," and she conceded that there was a great "feeling of insecurity." She said one worker came into her office and told her he just didn't care about his work anymore because he was so disheartened by what had happened in San Antonio.

In four interviews that we conducted with CEO Bob Haas and other top executives at Levi's headquarters in San Francisco, we heard no assurances that similar closings would not be forthcoming. Peter Jacobi, president of executive global sourcing, said he felt the company had not done a great job in closing the San Antonio plant: "We just did not manage it very well. It was a real tragedy. The decision [to close the plant] was made for a very good business reason. The problem was that we were not compassionate enough about the impact." CEO Haas expressed similar feelings, but he added that Levi's has made a strong effort to keep production in the United States: "If it were strictly on the basis of economic cost, plants in the U.S. are dead as a dodo."

Haas told us that Levi's U.S. facilities are becoming better places to work. He pointed particularly to experiments in gain-sharing and team-based manufacturing at plants in Georgia, Tennessee, and New Mexico. He acknowledged that such experiments affected only a relative handful of

Levi's workers, "in the low double digits," but he sees such efforts as the wave of the future for the company founded by his great-great granduncle.

When we included Levi Strauss in our original edition, the company had a listing on the New York Stock Exchange, although Haas family members still controlled 40 percent of the shares. In 1985, though, the Haas family members bought back from the public for $1.6 billion all the shares they did not own. This was done through what is called a leveraged buyout, meaning that it was financed by borrowing. Employees of the company were not invited to share in this buyout through any employee stock-ownership plan. So the company reverted to a family-owned company. It was a revival of paternalism, with employees depending on the generosity of the owners. One argument advanced in favor of the buyout was that the company would no longer have to kowtow to Wall Street security analysts and their short-term outlook. But as a privately owned firm, Levi Strauss proceeded to rack up record profits quarter after quarter, using much of these earnings to pay back debt and further enrich the Haas family members. And if the company was behaving differently from a publicly owned firm, it certainly wasn't obvious in the closing of the San Antonio plant.

As we considered what we had seen and heard at Levi's—in El Paso and San Francisco—we felt, on balance, that the company did not measure up to the other 100 companies on our list. We visited plants at many other companies where there was much greater employee involvement in decision-making. We were surprised to see that workers in El Paso did not even have enough pride in the product they were making to wear it. And the Hispanic work force had little chance to feel much sense of accomplishment in what they were doing since the work was organized in ways that went back to the sweatshop era. We were disturbed by the disparity in benefits between plant workers and headquarters employees. It seemed to reflect two different classes of citizens.

Levi Strauss is unquestionably a good place to work—and provides a better workplace than most of the other companies in the apparel industry. For us, however, looking at the best workplaces in the land, the negatives outweighed the positives. They have 1,500 people working in splendid, comfortable offices overlooking the San Francisco Bay. Another 20,000 people work in less commodious workplaces in plants scattered across the southern tier of the country. And there's little doubt that there are significant differences between those two environments. Ours is not a book saluting conditions at corporate headquarters.

THE 10 BEST COMPANIES TO WORK FOR IN AMERICA
(in alphabetical order)

Beth Israel Hospital Boston
Delta Air Lines
Donnelly
Federal Express
Fel-Pro
Hallmark Cards
Publix Super Markets
Rosenbluth International
Southwest Airlines
USAA

. . . AND 5 RUNNERS-UP
(in alphabetical order)

Acipco
Baptist Hospital of Miami
Merck
Motorola
Northwestern Mutual Life

Updates for
the Plume Edition

Companies never stand still; they are changing every day. Since the January 1993 publication of *The 100 Best Companies to Work for in America*, we have been monitoring the advances and setbacks of the companies on our roster. In most of these companies, no significant changes have occurred. In others, there were major developments, which we summarize here.

• **Ben & Jerry's Homemade** opened a temporary manufacturing line as they were finishing their new ice cream plant in St. Albans, Vermont, due to open in 1994. More than 600 people now work at Ben & Jerry's, but the company became quite concerned about rising injury rates on the production lines that put together their new flavor Wavy Gravy.

• Making money again, **Cummins Engine** hired 500 new employees and signed an 11-year contract with the Diesel Workers Union that establishes new team-based work systems for the entire company similar to the one we described at their Rocky Mount, North Carolina, plant.

• **Delta Air Lines** continued to fly through turbulence but avoided the mass layoffs ordered by some of its rivals. However, 3,000 workers were offered early retirement packages and 400 pilots were furloughed after the pilots' union refused to agree to pay cuts, as had other employees.

• **Du Pont**, which had shunned outright layoffs in the past, announced in late 1993 it would cut its payroll by 4,500 workers. Those being laid off were to receive one month's severance pay for every two years of employment with medical, dental, and life insurance continued for one year.

• **H.B. Fuller** introduced a new benefit that will enable employees who are first-time home buyers to borrow the down payment from the company—and then Fuller will gradually forgive the loan over five years.

• **Great Plains Software** nearly doubled its employee force to almost 600.

• **Hallmark Cards** closed two plants in 1992 but offered all affected employees a chance to relocate to other locations, and many did. CEO

Irv Hockaday reaffirmed Hallmark's policy not to "arbitrarily cut a percentage of our work force across the board," but he also insisted that the company can no longer "indulge poor performers." He said, "When we provide people with an opportunity and the appropriate training, we have a right to expect a high level of performance."

• Anxiety continued at **IBM**, where the world's largest (still) computer maker fought to maintain not its supremacy but its viability. With a new management team in place, the company was looking to reduce its work force by another 85,000 by the end of 1994 to slim down to a total of 225,000 (compared with 405,000 in 1985). Most of those leaving took early retirement packages. IBM will no longer say that it will not fire people, but it remains committed to treating all its people with respect, including those ticketed to leave, and it continues to offer one of the best benefits packages in American business.

• **Inland Steel** reached a precedent-setting agreement with the United Steelworkers, signing a six-year contract that calls for no layoffs, a seat on the board for the union, more flexible work rules and a voice for the union in management decisions. The Inland breakthrough set the pattern for similar agreements later signed by Bethlehem Steel and National Steel. Jack Parton, leader of the steelworkers' union at Inland, said: "I think this is the way of the future for the industry and all industries." And Maurice C. Nelson, president of Inland, declared: "We have dragons to slay together and this sets the context for very close company-union cooperation."

• **Johnson & Johnson** joined the legion of companies reducing their work forces as it moved to eliminate 3,000 jobs, many through early retirement. J&J also opened its fourth on-site child care center.

• Under fire from the Clinton White House, along with the rest of the pharmaceutical industry, for high prescription drug prices, **Merck** teamed up with the enemy, acquiring Medco Containment Services in a $6 billion deal. Medco is the nation's largest mail-order pharmacy (with 6,750 employees), selling drugs at cut-rate prices to medical plans. Merck also began offering early retirement programs to induce 1,000 people to leave.

• Not immune to the crunch in the corporate law field, **Morrison & Foerster** laid off 90 people.

• **Motorola** became the first recipient of the Opportunity 2000 award, the U.S. Labor Department's answer to the prestigious Baldridge Award. Motorola also opened its first on-site child care center.

• **Physio-Control** was virtually shut down by the Food and Drug Administration for violating rules governing manufacture of medical devices, and toward the end of 1993 it was still not shipping its main product, the LifePak9 defibrillator. Amazingly, not one of the 700 employees at its plant was laid off. It helps to have a rich, benevolent parent, Eli Lilly.

• **Preston Trucking** went through the most drastic change of any company on our list, having been bought out by Yellow Freight early in 1993. Preston's Teamster workers then voted by a nearly 80 percent margin for a 9 percent wage reduction in exchange for a profit-sharing plan. Yellow replaced Preston's chairman and president but retained the rest of the management team.

• **Procter & Gamble**, once known as a no-layoff company, started to whittle down operations in 1993. On the hit list were 30 plants around the world. Leaving the company: 13,000 employees. In *Soap Opera*, a new book by *Wall Street Journal* reporter Alecia Swasy, P&G is portrayed as a company that hires former FBI and CIA agents to monitor activities of employees.

• **Recreational Equipment Inc.** extended its profit-sharing program to include all employees regardless of how many hours they work.

• **Southwest Airlines**, now flying coast to coast as it extended service to Baltimore, hired 3,500 new employees, bringing its total to more than 13,000.

• **Syntex** is closing its lone U.S. drug manufacturing plant at the headquarters in Palo Alto, California. Nearly 2,000 people left the company in 1992 and 1993.

• **Tandem Computers** weighed in with a loss in mid-1993 and announced layoffs of up to 1,800.

• Facing a profit slide, **Tennant** asked everyone in the company, including CEO Roger Hale, to give up five days of pay during the summer of 1993. As a result, the company was able to avoid layoffs.

• Continuing its push to cover the nation, **Wal-Mart** added 80,000 new employees.

• Coming off a year in which two employees were killed and 17 injured while working, **Weyerhaeuser** made safety its Number 1 priority, declaring that "there's no acceptable reason for people being killed on the job."

• **Levi Strauss** announced major changes in the manufacturing processes described in our Epilogue. Workers will now be cross-trained in different operations and become part of self-directed work teams. The company said it would convert all 37 of its North American plants to this team manufacturing system.